COMPUTER DATA PROCESSING

McGRAW-HILL ACCOUNTING SERIES

NORTON M. BEDFORD, ROBERT K. JAEDICKE, AND

CHARLES E. JOHNSON, *Consulting Editors*

ANTON AND BOUTELL—Fortran and Business Data Processing

ARKIN—Handbook of Sampling and Accounting

BACKER AND JACOBSON—Cost Accounting: A Managerial Approach

BURNS AND HENDRICKSON—The Accounting Sampler: An Introduction

DAVIS—An Introduction to Electronic Computers

DAVIS—Computer Data Processing

EASTON AND NEWTON—Accounting and Analysis of Financial Data

EDWARDS AND RUSWINCKEL—The Professional CPA Examination: *Volume 1*, Text and Problems, *Volume 2*, Solutions

FOULKE—Practical Financial Statement Analysis

GRAWOIG—Decision Mathematics

GRANT AND BELL—Basic Accounting and Cost Accounting

HENRICI—Standard Costs for Manufacturing

KELLER AND FERRARA—Management Accounting for Profit Control

KELLER AND ZEFF—Financial Accounting Theory: II

KERRIGAN—Fund Accounting

LI—Accounting Computers Management Information Systems

LYNCH—Accounting for Management: Planning and Control

NICKERSON—Managerial Cost Accounting and Analysis

SAUNDERS—Computers in Business: An Introduction

SMITH AND ASHBURNE—Financial and Administrative Accounting

TEICHROEW, SMITH, AND SNELL—Computerized Practice Set

VANASSE—Statistical Sampling for Auditing and Accounting Decisions: A Simulation

WENTWORTH–MONTGOMERY–GOWEN–HARRELL—The Accounting Process: A Program for Self-instruction

ZEFF AND KELLER—Financial Accounting Theory: Issues and Controversies

COMPUTER DATA PROCESSING

GORDON B. DAVIS

PROFESSOR AND DIRECTOR
THE MANAGEMENT INFORMATION
SYSTEMS RESEARCH CENTER
UNIVERSITY OF MINNESOTA

McGRAW-HILL BOOK COMPANY
NEW YORK, ST. LOUIS, SAN FRANCISCO
LONDON, SYDNEY, TORONTO
MEXICO, PANAMA

COMPUTER DATA PROCESSING

Editor: Hiag Akmakjian
Cover Design and Photo: J. Paul Kirouac
Book Designer: J. Paul Kirouac
Illustrators: Edward Malsberg (Matthew-Lawrence Co., Inc.)
                John Cordes (J & R Technical Services, Inc.)
Editing Supervisor: Mary A. O'Callahan
Production Supervisor: Peter D. Guilmette

This book was set in Foto News Gothic by Westcott & Thomson, Inc.,
printed on 50 lb. McGraw-Hill Blade-coated Matte paper by
Halliday Lithograph Corp., and bound by The Book Press, Inc.

Library of Congress Catalog Card Number 69–18707

15775

1 2 3 4 5 6 7 8 9 0   HDBP   7 6 5 4 3 2 1 0 6 9

A man receives his paycheck; he writes a check to pay a bill received from his insurance company; he receives a notice that his income tax computation was in error and he will receive a refund; he calls his stock broker and receives a price quotation on stocks he owns; his child comes home from school and tells him of a "talking typewriter" used in instruction; he watches a news report of a rocket being sent to the moon; in his work as a construction supervisor, he receives a listing of each task to be done, the date it should be started, and the last day it can be completed without delaying the job; his credit record is checked when he purchases a new TV; and early in the evening while watching television on election night, he is given very accurate predictions of the outcome. The computer affects the life of each of us. The economic impact is significant—over 60,000 computers with a value of $20 billion were installed by the end of 1968. Annual operating expenses (based on 1968) were about $5 to $6 billion. New vocations have been created—computer systems analyst, computer programmer, and computer operator. The uses of the computer range from the most mundane data processing task to guiding a space craft to a landing zone. And yet the industry is not even 20 years old.

The student, no matter what his career choice, is likely to have substantial contact with the computer or the results of computer processing in his future job. Business administration, medicine, government, library science, teaching, engineering, research are a few examples of vocations in which the computer is having an impact. The trend is clearly toward increasing use of man-computer systems in which the computer performs certain well-defined functions and the man performs the judgmental functions. The forward-looking student will want to have an understanding of this important component of his future work environment. And even where the job influence may be small, the computer has become such an important element in the society in which we live that an introductory knowledge of computers should be a part of the knowledge of the well-educated man.

In the study of computers, there are two pedagogical problems: (1) how much to emphasize the characteristics of a specific computer and (2) how to handle concepts of computer programming. If the coverage is too brief and in insufficient depth, the student ends up with very little understanding other than that computers are "very fast." On the other hand, a concentration on the particular features of a single computer gives the student such a narrow view of the field that his knowledge will become obsolete as rapidly as the computer he studied.

This text avoids both the shallowness of the "gee whiz" introduction and the excessive detail and narrowness which comes from concentrating on the features of a single computer. The coverage includes an explanation of the major types of computers and the characteristics which are usually associated with each type. There are examples from different computers with emphasis on the most popular computer—the IBM System/360. The material may be used by an instructor as a general introduction to computers without reference to a specific computer, or it may be used in conjunction with the use of the specific computer available to the class. In the latter approach, the student has the advantage of the general explanation of the text and

PREFACE

can relate the specific computer to this general framework. Also, the broad coverage of the text provides the breadth of study that the student needs to keep a specific computer in perspective. Both of these teaching approaches—teaching the subject without reference to a specific computer and using the general material in conjunction with some instruction about a specific computer—have been successful, and the one chosen should reflect the availability of equipment and the needs of the group being taught. This text has been written to support both of these approaches.

The problems of teaching programming center on the depth of instruction and the programming language to use. The book presents the basic elements for understanding how a computer is programmed at the level of both the machine-oriented language and the higher-order machine-independent language. If an instructor wishes to increase the depth of study by having the student program in a specific language, supplementary material covering the rules for that language will be required. The trend in programming is clearly toward the use of higher-order machine-independent languages such as FORTRAN or COBOL, so the instructor may wish to have the students write and run problems in one of these languages. Chapter 14 provides a review of major higher-order languages and their characteristics. The instructor who wishes to teach the programming of one of the languages will need a manual for that language. A large number of different language manuals are available for this purpose.

There are similarities between this text and a previous book, *An Introduction to Electronic Computers.* In both, the explanations of computers are general and emphasize the major features found in computers. This book has more of an orientation to computers in data processing, so many topics have been expanded and new topics have been added. In general, this book will be easier for the student to use and more adapted to self-study. The extensive coverage of FORTRAN and COBOL contained in the prior book has not been included, allowing the instructor to select a specific language manual if he wishes to teach a language in connection with the use of this book.

The book is suitable as a text for a course covering an introduction to computers or an introduction to computer data processing. The length of the course may be one or two quarters (semesters) depending on the proficiency desired and the time devoted to a programming language. Three possible course uses are:

1 One quarter (semester) general introduction to computer data processing—little or no programming
2 Two quarter (semester) general introduction to computer data processing with programming (say in FORTRAN and/or COBOL) included in both terms of the sequence
3 Two quarter (semester) sequence with the first term being a general introduction and the second being a course emphasizing programming and other applications of the material from the first term

Although this is an introductory text, material has been offered for the student who wishes to investigate a topic in greater depth. This material includes selected references, a guide to computer organizations and periodicals, a glossary of terms, and information on the development of data processing standards.

In those cases where the coverage is too extensive and some chapters must be deleted from the formal course reading list, one or more of the following chapters may be considered for omission without seriously affecting comprehension of other chapters.

CHAPTER	CHAPTER SUBJECT	POSSIBLE REASON FOR OMISSION
2	A review of punched card data processing	If punched card data processing has been covered in a prior course
6	The internal operation of a computer	Where even a cursory look at circuitry is unnecessary
11	Computer instructions for processing	Where an introduction to types of instructions is not considered necessary
12	Program modification	
16	Data communications	Where time constraints or background of students make chapter coverage not feasible or unnecessary
20	Data processing service centers	
21	Time-sharing	

The material in the text has been used in conjunction with the computer courses offered by the School of Business Administration at the University of Minnesota and has proved very successful in teaching a solid understanding of computer data processing to students with a variety of educational backgrounds and many different vocational objectives.

Several chapters contain self-testing quizzes which aid the student in studying the topics in these chapters. A study guide is also available for use with the text. It contains an outline of the material in each chapter, a list of important terms used in the chapter, "test your knowledge" quizzes, and problems. There is also a supply of layout paper for use in class problems.

GORDON B. DAVIS

CONTENTS

PREFACE

CHAPTER

1   ELEMENTS OF A DATA PROCESSING SYSTEM   1

2   A REVIEW OF PUNCHED CARD DATA PROCESSING   21

3   A SURVEY OF COMPUTER DATA PROCESSING   57

4   A LOOK AT THE USE OF COMPUTERS   87

5   COMPUTER ARITHMETIC AND DATA REPRESENTATION   111

6   THE INTERNAL OPERATION OF A COMPUTER   139

7   STORAGE AND RETRIEVAL OF INFORMATION IN A
    COMPUTER   153

8   INSTRUCTING A COMPUTER   173

9   TOOLS FOR ANALYZING AND PLANNING COMPUTER
    PROGRAMS   193

10 PREPARING THE COMPUTER PROGRAM   219

11 COMPUTER INSTRUCTIONS FOR PROCESSING   235

12 PROGRAM MODIFICATION   265

13 INPUT/OUTPUT PROGRAMMING   291

14 PROCEDURE- AND PROBLEM-ORIENTED LANGUAGES   331

15 METHODS FOR ORGANIZING AND PROCESSING COMPUTER
    FILES   369

16 DATA COMMUNICATIONS IN DATA PROCESSING SYSTEMS   393

17 CONTROL OVER QUALITY OF COMPUTER PROCESSING   411

18 OPERATION AND MANAGEMENT OF THE COMPUTER
    INSTALLATION   439

19 EVALUATING AND INSTALLING A PROPOSED COMPUTER
    SYSTEM   461

20 DATA PROCESSING SERVICE CENTERS   483

21 TIME SHARING A REMOTE COMPUTER   499

22 LOOKING AHEAD: IMPACT OF CURRENT AND
    PROSPECTIVE DEVELOPMENTS IN HARDWARE/SOFTWARE
    AND SYSTEMS   521

APPENDIXES

I   HOW TO USE THE CARD PUNCH   537

II   GUIDE TO COMPUTER ORGANIZATIONS AND PERIODICALS   545

III THE DATA PROCESSING MANAGEMENT ASSOCIATION
     CERTIFICATE IN DATA PROCESSING   551

IV   STANDARDS FOR COMPUTERS AND INFORMATION
     PROCESSING   555

GLOSSARY   561

SELECTED REFERENCES   603

INDEX   609

❚ THE INFORMATION SYSTEM

❚ SOME DEFINITIONS
SYSTEM
DATA
INFORMATION

❚ THE DATA PROCESSING SYSTEM
DATA PROCESSING TASKS
THE DATA PROCESSING CYCLE

❚ MECHANIZATION OF DATA PROCESSING
MANUAL PROCESSING
ELECTROMECHANICAL PROCESSING
PUNCHED CARD DATA PROCESSING
COMPUTER DATA PROCESSING
SUMMARY OF ECONOMICS

❚ WHY LEARN ABOUT COMPUTERS?

❚ SUMMARY

❚ EXERCISES

ELEMENTS OF A DATA PROCESSING SYSTEM

A customer places an order for immediate delivery—are the goods available in inventory? Can they be shipped today? A decision must be made on the price to charge for a new model of a product—what are competitors charging, what does the product cost, and how is price expected to affect the total sales? The person making these and other decisions needs information. If he understands how to use it, the decision maker with the greatest amount of accurate information has a competitive edge in making the best decision.

The raw material for these decisions consists of data from a number of sources and from a large number of transactions. This raw data has limited use unless it is summarized, compared, analyzed, etc. The data processing system performs this activity. Data processing is similar to manufacturing in the sense that raw data is transformed into a valuable finished product—information for decisions and actions. The data processing system is therefore a vital part of the management information-decision system of an organization.

Data processing systems in organizations are currently in a period of major change. One reason for this is the use of the computer; a second reason is the application of mathematical and statistical techniques to decision making. These developments have made the analysis and design of new data processing systems an exciting and challenging occupation. They also mean that management and others in the organization need to understand the design and operation of the new systems in order to evaluate the changes and to use the system effectively.

▌ THE INFORMATION SYSTEM

The information system of an organization consists of the people, procedures, and facilities which supply the organization with information. This system consists of: (1) a central data processing system, (2) information processing in various parts of the organization, and (3) an informal process of collecting, processing, and disseminating information. The central data processing system has historically been operated in conjunction with the accounting function, but many computer-based systems have established a separate function for this activity. There are usually data processing activities closely identified with the various functions of an organization (e.g., finance, marketing, production, purchasing, personnel) which are handled separately by that function. Thus, for example, the personnel function probably has people, procedures, and facilities to provide it with the information needed to manage the personnel responsibility. The purchasing department has clerks, procedures, and files which provide information (sources of supply, specifications of merchandise, etc.) necessary for performing the purchasing function. The relationship of these components of an information system is illustrated by Figure 1–1.

The impact of the computer and the new systems concepts made possible by it has been to expand the central data processing activity and to shrink both the functional area information processing activities and the role of the informal information system.

In this text, we are concerned with the central data processing function and primarily with how this function is carried out using computers. In this chapter, the basic elements of a data processing system will be described in terms of manual, electromechanical, punched card, and computer processing. Chapter 2 reviews punched card data processing. The remainder of the text is on computer data processing.

▌ SOME DEFINITIONS

Before proceeding further, it may be helpful to define some basic terms—system, data, and information.

FIGURE 1-1 The information system in an organization

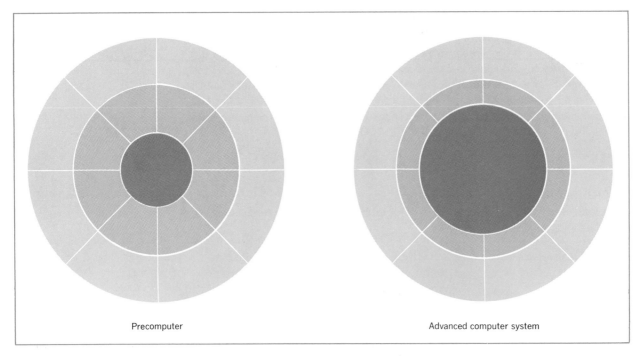

Precomputer

Advanced computer system

FIGURE 1–2 Changing emphasis for different components of the information system

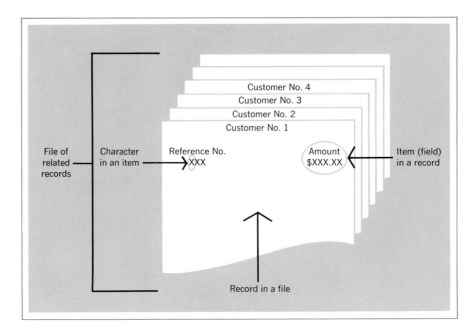

FIGURE 1–3 Relationship of character, item, record, and file

SYSTEM

A *system* is a group of physical and/or nonphysical components which accepts inputs and produces outputs in an organized ongoing process. Thus, a group of workers, procedures, and machines which accept raw material, power, etc. and convert them into a finished product form a production system; a heating system consists of an input of coal, gas, or other material and a processor to convert the material to heat, which is the output; and a data processing system accepts data and processes it into organized, meaningful output.

DATA

In data processing, *data*[1] refers to any set of characters which is accepted as input, is stored, processed, and produced as output. Data is further described by the following terms:

TERM	DEFINITION
Digit	A single numeric character 0, 1, 2 . . . 9
Character	A single alphabetic, numeric, or special symbol; e.g., A, Z, 1, 2, $, ;
Item (field)	A set of characters which are used together; e.g., a name item contains the characters in a name, and an amount item consists of the numbers representing the amount. Also called a field.
Record	All items related to an object of data processing; e.g., a payroll record for a man contains all fields relating to him for payroll processing, and an accounts receivable record will contain all data fields relating to the customer for accounts receivable processing.
File	All records of a given type. Files are classified as master files and detail (or transaction) files. The master files contain permanent records which are kept up to date by recording in them the transactions found in the detail file.

The relationship of a character, item, record, and file is given in Figure 1–3.

Files are frequently established according to a data processing function, so that a data processing installation will have a payroll file, an accounts receivable file, and so on. If the data is integrated so that a single file serves many data processing applications, it is referred to as a *data base*.

INFORMATION

The terms "data" and "information" are sometimes used interchangeably in the literature of data processing although information usually implies data that is organized and meaningful to the person getting it.

Communication theory (also termed information theory) distinguishes between data elements and information. A data element which is transmitted over a communication line has information content only if it is necessary to transmit the element in order to tell the receiver something he could not otherwise predict. Information is

[1] By common usage in data processing, data is singular as well as plural. The singular form, datum, is rarely used.

therefore synonymous with surprise, because the data element tells the receiver something he did not know. In communication theory, in other words, a message consisting of random digits has the maximum information content, since the value of each digit is completely independent of the preceding digits and cannot be predicted.

The communication theory definition of information is too narrow for data processing purposes. Information has meaning in addition to surprise. Thus, for a business report to have information value for a user, it must provide facts which were not known by the receiver (or add assurance to a tentative knowledge), and these must have meaning. A page of random digits has no meaning unless the user requested random digits.

▋ THE DATA PROCESSING SYSTEM

A data processing system consists of four elements—input, processing unit, data storage, and output. These components are part of every data processing system, whether manual, mechanical, or computer (Figure 1–4).

DATA PROCESSING TASKS

There are two types of data processing tasks—*facilitating tasks,* which are performed as support for *result tasks*, which are associated with the results or end product of data processing.

Facilitating tasks
    Input preparation
    File maintenance

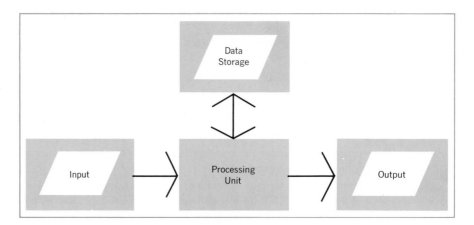

FIGURE 1–4 Components of a data processing system

Result tasks
   Transaction processing
   Inquiry processing
   Report preparation

Input preparation is required before other data processing tasks can begin. This task includes the recording of source data, putting codes on it for data processing (such as account numbers), checking it to eliminate errors and converting it, where applicable, to a machine-readable form.

File maintenance is a facilitating task because up-to-date files are required in the end result tasks. File maintenance includes the recording of transaction data affecting the file, the computing of new balances reflecting the effect of the transactions, and the purging of obsolete records. If the file is an accounts receivable file with the records of amounts due from customers, file maintenance includes recording new purchases and payments plus removing records of customers who close out their accounts. In terms of time spent, file maintenance is one of the major data processing tasks.

Transaction processing results in the preparation of documents recording the existence or effect of a transaction. The processing may include data manipulation, reference to files, recording of data for file maintenance, etc. An example is a credit sale transaction which requires the preparation of a sales invoice plus the recording of data for the preparation of sales analyses and accounts receivable file maintenance.

Handling of inquiries involves data retrieval and may include manipulation and analysis as well. In contrast to reports which are prepared at regular intervals and may be planned accordingly, inquiries occur at random intervals and cover a variety of topics. The handling of inquiries means that the system must provide for access to the records containing the data to be referenced and that the records must be arranged so that those being sought can be located within a reasonable time.

Report preparation is usually conducted at regular intervals, such as weekly or monthly. The manipulation and analyses performed in preparing a report may range from simple tallies of data in files to complex mathematical analysis. An example of a report is a monthly report of sales classified by product, customer, and sales territory.

THE DATA PROCESSING CYCLE

There is input into a data processing system, there is output from the system, and internally there is manipulation. Storage provides a temporary repository for data to be used again. These form a data processing cycle which can be further described by the activities performed.

PORTION OF CYCLE	ACTIVITY
Input	Originating and recording
	Classifying (coding)
	Editing and converting
	Retrieval from storage
Manipulation	Sorting
	Calculating and analyzing
	Summarizing
Output	Recording in storage
	Recording in report

In the input portion of the cycle, data is originated as activities occur and are recorded on source documents. The source documents are coded to classify them for data processing. Identification codes for transaction types, organization unit affected, accounting classification, etc. are added. The editing of the data consists of checking the source record for completeness and validity before it is allowed to proceed further in the cycle and, if necessary, be converted to machine-readable form. When data is converted, there are usually verification procedures to check the accuracy of the conversion. Where the data needed has previously been recorded in storage, the input will consist of retrieval from data storage.

The manipulation or processing activities rearrange the data, combine it in different ways, and perform computations or other types of analysis. The activities can be classified as sorting, calculating, summarizing, and analyzing.

MANIPULATION ACTIVITY	DESCRIPTION
Sorting	The sorting of items into an order and/or class is performed (1) to facilitate further processing, (2) for filing, and (3) for summarizing.
Calculating and analyzing	Calculating includes standard arithmetic operations. Analyzing is the manipulation of data to find meaningful relationships, and decision-impelling facts or indicators.
Summarizing	The summarizing activity counts, adds, or otherwise summarizes items in a class.

The output phase of the cycle is the recording of information obtained from the input and manipulation phases. The recording may be in data storage for subsequent retrieval or may be a report (regular or inquiry) which provides information for immediate distribution.

▌ MECHANIZATION OF DATA PROCESSING

Data processing systems differ in the amount of mechanization utilized. Four major categories can be identified:

1   Manual
2   Electromechanical
3   Punched card
4   Computer

Each of these will be examined in terms of a very simple data processing application—the recording (posting) of payments received from charge customers. In each case there is a file of customer accounts (accounts receivable) to be updated by posting the payments received from customers. In other words, the task is file maintenance.

MANUAL PROCESSING

The accounts receivable file, in a manual system, probably consists of sheets or ledger cards—one for each customer. They are usually filed in alphabetical order by customer name. The posting task begins with the receipt of a batch of remittance advices (i.e., receipts or other slips of paper indicating the customer name and the amount paid). These are first sorted into the same order as the file (alphabetical order in this case). The next step is to take each remittance slip, locate the corresponding customer record in the file, write in the payment, and compute the revised account balance. The manual processing procedure is illustrated in Figure 1–5.

There are many variations in manual processing. One of the most significant is the technique of using a writing board, overlapping forms, and carbon paper to simultaneously produce a listing (journal) and a posting to individual accounts.

The advantages of manual processing are a low setup cost for a processing job (the time required to get everything ready to begin processing) and flexibility. The disadvantages are a rather high variable cost per unit processed and a rather large chance for error in posting or computation.

ELECTROMECHANICAL PROCESSING

The likelihood of making an error when handwritten numbers are used and the possibility of errors in computing new balances when performing the work by hand suggest advantages from the use of a bookkeeping or posting machine. The process is similar to the manual method, as shown by Figure 1–6. In posting, the operator keys in the old balance, the reference such as check number for the payment, and the amount of the payment. The machine records these figures plus the new balance. For control purposes, the operator may be required to key in the old balance twice. The machine makes an error control comparison from these two to detect errors in picking up the old balance. In addition to legibility and accuracy of computation, the electromechanical bookkeeping machine produces, as a by-product, control listings of account balances and amounts posted.

FIGURE 1–5 Manual processing—example of posting payments to an accounts receivable file

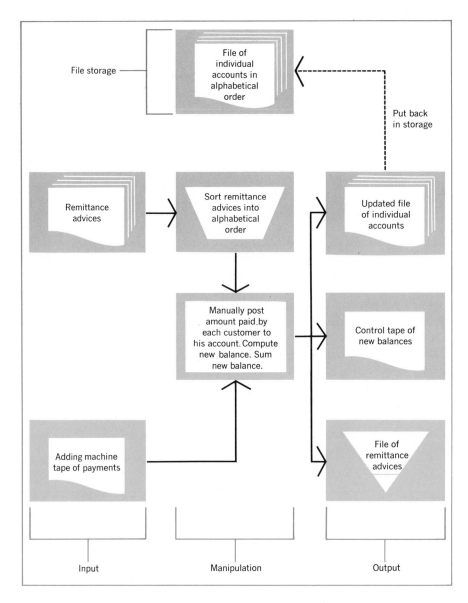

The advantages of a bookkeeping machine are a low setup cost, accuracy of processing, and the automatic preparation of control figures. The disadvantages are the cost of the machine and the fact that the machine is a potential bottleneck facility because it is limited to the speed of the operator. Processing volume cannot be increased without adding another machine for each new operator. Recent develop-

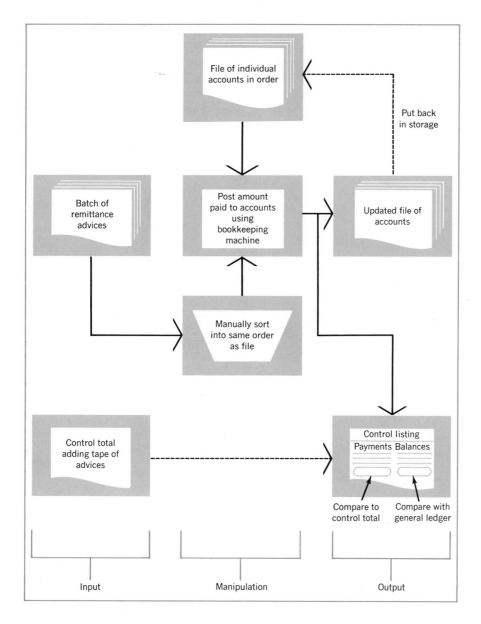

FIGURE 1–6 Use of bookkeeping machine—example of posting payments to an account receivable file

ments in bookkeeping machines have greatly improved their versatility and speed of operation. A magnetic strip on the back of the account card contains data such as the current balance. This data is read automatically by the machine, eliminating part of the work of the operator, decreasing the possibility of operator-based error and increasing the speed of operation.

PUNCHED CARD DATA PROCESSING

Punched card data processing is a substantial departure from manual or bookkeeping machine data processing. It is closely connected to computer data processing, so that it will receive further explanation in Chapter 2.

In punched card processing all input data and files are recorded on punched cards, which can be processed by punched card equipment. It is often called *unit record processing* because each record to be processed is put on a separate unit, i.e., a

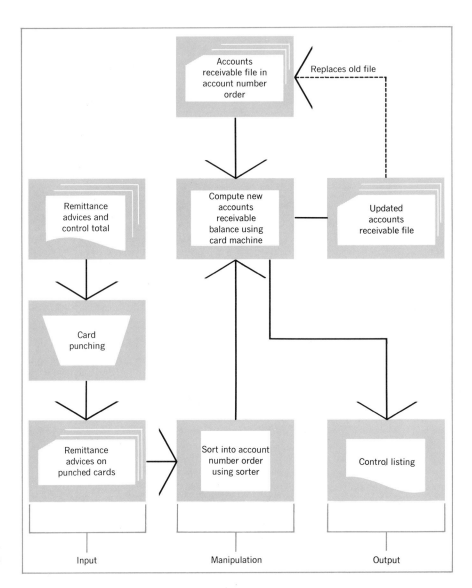

FIGURE 1–7　Punched card data processing—example of posting payments to an accounts receivable file

separate punched card. Figure 1–7 shows how punched card processing might be applied to the posting of receipts to the accounts receivable file and illustrates the difference between it and the preceding methods. Note that, for efficiency of processing, a numerical account number is now used.

The advantages of punched card processing are the speed and accuracy of processing and the low variable cost. Once the conversion to punched cards is made, additional processing can be performed with relatively little added cost. The disadvantages are the cost of converting transaction data to punched cards, the cost of setup for processing and the cost of converting a file to punched cards for a new application.

COMPUTER DATA PROCESSING

The use of the computer provides substantially increased processing capabilities. Figure 1–8 presents a computer approach to the same problem of recording payments on account. As will be explained later, the file media can vary—this example assumes magnetic tape.

The advantages of computer processing are versatility, very high speed, high level of accuracy, very low marginal cost, and the ability to perform several data processing tasks in one processing run. The disadvantages are a high fixed cost for equipment and programs, a high setup and conversion cost for an application, and the need for better-trained, higher-paid personnel than with the other methods.

SUMMARY OF ECONOMICS

The economic advantages and disadvantages of the different methods when used on a straightforward data processing task are related to the following cost factors:

1 Data conversion—cost of transcribing data into a machine-readable form for machine data processing.
2 Procedure design and implementation—cost (including personnel) of formulating and implementing the manual and machine steps for data processing. This includes the preparation of a program of processing steps for computer processing and file conversion to transfer a file to a machine-readable form.
3 Machine amortization or rental.
4 Personnel costs for operating.
5 Supplies.

The costs which are relatively fixed over a normal range of operations are machine costs and procedure design and implementation. The data conversion, operating personnel, and supplies are, to a great extent, variable. Given this rough breakdown in cost factors, the cost curves in Figures 1–10 and 1–11 are an indication of the relative cost behavior of the different processing methods. The general conclusion from these cost curves is that the manual method is most economical for low volumes of processing and that as volume becomes greater, an increased level of mechaniza-

14

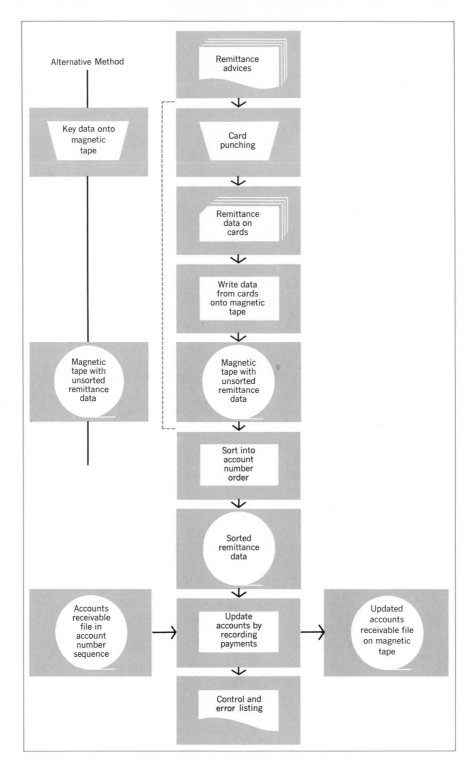

FIGURE 1–8 Computer data processing—example of posting payments to an accounts receivable file

Alternative Method

Key data onto magnetic tape

Magnetic tape with unsorted remittance data

Remittance advices

Card punching

Remittance data on cards

Write data from cards onto magnetic tape

Magnetic tape with unsorted remittance data

Sort into account number order

Sorted remittance data

Accounts receivable file in account number sequence

Update accounts by recording payments

Updated accounts receivable file on magnetic tape

Control and error listing

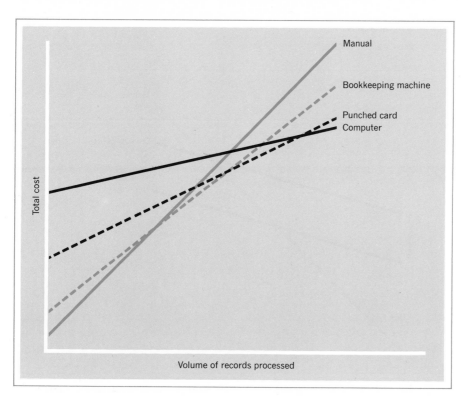

Manual

Bookkeeping machine

Punched card
Computer

Total cost

Volume of records processed

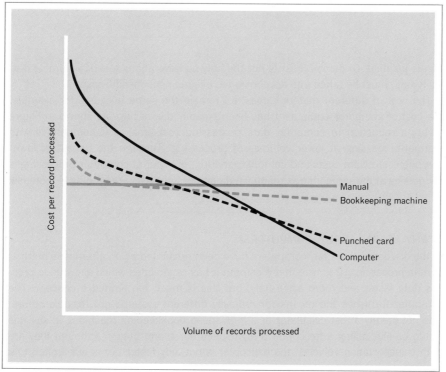

Cost per record processed

Manual

Bookkeeping machine

Punched card

Computer

Volume of records processed

FIGURE 1–11 Effect of a reduction in computer costs on volume of activity at which the computer is economical when compared to manual methods

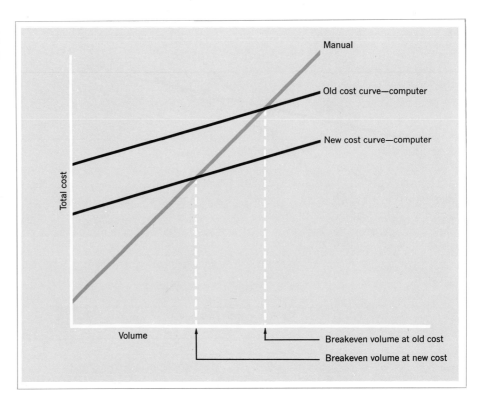

tion is justified. Of course, cost is not the only consideration; speed, accuracy, flexibility, etc. must be taken into account when evaluating a specific case.

The cost of different methods does not remain the same because, for example, the cost of computer equipment has been steadily decreasing. As shown in Figure 1–11, a reduction in computer data processing costs makes it competitive with manual processing at lower volumes of processing. Through the impact of lower computer hardware costs and computer sharing, the cost of computer processing is decreasing at the same time as manual data processing costs are tending to increase.

▌ WHY LEARN ABOUT COMPUTERS?

In the discussion thus far, computers have been presented as an alternative method of data processing. It is true that a computer has capabilities which allow us to process data faster and more accurately, but this is much too limited a concept. The computer furnishes the means for radically different systems not feasible before. It is not merely a fast calculator or a high-speed bookkeeping machine. To say this would be like calling a helicopter a high-speed horse and buggy. Although they are both transportation vehicles, the helicopter is not only faster but is not limited to a road or path. It overcomes the restrictions of topography. Similarly, the computer system has capabilities not found in any prior method.

Not only does the computer have important implications for data processing as traditionally defined for organizations such as businesses, but it is causing a change in information and intelligence systems of all types. The establishment of large data files (often called data banks) which centralize everything known by an organization about an individual or about another organization, when coupled with the exchange of information between such files, raises important political and sociological questions relating to privacy, liability for false information, etc. As another case in point, voting ceases on the East Coast of the United States three hours before the polls close on the West Coast. The computer vote projections now appear to be so accurate that the projections, based upon early returns in the East, may affect the voting in the West. The computer is thus an important element of any system of which it is a part.

Considering the impact of the computer, there are three main reasons for studying about it.

1 For general information, because it is an important element in our society.
2 For general understanding in order to work effectively in an environment where computers are used. A manager who utilizes computer-prepared reports and an engineer using the computer for computation are examples.
3 For specific understanding for persons directly connected with data processing or who intend to become data processing specialists.

This text is an introduction which may be used for any of these three purposes. Its orientation is toward the computer as a part of a data processing or information system rather than toward the computer as a device for statistical or numerical analysis. The text is divided into four sections plus appendixes:

1 Introduction (Chapters 1–7)
2 Programming a computer (Chapters 8–14)
3 Design and operation of the data processing system (Chapters 15–21)
4 Looking ahead (Chapter 22)

The organization of the book presents programming before systems design because the reader needs to understand programming before he can understand the way a computer can be used in a system. The last section, on looking ahead, is intended to provide a perspective on the future impact of computers and the expected future developments in the field.

▌ SUMMARY

The information system of an organization consists of the people, procedures, and facilities which supply the organization with information. The term "data processing system," less inclusive than the term "information system," is usually used to refer to those people, procedures, and facilities which are formally engaged in data processing activities.

The major data processing tasks are input preparation, file maintenance, transaction processing, inquiry processing, and report preparation. The phases in a data processing cycle are input, manipulation, and output. The chapter examined the different methods of data processing and illustrated with a simple example the difference between manual, electromechanical, punched card, and computer methods.

The general shape of the cost curves for the different methods shows that manual processing is most economical at a low volume of activity while computer processing is clearly indicated with high volume.

The importance of the computer and its impact on the individual suggests that an introductory knowledge of computer data processing is valuable general knowledge. This book will provide a good basic knowledge for the student who wishes a general understanding and will provide a foundation for the student who wishes to go on to advanced, specialized courses.

▌ EXERCISES

1 Define the following terms:
   a   Information system
   b   System
   c   Information
   d   Data
   e   File
   f   Record
2 What are the phases in a data processing cycle?
3 What are the major types of data processing tasks?
4 Why is the computer not usually economical for a low-volume data processing job?
5 What are the major advantages and disadvantages of data processing using manual, electromechanical, punched card, and computer methods?
6 How has the computer affected the role of central data processing compared to formal information systems maintained by functional areas (see Figures 1–1 and 1–2)?
7 Identify the file, record, and data items for purchase order processing and accounts payable processing.
8 The cost curves in Figure 1–10 are, for a given installation, likely to curve upward at some point. Why?

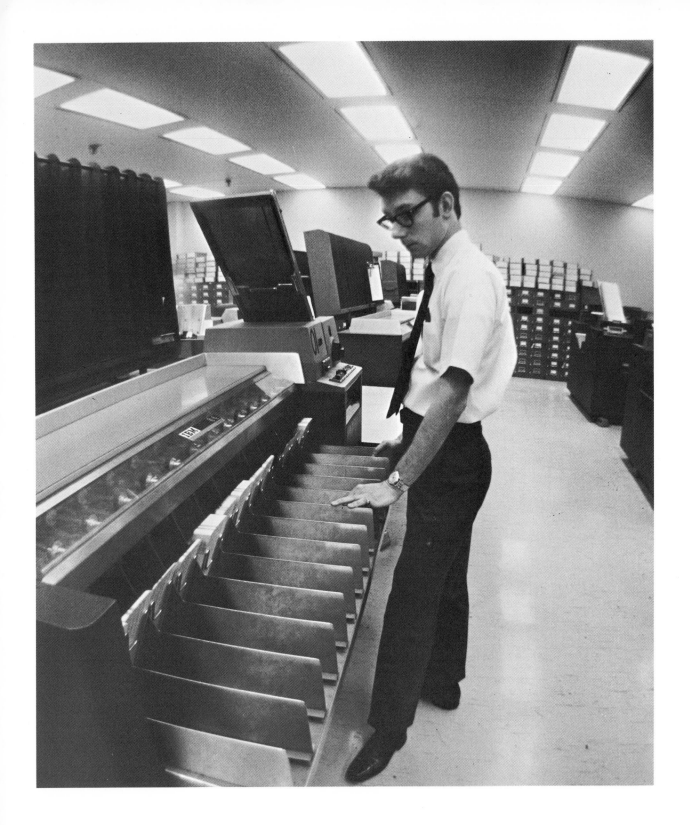

▌ DESCRIPTION OF THE PUNCHED CARD

HISTORY OF THE PUNCHED CARD

GENERAL CHARACTERISTICS OF PUNCHED CARDS

CODING DATA IN PUNCHED CARDS

ALTERNATIVE CARD TYPES AND SIZES

▌ PUNCHED CARD DATA PROCESSING EQUIPMENT
AND PROCEDURES

PREPARING THE PUNCHED CARDS

SORTING AND COLLATING

CONTROL PANELS

CALCULATING AND PRINTING

OTHER EQUIPMENT

▌ AN ILLUSTRATION OF PUNCHED CARD DATA
PROCESSING

▌ SUMMARY

▌ EXERCISES

A REVIEW
OF PUNCHED CARD
DATA PROCESSING

The importance of punched cards to data processing is indicated by the fact that billions of punched cards are used each year. For example, over 100 billion cards were estimated to have been used during the year 1966. Not only is punched card processing a significant method of data processing, but, in addition, punched cards are the most common input medium for computer processing, and many small computer systems use cards for file storage. These card-oriented computer systems constitute roughly one-third of all computer data processing installations. When a computer system uses punched cards as file storage, processing requires much of the same equipment as a punched card installation. In fact, one of the trends in computers is the emergence of the low-cost card-oriented computer system to replace punched card processing systems. An understanding of punched card data processing is therefore a desirable background for the study of computer data processing.

This chapter explains the preparation and use of punched cards, describes the major items of equipment used in punched card installations, and presents an illustration of the application of punched cards to business data processing.

▍ DESCRIPTION OF THE PUNCHED CARD

HISTORY OF THE PUNCHED CARD

The punched card was developed because of the difficulty of performing a massive data tabulation task—the United States census, which, by constitutional provision, must be taken every ten years. In the 1880s, the tabulation was moving so slowly on the 1880 census data that the Census Bureau sought mechanical aids for use with the 1890 census. In response to this need, Herman Hollerith developed a tabulating device which he called a census machine. The census data was punched into cards which were tabulated by the census machine. The approach worked so well that Hollerith left the Census Bureau in 1896 to form the Tabulating Machine Company to manufacture and sell his equipment. Through mergers, this company became a part of International Business Machines Corporation (usually referred to as IBM).

As shown in Figure 2–1, the Hollerith or IBM card has 80 columns and rectangular punches. An alternative type of card is the 90-column card using round holes. This was developed by James Powers, also of the Census Bureau. This approach was marketed by a company which became a part of Remington Rand (now a division of Sperry Rand Corporation). This 90-column card shown in Figure 2–2 is referred to as a Remington Rand card. The 80-column Hollerith card dominates the field, and will be used throughout the text.

GENERAL CHARACTERISTICS OF PUNCHED CARDS

The standard punched card, made from paper stock, is 7⅜ by 3¼ in. and .007 in. thick. The corners may either be sharp or rounded, and one corner is usually cut to help keep the cards right end up in processing.

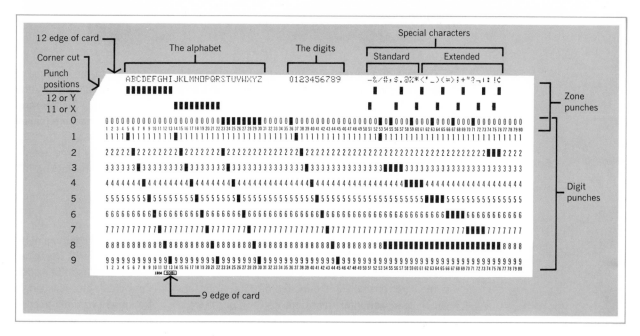

FIGURE 2–1   80-column punched card

FIGURE 2–2   90-column punched card

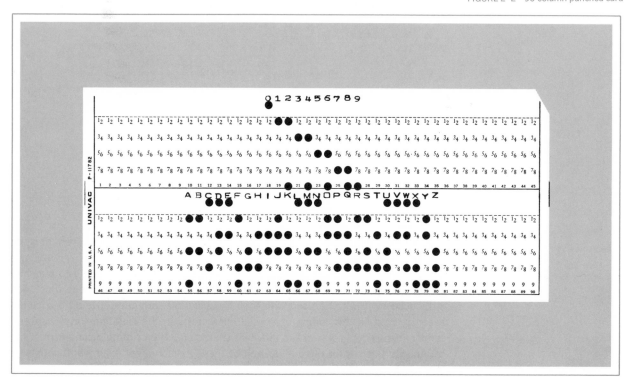

The face of a card may have any printing the customer desires. In the absence of special printing, the card usually has numbers on each column which identify the 0–9 punching positions. The area along the top edge is used for printing the interpretation of the punches in the column below. By the use of a special machine (called an interpreter) the printing can be placed elsewhere on the card.

The cost of standard punched cards, when purchased in reasonably large quantities, runs about $1.00 per 1,000 cards, or ⅒¢ each. Colored cards, special imprinting, etc., increase the cost slightly.

CODING DATA IN PUNCHED CARDS

As can be seen from Figure 2–1, a Hollerith card consists of 80 vertical columns numbered 1 to 80. There are 12 positions or rows in each column of the card. These are designated as the 12, 11, and 0 to 9 punch positions. If the number 2 is to be coded in the card, position 2 is punched out; if a 4, position 4 is punched, etc. This single punch code works for the numerics 0–9, but there are not enough positions to code the alphabetic and special characters. This coding is done by using two or three punches in the same column. The top three punch positions (12, 11, and 0) are designated as the zone for coding characters other than the numerics. The 0–9 positions are the numeric or digit punches (0 is used both as a zone or a numeric punch). An alphabetic is coded as one zone punch and one numeric punch. For example:

PUNCHES

LETTER	ZONE	NUMERIC
A	12	1
B	12	2
.		
.		
.		
K	11	2
L	11	3
.		
.		
.		
X	0	7
Y	0	8

Special characters—comma, period, dollar sign, etc.—are coded by one, two, or three punches.

There are two different codes (sets of punches) for encoding data into punched cards. The first is the standard code, and the second is an extended code which was introduced by IBM to be used with their System/360 computer. The difference between them is in the coding of special characters. In the traditional code, several combinations could refer to two different characters. The printing mechanism of the card punch was set for the one desired by the installation. For example, the installation could choose to have a pound sign (#) or an equal sign (=) but not both, since

TABLE 2-1   Punch Positions in Standard Code and Extended Code

| | SAME CODING—BOTH CODES | | | DIFFERENT PUNCH POSITIONS | | |
CHARACTER	PUNCH POSITION	CHARACTER	PUNCH POSITION	CHARACTER	STANDARD	EXTENDED
A	12, 1	1	1	<	—	12, 4, 8
B	12, 2	2	2	>	—	0, 6, 8
C	12, 3	3	3	+	12	12, 6, 8
D	12, 4	4	4	.	—	0, 5, 8
E	12, 5	5	5	)	12, 4, 8	11, 5, 8
F	12, 6	6	6	(	0, 4, 8	12, 5, 8
G	12, 7	7	7	¢	—	12, 2, 8
H	12, 8	8	8	:	—	2, 8
I	12, 9	9	9	;	—	11, 6, 8
J	11, 1	0	0	⌐	—	11, 7, 8
K	11, 2	—	11	'	4, 8	5, 8
L	11, 3	&	12	?	—	0, 7, 8
M	11, 4	.	12, 3, 8	"	—	7, 8
N	11, 5	$	11, 3, 8	=	3, 8	6, 8
O	11, 6	,	0, 3, 8	!	—	11, 2, 8
P	11, 7	#	3, 8	⌊	—	12, 7, 8
Q	11, 8	*	11, 4, 8	⊐	12, 4, 8	—
R	11, 9	%	0, 4, 8			
S	0, 2	@	4, 8			
T	0, 3	/	0, 1			
U	0, 4					
V	0, 5					
W	0, 6					
X	0, 7					
Y	0, 8					
Z	0, 9					

the coding for these is identical. The new, extended code has a unique set of punches for each special character. Both codes are shown in Table 2-1. It is not necessary to memorize these codes, but it is useful to understand the concept of encoding data on punched cards.

ALTERNATIVE CARD TYPES AND SIZES

Edge-notched cards (Figure 2-3) are an approach to using the unit record concept without mechanical sorting equipment. The card is encoded by notching the edge. Four positions labeled 7, 4, 2, and 1 are used for coding each digit. For example, the digit 3 is coded by a 2 and 1 notches and the digit 8 by a 7 and 1 notches. As shown in Figure 2-4, the cards are sorted by inserting a needle through the position being examined. All cards with the edge notched will fall out. By performing this operation in a specific order, the cards can be sorted or cards with specified characteristics coded in them can be located.

FIGURE 2–3 Edge-notched card (Courtesy of Litton Automated Business Systems)

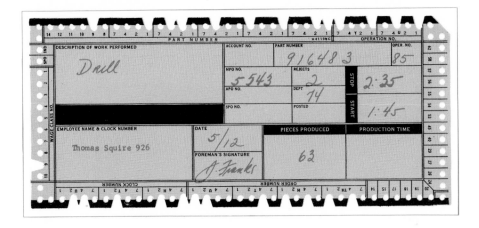

FIGURE 2–3 Edge-notched card (Courtesy of Litton Automated Business Systems)

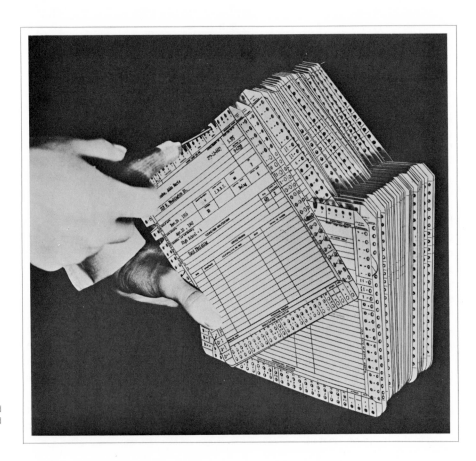

FIGURE 2–4 Sorting edge-notched cards (Courtesy of Litton Automated Business Systems)

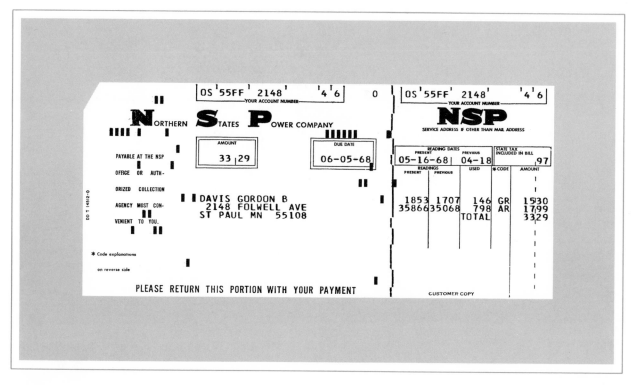

FIGURE 2–5 Perforated card used for customer billing

In addition to regular-size 80- or 90-column cards, there are small-size punched cards. One of the most popular is the 51-column card. This is used extensively in billing customers. A full-size 80-column card is prepared and sent to the customers. The billing information is printed on the face of the card in two sections—the one section for the customer, the other to be returned. The card is perforated so that the customer can separate the 51-column section to return with his payment. The 29-column section, with all relevant information on it, is retained by the customer. A typical perforated card is shown in Figure 2–5. When returned, the 51-column section is read by a special attachment to the card equipment. In some cases, as an alternative, a smaller 22-column section is the one which is returned.

A type of punched card used primarily in retailing is the price tag section. The price tag is divided into perforated sections. One section, in which information on size, color, etc. has been punched, is torn off when a sale is made (Figure 2–6). The information on the tag is read by a special reader and converted to other media, such as punched cards or magnetic tape for further processing.

Edge-punched cards are used for some applications (Figure 2–7). The card is punched along the edge with rows of small holes. These must be read by special equipment and converted to other media for further processing to take place.

FIGURE 2–6 Machine-readable tag (Courtesy of Dennison Manufacturing Company)

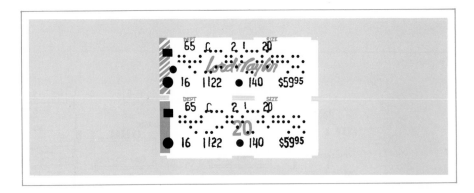

FIGURE 2–7 Edge-punched card (Courtesy of Friden, Inc.)

▍ PUNCHED CARD DATA PROCESSING EQUIPMENT AND PROCEDURES
Punched card data processing is based on the concept of the unit record—one card is used for encoding each transaction or for storing each master record (record containing permanent information). If the transaction data or master record data will not fit on one card, a set of two or more cards can be used, but this is avoided if

possible. The cards following the first card in the set are termed trailer cards. A group of the cards representing a given type of record or transaction is called a card deck.

In most applications, the data to be processed has been recorded on a written or typed source document. Examples are a sales invoice, a receiving report, a questionnaire, etc. The data on the document is coded into a punched card, and for processing purposes the punched card then takes the place of the original document. The main advantage of punched cards is that, once encoded into cards, data may then be processed by machine (Figure 2–8). The major processing steps are sorting, merging, calculating, and printing.

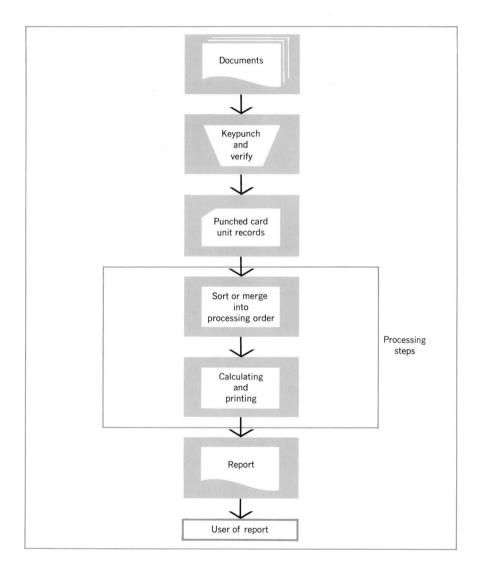

FIGURE 2–8 The unit record approach

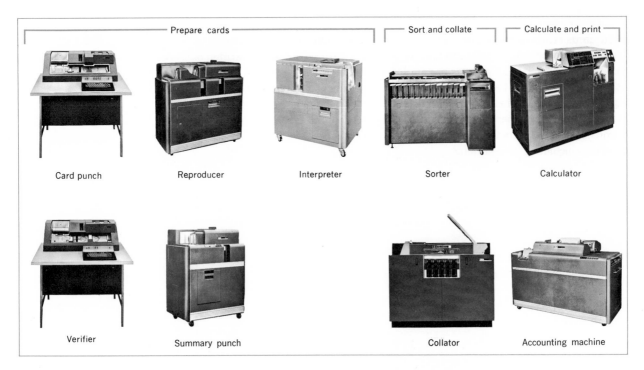

FIGURE 2–9 Equipment in a punched card data processing installation (Courtesy of International Business Machines Corporation)

In order to implement punched card data processing, there must be equipment to prepare the punched card, to sort and to merge (collate) decks of cards, and to calculate and print results. Figure 2–9 shows the basic equipment which is usually found in a punched card data processing installation.

This chapter will explain how the basic functions of card processing are performed and will describe the equipment used. Since IBM dominates the punched card processing field, the illustrations will use mainly IBM equipment.

PREPARING THE PUNCHED CARDS

The data to be processed by punched card equipment must be transcribed into a punched card. The most common way for doing this is with the card punch machine. Other methods are hand punching, punching as a by-product of other processing and mark sensing.

There are four 80-column card punches in common use. These are:

CARD PUNCH	CHARACTERISTIC
IBM model 24	Punching but no printing at top of card
IBM model 26	Prints interpretation of character being punched on top of card
IBM model 29	Has extended code related to IBM System/360 computer
UNIVAC model 1701	Allows correction of erroneous key strokes before card is punched

Since these units are very similar, the new IBM 29 printing card punch is used to illustrate this type of equipment. Figure 2–10 shows the model 29 punch and identifies its components. The card punch consists basically of an input hopper for cards to be punched, a mechanism for moving the card from the input hopper to the punching station, a keyboard for the operator to indicate the punches to be made, an output stacker for cards which have been punched, a reading station used in connection with reproducing part or all of a card, and various control keys, switches, etc.

It is useful for the student of data processing to understand how to operate a card punch. There are occasions when it may be necessary to personally punch a few cards for reasons such as replacing a damaged or incorrect card or preparing some

FIGURE 2–10 The IBM model 29 printing card punch (Courtesy of International Business Machines Corporation)

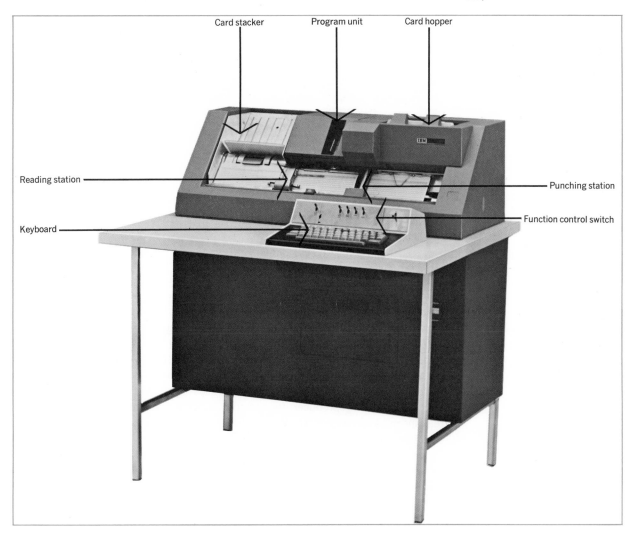

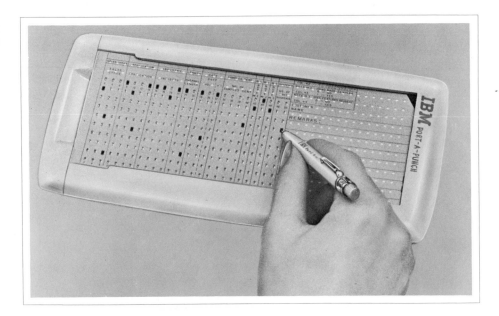

test data. Appendix I contains a short description of how to perform key punching and explains the use of the program card.

Although the mechanical card punch is the most common way of preparing punched cards, there are also other methods:

Manual punches
Mark sensing
Punching as a by-product
Conversion from another media to cards

In one manual punching approach the punching positions on the card are scored so that punching on a position with a pencil or stylus will cause the rectangular punch to fall out. IBM offers the Port-A-Punch, consisting of a holder and template to implement this method (Figure 2–11). Other small manual punches are also available.

The mark sensing approach requires the marking of a specific area of the card with a soft pencil (Figure 2–12). There are two methods for reading the marks. One method requires the mark to be made with a soft-leaded pencil so that the mark can be sensed electrically. The other method uses equipment which reads the mark optically. The IBM reproducer, for example, has an attachment which can electrically read the marks on a card. The data is then punched in selected columns of the same card from which it was read.

Cards are also prepared as a by-product of other processing steps. For example, several manufacturers provide an attachment to an electric typewriter or to electric bookkeeping machines which will produce a punched card containing selected data being typed on the typewriter or bookkeeping machine keyboard (Figure 2–13).

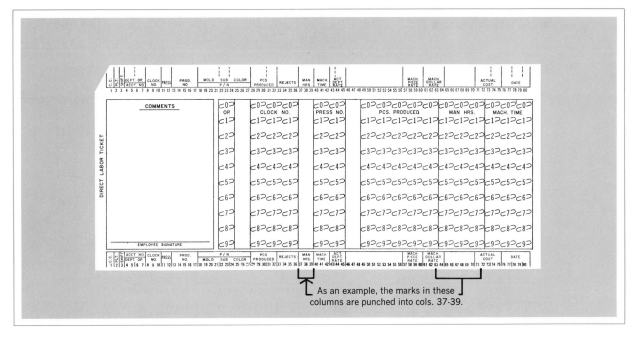

As an example, the marks in these columns are punched into cols. 37-39.

FIGURE 2–12 Mark-sense cards

FIGURE 2–13 Typewriter with edge-punched card attachment (Courtesy of Friden, Inc.)

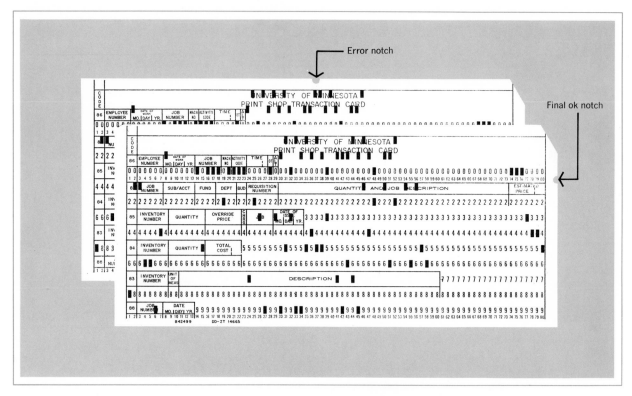

FIGURE 2–14 Illustration of verifier notch on incorrect card (top) and correct card (bottom)

When cards are punched on a keypunch, how can the user be assured that the punching was performed correctly? With only a few cards, the punching can be checked visually. However, for large volumes of cards, the most common method is to check the punching with a machine called a verifier. When using an IBM verifier, the cards which have been punched and the documents from which they were punched are given to a second operator who has a machine almost identical to the keypunch except it does no punching. The verifier operator puts the punched cards in the input hopper of the verifier and then keys the data from the input document just as if she were doing the original punching. If the operator keys a different character from the one punched, the keyboard locks. If this happens, the verifier operator checks her work and keys it again. If there is no agreement after three tries, the card is notched at the top directly above the column found to be in error. If the entire card is correct, a notch is automatically placed at the right hand edge, as shown by Figure 2–14.

SORTING AND COLLATING

Data for processing is not usually recorded in any order, so that the cards punched from the data must be put into a sequence before a report or analysis can be prepared. If data is classified one way for one report and a second way for another report, it will need to be sequenced for the first report and then sorted into a different sequence for the second report.

Sorting is the arranging of data into a sequence. Collating is a related operation— the comparing and merging of two or more card decks into a single combined deck. Sorting is performed with a sorter; collating requires a separate collator machine.

A card sorter can be used for three basic types of operations: sequencing, grouping, and selecting.

CLASSIFICATION	DESCRIPTION
Sequencing	Process of arranging data in alphabetic or numeric order. The order can be either ascending or descending. For example, inventory transaction cards might be arranged in part number order.
Grouping	Process of arranging like items together. For example, all sales for a period from each customer might be grouped together.
Selecting	Process of selecting a desired item or items from a file of data. For example, an analysis might require only those transactions from territory 4.

The basic procedure for sorting is quite simple. Using an IBM sorter (Figure 2–15) as the basis for an example, a sorter consists of an input hopper, a mechanism to select the column on which to sort, and thirteen pockets for the sorted cards. Twelve

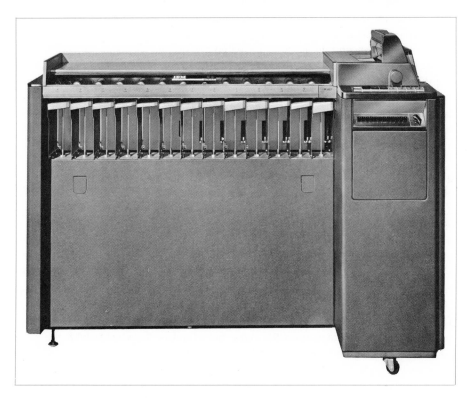

FIGURE 2–15 Card sorter (Courtesy of International Business Machines Corporation)

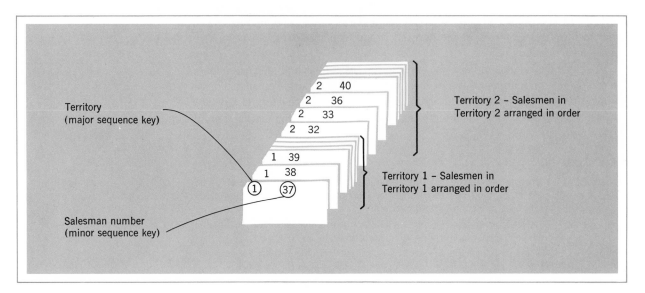

Territory
(major sequence key)

Salesman number
(minor sequence key)

Territory 2 – Salesmen in
Territory 2 arranged in order

Territory 1 – Salesmen in
Territory 1 arranged in order

FIGURE 2–16 Arrangement of card
deck based on two sort keys

of the pockets are for the 12 punch positions in a column on a punched card, and the thirteenth is for blanks or rejects. The sensing mechanisms are either wire brushes or photoelectric cells.

A card is sequenced into an order based on one or more fields in the cards to be sorted (called a sort key). As an example of sequencing on one field, payroll cards might be sorted on the employee identification field. At the end of the sort, the card deck will be in employee number order. As an example of sequencing on two fields, cards might be sorted into salesman identification number order (called the minor sort) within a larger classification by territory (major sort). This concept of major and minor sequence is illustrated by Figure 2–16.

To illustrate how sorting is performed, assume a payroll file which is to be sequenced by employee identification number. The identification field contains six digits. A typical employee might thus be numbered 376428. In order to sort the file, it is necessary to pass the cards through the sorter six times, once for each column of the field, because each pass sorts on only one column. The sorting is performed from right to left. The first pass (on the rightmost or units position) will sort all employee cards having a number ending in 0 into the 0 pocket of the sorter, all cards with a number ending in 1 into the 1 pocket, etc. To end up with a deck sorted in ascending order (0, 1, 2, 3, etc.), the cards are taken from the pockets so that the ones in the zero pocket are put face down on the bottom of the deck (Figure 2–17). The deck in the example is then placed back in the input hopper of the sorter and sorted on the second digit from the right, pulled out of the stacker with the zero pocket contents on the bottom, 1s next, etc. This process is continued for each digit of the sort field. After the sort on the last position of the field (in this case, the sixth), the deck is in numerical order. For a descending sort (in order 9, 8, 7, etc.) the only difference in procedure would be to put those in the 9s pocket face down on the bottom followed by the 8s, 7s, etc.

After each pass, the operator can test the accuracy of the sort by sighting through the cards from each pocket. Since all the cards in the 9s pocket should have a 9 punch in the position just sorted, one can see light through the deck at that position. One can also push a small sort needle through the position to test the sort. It is considered good practice to make such an eye or needle test of each sort pocket.

If the field on which the sort is made is alphabetic (such as a name), two passes are required for each column—once on the zone and once on the numeric portion. This means that it requires twice as many passes to sort on alphabetic data as to sort on numeric data. There are various sorting techniques which build upon the basic method presented here, but a description of these is beyond the scope of this chapter.

Collating is the comparing and merging together of two decks which are each in the same sequence. For example, if one card deck consists of all payroll cards for female employees sequenced by payroll number and another consists of all payroll cards for males, a single payroll deck for all employees, sequenced on payroll num-

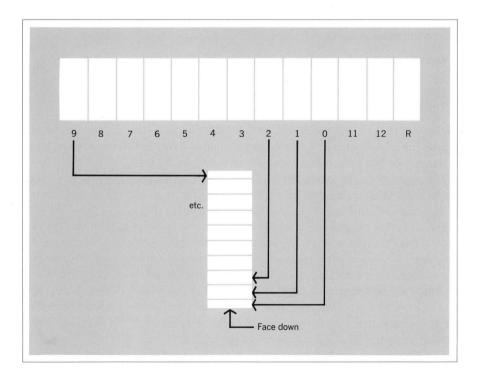

FIGURE 2-17 Taking the cards from the sorter in an ascending sort

ber, is formed by collating the two. This collation can be performed by resorting the combined decks with a sorter (if the payroll number fields are in the same column in both decks), but this is not as efficient or as fast as using a special device, a collator. Also, the use of the collator does not require the fields controlling the merging operation to be in the same columns.

The functions which can be performed by the collator are not limited to the simple merging of two decks. The following operations can be handled either individually or in combination by a collator.

OPERATION	DISCUSSION
Merging	An example is the merging of a customer data file with an address file in order to prepare a mailing.
Sequence checking	Checking to see if the file is in proper sequence. This can be used for verifying the correctness of a prior sort.
Matching	Checking for unmatched cards in files being merged in cases where there should be a matching card in each file to be merged, e.g., a data card and a corresponding address card.
Selection	The collator can be set to select cards meeting certain selection criteria, e.g., all sales greater than a specified amount to a specified class of customers.

An example will illustrate the way a collator is used. During the month of January, an employer must send to each employee who worked during the preceding calendar year, a statement showing:

The amount earned
The Federal taxes withheld
The amount earned that was subject to Social Security
The amount of the Social Security tax withheld (also called FICA)

Two copies (B and C) of this report, called a W-2 (Figure 2–18), are sent to the employee; the original, or copy A, is sent to the Internal Revenue Service. The employee attaches copy B to his tax return and retains copy C for his files.

The employer has two different files which must be merged. The first is a file of name and address cards, one for each employee (Figure 2–18); the second is a file of accumulated earnings cards, one for each employee (Figure 2–18), which were prepared during the processing of the employee pay. In order to print out the W-2 report, there must be a single file of cards in which the name and address card for an employee is immediately followed by his accumulated earnings card. The merging is performed on the collator, which will reject all unmatched cards, i.e., a name and address card with no accumulated earnings card or the reverse (Figure 2–19). Why should there be any unmatched cards? There should not, but they may be caused by cards having gotten out of order, by lost cards, or by errors in the punching of the field on which the cards are matched.

The IBM collator has two input hoppers for the two decks being merged (Figure 2–20). One is called the primary feed hopper and the other the secondary feed

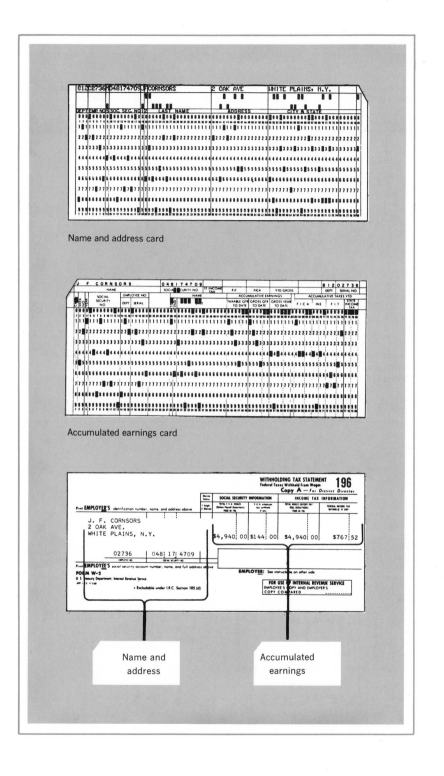

Name and address card

Accumulated earnings card

FIGURE 2–18 Name and address card, accumulated earnings card, and W-2 report (Courtesy of International Business Machines Corporation)

FIGURE 2–19 Merging of decks to prepare W-2 reports

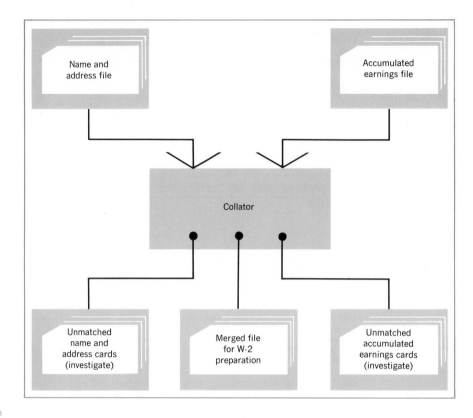

FIGURE 2–20 Path of cards through IBM collator

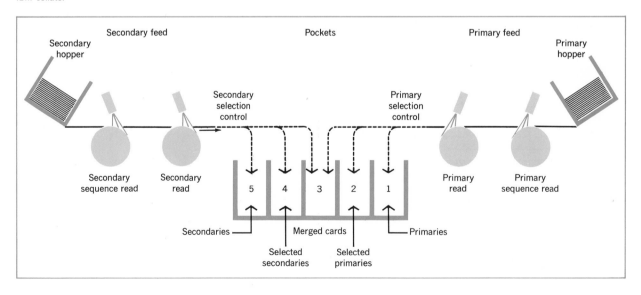

hopper. There are two sets of reading brushes for the cards from the primary feed hopper (the second set is used for sequence checking), and, depending on the model, one or two sets for the secondary feed hopper. There may, depending on the model, be four or five stacker pockets. In general these pockets will be used as follows:

STACKER NO.	CONTENTS
1	Unmatched items from primary feed hopper Out-of-sequence cards when doing sequence check only
2	Selected items fed from primary test hopper
3	Merged items from both feed hoppers or in-sequence cards from a sequence check
4	Selected items from secondary feed
5	Unmatched items from secondary feed

A card is put into one of the output stackers of the collator based on a test made by a small device in the collator called a selector-comparing unit. The brushes which read the data fields being compared are connected to the selector-comparing unit. Based on a comparison, the unit can indicate a result of equal, high, or low. The output of the selector-comparing unit is connected to the mechanism which determines which stacker the card will drop into. The wiring which connects the reading brushes to the selector-comparing unit and connects this unit to the stacker mechanism is done by means of a control panel.

CONTROL PANELS

The collator and other machines to be explained (reproducer, interpreter, and accounting machine) are instructed by means of a removable wired control panel (Figure 2–21). This panel provides flexibility to these machines because changing the control panel changes the set of instructions governing the machine. The panels range from a very simple one for an interpreter to fairly complex ones for some applications on accounting machines.

The panel contains rows of holes which pass through the panel. Each of these holes, called a hub, contains a metal socket into which a connecting wire can be plugged. When the control panel is inserted in the machine, each socket is connected to internal wiring. Thus, joining two hubs with a wire on the control panel has the effect of connecting two circuits in the machine. This connection causes various operations to be performed (Figure 2–22). In the case of the collator, for example, panel wires connect the reading brush circuits with the comparing unit and the comparing unit result circuits (low, equal, high) with the stacker pocket controls.

The process of control panel wiring or board wiring usually involves the preparation of a wiring diagram before the panel is wired. This diagram is drawn on a sheet which shows the hubs of the control panel. Not only is this drawing useful in the planning of the wiring, it is also a major part of the documentation describing the wiring panel (Figure 2–23). Complex panels in frequent use are not disassembled but are kept

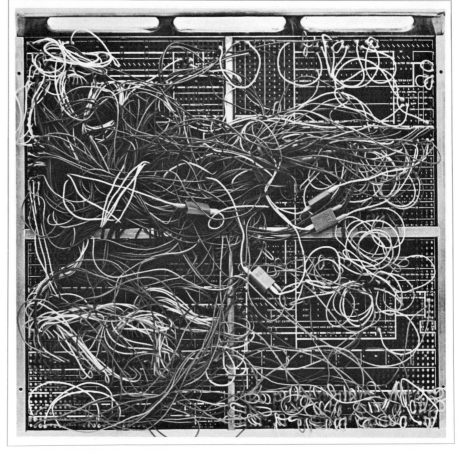

FIGURE 2–21 Wired control panel (Courtesy of International Business Machines Corporation)

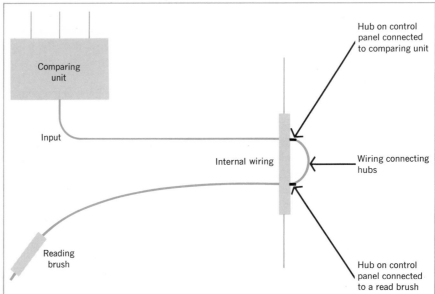

FIGURE 2–22 Example of use of panel wire to complete connection with internal circuits (on a collator)

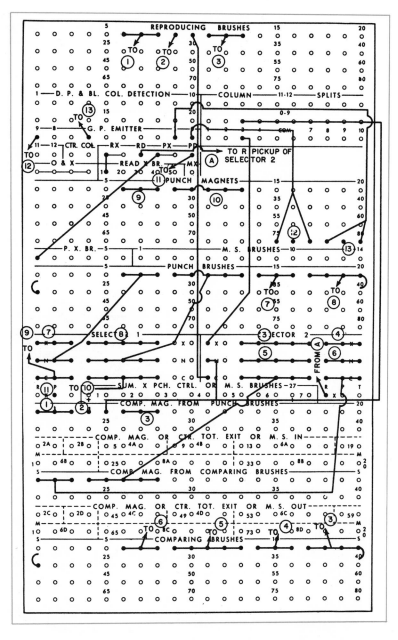

FIGURE 2-23 Wiring diagram (for reproducer) Courtesy of International Business Machines Corporation)

permanently wired. Panels that are used infrequently are disassembled and rewired for each use. The wiring diagram forms a means for restoring any wires which may come undone in a permanent panel and a basis for rewiring an infrequently used panel.

A panel can become fairly complex, and therefore many installations use different-colored connecting wires to help identify the wiring. The details of panel wiring are beyond the scope of this text. There are several programmed learning or self-study texts available for the wiring of the control panels for different machines.

CALCULATING AND PRINTING

In punched card data processing, separate machines have usually been used for calculating and printing. The calculating unit is typified by the IBM 602 or 604 calculating punch or the 609 calculator; the printing function is illustrated by an IBM 402 or 407 accounting machine. The operation of these is programmed by a wired control panel.

The calculating punch (Figure 2–24 shows the IBM 609) reads information from punched cards and performs addition, subtraction, multiplication, and division. It

FIGURE 2–24 IBM 609 calculating punch (Courtesy of International Business Machines Corporation)

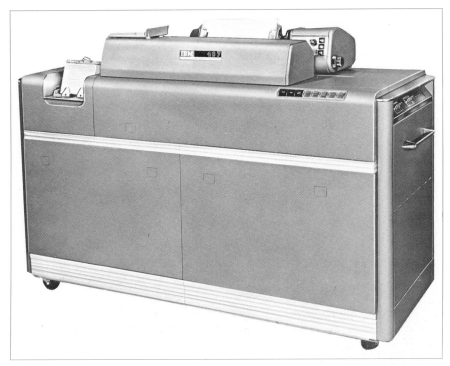

FIGURE 2–25 IBM 407 accounting machine (Courtesy of International Business Machines Corporation)

can also test the sign (positive or negative) of a value and perform alternate calculations depending on the result. The result of the calculations can be punched either in the same card from which the data was read or into cards which follow it.

The accounting machine prepares printed output from cards which have been punched and sequenced by the other machines—card punch, sorter, collator, calculator, etc. The printed output includes statements, invoices, checks, management reports, etc. The accounting machine (Figure 2–25 shows an IBM 407 accounting machine) can also be wired to summarize numerical data found on the cards and to print this summary information. The machine has internal counters which can add and subtract data read from the cards. The data from the card can be rearranged, using the wired control panel, so that it is printed in a meaningful way on a form or on a report.

Card equipment is very slow compared to the speeds associated with most computer systems. For example:

UNIT NO.	MAXIMUM SPEED
IBM 602 calculating punch	50 cards per minute
IBM 604 calculating punch	100 cards per minute
IBM 609 calculator	200 cards per minute
IBM 402 accounting machine	100–150 lines per minute (50–100 cards)
IBM 407 accounting machine	150 lines per minute (150 cards)

FIGURE 2-26 Electronic card processor (UNIVAC 1004) (Courtesy of UNIVAC Division of Sperry Rand Corporation)

FIGURE 2-26 Electronic card processor (UNIVAC 1004) (Courtesy of UNIVAC Division of Sperry Rand Corporation)

By way of contrast, a medium-speed computer system will read cards at from 600 to 1,200 per minute, punch cards at about 100–300 cards per minute, and print at from 300 to 1,200 lines per minute.

The electronic card processor combines many of the features of both card processing and computers. This class of equipment is illustrated by the UNIVAC 1004 electronic card processor (Figure 2–26). This unit is programmed with a wired panel but has limited internal storage. It can read cards, calculate, and print at speeds up to 600 cards and 600 lines per minute.

OTHER EQUIPMENT

In order to complete the review of punched card data processing three additional units will be described. These are the interpreter, reproducer, and summary punch.

When cards are punched with a printing card punch, the characters can be printed along the top of the card directly above the columns punched, but this may not always be satisfactory because the printing cannot be spaced or otherwise rearranged. Cards which are prepared on a reproducer or summary punch have no printing on them to identify the punches. The *interpreter* is used to print on the card part or all of the data punched in it. The data may be printed in a different sequence and with different spacing from that with which it is punched. Normally interpretation appears at the top of the card, although some models will print on any of 25 lines on the card (Figure 2–27). Typical speeds of operation range up to 100 lines per minute. The interpretation is controlled by a wired panel.

A *reproducer* performs three functions: reproducing, gang punching, and summary punching. In reproducing, part or all of one card may be reproduced in another. The sequence in which the data is punched may also be changed. Cards to be reproduced are placed in one input hopper and blank cards into a second input hopper. The reproduction, done at speeds up to 100 cards per minute, is directed by a wired control panel. A comparison feature examines the reproduced card to check for agreement with the card being copied.

Gang punching is the copying of punched information from a master card into each of a set of detail cards which follow it. For example, the detail transaction cards for a payroll, one for each man, may have been punched without inserting the date of the payroll. Since this is a constant for all of the detail cards, this can be added by gang punching.

Summary punching is the automatic punching of a summary card containing the total of a particular data item from a set of detail cards. Summary punching may be performed by a special summary punch machine or by a reproducer operating in conjunction with an accounting machine. The two machines are connected by a cable,

FIGURE 2–27 Example of interpreting cards

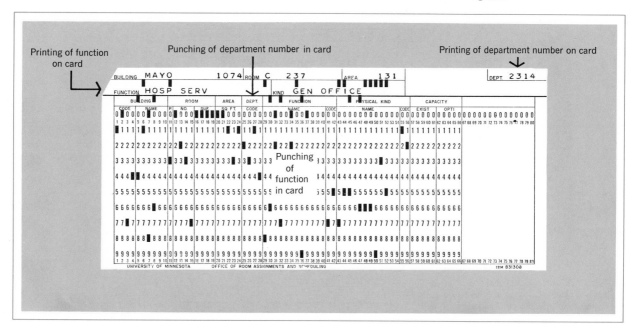

and when totals are accumulated for printing, they are also punched. The purpose of summary punching is to reduce card volume and obtain summary cards for processing.

▌ AN ILLUSTRATION OF PUNCHED CARD DATA PROCESSING

A simple accounts receivable application will illustrate the use of punched cards in data processing. Accounts receivable would probably be only one of several applications put on punched cards, but to simplify the illustration all other applications will be ignored.

Accounts receivable represent the money owed to a company by its customers who have received merchandise or service on credit. The accounts receivable procedure includes provisions for recording all sales, payments, and credits, for maintaining a current record of accounts due, and for preparing customer statements (if this procedure is followed). There must be a method for establishing new accounts and for identifying late-paying accounts.

There are two different approaches to accounts receivable files—open item and

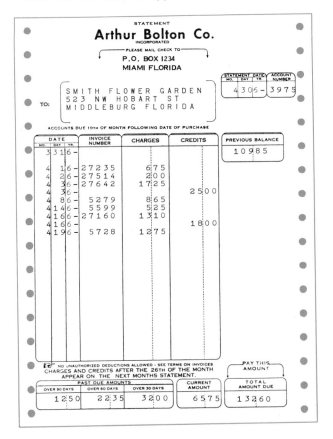

FIGURE 2-28 Example of balance forward statement (Courtesy of International Business Machines Corporation)

balance forward. Under the open item approach, the file contains a punched card for each unpaid invoice. This is used by many businesses because their customers pay individual invoices rather than a summary figure. When a payment is received, the related charge is removed from the files. Under the balance forward approach, used extensively for retail customers, a record is maintained of the balance owed at the beginning of the period and the new purchases or payments made during the period. Payments are applied against the balance rather than individual items. In other words, a payment reduces the amount the customer owes, and no attempt is made to identify which charge slips he is paying.

This example will use the balance forward approach. At the beginning of the period, there is a balance file created at the end of the prior period. This consists of punched cards, one per customer, giving the balance owing. For each transaction made during the period (purchase, payment, or credit) a punched card is added to the file. Thus, at the end of the period, the accounts receivable file contains the balance forward card (giving the balance at the beginning of the period) plus the transaction detail cards for the current period. The statement prepared at the end of the period shows the old balance, purchases, payments, and new balance (Figure 2–28). Special control procedures are necessary to make sure that no cards are lost or misplaced. An accounts receivable control sheet is maintained for this purpose. Each day's totals of charge purchases and payments or credits are posted to the control sheet (Figure 2–29). Periodically (or at the time of preparing the statements) the file is proved

FIGURE 2–29 Control sheet for accounts receivable file

Accounts Receivable Control Sheet						
						Month of _____
Date	Additions		Deductions				Balance
	Invoices billed	Miscellaneous	Payments received	Discounts allowed	Returns and allowances	Miscellaneous	

against this control by taking the total of the balance and detail cards and comparing this total control with the control sheet total.

Figure 2–30 illustrates the flow of work in preparing the detail cards for payments made by the customers. The symbols used in this flowchart and the one in Figure 2–31 will not be explained until Chapter 8. However, the simplicity of this flowchart and the detailed description of the process will make it understandable. The process consists of the following major steps:

1 Separation of checks and preparation of remittance advice for keypunching. The remittance advice, describing the payment made by a customer, may be a notice which the customer returns or a memo made out by the clerk opening the mail. If the customer is asked to return a punched card or a punched card stub, the steps for preparing detail cards would be a little different. Before sending the batch of remittance slips to keypunching, a total is taken of the payments represented by the batch of advices.
2 Preparation of detail payment cards. The data on the remittance advices is punched into payment cards, one card for each payment received.
3 Listing and proofing. The cards, punched and verified, are listed and a total prepared using an accounting machine. The list of all payments received that day represents the cash receipts register and is a reference in the event of inquiry. Therefore, the cards may be sorted in account number order before listing, or the remittance advices may be sorted in alphabetical order before being sent for punching. The control total taken before the remittance advices were punched is compared with the cash receipts register total. If they agree, the detail cards are approved for use with the accounts receivable file.

The preparation of the customer statements is diagrammed in Figure 2–31. The flowchart indicates that customer invoice and payment cards are sorted and merged at the time the statement is to be prepared. This sorting and merging could have taken place earlier, perhaps daily or weekly, depending on the volume of cards involved. The major steps in the statement procedure are the merging of the decks, the preparation of the statements, and the sorting and filing of the parts of the file.

1 Merging of the decks. The preparation of the statement for customers requires a separate set of cards for each one:
   a A name and address card
   b Balance forward card
   c The transaction cards for the period covered by the statement
   These are maintained as separate files prior to the statement preparation. The files are all in the customers' account number order (or sorted to be in that order), so that they can be merged using a collator.
2 Statement preparation. The statement (example in Figure 2–28) is prepared by an accounting machine which prints the name and address from the name and address card and the old balance from the balance forward card, lists the pur-

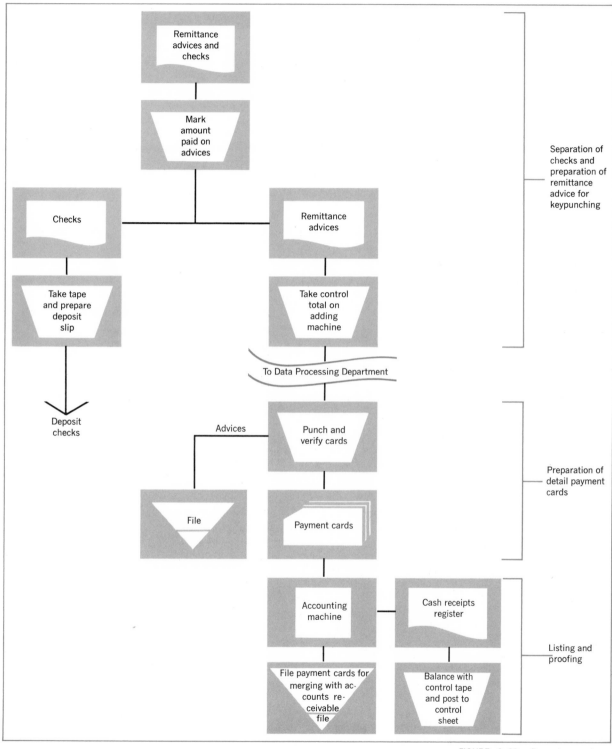

FIGURE 2–30 Preparing customer payment detail cards

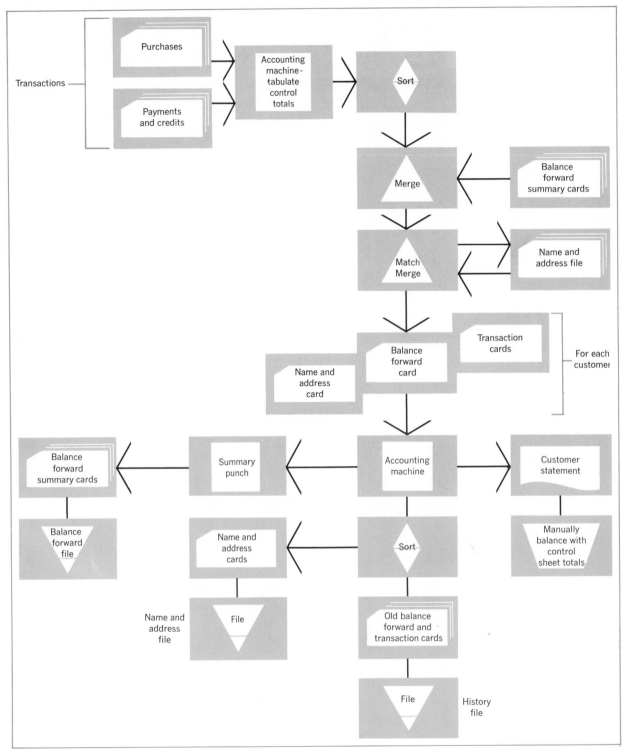

FIGURE 2-31 Preparation of customer statements

chases, payments, and credits, and totals these plus the old balance to give a new balance. The new balance is not only printed on the statement but is also punched, via a summary punch connected to the accounting machine, into a new balance forward summary card. The accounting machine keeps a total of all ending balances. At the end of the run this is checked against the total on the control sheet.

3 Sorting and filing. The summary cards are the new balance forward summary file. The name and address cards are removed with a sorter from the report preparation file and held for the next statement run or other use. The old balance and transaction cards are filed temporarily and then destroyed.

As part of the statement preparation, the account may have been aged to divide the balance into categories based on whether the amount owed is current, 30–60 days old, 60–90, 90–120, over 120, etc. This information could then be listed to provide an aged listing (trial balance) of customer accounts for use in credit followup, etc.

▌ SUMMARY

An understanding of unit record (punched card) data processing is a useful background for a study of computer-based data processing. This chapter has presented a review of punched cards, punched card processing equipment, and punched card processing procedures.

The equipment surveyed in the chapter included:

Card punch and verifier
Sorter
Collator
Calculator
Accounting machine
Interpreter
Reproducer
Summary punch

In order to show the sequence of steps in an actual data processing application, a simple statement preparation procedure was presented. This example covers the accumulation of detail transaction cards as well as the merging of these cards into a balance forward file for statement computation and printing.

▌ EXERCISES

1 Identify the card punches required to punch your name.
2 Identify the punch code to encode the following:
   MY DOG HAS 3,479 FLEAS.

3   How is the punch code for the IBM 29 keypunch different from the 26 punch?
4   What is the purpose of verification?
5   What are the major functions performed by the following punched card equipment:
    a   card punch
    b   verifier
    c   sorter
    d   collator
    e   calculating punch
    f   accounting machine
    g   interpreter
    h   reproducer
    i   summary punch
6   Describe the following and indicate which item of equipment is used:
    a   gang punching
    b   merging
    c   summarize data on cards
    d   check sequence of deck
    e   summary punching
    f   selection
7   Which of the units listed under question 5 use a wired control panel for specifying what the machine is to do?
8   Why is it important to maintain a control sheet such as the one described in the chapter for the accounts receivable application?
9   A data field of 6 digits is to be sorted into ascending order. There are 10,000 cards, and the card sorter to be used sorts at the rate of 1,000 cards per minute. Using a handling factor of 20 percent of the straight machine time, estimate the time required. Describe the steps in the sorting. How would the answer differ if the field were a 6-character name?
10 It has been estimated that there is, on the average, one sorting error in 10,000 cards passing through the sorter. What procedures can be used to detect these errors?
11 A keypunch operator makes a mistake. The cards are verified. What happens? Under what circumstances may the error not be detected in verification?
12 Describe the steps in wiring a control board.
13 What alternatives are there in the preparation of punched cards?

▌ DEFINITION OF A COMPUTER

▌ IMPORTANCE OF THE COMPUTER

▌ HISTORY OF COMPUTERS
CHARLES BABBAGE'S ANALYTIC ENGINE
BOOLEAN ALGEBRA
THE AUTOMATIC SEQUENCE CONTROLLED CALCULATOR—MARK I
THE ENIAC (ELECTRONIC NUMERICAL INTEGRATOR AND
CALCULATOR)
EDVAC, EDSAC, AND IAS
THE UNIVAC I (UNIVERSAL AUTOMATIC COMPUTER)
COMPUTERS SINCE THE UNIVAC I
SUMMARY OF EVENTS

▌ ELEMENTS OF A COMPUTER DATA PROCESSING
SYSTEM
HARDWARE
SOFTWARE
USER PROGRAMS
PROCEDURES
PERSONNEL
STEPS IN USING THE COMPUTER

▌ THE EQUIPMENT IN A COMPUTER CENTER
EQUIPMENT FOR COMPUTATION AND CONTROL
EQUIPMENT FOR SECONDARY STORAGE
INPUT DEVICES
OUTPUT DEVICES
DATA PREPARATION EQUIPMENT

▌ METHODS OF DATA PROCESSING
BATCH PROCESSING WITH SEQUENTIAL ACCESS FILE STORAGE
BATCH PROCESSING WITH DIRECT ACCESS FILE STORAGE
ONLINE PROCESSING

▌ SOME TYPICAL COMPUTER SYSTEM
CONFIGURATIONS
SMALL CARD-ORIENTED SYSTEM
SMALL MAGNETIC TAPE–ORIENTED SYSTEM
SMALL MAGNETIC DISC–ORIENTED SYSTEM
MEDIUM-SCALE BUSINESS SYSTEM

▌ SUMMARY

▌ EXERCISES

CHAPTER

3

A SURVEY OF COMPUTER DATA PROCESSING

One of the difficulties experienced when beginning to study computer data processing is understanding how the different operations and procedures fit together. The purpose of this chapter is to give an overview of computer data processing before proceeding, in the chapters which follow, to explain it in more detail. The chapter presents a short historical background along with the sequence of steps in using a computer, and it identifies the major items of equipment likely to be found in a computer installation.

▌ DEFINITION OF A COMPUTER

The term "computer" can logically be applied to any calculating device. However, in common usage, the term has come to refer rather specifically to an electronic computer. Early writers in the computer field frequently referred to the equipment as an automatic computer to differentiate it from other calculating devices. As generally understood, the computer has certain differentiating characteristics. These are:

1   *Electronic.* The computer uses electronic elements—transistors, resistors, diodes, etc. It operates with two-state logic based on two measurable states in these electronic components. This will be explained in Chapter 6.
2   *Internal storage.* The computer has an internal storage (frequently called memory) for storing both the program and data being processed by the program. The representation, storage, and retrieval of information in a computer is covered in Chapter 7.
3   *Stored program.* The program of instructions which specifies the sequence of operations to be followed is stored in the internal memory. It is the stored program which makes the computer "automatic" because the entire set of steps to be taken is determined in advance and no human intervention is required during execution. Principles of programming a computer are presented in Chapters 8 through 14.
4   *Program modification.* A distinguishing feature of computers is the ability to change the stored program of instructions during the execution of the program steps. The modification is usually based on the form, quantity, or value of the data being processed. Chapter 12 gives an explanation of concepts and methods of program modification.

In summary, a computer is an electronic computational device having internal storage, a stored program of instructions, and the capability for modification of the set of instructions during the execution of the program.

There are two main types of computers—*digital* and *analog*. The digital computer operates essentially by counting. All quantities are expressed as numbers. The analog computer operates by measuring rather than counting. Quantities are expressed as voltages which are read from meters. Computers which combine features of both analog and digital are called hybrid computers. Almost all electronic computers are digital and, for the purposes of this text, "computers" refers only to digital computers.

Digital computers may be categorized as to orientation:

1 Business data processing
2 Scientific computation
3 Process control

These distinctions do not always hold too clearly because the trend is to make a general-purpose computer which can be used for any of these purposes. In order to give some orientation to the reader, a brief summary of characteristics commonly associated with these categories is presented, but one should keep in mind that many computers are designed so that they can be used for any or all of these purposes.

Business data processing typically requires the processing of large numbers of records but with relatively little computation for each record. There is also a large volume of output in the form of reports. The computer that is oriented toward business data processing will therefore emphasize high-speed input and output and instructions to facilitate the conversion (editing) of stored data into report format.

Scientific computation is characterized by relatively little input or output but extensive internal computation. The scientific computer will emphasize high-speed internal processing but may have limited input and output capabilities.

Process control requires the computer to accept frequent inputs of data from the process being controlled (such as a chemical process), to test the data, and to make computations to adjust the process controls. The computer will usually be servicing several controls, so that the hardware is designed to accept and act on many concurrent or simultaneous inputs.

IMPORTANCE OF THE COMPUTER

In the short space of 18 years (1951 to 1969) the number of computers installed in the United States has grown to over 65,000. The value of these installations has been rising at a rapid rate and at the end of 1968 was about 20 billion dollars.

The computer is causing a revolution in the field of data processing. Not only is it allowing traditional data processing tasks to be performed much faster, but the computer also encourages the use of new and different methods. The impact of the computer on clerical workers may be seen in the fact that during the 1960s, when there was a rapid conversion to computers, there was a substantial reduction in the growth rate for numbers of clerical jobs. At the same time as the introduction of computers has reduced the numbers of clerical jobs, it has also created new job opportunities. These include the work of the systems analyst who designs the processing system, the programmer who writes the program of instructions, and the operator who runs the equipment.

Why is the computer such an important technological advance? The reason lies in

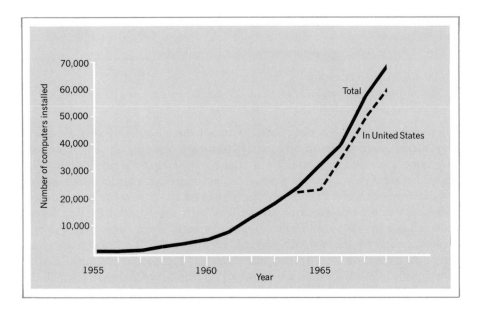

FIGURE 3–1 Number of computers installed by United States computer manufacturers
SOURCE: *Computers and Automation* monthly computer census

the fact that the computer is an extension of man's ability. Unaided, man is rather puny. He can lift perhaps 150–175 pounds, can move himself about at 5–10 miles per hour, and can perform on the order of 10 to 15 additions of 5-digit numbers per minute. Aided by equipment which extends his ability, a man may lift thousands of pounds, move himself about at speeds of thousands of miles per hour, and perform millions of computations per minute. The computer is not only an extension of man's ability to compute, it also expands his ability to store and retrieve data, to manipulate symbols, and to make decisions.

▌ HISTORY OF COMPUTERS

The history of computers starts in 1939 with Howard Aiken and the Mark I, but it is interesting to note that an inventor named Charles Babbage had conceived the design of an automatic computer well over a hundred years before. Another nineteenth-century event, the development of Boolean algebra, is important because of its application to the design of computers.

CHARLES BABBAGE'S ANALYTIC ENGINE

In 1812, Charles Babbage, Lucasian Professor of Mathematics at Cambridge University, devised a machine to automatically calculate trigonometric and logarithmic tables. It was called a *difference engine* because it used a difference method of computation. Babbage received a large government grant to develop his difference engine, but the project turned out to be something of a flop because the machine was beyond the technological capabilities of the time.

The difference engine was designed to carry out a single sequence of operations, but Babbage also conceived a different type of machine, an *analytic engine*, which would execute a changeable sequence of operations and would have internal storage for data. The design features of the analytic engine are remarkably close to the stored-program concepts of modern computers. Nothing came of this idea because, as with many of his ideas, it was too far advanced to be implemented with the existing technology.

BOOLEAN ALGEBRA

As will be explained in Chapters 5 and 6, a computer operates with two-state logic. Boolean algebra is applicable to the design of computers because it is a systematic method of analysis in which there are only two values. Developed by George Boole, who in 1854 published *The Laws of Thought*, Boolean algebra represents logic in mathematical symbols and provides rules for calculating the truth or falsity of statements. The two values in the algebra are *true*, which may be represented by 1, and *false*, represented by 0. The mathematical operations are:

OPERATION	SYMBOLS USED	COMMENT
NOT	$\sim$ or $-$	Negation. Reverses the value of what follows
AND	$\wedge$ or $\cap$	Similar to multiplication
OR	$\vee$ or $\cup$	Similar to addition

This concept of statement logic may be illustrated with some simple statements about an individual:

He is happy or he is rich
He is happy and he is rich

If "he is happy" is represented by A and "he is rich" by B, then the first statement can be symbolically represented as $A \vee B$ (A OR B) and the second by $A \wedge B$ (A AND B). A truth table is a tabular representation which summarizes the different combinations of truth values which may apply to the individual elements and shows the resulting truth values for the statement. The truth values for $A \wedge B$ and $A \vee B$ are shown in Table 3–1, with true being represented by 1 and false by 0. Note that the

TABLE 3–1   Truth Table

ALL COMBINATIONS OF TRUTH VALUES FOR ELEMENTS		TRUTH VALUE FOR STATEMENTS	
A	B	$A \wedge B$	$A \vee B$
1	1	1	1
1	0	0	1
0	1	0	1
0	0	0	0

statement $A \vee B$ (he is happy or he is rich) is false only if both ''he is happy'' and ''he is rich'' are false while the statement $A \wedge B$ (he is happy and he is rich) is false if either of the elements is false.

The Boolean analysis can be applied to networks of switches. If a switch is open, it can be described as false, and if it is closed, as true. A network is true if current flows through it to the output line. Therefore, two switches A and B which operate in series such that there is current at the output line C only if both switches are closed is described in Boolean terms as $A \wedge B$. If the two switches A and B present alternative paths to the output line C, the switching network is $A \vee B$. The analysis of these switching circuits as shown in Table 3–2 is identical to the truth tables using symbolic logic.

TABLE 3–2   Analysis of Switching Circuits

COMBINATION OF SWITCH POSITIONS		SWITCHES A $\wedge$ B		SWITCHES A $\vee$ B	
A	B	DIAGRAM	C	DIAGRAM	C
Closed	Closed		on		on
Closed	Open		off		on
Open	Closed		off		on
Open	Open		off		off

As will be explained further in Chapter 6, the circuitry of a computer is designed from combinations of rather simple AND, OR, NOT AND, and NOT OR logic modules. For this reason, the mathematics of symbolic logic are important to the design of computers.

THE AUTOMATIC SEQUENCE CONTROLLED CALCULATOR—MARK I

The preparation of mathematical tables, the task for which Babbage had designed his machines, is time-consuming and error-prone. In 1937 Howard Aiken of Harvard University designed a machine called an Automatic Sequence Controlled Calculator— Mark I, which would prepare mathematical tables by automatically performing a set sequence of arithmetic operations. It was not a computer, as the term is now used, because it was mechanical rather than electronic, and the program of instructions consisted of switch settings, wired control boards, and punched paper tape. Data was represented by patterns of open and closed mechanical relays.

The Mark I, completed in 1944, is historically important because it was the immediate predecessor of the electronic computer and contained many features such as the preestablished program of operations, now associated with computers.

THE ENIAC[1] (ELECTRONIC NUMERICAL INTEGRATOR AND CALCULATOR)

The ENIAC, designed by J. Presper Eckert and John W. Mauchly of the Moore School of Engineering of the University of Pennsylvania, was an electronic version of the Mark I. Completed in 1945, it used electronic components instead of mechanical relays and was therefore much faster than the Mark I. It was programmed by means of switches and plug-in connections but, because of its electronic components, is often identified as the first electronic computer. It was used mainly for calculating mathematical tables.

[1] ENIAC is an example of an acronym, i.e., a word formed from the initial letter or letters of the words describing some item. Acronyms are widely used in the computer field.

EDVAC, EDSAC, AND IAS

After the ENIAC, many research laboratories, most of them connected with universities, began to construct computers. One of the most active of these research groups was headed by Eckert and Mauchly at the Moore School of Engineering. They designed the EDVAC (Electronic Discrete Variable Automatic Computer), which differed fundamentally from the ENIAC in two ways—the use of binary numbers and the internal storage of instructions written in digital form. Because the completion of the EDVAC was delayed until 1952, another computer, the EDSAC, built at the University of Manchester in England, was the first stored program electronic computer.

John Von Neumann, a noted mathematician from the Institute for Advanced Study at Princeton University, became acquainted with the work of Eckert and Mauchly during a stay at the Moore School. As a result of this exchange, the IAS computer (named for the Institute for Advanced Study) was built as a joint project of IAS and the Moore School. The IAS, completed in 1952, is historically important because of innovations in its design. It incorporated the binary system and parallel arithmetic and provided the basis for subsequent parallel, binary computers. The EDVAC, on the other hand, is the prototype of serial computers. These concepts will be explained in Chapter 6.

THE UNIVAC I (UNIVERSAL AUTOMATIC COMPUTER)

The UNIVAC I is important because it was the first commercially available computer. Until UNIVAC I, computers were one-of-a-kind. The UNIVAC I was built by the Eckert and Mauchly Computer Company founded in 1946 by J. Presper Eckert and J. W. Mauchly. The company was purchased by Remington Rand in 1949 and subsequently became the UNIVAC division of Sperry Rand Corporation.

The first UNIVAC computer was installed at the United States Bureau of Census in 1951. The speed of technological change for computers can be appreciated by noting that only 13 years later this first UNIVAC I from the Census Bureau was turned over to the Smithsonian Institution for its historical value.

The initial reaction of many of the scientists who developed computers was that a very small number of computers would suffice for the entire country. However, business organizations recognized their potential data processing value. The first business use of a computer was in 1954 at General Electric Appliance Park in Louisville, Kentucky. The successful use of computers in business opened an entirely new field and became an important factor in the growth of the computer industry.

COMPUTERS SINCE THE UNIVAC I

Computers built during the period from the UNIVAC I to the late 1950s used vacuum tubes and are identified as first-generation computers. IBM, which had not been particularly active in the development of computers, entered the computer business with the IBM 701 in 1953. Late in 1954 IBM installed the first of the IBM 650 computers. This small- to medium-scale computer was the most popular computer during the next five years. In this period IBM obtained a dominant position in the computer field, with more than two-thirds of the market.

Second-generation computers are identified by the use of transistors instead of vacuum tubes. The transistor performs the same function as the vacuum tube but is smaller, is less expensive, generates almost no heat, and requires little power. Second-generation computers were therefore substantially reduced in size, required less power, needed little or even no air conditioning and were more reliable than the first-generation equipment. The most popular by far of the second-generation computers were IBM's small- to medium-scale business-oriented 1401 computer and small, scientific-oriented 1620 computer. IBM's 7090–7094 series dominated the large-scale computer market.

The third generation of computers is characterized by miniaturized circuits, the integration of hardware with software (programming and operating aids), and an orientation to data communication and the handling of more than one operation simultaneously. The speeds of the third-generation equipment are faster than comparable second-generation equipment, and prices are generally lower. The change to third-generation characteristics began in 1963–1964, but the major transition was in 1965 when IBM began deliveries of its third-generation System/360.

The price of computers relative to performance has decreased steadily since the UNIVAC I. As shown by Figure 3–2, there has been an average decrease in cost of 20 percent per year. The chart also illustrates graphically a rule of thumb which states the relationship of the price of computers and their performance. This rule, known as Grosch's law, is that the relative performance of computer systems varies according to the square of their prices. This means that, for double the price, one obtains four times the power. This rule has far-reaching implications because it means that the largest and most expensive computers are by far the cheapest in terms of price per computation, etc.

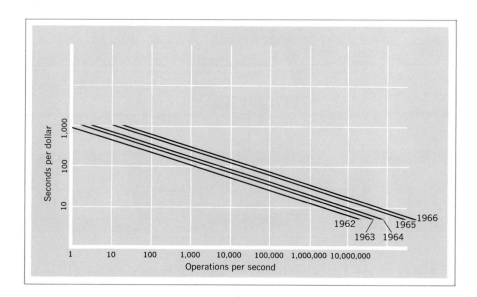

FIGURE 3–2 Changes in price and performance for commercial computers 1962–1967
SOURCE: Kenneth E. Knight, "Evolving Computer Performance 1963–1967," *Datamation*, January, 1968, p. 34.

SUMMARY OF EVENTS

1937	Howard Aiken proposes automatic calculator (completed 1944)
1943	Eckert and Mauchly begin the ENIAC (completed 1947)
1944–45	EDVAC and IAS begun (completed 1952)
1949	EDSAC completed in England
1951	UNIVAC I installed in Census Bureau
1954	First installation of computer for business use; first installation of IBM 650, most popular first-generation computer
1959–60	Second-generation computers available
1965	Third-generation computers available

▮ ELEMENTS OF A COMPUTER DATA PROCESSING SYSTEM

There are five basic elements in a computer data processing system. These are the hardware, the software, the programs, the procedures, and the personnel. Each of these will be described briefly in this chapter and receive further explanations in subsequent chapters. Hardware is explained in Chapters 6, 7, 13, 19, and 22; software is described in Chapters 8, 14, and 22; programming is covered in Chapters 8 to 14; the procedures are discussed in Chapters 15 to 18; and personnel requirements are treated in Chapter 17.

HARDWARE

Hardware for computer data processing involves equipment which can perform the following functions: data preparation; input to the computer; computation, control,

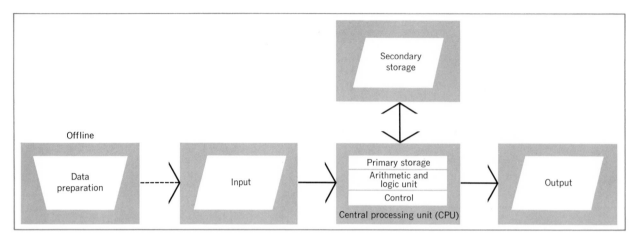

FIGURE 3-3   Functions in a computer
system

and primary storage; secondary storage; and output from the computer. Equipment which is connected directly to the computer is termed "online" whereas equipment which is used separately and is not connected is called "offline." The relationship of these equipment functions is shown in Figure 3–3.

SOFTWARE

Software consists of programs and routines whose purpose is to facilitate the use of the computer by the user installations. The term can include applications programs and routines written for a specific installation but more commonly refers only to general programming and operating aids which are usually furnished by the manufacturer. These aids consist of computer programs utilized in such tasks as printout of machine-readable records, sorting records, organizing and maintaining files, translating of programs written in a symbolic language into machine language instructions, and scheduling jobs through the computer. Software extends the capabilities of the computer and is therefore as critical to effective use of a computer as the hardware.

USER PROGRAMS

A program consists of a set of instructions for performing a data processing task. A complete data processing job usually requires a number of programs. Although the computer manufacturer supplies, as part of the software, generalized programs for some common tasks, it is necessary for the user to write most of the programs needed to meet his own processing requirements.

PROCEDURES

The operation of a data processing system requires procedures for use in obtaining and preparing data, for operating the computer, and for distributing the output from computer processing. These procedures include control steps such as actions to be taken in the event there are errors in the data or there is a malfunctioning of the equipment.

PERSONNEL

Computer data processing requires new skills. Three major jobs are found in data processing installations:

JOB TITLE	JOB DESCRIPTION
Systems analyst	Study information needs and data processing requirements. Design a data processing system. Prepare specifications and broad outline of the system
Programmer	Prepare computer programs based on specifications prepared by the systems analyst
Computer operator	Operate the computer

Of these jobs, the systems analyst requires the broadest background in terms of education and understanding of organizations. The programmer has to have the specialized skill of writing computer instructions. The computer operator requires considerably less training than is needed for the other jobs because the equipment is for the most part automatic and the operator function involves well-defined tasks which do not require knowledge of the internal workings of the equipment or the program.

STEPS IN USING THE COMPUTER

The steps, beginning with the analysis of information requirements and ending with the use of the output, are described in Figure 3–4.

▌ THE EQUIPMENT IN A COMPUTER CENTER

The exact selection of equipment in a computer center will depend on the amount and type of processing being performed and the types of equipment available with the computer system being used. In general, a center will have one or more pieces of equipment for each of the five equipment functions described earlier in this chapter. The equipment for each function is summarized in Table 3–3.

EQUIPMENT FOR COMPUTATION AND CONTROL

The central processing unit, or CPU, is the "computer" part of the computer system. It contains an arithmetic unit for computation, a control unit, and the primary storage (frequently termed the internal memory) for storing the program being used and the data being processed. The primary storage and control units may be in the same or

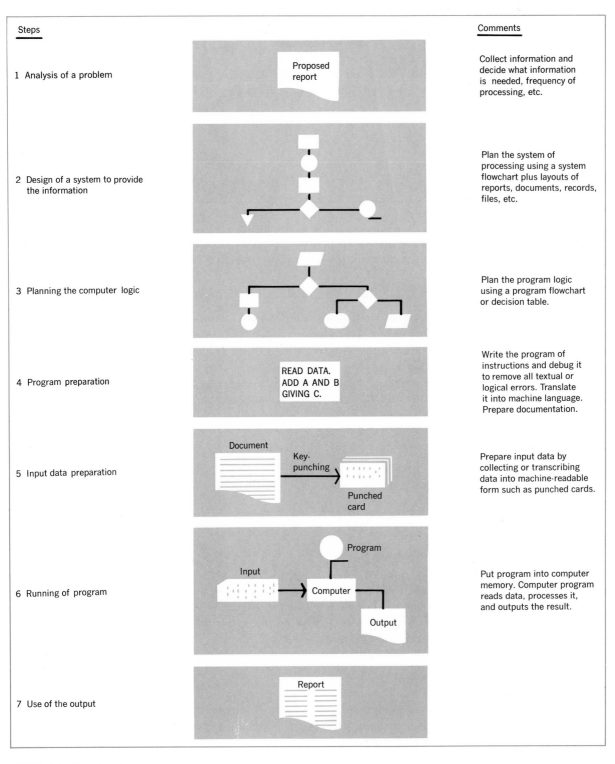

Steps		Comments
1 Analysis of a problem	Proposed report	Collect information and decide what information is needed, frequency of processing, etc.
2 Design of a system to provide the information		Plan the system of processing using a system flowchart plus layouts of reports, documents, records, files, etc.
3 Planning the computer logic		Plan the program logic using a program flowchart or decision table.
4 Program preparation	READ DATA. ADD A AND B GIVING C.	Write the program of instructions and debug it to remove all textual or logical errors. Translate it into machine language. Prepare documentation.
5 Input data preparation	Document — Key-punching → Punched card	Prepare input data by collecting or transcribing data into machine-readable form such as punched cards.
6 Running of program	Input → Computer → Output / Program	Put program into computer memory. Computer program reads data, processes it, and outputs the result.
7 Use of the output	Report	

FIGURE 3–4 Steps in using a computer for data processing

separate cabinet. The CPU has a control console for operator use, which may be a panel on the CPU cabinet or a separate console with a typewriter or visual display device. Figure 3–5 shows a central processor with an attached console typewriter.

TABLE 3–3 Type of Equipment for Each Computer Data Processing Function

FUNCTION	TYPE OF EQUIPMENT USED
Data preparation	Key-driven card punch
	Key-driven card verifier
	Paper tape punch
	Magnetic tape encoder
	Magnetic ink enscriber
	Optical character enscriber
	Data collection devices with keyboard, plastic card sensor, etc., which transcribe onto some machine-readable medium
	Devices to prepare cards, paper tape, or optical tape as a by-product of another operation
	Conversion devices, such as paper tape to magnetic tape converter and paper tape to punched card converter
Input	Card reader
	Magnetic tape unit
	Paper tape reader
	Magnetic-ink character reader
	Optical scanner
	Console typewriter
	Online data collection devices
Computation, control, and primary storage	Central processing unit (CPU)
Secondary storage	Storage devices using the following file media:
	Magnetic tape
	Magnetic disc
	Magnetic drum
	Magnetic card or strip
Output	Printer
	Card punch
	Paper tape punch
	Console typewriter
	Visual display (CRT)
	Graph plotter
	Audio response unit

EQUIPMENT FOR SECONDARY STORAGE

Secondary storage (also called mass or auxiliary storage) is used to hold programs not currently in use and data files. Since the main use is for data files, this equipment can be considered as file storage. Punched cards are used for file storage with small data processing systems, but the speed and capacity of storage devices with reusable, magnetically encoded storage media put the latter devices in a different class. Data can be written on a magnetic surface, read as many times as necessary, and then used again by writing over the old records. The concept is identical to that of the home tape recorder—once recorded, a program may be played as often as desired and the tape may be reused by recording on it again. The most popular magnetic storage media is magnetic tape; the next most common is the magnetic disc. The different file storage devices are illustrated in Figure 3-6.

INPUT DEVICES

The most commonly used input device (Figure 3-7) is the punched card reader. Paper tape readers are used when input data has been placed on punched paper

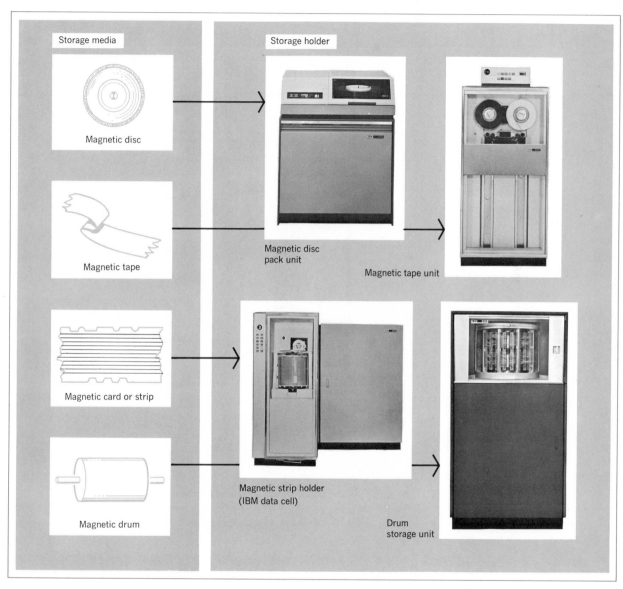

Storage media

Magnetic disc

Magnetic tape

Magnetic card or strip

Magnetic drum

Storage holder

Magnetic disc pack unit

Magnetic tape unit

Magnetic strip holder (IBM data cell)

Drum storage unit

FIGURE 3-6 Secondary storage devices

tape by devices such as an add punch, cash register attachment, or typewriter attachment. Magnetic character readers are used mainly in banks for check processing. Optical scanners are becoming more popular, especially for reading ticket-type data such as gasoline charge tickets and airline tickets.

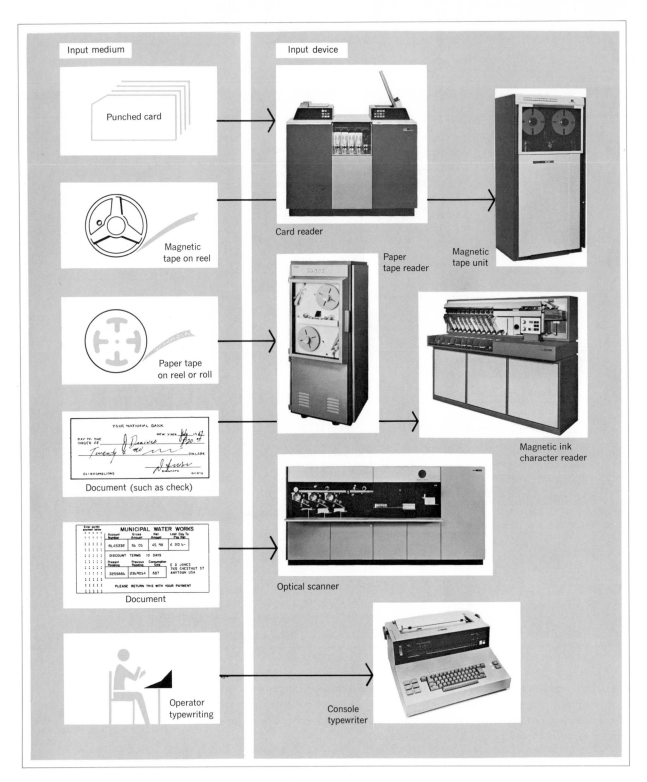

Input medium

Input device

Punched card

Magnetic tape on reel

Card reader

Magnetic tape unit

Paper tape on reel or roll

Paper tape reader

Document (such as check)

Magnetic ink character reader

MUNICIPAL WATER WORKS

Document

Optical scanner

Operator typewriting

Console typewriter

FIGURE 3–7 Input devices

OUTPUT DEVICES

The printer dominates the list of output devices (Figure 3–8). To be usable, except for further machine processing, data for output must be put into a form readable by humans. The line printer performs this function. The cathode ray tube (CRT) display device is expected to receive more use in systems requiring many persons at various remote locations to interrogate the computer or look at records in a file.

DATA PREPARATION EQUIPMENT

Since punched cards are the most common input media, the data preparation equipment (Figure 3–9) will include keypunches and possibly other card handling equipment described in Chapter 2, such as sorters, collators, interpreters, and reproducers. However, data preparation is time-consuming and expensive, and there is a trend toward elimination of this step either by encoding on the source document for direct input to the computer or creating a machine-readable by-product while making the source document. Direct readin of data from online input devices such as a teller window machine also eliminates the data preparation step.

█ METHODS OF DATA PROCESSING

Two major data processing approaches are used—batch processing (periodic processing of an accumulated batch of items) and online processing (immediate processing of unbatched items). The items in a batch may be in sequential order or in random order. File storage devices offer two types of access—sequential access and direct access.

In sequential access files, the records are stored in order on the file media and are read one at a time starting at the first of the file. In order to read a record in the middle of the file, all preceding records must first be read. Examples of sequential access file storage are punched cards and magnetic tape. In direct (or random) access, the reading mechanism can locate and read any record without reading other records. Examples are the magnetic disc, magnetic drum, and magnetic strips. The type of access afforded by the file devices will, in part, determine the processing approach.

TYPE OF ACCESS	PROCESSING APPROACH
Sequential access	Batch—sequential
Direct access	Batch—sequential
	Batch—random
	Online (random)

BATCH PROCESSING WITH SEQUENTIAL ACCESS FILE STORAGE

Batch processing is characterized by the accumulation of transactions over a period of time and the periodic processing of the batch. Sequential access batch processing

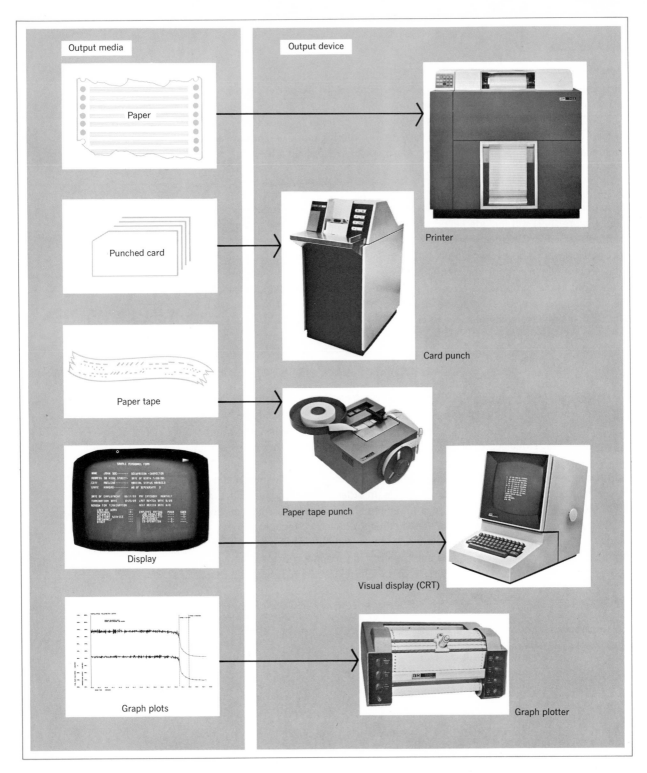

FIGURE 3–8   Output devices

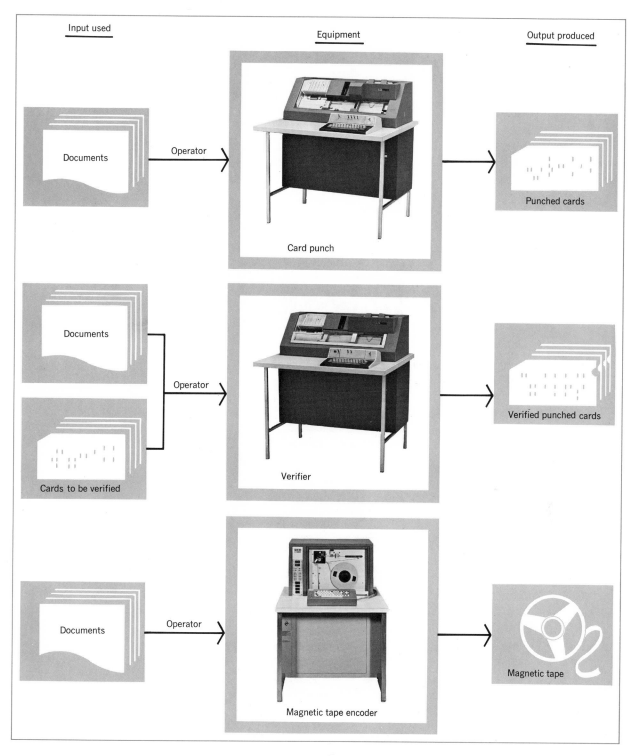

Input used	Equipment	Output produced
Documents	Card punch	Punched cards
Documents / Cards to be verified	Verifier	Verified punched cards
Documents	Magnetic tape encoder	Magnetic tape

FIGURE 3–9 Data preparation equipment

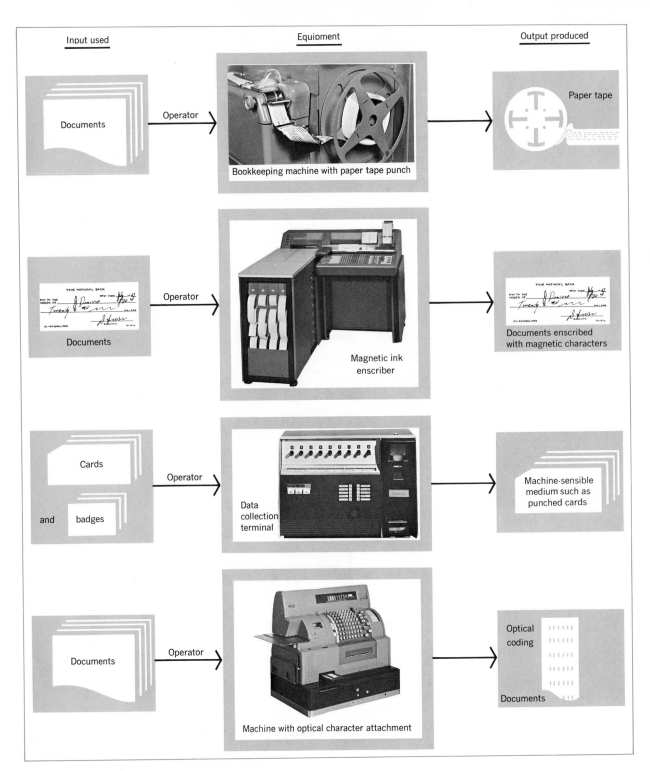

FIGURE 3-9 (Continued)

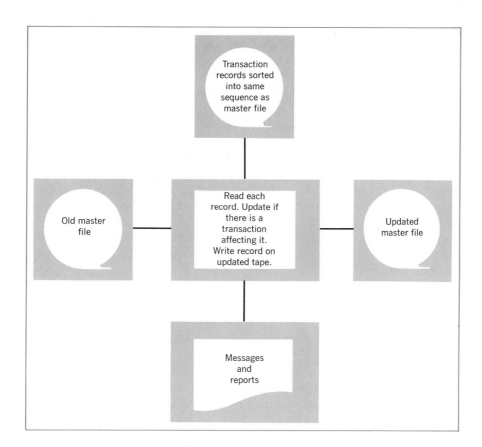

FIGURE 3–10 Batch-sequential data processing using sequential access storage (magnetic tape)

is normally used when records are maintained on punched cards or magnetic tape. The distinguishing feature of batch-sequential processing using sequential access file storage is that the entire master file is put through the computer each time the master file is updated (Figure 3–10) and an entirely new updated master file is written. The user sorts the transactions into the same sequence as the master file so that each record on the master file will have to be read only once for the updating process. Since the entire file must be read each time, it is desirable to accumulate the transactions into batches of fair size before processing them in order to reduce the frequency of processing. The time to read a record, whether or not it is updated, represents a fixed time element each time the file is processed. Each transaction to be processed represents a variable time element, but this may overlap, at least in part, the fixed time for reading the record. In many processing applications, the nature of the job is such that batching and sequencing requirements are not actually restrictions. For applications such as payroll and accounts payable, batch processing is ideal. It also usually costs less to process batches than to process each transaction immediately online.

BATCH PROCESSING WITH DIRECT ACCESS FILE STORAGE

A direct access file device is one in which each record is accessible without reading any of the other records. Also termed a random access file, the most popular direct access file device is the disc file. Even though it is not necessary to sequence data when using a direct access file, the speed and cost advantages obtained from batching transactions for periodic processing make it applicable in many cases. For example, in using the magnetic disc, the processing can frequently be done faster if the input data is sequenced to minimize the mechanical movement of the disc in locating the records.

For applications involving relatively few transactions compared to the total number of file records, the batch of transactions may be left in random order for processing. The extra time to sort them into a sequence is, in such cases, not justified by the savings in direct access seek time.

The direct access processing approach does not write an entire new file. Instead, only those records affected by the transactions are updated. All others are left untouched (Figure 3–11).

ONLINE PROCESSING

In applications such as production control and some inventory control, records need to be kept up to date. Transactions and inquiries are processed randomly as received rather than being batched. Online processing requires direct access storage devices in order to locate any record at random.

An advanced type of online processing system is an online realtime (OLRT) system. In this system, transactions and inquiries are recorded and processed as they occur. The processing is fast enough that the results can influence the transaction rather

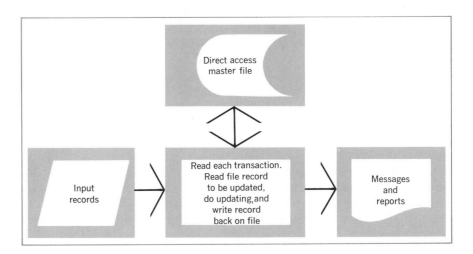

FIGURE 3–11 Data processing using direct access storage

than merely be a passive recording. Each point of origin of transactions in the organizations has a point of origin device (POD) connected to the computer with which to communicate with the system—originating data and receiving responses. All information with which the person or computer must deal is stored in direct access files. On-line realtime applications presently include airlines' reservation systems; savings and loan deposit accounting; stock market information systems; law enforcement intelligence systems in state and local government; guest accounting and reservations systems in hotels; and patient service records in hospitals.

▌ SOME TYPICAL COMPUTER SYSTEM CONFIGURATIONS

A computer system may range in size from a small-equipment configuration renting for less than $1,000 per month to a large-scale system with a monthly rental of over $100,000. In order to provide some concept of what equipment is found in a typical system and the cost range of such a system, four typical configurations will be diagrammed—small card, small magnetic tape, small magnetic disc, and a medium-scale system. Illustrations of more complex systems must wait until later in the text. The descriptions do not include data preparation or offline equipment.

SMALL CARD-ORIENTED SYSTEM

In this type of arrangement, the transaction and master files and programs not in use are all stored on punched cards. Processing is of the batch type which uses sequentially organized data and files and requires the performing of many card-handling operations (sorting, merging, etc.) as well as computer computation. The card handling is usually done with sorters and collators, although some manufacturers offer a multifunction card handler attached to the computer which performs collating, gang punching, reproducing, interpreting, etc. Memory size is small, probably $4K^2$ (4,000) character positions of storage. The monthly rental for a small card-oriented system such as shown in Figure 3–12 is on the order of $1,200 to $2,500. More powerful card-oriented systems may cost up to $4,000 per month.

SMALL MAGNETIC TAPE–ORIENTED SYSTEM

The keeping of files on punched cards severely limits the speed and versatility of a computer system. The next step up in computers is to use magnetic tape or magnetic discs as file storage. When using magnetic tapes, it is necessary to sort transactions to be processed into the same order as the file to which they relate. This sorting requirement takes at least three and usually four magnetic tape drives, so most systems have at least this many tape units. Memory size for a small tape system will usually be at least sufficient to store $8K$ characters. The monthly rental for a system of the type diagrammed in Figure 3–13 will range from $3,000 to $5,000.

[2] K is used in computer circles to refer to thousands of addressable storage locations. The number of storage locations are truncated to the thousands. 32K probably refers to 32,768 storage locations.

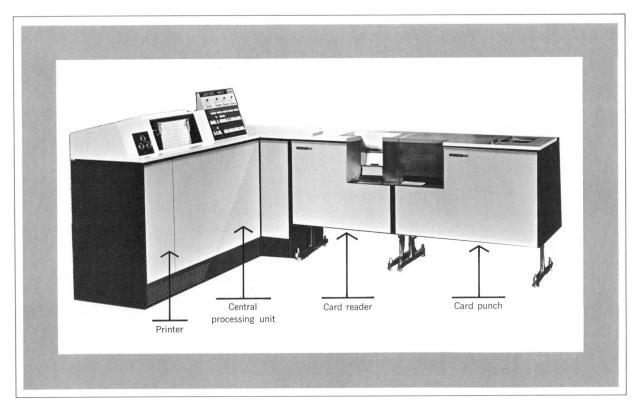

FIGURE 3–12 Small card-oriented system (UNIVAC 9200) (Courtesy of Sperry Rand Corporation)

SMALL MAGNETIC DISC–ORIENTED SYSTEM

As an alternative to magnetic tape, the user may elect to use removable disc pack storage. Because of the problems of file protection and reconstruction (described in Chapter 17), it is usually desirable to have at least two disc storage drives. The price for this alternative, as shown in Figure 3–14, is $3,000 to $5,000 per month. By way of contrast, the price of a disc pack is about $400, while a reel of magnetic tape costs about $20.

MEDIUM-SCALE BUSINESS SYSTEM

As a system expands in size, the central processor chosen is a faster one, the peripheral equipment is also faster, and the number of attached units increases. A configuration on the order of the one shown in Figure 3–15 will cost in the neighborhood of $4,000 to $7,000 per month. The storage size will be larger, say enough to store 16 to 32,000 characters.

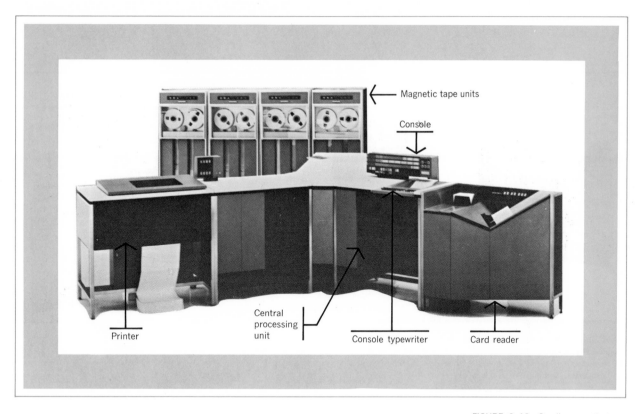

Magnetic tape units

Console

Printer

Central processing unit

Console typewriter

Card reader

FIGURE 3–13 Small magnetic tape-oriented system (Honeywell 200)

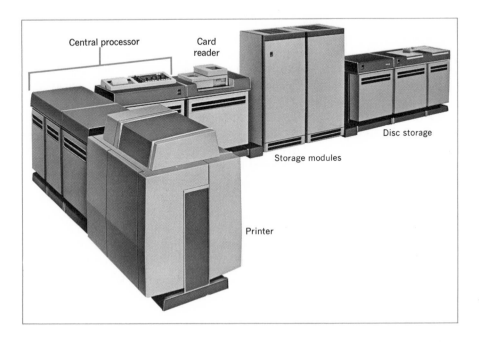

Central processor

Card reader

Disc storage

Storage modules

Printer

FIGURE 3–14 Small magnetic disc-oriented system (NCR Century 200 System) (Courtesy of the National Cash Register Company)

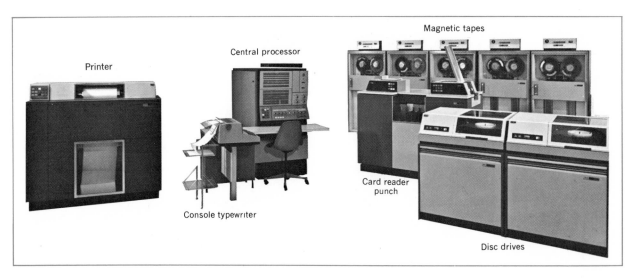

Printer

Central processor

Magnetic tapes

Card reader punch

Console typewriter

Disc drives

FIGURE 3–15   Medium-scale business data processing system (IBM System/ 360 model 30) (Courtesy of International Business Machines Corporation)

▌ SUMMARY

This chapter has contained an overview of computer data processing. A computer was defined as a device having electronic construction, internal storage, a stored program, and program modification capabilities. Although the history of computers begins in the 1940s with Howard Aiken's automatic sequence controlled calculator, Charles Babbage had thought of the idea a hundred years before. The Boolean algebra, developed to apply to truth or falsity of statements, is important to computers because the two states in Boolean analysis can be applied to the two states in computer circuitry. The development of computers was "one of a kind" until the advent of the UNIVAC I, first installed in 1951. In 1954, the first business computer was installed. The first generation of tube-type machines lasted until 1959–1960, when the second generation of transistorized computers were introduced. These were superseded by third-generation hardware in the mid-1960s. During this period, there have been large increases in speed and significant reductions in cost.

The elements in a computer data processing system are hardware, software, programs, procedures, and personnel. Each of these elements was surveyed in this chapter; they will be explained in more detail in subsequent chapters. Also described were the hardware functions of computation and control, secondary storage, input, output, and data preparation. As part of the general overview of this chapter, the two major methods of data processing, batch and direct access, were presented, and four typical configurations were illustrated.

▌ EXERCISES

1   Fill in the following table of historical events:

EVENT	YEAR	SIGNIFICANCE
a		An ahead-of-its-time description of a computer
b Boolean algebra		
c Automatic sequence controlled calculator		
d		First electronic calculator
e EDVAC and IAS		
f EDSAC at Manchester, England		
g		First commercially available computer
h UNIVAC I at General Electric in Kentucky		

2   What is the difference between first-, second-, and third-generation computers?
3   What are the essential functions of the equipment in a computer center?
4   List the equipment in your computer center, classifying it by function.
5   Define the following terms:
     a   Computer
     b   Analog computer
     c   Digital computer
     d   Hybrid computer
     e   Software
     f   Program
     g   Offline
     h   Acronym
6   Outline the steps in utilizing a computer in data processing.
7   What is the difference between batch processing and direct access processing?
8   Define the following abbreviations used in data processing:
     a   CPU
     b   POD
     c   EDP
     d   OLRT
     e   I/O
9   Prepare a truth table for each of the following statements:
     a   It is raining or the sun is shining.

  b I get a B in History 201 and I get a C in Sociology 265 or I will be suspended
       from college.
10 Prepare a truth table for the following circuits.

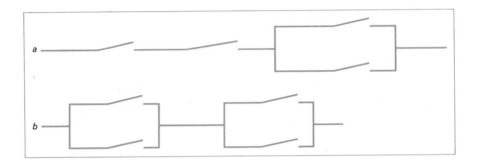

❚ CAPABILITIES OF COMPUTERS
ADVANTAGES POSSESSED BY THE COMPUTER
ADVANTAGES POSSESSED BY MAN

❚ RECORD KEEPING

❚ METHODS OF ANALYSIS AND PROCESSING MADE
FEASIBLE BY THE COMPUTER
LINEAR PROGRAMMING
CRITICAL PATH ANALYSIS (PERT/CPM)
FORECASTING MODELS
SYSTEM SIMULATION IN OPERATIONS RESEARCH
INFORMATION RETRIEVAL

❚ ADVANCED APPROACHES TO INFORMATION
SYSTEMS
REALTIME PROCESSING
INTEGRATED DATA PROCESSING
MANAGEMENT INFORMATION SYSTEM

❚ SOME INTERESTING EXAMPLES OF COMPUTER USE
GUIDANCE AND CONTROL OF SPACECRAFT
PREDICTION OF ELECTIONS
COMPUTER-ASSISTED INSTRUCTION

❚ SUMMARY

❚ EXERCISES

A LOOK AT THE
USE OF COMPUTERS

This chapter provides background for the chapters to follow by surveying the capabilities of computers and the ways in which computers are being used. These uses include simple record keeping, computer-based methods of analysis and processing, and advanced information systems. The computer has been applied to a variety of other interesting and unusual tasks, a few of which are described briefly.

▍ CAPABILITIES OF COMPUTERS

A computer cannot perform any new operation which cannot also be performed by a human, but the computer executes operations with such speed that it is in a different class. This speed also opens new approaches to problem solving and data processing. The speed of execution by computers is illustrated by the fact that a very large computer can perform several million addition operations per second and even a small, rather slow computer can do tens of thousands of addition operations per second. The concept that the basic operations performed by a computer can also be performed by a human is illustrated by a comparison of computer operations with human actions in Table 4–1.

TABLE 4–1   What a Computer Can Do

OPERATION PERFORMED BY COMPUTER	CORRESPONDING ACTION PERFORMED BY A HUMAN
1 Hold a program of instructions in internal storage.	1 Remember a set of instructions.
2 Read data in machine-readable form and store in internal memory or in secondary storage.	2 Read data in written or printed form and memorize it or file it.
3 Perform arithmetic computations.	3 Perform arithmetic computations.
4 Manipulate symbols.	4 Manipulate symbols.
5 Make comparisons.	5 Make comparisons.
6 Choose a path of instruction based on a comparison or an examination of the results to that point.	6 Make a decision as to further processing based on results to that point.
7 Retrieve any data from internal memory or secondary storage.	7 Remember data or retrieve data from a file.
8 Output the results on an output device.	8 Write or speak the results.

Although Table 4–1 indicates the ability of a man to do anything a computer can do, the reverse is not true—a computer cannot do everything a man can do. Some people have characterized the computer as a very fast but somewhat moronic assistant. The computer does only what it is instructed, and these instructions must take into account every possible set of conditions relating to the action. Take, as an example, the instructions we would have to give an assistant relative to dispensing change at a newsstand selling magazines, newspapers, candy, and cigarettes if the assistant had to be completely instructed:

STEP	INSTRUCTION
1	Add sales price of items purchased to give amount of sale.
2	Accept payment amount. Open cash box and put payment amount in box.
3	Subtract amount of sale from amount given as payment to arrive at amount of change.
4	If amount of change is: a Negative—Ask for additional payments, add to amount already received, and start again at step 3. b Zero—Go to step 10. c Positive—Continue with step 5.
5	Select largest bill or coin available in cash box which is also less than amount of change. If no bills or coins are available, go to step 11.
6	Put selected bill or coin in left hand (change hand); subtract amount of bill or coin from amount of change to obtain a new change amount.
7	If new change amount is: a Positive—Go to step 5 and continue. b Negative—There has been an error. Replace money in change hand and begin over with step 4. c Zero—Continue with step 8.
8	Close cash box and count out change in change hand to customer. Starting with the amount of the sale and using smallest bill or coin left in the change, add each bill or coin to the accumulated count as it is given to the customer.
9	When all coins and bills are counted out to the customer, compare accumulated count to amount given as payment. If a Unequal—Take back all change and start again with step 8. If this happens twice, replace change and start over at step 5. b Equal—Go on to step 10.
10	Thank customer and go to step 12.
11	Refuse sale, return purchase price, take back merchandise, and express regret at inability to make change. If customer tenders a smaller payment, start at step 2.
12	Go to next customer.

The steps in making change are much more detailed than any human supervisor would feel it necessary to give an employee. But these are barely detailed enough to instruct a computer. This example reflects the fact that although a computer exceeds human capability in some respects, a human has other inherent advantages over a computer. This suggests that data processing and information systems should be designed as man-machine systems in which each is assigned the part for which it is most suited. The capabilities of computers and human clerks in data processing are summarized in Table 4–2.

TABLE 4–2   Comparison of Computers and Clerks in Performing Data Processing Tasks

BASIS FOR COMPARISON	CLERK	COMPUTER
Speed of execution	Relatively slow	Extremely fast
Ability to continue processing over an extended period	Poor	Very good
Ability to remember or retrieve information	Relatively inaccurate	Accurate
Accuracy of work	Make errors	Makes virtually no errors
Ability to consistently follow instructions	Imperfect	Perfect
Ability to innovate in new situation	Fairly good	Lacking
Ability to learn by trial and error	Fairly good	Lacking

ADVANTAGES POSSESSED BY THE COMPUTER

As seen from Table 4–2, the computer is extremely fast, and almost perfect in reliability and accuracy. Once provided with a program of instructions, it will accurately retrieve information and will follow the set of directions perfectly. In substance, then, the computer is suited to any task which involves large amounts of retrieval, computation, manipulation, and comparison so long as the procedures can be completely described in advance by a set of instructions.

ADVANTAGES POSSESSED BY MAN

Man is a rather poor data processor. He is slow and not completely accurate. But he has two advantages—he can innovate or adapt, and he can reason heuristically. The ability to innovate and adapt means that his set of instructions does not have to anticipate everything that could happen because he can relate the new situation to old ones and make and execute a new procedure immediately.

Man can reason heuristically. This means that he can learn by trial and error discovery. Man does not usually reason in a simple step-by-step manner, but, in some fashion, he reaches a conclusion based on trial and error, taking into account incomplete information and the effect of past experiences. A computer does not learn from past experience; a man does. (As explained in Chapter 22, attempts are being made to develop an adaptive computer, but this is in early stages of research.) A man is aware of his environment and has his entire past experience always available; a computer has only the information which the program of instructions has made available. A man is best suited to think, reason, and discover; a computer is best adapted to calculate, manipulate, and compare.

The computer can thus extend the power of man by performing tasks perfectly which man performs imperfectly and by providing the raw material (data, results of processing, etc.) with which man may reason and discover. In the sections which follow in this chapter, the text will explore some of the ways in which the capabilities of the computer are applied.

▌ RECORD KEEPING

The first commercial application of a computer was the preparation of the payroll. Simple record-keeping tasks such as payroll, customer accounts receivable, and inventory accounting are usually the first applications to be put on the computer. The reasons for this are that these tasks use well-defined procedures with few exceptions and involve large volumes of records. One of these applications, payroll, will be described in some detail, as an illustration of the record-keeping use of computers.

Processing of the payroll essentially requires the preparation of a payroll check for the employee and an updating of the historical pay record for each employee. It is typically necessary also to prepare a listing of the payroll for the period. In terms of accounting terminology, the individual pay records constitute the payroll ledger, and the payroll listings are the payroll journal. The input and output for payroll processing are shown in Figure 4–1. Government reports must be prepared periodically for each employee.

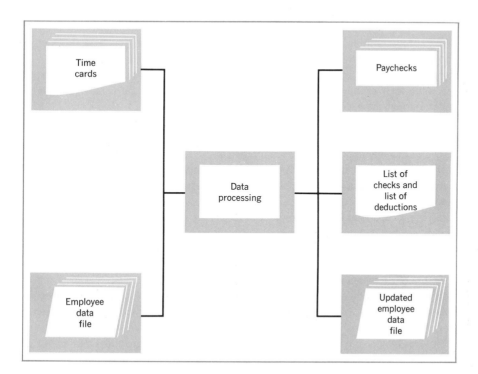

FIGURE 4–1 Elements of input/output for payroll data processing

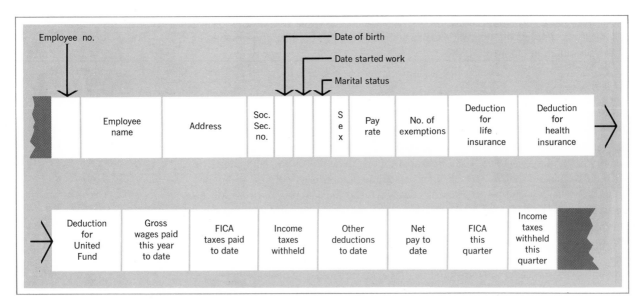

FIGURE 4–2 A payroll record for the master payroll file

The computations for each employee are fairly simple. The gross pay (for an hourly employee) is computed as hours × rate. Withholding tax and social security are calculated from formulas. These and other agreed-upon deductions are subtracted from gross pay to arrive at net pay. Just as in the newsstand example, however, the computer must take into account all possible conditions such as overtime, different pay rates for weekdays and Sundays, minimum work days, garnishments against wages, deductions exceeding gross pay, etc.

In order to illustrate how a computer is applied to record-keeping applications, the steps in processing payroll with a computer will be described. The computer is assumed to use magnetic tape for file storage.

The preparation of the payroll begins when the new employee fills out an employment form and is assigned a payroll number. The form asks for name, address, social security number, number of exemptions for income tax purposes, and other pertinent data. The company may allow employees to have amounts deducted from their pay. Examples are directions for purchase of government bonds, union dues, United Fund contributions, group life insurance, and group health insurance. The authorization for these deductions was obtained when the employee was hired or at a later time when the employee changed a deduction.

The data about the employee is written on a master payroll tape. There is a record for each employee which contains information necessary to process the payroll. On magnetic tape, a record is stored on a length of the tape as a series of magnetized spots. The master payroll file consists of the magnetic tape (or tapes) containing all of the payroll records. Since the magnetized spots are read automatically and con-

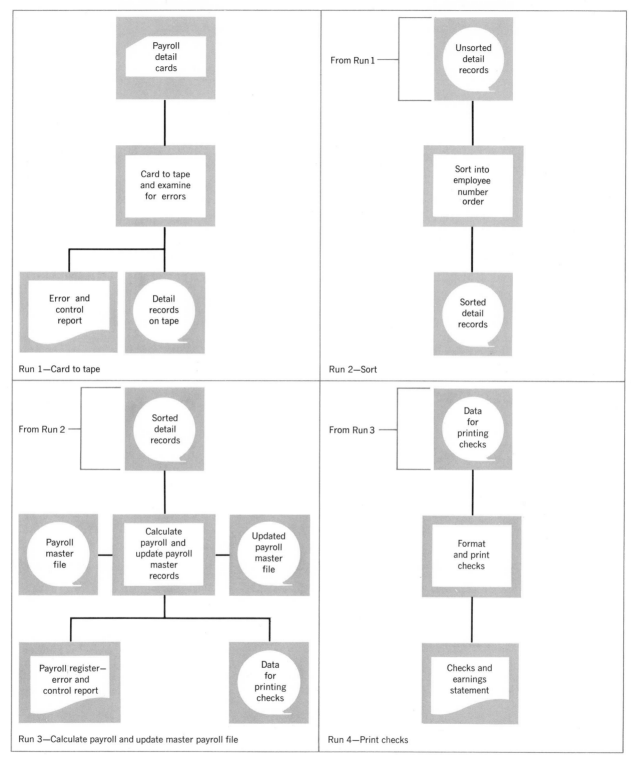

FIGURE 4-3 Computer runs for payroll processing

Employee no.	Dept.	Payroll date	Hours worked							
			M	T	W	Th	F	Sa	Su	

5084

FIGURE 4-4 Card layout for payroll
detail card

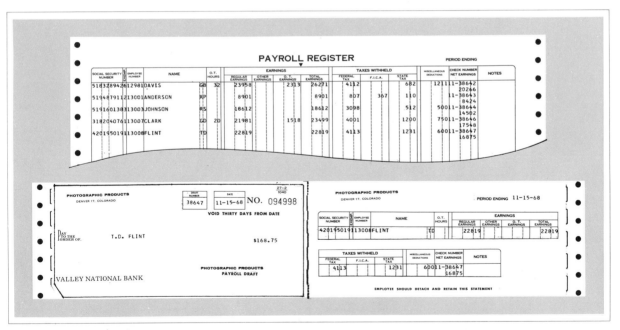

FIGURE 4-5 Printed output from payroll runs

verted to computer code, the explanation will use the format of the record in terms of alphabetic and numeric characters. A new record is added to the file for each new employee hired, and records are dropped (purged) from the file for all employees who have stopped working for the organization (after the final annual tax reports have been made). A record on magnetic tape is shown by Figure 4–2. This master payroll file was prepared when the payroll application was begun.

The payroll application includes periodic government reports, yearly reports to the individual for income tax purposes, and management reports. This description will cover only the major processing task—preparation of the weekly payroll. This task consists of five subtasks. The computer subtasks, called runs, are diagrammed in Figure 4–3. The subtasks consist of the following actions:

SUBTASK	DESCRIPTION
Data preparation	The data on hours worked, taken from the time sheets, is punched into cards. These are the payroll detail cards. The card layout is shown in Figure 4–4. The cards are first keypunched and then verified.
Run 1: Card to tape	The payroll detail cards are read, examined by the computer program for errors in format (missing data, illogical data, etc.), and written on magnetic tape.
Run 2: Sort	The master payroll file is arranged in sequence by employee number. The payroll detail file is sorted into this same order for efficiency of processing.
Run 3: Calculate payroll and update master payroll file	Each transaction record is processed in connection with a master record. The gross pay, deductions and net pay are computed and written on a data tape from which the checks will be written. The amounts are also added to the payroll master record and this is written to form an updated master file. A listing of the pay and a control report are printed out.
Run 4: Print checks	The checks and the earnings statements are written from the data prepared by Run 3.

The printed output from the payroll preparation runs consists of (1) a payroll register listing all of the employees together with the details of their pay (hours, gross pay, deductions, net pay, check number, etc.), (2) the employee checks and earnings statements, and (3) control figures and error lists. The first two of these reports are illustrated in Figure 4–5. The error and control listings wil be explained and illustrated in Chapter 17.

▌ METHODS OF ANALYSIS AND PROCESSING MADE FEASIBLE BY THE COMPUTER

Not only has the computer been used for traditional data processing, it has made feasible new approaches to numerical analysis and data processing. When computations must be performed manually or with a desk calculator, the cost and time for doing a complex technique tend to be prohibitive. The cost of computer computation is extremely low by comparison with manual processing, and the accuracy of the machine is, for all practical purposes, perfect. For example, the cost of computer computation time equivalent to one man-year of manual calculating is less than $1 on the fastest computer. A thousand additions cost only a fraction of a cent. These cost factors make new techniques economically feasible; the high speeds make them feasible timewise. Linear programming, critical path analyses, forecasting models, systems simulation in operations research, and information retrieval are examples of the new techniques and approaches made feasible by the computer.

LINEAR PROGRAMMING

Linear programming, as applied to business problems, is a mathematical method for allocating the resources of an organization to achieve some optimum result (such as minimizing cost or maximizing profit). The solution to a linear programming problem of any size and complexity involves hundreds of thousands of simple repetitive calculations which would be impractical without a computer. In fact, linear programming methods were developed specifically to take advantage of computer technology. The concepts underlying these methods were known previously but could not be economically utilized because of the volume of calculations involved. Linear programming is used by business firms to find the optimum solution to such problems as the least-cost blend of ingredients for feed, the most profitable combination of oil refinery production, and the most economical shipping schedules. Special computer programs for solving linear programming problems are usually available from the manufacturer.

CRITICAL PATH ANALYSIS (PERT/CPM)

The scheduling of large-scale development projects, construction projects, etc., is difficult because of the number of interrelationships among the activities to be carried out. Some activities must be performed serially (an activity cannot begin until the prior one is completed) or in parallel (more than one activity can be carried out at the same time). This means that there is a critical path of activities which define the least time to completion. If any activity on the critical path is delayed, the project completion will be delayed. A delay of an activity not on the critical path will not cause a project delay unless the delay is so great as to alter the critical path. Computer programs are available for most computers to perform critical path analysis. Both at the beginning of the project and on a continuing basis, the activities and events critical to timely completion, the "slack" available for completion of noncritical activities and events, and estimates of completion time are computed. The technique is called by a variety of names, e.g., PERT, CPM, PERT/CPM, and critical path scheduling. The computer is used for all large-scale critical path analysis because of the number of computations required for updating the network and producing a new analysis.

FORECASTING MODELS

Mathematical forecasting is based on an assumption that the future will tend to follow the pattern of the past. A forecasting model is a mathematical description of the past relationship. The computer is used initially to discover the past relationship, using statistical analysis techniques. On a continuing basis, the computer is used to make the computations to apply the model to current conditions. A computer is required if the forecasting model is complex and also if the model is applied to many different items, such as inventory items. A computer-oriented forecasting technique, exponential smoothing, is frequently used for item forecasting.

The value of a computer in applying even fairly simple forecasting techniques is demonstrated by the computations required for exponential smoothing. The exponential smoothing formula is shown in the margin. This means that a new forecast is computed by taking the old forecast and adjusting it by a fraction of the difference by which the old forecast deviated from the actual performance. This smoothing fraction is often called Alpha. This is a simple computation, but, if performed manually for large numbers of items, it would be time consuming and likely to result in errors. For example, if actual usage was 193 and the old forecast was 180, given an Alpha fraction of .15, the computation would be as shown in the margin. These computations are easily and accurately performed on a computer.

New forecast = old forecast + Alpha (actual − old forecast)

$$\text{New forecast} = 180 + .15(193 - 180)$$
$$= 182 \quad (181.95 \text{ rounded})$$

SYSTEM SIMULATION IN OPERATIONS RESEARCH

The term "system simulation" refers to duplicating the essence of a system in a way that allows an investigator to study and work with it. The mathematical or symbolic representation of a system is called the model. This approach to problem solving is not new; investigators have frequently made models or representations of reality in order to learn, to test ideas, and to predict the effect of introducing changes. However, the computer has made possible systems studies that heretofore were impractical. Even a modestly scaled system simulation usually requires more computations than can be efficiently performed by hand.

Simulation is used in the sciences for simulating behavior, and by business for simulating business systems. The latter application is one of the most promising business uses for computers. The simulation approach requires a quantitative description of the business system and the programming of the model for a computer. The model allows those using it to compress real time, so that years of operation can be studied in a few minutes. Alternatively, the process may be slowed down to study problem areas in detail. Simulation can thus offer a basis for decisions about a new system without the disruptions and the costs associated with trying a system which may fail. Three examples of the use of simulation are budgetary planning, inventory management, and industrial dynamics.

In simulation for budgetary planning, the budgetary relationships are described mathematically and programmed on the computer. A budget document is prepared by the computer from information provided by the user. If the result is not satisfactory, the assumption and relationships are examined to find out which ones can be changed. After changes in the variables are made, a new budget is run off. This process continues until a satisfactory plan is achieved. The approach concentrates the attention of the planner on the assumptions and estimates rather than on the computations necessary to prepare the planning document.

As an example of the use of budgetary simulation, a company facing a decision whether it should form its own financing subsidiary constructed a mathematical model of the revenue and expense factors expected to be present if the project were undertaken. Using the computer, five years of operation were simulated in a few minutes and projected results printed out for each year. When using the computer model, the executives had only to examine the 28 items which determined the results (cost of funds, interest rate charged, length of contracts, etc.). Each executive connected with the decision could ask ''what if'' questions based on his own estimates for each of these variables. Figure 4–6 shows the results of three different executives using the model—one an optimist, one a pessimist, and the third in a

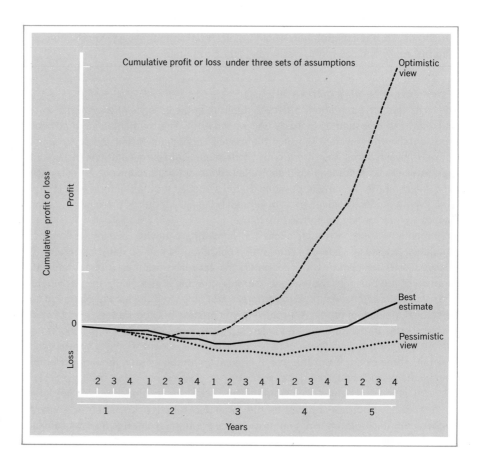

FIGURE 4–6 Results of computer simulation for budgetary planning

middle position. Without the computer, such simulation would have been too expensive to perform.

In deciding on an inventory management plan, it is frequently desirable to test out several alternatives before installing a new system. A computer simulation provides this facility. Several computer programs are available which were written specifically for inventory simulation. Actual past data is used as input into the simulation. The results that would have been achieved with different decision rules can be compared with each other and with actual results.

Industrial dynamics is the name given to an integrated simulation which seeks to discover the best set of decision rules and the best systems design in terms of the organization as a whole. For example, a set of inventory reorder rules may be designed giving a low inventory but possibly causing serious difficulties in the production departments; thus, these inventory reorder rules should be designed in the context of a simulation which includes production, sales, etc. The computer makes it feasible to do so.

INFORMATION RETRIEVAL

Information retrieval illustrates the use of the computer as a symbol manipulator rather than as a computational device. This is potentially one of the most fruitful uses for the computer because the growth in the amount of available information has made it difficult and time consuming to locate and retrieve information using traditional methods. The cost of inadequate retrieval is large. It is estimated that billions of dollars are spent each year in duplicating research which has already been completed and reported in the scientific journals. Three examples of information retrieval applications will illustrate the use of the computer and will suggest possibilities for future use. These examples are selective dissemination of information, technical information retrieval, and legal research.

In a large organization, more information is available than can be read by a single individual, even if he did nothing else. The flood of inside reports, technical memoranda, etc. plus large numbers of outside journals, pamphlets, reports, etc. is more than an individual can handle, and, in fact, any given individual is probably interested in only a small fraction of the available information. The problem is to identify these needs. The individual himself, given the stack of literature, could make a quick decision as to how much of it he wished to read. But in a large organization, this method is not feasible. It might take years for the whole stack of literature to circulate, thereby negating the need for a timely distribution. In addition, the repeated search would represent a huge expenditure of time. With a computer, however, each individual can indicate beforehand the subject areas in which he has an interest, and the computer performs the search for all individuals simultaneously. The computer prepares a small abstract of each article thought to be of interest to an individual. The abstracts are sent out, and the individual then makes the final selection of those items he wishes to read (Figure 4–7). The entire process is performed quickly and uses the capabilities of the computer to make the initial time-consuming search, but the indi-

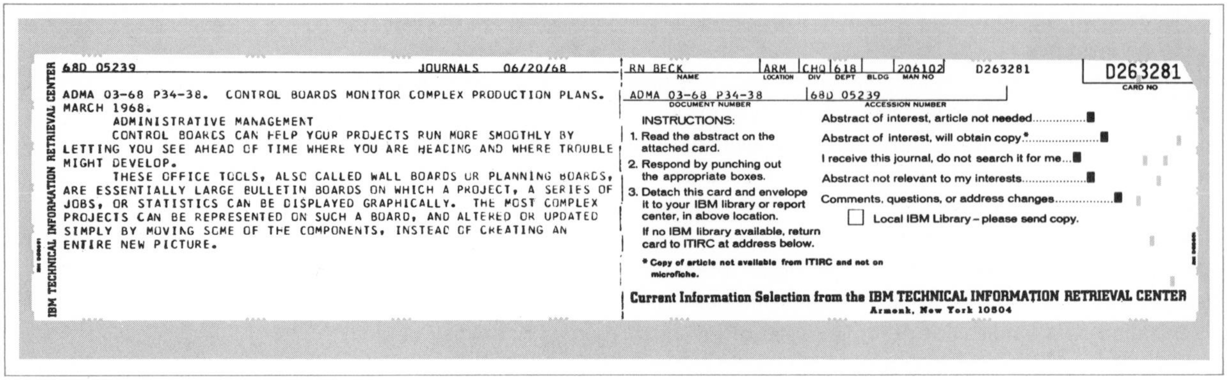

IBM TECHNICAL INFORMATION RETRIEVAL CENTER

68D 05239 JOURNALS 06/20/68

ADMA 03-68 P34-38. CONTROL BOARDS MONITOR COMPLEX PRODUCTION PLANS.
MARCH 1968.
ADMINISTRATIVE MANAGEMENT
CONTROL BOARCS CAN FELP YOUR PROJECTS RUN MORE SMOOTHLY BY LETTING YOU SEE AHEAD OF TIME WHERE YOU ARE HEACING AND WHERE TROUBLE MIGHT DEVELOP.
THESE OFFICE TOCLS, ALSC CALLED WALL BOARDS OR PLANNING BOARCS, ARE ESSENTIALLY LARGE BULLETIN BOARDS ON WHICH A PROJECT, A SERIES OF JOBS, OR STATISTICS CAN BE DISPLAYED GRAPHICALLY. THE MOST COMPLEX PROJECTS CAN BE REPRESENTED ON SUCH A BOARD, AND ALTERED OR UPDATED SIMPLY BY MOVING SCME OF THE COMPONENTS, INSTEAC CF CREATING AN ENTIRE NEW PICTURE.

RN BECK (NAME) | ARM (LOCATION) | CHQ (DIV) | 618 (DEPT) | (BLDG) | 206102 (MAN NO) D263281

D263281 (CARD NO)

ADMA 03-68 P34-38 (DOCUMENT NUMBER) | 68D 05239 (ACCESSION NUMBER)

INSTRUCTIONS:
1. Read the abstract on the attached card.
2. Respond by punching out the appropriate boxes.
3. Detach this card and envelope it to your IBM library or report center, in above location.
If no IBM library available, return card to ITIRC at address below.

Abstract of interest, article not needed...............
Abstract of interest, will obtain copy*...................
I receive this journal, do not search it for me...
Abstract not relevant to my interests..................
Comments, questions, or address changes................
☐ Local IBM Library – please send copy.

* Copy of article not available from ITIRC and not on microfiche.

Current Information Selection from the IBM TECHNICAL INFORMATION RETRIEVAL CENTER
Armonk, New York 10504

FIGURE 4–7 Notice used in IBM Current Information Selection system. Abstract is printed on left-hand card; right-hand card is for response. (Courtesy of International Business Machines Corporation)

vidual himself makes the final judgmental decision. The method works by the use of a set of identifiers by which the individual describes his interests and which are also found in the text of articles, reports, memoranda, etc. The computer compares the identifiers in the profile of each individual against identifiers taken by the computer from abstracts of articles in order to select those that match.

Technical information retrieval can use several different approaches. The most common is the key word approach, in which the contents of each technical paper are identified by key words. For example, a technical article on the effect on metals of radiation in space might be identified by the key words "metals," "radiation," and "space." In addition to the key-words identifier, a short abstract is prepared and stored on a medium such as magnetic tape. In order to obtain information on a topic, the topic is defined by a set of key words which best describe it. The computer compares this set of topic identifiers with the list of identifiers for each article and selects those papers which have one or more identifiers in common. The abstracts of these papers are then printed out, together with an identifying number through which the article may be located. A second method, used in IBM's Current Information Selection system illustrated in Figure 4–7, examines the entire text of the abstract as the basis for matching and selection. The computer can therefore search not only for key words but also for words in context. Requests can indicate single terms, combinations of terms, exclusions, etc.

The determination of legal questions depends heavily upon legal precedent—what has been decided previously in similar cases. It is therefore necessary for the lawyer to examine all such precedents in order to prepare his opinion or his case. A service[1] is available through which a lawyer may use the computer to search for the legal citations to be examined. The lawyer, using a teletypewriter, types a term which describes the problem he is researching. The computer searches the descriptions for all cases and provides, via the teletypewriter, an immediate response by listing the case

[1] Offered by Law Research, Inc., New York City, over the Western Union Telex network.

citations. The lawyer must then look up the cases in his own law books. The computer search is usually used to speed up the search process or to check prior manual research. The lawyer may still do additional manual searching, but the computer has provided a basis from which to proceed.

▌ADVANCED APPROACHES TO INFORMATION SYSTEMS

Many computer systems are merely copies of a prior manual or punched-card system and do not take advantage of the unique capabilities of the computer. Especially when third-generation hardware is used, the computer allows new dimensions in processing methods and systems design. The advanced information systems now being designed and installed therefore differ radically from the systems in common use. Three important concepts will serve as an introduction to the way computers are being applied in advanced approaches to information systems. These are realtime processing, partially integrated systems, and the management information system.

REALTIME PROCESSING

Realtime processing is immediate response processing, which for effective performance requires a computer designed to handle such an approach. Most general-purpose medium and large third-generation equipment can handle realtime processing. There are also computers especially designed for realtime work.

A realtime system, also referred to as an online realtime (OLRT) system, consists of a computer to which are connected a number of remote devices for sending data to the computer and for receiving responses back from the computer. These devices are provided to each person or machine having a need to originate, retrieve, or utilize information on an immediate response basis. A computer system is described as "realtime" if the complete cycle of transmission of data to the computer, processing, and sending out of results takes place within the time allowed for influencing a process or transaction. If the process being controlled is the flight of a guided missile, there is a very short interval of time allowed for computing changes to be made in the guidance controls if the course of the missile is to be influenced. For a check-cashing transaction in which the bank balance or credit standing of a customer is to be approved before his check will be cashed, realtime is the interval of time, perhaps 1 to 2 minutes, the customer is willing to wait for the transaction to be completed. In other words, realtime data processing is concurrent with the transaction or process such that the results of the data processing can influence the course of the action taking place. Although this definition would allow realtime processing, in some cases, to extend over several days, the term is limited to data processing which is performed immediately.

The term online refers to the fact that all data files, input/output devices, etc., are connected directly to the computer so that a request for a response may be made at any time. In fact, there may be several concurrent requests which the computer

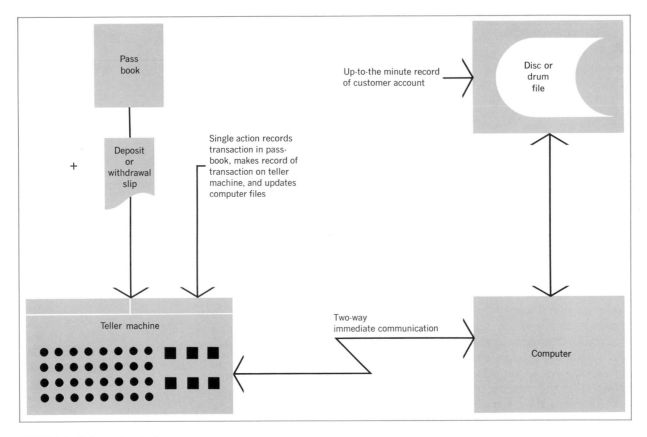

Pass book

Deposit or withdrawal slip

+

Single action records transaction in pass-book, makes record of transaction on teller machine, and updates computer files

Teller machine

Up-to-the minute record of customer account

Disc or drum file

Two-way immediate communication

Computer

FIGURE 4–8 Online savings bank application

must be able to accept and act upon. Four examples of realtime applications will illustrate this data processing concept.

The first example is an airlines reservation system, in which a central computer maintains a record of all scheduled flights for several weeks into the future. Each reservation agent has a device for interrogating the computer to determine if the space that a customer is requesting is available. If a customer makes a reservation, the computer records this fact in storage and reduces the number of seats available for the flight. The interrogation of the computer and the recording of the reservation occur in a few seconds. It occurs in realtime because the request and reply are processed in the time the customer is willing to wait.

A second example is a savings bank system. In this system, customer records are maintained on a central computer and input/output devices are installed at each branch of the savings bank. Thus, every deposit, withdrawal, payment, etc., is recorded at the time of the transaction, and current customer balances are available at all times at all branches (Figure 4–8).

Another realtime application is process control. A special process control computer is frequently used for this purpose because the full capabilities of a general-purpose computer are not always required. Continuous manufacturing processes such as oil refining and chemical production have measuring and regulating devices at various points in the process. When the measurements indicate that the process is deviating from the desired norm by more than an allowable limit, the regulating devices are adjusted. Computers have been programmed to run such plants by having the measurement devices connected to the computer, which makes continuous comparison. Necessary changes in controls are made directly by the computer. The measurements and the setting of the controls are carried out faster and more accurately than when performed by human operators (Figure 4–9).

Any large organization with geographically dispersed units has a problem in the control of teletype message traffic. This problem can be solved by a communications system equipped with transmitting and receiving terminals linked to a switching center, which makes the connections between the receiving and sending terminals. Computers are being used to perform the switching function. The largest of such computer-controlled communications systems is the United States Air Force AUTO-DIN (Automatic Digital Network) system. In this system, five regional computer-controlled switching centers connect to terminals in each region and then to each other. The system has a capacity of 500 terminals. The computers switch messages on the basis of priority and security classification. They also make a record of all messages for reference and do statistical analysis.

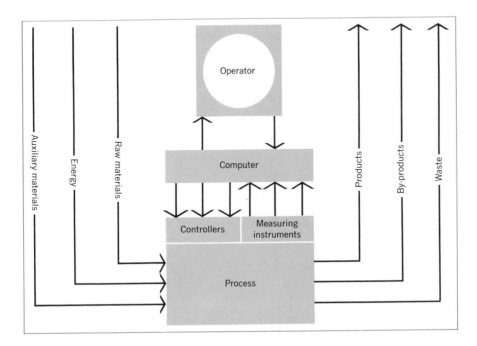

FIGURE 4–9 Use of computer to control an industrial process

INTEGRATED DATA PROCESSING

Integrated data processing is an approach to system design in which the collection, coding, and filing of data are coordinated in order to minimize duplicate operations and duplicate files. Transcribing of the same data more than once is avoided. This concept can be illustrated by the recording which takes place when a manufacturing company sells an item.

DOCUMENT	DATA ITEMS
Order confirmation	Name, address, quantity, description, and price
Shipping instructions	Name, address, order quantity, and description
Shipping advice	Name, address, actual quantity, and description
Sales invoice	Name, address, quantity, description, price, and amount
Sales record	Customer number and amount
Receivable record	Customer number and amount
Physical inventory record	Quantity and description
Dollar inventory record	Quantity, description, and cost of item
Cost of sales record	Quantity and cost of item

In a nonintegrated data processing approach, there is a separate preparation of the documents, and the common information must be recorded separately on each to make the documents complete. The integrated system prepares all documents and updates all files from an initial input of the data items. In the example given, the initial inputs might come from a typing of the order confirmation plus a recording of the amount shipped. All document preparation and file updating is then performed without further transcriptions of data (Figure 4–10).

FIGURE 4–10   Example of integrated data processing approach

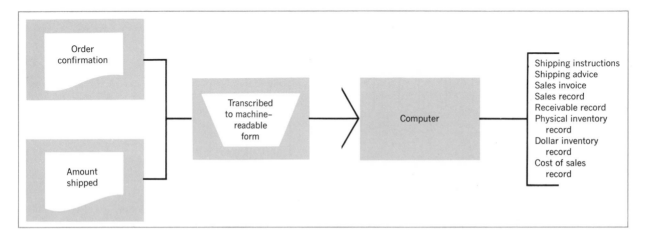

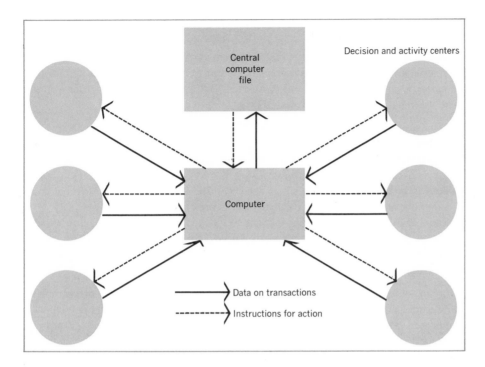

FIGURE 4–11 The total computer-based management information system

From this example, two characteristics of integrated systems can be seen:

1 The parts of the system are interrelated.
2 A single source document, once entered into the system, initiates the updating of all master files and records associated with the transaction.

The data processing in an organization can be partially integrated or fully integrated. A complex, fully integrated system has also been referred to as a management information system (MIS), or as a total system.

MANAGEMENT INFORMATION SYSTEM

There is not unanimity on what is meant by a management information system, but in general the term is used to refer to a highly integrated, all-encompassing computer-based system for processing data and providing information for operating and managing an organization. The MIS system is based on the concept that the organization is an integrated entity in which all economic functions are interrelated and dependent upon one another, and therefore the data processing system should likewise be interlocked. In this type of total system, data generated anywhere in the organization is available to the central computer, which then makes the data accessible to all decision points having a need for it (Figure 4–11). All data inputs are analyzed in terms of the organization as a whole, so that decisions resulting from this analysis will maximize the efficiency of the entire concern. The computer analysis makes use of quantitative analysis methods from statistics and operations research.

Achievement of any degree of sophistication in the design of an MIS system requires an advanced online realtime computer. The total system, using such equipment, will have the following characteristics:

1 All environmental changes and transactions are recorded immediately and transmitted to the computer.
2 The computer maintains central files containing all history, current data, and decision rules.
3 Data is processed continuously as received. The overall impact of internal and external events is evaluated as these events are reported.
4 Periodic information reports are produced at appropriate intervals. Special reports are transmitted automatically to inform individuals of actions to be taken or of information vital to their function. Up-to-date minute reports are available on request.

The implementation of systems with these characteristics is much more complex than computerizing single data processing application modules such as payroll, accounts receivable, etc. These application modules were convenient for data processing when it was performed manually, with punched cards, or by a simple computer, but the advanced computer system allows the system design to break from this pattern and make the processing of data mirror the interrelationship found in the organization. The implementation of such total systems is one of the most challenging problems in data processing today.

SOME INTERESTING EXAMPLES OF COMPUTER USE

The preceding discussion has concentrated on the use of computers in commercial data processing applications. Computers are also being applied to a wide range of other types of problems involving processing of data and manipulation of symbols. Some examples are guidance and control of spacecraft, prediction of elections, and computer-aided instruction.

GUIDANCE AND CONTROL OF SPACECRAFT

A spacecraft is monitored as to speed, velocity, orbit, etc. by computers at tracking stations. In addition, a miniaturized but powerful computer is contained in the spacecraft itself. This computer accepts data from the various controls and measuring devices and computes the actions to be taken to achieve changes in speed, direction, orbit, etc. The reliance placed upon the computers in guidance and control is illustrated by the fact that a malfunction in the computer aboard a spacecraft in 1966 led to the flight being terminated ahead of schedule.

PREDICTION OF ELECTIONS

Each of the major television networks in the United States has a computer as part of the national election coverage. Based on early returns representing as little as 1 percent of the total vote, the computer programs forecast the final winner. No longer need election watchers stay up through the night to find out which candidate in the major contests is the winner—by the time the polls close in California, there is already a firm computer-based prediction for the office of President and much of the Congress.

Conceptually, the computer is programmed to perform the same task as political commentators, but to do it much faster, more precisely, more comprehensively, and more accurately. The prediction of final results is based on the relationship between early, scattered returns and the complete tally. The predictive relationship is computed by a statistical analysis of historical patterns. The astute political observer may have a gross idea of a few predictive relationships; the computer analysis provides thousands of precise, mathematically defined ones. On election night these previously computed relationships are applied to the early returns to formulate the prediction of final results. The accuracy of these predictions has been excellent. Only where there were major elements present which could not be estimated from historical data have the predictions been wrong.

COMPUTER-ASSISTED INSTRUCTION

A major problem in education is the fact that students learn best when they must respond at frequent intervals to questions about the content and meaning of that

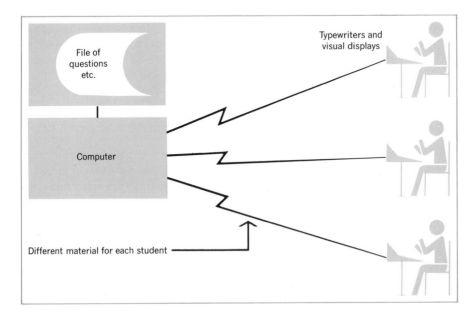

FIGURE 4–12 Computer-aided instruction

which they are studying, yet to do this is impossible in the typical classroom situation. The ideal situation consists of one teacher for each student, with the teacher pacing the presentation of the material to suit the background and learning capability of the student. The computer is being used in exactly this way. Either through a type-writer or display device (similar to a television screen), the computer presents short instructional steps followed by a question requiring a response. If a student has grasped a concept, as evidenced by a correct response, he proceeds to the next step in the material. If a mistake is made at some point, the student is given additional material to explain the topic again. The computer can handle many students con-currently with each student following a different, individualized sequence of instructions (Figure 4–12).

▌ SUMMARY

As a data processor, the capabilities of the computer exceed those of the human in speed, accuracy, retrieval, continuance, and ability to follow directions, but the human has capabilities of innovation and heuristic reasoning which are lacking in the computer. This suggests the characteristics which make an application suitable for a computer—much volume of processing (either in numbers of computations or in numbers of records to be handled) and a well-defined, explicit processing procedure.

The applications described in the chapter fit this description. The first category, traditional record keeping, consists of well-defined procedures which are easily transferred to a computer, the major economic requirement being a sufficient volume to justify the costs of setting up and converting to a computer system. The second group were methods of analysis that are made feasible by the computer. There would be no linear programming, system simulation, etc., without a computer. The low cost of computer computations makes economical a new range of techniques. The third use is in advanced approaches to information systems. Manual and punched card data processing are usually economical only if there is a batch mode of operation. Realtime processing, integrated processing, and such concepts as the management information system are possible because of the capabilities of computer hardware. The computer thus opens up new methods of processing and new system design concepts. The last category of uses is a reminder that there are myriads of possibilities for using the computer. The three interesting uses presented are only indications of these applications.

▌ EXERCISES

1   Define:

    a   Heuristic reasoning

  b   System simulation
  c   Realtime processing
  d   Total management information system
  e   Integrated data processing

2 What characteristics make each of the following a widely used application for computer processing:
  a   Payroll
  b   Accounts receivable
  c   Linear programming
  d   Forecasting
  e   Simulation

3 Based on the material presented thus far in the text, what are the characteristics of a processing problem which will be suitable and economically justified for computer processing?

4 The chapter described the relative capabilities of both man and the computer. What would be the general characteristics of a system which will make use of the capabilities of both? What types of problems would the man-machine system be equipped to handle?

5 What might be some of the difficulties with two of the information retrieval methods explained in the chapter?
  a   Selective distribution of information
  b   Technical retrieval using keyword

6 What are the social implications of computer forecasting of results of elections while the polls are still open in part of the country?

7 What might be some disadvantages from a total management information system?

8 What competitive advantage would a realtime system give:
  a   A savings and loan association with several branch locations
  b   An airline

9 Using exponential smoothing, calculate for each point the forecasted usage for an item with the following usage by period. Use a smoothing factor of .15.

ACTUAL USAGE	FORECAST
104	108
110	
102	
100	
112	

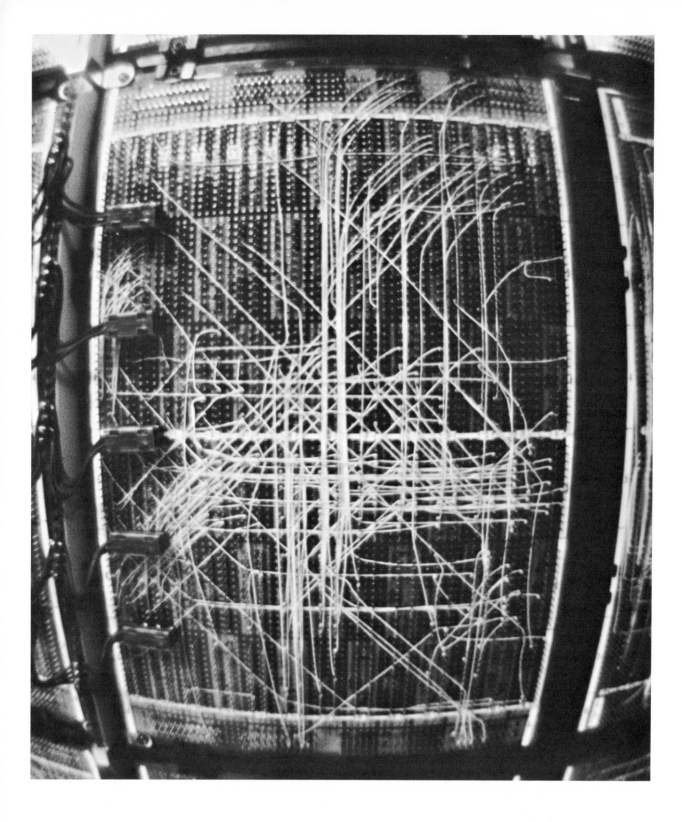

▮ TWO-STATE REPRESENTATION OF DATA
OVERVIEW
CONCEPTS OF A NUMBER SYSTEM
CONCEPT OF STATE FOR REPRESENTING INFORMATION

▮ BINARY ARITHMETIC
THE BINARY SYSTEM
SELF-TESTING QUIZ 5–1
SELF-TESTING QUIZ 5–2
SELF-TESTING QUIZ 5–3
ARITHMETIC OPERATIONS IN BINARY
SELF-TESTING QUIZ 5–4
SELF-TESTING QUIZ 5–5
BINARY ARITHMETIC USING COMPLEMENTS
SELF-TESTING QUIZ 5–6

▮ OPERATOR NOTATION
THE OCTAL SYSTEM
SELF-TESTING QUIZ 5–7
THE HEXADECIMAL SYSTEM
SELF-TESTING QUIZ 5–8

▮ BINARY CODED DECIMAL

▮ REPRESENTING ALPHANUMERIC INFORMATION
REPRESENTING ALPHANUMERICS IN A BINARY COMPUTER
REPRESENTING ALPHANUMERICS AS BINARY CODED CHARACTERS
CONTROL BITS

▮ SUMMARY

▮ ANSWERS TO SELF-TESTING QUIZZES
SELF-TESTING QUIZ 5–1
SELF-TESTING QUIZ 5–2
SELF-TESTING QUIZ 5–3
SELF-TESTING QUIZ 5–4
SELF-TESTING QUIZ 5–5
SELF-TESTING QUIZ 5–6
SELF-TESTING QUIZ 5–7
SELF-TESTING QUIZ 5–8

▮ EXERCISES

CHAPTER

5

COMPUTER
ARITHMETIC
AND DATA
REPRESENTATION

In written communication, we normally use symbols consisting of the decimal number system, a set of 26 alphabetic characters, and a number of special characters such as period, equals sign, semicolon, etc. When using the computer, the data input to computer processing consists of these alphanumeric characters; the reports and documents prepared as computer output also use this set of symbols. Internally in the computer, however, numbers and alphabetic or other characters are represented by a special computer notation. This chapter explains the computer data representa-

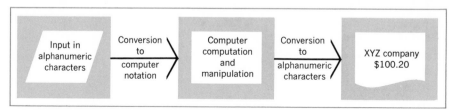

tion and how a computer can manipulate it for arithmetic. Self-testing quizzes are used in the chapter to aid in learning these topics. The answers to these quizzes are at the end of the chapter.

❚ TWO-STATE REPRESENTATION OF DATA

OVERVIEW

The computer does not have a large number of symbols for representing data. It has only two, 0 and 1 (called binary digits or bits.) These correspond to the two electronic or magnetic states used in computer circuits and storage. If the computer can only represent 0 and 1, how can it store and manipulate the 60 or so alphanumeric characters used to represent data? This is done by using a set of binary digits (0s and 1s) to identify which data character is being represented. If, for example, a set of three bits were used, it would be possible to encode eight different characters because there are eight different combinations of the bits in the set, each of which could be assigned to represent a different character. Eight combinations are of course not sufficient. It takes at least a set of 6 bits (64 combinations), and many third-generation computers use a set of 8 bits (256 combinations).

000	011	110
001	100	111
010	101	

   The coding of each alphanumeric character by a separate set of bits is used in connection with all input and output by the computer. This coding is termed *binary coded decimal* or BCD. Many computers perform an additional conversion from BCD into a straight binary representation for all numeric quantities to be used in arithmetic. After computation, the binary numbers must be converted to the BCD character coding for output. Computers which use binary coded numbers in arithmetic need not make these conversions (Figure 5–1). Straight binary arithmetic is much faster and is therefore used on most high-speed computers.

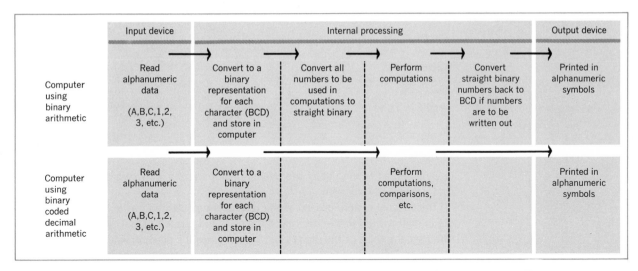

FIGURE 5–1 Data representation in computer processing

Up to this point in the discussion the representation of alphanumeric data in the computer by a set of binary digits has been viewed as a simple matter of making a code, i.e., deciding which 0 and 1 combinations would be used to represent each character. Since numeric data must be used in computations, the coded representations must also be suited for arithmetic. This is accomplished by using the binary system as a basis for coding and for arithmetic. The remainder of this section will explain the concept of a number system and how this relates to use of a binary (0 and 1) representation in computers. The sections that follow will explain binary arithmetic, binary coded decimal, operator notations and the representation of alphanumeric data.

CONCEPTS OF A NUMBER SYSTEM

The number systems we shall be dealing with are based on an absolute value and a positional value. The base (also called radix) of the number system indicates how many absolute values are used in that system. The positional values are found by raising the base of the number system to the power of the position.[1] This is illustrated in Table 5–1 for the decimal system, which has a radix of 10. Note that the positions

[1] As a reminder to readers who may have forgotten, the value resulting from raising a number to a power (i.e., the value resulting from exponentiation) is the product of successive multiplications by the number, with the number of multiplications being equal to the exponent. Thus, $3^4 = 3 \times 3 \times 3 \times 3 = 81$. A number to the 0 power is equal to 1. Therefore, $1^0 = 1$, $2^0 = 1$, $3^0 = 1$, etc. A minus exponent represents a fraction. For example, $4^{-3} = \frac{1}{4^3} = 1/64$.

TABLE 5–1 Some of the Positional Values in the Decimal System

Position number	3	2	1	0		−1	−2
Position value (base of 10)	10^3	10^2	10^1	10^0	Decimal point	10^{-1}	10^{-2}
Quantity represented by position value	1,000 thousands	100 hundreds	10 tens	1 units		1/10 tenths	1/100 hundredths

FIGURE 5–2 Two examples of the decimal system

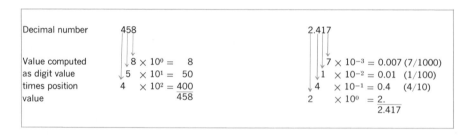

are numbered to the left of the decimal point starting with zero and to the right of the decimal starting with -1.

The decimal system has 10 absolute values represented by the digits 0 through 9. Each digit written in the decimal notation is interpreted as having a value equal to the absolute value of the digit (1, 2, 3, etc.) times the position value of the position it occupies. This is illustrated in Figure 5–2 for two examples.

Many number systems are possible using different sets of absolute values and different bases. Three of the most important for computers are the binary, the octal, and the hexadecimal systems:

NAME	BASE	ABSOLUTE VALUES
Binary	2	0, 1
Octal	8	0, 1, 2, 3, 4, 5, 6, 7
Hexadecimal	16	0 through 9, A, B, C, D, E, F

Each of these will be discussed later in the chapter.

CONCEPT OF STATE FOR REPRESENTING INFORMATION

Since these number systems use the two concepts of position value and absolute values, a mechanical or electronic device can represent a number only if it can represent a position and can have different recognizable states each of which can be identified with a separate absolute value. This concept is illustrated by a mechanical adding machine or by an odometer (mileage indicator) in an automobile (Figure 5–3). There is a wheel for each position value, and each wheel has 10 notches or other markings identifying the 10 absolute values of the decimal system. The wheels are connected so that when the units wheel turns past 9, it moves the 10s wheel one position, and when the 10s wheel moves past 9, it moves the 100s wheel one position, and so on.

A device for representing numbers in a given number system must have as many different states as there are absolute values in the number system. A device for the decimal system must have 10 states, whereas a device for the binary system requires only two states since it has only two absolute values. The 10-state wheel is satisfactory for a mechanical calculator or odometer, but for the electronic devices used in

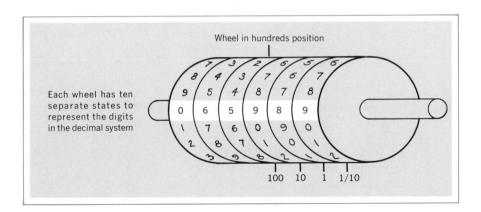

Each wheel has ten separate states to represent the digits in the decimal system

Wheel in hundreds position

100 10 1 1/10

computers 10 recognizable states are not feasible. There are, however, two well-defined states—on and off, or magnetized in one of two directions.

The use of two-state devices in computers suggests the use of the binary system. However, variations from straight binary are possible by the simple approach of using a set of binary devices to represent each position value. The set provides a number of absolute values and allows a binary-based decimal system. The same binary coded decimal approach is used for representing alphabetic characters.

❚ BINARY ARITHMETIC

THE BINARY SYSTEM

The binary system uses the concepts of absolute value and positional value in the same way as the decimal. The difference is that the binary system uses only two absolute values, 0 and 1, and the positional values are powers of 2. Numbers are thus expressed in binary notations as a series of 0s and 1s. The term "bit" is an abbreviation of binary digit. The two values of binary digits are called "0 bit" and "1 bit." The binary point serves the same purpose as the decimal point.

TABLE 5–2   Some of the Positional Values in the Binary System

Position	4	3	2	1	0	•	−1	−2	−3	−4
Position value	2^4	2^3	2^2	2^1	2^0	Binary point	2^{-1}	2^{-2}	2^{-3}	2^{-4}
Quantity represented by position value	16	8	4	2	1		$\frac{1}{2}$	$\frac{1}{4}$	$\frac{1}{8}$	$\frac{1}{16}$

FIGURE 5–4   Example of converting a binary number to the decimal equivalent

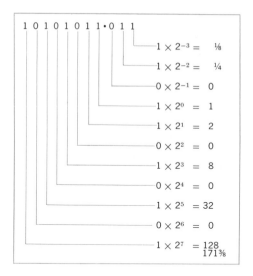

The decimal equivalent of a number written in binary is found by adding the products of the absolute and positional values. For example, the binary 10101011.011 is interpreted as 171⅜, as shown in Figure 5–4.

SELF-TESTING QUIZ 5-1

Before proceeding, we should test our understanding of the basic concepts of the binary system. Do the following self-testing quizzes—the answers are found at the end of the chapter.

1   What is the decimal equivalent of each of the following binary numbers?
    a   1011   *c*   1.0111
    b   10001   *d*   10.1
2   What is the binary number equivalent to the decimal?
    a   3   *c*   15
    b   7   *d*   16

Although most conversion to and from binary is performed by the computer, it is sometimes helpful to be able to interpret a binary number or convert a decimal number to binary. The method of converting from binary to decimal (just shown) is cumbersome; a shortcut method takes advantage of a simple doubling operation (shown in margin). Note, in the conversion shown in Figure 5–4, that the value of a 1 in any position to the left of the binary point can be found by starting with the 1 and doubling it for each position to the left of the binary point.

The shortcut method combines the doubling operation for the different positions. Starting at the leftmost 1 bit, and moving from left to right, double the 1 and add the value of the binary digit in the next position (0 or 1). Take this sum, double it, and add the value in the succeeding position. This sequence of operations is continued,

Value of position = 16

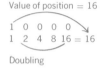

Doubling

Binary number	1	0	1	0	1	0	1	1.	
Conversion sums from doubling and adding			1	2	5	10	21	42	85 (171) answer

FIGURE 5-5 Example of conversion of a binary number by doubling and adding

Binary number	.0	1	1	0	1	
Conversion sums	½	¼	⅜	⁵⁄₁₆	(¹³⁄₃₂) answer	

FIGURE 5-6 Example of conversion of a binary fraction to a decimal fraction by doubling and adding

doubling the new sum and adding the 1 or 0 in the next position, until the binary point is reached. For example, the binary number 10101011 from the example in Figure 5-4 would be handled as shown in Figure 5-5. This process can also be used for binary digits to the right of the binary point, except that the denominator starts with 2 and doubles for each position to the right. The numerator is found by doubling and adding, starting with the first 1 bit to the right of the binary point. The conversion of .01101 is shown in Figure 5-6.

SELF-TESTING QUIZ 5-2

Use the doubling and addition method to convert the following binary numbers to decimal:

1 10111   3 .101101
2 100001   4 1110.111

The conversion of a decimal number to a binary number requires finding the different powers of 2 which represent the number. For an integer (whole) number or for the integral (whole number) portion of a mixed number, this can be accomplished by successive divisions by 2. The division from each division is recorded. This will be either a 1 or a 0. A decimal fraction is converted to binary by doubling the digits to the right of the decimal. The whole number (a 0 or 1) which results from the doubling is the digit for the binary number. The fractional portion resulting from the doubling is saved and the process repeated until the fraction becomes zero or until the required number of binary digits has been obtained. As examples, the conversion of the numbers 141 and .375 are shown in Figure 5-7.

SELF-TESTING QUIZ 5-3

Convert the following decimal numbers to binary. Do not carry the fractions beyond six binary digits.

1 89   3 .828125
2 104   4 .0774

FIGURE 5-7 Examples of converting decimal numbers to binary

```
                    Remainder
2 | 141
2 |  70        1
2 |  35        0

2 |  17        1
2 |   8        1
2 |   4        0
2 |   2        0
2 |   1        0
  |   0        1    Start binary number with last digit. The binary
                    equivalent of 141 is 10001101.

    .375
    × 2
  ⓪.750        0  ⎫
    × 2           ⎬
  ①.500        1  ⎬ Integers resulting from doubling.
    × 2           ⎪
  ①.000        1  ⎭

      ↑
                      Start binary fraction at first digit. The binary
                      equivalent of .375 is .011.
```

ARITHMETIC OPERATIONS IN BINARY

Arithmetic operations with decimal numbers depend on several rules which are usually learned at such an early age that the process seems "natural" rather than dependent on a set of rules and tables. For example, we learn to add by memorizing the add table for the decimal system (Figure 5-8). This is a table expressing the re-

FIGURE 5-8 Addition tables for decimal and binary systems

Decimal addition table

	0	1	2	3	4	5	6	7	8	9
0	0	1	2	3	4	5	6	7	8	9
1		2	3	4	5	6	7	8	9	10
2			4	5	6	7	8	9	10	11
3				6	7	8	9	10	11	12
4	Example:				8	9	10	11	12	13
5	3 + 4 = 7					10	11	12	13	14
6							12	13	14	15
7								14	15	16
8									16	17
9										18

Binary addition table

	0	1
0	0	1
1	1	10

sults of all possible addition combinations of two numbers. Only half the table is needed, since it is symmetrical. The sum of two numbers is shown at the intersection of one of the numbers from the row and the other from the column.

The rules and add table for binary arithmetic are much simpler than for decimal arithmetic. For example, the addition table for binary arithmetic (Figure 5–8) consists of only four entries. The table is used in the same way as the decimal addition table. Similar tables can be made for multiplication and subtraction.

As with binary to decimal or decimal to binary conversion, the computer programmer or computer user does not usually need to be able to perform binary arithmetic. However, binary arithmetic is useful background for understanding computers. The explanations in this chapter will present a short introduction to arithmetic in binary.

RULES FOR BINARY ADDITION

$1 + 1 = 0$ and carry 1 to add to next column
$1 + 0 = 1$
$0 + 1 = 1$
$0 + 0 = 0$

Examples:

Binary	Decimal equivalent	Binary	Decimal equivalent
1011	11	1110.01	14.25
1001	9	11010.11	26.75
10100	20	101001.00	41.00

RULES FOR BINARY SUBTRACTION

$1 - 1 = 0$
$1 - 0 = 1$
$0 - 1 = 1$ with a borrow from the next column of the minuend
$0 - 0 = 0$

Examples:

	Binary	Decimal equivalent	Binary	Decimal equivalent
Minuend	10100	20	101001.00	41.00
Subtrahend	−01001	−9	−011010.11	−26.75
Remainder	01011	11	001110.01	14.25

In subtraction, the borrow reduces the remaining minuend by 1. A borrow will cause a 1 in the next column to the left in the minuend to become 0. If the next column contains a 0, it is changed to a 1 and the succeeding 0s in the minuend are changed to 1s until a 1 can be changed to a 0. For example, 001 from 1100 will cause a borrow when the first position is subtracted:

PROBLEM	STEP 1	STEP 2	STEP 3	STEP 4
	*	*	*	
	1	11	011	011
11000	110̸0̸0	11̸0̸0̸0	1̸1̸0̸0̸0	1̸1̸0̸0̸0
−00001	−00001	−00001	−00001	−00001
	1	1	1	10111
	*Carry changes 0 to 1	*Continue changing 0s to 1s	*Until a 1 can be changed to a 0, then proceed with problem	

From a computational standpoint, the borrow can also be accomplished by an "add back method" in which the carry is handled by adding a 1 to the next column of the subtrahend. In the case of the preceding example, the add back method would be:

PROBLEM	STEP 1	STEP 2	STEP 3	STEP 4
11000	11000	11000	11000	11000
−00001	−0000̸1	−000̸0̸1	−00̸0̸0̸1	−00̸0̸0̸1
	1	11	111	111
	1	11	111	10111
	0 − 1 = 1 and add 1 to next column to left in subtrahend	0 − 1 = 1 so add 1 to next column	0 − 1 = 1 so add 1 to next column	Complete subtraction— no more carries

SELF-TESTING QUIZ 5-4
Perform the following binary arithmetic:

1   10110
    +10011

2   10111
    +10011

3   101101
   − 10011

4   100000
   −   11

RULES FOR BINARY MULTIPLICATION

Copy multiplicand when multiplier digit is 1; do not when it is 0.

Shift as in decimal multiplication.

Add the resulting binary numbers according to the binary addition rules.

Examples:

Binary	Decimal equivalent	Binary	Decimal equivalent
1101	13	101	5
1100	$\times 12$	111	$\times 7$
0	26	101	35
0	13	101	
1101	156	101	
1101		100011	
10011100			

It may not be obvious how to handle the addition if the result of the multiplication gives columns with more than two 1s. They can be handled as pairs or by adjusting the column to which the carry is placed, as shown by the following example.

SAMPLE MULTIPLI-CATION PROBLEM	ADDITION HANDLED AS PAIRS (COL. 3)	HANDLE AS SINGLE CARRY

RULES FOR BINARY DIVISION

Start from the left on the dividend.

Perform a series of subtractions in which the divisor is subtracted from the dividend.

If subtraction is possible, put a 1 in the quotient and subtract the divisor from the corresponding digits of the dividend.

If subtraction is not possible (divisor greater than remainder), record a 0 in the quotient.

Bring down the next digit to add to the remainder digits. Proceed as before in a manner similar to long division.

Example:

Binary

```
        0101 1
110)100001^0
    110 ←——— Divisor greater than 100, so put 0 in quotient
   1000 ←——— Add digit from dividend to group used above
    110 ←——— Subtraction possible, so put 1 in quotient
    100 ←——— Remainder from subtraction plus digit from dividend
    110 ←——— Divisor greater, so put 0 in quotient
   1001 ←— Add digit from dividend to group
    110 ←— Subtraction possible, so put 1 in quotient
    110 ←— Perform subtraction, and add digit from dividend to remainder
    110 ←— Subtraction possible, so put 1 in quotient
      ←— No remainder, so stop
```

Decimal equivalent
```
  5 5
6)33^
  30
  30
  30
```

Perform the following binary arithmetic:

1   10111
    ×101

2   1110
    ×111

3   101)$\overline{1110011}$

4   111)$\overline{1100010}$

BINARY ARITHMETIC USING COMPLEMENTS

One of the problems of the computer hardware designer is to simplify the computer circuitry. Subtraction is usually performed by complementing the number to be subtracted and then adding the complement. This simplifies circuitry because subtraction can make use of the addition circuitry. The complementing process itself is very simple. Since multiplication is basically addition and division involves subtraction, the change to the complement method of subtraction reduces all computer arithmetic to forms of addition. Negative numbers are usually also handled by complementing.

In the decimal system, also, subtraction may be performed by adding of complements. The 9s complement of a decimal number is found by subtracting each digit from 9, and the 10s by adding 1 to the 9s complement. The corresponding binary number complements are the 1s and 2s complements. The 1s complement of a binary number is the number obtained by making each 0 into a 1 and each 1 into a 0. The 2s complement is the 1s complement plus 1.

The rules for complement subtraction of decimal numbers, with the exception of the manner of forming the complement, are the same as for binary numbers.

Number	346	799	192
9s complement	653	200	807
10s complement	654	201	808
Binary number	1011	1111	1010
1s complement	0100	0000	0101
2d complement	0101	0001	0110

RULES FOR COMPLEMENT SUBTRACTION—1S COMPLEMENT

Compute the 1s complement of the subtrahend by changing 1s to 0s and all 0s to 1s.

Add the complement to the minuend.

Perform an end-around carry of 1 or 0.

If the end-around carry is 0, the result must be recomplemented and a negative sign attached. If the end-around carry is 1, no recomplementing is necessary.

Problem	Decimal using 9s complement	Binary using 1s complement
14 −06 08	14 +93 ①07 {End-around carry of 1} →1 08	1110 +1001 ①0111 →1 1000
06 −14 −08	06 85 ⓪91 {End-around carry of 0} →0 91 {Recomplement and attach negative sign} −08	0110 0001 ⓪0111 →0 0111 −1000

If the 2s and 10s complements were used in the examples, the end-around carry would be unnecessary, but recomplementing would still be determined by a carry of 0.

SELF-TESTING QUIZ 5–6

Perform the following arithmetic using the complements indicated:

1	140 (9s complement) −270		4	10110 (1s complement) −11000	
2	374 (9s complement) −280		5	11100 (1s complement) −01011	
3	853 (10s complement) −127		6	11001 (2s complement) −01101	

▌OPERATOR NOTATION

The preceding discussion of the binary system showed how a number can be represented by a string of binary digits (bits). By having a sufficiently large number of bit positions any binary number can be represented. The requirements of computer storage and computer circuitry are such that the number of bits to be used by a number must be specified in advance. There are two basic approaches to this specification:

1 A fixed number of bits is always used to represent a number, and any extra bit positions are set to 0s. A common size is 32 to 36 bits. However, sizes range from 16 to 60 bits.
2 A variable number of small bit sets is used. Each of the small bit sets encodes a character. These sets vary in size from 4 to 8 bits.

These two approaches form the basis for the fixed and variable word length computer designs to be discussed in Chapter 7. In this chapter, the approaches are important because they are the reason for different binary-based notations.

When a fixed set of bits is used to represent a number, there is a need for a computer operator notation. If the computer programmer or computer operator had to write down a set of 32 bits when representing the contents of a storage location, the chances for error would be great. This is illustrated by the following example of a 32-bit set expressed in binary and the corresponding octal and hexadecimal shorthand for programmer and operator use:

Binary	10010111101000110111011101110111
Octal	2 2 7 5 0 6 7 3 5 6 7
Hexadecimal	9 7 A 3 7 7 7 7

It can readily be seen that using either octal or hexadecimal notation to describe the underlying binary digits is less error prone and more efficient. When a binary computer uses one of these number systems for operator and programmer purposes, the computer messages regarding the instructions and data stored in memory are in that notation rather than straight binary. Many of the computer console displays on the operator panel may show a light for each binary digit, but the lights are marked off in groups of 3 or 4 bits so that the operator can read them off in octal or hexadecimal notation.

The approach of using a variable number of small bit sets is the basis for a binary-based system of coding in which each numeric digit is represented by a separate bit set. This coding, called binary coded decimal, will be explained in the next section.

THE OCTAL SYSTEM

The octal system has a base (radix) of 8. It therefore uses the absolute values from 0 through 7 and positional values which are powers of 8. This is shown by the octal notation for a group of decimal numbers.

DECIMAL	OCTAL	DECIMAL	OCTAL
1	1	11	13
2	2	12	14
3	3	13	15
4	4	14	16
5	5	15	17
6	6	16	20
7	7	17	21
8	10	18	22
9	11	19	23
10	12	20	24

$$
\begin{array}{r}
2\ 2\ 4 \\
4 \times 8^0 = \ \ 4 \\
2 \times 8^1 = \ 16 \\
2 \times 8^2 = 128 \\
\hline
148
\end{array}
$$

The number 224 in octal (written 224_8) is converted to decimal by taking the absolute values times the position values.

A method similar to the doubling and adding method for binary can be used in converting from octal to decimal. Starting with the leftmost digit, multiply by 8, add the next octal digit, multiply by 8, etc. until the last digit is added. We use the same example of 224_8.

A number to the base 10 (decimal number) is translated into octal by dividing successively by 8 and saving the remainders. The remainders are the digits in the octal number. This procedure is the same as the successive division by 2 procedure for translating from decimal to binary. For example, the translation of decimal 247 to octal is shown in the margin.

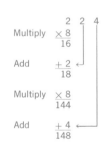

		2	2	4
Multiply	$\times 8$			
	16			
Add	$+2$			
	18			
Multiply	$\times 8$			
	144			
Add	$+4$			
	148			

Octal to binary and binary to octal may be performed easily without computation. To convert a binary number to octal, begin at the binary point and block off groups of three binary digits. Replace each group of three binary digits with its equivalent decimal digit. The digit will range from 0 to 7. To convert from octal to binary, replace each octal digit with the equivalent three binary digits.

```
            Remainder
8 | 247        7
  8 | 30       6   The octal equivalent
    8 | 3      3   of 247 is 367.
        0
```

Octal	761	365	6437101
Binary	111 110 001	011 110 101	110 100 011 111 001 000 001

For converting short binary numbers, it is frequently simpler to convert first to octal and then mentally to convert octal to decimal. The binary number 110111101, for example, is easily converted to octal 675, which is $(6 \times 64) + (7 \times 8) + 5 = 445$.

1 Convert 3769 to octal.
2 Convert 327_8 to decimal.
3 Convert binary 1110111101100 to octal.
4 Convert 427_8 to binary.
5 Convert the fraction $.36_8$ to decimal.
6 Convert the fraction .45 to an octal fraction (4 digits).

THE HEXADECIMAL SYSTEM

The hexadecimal system has a base of 16. It uses characters representing the values from 0 to 15 for absolute values and powers of 16 for positional values. Because only a single character is allowed for each absolute value, the hexadecimal system uses the characters A through F to represent the values of 10 through 15. (Although one may find many different characters used in mathematics texts, the A–F are the accepted characters for computers.)

DECIMAL VALUE	HEXADECIMAL CHARACTER	DECIMAL VALUE	HEXADECIMAL CHARACTER
0	0	8	8
1	1	9	9
2	2	10	A
3	3	11	B
4	4	12	C
5	5	13	D
6	6	14	E
7	7	15	F

Remainder

16/929

16/58   1

16/3   10 (expressed as A)

0   3

The hexadecimal equivalent of 929 is 3A1.

Conversion from and to hexadecimal is similar to binary and octal conversion. The decimal number is divided by 16 and the remainder saved. For example, 929 in decimal is converted to 3A1 in hexadecimal as shown.

3A1 is converted to decimal as $(3 \times 16^2) + (10 \times 16^1) + (1 \times 16^0) = 929$. The multiply and add procedure can also be used. For the same hexadecimal number, the steps are shown in the margin. When hexadecimal is used to represent a binary number, the individual hexadecimal digits represent successive groups of four binary digits starting at the point. This is similar to the conversion from binary to octal, in

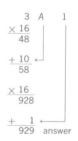

$$\begin{array}{r} 3 \quad A \quad 1 \\ \times\,16 \\ \hline 48 \\ +\,10 \\ \hline 58 \\ \times\,16 \\ \hline 928 \\ +\quad 1 \\ \hline 929 \quad \text{answer} \end{array}$$

which each set of three bits is translated to an octal digit. The hexadecimal 3A1 is equal to the binary $\overline{0011}\overline{1010}\overline{0001}$. Conversion of hexadecimal to or from binary is by inspection, but conversion from or to decimal frequently makes use of a table.

SELF-TESTING QUIZ 5-8

1 Convert 376 to hexadecimal.
2 Convert $1F2_{16}$ to decimal.
3 Convert 10110111101100011 to hexadecimal.
4 Convert $2B6F_{16}$ to binary.
5 Convert $.21_{16}$ to decimal.

▌ BINARY CODED DECIMAL

In straight binary, a number is represented by a string of binary digits. Another approach to representing data in storage is to use individual bit sets for each decimal digit. This modification of the binary system, called binary coded decimal, is used for many business-oriented computers since it simplifies the programming of commercial applications. Straight binary computer design usually provides faster operating speeds and is therefore emphasized in scientific computers, where internal computational speeds are important. Commercial applications typically involve much input and output but very little computation on each record. Therefore, the business computer is oriented to fast conversion from and to decimal form and ease of programming data handling. The use of binary coded decimal or the related binary coded character codes can simplify the input/output conversion and input/output programming, but this occurs at the expense of internal operating speeds.

The binary coded decimal form uses a separate set of four binary digits to represent each decimal digit. As will be explained, the bit set may be larger but the extra bits serve other purposes. The four bit positions are interpreted as in straight binary. This coding, often termed natural binary coded decimal, is the most common code; but variations of this have also been used.

4-BIT SET	DECIMAL VALUE	4-BIT SET	DECIMAL VALUE
0000	0	0101	5
0001	1	0110	6
0010	2	0111	7
0011	3	1000	8
0100	4	1001	9

Note that there are bit combinations that are not used. The number of combinations which can be represented by a set of bits is 2 exponentiated by the number of

Binary coded decimal				Binary
Position value				
8	0	0	0	
4	1	1	0	
2	1	1	1	Bit sets 1011111011
1	1	0	1	
	7	6	3	

FIGURE 5–9 Comparison of binary coded decimal and binary representation of the decimal number 763

bits in the set (2 because there are two absolute values). This means a 4-bit set has 16 zero and one bit combinations. Since only 10 of these can be used to represent decimal digits, the remainder are available for other purposes.

Figure 5–9 illustrates the difference between a binary coded decimal representation and a straight binary for the number 763.

Binary coded decimal arithmetic is slightly different from binary arithmetic. The rules provide for a decimal-type carry when the results from adding two digits exceed 9. Arithmetic using binary coded decimal is often referred to as decimal arithmetic or packed decimal to distinguish it from straight binary.

▌ REPRESENTING ALPHANUMERIC INFORMATION

Up to this point, all discussion has related only to the representing of numbers. Since computers must also be able to accept alphabetic information, there is provision for encoding alphabetic and other characters as well. All methods use a separate set of binary bits for encoding each character. Since each combination of 0 bits and 1 bits in the set can represent a single character, the number of bits needed in the set is determined by the number of different characters to be encoded. As a minimum, for example, the characters to be encoded would include:

10 numeric characters
26 alphabetic characters (capital letters)
16 special characters ($, ; : % etc.)
52 Total

Since computers have become more complex, there is also a need for control characters and more special characters ([ ] $>$ $<$, etc.) plus the potential for lowercase alphabetics. This increases substantially the number of characters to be encoded.

As explained previously, the number of different combinations of 0 bits and 1 bits in a set is 2 raised to a power equal to the number of bits in the set.

BITS IN SET	NUMBER OF COMBINATIONS	POSSIBLE NUMBER OF CHARACTERS ENCODED
4	2^4	16
5	2^5	32
6	2^6	64
7	2^7	128
8	2^8	256

Thus, it can be seen that a 6-bit set is a minimum-size set for representing alphanumerics (combination of alphabetics, numerics and special characters, also called alphamerics).

REPRESENTING ALPHANUMERICS IN A BINARY COMPUTER

The basic approach to representing alphanumerics is a binary computer to break down the large set of bits into smaller groups called bytes, each of which can encode one character. For example, a computer using a 36-bit set might encode alphanumeric information using six 6-bit bytes within the 36 bits. Several popular computers have a 32-bit binary set which can be subdivided into four 8-bit bytes. This approach requires that the computer circuitry be designed to encode alphanumeric information into these groups.

The binary computer uses binary, not binary coded character code, for computational purposes. This means that all numeric data must be converted from the byte coding to binary. All data to be printed out must be coded in the 6- or 8-bit byte code, so, after computation, the binary computational data must be converted to this coding. The different handling in a binary computer of data for computation is illustrated by Figure 5–10.

The encoding of alphanumerics within the bytes uses the same approach as for binary coded decimal explained previously, except that the basic set of four bits is expanded by adding two (or more) zone bits. This is explained in the discussion to follow on binary coded characters.

REPRESENTING ALPHANUMERICS AS BINARY CODED CHARACTERS

The representing of alphanumeric characters is handled in two ways. One method is to expand the binary coded decimal bit set to include zone bits. The other method is to use two separate numeric bit sets to represent alphabetic and special characters. One of the bit sets is designated as the zone set and the other as the numeric set.

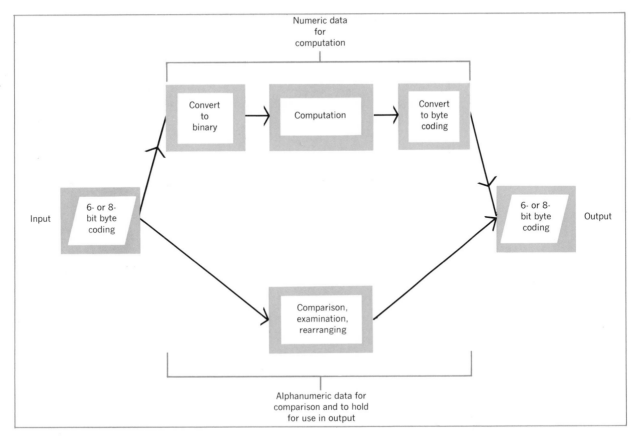

FIGURE 5–10 Handling of alphanumeric data compared to numeric, computational data in a binary computer

A variation of these methods which is quite common in third-generation computers is the use of an 8-bit byte which can represent either two numeric digits or one alphanumeric character. For encoding alphanumerics, one of the 4-bit sets codes the zone and the other the numeric. For internal binary coded decimal processing each of the two 4-bit sets can hold a numeric digit. The latter form is termed "packed decimal." Figure 5–11 illustrates the different methods. Figure 5–12 gives sample codes for the letter A. For numerics, the zone bits may be zero or there may be a special zone to accompany numerics (for input and output). The examples use codes from three different popular computers. Note that the numeric portion in each case is 1 for A, but the zone bits are different. This reflects the different design characteristics of the computer. The codes used also define the collating sequence. When sorting data, an A is smaller than a B, and so on, but the number 1 may be smaller or larger than an A depending on the zone code for the particular computer.

FIGURE 5–11 Methods for representing alphanumerics as binary coded characters

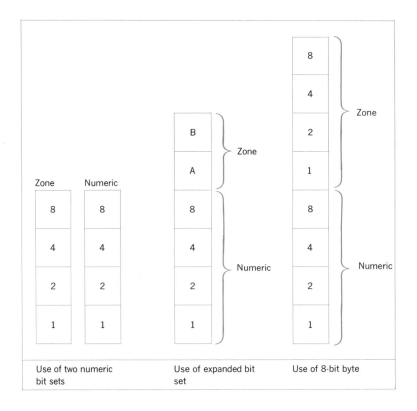

CONTROL BITS

Two control bits need to be mentioned; they will be explained further in subsequent chapters. These are the parity bit and the word mark bit.

A *parity bit* is generally used with either the fixed binary group, the byte, or binary coded character bit set as an error control bit. Its purpose is to detect a malfunction in the equipment which results in the loss or destruction of bits. Any data representation will have a certain number of 1-bits. This number will be either an odd or an even number. The check bit is added (or not added) to the bit set in order to make the total number of bits odd (for an odd-parity check) or even (for an even-parity check). The most common parity check is odd. The parity check is made by recomputing the number of 1-bits whenever a bit set is processed to make sure the number of 1-bits is still odd (or even).

The *word mark bit* is a bit added to a binary coded bit set. It is used for defining a group of the bit sets which are to be handled as a unit. In one common second-generation computer (the IBM 1620), the word mark bit, also used as an arithmetic sign designator, is called a flag bit. The use of the word mark bit will be explained further in Chapter 7 in the discussion of computer words.

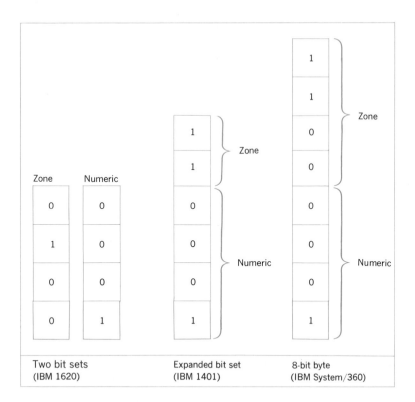

FIGURE 5–12   Sample coding of letter
A—control bits not shown

Zone

Zone

Zone

Numeric

Numeric

Zone | Numeric

0	0
1	0
0	0
0	1

Two bit sets
(IBM 1620)

Expanded bit set
(IBM 1401)

8-bit byte
(IBM System/360)

▌ SUMMARY

An understanding of computer arithmetic is helpful in understanding the differences between different computers. When programming or operating a computer, it is necessary to understand the operator notation used by the computer. This may be binary coded character, hexadecimal, or octal.

It is not necessary to be expert in binary arithmetic but an overview such as has been presented in this chapter is helpful in understanding how computers work.

Although a binary computer performs computations using binary data and binary arithmetic, the data, when originally read from cards, is coded as individual characters each encoded by a 6- or 8-bit set. Computational data is converted from this individual character coding into straight binary coding for computational purposes. When the data is ready for display as printed output, it is encoded again into bit sets, one for each character. Each character for the line to be printed out is represented by a separate bit set.

▌ ANSWERS TO SELF-TESTING QUIZZES

SELF-TESTING QUIZ 5–1

1   *a*   11   **2**   *a*   11

      b   17   *b*   111

      c $1\frac{7}{16}$ *c*   1111

      d $2\frac{1}{2}$ *d*   10000

SELF-TESTING QUIZ 5–2

1   Binary number   1   0   1   1   1

     Sum from doubling   2   4   10   22

     Sum from adding   2   5   11   (23)   answer

2   33

3   Binary number   1   0   1   1   0   1

     Sum from doubling and adding

     numerator   1   2   5   11   22   (43)

     Sum from doubling of denominator   2   4   8   16   32   (64)

                                 answer = 43/64

4 $14\frac{7}{8}$

SELF-TESTING QUIZ 5–3

1   1011001   **3**   .110101

2   1101000   **4**   .000101

SELF-TESTING QUIZ 5–4

        11   0   0

1   10110   22   **3**   1̸01̸01   45

     10011   +19   − 10011   −19

    ‾‾‾‾‾‾‾‾‾‾‾‾‾   ‾‾‾‾‾‾‾‾‾‾‾‾‾

    101001   41   011010   26

       111   01111

2   10111   23   **4**   100000   32

     10011   19   11   −3

    ‾‾‾‾‾‾‾‾‾‾‾‾‾   ‾‾‾‾‾‾‾‾‾‾‾‾‾

    101010   42   011101   29

SELF-TESTING QUIZ 5–5

1
```
   10111      23
    101      × 5
   10111      115
  101110
 1110011
```

2
```
    1110      14
     111     × 7
    ①         98
    1110
    ①
    1110
    ①
   .1110
  1100010
```

3
```
           10111.
  101)1110011
      101
      1000
       101
       111
       101
       101
       101
```

4
```
           1110
  111)1100010
      111
      1010
       111
       111
       111
```

SELF-TESTING QUIZ 5–6

	Problem	*Complement*
1	140	140
	−270	729
		869

Recomplement −130

2	374	374
	−280	719
		① 093

End-around
carry   ↘1
                 ㊽4

3	853	853
	−127	873
		① 726

	Problem	*Complement*
4	10110	10110
	−11000	00111
		11101

Recomplement −00010

5	11100	11100
	−01011	10100
		① 10000

                 ↘1
              ⟨10001⟩

6	11001	11001
	−01101	10011
		① 01100

SELF-TESTING QUIZ 5-7

1   8⌐3769

    8⌐471   1

      8⌐58   7

       8⌐7   2

           7   Answer = 7271

2 327_8

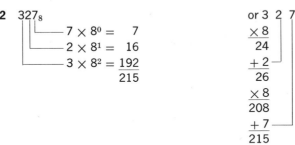

$$7 \times 8^0 = 7$$
$$2 \times 8^1 = 16$$
$$3 \times 8^2 = \underline{192}$$
$$215$$

or 3   2   7

$$\times 8$$
$$24$$
$$+2$$
$$26$$
$$\times 8$$
$$208$$
$$+7$$
$$215$$

3   1 1 1 0 1 1 1 1 0 1 1 0 0   Binary

   1   6   7   5   4   Octal

4   4   2   7   Octal

   1 0 0 0 1 0 1 1 1   Binary

5 $.36_8$

   $3 \times \frac{1}{8} = \frac{3}{8}$

   $6 \times \frac{1}{64} = \frac{6}{64}$

   $\frac{30}{64}$

6 $.45_8$

   $\times 8$

   ③.60

     8   Answer = .3463

   ④.80

     8

   ⑥.40

     8

   ③.20

SELF-TESTING QUIZ 5-8

1   16⌐376

   16⌐23   8

    16⌐1   7   Answer = 178_{16}

      0   1

2 1F2

$2 \times 16^0 = 2$ or

$F \times 16^1 = 240$

$1 \times 16^2 = \underline{256}$

498

$$\begin{array}{r} 1 \quad F \quad 2 \\ \times 16 \\ \hline 16 \\ +15 \\ \hline 31 \\ \times 16 \\ \hline 496 \\ +2 \\ \hline 498 \end{array}$$

3 $\underline{1\,0\,1\,1\,0}\,\underline{1\,1\,1\,1}\,\underline{0\,1\,1\,0}\,\underline{0\,0\,1\,1}$ Binary

$16F63$ Hexadecimal

4 $2B6F$

$\overline{1\,0}\,\overline{1\,0\,1\,1}\,\overline{0\,1\,1\,0}\,\overline{1\,1\,1\,1}$ Binary

5 .21

$2 \times \frac{1}{16}^1 = \frac{2}{16}$

$1 \times \frac{1}{16}^2 = \frac{1}{256}$

$\overline{\frac{33}{256}}$

▌ EXERCISES

1 In what form is data after it has been read into the computer from a punched card? If the computer is a binary computer, what must be done to computational data? If computations are to be printed out, what form must the numbers be in?

2 Using the concepts explained in the chapter, interpret the following in terms of the duodecimal system (base 12). Make $A = 10$ and $B = 11$.

   a Name the absolute values and first three position values.

   b Convert decimal numbers to duodecimal:

      (1) 12 (2) 15 (3) 150

   c Convert duodecimal numbers to decimal:

      (1) 16 (2) 23 (3) 201

3 Name the position value for each of the positions in the following binary number: 101111.1001

4 Convert the following decimal numbers to binary:

   a 105   *b* 99   *c* 127

   d 15.5   *e* 69.875   *f* 17.59375

5 Convert the following binary numbers to decimal:

   a 101110   *b* 110111001

   c 1011.11101   *d* 11101000.000101

6 Convert the binary numbers in question 5 to:

   a Octal   *b* Hexadecimal

7 Convert the following octal numbers to binary:
   a 313   *b* 202   *c* 372.5
8 Convert the octal numbers in question 7 to decimal.
9 Convert the following hexadecimal numbers to binary:
   a CB   *b* 82   *c* FA.A
10 Convert the hexadecimal numbers in question 9 to decimal.
11 Interpret the number represented by the following binary coded decimal bit sets:
   a 1001   0110   0111   1001
   b 0011   0101   0010   0100   0000
12 Perform the following binary arithmetic:

a	11101	*b*	100011	*c*	1011	*d*	$110111 \div 100$
	+ 1100		+110101		×101		

13 Perform the following binary subtraction using:
   a Regular binary subtraction
   b 1s complement subtraction
   c 2s complement subtraction

(1)	10111	(2)	010001
	−01011		−101100

14 How are alphabetics represented in a computer?
   a In a computer using binary
   b In a binary coded computer (2 ways)

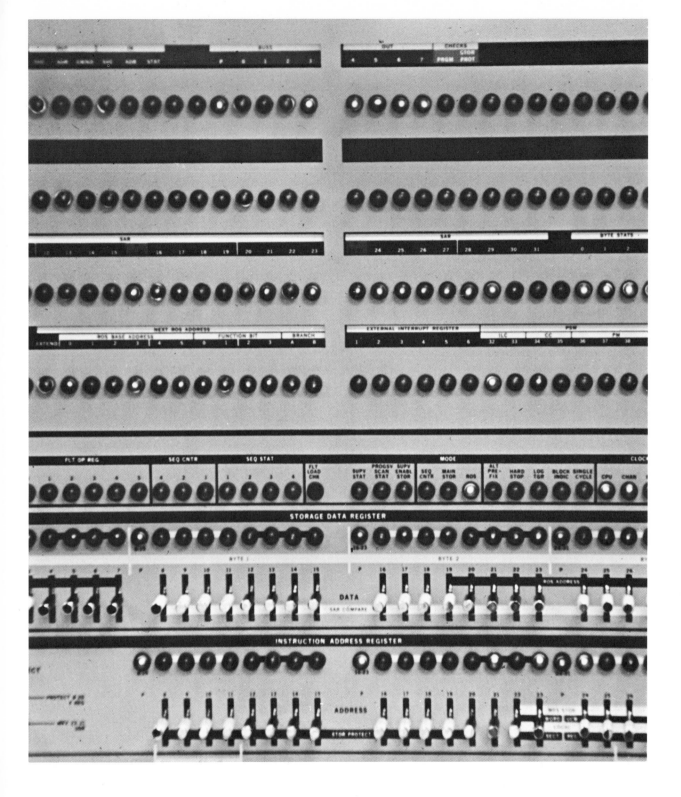

▍ AN OVERVIEW OF THE INTERNAL OPERATION OF A
COMPUTER

▍ ELECTRONIC COMPONENTS OF THE COMPUTER
BASIC COMPONENTS
MICROELECTRONICS

▍ COMPUTER CIRCUITS
LOGICAL CIRCUITS
BIT STORAGE CIRCUITS
TIMING OR CLOCK CIRCUITS

▍ FUNCTIONAL UNITS
REGISTERS
ACCUMULATOR
ENCODER AND DECODER
COMPLEMENTER AND COMPARATOR

▍ A COMPUTER OPERATING CYCLE

▍ SUMMARY

▍ EXERCISES

THE INTERNAL
OPERATION
OF A COMPUTER

A programmer can write programs, an operator can perform his duties, and a manager can supervise computer operations—without understanding the internal workings of the computer. However, a general understanding of the internal operations of a computer is a useful background for understanding why computers are designed as they are. This understanding may also help in comprehending how most effectively to program and operate the equipment. This chapter presents a survey of the circuitry and other internal operating features of computers.

▌ AN OVERVIEW OF THE INTERNAL OPERATION OF A COMPUTER

A computer must be able to perform certain fundamental operations internally:

Represent data and instructions
Hold (store) data and instructions
Move the data and instructions internally
Interpret and execute the commands of the instructions

These internal operations are carried out by the central processing unit (CPU) of the computer. The CPU contains three subunits—the control unit, the processing or arithmetic unit (pronounced arith-met'ic), and the storage unit. As explained in Chapter 3, these three units plus the input and output subsystems form the elements of a simple computer system (Figure 6–1).

There is no mechanical movement in the central processing unit such as one finds in an adding machine or mechanical calculator. It performs all operations electronically. The operations are directed by a program of instructions in the storage unit, in which the data to be operated upon is also held. However, the storage unit is passive in that the data and instructions are merely held there. To be acted upon, the data and instructions must be moved into the control and processing units.

The information held in the storage unit is represented by the polarity in one of two directions of sets of ferrite (iron) cores or similar storage media. When data or instructions are moved from storage into the processing or control unit, the information being moved is represented by the two electrical states: pulse and no pulse. While being operated upon in the processing or control units, the data and instructions are held in registers.

FIGURE 6–1 A computer system

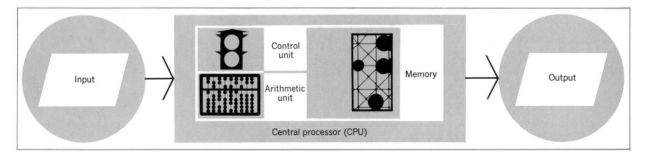

Input   Control unit   Arithmetic unit   Memory   Output

Central processor (CPU)

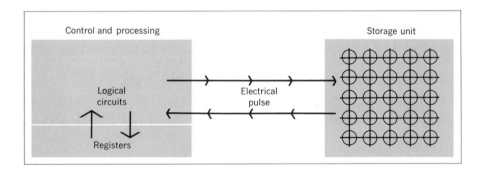

FIGURE 6-2 Relationship between storage and registers

The registers are devices designed to accept electrical pulse representations, temporarily hold the information, and then release the information in the form of electrical pulses when directed by control circuits. Computer operations such as comparison, arithmetic, etc. are performed by groups of logic (switching) circuits. This relationship is illustrated in Figure 6-2. It also suggests that much of the computer circuitry is for the purpose of controlling and counting the movement of the electrical pulses. The circuits of the computer are designed to react to two electrical states of pulse and no pulse. Because they are using only two states, the switching logic can be described with Boolean algebra, the arithmetic of logic. The "truth" and "falsity" conditions of the Boolean analysis are identified with "closed" or "open" states in computer circuits which allow an electrical pulse to pass or not pass.

The computer is directed to perform actions by an instruction. The instruction is brought from main storage to the central processing unit and decoded. One part of the instruction specifies what the computer is to do. The other part, the operand, specifies what the computer is to use (data from storage or a device).

▌ ELECTRONIC COMPONENTS OF THE COMPUTER

The computer circuits of the control and arithmetic units perform two basic tasks: (1) control the flow of electrical pulses and (2) provide temporary bit storage. The logical and bit storage circuits will be described in the next section of this chapter. This section will describe briefly the elements from which the circuits are formed. In both of these sections the explanations will be brief, since they are intended only as surveys to acquaint the reader with a general idea of the electronic components and circuits in a computer.

BASIC COMPONENTS

The computer uses the same type of basic components as a television receiver or radio. These are diodes, transistors, capacitors, and resistors. Each of these is important in controlling the flow of electrical current:

Diode	Essentially an electronic switch in which current flows well in one direction only.
Transistor	A small crystal device that controls the flow of electricity. It performs the same function as a vacuum tube.
Capacitor	Used for modifying the electrical capacity in a circuit.
Resistor	Controls the amount of current by "resisting" current flow.

Early computers used vacuum tubes instead of transistors. These "first-generation" computers required much more power, generated much more heat, and were less reliable than second-generation equipment, which used transistors. Since the computer operates with electrical current which is moved and switched, the speed of the computer depends on the speed at which the components will operate plus the length of the interconnections. The speed of computers is expressed in one of the following terms.

TERM	FRACTION OF A SECOND	ABBREVIATION
Millisecond	thousandths (1/1000)	ms or msec
Microsecond	millionths (1/1,000,000)	μs or microsec
Nanosecond	billionths (1/1,000,000,000)	ns or nanosec
Picosecond	trillionth (1/10^{12})	ps or psec

The speed of electricity is 186,000 miles per second, which is about 1 ft per nanosecond. This is the limit on the speed of a computer; in fact, a practical limit is about two-thirds of this, or 8 in. per nanosecond. Reducing the length of interconnecting wiring in computers is therefore a factor in achieving higher internal speeds.

MICROELECTRONICS

The trend in computer circuitry has been to smaller, faster, and more reliable components. The circuits are typically packaged into modules. There are hundreds or even thousands of modules in a computer but only a small number of different types. When a module fails, it can be replaced in minutes because the modules are mounted on a base with pins which plug into a board containing the connecting wires. Two techniques are currently used for miniature modules. These result in partially integrated (hybrid) circuits and monolithic integrated circuits.

In the hybrid circuit approach (called solid-logic technology by IBM), transistors and diodes composed of tiny silicon chips are placed on a ceramic base on which a circuit containing all connections and resistors has been printed. The completed module, encased in plastic, is 1/2 in. square (Figure 6–3).

The monolithic integrated circuit is smaller because the entire circuit is produced on a silicon wafer. Through a process of photomasking, etching, diffusions, and firings, the transistors, resistors, and diodes are made and interconnected (Figure 6–4).

One of the newer developments is the use of large-scale integrated circuits (LSI) for the logic and switching purposes and also for part or all of the primary storage. Large-scale integrated circuits are an extension of integrated circuitry to include large

FIGURE 6-3 Hybrid integrated circuit module for IBM System/360 (Courtesy of International Business Machines Corporation)

numbers of circuits (more than 50) on a single chip. The advantage of the use of LSI for memory is very fast access speed.

▌ COMPUTER CIRCUITS

The computer operates with electrical pulses. A binary 1 is represented by a sharp voltage pulse; a binary 0 by the lack of the voltage rise. A timing arrangement is used to distinguish the different binary digits being moved.

In order to form the pulses correctly, the computer will have amplifier circuits, which produce pulses of correct amplitude, and shaper circuits, which produce pulses of proper length. In general, the pulses will move through two basic kinds of circuits—switching or logic elements and bit storage elements or flip-flops. These basic circuits are the building blocks for the registers which hold information being processed and for the other functional units of the computer which encode, decode, accumulate, complement and compare.

LOGICAL CIRCUITS

The logical or switching circuits can be described using mathematical logic (also called Boolean algebra) described in Chapter 3. The two states in logic, true and false, are represented by open and closed switches in the electronic equipment. To produce

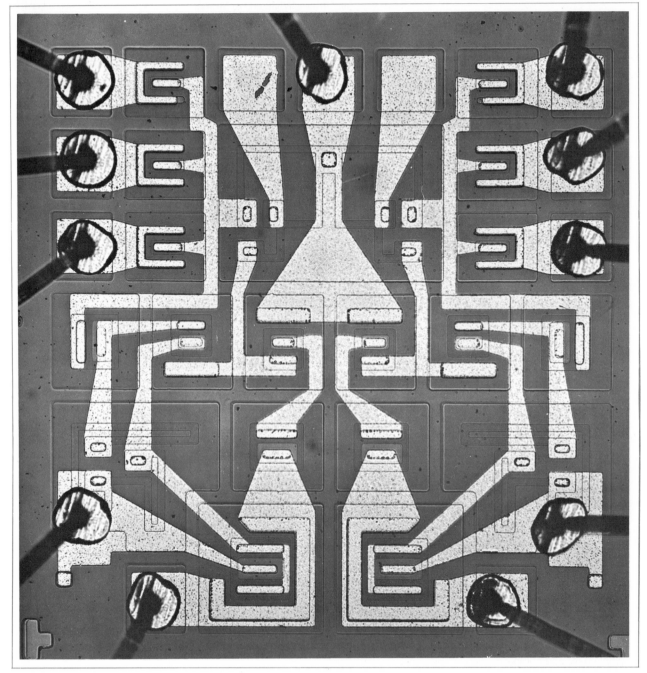

FIGURE 6-4 Monolithic integrated circuit (Courtesy of UNIVAC Division, Sperry Rand Corporation)

all possible logical functions, only three logical circuits are used—AND, OR, and NOT circuits. These names are taken from mathematical logic, and the circuits exhibit the same characteristics as the logical AND, OR, and NOT. The basic circuits are combined in complex groupings to perform the switching for computer operation logic.

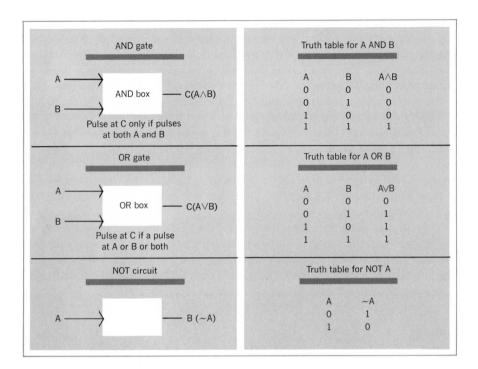

FIGURE 6-5 Logical circuits and corresponding truth tables

The AND gate (also called & gate, ∧ gate, and AND block) can be thought of as an electronic element into which two (or more) wires enter and one wire exits. The logic statement $A \wedge B$ (A AND B) is represented by the AND gate; i.e., for a pulse to come out on the exit wire, pulses must be sent into the element on *both* input wires. The truth table for $A \wedge B$ presents the operating characteristics of the AND gate when 1 is used to represent a pulse, and 0 a no-pulse.

The OR gate (also called ∨ gate, OR block, and mixer) represents the logic statement $A \vee B$ (A OR B). Like the AND gate, it has two (or more) input wires and one output wire. However, the OR gate will allow an output pulse if either or both of the input lines receive an electrical pulse. The truth table $A \vee B$ specifies the operating characteristics of the OR gate.

The NOT circuit is very simple—the output is the opposite of the input. There are several common NOT notations, e.g., $\sim A$ and $\overline{A}$ are two different ways of writing the opposite of A.

In the design of computers it is desirable to standardize as much as possible. If a single logic module could be used for forming any logical function, this would simplify production. Two common modules are the NAND circuit (NOT AND) and the NOR circuit (NOT OR). The truth tables are not given since the inputs are the same as the AND and OR and the outputs are just the opposite.

BIT STORAGE CIRCUITS

The two-state storage devices used in the storage unit will be described in the next chapter; the storage devices used in the arithmetic and control units will be explained here. These devices, referred to as flip-flops, are used for remembering bit values during processing. They are the basic elements from which most registers are built.

The term "flip-flop" can refer to any two-state circuit, but it is usually used to refer to a device having two inputs (represented as 0 and 1, or "set" and "restore"), two outputs, and two stable states. When a pulse is applied to the set input, the flip-flop is set; when applied to the restore input, the flip-flop is cleared, or restored. If the flip-flop is in one or the other of the two states, the corresponding output signal will be emitted, and the other output will be at the no-signal level. The output signal thus provides information on the most recent input of the flip-flop. The flip-flop maintains its state until altered by an input.

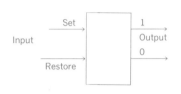

Other bit storage circuits used in developing the basic circuits of the computer are the trigger, or inverter, which is set by a pulse to the state opposite to its state before the pulse, and the delay flop, which has an output signal which is the same as the input signal but only after a delay. The delay is used to slow down an electrical signal so that the bit represented by the signal appears one cycle later.

TIMING OR CLOCK CIRCUITS

It takes time for electrical pulses to reach the proper level for representing a bit and time for the pulse to travel through the computer. Also operations in the computer must be performed in an orderly, timed sequence. The control of timing is performed by the use of control signals called clock pulses which are emitted from a central device called the master clock. These timing signals are sent to all of the logical components to keep them synchronized with each other.

To illustrate the use of the clock pulse, assume a pulse A which must arrive at a point B at an exact time. By inserting an AND gate and a clock pulse, the pulse at A cannot pass until the clock pulse is also received.

▌ FUNCTIONAL UNITS

The circuits just described—gates, flip-flops, delays, etc.—are combined to form assemblies which perform specified functions necessary to computer operation. Examples of functional units are registers, accumulator, encoder, decoder, complementer, and comparator.

REGISTERS

Registers are used to receive, hold, and transfer information used by the processing unit. A register is an assembly of bistable circuits (typically flip-flops, but magnetic cores are sometimes used). It acts as a temporary memory for the processing unit.

There are usually several registers which have different functions. An accumulator register accumulates results; a multiplier-divider register holds the multiplier for multiplication and the divisor (or possibly quotient) for division. In some computers, any general register can be used for arithmetic operations. Other registers are an instruction register, which holds the instruction being executed, an address register, which holds the address of a storage location or device, and a storage register, which holds data taken from or being sent to storage.

The important registers in the system are frequently connected to small lights on the computer console which display the contents of the registers. As will be seen in Chapter 17, the register contents are important aids in diagnosing errors.

ACCUMULATOR

An accumulator is an assembly used for addition. The design of the accumulator will depend on whether the computer uses a binary or a binary coded decimal code and on whether the arithmetic is to be serial (one digit at a time) or parallel (all digits at once). The difference between a binary and a binary coded decimal accumulator results from the difference in the rules for addition for these two systems. The major difference between serial and parallel arithmetic is in the number of adder units required. Serial addition uses only one 1-digit adder and adds successive pairs of digits one at a time. Parallel addition adds all pairs simultaneously, using a different adder for each pair of digits (Figure 6-6). The serial accumulator is slower than the parallel accumulator, but requires less hardware.

The binary half adder, composed of logic elements, is the basic addition circuit. There are several possible half-adder designs, all of which arrive at the result shown in Figure 6-7. In the half adder, if there are pulse (1) inputs at A and B (but not both), the sum is 1 (a pulse). When both inputs are 1, the sum is 0 and there is a carry.

The half adder is incomplete for addition purposes because it does not provide a carry to the next pair of digits to be added. The combination of circuits which correctly adds and carries is called a full adder. It is essentially two half adders linked together by a delay circuit. The delay flip-flop holds the carry bit and delays it one timing pulse so it can be added to the sum of the next pair of digits which have then entered the adder.

Serial		Parallel	
01011		01011	
01010		01010	
1		00001	Sums
10	Results of adding	1 1	Carries
0	a pair at a time	10101	Final sum
10			
0			
10101			

FIGURE 6-6 Comparison of serial and parallel addition

FIGURE 6-7 Half-adder logic

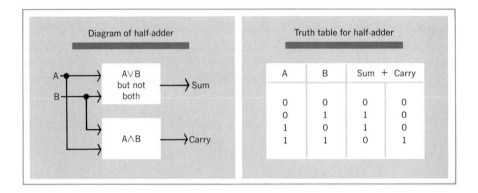

The net effect of the two half adders and the delay is to produce a sum and carry (if any) from each pair of binary digits and the transmitting of any carry for combining with the next pair to be added. A simplified diagram of a full adder is shown in Figure 6-8.

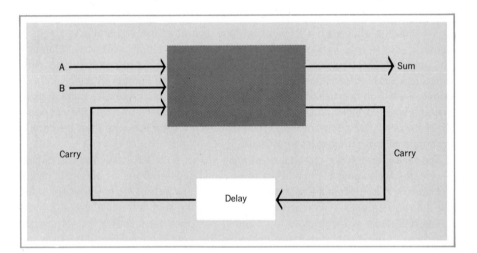

FIGURE 6-8 Simplified diagram of full adder

ENCODER AND DECODER

The encoder translates data from decimal form into binary coded character form. The decoder translates the internal code into decimal equivalents. Illustrative of the encoding function is the conversion from decimal to binary coded decimal. Each input pulse (corresponding to a decimal digit) is converted into one or more binary digits. The logic of the encoder for binary coded decimal is illustrated by Figure 6-9. The decoder is essentially the reverse of an encoder.

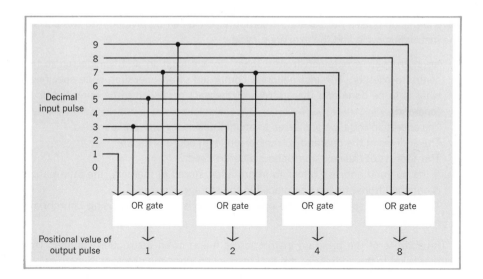

FIGURE 6-9 Binary coded decimal encoder logic

COMPLEMENTER AND COMPARATOR

Since computer subtraction consists of complementing the subtrahend and then adding, the subtraction operation requires special circuitry to perform complementing. Complementing is quite simple, since the 1s complement of a binary number is each 1 replaced by a 0 and each 0 replaced by a 1. The inverter circuit performs exactly in this manner. If the 2s complement is used, a 1 bit is added to the 1s complement.

Computer compare instructions form the basis for variable-path stored programs and are therefore an important element in the modern digital computer. Several methods can be used in designing the comparison assembly. One common method compares pairs (or small groups of bits) until the larger of two quantities has been determined. For example, if 011011 and 010111 are to be compared, the comparison might proceed as shown in the margin.

▌ A COMPUTER OPERATING CYCLE

Most computers are designed so that a fixed interval of time is allowed for each computer operation. A computer which uses fixed time intervals to determine when to initiate the next operation is known as synchronous. A less common design, the asynchronous computer, initiates the next operation when a signal from the current operation indicates a completion. In both cases, exact timing is necessary to proper operation. The basic timing interval is a pulse emitted by the electronic clock circuits. Since each operation takes a specified number of pulse times, the control circuitry will initiate the proper commands at the correct intervals. Pulse times range up to several million pulses per second. A computer cycle can be divided into two parts—the instruction cycle and the execution cycle.

Instruction cycle

1   An instruction is obtained from a main storage location and transferred to the central processor. The instruction is composed of an operation code specifying what is to be done and the address of the data or device to be operated upon (operand).
2   The operation code is transferred to an instruction register and decoded.
3   The address of the operand is transferred to an address register.
4   The address of the next instruction is determined.

Execution cycle

5   If the operand address refers to information stored in memory, the information is obtained from storage and placed in the storage register.
6   The operation specified by the operation code is performed, using appropriate registers.

The address of the program instruction is found in an instruction counter. This counter is set to the address of the first instruction when the program of instructions is begun. When an instruction is brought from storage, the counter automatically advances to the address of the next instruction. If an instruction occupies one storage location, the counter will advance by one; if two locations, by two, etc. This procedure assumes that instructions are stored in sequence in main memory. For many of the instructions, this sequence assumption is correct. However, the program itself may specify a break in the sequence. In this case, the instruction counter is reset to the instruction address specified.

▌ SUMMARY

The internal operation of the computer is binary, i.e., based on two values or conditions. Examples of the two-valued orientation are:

1   Data is represented in binary or a variation based on binary.
2   Temporary storage in the processing and control units makes use of a bistable (two stable states) device, the flip-flop.
3   Information being moved is encoded by having an electrical pulse represent a binary 1 and a no pulse a binary 0.
4   The switching circuits are two-valued and can be described using the two-valued arithmetic of Boolean algebra.

The survey of the internal operation of a computer has described design alternatives for timing and arithmetic. The timing may be either synchronous or asynchronous timing. Synchronous timing assigns fixed times to operations; the end of the fixed time for the current operation is the basis for initiating the next operation. Asynchronous timing initiates the next operation after a signal is received that the previous operation is completed. The asynchronous computer can be faster but is more complicated than the synchronous computer. Most computers are synchronous. The basic operation of addition can be performed serially (digit by digit) or in parallel (all digits at once). The parallel mode requires more circuitry than the serial mode but is faster.

The chapter has surveyed the circuits and functional assemblies from which a computer is built, providing a background for understanding how to program and operate a computer.

▌ EXERCISES

1 In the processing unit, data is either being moved or being held in temporary, operating storage. How are binary digits represented in these two cases?
2 Give the truth table for:
   a A NOR circuit
   b A NAND circuit
3 Define the following terms:
   a Flip-flop
   b Register
   c Encoder
   d Monolithic integrated circuit
   e Half adder
   f Clock circuit
4 Explain the difference between:
   a Synchronous and asynchronous timing
   b Parallel and serial addition

CHAPTER 7

▎ CHARACTERISTICS OF COMPUTER STORAGE
PURPOSE OF STORAGE
LOCATION OF STORAGE
METHOD OF ACCESS
OTHER CHARACTERISTICS

▎ DEVICES AND MEDIA FOR STORAGE
MAGNETIC CORE
THIN FILM
PLATED WIRE MEMORY
MAGNETIC RECORDINGS

▎ CONCEPT OF ADDRESS

▎ CONCEPT OF A COMPUTER WORD
FIXED WORD LENGTH
VARIABLE WORD LENGTH
THE BYTE ADDRESSABLE COMBINATION

▎ CHARACTERISTICS OF COMPUTERS BASED ON
WORD STRUCTURE
THE USE OF ADDRESSABLE REGISTERS
THE STORAGE-TO-STORAGE APPROACH
THE PROBLEM OF PRECISION
SUMMARY OF DIFFERENCES

▎ COMPARING MEMORY SIZES
COMPARING STORAGE OF ALPHANUMERIC CHARACTERS
COMPARING STORAGE OF NUMERIC DATA
COMPARING STORAGE SPACE FOR INSTRUCTIONS

▎ SUMMARY

▎ EXERCISES

STORAGE AND RETRIEVAL OF INFORMATION IN A COMPUTER

There is a requirement for storage both inside and outside the computer system. A report, a book, and a file of letters all are forms of storage, and even a small organization will utilize billions of characters of storage for its records. A typical textbook, for example, contains well over a million characters. Although the printed or written document is important for storage, this chapter deals only with storage which is used by the computer system.

▮ CHARACTERISTICS OF COMPUTER STORAGE

There is storage in many different parts of the computer system. When one speaks of "computer memory," the primary or main storage is often implied. However, there are many different types of storage media and devices. Figure 7–1 identifies the different types of storage as (1) temporary storage occurring in the processing and control units, (2) primary storage, (3) secondary storage, and (4) offline, low-speed storage. For the purpose of explaining storage, the classifications summarized in Table 7–1 will be used.

PURPOSE OF STORAGE

The purposes for which storage is available are either for operating purposes by the central processor or for holding programs and data. The storage for holding programs and data includes both primary and secondary storage. This type will receive most of our attention. The operating storage consists of small storage elements used by the processing and control units of the central processor. One type of temporary operating storage (called registers) was described in Chapter 6. The second type of temporary operating storage is sometimes referred to as a scratch pad memory. This is a separate, high-speed storage, usually small in size, which is available for holding

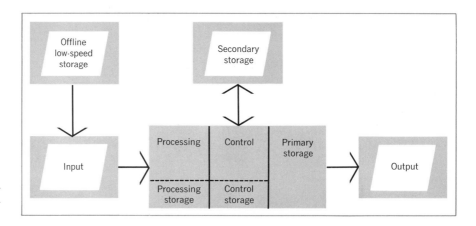

FIGURE 7–1 Elements of a computer system showing different types of storage

TABLE 7–1   Classification of Storage

CHARACTERISTICS	ALTERNATIVES	
Purpose	Temporary operating storage	Program and data storage
Location	Primary	Secondary
Method of access	Sequential *a* Reversible *b* Forward only	Direct
Recording method	Magnetic	Nonmagnetic
Permanency	Permanent until changed	Requires regeneration
Effect of readout	Nondestructive	Destructive
Alterability	Read and write	Read only

data and instructions temporarily during operations. A scratch pad memory can be regarded as fulfilling many of the same purposes as registers. Another type of storage in some computers is a control memory unit which contains a permanently wired program for interpreting computer instructions. This is also referred to as read-only storage. It is a substitute for circuitry, and the programmer or operator is not normally concerned with it.

LOCATION OF STORAGE

The program and data storage can be classified as either primary or secondary. The primary storage is often referred to as internal or main storage because this is the storage in the central processing unit. The secondary storage, frequently referred to as auxiliary or mass storage, extends the storage capabilities of the system. Although programs are also stored on the secondary storage media, the major use of the secondary storage is for data.

METHOD OF ACCESS

Data is stored at separate locations on a storage medium. Access refers to the method by which the computer obtains access to a storage location in order to read or write. Access is either direct or sequential. If access is direct, this means that the computer can read or write at any storage location without having to read other locations to get to the one desired. Direct access is also referred to as random access.

The sequential method of access means that the media must be read sequentially and all locations preceding the one desired must first be read before it can be obtained. This is similar in concept to viewing a reel of movie film. If the frames one wishes to see are near the end of the reel of film, one must nevertheless run all preceding frames through the projector before being able to view the ones selected. Information stored on magnetic tape must be read sequentially. Likewise, information stored on a deck of punched cards must be read sequentially, but there is a difference between these two media. In the case of magnetic tape, the tape is continuous, and the computer can reverse the movement of the tape in order to go back to a prior record. However, a card, once read, cannot be retrieved by the computer without being physically removed by the operator from the output bin and again placed in the reader. In other words, sequential access media can be divided into two categories, those that are reversible and can therefore be moved backward under control from computer instructions, and those that can move forward only and, once read, cannot be called back.

OTHER CHARACTERISTICS

The storage of information on the different primary and secondary storage media is based on magnetic recording. Some new types of storage described in Chapter 22 use a different approach, but magnetic recording now dominates the field. Slow-speed storage media (punched cards, paper tape, documents) use different methods of recording, and their slow speed and other limitations put them in a different category from magnetically encoded media. These are therefore handled in a later chapter.

Almost all currently used storage media are permanent in the sense that what is recorded will remain until it is changed. It is magnetically recorded, and a power failure will not change the recording. There are, however, a few seldom used storage devices which use a nonpermanent method of storage requiring continuous regeneration, and a power failure will cause the loss of all information held in that type of storage.

When a storage element is read, this may be performed in a nondestructive or destructive mode. The characteristics of the media and requirements of the overall design will determine which mode is to be used. In the destructive readout mode (DRO) the reading operation may alter the data at the location being read, and it must be restored. The restoration is performed automatically so that, from the user's view, reading a location does not alter its contents. The nondestructive readout does not alter the recorded data, and no restore mechanism is required.

The necessity for specialized never-altered programs and for control instructions has led to the use of read-only internal storage. This storage, which can be read but is not available for writing, is used for specialized, wired programs. Most storage is general-purpose and can be used for both reading and writing.

▌ DEVICES AND MEDIA FOR STORAGE

Table 7–2 presents a summary of devices and media used for program and file storage. This chapter is concerned only with the primary storage using magnetic recording. Punched cards, which are the major nonmagnetic storage medium, were discussed in Chapter 2. The remaining media will be discussed in Chapter 13.

TABLE 7–2 Characteristics of Devices and Media for Storage in Electronic Data Processing

| | TYPE OF STORAGE | | | TYPE OF ACCESS | |
MEDIA	PRIMARY	SECONDARY	SEQUENTIAL-REVERSIBLE	SEQUENTIAL-FORWARD ONLY	DIRECT (RANDOM)
High Speed (magnetic recording only)					
Magnetic core	X				X
Thin film	X				X
Plated wire	X				X
Drum		X			X
Disc		X			X
Magnetic tape		X	X		
Magnetic strip or card		X	X		
Low Speed (nonmagnetic or mixed recording)					
Punched cards		X		X	
Punched paper tape		X		X	
Magnetic ink characters on documents		X		X	
Ledger card with magnetic strip		X		X	
Optical characters on documents		X		X	

MAGNETIC CORE

Cores are the most common internal storage device. A core is molded from a ferrite (iron) powder into a doughnut shape about the size of the head of a pin. The individual cores are strung on wires to form core planes. Several core planes stacked one on top of another form a core stack (Figure 7–2).

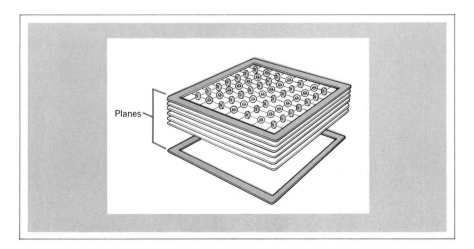

Planes

FIGURE 7–2 Core stack

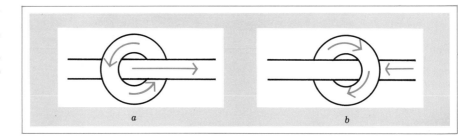

One of the experiments commonly carried out in an elementary physics course demonstrates that an iron bar can be magnetized in one of two directions, north-south or south-north. Similarly, a ferrite core can be polarized in two directions. These two directions of polarity form the two states of the core. A core can be placed in either state by the application of a magnetizing force. The direction of polarity will depend on the direction of magnetizing current. The computer designer selects one direction to represent a 0 bit and the other to represent a 1 bit. Once polarized in one direction, a core will retain that polarity until changed.

Figure 7-3 shows a single wire being used to apply current to the core. The typical arrangement uses two wires strung through the core. This arrangement is termed a coincident-current core memory. One-half of the current required to switch the core is applied to each of the wires when the core is to be "flipped." The cores are arranged in the planes with the intersection of two wires applying full current to only one core. This arrangement, shown in Figure 7-4, allows the computer to control the state of each individual core. These two wires will write on a selected core, but reading requires more wiring. Although there are several different design possibilities, the

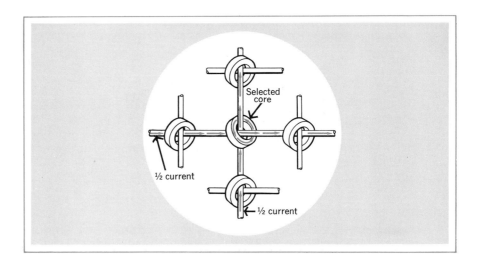

FIGURE 7-4   Selecting a core

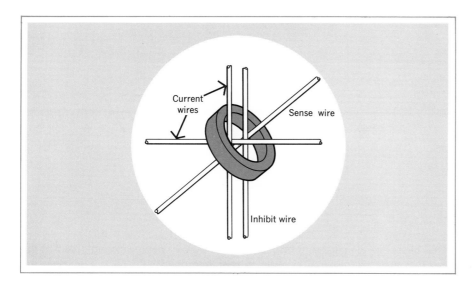

FIGURE 7–5 Closeup of a single core

most common organization of a core memory uses four wires through each core to accomplish reading and writing. In addition to the two wires for applying the magnetizing current there is an inhibit wire and a sense wire (Figure 7–5).

A core is read by sending a current to polarize the core in a particular direction. If the core is already magnetized in that direction, nothing happens. If it is not, the core changes state. This changing or "flipping" induces a current. The sense wire picks up this current indicating that the core was in the opposite state prior to being changed. For example, if an electrical pulse is sent to write a 0 at that core position and the core is already in the 1 state, the writing of a 0 will flip the core. If a 0 is already there, no change will occur. The "flipping" induces a current which is picked up by the sense wire running through the plane. Only one sense wire is needed for an entire plane, since only one core is sensed at a time. In this case, if the core represented a 1, the sense wire will pick up a current, and if a 0 there will be no current. Note, however, that reading by the writing of a 0 left the core position with a 0. In other words, a 1 would have been replaced by a 0 and a 0 would have remained a 0. Reading a core in this way is destructive of the prior information, and, to remedy this, the core must be restored to its former state. This is done by attempting to write a 1 at the position (the opposite current from that used to read the core). If no current was sensed during the read cycle, the restore cycle will simultaneously put an inhibit current in the inhibit wire. If the sense wire picked up a current during the read, no current will be used during the restore cycle. The result of this approach is to inhibit the writing of a 1 if the core was 0 and should therefore remain 0, and the writing of a 1 with no interference from an inhibit current if the core was flipped from 1 to 0 during the read cycle and is to be restored.

In summary, writing on a core is achieved by having one-half of the current re-

FIGURE 7-6 Thin film memory

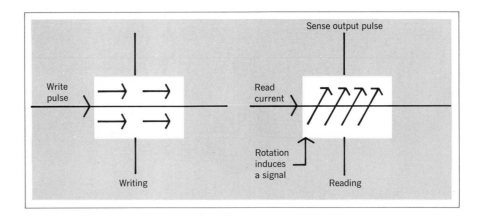

quired to change the core sent through each of the two wires which intersect at the core. Two steps are required in order to read from the core. The first involves the writing of a bit and sensing if this caused the core to flip. If a 0 is written and a 1 was already there, the sense wire will pick up a current caused by switching. If the core was in a 0 polarity, no current will be generated. The second step is to restore the core by attempting to write the opposite state from that used in the read cycle. The inhibit wire will contain a current to prevent the change if the core was not previously switched. Otherwise, the core will be restored to its former state.

THIN FILM

Thin film memory is produced by depositing very thin spots of metallic alloy on a ceramic or metal plate. This spot performs in the same manner as the core except that only two wires are required. A typical thin film element consists of a rectangle about 0.025 by 0.050 in. with a thickness of about 1,000 angstroms (0.0000004 in.). This rectangle can be thought of as a bar magnet. Applying a current which causes the polarity to rotate but not to flip induces a current which indicates whether a 1 or 0 was stored (Figure 7-6). After the sense field is removed, the polarity is returned to its prior state by a digit pulse which "steers" the polarity back to a 1 or 0 state. An overlay of etched copper wires provides the circuitry necessary to connect the individual elements with the circuits which read and write (Figure 7-7). The magnetic properties of film elements allow much faster switching times than can be achieved with cores. This provides faster memory cycle speeds, but the technical difficulties of thin films have, up to now, discouraged their use.

PLATED WIRE MEMORY

Plated wire memory or woven wire memory is a thin film which is deposited around a fine wire. This wire carries the write current during a write operation and is the sense line in a read operation. Insulated wires are woven across the plated wire in a

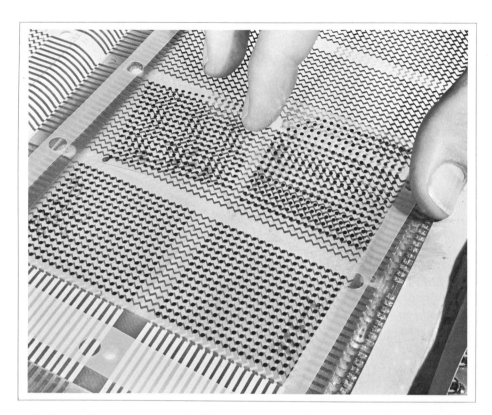

FIGURE 7-7 Thin film memory plane with overlay (Courtesy of UNIVAC Division, Sperry Rand Corporation)

fashion similar to weaving cloth. The area where the insulated wires loop around the plated wire (Figure 7-8) forms a bit storage location. Reading is nondestructive.

MAGNETIC RECORDINGS

The remaining storage devices in Table 7-2 are used in secondary storage and will be discussed in Chapter 12, but the principle of magnetic recording for storage will

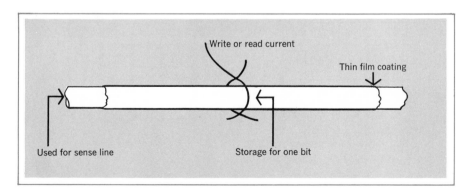

FIGURE 7-8 Plated wire memory

FIGURE 7-9 Magnetic recording

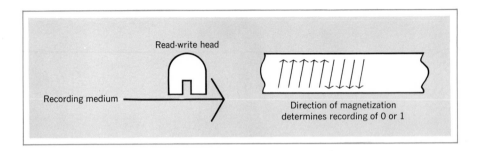

Read-write head

Recording medium →

Direction of magnetization
determines recording of 0 or 1

be discussed in this section. The recording surface is a base coated with a thin layer of iron oxide which can be magnetized. The base is a metal drum for a drum memory, a metal disc for a disc memory, and plastic for magnetic tape and strip storage. The recording is performed by a magnetic recording head as the recording surface is moved past it. A current is sent through a coil on the write head which causes a tiny surface just beneath the head to be magnetized. The surface will be polarized in one direction for recording 1s and the other direction for 0s. For reading, the surface of the recording medium is drawn past the read head. This induces a signal in the head corresponding to a 1 or 0 recording (Figure 7-9).

▌ CONCEPT OF ADDRESS

Ferrite cores, thin film, and other direct access storage devices are not usable unless data stored there can be retrieved when needed. In order to accomplish this, each storage location has an address which identifies it just as a house address identifies a

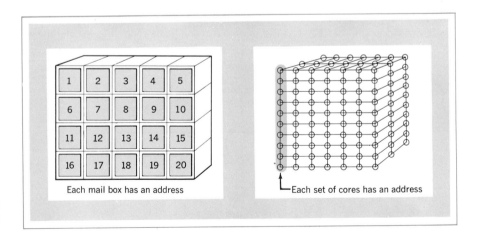

Each mail box has an address

Each set of cores has an address

FIGURE 7-10 Comparison of mail box number and core storage address

dwelling. Another comparison is a set of mailboxes in a post office. Each has a unique number which identifies the storage location. If a person wishes to store a letter in the box, he specifies the box number; if he wishes to retrieve the mail that is stored there, he identifies the location by the box number. Likewise, each set of cores in a core storage unit has an address. The address identifies the location so that data may be stored there and data so stored may be retrieved. The address is a code which identifies the location for the computer circuitry. In other words, the computer cir-cuitry associates a separate set of storage devices with each location designation. There is, for example, a set of ferrite cores which are identified by the location 347, another set associated with location 348, etc. Each address refers to a set of storage devices, but how large the set is and what can be stored there depends on the word structure of the particular computer.

▌ CONCEPT OF A COMPUTER WORD

A computer word consists of the data which is stored or retrieved when a memory location is specified. There are two basic approaches—fixed-length word and variable-length word. In addition, there is a byte-addressable word structure which combines many of the features of both.

FIXED WORD LENGTH

In a fixed word length computer, every storage location identified by an address con-sists of a fixed number of cores or other storage representations. Some popular word sizes for fixed word length machines are 24, 30, 32, 36, 48, and 54 bits. The com-puter designer makes a choice of word size, and all addresses then reference that number of bits. If the computer is designed with a 48-bit word, each reference to a memory location will access 48 bits.

VARIABLE WORD LENGTH

The variable word length or character computer has an address for each set of bits which can encode one character. If it requires 6 bits to encode a character, each 6-bit set (not counting control bits) will have an address assigned to it. Thus, if the number 39 is in storage, the 3 will occupy one storage location having an address, the 9 is in another contiguous storage location with a separate address.

If each character is stored in a separate storage location having a separate ad-dress, how is a number such as 945823, which takes up six separate storage loca-tions, accessible? If it were necessary to specify each of these six locations in order to access the number stored there, it would become quite cumbersome. This is, however, not necessary. A group of storage locations can be accessed by specifying only a single storage location which defines the starting location for the group of characters which make up the word. Since the number of characters in the group can vary, the number of memory locations accessed is variable. Or, to put it another way, the word length is variable. Since the computer begins at the starting location given and picks up all succeeding bit sets until the end of the word is indicated, there must be a method of specifying the end of the word. Two methods are in common use:

1 *A word mark bit.* A special control bit called a word mark bit is added to the set of bits which encode a character. This bit is set to 1 in the bit set of the character which ends the word. Thus, the instruction defines one end of the word, and the word mark defines the other.

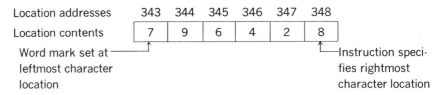

2 *Specification of length.* In this approach, any instruction which specifies a variable-length word gives the leftmost starting address plus the number of locations to be included in the word. The word mark control bit is not required.

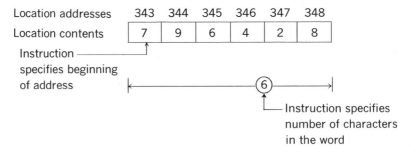

THE BYTE-ADDRESSABLE COMBINATION

Several third-generation computer systems are designed so that both fixed and variable words can be used in the same computer. This is done by having a byte-addressable organization. As explained previously, a byte is a group of bits which form a subunit of a computer word. In IBM's System/360, an example of a byte-addressable computer, each 8-bit byte has an address. Four such bytes make up a 32-bit fixed binary word, the address of which is the address of the first byte. When an instruction references a fixed binary word, the computer automatically stores or retrieves 4 bytes. The computer also has instructions which specify a fixed length of 2 bytes (half-word) and 8 bytes (double word). In addition to these fixed word length instructions, there are variable word length instructions which operate upon binary coded characters. Instructions using variable-length words specify the first byte of the word and the number of bytes to be included.

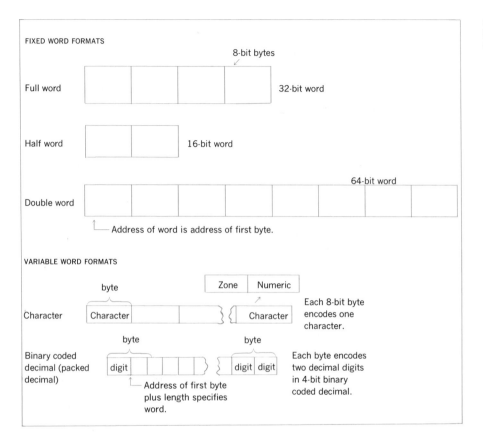

FIXED WORD FORMATS

8-bit bytes

Full word   32-bit word

Half word   16-bit word

                                        64-bit word
Double word

⌐— Address of word is address of first byte.

VARIABLE WORD FORMATS

                        Zone   Numeric

                byte

Character   Character   {   Character   Each 8-bit byte
                                                     encodes one
                                                     character.

Binary coded   byte   byte
decimal (packed   digit   { digit digit   Each byte encodes
decimal)   two decimal digits
              ⌐— Address of first byte   in 4-bit binary
                 plus length specifies   coded decimal.
                 word.

FIGURE 7–11 Address formats in byte-addressable computer (IBM System/360)

CHARACTERISTICS OF COMPUTERS BASED ON WORD STRUCTURE

In terms of understanding the difference between computers, the word organization is an important distinction. The differences between fixed word length, variable word length, and byte-addressable computers are, for the most part, a natural consequence of the different word organizations. One of the important distinctions is the use of addressable registers versus the use of a storage-to-storage approach. This leads also to other important differences.

THE USE OF ADDRESSABLE REGISTERS

As explained in Chapter 6, a register is a set of storage devices where data or instructions are moved in order to be operated upon. The main storage is passive, merely holding the data and instructions; the register is active storage. A register may be addressable, so that the programmer can write an instruction to load it with the contents of a storage location or to copy its contents into a regular storage location. Or

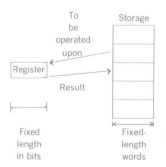

To
be
operated
upon

Storage

Register

Result

Fixed
length
in bits

Fixed-
length
words

a register may not be addressable, being called into use automatically by the circuitry of the computer.

The use of addressable registers requires a fixed-length word because the register is designed to accept and hold a specified number of bits. When addressable registers are used, data is moved into a register, operated upon, and then moved back to a storage location. The trend in the design of fixed word length computers is for several addressable registers. For example, IBM's System/360 computers have 16 general-purpose registers for fixed word length instructions.

The advantage of a register approach is the speed which can be attained. Data can be transferred from storage to register in parallel, i.e., all bits simultaneously. This is possible because all words contain the same number of bits no matter how small or large the value. If a 32-bit memory location, for example, is storing the number 1, it will have 31 leading 0 bits and one 1 bit. This can be transferred in parallel from storage to a register in exactly the same time as a 32-bit number. Once in a register the arithmetic operations can also be performed in parallel as described in Chapter 6.

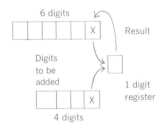

6 digits

Digits to be added

4 digits

Result

1 digit register

THE STORAGE-TO-STORAGE APPROACH

When the word length is variable, this precludes transferring the entire word into a register because the register size cannot be exactly specified. Instead of using an addressable register, the variable-length instructions are executed in a storage-to-storage approach in which a single character or byte is read from storage into a nonaddressable register, operated upon, and the result stored back in a character or byte location. For example, if a 6-digit and a 4-digit number are to be added in a character machine, the addition will be performed serially, a pair of digits at a time. The result will be stored a digit at a time in memory, replacing one of the operands.

This approach removes the limitation imposed by a fixed-length word. Operands may be as small or as large as necessary. However, this flexibility is achieved at a loss in speed. The storage-to-storage approach must operate in serial fashion.

THE PROBLEM OF PRECISION

Precision refers to the number of significant digits which are used to express a quantity. The precision for a fixed word length computer is the size of the word. If, for example, a 32-bit binary word is used, the largest quantity which can be represented is 2,147,483,647. If a larger number is to be stored, two words can be used as if they were a single location. This is known as double precision. Double precision hardware is available on many large-scale computers; for small computers, the use of two words for one quantity is handled by program instructions. Another approach to representing very large or very small numbers will be explained in a later chapter in connection with floating point arithmetic.

SUMMARY OF DIFFERENCES

In the fixed word length computer, every instruction or data word has exactly the

TABLE 7-3   Hardware Characteristics for Different Word Length Designs

CHARACTERISTIC	FIXED WORD LENGTH	VARIABLE WORD LENGTH	MIXED BYTE-ADDRESSABLE
Length of word	Specified	Variable	Both
Registers	Addressable	Storage-to-storage	Both
Arithmetic	Usually binary	Binary coded decimal	Both
Transfer for data	Parallel	Serial	Both

same number of bits. All of the circuitry is designed to accept this basic block. The variable word length computer word can range from one character up to many characters. Computer circuitry cannot therefore be designed to handle a fixed group of bits other than the small number associated with a single character. These two approaches lead to the hardware characteristics (Table 7–3) usually found in computers using these word organizations.

▌ COMPARING MEMORY SIZES

When referring to a computer, the primary storage is designated in terms of the number of addressable storage locations. Yet an addressable location may range from a large fixed word to a group of bits encoding a single decimal digit. Frequently, memory sizes will come in rather odd numbers—multiples of 4,096, which represents a 64×64 core array. The term K is used to refer to thousands of addressable locations rounded to the thousands. Thus, 4,096 storage locations are termed $4K$ memory. A $32K$ memory may actually be 32,768 locations.

Since the storage is described in terms of addressable storage locations and these locations vary widely in their capacity and versatility, the comparison of memory sizes requires some analysis. An initial analysis can be made in terms of the capacity of the storage with respect to alphanumeric characters, decimal digits, and instructions.

COMPARING STORAGE OF ALPHANUMERIC CHARACTERS

In Chapter 5, the methods of encoding alphanumeric characters were explained. In summary, these are:

WORD ORIENTATION OF COMPUTER	METHOD OF REPRESENTING ALPHANUMERICS
Binary	Groups (bytes) of 6 bits within a binary word
Binary coded decimal	Two BCD sets for each character—one for zone and one for numeric positions
Binary coded character	One character per bit set
Byte-addressable	One character per byte

As examples, a Control Data 6600 60-bit fixed word length computer stores 10 alpha-numeric characters in each word, the binary coded decimal IBM 1620 takes two storage locations for each character, the Honeywell 200 character code uses one location to encode each character, and the byte-oriented UNIVAC 9000 series stores one character in each 8-bit byte.

COMPARING STORAGE OF NUMERIC DATA

There are two problems in comparing storage of numeric data. The first arises from the difference between encoding numeric data in binary versus binary coded decimal and the second because of the unused bits in a fixed-word format. In binary coded decimal, each digit requires one bit set, so that a 10-digit number takes 10 bit sets in storage. A binary representation will take roughly 3.36 bits to encode each numeric digit. The number of decimal digits which can be represented by a 32-bit computer word, for example, is computed as $31 \div 3.36$ (31 because one bit is reserved for the arithmetic sign), or 9.2. One can either round down this answer to 9 for comparison purposes, since we shall not be encoding a fraction of a digit, or express the 9.2 digits as the largest number which can be encoded, if this is more relevant. A 32-bit word (31 bits plus sign) can, for example, encode any number up to and including 2,147,483,647.

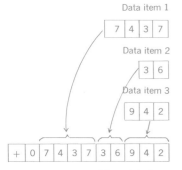

Data item 1

7 4 3 7

Data item 2

3 6

Data item 3

9 4 2

+ 0 7 4 3 7 3 6 9 4 2

Three data items packed into a 10-digit fixed-length word

The character computer uses only the storage needed to encode the data words; the fixed-word computer must use an entire word even if only a single digit is to be stored. This leads to unused storage space compared to the character machine. There are ways of partially overcoming this disadvantage. The programmer may put several data items in a single computer word. This process is known as packing. When part of the data is needed, it is unpacked. The packing and unpacking require several instructions so that it is not usually worthwhile unless these are a number of like items to be packed and unpacked.

COMPARING STORAGE SPACE FOR INSTRUCTIONS

In the simplest case, all instructions are the same size in terms of storage, and one instruction, in a fixed word length computer, will occupy one memory location. Although many computers follow this simple approach, most of the newer computers put more than one instruction in a fixed memory location, and, especially in the case of variable word length or byte-oriented computers, the different instruction can vary in length. In IBM's System/360, for example, an instruction occupies either 2, 4, or 6 bytes, depending on the type of instruction. As will be seen in succeeding chapters, the instruction repertoires of different computers vary in power, so that a single instruction in one computer may suffice for what it takes several instructions to do in another computer.

The comparison of memory sizes is not a simple matter when all factors are considered properly. In order to make a meaningful comparison, one must know something about the data to be stored, the program to be run, etc. Such an evaluation is

TABLE 7-4   Example of Comparing Memory Sizes

COMPUTER	ORIENTATION	CODE	MEMORY SIZE BEING COMPARED*	MAXIMUM STORAGE IF ALL DEVOTED TO		LOCATIONS TO ENCODE ONE INSTRUCTION
				ALPHABETICS	NUMERICS	
IBM 1620	Small scientific	BCD	40K	20,000	40,000	12
IBM 1130	Small scientific	16-bit binary	8K	16,000	32,000	1 or 2
IBM System/360	Model 30 medium general-purpose	Byte-binary	16K	16,000	32,000	2, 4, or 6
Honeywell 200	Medium commercial	BCD	16K	16,000	16,000	1 to 12
UNIVAC 1108	Large general-purpose	36-bit binary	65K	390,000	390,000	1

* These sizes are chosen from many available but are typical for these computers.

beyond the scope of this text, but with the background obtained in these chapters a rough evaluation can be made, and this is usually satisfactory considering the fact that there are many uncertainties in any computer comparison. To illustrate the effect of the three elements to consider in looking at memory size, Table 7-4 gives these measures for four popular computers.

Most computer systems can be obtained with a storage chosen from a large range of possible memory sizes. In the usual case, the storage can be increased by later addition of storage modules. In choosing the size of memory to be installed, one must consider not only the probable necessity for data and program storage but also the storage requirements of the various programming and operating aids to be described in Chapter 8.

❚ SUMMARY

The chapter explored the characteristics of computer storage. These were purpose, location, method of access, recording method, permanency, effect of readout, and alterability. The major emphasis of this chapter has been on the primary, internal storage. Other storage will be discussed in Chapter 13.

The dominant form for primary storage is magnetic core. The method of reading and writing on a core were explained, as was the necessity for restoring after reading. Thin film and plated wire memory, although much less common, were also reviewed.

The concept of address is a means for identifying storage locations to be used. It must be understood in the context of the word structure for the computer being used. The fixed and variable word length organizations are basic alternatives, while a byte-addressable structure is being used to provide both methods in a single computer.

The word structure leads to a number of alternative design concepts. The fixed word length computer will use addressable registers for performing arithmetic and logic operations; the variable word length computer will use a storage-to-storage approach. The decision to use addressable registers results in fixed precision but allows parallel transfer of data and parallel arithmetic. The storage-to-storage method uses serial transfer and serial arithmetic, and it has variable precision.

The addressing differences make it difficult to compare memory sizes of different computers without some analysis. This analysis will usually include a comparison of the capacity for storage of alphanumeric characters, numeric digits, and instructions. Differences in storage of alphanumerics and numerics were discussed in this chapter. Subsequent chapters will provide an understanding of the capabilities of different instruction formats.

‖ EXERCISES

1   What is the difference between primary and secondary storage?
2   Define the following terms with respect to storage:

    a Scratch pad   *d* Plated wire
    b Register   *e* Address
    c Thin film   *f* Byte

3   What is the difference between a fixed word and a variable word structure?
4   In what two ways can the end of a variable word be specified?
5   What is the storage-to-storage method?
6   What is the difference in the precision obtainable in a fixed- versus a variable-length word?
7   Identify each of the following characteristics with either a fixed or variable word length computer:

    a Register   *c* Parallel arithmetic
    b Parallel transfer   *d* Binary representation
                             of number

8   A salesman indicates a computer has 16*K* memory. It is probably not exactly 16,000, but is much more likely to be how many?
9   Two executives are talking, and one boasts that his firm has a 65*K* computer while the other admits that they only have a 32*K* machine. What information would you need to have in order to evaluate these two computers?
10 One of the largest available computers, the CDC 6600, has a 60-bit word. How many numeric digits would there be in the largest number the word can encode? How many alphanumerics can it probably encode?
11 What is "packing" a fixed word?
12 Refer to Table 7–4. The IBM 1130 is being sold to replace the slower and older IBM 1620 as a small scientific computer (although it is also used for some commercial purposes). Compare an 8*K* 1130 with a 40*K* 1620, with respect to storage, assuming that the larger programs which strain storage capacity will

require about 2,000 characters of alphabetic storage and 12,000 numeric digits in words of three digits. How much storage does this leave in each case for instructions?

13 How is a core ''read''?

14 If you have a computer available to you, make the analysis on storage in the same format as Table 7–4.

▮ CHARACTERISTICS OF A COMPUTER PROGRAM

▮ STEPS IN PREPARING A COMPUTER PROGRAM
SYSTEM DESIGN
PLANNING THE PROGRAM
CODING
ASSEMBLY OR COMPILATION
DEBUGGING
DOCUMENTATION

▮ FORM OF AN INSTRUCTION

▮ CODING AN INSTRUCTION
MACHINE LANGUAGE CODING
SYMBOLIC CODING
MACRO INSTRUCTIONS
PROCEDURE-ORIENTED AND PROBLEM-ORIENTED LANGUAGES

▮ AIDS TO PROGRAMMING
PROGRAMMING LANGUAGES
LIBRARY ROUTINES
UTILITY PROGRAMS
PROGRAM GENERATORS
APPLICATIONS PROGRAMS
CONVERSION PROGRAMS
OPERATING SYSTEM

▮ SUMMARY

▮ EXERCISES

INSTRUCTING
A COMPUTER

The purpose of this chapter is to provide an overview of computer programming before proceeding to the detailed explanations of succeeding chapters. This should help in understanding how the individual topics fit into the overall process of programming a computer.

CHARACTERISTICS OF A COMPUTER PROGRAM

A computer program is a set of instructions to direct the operation of a computer system. Because it is a set of instructions, it bears a resemblance to other types of instructions used in organizations—procedures manuals, equipment operating instructions, etc. The major difference is the precision and amount of detail required in the computer program. When writing a set of instructions to direct a human operator, one can typically assume that the human has a certain background knowledge, and therefore one need not specify every single detail. If a document is to be worked on, one need not say:

Step 1   Pick up the document
Step 2   Pick up the pencil
Step 3   Put the pencil on line 1

When exceptions to the written procedures occur, the human operator and his supervisor can be expected to work out new or revised procedures for handling these. The steps in a computer program must be specified exactly, and all possible conditions which can occur must be provided for.

A computer program, consisting of machine language steps for directing the computer, has three salient features:

1   Each computer instruction specifies the execution of an elementary step or operation in data processing.
2   The sequence of instructions specifies what should be done under all possible conditions during data processing.
3   Instructions can be altered by other instructions as the program is run.

Some examples of program instructions are: read a punched card and put the contents in the storage, move the contents of one memory location to another memory location, print one line of output, and add the contents of one memory location to the contents of another. As will be explained later, the trend in computer programming is for the programmer to use macro instructions which encompass several elementary instructions. Since at the operating level of the computer only the elementary instructions are used, the macro instructions must be translated into the basic computer instructions before the computer can execute them.

A basic concept underlying the use of the computer program is that no human intervention is to be required once processing has begun. This means that if there is only one possible condition or decision, the program will be a single-path program

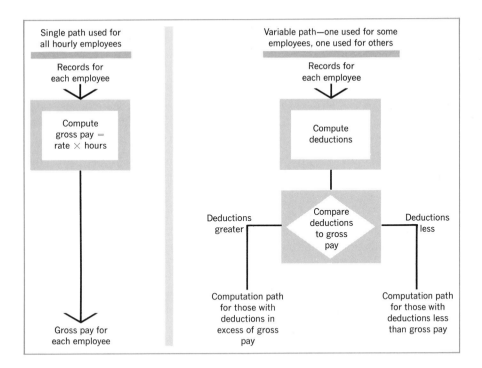

FIGURE 8–1 Variable versus single path for steps in a program

in which all processing follows the same steps. If there are alternatives, different program paths must be provided for each of the conditions or alternatives and a test made to determine which condition or alternative exists. A program may contain both single paths and alternative paths. For example, a program to calculate pay for hourly employees will follow the same computation (hours × rate) for determining the gross pay of each employee, but when calculating net pay, each employee may have different deductions from gross pay in order to arrive at net pay, and in addition, certain error-type conditions must be handled. If an employee does not earn sufficient pay to cover his deductions, such as Blue Cross, union dues, community chest, savings bonds, etc., then the program must have within it a set of instructions for handling this possibility (Figure 8–1).

STEPS IN PREPARING A COMPUTER PROGRAM

The general steps in preparing a computer program are:

1 System design
2 Program planning
3 Coding

4   Assembly or compilation
5   Debugging
6   Documentation

These steps will be described briefly as part of this overview chapter and described in more detail in succeeding chapters.

SYSTEM DESIGN

The first step in preparing a program is to design the framework in which data processing will occur. Some of the questions which are answered in the system design phase are:

What reports or analyses are to be prepared?
What source documents must be provided, how often, and by whom?
How will information on the source document be transcribed to machine-readable form?
What computer files will be maintained?
What type of file media and file organization will be used?
What is the layout of the source document, the computer record, the computer file and the report?
What processing, computer and noncomputer, is required?
How frequently must processing be performed?
What processing approach will be used?
What offline equipment will be necessary?
To whom will the report be distributed?

These and similar questions are answered in the system design phase. Important tools of system design are (1) layouts (sketches showing form and location of data items) of reports, source documents, files, and records, and (2) system flowcharts showing the flow of work through all steps of the data processing including manual, noncomputer machines, computer processing, report distribution, etc. The end result of the system design phase will thus be a description of the processing required for the particular application documented by system flowcharts and layouts.

PLANNING THE PROGRAM

A program of even modest complexity can rarely be written without preplanning. This planning usually takes the form of a programming flowchart. In some cases, a decision table is used as an alternative. A set of program flowcharts typically begins with flowcharts showing the overall flow of program steps. This macro or overall flowchart is then supported by one or more levels of detail (micro) program flowcharts. The macro flowchart allows the reader and programmer to keep in mind the overall flow of work, while the micro flowchart has sufficient detail to be useful as a guide in the coding of the computer instructions.

CODING

Coding is the writing of the actual computer instructions. Although the computer will accept only instructions written in the absolute or machine language form, the programmer typically codes in a symbolic format more suitable for human use. The symbolic instructions must follow rather rigid rules with respect to format, punctuation, etc. The conversion of the symbolic coding to machine language instructions accepted by the computer is done by the assembly or compilation process.

ASSEMBLY OR COMPILATION

Assembly is the translation of a program written in symbolic machine-oriented coding into machine language instructions. Compilation is the term given to the translation or preparation of a machine language program based on a procedure-oriented or macro instruction language. The terms are sometimes used interchangeably although they do have slightly different meanings. One *assembles* a program written in AUTO-CODER, SPS, BAL (names of symbolic languages), whereas one *compiles* a program written in FORTRAN, COBOL, ALGOL (names of procedure-oriented languages). In both cases, the assembly or compilation process is carried out by a computer program furnished by the manufacturer. The result is a machine language program which performs the steps represented by the symbolic coding.

DEBUGGING

Once a program has been coded and translated by assembly or compilation, the next step is debugging the program to remove all errors. Errors in following the coding format rules are detected during assembly or compilation. Logical errors and errors caused by omitting certain program paths are detected through testing the program by running it with data items which test the various paths the program can take.

DOCUMENTATION

The documentation phase consists of pulling together all the documents associated with the program and assembling them into a run manual and operating instructions. The run manual contains the complete set of documentation for the program. A typical run manual might contain the following: problem description; system flow-charts, layouts of records, files, reports, etc.; program flowcharts and/or decision tables; copy of the symbolic coding and results of the assembly; test data used in debugging; program approvals; and change records. The operating instructions used by the computer operator contain a portion of the run manual giving all information necessary for the operator.

▮ FORM OF AN INSTRUCTION

A computer is instructed by a program. The program is written by coding a sequence of instructions which, when executed, will produce a desired result. The instructions, when translated to machine language from the symbolic language used in coding, are stored in identifiable locations within the main storage of the computer. The data to be operated upon will also be stored in the internal memory. There is no particular identification which differentiates an instruction from a data word. An instruction is called upon by specifying either directly or indirectly the address at which it will be found. If, by an error in programming, a data word were called from memory when an instruction word was intended, the computer would attempt to translate the data into an operating command. This lack of differentiation between data words and instructions is useful in program modification, to be described in Chapter 12. Each computer has its own repertoire of instructions based on its circuitry and design. The instructions of one computer will therefore not usually work on another computer, even though there is considerable similarity among all digital computers.

In general, an instruction must specify or imply three things:

1 The operation to be performed
2 The operands (registers, storage location, channels, input/output devices, etc.) to be used
3 The location of the next instruction

The general format of an instruction is operation code plus operands. The operation code determines how the operand to be operated upon is to be interpreted. With different operation codes, the same operand might be interpreted as (1) a data storage address, (2) an addressable register, (3) an instruction storage address, (4) an input/output unit, or (5) a literal number.

The operation code, or "op code," specifies an operation such as load (copy) the contents of a storage location into a register, add the contents of a storage location to the contents of a register, add the contents of a storage location to the contents of another storage location, and initiate an input/ouput operation.

Two operands, either specified or implied, are usually required for an instruction because the instruction must specify what device or which storage location contents are to be operated upon and also the register or storage location to be used in obtaining or holding the result. Some examples of the two specifications are:

OPERATION	REGISTER, STORAGE LOCATION, OR DEVICE OPERATED UPON	REGISTER OR STORAGE LOCATION USED IN HOLDING OR OBTAINING RESULT
Add	Contents of a register or storage location	A receiving register or a receiving storage location
Move or load	Contents of a register or storage location	A receiving register or a receiving storage location
Read (a card)	The card reader	Specified or implied locations in storage where card contents are stored
Compare	Contents of a register or storage location to be compared	Contents of a register or storage location with which compared

The two most common instruction formats are classed as one- (or single) address and two-address. The single address is usually associated with a fixed word length computer, in which the instruction length is fixed at one or perhaps one-half of a computer word. The two-address format is used with variable word length computers, which must specify two storage addresses. The instruction length may be fixed, or it may vary for different types of instructions, since some operands need not be specified if they are implied by the instruction or are made part of the operation code.

	OPERATION CODE	OPERAND	OPERAND
Single-address	XX	XXXX	
Two-address	XX	XXXX	XXXX

The fixed word length computer, using addressable registers, will have an instruction format which specifies the register to be used as well as the storage location or other operand. The register specification may be part of the operation code or may be separately specified if there are several general-purpose registers. For example, an instruction to load a register with the contents of storage location 3768 might take one of two forms, depending on the computer.

Case 1	LOAD ACCUMULATOR REGISTER	STORAGE LOCATION TO BE LOADED
	LDA	3768

Case 2	LOAD REGISTER	REGISTER NO.	STORAGE LOCATION TO BE LOADED
	L	2	3768

The two-address format is used for all storage-to-storage instructions where two storage addresses must be specified. For example, an instruction to add two numbers at locations 3457 and 3480 will have a form such as the one shown in the margin. The answer will be developed in one of the locations. In one popular computer, it is developed in the first; in another, the answer replaces the contents of the second location.

| Op code to add | 3480 | 3457 |

Some instruction operands can be implied or made part of the operation code, thereby reducing their size. For example, only a single character (1) is used to instruct the IBM 1401 to read a card because a separate operation code is used for each of the input/output devices so that the device operand is part of the op code and because, in that computer, the contents of a card are always read into the same section of memory, thereby eliminating the need to specify a receiving location for the read-a-card operation.

The two-address storage-to-storage instruction format has some advantage over the register-based single-address format because the register need not be used as an intermediate step and this reduces the number of instructions. The disadvantages of the storage-to-storage approach are that a higher speed is usually obtainable from a register approach and that the storage-to-storage arithmetic destroys one of the operands by putting the answer in its place.

The effect of having a single-address register approach versus a two-address storage-to-storage format is illustrated for a set of instructions to add two numbers and store the result. Assume the numbers are stored in locations 3437 and 3458 and that the result is to be stored at 3470. The instructions, using an accumulator register specified by the operation code, would be as follows:

OPERATION CODE	OPERAND	EXPLANATION
XX (LDA)	3437	Copy the number found in location 3437 into the accumulator register
XX (ADD)	3458	Add the contents of location 3458 to the number in the accumulator register
XX (STA)	3470	Store (copy) the contents of the accumulator register into storage location 3470

The two-address storage-to-storage approach requires only one instruction if the result can destroy one of the factors.

OPERATION CODE	1ST OPERAND	2D OPERAND	EXPLANATION
XX (ADD)	3458	3437	Add the data at location 3437 to the data at location 3458. The result is automatically stored at location 3458, destroying the previous contents

If one of the arithmetic factors must be saved, there would need to be two instructions, the first one copying one of the factors in the location selected for the result and the second specifying the storage-to-storage instruction to add the two numbers in this location.

OP CODE	1ST OPERAND	2D OPERAND	EXPLANATION
XX (MVC)	3470	3437	Copy contents of location 3437 into location 3470
XX (ADD)	3470	3458	Add contents of 3458 to contents of 3470 with the answer at 3470

There are other operation code variations, such as a three-address structure which specifies both factors in an arithmetic computation and the address where the result is to be stored.

After an instruction is executed, the next instruction must be located. Two methods are used to determine the next instruction—sequential location and explicit specification. Instructions are normally stored sequentially in memory and follow one after the other until a specific instruction breaks the sequence. This means that the location of the next instruction is understood to be the next in the sequence unless there is a transfer of control instruction.

In summary, an instruction is required to give the following information either explicitly or implicitly:

ITEM	SOURCE
Operation to be performed	Operation code
Operand	One or more specified
Location for storage of results	Defined by an instruction or defined by computer design
Location of next instruction	Next location in sequence or specified by instruction when sequence is to be broken

▌ CODING AN INSTRUCTION

Writing sequences of computer instructions which will execute the desired steps is known as coding. Coding can be written at different levels, ranging from machine language to languages which are procedure- or problem-oriented, not machine-oriented. These different levels are:

Machine language (absolute)
Symbolic language
Symbolic with macro instructions
Procedure and problem-oriented language (higher-order language)

The general form for instruction at all levels except the higher-order language is operation code plus operand. The first level, machine language, is the form required by the computer. In the computer, the absolute instruction is represented in binary form, but for operator purposes, notations such as octal, hexadecimal, and binary coded character are used. The other levels are written in a form more convenient to the programmer and must be translated into the absolute machine language instructions by an assembler or compiler. The program coded in a symbolic form is known as a source program; the machine language program is referred to as the object program. The following examples illustrate the coding to perform $C = A + B$ in machine code and symbolic and procedure-oriented language.

Machine language in binary as stored in the computer	0101100000100000000100001110000
	0101101000100000000100001110001
	0101000000100000000100001110010
Symbolic assembly language	L 2,A
	A 2,B
	ST 2,C
Procedure-oriented language (COBOL)	ADD A AND B GIVING C.

MACHINE LANGUAGE CODING

The machine language instruction typically contains one or two digits (or the equivalent in binary) for the operation code and four or five digits to identify an operand. Thus, a machine language instruction may look like 563603 where 56 is the operation code for addition and 3603 is the address of the memory location where the number to be added is stored. The instruction is itself stored in a memory location and is therefore coded in the binary or binary coded decimal code used by the computer. Using the operator notation (hexadecimal and binary coded characters), some examples of machine language coding are:

MACHINE-LEVEL INSTRUCTION	OPERATOR NOTATION	COMPUTER	EXPLANATION
M372337	BCD	IBM 1401	Move contents of 372 to 337
060100000035	Octal	IBM 7094	Store contents of accumulator register in location 35_8
210111601009	BCD	IBM 1620	Add contents of location 1009 to contents of 1116
FA6541EF41E9	Hexadecimal	IBM 360	Add contents of location $1E9_{16}$ to location $1EF_{16}$

SYMBOLIC CODING

The machine language form necessary for computer operation is not well suited to the person who must write the instructions. The reason for this is the problem of keeping track of where everything is stored. Since each instruction and each data word must be given a unique address, writing instructions in absolute code necessitates keeping track of all memory locations. In addition, the numeric memory location identifiers and numeric operation codes are difficult to remember.

Computer manufacturers have met this problem by the use of coding which is symbolic rather than absolute. Mnemonic codes (i.e., codes to assist the memory) are used in place of numeric operation codes. For example, ADD or A is used as a symbolic operation code for addition instead of a numeric code such as 12. Each symbolic coding system has a more or less unique set of mnemonic operation codes. The programmer may also use symbolic addresses for identifying storage locations holding data or instructions. The programmer chooses his own symbolic addresses, subject only to the naming restrictions of the particular symbolic system. For example, a programmer writing a program to compute a payroll might refer to the memory location by using mnemonics which suggest the contents of the locations.

CONTENTS	SYMBOLIC ADDRESS
Gross pay	GROSS
FICA tax rate	FICAR
Cumulative FICA tax	FICAC
Net pay	NET

The symbolic coding might look like the following:

| INSTRUCTION STORED AT | INSTRUCTION | |
	OPERATION CODE	OPERAND
PAY	ADD	GROSS
	MUL	FICAR

Each instruction must be stored in a memory location, yet note that the second of the two illustrative lines of symbolic coding has no symbolic tag to identify the memory location where that instruction is to be stored. The location of the instruction needs a symbolic tag only if the instruction is to be referenced during the program, as, for example, by a subsequent instruction which loops back to this instruction. In other words, although an absolute storage location must be associated with each instruction, it is not necessary to have a symbolic tag for each when coding in symbolic because the instructions are assumed to be stored sequentially unless otherwise specified. Coding of instructions is usually done on coding paper which assists the programmer in following the correct coding format. Figure 8–2 illustrates symbolic coding.

Since the computer will not operate using mnemonic codes and symbolic addresses, these must be translated to absolute codes and absolute addresses. This translation is done by a computer program referred to as an assembly system. The assembly routine reads the symbolic program which has been put on punched cards, translates the mnemonic operation codes to machine operation codes, and assigns memory locations for storing instructions and data. The assembly program then punches out (or records on some other memory media) a machine language program. The translation from symbolic is one for one—one symbolic instruction results in one machine language instruction. The assembly routine keeps track of all memory locations used and of all symbolic tags associated with the memory locations. Once a memory location is assigned to a particular symbolic address, the same memory location will be assigned to all subsequent uses of that symbolic tag. The process of using a symbolic assembly system is illustrated in Figure 8–3. The translation process includes error diagnostics to detect certain types of coding errors.

The advantages of symbolic coding and conversion by the assembly program compared with coding directly in machine language are:

1 Coding is easier, since the programmer can use easy-to-remember mnemonics and symbolic address tags.
2 If a program is changed later or if two programs are combined, machine language programming would require extensive checking to prevent incompatible use of memory locations. Programs written in symbolic code are merely reassembled to provide a reassignment of memory locations.
3 The assembly routine provides diagnostic procedures to detect errors.

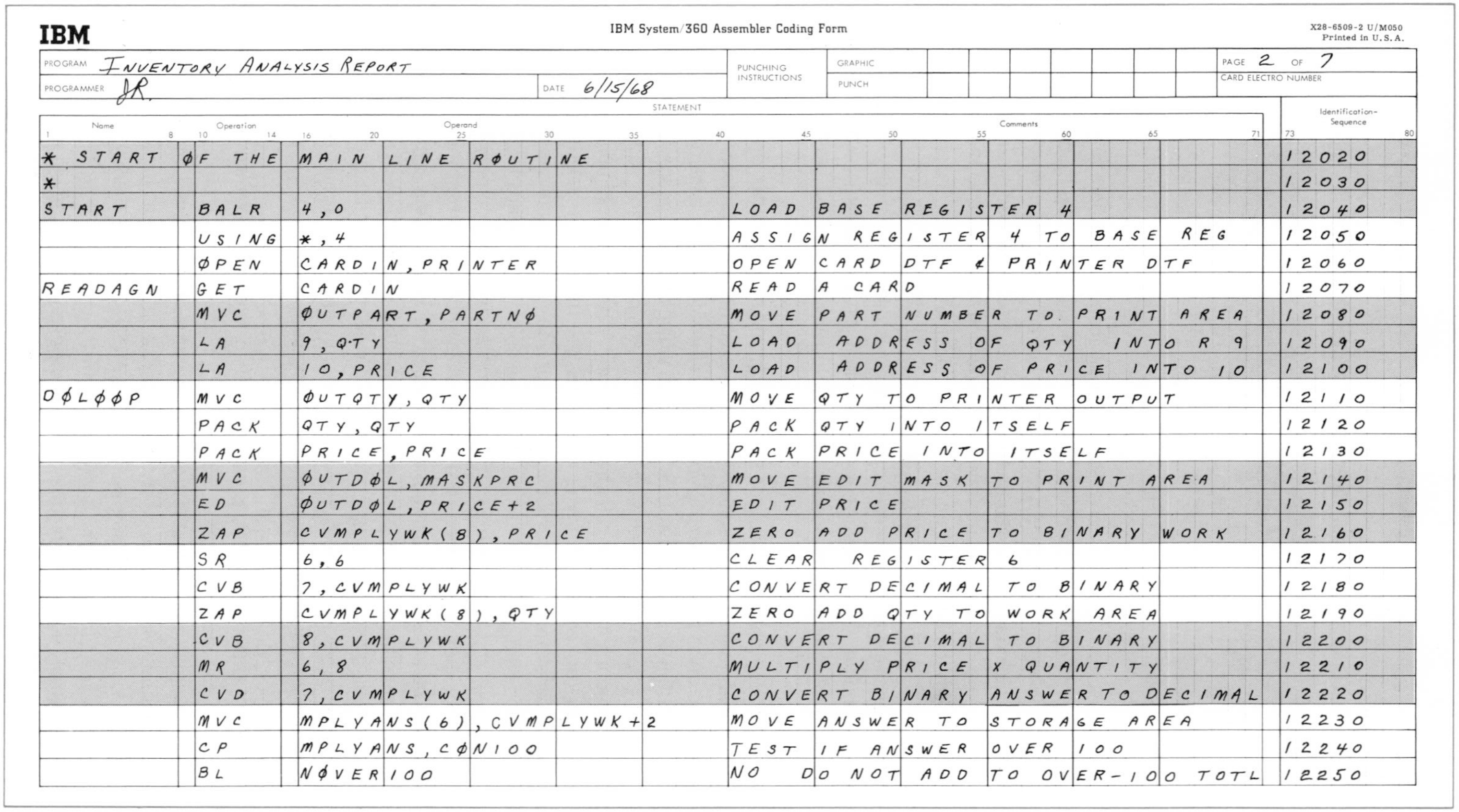

FIGURE 8-2 Example of symbolic coding

IBM System/360 Assembler Coding Form — X28-6509-2 U/M050 Printed in U.S.A.

PROGRAM: INVENTORY ANALYSIS REPORT PROGRAMMER: JR DATE 6/15/68 PAGE 2 OF 7

Name	Operation	Operand	Comments	Identification-Sequence
* START ØF THE MAIN LINE RØUTINE				1 2 0 2 0
*				1 2 0 3 0
START	BALR	4,0	LOAD BASE REGISTER 4	1 2 0 4 0
	USING	*,4	ASSIGN REGISTER 4 TO BASE REG	1 2 0 5 0
	ØPEN	CARDIN,PRINTER	OPEN CARD DTF & PRINTER DTF	1 2 0 6 0
READAGN	GET	CARDIN	READ A CARD	1 2 0 7 0
	MVC	ØUTPART,PARTNØ	MOVE PART NUMBER TO PRINT AREA	1 2 0 8 0
	LA	9,QTY	LOAD ADDRESS OF QTY INTO R 9	1 2 0 9 0
	LA	10,PRICE	LOAD ADDRESS OF PRICE INTO 10	1 2 1 0 0
ØØLØØP	MVC	ØUTQTY,QTY	MOVE QTY TO PRINTER OUTPUT	1 2 1 1 0
	PACK	QTY,QTY	PACK QTY INTO ITSELF	1 2 1 2 0
	PACK	PRICE,PRICE	PACK PRICE INTO ITSELF	1 2 1 3 0
	MVC	ØUTDØL,MASKPRC	MOVE EDIT MASK TO PRINT AREA	1 2 1 4 0
	ED	ØUTDØL,PRICE+2	EDIT PRICE	1 2 1 5 0
	ZAP	CVMPLYWK(8),PRICE	ADD PRICE TO BINARY WORK	1 2 1 6 0
	SR	6,6	CLEAR REGISTER 6	1 2 1 7 0
	CVB	7,CVMPLYWK	CONVERT DECIMAL TO BINARY	1 2 1 8 0
	ZAP	CVMPLYWK(8),QTY	ZERO ADD QTY TO WORK AREA	1 2 1 9 0
	CVB	8,CVMPLYWK	CONVERT DECIMAL TO BINARY	1 2 2 0 0
	MR	6,8	MULTIPLY PRICE x QUANTITY	1 2 2 1 0
	CVD	7,CVMPLYWK	CONVERT BINARY ANSWER TO DECIMAL	1 2 2 2 0
	MVC	MPLYANS(6),CVMPLYWK+2	MOVE ANSWER TO STORAGE AREA	1 2 2 3 0
	CP	MPLYANS,CØN100	TEST IF ANSWER OVER 100	1 2 2 4 0
	BL	NØVER100	NO DO NOT ADD TO OVER-100 TOTL	1 2 2 5 0

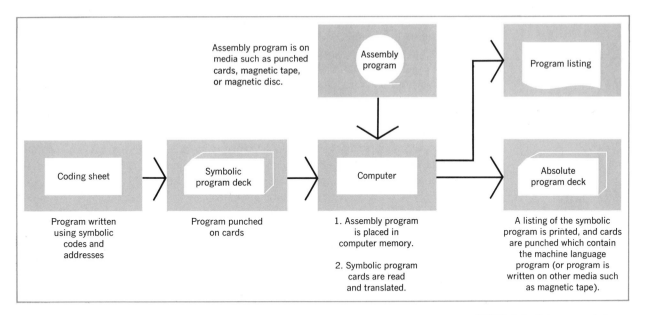

Assembly program is on media such as punched cards, magnetic tape, or magnetic disc.

Assembly program

Program listing

Coding sheet

Symbolic program deck

Computer

Absolute program deck

Program written using symbolic codes and addresses

Program punched on cards

1. Assembly program is placed in computer memory.

2. Symbolic program cards are read and translated.

A listing of the symbolic program is printed, and cards are punched which contain the machine language program (or program is written on other media such as magnetic tape).

FIGURE 8-3 Using a symbolic assembly system

MACRO INSTRUCTIONS

The use of symbolic assembly systems does not reduce the amount of coding for the programmer. There is still one symbolic instruction for each machine language instruction. But many programs have small segments in common. Examples are the steps in reading and writing records, error checking, and scaling numbers. Since these operations are common to many different programs, it is possible to write short program segments which can be spliced into any program which calls for performing these operations. To accomplish this, an instruction is added to the symbolic system which indicates that this program segment is to be added. When this instruction is used, the assembly system inserts the set of computer instructions. Macro instructions are available with many symbolic programming systems. The macro instruction relieves the programmer from writing repetitious, standard routines and thereby lessens the chance of coding errors. Macro instructions are used especially in connection with input and output coding.

PROCEDURE-ORIENTED AND PROBLEM-ORIENTED LANGUAGES

The logic of using macro instructions can be carried one step further to build an entire coding system using them. Since macro instructions are translated by a computer program into machine language, the instructions themselves can be independent of any particular computer. There must then be a separate translator for each computer on which the macro instruction language is to be used. The macro instruction language, being machine-independent, can be oriented toward the problem or procedure for which the language will be used. These languages are frequently referred to as pseudo codes, compiler codes, or automatic coding systems. The compiler consists of the translator program and other programs necessary to convert the pseudo-code statements into a machine language program.

A distinction is frequently made between two types of automatic coding systems, procedure-oriented languages and problem-oriented languages. Both are included in the abbreviation POL, and both types are often referred to as problem-oriented. The distinction is that, although both are user-oriented, a procedure-oriented language describes the computational procedures to be followed while a problem-oriented language describes the problem itself. The most common POLs are two procedure-oriented languages—FORTRAN and COBOL. FORTRAN is a language especially suited for writing arithmetic procedures for solving statistical and mathematical problems. COBOL is written for business-type file processing. These languages are surveyed in Chapter 14. The nature of the languages is illustrated in Figure 8–4 by sample lines of coding from FORTRAN and COBOL.

A compiler language such as FORTRAN or COBOL consists of a set of simple rules for writing steps to solve a problem. The compiler program translates these statements and creates a machine language program. The compiler language is problem- or procedure-oriented rather than computer-oriented and is therefore much easier to use than symbolic or machine language. Reasonable proficiency in FORTRAN or COBOL can be attained in a small fraction of the time required to develop proficiency in symbolic or machine coding. The resulting programs are also easier to revise because the coding is more understandable and closely related to the procedure being performed.

The advantages of macro instruction languages would seem to be so overwhelming as to preclude the use of absolute or symbolic coding. This would be true except for two reasons. The first is the amount of storage required for the compiler. The compiler program is sufficiently complex that it usually requires a medium-size storage capacity to make use of the compiler. Also, the program resulting from the compiler is typically considerably larger than one which is coded directly in symbolic coding. Therefore, the computer with a minimum-size storage may not be able to make use of the less compact compiler coding. The second is the fact that the translation routine to convert from macro to absolute coding must be general enough to handle all possible cases, therefore the result of programming is not so efficient in terms of running time as one which is programmed specifically for the particular problem. The disparity in running time may not be important for once-only scientific problems but may become significant for commercial problems that are run day in and day out. If the inventory-updating run takes 3 hr per day using machine-oriented programming and 4 hr using a compiler language, the difference in running time may preclude the use of the macro language. As computers and compilers have become more efficient, this disparity in running time has been narrowed. Also, internal speeds are now so fast that even with relatively inefficient coding, the input/output devices may still operate at maximum speeds.

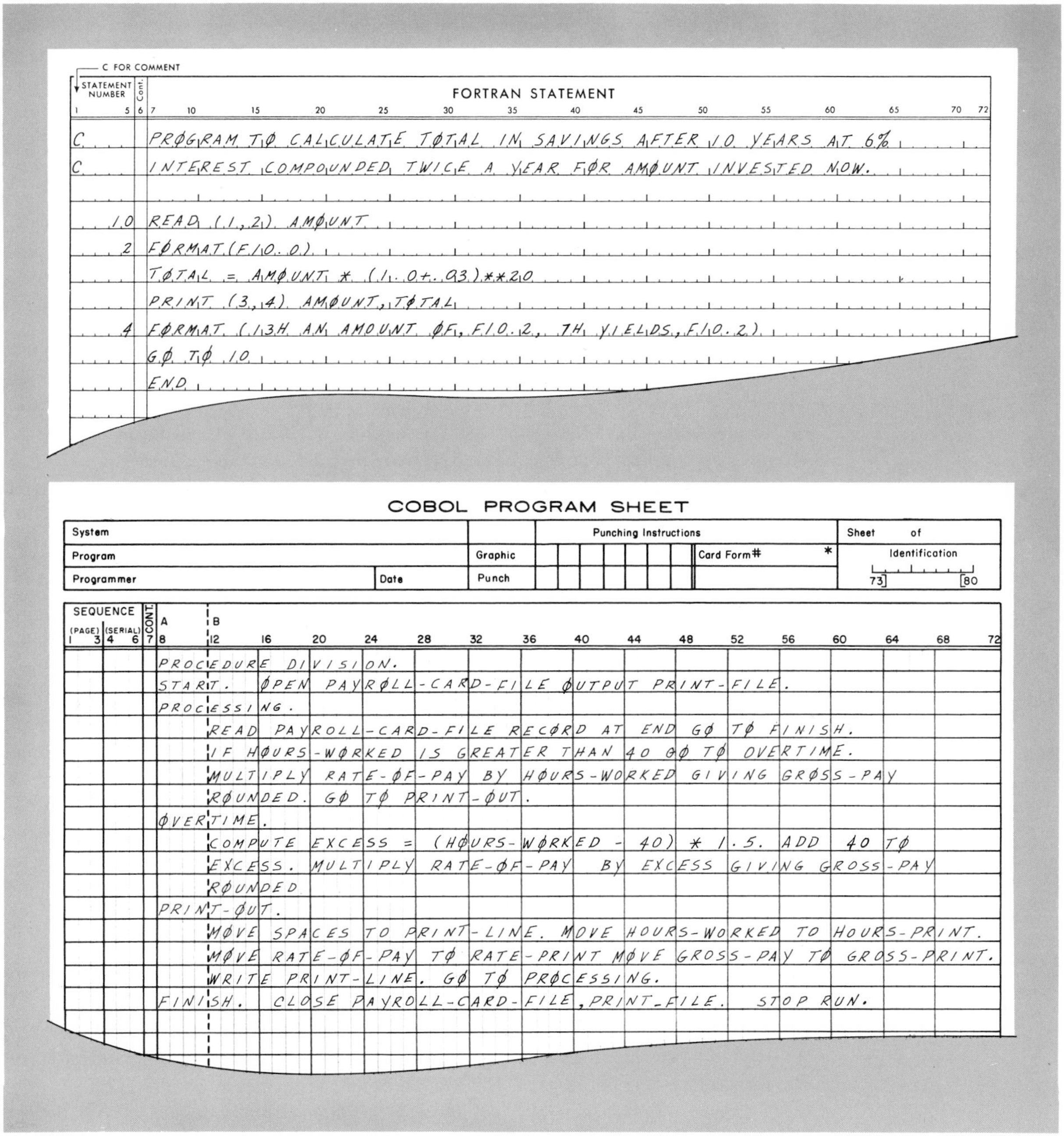

FORTRAN STATEMENT

```
C    PROGRAM TO CALCULATE TOTAL IN SAVINGS AFTER 10 YEARS AT 6%
C    INTEREST COMPOUNDED TWICE A YEAR FOR AMOUNT INVESTED NOW.

  10 READ (1,2) AMOUNT
   2 FORMAT (F10.0)
     TOTAL = AMOUNT * (1.0 + .03) ** 20
     PRINT (3,4) AMOUNT, TOTAL
   4 FORMAT (13H AN AMOUNT OF, F10.2, 7H YIELDS, F10.2)
     GO TO 10
     END
```

COBOL PROGRAM SHEET

System				Punching Instructions				Sheet of
Program				Graphic				Card Form #	*	Identification
Programmer		Date		Punch						73 80

```
     PROCEDURE DIVISION.
     START.  OPEN PAYROLL-CARD-FILE OUTPUT PRINT-FILE.
     PROCESSING.
         READ PAYROLL-CARD-FILE RECORD AT END GO TO FINISH.
         IF HOURS-WORKED IS GREATER THAN 40 GO TO OVERTIME.
         MULTIPLY RATE-OF-PAY BY HOURS-WORKED GIVING GROSS-PAY
         ROUNDED. GO TO PRINT-OUT.
     OVERTIME.
         COMPUTE EXCESS = (HOURS-WORKED - 40) * 1.5. ADD 40 TO
         EXCESS. MULTIPLY RATE-OF-PAY BY EXCESS GIVING GROSS-PAY
         ROUNDED
     PRINT-OUT.
         MOVE SPACES TO PRINT-LINE. MOVE HOURS-WORKED TO HOURS-PRINT.
         MOVE RATE-OF-PAY TO RATE-PRINT MOVE GROSS-PAY TO GROSS-PRINT.
         WRITE PRINT-LINE. GO TO PROCESSING.
     FINISH.  CLOSE PAYROLL-CARD-FILE, PRINT-FILE.  STOP RUN.
```

FIGURE 8–4 Examples of FORTRAN and COBOL coding

▌ AIDS TO PROGRAMMING

As may be apparent, the success of programming efforts depends not only on the hardware on which the application is to be run, but also on the software, or aids to programming. Software is typically provided without charge by the manufacturer, although some software is developed by independent concerns which sell the use of it. In addition, most computer users belong to a users' association which promotes the exchange of programs written by the users themselves. Programming aids furnished to users include, in addition to the symbolic assembly systems and compilers already discussed, library routines, utility programs, program generators, applications programs, and conversion routines.

PROGRAMMING LANGUAGES

The programming languages described previously are part of the software or program aids provided by the manufacturer. As a minimum, the user can expect a symbolic programming language with a related assembly routine to perform the conversion to absolute machine language and one or more procedure-oriented or problem-oriented languages. For a general-purpose computer, there should be a FORTRAN compiler for formula problems and a COBOL compiler for business-type processing.

LIBRARY ROUTINES

Library routines are program sections which solve a common computational problem. They are written to be spliced into any program being written by a user. For example, a routine to calculate the square root of a number is prepared once by a manufacturer and can be inserted in a user's program where he needs to calculate a square root. When the routine is spliced directly into the main program, it is termed an open subroutine; when it is attached to the main program but remains a separate program, it is termed a closed subroutine.

The technique of using closed subroutines is very important in programming. It consists of writing a routine (or using a library routine as a separate program) which is entered at various times by a transfer from the main program. After using the subroutine, control is returned to the main program at the same point as it left. The use of closed subroutines may be illustrated by the same problem of calculating a square root, but this time assume that there are many points in the program at which a square root must be taken. Rather than putting this routine into the program several times, the routine is put in once as a closed subroutine. When a square root is to be calculated, control is transferred to the square root routine. After the square root is taken, the answer is placed in a predetermined location, and control is returned to the main program. This will be explained further in Chapter 12.

Library routines generally include a wide range of mathematical and statistical routines.

UTILITY PROGRAMS

Utility programs are routines for performing operating and testing functions usually necessary in the operations of a particular computer. Examples are:

Program to load a program into memory
Program to clear the entire storage by inserting zeros in all locations
Program to duplicate magnetic tapes
Program to dump memory (output the entire contents of storage using printer or other output device)
Program to trace the operation of a program (print the results of each step)
Program to sort data

PROGRAM GENERATORS

A program generator is a routine that will write a simple program based on the specifications for a particular type of problem. For example, a report program generator (often termed RPG) will write a complete program for producing a report from a description of the desired report. RPG routines allow the user to specify simple manipulation of the data as well as printing the report. For many small computers, the RPG may be the most significant user-oriented programming aid for that computer.

APPLICATIONS PROGRAMS

These are complete programs which solve problems common to many users. The applications programs are typically all ready to use, requiring only a set of data prepared according to the specifications. Examples are linear programming, critical path (PERT) analysis, sales analysis, and inventory simulation. There is also a trend to applications programs that are suitable for a whole industry, such as a complete billing program for electric and gas utilities or an analysis program for brokerage firms.

CONVERSION PROGRAMS

Manufacturers of computers provide users with considerable assistance. For customers changing to a new computer from an old one, conversion routines have been written to assist in the conversion process. Since a major problem in conversion is the rewriting of old programs for the new computer, a major difficulty is removed by having a program for the new machine that will accept instructions written for the old. This is done by having the new computer simulate the operation of the old. Programs run through simulation of one computer by another are not as efficient as the programs written for the new computer, but the approach is helpful during the period of conversion. The simulation approach to conversion uses a simulator program. This is in contrast to the use of a stored hardware routine called an emulator, described in Chapter 6. Another approach to conversion is a program which codes a program for a new computer from the machine level coding for the old computer. Although the coding is not usually completed without some additional work by a programmer, it reduces the time and effort of conversion.

OPERATING SYSTEM

The operating system is a set of routines which directs the operation of the computer. These routines are more an aid to computer operating rather than programming, but they do have features which assist in the programming function. For example, the operating system will manage all compilers and assemblers that perform the task of translating from the symbolic coding to absolute instructions.

▮ SUMMARY

The chapter has surveyed the steps in programming a computer. These steps begin with system design, which develops the specifications, and continue with procedures to plan the program, code the instructions, assemble or compile into machine language, debug and test, and finally to document the result.

There are two basic instruction formats reflecting the difference between a binary computer using registers and a computer using a storage-to-storage approach. Although the computer runs only with machine language instructions, the programmer codes in a symbolic-level language or a higher-level procedure or problem-oriented language. These languages are converted to absolute, machine-level coding by special programs called assembly routines and compilers.

Each level of programming has advantages and disadvantages. Although lower-level languages generally are more efficient in terms of running time, higher-level languages are easier to use, reduce programming time, and introduce compatibility for use on different computers. Documentation is also improved. In general, the trend is toward the use of higher-order languages. Depending on the efficiency of the compiler, improving the effectiveness of programming will usually be a more significant factor than possible inefficiencies which are reflected in extra machine running time. For single-use or infrequently used programs, the compiler language is usually preferred; for programs to be run day in day out, the choice depends on the cost advantages and disadvantages mentioned.

The manufacturer usually provides an extensive number of aids to programming. These include programming languages, library routines, utility programs, report program generators, applications programs, and conversion routines. Operating systems, because they manage the running of programs, relieve the programmer from coding some housekeeping tasks related to the programs.

▌EXERCISES

1 What is the difference between the following:

   a Assembly and compilation
   b Procedure-oriented and problem-oriented languages
   c FORTRAN and COBOL

2 Define the following terms:

   a RPG   d Macro instruction
   b Library programs   e Operand
   c Applications program

3 What must an instruction specify—either explicitly or implicitly?

4 What is the difference between the one- and two-address instruction formats?

5 Based on your answer to question 4, how could the IBM 401 computer use a single character "2" to print a line from data stored in the main storage?

6 If you have a computer available for your use, determine:

   a The name of the symbolic assembly system
   b The names of compilers available for use
   c Whether or not there are macro instructions for use with input and output
   d Whether or not there is a report program generator
   e Whether or not the computer runs under the control of an operating system
   f The name of one applications program

7 Why is all coding not done using a compiler language?

▌ LAYOUT CHARTS
CARD LAYOUT
TAPE AND DISC LAYOUT
PRINTER LAYOUT
STORAGE LAYOUT

▌ GRID CHARTS

▌ FLOWCHARTS
FLOWCHART STANDARDIZATION
EXPLANATION OF SYMBOLS
ADDITIONAL INTERNATIONAL SYMBOLS
SYMBOLS PRIOR TO 1966
FLOWCHART USAGE CONVENTIONS
TYPES OF FLOWCHARTS
FLOWCHARTING SOFTWARE

▌ DECISION TABLES

▌ SUMMARY

▌ EXERCISES

TOOLS FOR
ANALYZING
AND PLANNING
COMPUTER
PROGRAMS

This chapter will describe some of the tools used by the systems analyst and computer programmer in analyzing and planning the computer programs for a computer application. The tools are layout charts, grid charts, flowcharts, and decision tables. These tools help the systems analyst and programmer to organize their thinking and to visualize the job which must be done. When a program is completed, the various charts used in designing and planning the program are included with the program documentation.

▌ LAYOUT CHARTS

A layout is a drawing which shows the format of an input/output record or the placement of data in storage. Preprinted forms are generally used for this purpose. Computer manufacturers make these forms available as part of their service to users of their equipment. The major layout forms in use are card layout, tape or disc layout, printer layout, and storage layout. Each of these will be described and illustrated.

CARD LAYOUT

Each type of input or output card is described by the use of a card layout form (Figure 9-1). The fields on the card are marked off and described by noting the name of the field, the type of characters (alphabetic, numeric, or alphanumeric), and the location of the decimal point where appropriate.

FIGURE 9-1 Card layout

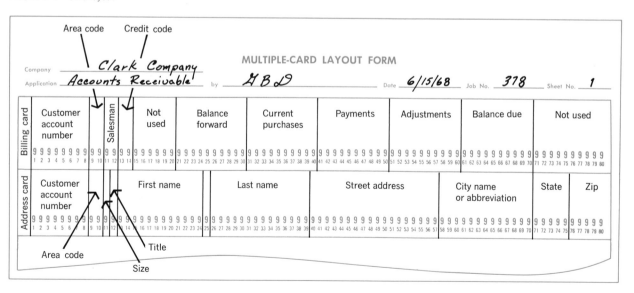

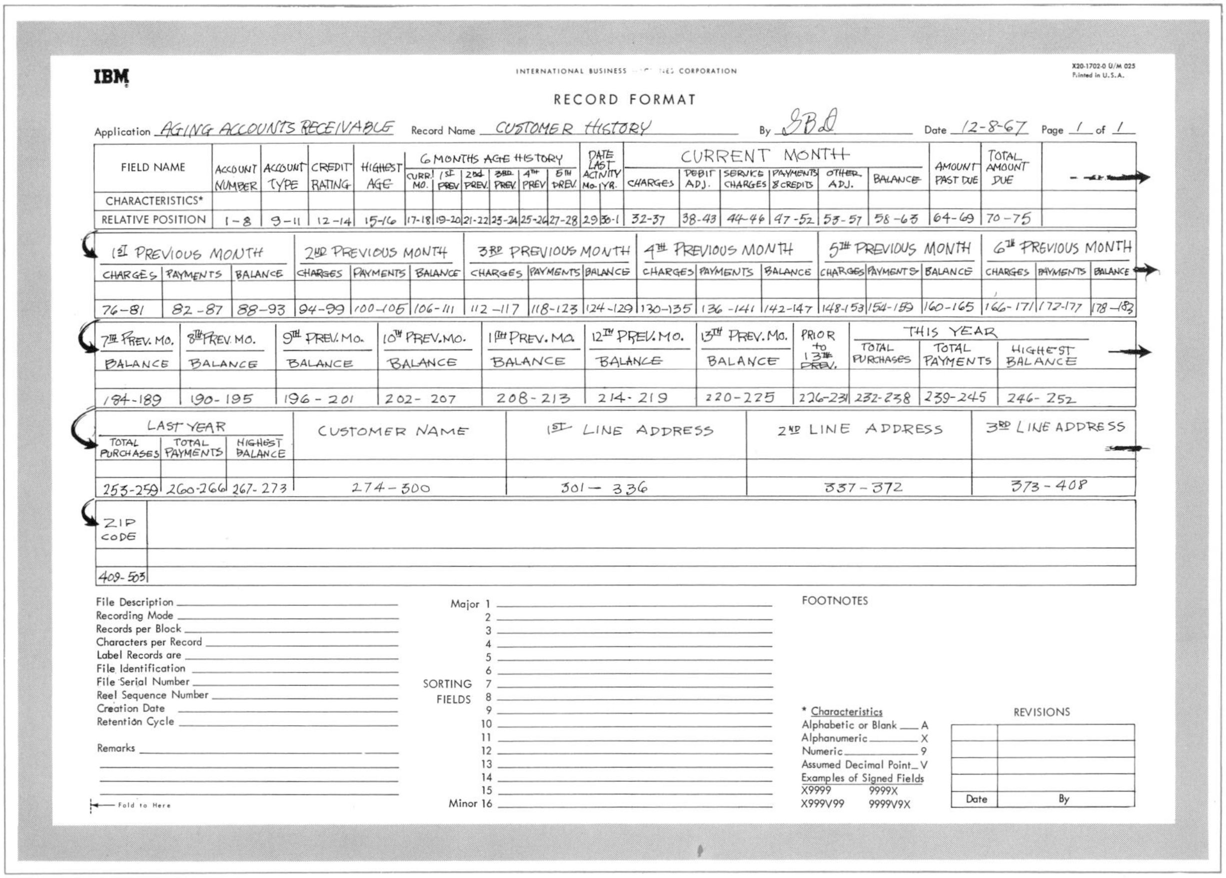

IBM INTERNATIONAL BUSINESS MACHINES CORPORATION X20-1702-0 U/M 025 Printed in U.S.A.

RECORD FORMAT

Application AGING ACCOUNTS RECEIVABLE Record Name CUSTOMER HISTORY By JBD Date 12-8-67 Page 1 of 1

FIELD NAME	ACCOUNT NUMBER	ACCOUNT TYPE	CREDIT RATING	HIGHEST AGE	6 MONTHS AGE HISTORY: CURR. MO.	1ST PREV	2ND PREV.	3RD PREV.	4TH PREV	5TH PREV.	DATE LAST ACTIVITY MO.	YR.	CURRENT MONTH: CHARGES	DEBIT ADJ.	SERVICE CHARGES	PAYMENTS & CREDITS	OTHER ADJ.	BALANCE	AMOUNT PAST DUE	TOTAL AMOUNT DUE
CHARACTERISTICS*																				
RELATIVE POSITION	1-8	9-11	12-14	15-16	17-18	19-20	21-22	23-24	25-26	27-28	29	30-1	32-37	38-43	44-46	47-52	53-57	58-63	64-69	70-75

1ST PREVIOUS MONTH: CHARGES	PAYMENTS	BALANCE	2ND PREVIOUS MONTH: CHARGES	PAYMENTS	BALANCE	3RD PREVIOUS MONTH: CHARGES	PAYMENTS	BALANCE	4TH PREVIOUS MONTH: CHARGES	PAYMENTS	BALANCE	5TH PREVIOUS MONTH: CHARGES	PAYMENTS	BALANCE	6TH PREVIOUS MONTH: CHARGES	PAYMENTS	BALANCE
76-81	82-87	88-93	94-99	100-105	106-111	112-117	118-123	124-129	130-135	136-141	142-147	148-153	154-159	160-165	166-171	172-177	178-183

7TH PREV. MO. BALANCE	8TH PREV. MO. BALANCE	9TH PREV. MO. BALANCE	10TH PREV. MO. BALANCE	11TH PREV. MO. BALANCE	12TH PREV. MO. BALANCE	13TH PREV. MO. BALANCE	PRIOR to 13TH PREV.	THIS YEAR: TOTAL PURCHASES	TOTAL PAYMENTS	HIGHEST BALANCE
184-189	190-195	196-201	202-207	208-213	214-219	220-225	226-231	232-238	239-245	246-252

LAST YEAR: TOTAL PURCHASES	TOTAL PAYMENTS	HIGHEST BALANCE	CUSTOMER NAME	1ST LINE ADDRESS	2ND LINE ADDRESS	3RD LINE ADDRESS
253-259	260-266	267-273	274-300	301-336	337-372	373-408

ZIP CODE
409-503

File Description
Recording Mode
Records per Block
Characters per Record
Label Records are
File Identification
File Serial Number
Reel Sequence Number
Creation Date
Retention Cycle

Remarks

Fold to Here

SORTING FIELDS: Major 1, 2, 3, 4, 5, 6, 7, 8, 9, 10, 11, 12, 13, 14, 15, Minor 16

FOOTNOTES

* Characteristics
Alphabetic or Blank — A
Alphanumeric — X
Numeric — 9
Assumed Decimal Point — V
Examples of Signed Fields
X9999 9999X
X999V99 9999V9X

REVISIONS

Date	By

FIGURE 9-2 Magnetic tape layout

TAPE AND DISC LAYOUT

The tape layout shows the format of records written on magnetic tape. It is similar to the card layout except that a card is limited to 80 characters and a tape record can be as many characters as desired, limited primarily by the main storage space available for holding a tape block during processing (Figure 9-2). A tape layout may also specify tape characteristics such as density, number of records in a block, etc. A disc layout is similar except that the disc is divided into fixed-length segments.

PRINTER LAYOUT

The printer layout assists the programmer in planning the exact placement of data for a printed output. Headings are shown on the form as well as Xs or other notation indicating the data field locations. The vertical spacing of printer paper is controlled by holes in a short paper or plastic tape. This carriage control tape is planned using the side of the printer layout sheet (Figure 9–3).

STORAGE LAYOUT

Some computers (such as the IBM 1401) have fixed areas of storage for use by the card reader, printer, and punch. Other computers may utilize any portion of storage. Depending on the particular computer and the programming language used, it may be valuable to have a storage layout (also called a memory map) showing the position of input/output records, constants, etc. for use in analyzing storage dumps (listings of the contents of storage) when an error is found (Figure 9–4).

FIGURE 9–3 Printer layout

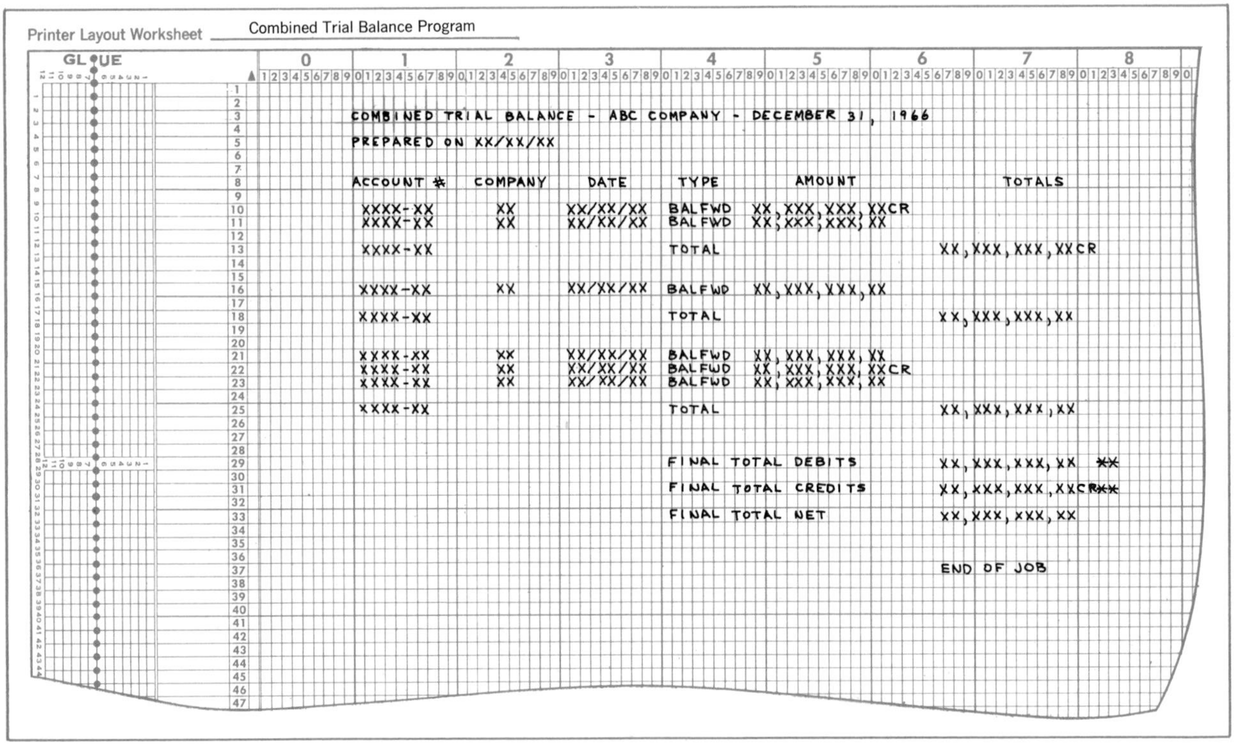
Printer Layout Worksheet Combined Trial Balance Program

GLUE

COMBINED TRIAL BALANCE - ABC COMPANY - DECEMBER 31, 1966
PREPARED ON XX/XX/XX
ACCOUNT # COMPANY DATE TYPE AMOUNT TOTALS
XXXX-XX XX XX/XX/XX BALFWD XX,XXX,XXX,XXCR
XXXX-XX XX XX/XX/XX BALFWD XX,XXX,XXX,XX
XXXX-XX TOTAL XX,XXX,XXX,XXCR
XXXX-XX XX XX/XX/XX BALFWD XX,XXX,XXX,XX
XXXX-XX TOTAL XX,XXX,XXX,XX
XXXX-XX XX XX/XX/XX BALFWD XX,XXX,XXX,XX
XXXX-XX XX XX/XX/XX BALFWD XX,XXX,XXX,XXCR
XXXX-XX XX XX/XX/XX BALFWD XX,XXX,XXX,XX
XXXX-XX TOTAL XX,XXX,XXX,XX
FINAL TOTAL DEBITS XX,XXX,XXX,XX **
FINAL TOTAL CREDITS XX,XXX,XXX,XXCR**
FINAL TOTAL NET XX,XXX,XXX,XX
END OF JOB

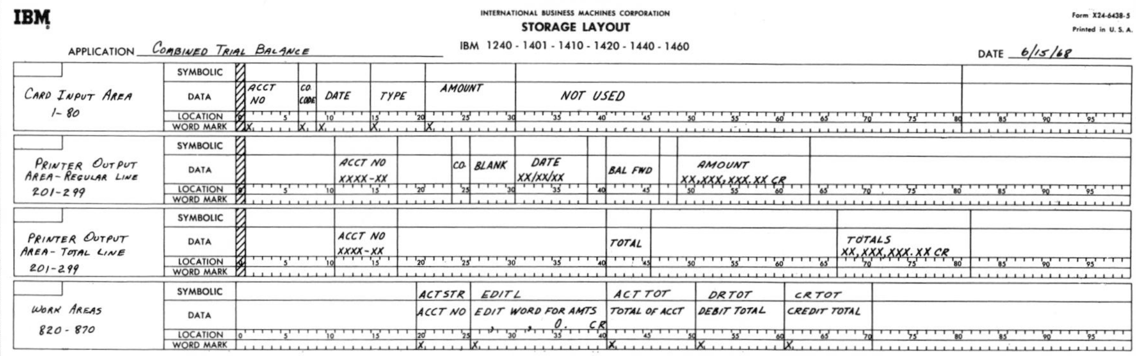
IBM
INTERNATIONAL BUSINESS MACHINES CORPORATION
STORAGE LAYOUT
Form X24-6438-5
Printed in U. S. A.
APPLICATION Combined Trial Balance
IBM 1240 - 1401 - 1410 - 1420 - 1440 - 1460
DATE 6/15/68

Card Input Area 1-80 — DATA: ACCT NO | CO CODE | DATE | TYPE | AMOUNT | NOT USED

Printer Output Area - Regular Line 201-299 — DATA: ACCT NO XXXX-XX | CO | BLANK | DATE XX/XX/XX | BAL FWD | AMOUNT XX,XXX,XXX.XX CR

Printer Output Area - Total Line 201-299 — DATA: ACCT NO XXXX-XX | TOTAL | TOTALS XX,XXX,XXX.XX CR

Work Areas 820 - 870 — SYMBOLIC: ACTSTR | EDITL | ACTTOT | DRTOT | CRTOT — DATA: ACCT NO | EDIT WORD FOR AMTS | TOTAL OF ACCT | DEBIT TOTAL | CREDIT TOTAL

FIGURE 9-4 Storage layout

GRID CHARTS

Grid charts are a tabular method of summarizing the connections or relationships between two sets of factors. For example, in planning the organization of a set of interrelated programs, which use the same set of data, it may be necessary to summarize which programs use which data items. A grid chart form is useful for this and similar purposes (Figure 9-5).

A grid chart analysis is often useful in eliminating unnecessary reports or simplifying reports by eliminating redundant data items. All of the data items are listed on the

FIGURE 9-5 Grid charts

Grid chart to analyze use of data items by different programs

Data items \ Programs	Sales analysis	Sales forecast	Sales budget	Salesman evaluation	Warehouse analysis	Product evaluation	Other
Customer name				/			
Customer address					/		
Credit code	/						
Territory code	/	/	/	/	(/)		
etc.							

Indicates use of territory code by warehouse analysis

Grid chart to analyze the use of data items for preparation of reports

Data items \ Reports	Attendance report	Foreman's production report	Payroll register	FICA quarterly report	Income tax withheld report	W-2 reports	Other
Employee no.	/	/	/				
Employee name			/	/	/	/	
Employee address						/	
Social Security no.			/	/	/	/	
etc.							

side of the chart; the reports are listed across the top (Figure 9–5). An entry of 1 indicates that the data item appears on the report. By analyzing the redundancies, the systems analyst may be able to reduce the number or complexity of reports.

▌ FLOWCHARTS

The flowchart is a method for representing with symbols the operations and flow of data in information processing. It is used for communicating information about a data processing system or a program. Therefore the reader must understand the meaning attached to the symbols used in drawing the chart. Every flowchart could have a dictionary of symbols which would explain the symbols for that flowchart. But a much better approach is to have agreement on a standard set of flowchart symbols.

FLOWCHART STANDARDIZATION

In the United States, groups desiring to develop industry-wide standards usually work through the United States of America Standards Institute (USASI). This organization was formerly the American Standards Association (ASA). (See Appendix IV for a description of data processing standards.) A USASI subcommittee on problem definition and analysis (X3.6) developed a standard set of flowchart symbols. The first USASI flowchart standards were approved in 1965 but not published because of conflicts with a proposed international standard. A revised set of standard flowchart symbols was approved and published in June, 1966 (Figure 9–6). Even though not published, the early efforts received wide acceptance in the period from 1964–1966. This pre-adoption may create some confusion, so a description of these changes will also be presented in this chapter.

Drawing flowcharts is sufficiently creative that no two people will draw them exactly alike. The main point is clarity of presentation. This is enhanced by using the USA standards. Since they are relatively new, one should expect to find variations. Some installations may ignore USA flowchart standards and use their own set of symbols.

EXPLANATION OF SYMBOLS

There are four basic symbols which are sufficient to describe a data processing system or a program. These are (1) the input/output symbol, (2) the process symbol, (3) the flowline, and (4) the annotation symbol. In addition to the basic symbols, there are 13 specialized and 2 other symbols which can be used. These additional symbols are optional, and if there is no specialized symbol, the general symbol is used. For example, an input from punched cards may be diagrammed either with the basic input/output symbol or by the specialized punched card symbol. Templates are available for drawing the flowchart symbols. Most computer manufacturers stock them.

Each of the standard symbols together with an example of use will be described in Figure 9–7. A short description of the document, file, or process is usually written inside the symbol. If additional description or explanatory notes are required, the annotation symbol is used.

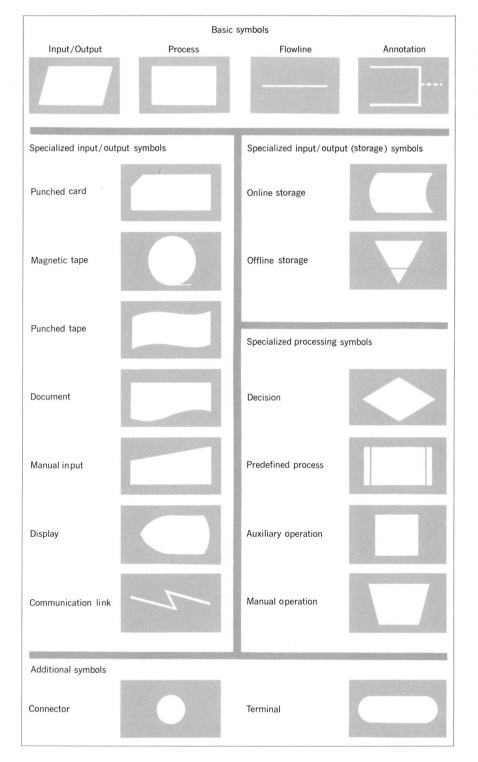

FIGURE 9–6 Summary of flowchart symbols

SOURCE: Section 5, "Summary of Flow-chart Symbols," from USA Standard X3.5-1966, *Flowchart Symbols for Information Processing*, p. 9.

FIGURE 9–7

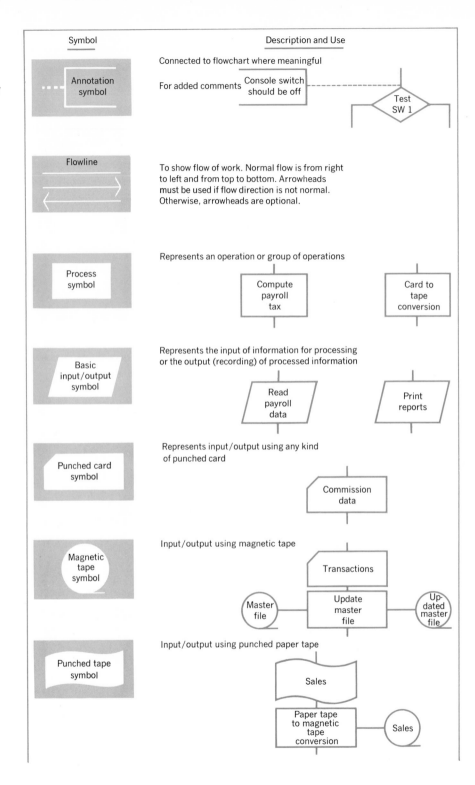

Symbol	Description and Use
Annotation symbol	Connected to flowchart where meaningful For added comments
Flowline	To show flow of work. Normal flow is from right to left and from top to bottom. Arrowheads must be used if flow direction is not normal. Otherwise, arrowheads are optional.
Process symbol	Represents an operation or group of operations
Basic input/output symbol	Represents the input of information for processing or the output (recording) of processed information
Punched card symbol	Represents input/output using any kind of punched card
Magnetic tape symbol	Input/output using magnetic tape
Punched tape symbol	Input/output using punched paper tape

FIGURE 9-7 (Continued)

Symbol	Description and Use

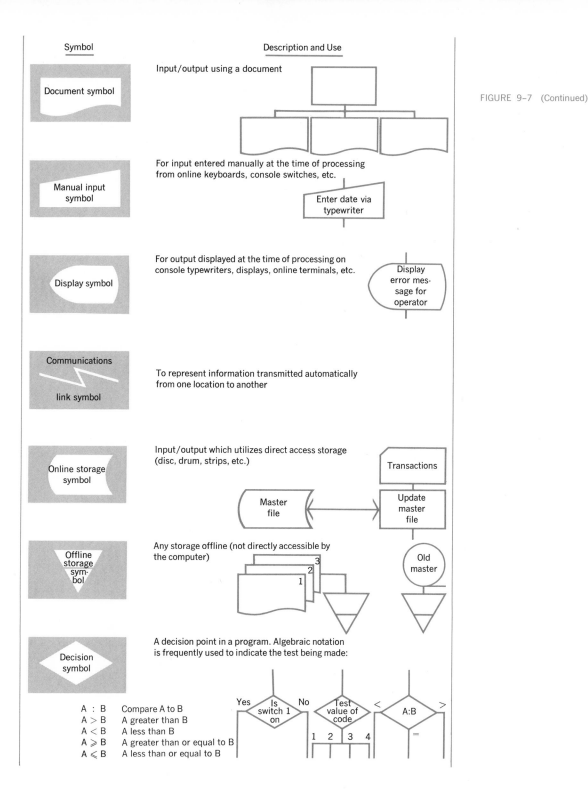

Document symbol — Input/output using a document

Manual input symbol — For input entered manually at the time of processing from online keyboards, console switches, etc.

Enter date via typewriter

Display symbol — For output displayed at the time of processing on console typewriters, displays, online terminals, etc.

Display error message for operator

Communications link symbol — To represent information transmitted automatically from one location to another

Online storage symbol — Input/output which utilizes direct access storage (disc, drum, strips, etc.)

Transactions

Master file

Update master file

Offline storage symbol — Any storage offline (not directly accessible by the computer)

Old master

Decision symbol — A decision point in a program. Algebraic notation is frequently used to indicate the test being made:

A : B   Compare A to B
A > B   A greater than B
A < B   A less than B
A ≥ B   A greater than or equal to B
A ≤ B   A less than or equal to B

Yes   Is switch 1 on   No

Test value of code   1   2   3   4

A:B   <   >   =

FIGURE 9-7 (Continued)

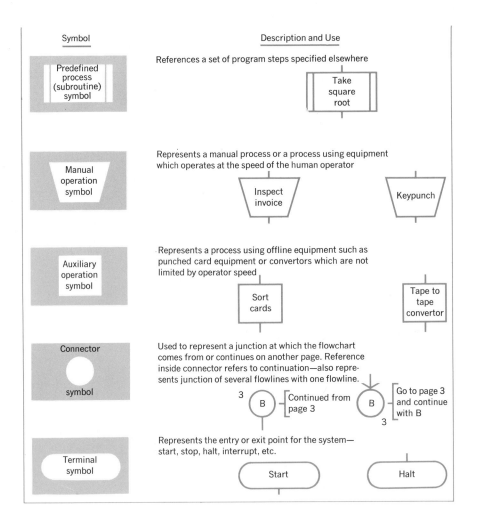

Symbol	Description and Use
Predefined process (subroutine) symbol	References a set of program steps specified elsewhere — Take square root
Manual operation symbol	Represents a manual process or a process using equipment which operates at the speed of the human operator — Inspect invoice, Keypunch
Auxiliary operation symbol	Represents a process using offline equipment such as punched card equipment or convertors which are not limited by operator speed — Sort cards, Tape to tape convertor
Connector symbol	Used to represent a junction at which the flowchart comes from or continues on another page. Reference inside connector refers to continuation—also represents junction of several flowlines with one flowline. 3 B Continued from page 3, B Go to page 3 and continue with B 3
Terminal symbol	Represents the entry or exit point for the system—start, stop, halt, interrupt, etc. Start, Halt

ADDITIONAL INTERNATIONAL SYMBOLS

The international counterpart of the United States of America Standards Institute (International Standards Organization) has proposed additional symbols which, when adopted, will supplement the USA standard symbols (Figure 9–8). Noteworthy is the addition of a preparation symbol and symbols for merging, extracting, sorting, and collating.

SYMBOLS PRIOR TO 1966

Before 1964, each manufacturer prepared his own symbols. These differed in many cases. For example, the decision symbol of one manufacturer was an oval and of an-

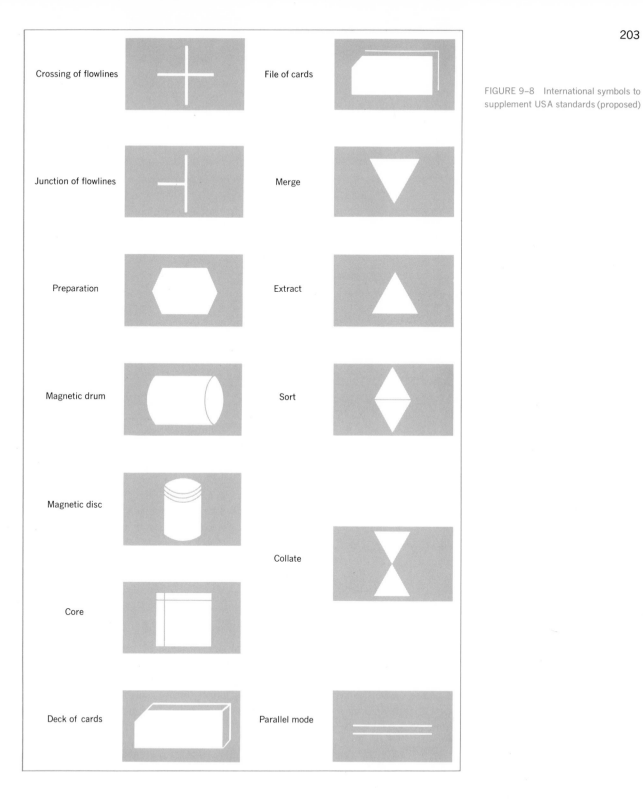

Crossing of flowlines

Junction of flowlines

Preparation

Magnetic drum

Magnetic disc

Core

Deck of cards

File of cards

Merge

Extract

Sort

Collate

Parallel mode

FIGURE 9–8 International symbols to supplement USA standards (proposed)

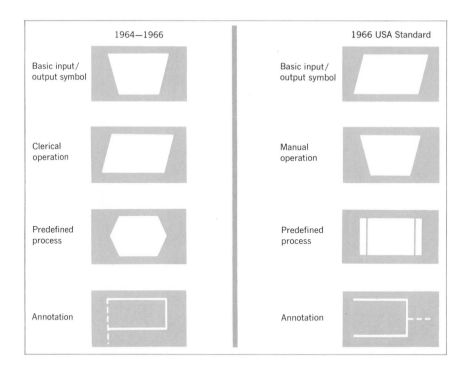

other a diamond. The work of the American Standards group was reflected in the 1964 adoption of revised templates by most manufacturers. Since the differences between those symbols and the final USA standards may cause some confusion, symbols in common use during this period which were changed are compared to the 1966 USA standards in Figure 9-9.

FLOWCHART USAGE CONVENTIONS

It is customary to draw flowcharts so that they read from left to right and top to bottom. If the flow goes in a reverse direction, arrowheads are used. Arrowheads can, of course, be used in normal flow to increase clarity or readability.

When it is desirable to identify a symbol for the purpose of referencing it, a notation is placed above the symbol to the right or left of the vertical bisector or inside the symbol separated by a stripe. USA standards for the use of the flowcharts specify a standard use for each:

Standard Use
Notation at top to right of bisector. Identifies the symbol.

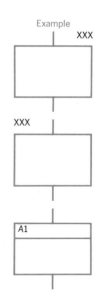

Notation at top to left of bisector. Identifies location, such as page number, of other documentation relating to the symbol. For example, the page number of a detailed representation of the processing step.

Striping—a line drawn inside the symbol near top. The reference inside the stripe identifies the processing. The symbol acts as a cross reference to the detailed micro flowcharts for the function.

The symbol identifier and striping code can be constituted so as to reflect other information important for the reader, e.g., department involved.

TYPES OF FLOWCHARTS

Although the same set of symbols is used for both, it is convenient to separate flowcharts into two types—system flowcharts and program flowcharts. A system flowchart describes the data flow and operations for a data processing system. The flowchart shows how the data processing is to be accomplished. A program flowchart describes the sequence of operations and decisions for a particular program. Program flowcharts are sometimes referred to as block or logic diagrams.

A system flowchart defines the broad flow of work in the organization, showing where data originates, when it is filed, what processing is to be performed, and whether it is to be done by a computer program or by using an offline device such as a mechanical sorter. Figure 9–10 illustrates a part of a system flowchart for processing of accounts receivable transactions.

The program flowchart is a blueprint for a program, and just as one can construct simple structures without a blueprint, one can write very simple programs without drawing a flowchart. When the problem becomes more complex, it is necessary to have formal plans. Program flowcharts serve two purposes. The first is the planning of the program structure as an aid in writing the computer program steps. The second is the documenting of the program logic and work flow for communicating it to others and for recall at a later date if the program needs to be altered. The latter purpose is extremely important because it is very difficult to grasp the logic of a program from a perusal of the detailed computer coding.

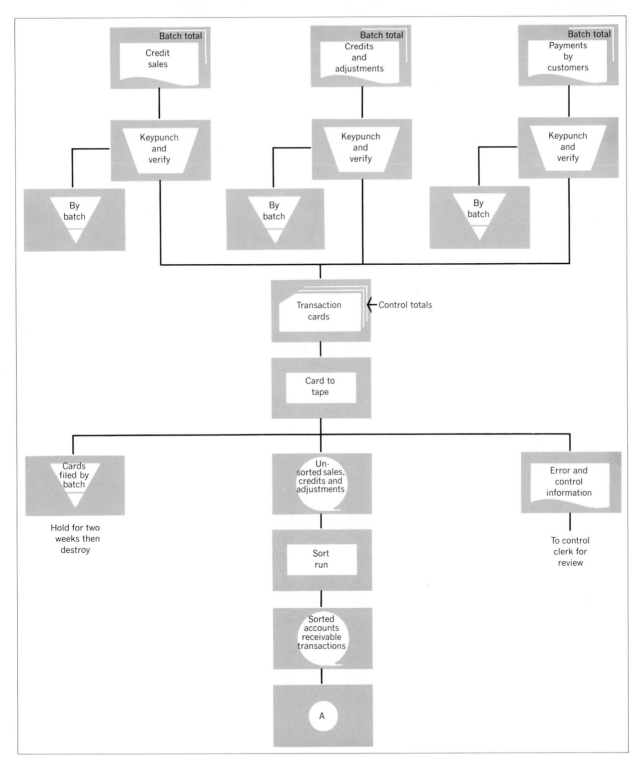

FIGURE 9-10 Example of system flowchart (accounts receivable processing)

There are no formal rules governing the amount of detail to include in a program flowchart. This will depend on the purpose for which the diagram will be used. In order to see the overall logic, programmers will frequently draw an overall or macro flowchart to describe the logic for a particular application. The overall flowchart will then be supported by detailed micro flowcharts. The "exploding" of sections of a flowchart into more detailed flowcharts may be continued until sufficient detail is available for the coding of instructions. The use of different levels of detail is illustrated in Figure 9–11. The overall flow is given by the macro flowchart, the detailed logic of the FICA tax (old-age survivors' insurance or social security) is given by a micro flowchart.

The logic for the FICA computation is not simply multiplying the rate times the gross pay, because there is a limit on the total amount to be deducted from an employee. For 1968, this amount was 4.4 percent of the first $7,800 of salary or wages, which gives a maximum tax of $343.20. There are thus three paths the program may take: (1) regular deduction of 4.4 percent, (2) no deduction because the employee is fully paid, and (3) partial deduction because the employee is almost fully paid and a deduction of 4.4 percent would be too much. Since no more than $343.20 should be deducted, any error which allowed this should be detected and noted for correction. There are many approaches which can be taken; the one illustrated calculates the regular rate using the 4.4 percentage (called FICA-REGULAR) and an alternative amount which is the maximum that can be paid without overpaying (FICA-MAX). FICA-MAX is used as the FICA-TAX if it is less than FICA-REGULAR; otherwise FICA-REGULAR is used. If equal, either will do and FICA-MAX is arbitrarily chosen. Note that this logic can be easily followed via the flowchart. If there is a change in rate or in wages to which the rate is applicable, the flowchart tells at a glance the way the program must be changed—both the rate and the maximum amount figures. Likewise, another programmer can understand what has been done.

The handling of the error condition illustrates an important concept. If the program logic is followed, it should never be possible for FICA-MAX to be less than zero, indicating an overwithholding by the employer. Despite the fact that it should never happen, the contingency is provided for by having an error routine to which the program transfers if it should occur.

The second illustration flowcharted in Figure 9–12 is a program segment dealing with the logic of issuing an airline ticket. Assuming there is one flight under consideration with two classes of service, the program has available to it data on which class is desired and whether or not the other class is acceptable in case the first is sold out. The logic is straightforward and covers all combinations of conditions. Note the use of the connectors to avoid having too many flowlines.

FLOWCHARTING SOFTWARE

One of the problems about preparing flowcharts is that it is time consuming, especially when substantial changes are made in the logic so that the flowchart must be redrawn. Under the pressure of getting a program to run, the flowcharts may not be kept current and may, in fact, become so messy as to be unreadable.

Various approaches have been taken to assist in the preparation of the flowcharts

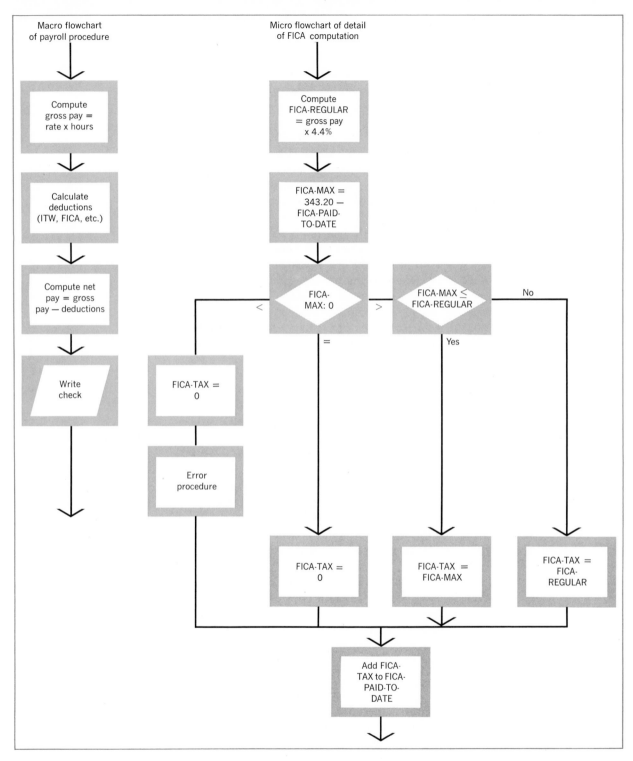

FIGURE 9–11 Use of macro and micro flowcharts

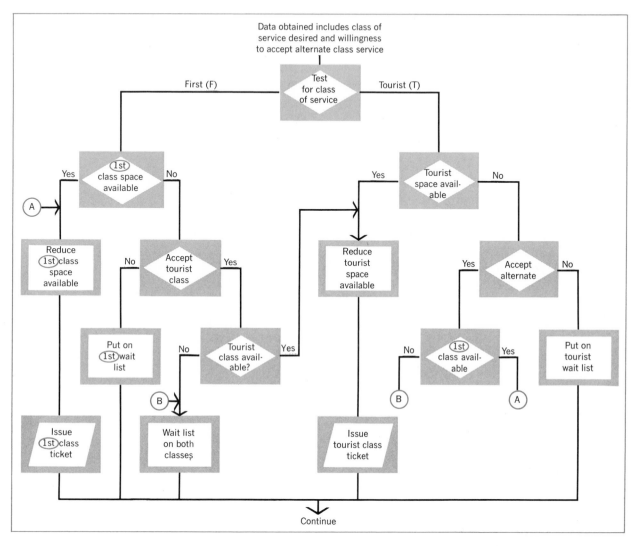

FIGURE 9–12 Flowchart of logic for issuing airline tickets

since these are important for communicating the design and logic of the data processing application. One approach is to assign a clerk to draw the flowcharts in good form from the rough sketches of the programmer and systems designer.

Another approach utilizes the computer. The flowchart is drawn on paper marked out in numbered squares. Data identifying the symbols, the squares in which they are placed, and the squares (containing symbols) to which they connect is read into a special flowchart writing program. Using asterisks and other symbols, the printer draws the outlines of the symbols and interconnects them. The advantage of this method is the ease of revision once the initial chart is prepared. One or more input cards are changed, and the problem is rerun. For this reason, the programs are useful primarily for complex charts which would require considerable effort to revise.

▌ DECISION TABLES

The decision table is another method of describing the logic of a computer program. It may be used in place of a program flowchart or as a supplement. While not as widely used as the flowchart, the decision table is useful for describing processing logic for those cases in which different sets of conditions will lead to different sets of actions.

The decision table, as shown in Figure 9–13, is a tabular form divided into four areas:

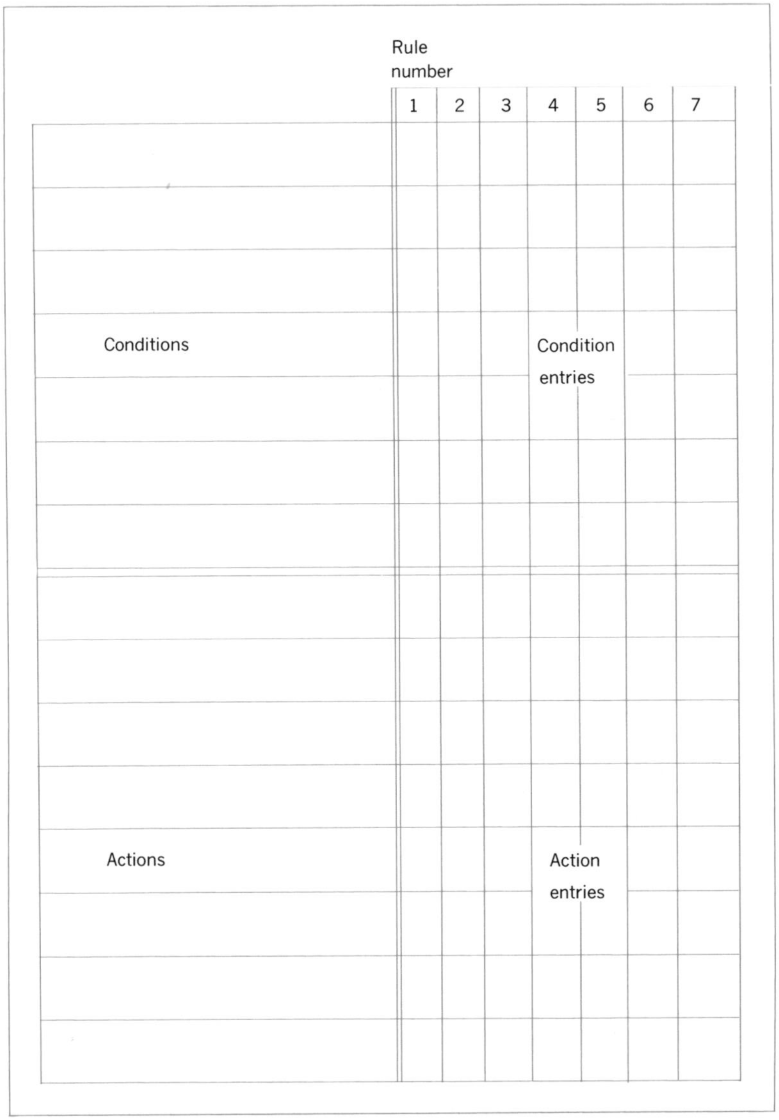

	Rule number						
	1	2	3	4	5	6	7
Conditions			Condition entries				
Actions			Action entries				

FIGURE 9–13 General form of the decision table

1 Condition stub
2 Condition entry
3 Action stub
4 Action entry

Conditions and actions are separated by an "if . . . then . . ." relationship. The table can be read; "*if* a set of conditions exists *then* perform the indicated actions." The stubs describe the conditions or actions, and the entries indicate whether or not the element exists, or other data such as values for the element. Each rule expresses a different set of conditions and actions. There are theoretically 2^n rules for n separate conditions. In other words, four conditions would result in 2^4 or 16 rules. But, in practice, many of the combinations are not feasible, and some conditions are actually the opposite of other conditions. For example, two conditions such as A = B and A $\neq$ B (A not equal to B) represent 2^2 or four rules, but they cannot both be true at the same time nor both false at the same time. Also, A $\neq$ B is the opposite of A = B, so that it is necessary to state only one condition A = B, which has only two entries— yes and no. By eliminating such redundancies, the decision table is a succinct method of presenting rather complex program decision logic.

To illustrate the use of decision tables, the logic in the two flowcharts in Figures 9–11 and 9–12 have been put into decision table form (Figures 9–14 and 9–15). In the FICA tax decision table, for example, there are four rules:

1 If FICA-MAX is less than zero, then set FICA-TAX to zero and to go an error routine.
2 If FICA-MAX is equal to zero, then set FICA-TAX to zero.
3 If FICA-MAX is greater than zero and FICA-MAX is less than or equal to FICA-REGULAR, set FICA-TAX equal to FICA-MAX.
4 If FICA-MAX is greater than FICA-REGULAR, use FICA-REGULAR as the FICA-TAX.

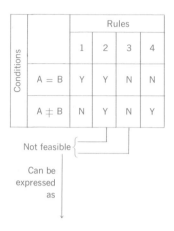

FICA computation		Rule number			
		1	2	3	4
Conditions	FICA-MAX compared to zero	$<$	$=$	$>$	$>$
	FICA-MAX $\leq$ FICA-REGULAR			Y	N
Actions	Go to error routine	x			
	FICA-TAX = 0	x	x		
	FICA-TAX = FICA-MAX			x	
	FICA-TAX = FICA-REGULAR				x

FIGURE 9–14 Decision table for FICA-TAX decision

FIGURE 9–15 Decision table of logic for issuing airline tickets

Airline ticketing		Rule number							
		1	2	3	4	5	6	7	8
Conditions	Request for first class ticket	Y	Y	Y	Y				
	Request for tourist class ticket					Y	Y	Y	Y
	First class space open	Y	N	N	N		Y	N	
	Tourist class space open		Y	N		Y	N	N	N
	Alternate class acceptable		Y	Y	N		Y	Y	N
Actions	Issue first class ticket	x					x		
	Issue tourist ticket		x			x			
	Reduce first class space available by 1	x					x		
	Reduce tourist class space available by 1		x			x			
	Place name on tourist wait list			x				x	x
	Place name on first class wait list			x	x		x		

Problems which have complex logic involving many conditions and actions are analyzed more easily using a decision table than a flowchart. The two can also be used together, with the flowchart providing the general structure of the solution and the decision table being used for the detailed description of the decision logic.

▌ SUMMARY

When a computer application is being designed, it is necessary to define explicitly the form and content of input/output documents and files and to describe both the overall flow of work and the processing logic. The tools which are used have been described. These are layout charts, grid charts, flowcharts, and decision tables.

Layout charts are used to describe the form and content of input, files, storage, and output. Examples are card, magnetic tape, and printer layouts. The layouts usually are drawn on printed forms prepared for this purpose.

Flowcharting is the most common method of planning the logic and flow of a computer application. Two types of flowcharts are used—the system flowchart, which describes the flow of documents and major processing tasks, and the program flowchart, which describes the logic of a computer program. The decision table is used as a supplement or in place of a program flowchart for problems with complex sets of conditions and actions.

The solution to a problem may be flowcharted in many different ways. There are individual differences in the way a flowchart is prepared in much the same way that there are individual differences in the way different individuals will write a description. The main objective of the flowchart is to communicate the logic and flow of processing in such a way that it is as understandable as possible to the reader. Clarity is enhanced by using standard symbols which have an agreed-upon meaning. Therefore, it is recommended that the USA standard symbols presented in the chapter be used.

▌ EXERCISES

1   What is the difference between the planning of the system and the planning of the program?
2   Using only a knowledge of the meaning of the flowchart symbols, explain what is probably being described by the following flowchart segments which have no description in them:

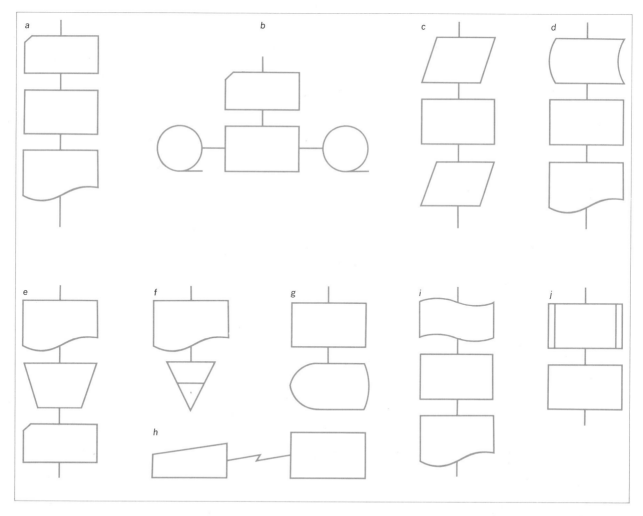

3   Reference the proposed international symbols and answer as in problem 2.

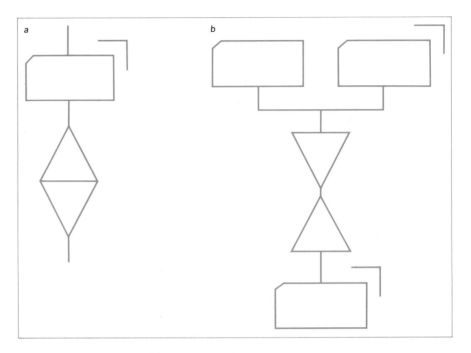

4   The following chart segment was drawn using the 1964–1966 conventions. Redraw it using USA standard symbols.

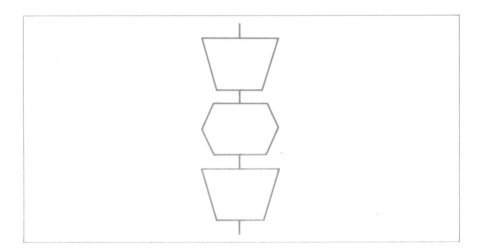

5   Label the parts of the decision table:

		e					
a		c					
b		d					

6   Draw flowcharts or flowchart segments for the following problems:
  a   Computer run to transfer data from punched tape to punched cards.
  b   Computer run to sort punched cards into order offline on the sorter and then, using the computer, transfer the data to magnetic tape.
  c   Logic to determine which of three numbers is the larger. Call the numbers A, B, and C.
  d   Logic of decision to reorder an item when:
    (1)   the stock on hand plus on order is equal to or below the reorder point
    (2)   the item is not obsolete
  e   Logic of a decision as to which Federal income tax return form to use (1040 or 1040A). A person must file a return if:
    (1)   Citizen or resident of the United States
    (2) $600 or more income if under 65 years of age
    (3) $1,200 or more income if 65 or over in age
    (4)   Desire to get a refund of tax withheld
    A person may use form 1040A (simple punch card form) if:
    (1)   Income was less than $10,000 and
    (2)   Income consisted of wages subject to withholding tax and not more than $200 total of other wages, interest, and dividends, *and*
    (3)   Instead of itemizing deductions, the taxpayer wishes to use the tax table or take the standard deduction.
  f   The logic of computing the different denomination bills and coins to give as change.
      Assume the change will not exceed $5.00. If not enough money is tendered to pay the amount due, an error message should be written.
  g   The logic of computing the factorial of a number. The factorial of *n* (*n*!) is:
    (1)   1 if *n* = 0.
    (2)   Otherwise, it is the product of the positive integers from 1 to *n*. For example, 4! = 1 × 2 × 3 × 4 = 24.
  h   The logic of selecting charge accounts for audit examination. A positive confirmation form requesting the customer to check the balance as reported against his records and report whether or not it is correct will be sent to all accounts which are over $300 and over 60 days old, and to all accounts showing a credit balance greater than $10. A negative confirmation requesting

an answer only if there is an error will be sent to all accounts owing less than $300 and over 60 days old, to every 10th account for accounts not over 60 days old, but greater than $200 owing, and to every 50th account which is not over 60 days old and has a balance owing not greater than $200.

7   Do the following problems in question 6 as decision tables:

    a 6c   c 6f

    b 6e   d 6h

8   What is the purpose of the card, tape, and printer layouts?

9   Describe in words the content of a card described by the following card layout:

1. General Ledger Year-end Balance Forward Cards

Account #	Company Code	Date (123166)	Type (BALFWD)	Amount	Note: X punch in column 30 means credit amount

```
9 9 9 9 9 9 9 9 9 9 9 9 9 9 9 9 9 9 9 9 9 9 9 9 9 9 9 9 9 9 9 9 9 9 9 9 9 9 9 9 9 9 9 9 9 9 9 9 9 9 9 9 9 9 9 9 9 9 9 9 9 9 9 9 9 9 9 9 9 9 9 9 9 9 9 9 9 9 9 9
1 2 3 4 5 6 7 8 9 10 11 12 13 14 15 16 17 18 19 20 21 22 23 24 25 26 27 28 29 30 31 32 33 34 35 36 37 38 39 40 41 42 43 44 45 46 47 48 49 50 51 52 53 54 55 56 57 58 59 60 61 62 63 64 65 66 67 68 69 70 71 72 73 74 75 76 77 78 79 80
```

▌ SYSTEMS ANALYSIS AND DESIGN
ANALYSIS OF NEED FOR INFORMATION
DESIGN OF A DATA PROCESSING SYSTEM
DESIGN OF INPUT, OUTPUT, AND FILE LAYOUTS
SPECIFICATION OF INDIVIDUAL COMPUTER RUNS
SPECIFICATION OF PROCEDURES

▌ PLANNING THE PROGRAM

▌ CODING
SYMBOLIC NAMES
LITERALS IN A PROGRAM
STORAGE DEFINITION FOR SYMBOLIC DATA NAMES
STORAGE DEFINITION FOR CONSTANTS
CONTROL INSTRUCTIONS

▌ ASSEMBLY

▌ DEBUGGING A PROGRAM
DESK CHECKING
ASSEMBLY SYSTEM CHECKING
PROGRAM RUN WITH TEST DATA
DIAGNOSTIC PROCEDURES
RUNNING DURING A TEST PERIOD

▌ DOCUMENTATION OF PROGRAMS
RUN MANUAL
COMPUTER OPERATOR INSTRUCTIONS

▌ SUMMARY

▌ EXERCISES

PREPARING A COMPUTER PROGRAM

The steps in preparing a computer program were summarized in Chapter 8 as: system design, planning the program, coding, assembly or compilation, debugging, and documentation. This chapter will describe these steps in more detail and provide the framework for understanding the chapters to follow.

▌SYSTEMS ANALYSIS AND DESIGN

The first event leading to the preparation of a computer program is someone's decision that there is a need for information—perhaps management requests the preparation of a report, or operating personnel may request a new or improved record-keeping procedure to provide data for decision making. The request for or identification of a need for information leads to an analysis of how the information can best be provided. The general steps in systems analysis and design are:

1   Definition of problem or definition of need for a new or improved system for providing information. This definition should come after an analysis of the actions and decisions requiring information and a definition of information required for these activities.
2   Design of a data processing system to record, collect, process, and disseminate the required information.
3   Design of format of input, files, reports, and other output.
4   Specification of individual computer runs.
5   Specification of procedures.

Many computer installations separate the system design from the programming function; in others, the same person does both. The system design function has broader scope because the systems analyst designs the entire process, while the programmer designs only the computer program portion.

ANALYSIS OF NEED FOR INFORMATION

Information is the basis for action both by personnel within an organization and by persons outside (e.g., customers, suppliers, government agencies). The analysis of need and development of specifications should involve both a systems analyst and the people who will use the information. The participation of those who need the data is important because of their knowledge of the function being studied and because of the human relations problems which develop if a system is designed for their use without their having a hand in it. Participation by a systems analyst early in the definition stage is important because he has the background to perceive ways in which the full power of the computer may be used to assist the decision process. Frequently, a system is designed from the specifications furnished by the users without considering the decisions to be made and other uses for the output. The resulting systems have frequently been found to be inadequate because the definition was incomplete or did not consider the use of new computer-based analytical and computational techniques.

The result of this analysis of need is a set of specifications for the application. The specifications describe the problem, the data to be provided, the persons to receive the output, the frequency of output, the required speed and frequency of processing, and an estimate of the volume of transactions to be processed.

DESIGN OF DATA PROCESSING SYSTEM

Based on the specifications for the application, the systems analyst designs a data processing system which best meets the need considering the limits imposed by the facilities and personnel which can be used and the costs which can be justified by the value of the results to be achieved. He must make decisions with respect to processing method, types of file media, frequency of processing, etc. to balance the cost and value of alternative approaches.

The result of the design phase will be systems flowcharts showing the flow of processing, both computer and noncomputer. The flowcharts and accompanying notes specify the preparation and handling of source documents, the distribution of output, the processing method, and frequency of processing.

DESIGN OF INPUT, OUTPUT, AND FILE LAYOUTS

The next step, which is really an extension of the design of the processing system, is the preparation of specifications for input documents, output documents, and computer files. This activity makes use of the layout forms described in Chapter 9. Additional information may be specified for files such as retention requirements, how sequenced, average and peak volumes of file records, and transactions to be processed.

SPECIFICATION OF INDIVIDUAL COMPUTER RUNS

As part of the design phase or as a separate step, the processing to be performed by the computer is separated into computer runs. A run is the performance of a specific process on a given set of data. There may, for example, be a separate computer run to edit the input data, a computation run, and a run to print out the results. Each computer run requires a computer program. Before a computer run can be planned, therefore, the requirements of the entire application must be known. The run is then planned within the framework of the other runs (if there are more than one), the record and file descriptions, and the application procedures.

In the terminology of data processing, an application will have one or more runs and each run will consist of a program. The term "routine" is frequently used in place of program to describe a set of instructions to perform a processing task. Although the terminology is not always precisely followed, a program may therefore encompass more than one routine. In terms of the computer operator, a run is a separate activity performed on the computer.

The data processing system will not work unless each person in the organization who must furnish or process data knows exactly how to perform his work. This means that a necessary part of the design of a system is the planning of procedures for preparation of source documents, for collecting the documents, for controlling them to prevent loss, for converting them to a machine-readable medium, and for filing them. This part of systems analysis and design may include the design of new or revised forms to improve the speed and accuracy of data recording and to increase the understandability of reports to management.

The design of forms is an important element in achieving accuracy and reducing unnecessary work in a data processing system. For example, if a code number is to be placed on a document, the printing of a box with a separate space for each digit of the code will reduce the number of errors from writing the code incorrectly. If the code were the social security number of an employee, there might be a box divided into nine spaces rather than merely a blank.

PLANNING THE PROGRAM

The run description, system flowchart, input, output, and file layouts form a set of specifications for a program. The programmer then proceeds to prepare a description of the processing logic. This is done using a program flowchart and perhaps also a decision table. The programmer may prepare several levels of flowcharts—macro program flowcharts showing the main logic of the computer program and micro flowcharts detailing the logic of portions of the program.

CODING

The form of the coding will depend on the language used—whether a machine-oriented symbolic assembly language or a problem-oriented language. Problem-oriented languages are described in Chapter 14, so this chapter will emphasize the machine-oriented symbolic coding.

The coding is done on coding paper usually obtained from the computer manufacturer. An example is shown in Figure 10–1. The coding form is laid out to assist the programmer to follow the rules for coding.

Each symbolic assembly system for coding has a set of rules associated with it. These include rules for the form of the coding, rules for symbolic names, rules for using literals in programming (i.e., characters which are to be used as numbers or characters rather than as references to storage locations), rules for defining the size and form of symbolic names, and rules for defining the value of constants referred to by name.

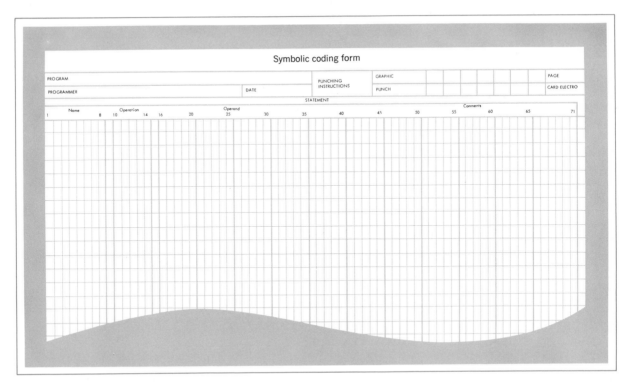

FIGURE 10–1 Symbolic coding form

SYMBOLIC NAMES

The programmer can formulate symbolic names which help him to remember the data which is being referenced. There is usually a limit (say, six or eight characters) to the size of the name. Examples of acceptable names are:

NAME	REFERRING TO
GRPAY	the value of gross pay
NETPAY	the value of net pay
D1	the first of a set of data

Names are not only used for data; an instruction is given a name if it needs to be referred to by another instruction. Names for instructions are similar to data names. For example, an instruction to read a card might be given a name READCD. Since each instruction, when converted to machine language, is stored in a memory location, the symbolic name given to the instruction actually refers to the address where the instruction will be stored. As an example of symbolic coding with symbolic names,

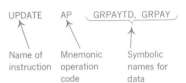

UPDATE AP GRPAYTD, GRPAY

Name of instruction   Mnemonic operation code   Symbolic names for data

IBM   IBM System/360 Assembler Coding Form   X28-6509-2 U/M050
                                                                                                                     Printed in U.S.A.

| PROGRAM | PRICING PROGRAM | | | PUNCHING INSTRUCTIONS | GRAPHIC | | | | | | PAGE 3 OF 5 | |
| PROGRAMMER | G. B. DAVIS | | DATE 6/22/68 | | PUNCH | | | | | | CARD ELECTRO NUMBER | |

Name	Operation	Operand	Comments	Identification-Sequence
	UNPK	UNITOTAL,MPLYANS	UNPACK ANSWER INTO TOTAL PRINT	14010
	CP	MPLYANS,CON100	ANSWER OVER$100?	14020
	BL	NOVER100	NO, DO NOT ADD OVER $100 TOTAL	14030
	AP	WK100TOT,MPLYANS	YES, ADD TO OVER $100 TOTAL	14040
NOVER100	AP	WKGRDTOT,MPLYANS	ADD ANSWER TO GRAND TOTAL	14050
	MVC	PRTOUT,WORK1	MOVE PRINT WORK TO OUTPUT PRINT	14060
	PUT	PRINTER	PRINT A LINE	14070
	B	READAGN	READ ANOTHER CARD	14080
ENDCDFL	UNPK	GRDTOTAL,WKGRDTOT	END OF ADDRESS UNPACK GRAND TOT	14090
	UNPK	OV100TOT,WK100TOT	UNPACK OVER $100 TOTAL	14100
	MVC	PRTOUT,WORK2	MOVE TOTAL WORK TO OUTPUT PRINT	14110
	PUT	PRINTER	PRINT TOTALS	14120
	CLOSE	CARDIN,PRINTER	CLOSE CARD DTF & PRINTER DTF	14130
	EOJ		CALL SUPERVISOR END OF JOB	14140
*				16010
* WORK AREAS FOR THE PRINTER				16020
*				16030
WORK1	DS	0CL132		16040
OUTPART	DC	CL6' '		16050
	DC	CL4' '		16060
OUTQTY	DC	CL4' '		16070
	DC	CL6' '		16080
OUTDOL	DC	CL6' '		16090
	DC	CL10' '		16100

FIGURE 10-2 Sample page of symbolic coding

an instruction to add GRPAY (gross pay) to GRPAYTD (gross pay to date) might look as shown in the margin. A sample page of symbolic coding is shown in Figure 10-2.

LITERALS IN A PROGRAM

Most symbolic coding systems allow the programmer to write a literal (or a set of characters to be used as written) in an instruction. This simplifies programming. For example, there may need to be a comparison between a data item and the number 594. An instruction might be written as shown. Although the actual format will vary between computers, it is common to use apostrophes as the characters which define the beginning and end of a literal. When the instruction with a literal in it is decoded, the assembly program prepares the constant and assigns it to a storage location. This storage location reference is put into the machine coded instruction in place of the literal.

CLC   DATA1, = C'594'

Compare   Literal
code

STORAGE DEFINITION FOR SYMBOLIC DATA NAMES

The programmer must make up names to reference all data locations. In order for the assembly program to assign storage locations to each of these data names, they must be defined by a special assembler definition instruction. This instruction is for assembly purposes only and is not an instruction to be executed. The assembler definition instruction usually contains a data name to be defined, its storage requirements, and possibly other storage characteristics. The following are examples of storage definition instructions for one computer; other computers will use slightly different formats. From the definition the assembly program is able to assign the proper number of storage locations to each data name.

DATA NAME	OPERATION	DEFINITION	
OUTNO	DS	CL2	Define OUTNO as 2 unsigned characters
ANSWER	DS	F	Define ANSWER as a full binary word

STORAGE DEFINITION FOR CONSTANTS

The use of literals as part of the symbolic instruction has already been explained. If a constant (a number, a set of alphanumeric characters, etc.) is to be used by a program, it may be more convenient to define a name for the constant. Any time the constant is to be used in a program instruction, the name is used. The "define constant" instruction tells the assembly program to include a constant with the program, and this constant will be loaded into storage along with the program steps. The following coding is an example of a storage definition and the use of the constant name in an instruction.

NAME	OP	OPERAND	
FORTY	DC	F'40'	(Define the name FORTY as referring to a constant of 40)
	A	2, FORTY	(Add 40 to the contents of register 2)

CONTROL INSTRUCTIONS

The assembler language defines certain instructions for control of the translation process. An instruction such as START may signal the start of the assembly, END may indicate the end of the statements to be assembled, etc. In addition to these assembler control instructions, there are usually a number of control cards which are necessary when the program is to be assembled. Examples of control cards are a job card, a date card, and an "execute" card.

▌ ASSEMBLY

The translation of the source program written in symbolic assembly language into a machine language program (absolute coding) for running on the computer makes

FIGURE 10–3 Preparing a program using a symbolic assembly system

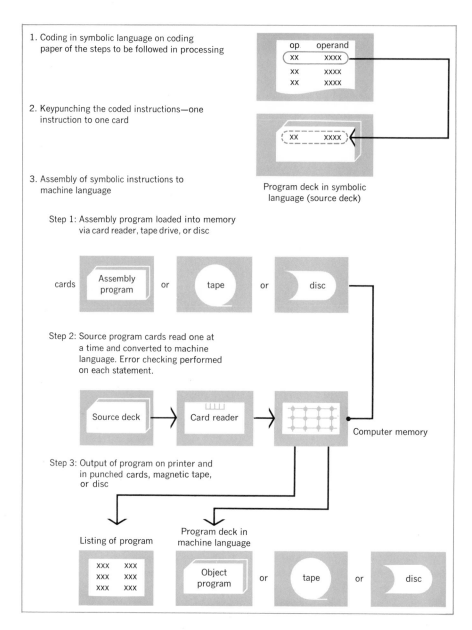

1. Coding in symbolic language on coding paper of the steps to be followed in processing

2. Keypunching the coded instructions—one instruction to one card

Program deck in symbolic language (source deck)

3. Assembly of symbolic instructions to machine language

Step 1: Assembly program loaded into memory via card reader, tape drive, or disc

cards   Assembly program   or   tape   or   disc

Step 2: Source program cards read one at a time and converted to machine language. Error checking performed on each statement.

Source deck   →   Card reader   →   Computer memory

Step 3: Output of program on printer and in punched cards, magnetic tape, or disc

Listing of program

Program deck in machine language

Object program   or   tape   or   disc

use of an assembly program furnished by the manufacturer. The steps in translating (assembling) a program are summarized in Figure 10–3.

The statements written on the coding sheets are punched into punched cards, one statement to a card. The cards form the source deck. The translator program is loaded into storage, and this program then takes control, reading and translating each card. As it reads each card, the translator program examines the operation code and from a table stored in memory finds the proper machine language equivalent. A storage location is assigned to each symbolic data name and each symbolic instruction name. A table of names and addresses is built up in storage. Based on this table and the operation code, a machine language instruction is prepared.

There is some error checking by the assembly program, primarily for errors of form such as referencing an instruction which does not exist, etc.

The results of the assembly process are (1) a listing with the symbolic source program and the machine language object program and (2) an object program on a machine-readable form such as punched cards, magnetic tape, or a magnetic disc. A sample of a listing from an assembly is given in Figure 10–4.

▌ DEBUGGING A PROGRAM

Rarely does a program run perfectly the first time. There are usually errors in it. The removing of these errors (bugs) is known as *debugging*. Errors in programming can occur both from mistakes in writing the symbolic instructions and from errors in the logic. In terms of a system of procedures for producing programs with a minimum of errors, program testing should occur at several stages as follows:

1   Desk checking.
2   Assembly system checking.
3   Program testing using test data.
4   Using of error diagnostic procedures, if necessary.
5   Running of program, using actual data. This may include running parallel with the old program or old system.

DESK CHECKING

When a program is completed, it should be checked by the programmer before being released for keypunching. This check should include a review by the programming supervisor. The programmer review consists of going over the program logic to see that the program is complete. Having done this, the programmer should take some sample data and manually step through the program.

ASSEMBLY SYSTEM CHECKING

As mentioned, a symbolic system has certain rules which must be followed, such as rules for naming variables and for using symbolic addresses. If these rules are not followed or if the instructions are not coded in proper form, the assembly system will detect these errors during the assembly process. When an error is detected, an error printout will describe the nature of the error. An error-free assembly does not indicate that the program is debugged, only that certain types of coding errors have been eliminated. Examples of errors which will be detected by the assembly program are

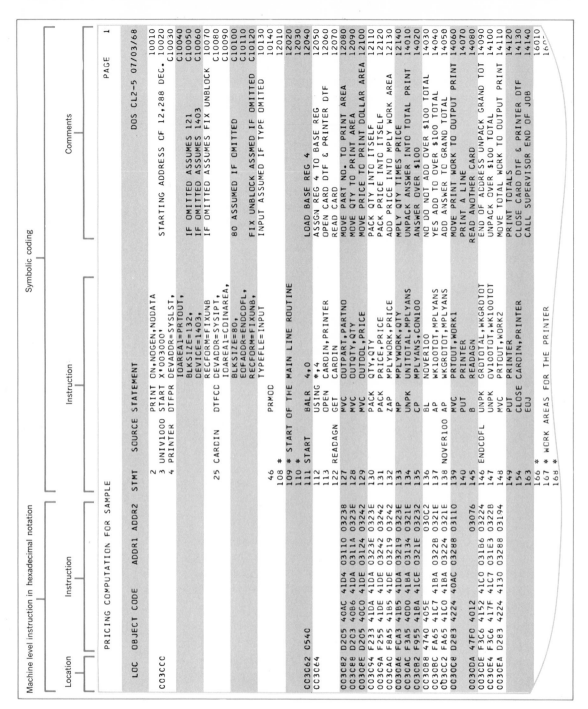

FIGURE 10-4 Listing of assembly of a symbolic program—IBM System/360. Object code is in hexadecimal notation.

invalid operation codes, invalid operands, and invalid addresses (such as an address which exceeds the highest address in the memory).

PROGRAM RUN WITH TEST DATA

The programmer (or other person assigned to such tasks) should prepare test data with which to test the actions of the program on a trial run using the computer. The results to be expected from the test data are known and can be compared with actual results. The test data should include all forms of errors in input data in order to test the handling of error conditions by the program. If the test program runs into difficulty, error diagnostic procedures may be called for.

DIAGNOSTIC PROCEDURES

If, after an error-free assembly, a program does not operate properly using test data, the correction of errors may include one or more diagnostic procedures. The need for diagnostic procedures results from the existence of errors for which the remedy may not be obvious. A program may modify data or destroy instructions, thus creating invalid addresses or illegal operation codes. When the machine attempts to execute these invalid instructions, it will hang up (stop). The following are some diagnostic procedures that may be followed:

1 Step through the program one instruction at a time, checking the contents of registers after each step in order to find the errors. This console debugging is not allowed in large-scale systems where machine time is expensive.
2 Run the program with a trace routine. A trace routine is a program which prints out such diagnostic information as the contents of all registers after each instruction. This is the same concept as stepping through the program, but it takes up less computer time and provides a diagnostic record.
3 Run the program until it hangs up and then obtain information on contents of registers, contents of important memory locations, etc., to locate the reason for the program's stopping. The entire memory may, in certain instances, be listed, or dumped.
4 Insert in the program temporary diagnostic instructions which will print out or display the results of the program at various stages of the program.
5 Run the program with test data which reflects several possible conditions the program is to handle in order to find which condition is giving difficulty.

RUNNING DURING A TEST PERIOD

When debugged so that it appears to be operating properly, the program may receive an additional period of testing by running parallel to the old program or old system. The introduction of live conditions gives the program the final test. This period of testing will give the operator experience in the error-recovery procedures built into the system. On a program of any consequence, it is undesirable to have to go back to the beginning when an error condition appears. A good program will therefore provide restart points (break points) from which the program can be started after an error stop.

▌ DOCUMENTATION OF PROGRAMS

Documentation consists of all documents and records which describe the data processing system. The preparation of documentation is a necessary, although frequently poorly handled phase of computer data processing. Documentation serves the following purposes:

1   Provides explanatory material necessary for a supervisory review of proposed systems and programs.
2   Simplifies program revision by providing full detail in support of each program.
3   Provides the data necessary for answering inquiries regarding the operation of a program.
4   Aids in instructing new personnel by providing background on previous programs and serving as a guideline for new programs.
5   Provides operator with current operating instructions.

In cases where documentation has not been maintained, organizations have been involved in considerable extra expense when it has become necessary to modify a program. A change in withholding rates or the addition of a city income tax has, in some cases, necessitated a substantial rewriting of a payroll program because documentation did not contain the information needed to make the requested modification. As an example of the danger inherent in poor documentation, an insurance company, which had employed a very competent programmer, did not enforce program documentation. Shortly after the programmer left the company, the state insurance authority asked the company for copies of all formulas used in computing agents' commissions. The commissions had been computerized for several years, and no one in the company knew the exact way the computer performed the computations. To recreate the documentation, the company had to hire a consultant who worked for three months to build up the data by working backward from a machine language object deck.

Documentation can take many different acceptable forms. The two documents which fulfill basic requirements are the run manual and the computer operator instructions.

RUN MANUAL

The run manual is prepared by the systems analysts and/or programmers. It is a complete documentation of the program used in a data processing run. For example, the program or set of programs to perform sales analysis would have a run manual associated with it. The sections of the run manual are, in general, the following:

SECTION	DESCRIPTION OF CONTENTS
Problem definition	A description of the reason why the program was prepared, the problem statement, and documentation of approvals both by department requesting the program and by data processing department.
System description	A general outline of the new program and the related environment or system in which the program operates. The section contains the system flowcharts and record layouts.
Program description	The documentation of the program portion of the system. Contains the program flowcharts, decision tables, program listing, and other descriptions which document the contents of the program.
Operating instructions	The instructions required to run the program on the computer. This is the same as the computer operator instructions provided to the equipment operator and will be described later in the chapter.
Summary of controls	Summarizes the controls built into the program to detect errors.
Acceptance record	Contains a documentation of steps taken to test the program before acceptance, the program change record, and record of approvals.

The documentation in the run manual is kept up to date by recording all changes in it. When a change is made in the program, a change record is placed in the acceptance record section and a reference noted on the appropriate flowchart. It is not necessary, with this procedure, to redraw the flowchart after each change. If the change is made directly in the machine language program (a patch), it is noted on the program listing. If several changes are to be made or after several patches have been made, it is desirable to make the changes in the symbolic source program and reassemble it to produce a "clean" object program. The new program listing is then placed in the run manual.

COMPUTER OPERATOR INSTRUCTIONS

The computer operator instructions for a run, sometimes called a console run book, are a copy of the operating section of the complete documentation of the run manual. The relationship of these two is shown in Figure 10–5. The operator instructions for a run may be placed in a separate cover or may be a section in one or more notebooks containing the operator instructions for all runs.

The computer operator instructions provide all information necessary for the running of the program. The types of coverage are indicated by the following items:

Brief description of program
Card layouts and keypunch instructions
System setup and takedown instructions
Deck setup (for card input)
Computer switch settings

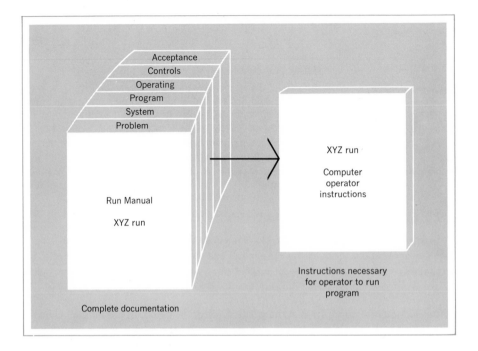

Operator duties in starting, running, and terminating the program
Console messages and halts

These instructions define completely what the operator should do and the sequencing of his jobs. Careful sequencing of setup and takedown instructions can usually reduce total job time if, for example, the printer is made ready while the computer is reading program cards, the printer is unloaded while tapes are rewinding, etc. The list of console messages and halts essentially defines what the operator is to do when there is some difficulty with the program.

▌ SUMMARY

This chapter provides a framework for understanding the chapters to follow by describing the steps in preparing a computer program.

This preparation is preceded by a recognition of the need for information and the preparation of specifications which describe the problem or need. This set of specifications is the basis for a systems analysis and the design of a data processing system. Systems flowcharts are used in this activity. Other specifications prepared are input, file, and output layouts. The application is divided, if appropriate, into several computer runs. Each of these runs becomes a computer program. A complete system design does not stop with preparation of these specifications but should also include the preparation of procedures such as those for creating source data and retaining of documents, and the design of new or revised forms.

The work of the programmer begins with the preparation of program flowcharts and possibly decision tables. From these planning documents, the program is coded in a symbolic form—either in an assembly language or a higher-order compiler language. This source coding is assembled or compiled to produce an object language program which is ready to run. Rarely will a program be ready for use without undergoing debugging. This phase includes checking through the program without using the computer, the use of test data, the use of diagnostic procedures, and running in parallel with live data.

The documentation of a computer program is an important part of the steps in program preparation, and the job is not completed until documentation is prepared. The basic documentation is the run manual. A section of the run manual is also used as the operator instructions. Documentation is kept up to date by change notices and making notations on the flowcharts and program listings.

▌ EXERCISES

1   Trace a computer application from its inception as a request from the president to its implementation as a program operating on the computer.
2   Name two ways a constant of 25 might be specified for use in a computer instruction.
3   What is the purpose of:
   a   The storage definition
   b   The constant definition
4   Describe what the assembly system translator will do in order to translate the following line of symbolic coding to absolute coding:
   NEXT1   A   ALPHA, BETA
5   Define the following terms:
   a   Debugging   c   Assembly system
   b   Desk checking   d   Hang up (for computer)
6   What are the reasons for documentation?
7   What are the major sections of a satisfactory computer run manual?
8   If a computer is available to you, examine the symbolic assembly system instructions to identify those which define storage and define constants. Also identify control instructions.

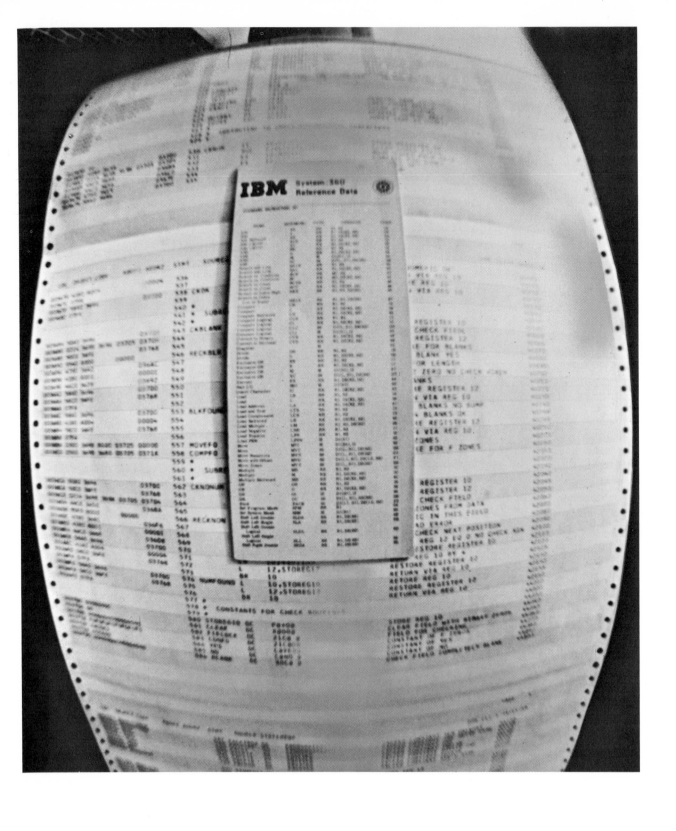

▌ MOVE INSTRUCTIONS
DATA TRANSFER USING REGISTERS
STORAGE-TO-STORAGE MOVE
FILLING A REGISTER OR STORAGE LOCATION WITH ZEROS
SELF-TESTING QUIZ 11–1

▌ ARITHMETIC INSTRUCTIONS
SCALING
ARITHMETIC PRECISION
ADDITION AND SUBTRACTION
SELF-TESTING QUIZ 11–2
MULTIPLICATION
SELF-TESTING QUIZ 11–3
DIVISION
SELF-TESTING QUIZ 11–4
OVERFLOW
THE SCALE FACTOR METHOD
SELF-TESTING QUIZ 11–5
FLOATING POINT ARITHMETIC

▌ TRANSFER OF CONTROL INSTRUCTIONS
UNCONDITIONAL TRANSFER
CONDITIONAL TRANSFER BASED ON COMPARISON
CONDITIONAL TRANSFER BASED ON ABSENCE OR
  EXISTENCE OF A CONDITION
INTERRUPTS
SELF-TESTING QUIZ 11–6

▌ EDITING
SHIFTING
LOGICAL OR BIT ALTERATION
DATA CONVERSION
OUTPUT EDITING

▌ SUMMARY

▌ ANSWERS TO SELF-TESTING QUIZZES
SELF-TESTING QUIZ 11–1
SELF-TESTING QUIZ 11–2
SELF-TESTING QUIZ 11–3
SELF-TESTING QUIZ 11–4
SELF-TESTING QUIZ 11–5
SELF-TESTING QUIZ 11–6

▌ EXERCISES

CHAPTER

11

COMPUTER INSTRUCTIONS FOR PROCESSING

There are a small number of basic instructions for programming a computer. The instruction repertoire of a particular computer may be extensive, but included in it are many instructions which are variations of the basic set of instructions and simplify programming by automatically executing two or more basic instructions. The number and variety will vary considerably with different computers. For example, one small general-purpose computer has 23 separate instructions available for programming; a larger compatible family of computers uses a set of 142 instructions. For all practical purposes, the small set can program anything which can be programmed for the larger, but a single instruction on the larger machine may perform the same action as several instructions using the more limited set.

Computer instructions can conveniently be divided into input/output and processing. Input/output instructions are discussed separately in Chapter 13. The basic processing instructions to be explained in this chapter are classified as move, arithmetic, transfer of control, and editing.

Short self-testing quizzes are included in the chapter as an aid to study. The answers are found at the end of the chapter.

▌ MOVE INSTRUCTIONS

The purpose of the data transfer or move instructions is to transfer data from one location in storage to another storage location. Moving data from one location to another might be termed copying, because the sending location is not changed; it is merely copied into the receiving location. The receiving location is, of course, changed. The previous contents of that location are destroyed by being replaced by the data being moved in.

For example, to transfer the contents of memory location 1026 to location 1214 will result in the word being found in an identical form in both locations.

Since data transfer results in the word being found in an identical form in two separate memory locations, why should it be necessary to move data or instruction words? The major reasons are:

1   The word in the original location may be destroyed by subsequent operations. Moving (copying) it in another location preserves the data or instruction word. Examples of this situation are:

   a   The results of an arithmetic operation are in some computers automatically written at the location of one of the operands, replacing the operand data. If this operand data is needed later in the program, it must be copied into another location before the arithmetic command is executed.

   b   Data from an input operation is usually brought into a specified section of memory. Each input operation will bring additional data to occupy the same memory locations. Data must therefore be moved from the input/output area in order to retain it for subsequent use.

2   Data may have to be in specified locations for subsequent instructions to be

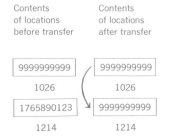

Contents of locations before transfer

Contents of locations after transfer

9999999999
1026

9999999999
1026

1765890123
1214

9999999999
1214

executed properly. For example, output operations frequently require that data be located in a specified section of memory. Data to be printed, etc. are moved into this output area.

3 Data may have to be rearranged. For example, data read in one format may be rearranged before writing it on output media.

4 In fixed-word computers, it is necessary to transfer data to a register before an operation can be performed on it. When the operation is completed, the results are transferred back to a storage location.

Transfer instructions are of two types—register transfer instructions for computers which use addressable registers and storage-to-storage transfer instructions for computers with character-addressable storage. Both types will be discussed, and in addition this section will explain the need, in some circumstances, to clear or zero memory locations.

DATA TRANSFER USING REGISTERS

As explained in Chapter 7, a register is a hardware device used to store a certain number of bits or characters which are being operated upon. Fixed word length computers make use of addressable registers which can be referenced as an operand in an instruction. Data to be operated upon is moved from the primary storage to a register in which the operation is to be performed. The result is held in a register, and a separate instruction is used to store it in a regular storage location. The registers may be specifically assigned to certain functions and named accordingly (e.g., accumulator register) or may be general-purpose. The number of registers will vary with the computer system being used. On a small computer, for example, three registers might suffice, while 16 or more can be expected in a larger computer.

For a fixed-word computer, the register serves as an intermediate storage in the transfer of data between two storage locations. The amount of data transferred is usually a computer word. The transfer consists of a pair of instructions—the first one loads the register (copies the contents of a memory location into a register), and the second puts the register contents in a storage location. The instructions specify or imply three things—the operation (load or store), the register, and the memory location to be used. Because these are copy instructions, the sequence will result in the same data being found in two separate locations and the register.

DESCRIPTION OF INSTRUCTION	REGISTER 8	MEMORY LOCATIONS	
		1006	1007
Contents before instruction	8496652	9643001	XXXXXXX
Load register 8 with contents of 1006	9643001	9643001	XXXXXXX
Store contents of register 8 in 1007	9643001	9643001	9643001

In addition to the basic load and store instructions for data transfer with registers, there may be variation such as a register-to-register transfer or a multiple-register load or store in which a single instruction will load consecutive memory locations into consecutive registers (or the reverse as a store instruction). There may be instructions to load or store half a word or to load or store a double word using two consecutive memory locations and two registers.

STORAGE-TO-STORAGE MOVE

In contrast to the fixed-word approach of registers, a storage-to-storage transfer usually involves a variable word containing from one to a large number of characters. A data transfer instruction will copy a number of characters from one series of locations in storage to another. Since, as pointed out in Chapter 7, each bit set for encoding a character is addressable, the move instruction must specify the locations from which the data is to be moved and the locations to which it is to be copied. There are two methods for specifying length of operand, so that the move instructions may take one of two forms, depending on the design of the computer. One method addresses the data fields by the rightmost location. The computer word starts at that location and includes the digits in successively lower-numbered locations until an end-of-word bit signals the end of the word. The word is thus defined by an address for one end and a word mark bit for the other. The word mark bit is a special bit in the set for this purpose. An instruction to move the data from locations 963–966 in the following example to locations 968–971 would give a move operation code and the addresses of both fields, say M 966 971.

Bit sets—each capable of storing a character and each having an address

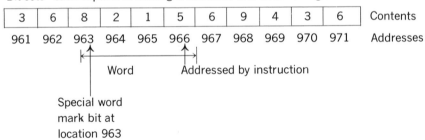

Prior to the move, an instruction was executed to set a word mark bit (make the word mark bit a 1) at location 963. A separate instruction is used to clear (set to 0) the word mark bit. The word mark bit need be set only at one of the locations since the end of either the sending or receiving field will terminate the transfer. A complete set of data transfer instructions in this approach thus includes set word mark, clear word mark, and move. A variation of the move instruction copies the word mark bit also and terminates transfer when a word mark is found in a sending field character. As with the register instructions, the result of a data transfer instruction is the same data in two locations. In the example given of a transfer from 963 to 971, the result would be:

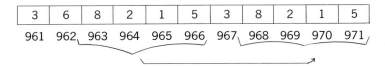

The second method for variable word addressing specifies the leftmost location of the field, and the instruction itself gives the length of the field to be transferred. In the example of a data transfer from 963–966 to 968–971, the sending field will have an address of 963 and a length of 4. The receiving field begins at 968, and no length specification is required. No word mark bits are necessary in this approach.

FILLING A REGISTER OR STORAGE LOCATION WITH ZEROS

The programmer does not need to zero out the previous contents of a memory location before storing new data at that location. The storing of data in a location automatically destroys the previous contents. There are, however, several reasons for zeroing (clearing) a location. One of these is when a memory location will be used to tally a count or accumulate a sum in an add-to-prior-sum fashion. Before beginning, the location must be cleared to zero for the same reason that an adding machine operator totals the adding machine before beginning to add.

The clearing operation can take several forms. If a "clear register" instruction is available in a computer using addressable registers, this will fill a register with zeros. To clear a memory location, the register contents are stored there. If a clear register instruction is not available, an alternative such as subtract the register contents from itself accomplishes the same purpose. In a storage-to-storage logic, a field of zeros is moved into the location to be zeroed. Frequently these are combination instructions available to zero and perform an operation—such as zero and add.

SELF-TESTING QUIZ 11-1

1 Assume a computer with seven registers. The load and store instructions take the following form:

OPERATION	OPERATION CODE	OPERANDS
Load register	L	register, storage address
Store register	ST	register, storage address

  a Move the contents of location ALPHA to location BETA. Use register 3.
  b Move the contents of location ALPHA to D1, D2, D3, and D4. Use register 6.
2 Assume a character computer using word marks and the following instruction formats:

OPERATION	OPERATION CODE	OPERANDS
Set word mark	SW	Storage address
Clear word mark	CW	Storage address
Move a field	MCW	Sending field address, Receiving field address

a Set a word mark at location BETA.

b Set a word mark at a location two positions lower than BETA (*Hint:* use relative addressing, i.e., specify BETA and + or − the number of locations).

c Move a 4-character field from DATA1 to DATA5. No word marks have been set in either field.

▌ARITHMETIC INSTRUCTIONS

For internal processing, a computer has one basic arithmetic operation—addition. All other arithmetic can be performed as addition. Subtraction can be done by complementing the number to be subtracted (subtrahend) and adding it to the minuend. Multiplication is performed as successive addition, and division is in essence performed as successive subtractions (complement additions).

However, for programming, each of the different arithmetic operations is specified by an instruction. When a computer is instructed to perform arithmetic, two operands must be specified in order to complete an arithmetic command. The result may be one or two data words.

ADDITION

$\left.\begin{array}{l}\text{Augend}\\ +\text{ Addend}\end{array}\right\}$ 2 operands

$\left.\text{Sum}\right\}$ 1 result

SUBTRACTION

$\left.\begin{array}{l}\text{Minuend}\\ \text{Subtrahend}\end{array}\right\}$ 2 operands

$\left.\text{Remainder}\right\}$ 1 result

MULTIPLICATION

$\left.\begin{array}{l}\text{Multiplicand}\\ \times\text{ Multiplier}\end{array}\right\}$ 2 operands

$\left.\text{Product}\right\}$ 1 result[1]

DIVISION

Divisor Dividend   2 operands

$\left.\begin{array}{l}\text{Quotient}\\ +\text{ Remainder}\end{array}\right\}$ 2 results

[1] The number of digits in the product is the sum of the digits in the multiplicand and the multiplier. If two data words of fixed length are multiplied, the product will consist of two words. For example, in a fixed word length computer using 10-digit words, a multiplication will result in a 20-digit product. This product consists of two 10-digit words. In a variable word length computer, this is not a problem since a word can contain a large number of digits.

SCALING

The decimal point is not part of the data word for arithmetic processing. Integral digits (1, 7, 95) and fractional digits (0.1, 0.7, 0.095) are all alike to the computer circuits. It is necessary, therefore, to keep track of the scaling (decimal locations) of a number for the following reasons:

1 To be able to locate and insert the decimal point in the printed output.

2 To line up numbers being added or subtracted so that digits with like positional values are paired.

3 To prevent or control arithmetic overflow, in which the result of an addition, sub-

traction, or division is greater than the capacity of the register or field where the result is to be stored.

4 To be able to locate the decimal point in the result of multiplication or division in order to save the significant digits.

Two methods are available for keeping track of the decimal point—the fixed decimal system and the floating point system. The floating point system can be implemented either as a hardware feature or by software using a series of program steps. Floating point arithmetic will be explained later in this chapter. Most data processing problems are run using the fixed decimal system, in which the computer circuitry operates on fixed, assumed decimal points and the programmer must keep track of the actual decimal point locations.

For circuitry purposes, the computer assumes all numbers are either whole numbers or fractions. In a fractional computer, all numbers are assumed to be less than 1.0; in an integral computer, all numbers are assumed to be greater than or equal to 1. The programmer must in both cases keep track of the actual decimal point position.

In a fixed decimal system, the programmer may use rules which involve counting the number of digits before and after the decimal point of the operands. From this count, the decimal point may be calculated for the results, or the scale factor method to be discussed later in the chapter may be used.

The computer performs arithmetic either in binary, in binary coded decimal, or in both. The binary coded decimal is, for purposes of scaling, rounding, etc., the same as decimal arithmetic since the computer encodes each decimal digit using a separate set of bits.

In a computer using decimal arithmetic, the programmer can line up decimal points for arithmetic by shifting. $36750_\wedge$ is turned into $03675_\wedge$ by shifting one place to the right. If the computer uses a fixed binary word, the lining up of decimal points can be accomplished by multiplying or dividing by powers of 10. For example, if 24 and 2.4 (both identical in storage) are to be added, the 24 might be multiplied by 10 to give a number which is understood to be 24.0 even though the computer (an integral computer) treats it as 240. 24 (11000) multiplied by 10 (1010) gives 240 (11110000).

Before scaling

| 0000011000 | = 24 |

| 0000011000 | = 2.4 |

After scaling

| 0011110000 | 24.0 |

| 0000011000 | 2.4 |

| 0100001000 | 26.4 (sum) |

ARITHMETIC PRECISION

A fixed word length computer performs arithmetic on words which contain a set number of bits. A 32-bit word can represent a number as large as 2,147,483,647, but what happens if the number to be represented is larger? Two approaches are taken. In the first, some of the low-order digits at the right are dropped in order to allow more significant digits to be added at the left. The programmer keeps track of the lost digit positions and will, when the number is printed out, print some zeros for these positions. In other words, the exact digits are lost, but the scaling is preserved and will be represented by zeros or other notation. The number of digits the computer can retain is the precision.

A second approach mentioned earlier is to use two computer words together to achieve a double precision. This is done usually with special routines, but some computers provide for double-precision arithmetic as part of the instruction repertoire. The double words are stored in adjacent memory locations, one containing the most significant digits and the other the least significant digits of the number.

ADDITION AND SUBTRACTION

The instructions to add or subtract must specify the memory locations of the operands and the location where the results are to be stored. The data words to be added or subtracted must be arranged so that the corresponding units, tens, etc. positions are paired. This may be thought of as lining up the decimal (or binary) points, even though there are no decimal or binary points in the data themselves.

For example, assume two quantities, A (497.65) and B (1.3760), are stored in two separate memory locations. If a command were given to add them without considering the calculated position of the decimal points, the answer would be incorrect.

MANUAL ARITHMETIC		INCORRECT COMPUTER		CORRECT COMPUTER	
A	497.65	A	4976500	A	4976500
B	1.3760	B	1376000	B	0013760
A + B	499.0260	A + B	6352500	A + B	4990260

The instructions to perform arithmetic will differ depending on whether the arithmetic is performed on fixed words by registers or by a storage-to-storage approach on individual characters. The register method will typically use three instructions to load the augend into a register, add the addend, and store the sum back in a memory location. For example, assuming a 10-digit size for registers and storage locations, the instruction sequence and contents of the locations would be:

	LOCATIONS			ACCUMULATOR REGISTER
	1003	1006	1029	
Initial conditions	3250000000	1260000000	1898998792	4287658721
Instructions Load accumulator with 1003	same	same	same	3250000000
Add 1006 to accumulator register	same	same	same	4510000000
Store accumulator in 1029	same	same	4510000000	same

If the assumed decimal or binary points are not already lined up, the scaling of the fixed words may be adjusted either by shifting, multiplying, or dividing.

The storage-to-storage method for addition and subtraction will typically require only a single instruction to execute an addition or subtraction. An additional instruction is sometimes necessary in order to have the result stored where desired. Since storage-to-storage arithmetic is performed by computers which can address each character in storage, the operands are not of a fixed length. The programmer can add together two 2-digit numbers, a 20- and a 30-digit number, etc. The result is put directly in storage, so that the result field must be large enough to receive it. The usual instruction for addition is to add the contents of one of the specified operands to the contents of the other. This "add-to-one-of-operands" logic means that the contents of one of the operands will be automatically replaced by the result field, thereby destroying the data in that operand. If that operand should not be destroyed, it must be removed prior to executing the instruction. If there is a specific location where the result is to be stored, one of the factors is moved into this location and the other factor added to it. If the fields to be added are of unequal length, the operand field to be used for the result field must be the larger of the two because addition will cease when all of the digits in the smallest operand have been processed.

For the purpose of examples of storage-to-storage addition and subtraction, assume the following data in storage, using a word mark (–) to define the left end of a word field (as in an IBM 1401) and addressing the rightmost digit of the word field. The examples are independent of each other. The decimal point is shown by a caret ($_\wedge$). For these two examples, based on an IBM 1401, the second operand is the receiving field.

	R				ALPHA			BETA			GAMMA			
9	3	7	2	0	5	4	8	6	2	7	2	8	1	4	2

EXAMPLE 1

The program is to subtract the contents of ALPHA from BETA (notice the scaling is the same on both three-digit fields). The result will be in BETA.

BETA

S   ALPHA, BETA | 0 | 7 | 9 |

EXAMPLE 2

The program is to preserve all factors and the answer is to be stored in R. Add BETA and GAMMA and then subtract ALPHA. Note the differences in scaling which require lining up the decimal location (the caret $\wedge$ marks the decimal point). The lining up is performed by adjusting the address at which the joining of the two factors begins.

MCW   GAMMA, R   Move GAMMA to R

R

| 2 $_\wedge$ 8 | 1 | 4 | 2 |

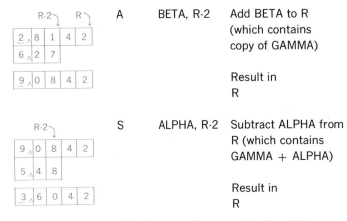

A   BETA, R-2   Add BETA to R
                    (which contains
                    copy of GAMMA)

                    Result in
                    R

S   ALPHA, R-2   Subtract ALPHA from
                    R (which contains
                    GAMMA + ALPHA)

                    Result in
                    R

In the preceding examples, the fields were addressed by the rightmost storage locations, and the field lengths were defined by word marks. In the second type of character storage addressing (as typified by the IBM System/360), there is an address
for each pair of decimal digits, namely, the leftmost storage location. The first oper-
and is the receiving field. As an example, assume storage as follows:

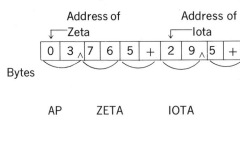

Bytes

AP   ZETA   IOTA

Add the data in two bytes of
IOTA to the data in the three
bytes of ZETA. ZETA then
appears as

| 3 | 3 | ∧2 | 6 | 5 | + |

1   Assume a binary computer with general registers and the following instruction
    formats:
        Op code   Register   Storage operand
    Given mnemonic operation codes of A (add), S (subtract), L (load), and ST
    (store), write instructions to:
    a   Add ZETA to BETA and store the result in SUM1. Use register 3.
    b   Add ALPHA to itself, subtract DATA1 and store the result in EX12. Use regis-
        ter 4.
2   Assume a character computer with an instruction format like examples 1 and 2:
    Op code, 1st operand, 2d operand. The second operand is the result operand.
    Write instructions to add and subtract the following data. Word marks are al-
    ready in place. The carets (∧) show scaling.

   a Add B2 and X4 and store the result in X4.

   b Add B2 and G1 and store the result in X4 (use MCW for a move instruction operation code).

3 Assume a byte-addressable computer, no word marks, the first field being the receiving field, and an addition code of AP (add packed decimal). Write an instruction to add ZX to BX with the result in BX.

AX						BX					
1	2	3	1	2	+	4	5	6	4	5	+

MULTIPLICATION

The instructions to multiply specify the multiplier and multiplicand. The location of the result is usually specified by the computer design. The maximum number of significant digits in the result is equal to the sum of the number of digits in the multiplier and multiplicand. The minimum number is one less than the maximum, as shown in the margin. This means that, for a fixed word length computer using registers, the resulting product will occupy two registers. In a variable word length computer, the product will occupy a number of adjacent storage locations equal, at a maximum, to the number of digits in the multiplicand and multiplier.

MAXIMUM
781 (3)
68 (2)
52108 (5)

MINIMUM
321 (3)
25 (2)
8025 (4)

As an example of the instruction sequence (for IBM System/360) using fixed words and addressable registers, assume the following two factors in storage (binary words expressed in hexadecimal notation), using registers 2 and 3 for the computation:

	SYMBOLIC NAME	CONTENTS	DECIMAL VALUE
Multiplier	location F1	+ 00000118	280
Multiplicand	location F2	+ 00000431	1073

SR	2, 2	Clear register 2 by subtracting it from itself
L	3, F2	Load multiplicand F2 into register 3
M	2, F1	Multiply using F1 as multiplier

The result will appear as two words in the two adjacent registers 2 and 3 (expressed in hexadecimal notation). Because of leading zeros in the factors, the entire result to be saved is, in this case, in register 3.

Register 2   Register 3

00000000   00049598 =

300440
in decimal

The variable-length instructions develop the answer in a product field set up for this purpose by the programmer. The steps in programming and multiplication are typically:

1 Move the multiplicand into the product area.

2 Execute multiply instruction using product area and multiplier field as operands.

The result is found in the product area. For example, using IBM System/360 character instructions, a field NIX containing 00625+ (3 bytes) is multiplied by a field called JIX containing 025+ (2 bytes), and the result found in location KIX (5 bytes) is 000015625+.

ZAP   KIX, NIX   Move contents of location NIX to KIX and zero out rest of KIX.

MP   KIX, JIX   Multiply contents of KIX (which contains copy of multiplicand) by contents of JIX, which is the multiplier. Result is located in KIX, writing over the previous contents.

The scaling of multiplication follows the rule that the number of digits to the right of the decimal location in the product is the sum of the number of places to the right of the decimal position in the multiplier and multiplicand. The number of places to the left of the decimal is equal to the number of places to the left in the multiplier and multiplicand except that the first digit in the product area may be zero. For example:

	SCALING			SCALING	
	LEFT	RIGHT		LEFT	RIGHT
$110_\wedge 01$	3	2	$2011_\wedge 2$	4	1
$\times\ 91_\wedge 31$	2	2	$3_\wedge 14$	1	2
$10045_\wedge 6131$	5	4	$06315_\wedge 168$	5	3

This approach to scaling, while satisfactory for simple problems or hand computations, is not always so, and the scale factor method or floating point arithmetic explained later in the chapter is used.

1   Using the IBM System/360 binary word instructions in the chapter example, write an instruction sequence to multiply HOURS × RATE and store the results in GPAY. The result of the multiplication (use registers 2 and 3) will be in register 3.

2   Using the IBM System/360 character instructions in the chapter example, write an instruction to multiply 03765+ found in DATAX by DATAY having contents of 024+. Use MULTAREA as a product area.

DIVISION

The instructions to divide must specify a divisor and a dividend. The location of the two results, the quotient and the remainder, is specified by the instructions for the computer being programmed. The size in digits of the quotient and remainder is usually limited to the size of a computer word register in a fixed-word computer using registers. When using a character logic, the quotient size is usually equal to the number of digits in the dividend, and the remainder is equal in size to the number of digits in the divisor. The remainder, as in manual arithmetic, is the numerator of a fraction which has the divisor as the denominator.

```
                007  Quotient
Divisor  14)100  Dividend
            02 14 = Remainder
```

The System/360 fixed-word divide instructions are used as an example of instructions using registers. Assume a dividend in a location called EENY containing a 32-bit binary word equal to 300440 (+ 00049598 in hexadecimal notation) and a divisor of 1073 (+ 00000436 in hexadecimal notation) located in MEENY. The instructions are:

L	3, EENY	Load dividend
SR	2, 2	Clear other register used in division
D	2, MEENY	Divide by contents of location MEENY

The result of the division will be (hexadecimal):

Register 2

| 00000000 |

Remainder

Register 3

| 00000118 |

Quotient   = 280 in decimal

The System/360 decimal instructions will be used to illustrate division using variable word length logic. A divide area is specified which will hold both the quotient and the remainder. The first step is to move the dividend into this divide area and zero out the remaining locations. The next instruction is "divide," with the operands being the divide area and the location of the divisor. Both the quotient and remainder appear in the divide area. For an example, if the contents of NUTS is to be divided by the contents of BOLTS using DVSN as a divide area, the following instructions will be used:

SYMBOLIC NAME	CONTENTS (DECIMAL)	LENGTH IN BYTES
NUTS	10365+	3
BOLTS	072+	2
DVSN	unknown	5

CODING	CONTENTS OF DVSN
ZAP DVSN, NUTS	000010365+
Load dividend (NUTS) into divide area and zero out rest of area (DVSN)	
DP DVSN, BOLTS	00143+069+
Divide by contents of BOLTS	Quotient remainder

The scaling rules for division differ depending on whether the arithmetic division is character or word and whether the word is interpreted as integers or as a fraction. The number of places to the right of the assumed decimal or binary point will be the number of places in the dividend minus the number in the divisor. The number of significant digits in the quotient is, at a minimum, equal to the number of digits other than leading zeros in the dividend minus the number of digits in the divisor. The maximum number of digits other than leading zeros is one greater than the minimum.

SELF-TESTING QUIZ 11-4

1   Using the IBM System/360 fixed binary word instructions presented in the text sample, write a sequence to divide ALPHA by BETA and store the quotient in RSLT. Use registers 2 and 3.

2   Using the IBM System/360 character instructions presented in the text example, write instructions to divide GRADES by CREDITS. Assume that GRADES is three bytes, CREDITS is two bytes, and the divide area called DAREA is five bytes in length.

OVERFLOW

Overflow describes a size error condition in which the storage locations which are assigned to hold a result are not large enough to hold all of the digits. Overflow generally refers to loss of digits at the left end of a group of digits. These are the most significant digits. If digits at the right end of a group are not to be stored for some reason, either truncation or rounding can occur. In truncation, the digits are merely dropped, whereas in rounding, the rightmost digit that is retained is increased by one if the digit dropped is 6 or greater.

Most significant digit lost through overflow → (1) | 7 | 9 | 6 | 5 | 4 | 3 | 7 | 5 | (2) ← digits lost in truncation or rounding

Overflow occurs in arithmetic in addition, subtraction, and division.

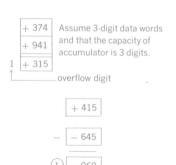

+ 374
+ 941
1 + 315

Assume 3-digit data words and that the capacity of accumulator is 3 digits.

overflow digit

+ 415
− 645
(1) − 060

overflow digit

1   In addition, overflow occurs when the sum of the most significant (leftmost) digits in the accumulator register or accumulator field exceeds 9.

2   In subtraction, overflow occurs when the remainder exceeds the number of digits in the accumulator. This can occur only if one of the quantities is negative.

3   Overflow will occur in division in different ways in a fractional computer and an integer computer. In a fractional computer, for example, overflow will occur whenever the dividend is greater in absolute value than the divisor. This would result in a number greater than 0.9, which would exceed the capacity of the register.

Overflow creates a problem because the overflow digit is usually lost. The existence of overflow is usually signaled by some sort of error indicator or error interruption. If the overflow indicator or interrupt shows overflow during addition or subtraction, it is a relatively simple matter to shift the number and replace the digit that has been lost, because the lost digit will always be 1. Overflow in division is more difficult, and the remedy does not necessarily follow automatically, as in addition and subtraction.

In some computers, the programmer must program tests for overflow and write routines to make adjustments; in others, the interrupt handling routine in the programs which operate the system take care of detecting overflow and making adjustments if necessary.

THE SCALE FACTOR METHOD

The various rules for scaling results of an arithmetic operation (locating the position of the decimal point) are sometimes ambiguous and difficult to implement. The scale factor method is an alternative approach. This method involves converting all numbers used in computation to a common base, such as whole numbers or fractions. The programmer records the number of places the decimal point had to be shifted to the right or left when the number was converted to the common basis. This number (+ for places shifted to left and − for shift to right) is the scale factor.

ORIGINAL NUMBER	SCALING BETWEEN 0 AND 1		SCALING AS INTEGRAL NUMBER	
	SCALED NUMBER	SCALE FACTOR	SCALED NUMBER	SCALE FACTOR
73.21	0.7321	2	7321.0	−2
0.07321	0.7321	−1	7321.0	−5
0.007321	0.7321	−2	7321.0	−6
7321.0	0.7321	4	7321.0	0

Any common basis may be used. The scale factor represents the power of 10 by which the scaled number must be multiplied to obtain the number as originally scaled. Thus, 0.7321 with a scale factor of 2 means 0.7321×10^2 or $0.7321 \times 100 = 73.21$. The scale factor is used in programming; it is not stored in the computer. The programmer keeps track of the scale factor in order to know how to position the data for arithmetic.

For addition or subtraction, the numbers to be added or subtracted must have the same scale factor. To accomplish this, the operands should be adjusted to the largest scale factor. The scale factor of the sum or remainder will be the same as the scale factor of the operands.

ORIGINAL NUMBER	SCALED NUMBER	SCALE FACTOR	SCALED NUMBERS FOR ADDITION	SCALE FACTOR
149.21	0.149210	3	0.149210	3
1.213	0.121300	1	0.001213	3
49.20	0.492000	2	0.049200	3
		Result of addition	0.199623	3
		or	199.623	

The scale factor method for keeping track of the decimal point in multiplication involves multiplying the two-scaled numbers and adding the two-scale factors. The product is scaled by the new scale factor.

EXAMPLE

Multiply 3.475 by 412.64.

Scaled number	Scaled factor
0.3475	1
× 0.41264	+ 3
0.143392400	4

$0.143392400 \times 10^4 = 1433.92400$

When the scale factor method is used for keeping track of the decimal point in division, the scaled divisor is divided into the scaled dividend, and the quotient has a scale factor formed by subtracting the scale factor of the divisor from the scale factor of the dividend.

EXAMPLE

Divide 370.36 by 15.76.

$$0.235 \times 10^2 = 23.5$$
$$0.1576\overline{)0.037036}$$

Scale   ↑   ↑

factors   (2)   (4) $4 - 2 =$ scale factor of 2 for quotient

SELF-TESTING QUIZ 11-5

Using the scale factor method, perform the following operations after scaling all numbers initially between 0 and 1:

1 Multiply 47.01 by 1.1.
2 Divide 100.25 by 2.5.
3 Add 38.01, 3.801 and 380.1.

FLOATING POINT ARITHMETIC

As has been explained, the computer does not keep track of the decimal point in data words. The programmer must do this and write the computational program accordingly. The task of keeping track of scaling is not too difficult for the uncomplicated data processing typical of business applications. But for complicated scientific problems, it becomes much more troublesome. The reader may have noticed that the scale factor method of scaling results depends on rather simple rules. It is possible for the computer to develop and keep track of its own scale factors. Arithmetic in which the computer does this is called floating point arithmetic.

In floating point arithmetic, the computer program converts all numbers to be used by the program to a form consisting of a fraction (or mantissa) and an exponent (or characteristic). The exponent is the power of 10 (or other radix) required to change the mantissa back to the original form. It corresponds to the scale factor in the scale factor method. The mantissa may be expressed in many forms, but the scientific or normal form has one place to the left of the decimal (absolute value greater than 1 but less than 10). The standard form of the mantissa for 12.41 is therefore 1.241 with an exponent of 1.

In computer computation, it is desirable to avoid a negative exponent. Therefore, the exponent is frequently written in an excess form, such as excess-50, in which 50 is added to the exponent. In excess-50 notation, an exponent of 00 is equivalent to 10^{-50}, and an exponent of 99 is equivalent to 10^{+49}. The same principles can be used for a notation with different limits and different radices. The exponent, for example, can represent in binary a negative 128 or a positive 127 exponent by using an excess-128 form.

In floating point arithmetic, the combination of fraction and exponent is stored in memory as a single data word. In order to perform arithmetic using two floating point words, the words are first separated into the two elements. Arithmetic is performed on the mantissas to obtain the result, then arithmetic is performed on the characteristics to obtain the exponent for the result. The fraction and exponent for the result are then combined into a data word and stored in memory.

Floating point arithmetic may be implemented either by hardware or software. Programming is performed as with other instructions, except that the scaling can be completely ignored because the floating point instructions keep track of the scale factor and automatically adjust for it.

▌ TRANSFER OF CONTROL INSTRUCTIONS

A computer program is a sequence of steps. The program executes the instructions one after another in the order in which they are found in memory unless a transfer of control instruction breaks the sequence. This break in the sequence, often called branching, is necessary because the computer program must usually provide not one but many possible program paths. One of these paths is selected during the running of the program based on the results obtained to that point, or on some other condition. For example, the path a program is to follow may depend on whether or not a numerical result is positive, zero, or negative. This is programmed as a test of the number followed by three different sets of instructions to handle the three outcomes (Figure 11–1). When programming this example, there must be a transfer of control to specify which of the three sequences of instructions will be used. When one of these sequences has been used, there must be a branching from the sequence up to the coding which is common to all processing. There are three general types of transfer of control instructions:

1 Unconditional transfer
2 Conditional transfer based on comparison
3 Conditional transfer based on absence or existence of a condition

FIGURE 11-1 Programming of three
alternative program paths

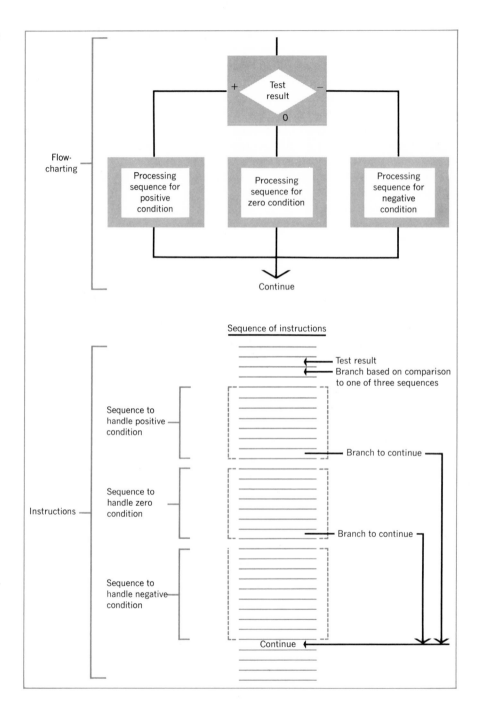

UNCONDITIONAL TRANSFER

Normally, the instructions are stored in consecutive locations and executed sequentially. An instruction counter keeps track of the location of the next instruction. However, there are occasions in programming when a straight sequence of instructions cannot be maintained. The jump or branch instruction provides for an unconditional transfer of control. This directs the processor to find the next instruction at a location other than the next location established by the instruction counter. The branching does not depend on a comparison or test of condition. An example of the use of unconditional transfer of control is branching to the main line flow after performing an alternative sequence of instructions.

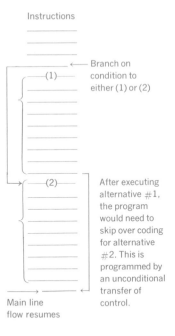

Instructions

Branch on condition to either (1) or (2)

After executing alternative #1, the program would need to skip over coding for alternative #2. This is programmed by an unconditional transfer of control.

Main line flow resumes

CONDITIONAL TRANSFER BASED ON COMPARISON

Branching based on a comparison involves the comparison of two data words or fields. The result of the comparison determines the path the program takes. The instructions for branching based on a comparison usually require two instructions:

1 Compare instruction. The instruction compares two data words (either numeric or alphanumeric) and sets a condition code or indicator.
2 The conditional branching instruction. The instruction specifies the location to which the program should branch if the condition code or indicator is equal to the specified code in the instruction or one of a group of specified codes. If not equal, the program does not branch.

By use of the compare instruction and related branch on condition instruction, branching may be programmed for the three branching possibilities shown in Figure 11-2 or variations of these. An example of a pair of instructions in symbolic coding is:

C   3, PAY   Compare the contents of register 3 with contents of location PAY

BH   FUNNY   Branch if the register contents were greater than PAY

FIGURE 11-2 Conditional branching possibilities

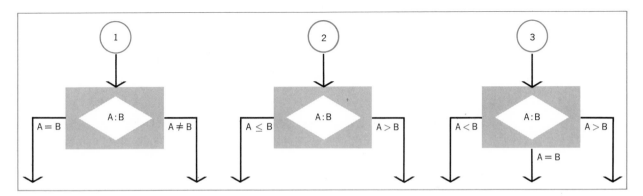

FIGURE 11–3 Example of flowchart of conditional branching required in billing procedure when there is a 5 percent quantity discount on orders in excess of $500

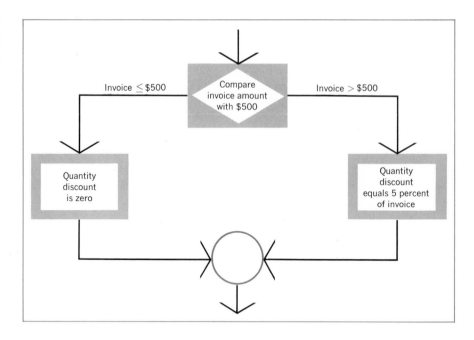

FIGURE 11–3 Example of flowchart of conditional branching required in billing procedure when there is a 5 percent quantity discount on orders in excess of $500

The use of the conditional branching based on a comparison is illustrated by the processing of a billing invoice for which a 5 percent quantity discount is allowed on orders in excess of $500 (Figure 11–3).

CONDITIONAL TRANSFER BASED ON ABSENCE OR EXISTENCE OF A CONDITION

The conditions on which the branching is based are usually a data condition, overflow from arithmetic, and equipment status. Examples of conditions which might be tested and thus be the basis for a conditional transfer of control are:

1   Whether a data word is zero, positive or negative
2   Overflow
3   The "on" or "off" condition of a console switch
4   The condition of an input/output unit, i.e., whether it is busy and therefore not ready for an instruction
5   The existence of various types of errors during processing (such as a read error)

These conditions usually set a condition or error indicator which is specified by the instruction as the reason for branching to occur. If the condition code or indicator is not set (i.e. the condition has not occurred), the conditional branching will not be performed. If the programmer does not write the conditional branching test, the condition will not be acted upon.

INTERRUPTS

Many computers have provisions for automatic transfer of control if certain conditions occur, rather than relying on the programmer to insert conditional branching instructions to test for them. The interrupt, or "trap," transfers control to a fixed location when a condition such as overflow, parity error, or I/O device needing attention is detected. In addition the interrupt process provides a record of the instruction to which control should go after the interrupt is handled, codes describing the reason for the interrupt, and various other status information.

When an interrupt occurs, control is transferred to a specified location which in turn transfers control to a routine to interpret the cause of the interrupt and take appropriate action. The interrupt handling routine is usually a part of the software provided by the manufacturer in the operating system, so that the programmer does not need to write this routine. After the error message or other action has been taken, the computer transfers control back to the next instruction following the one during which the interrupt occurred. In essence, an interrupt system provides an automatic transfer of control based on a condition with the action to be taken being based on an analysis of the interrupt code.

SELF-TESTING QUIZ 11-6

1 In the following flowchart, identify where branching instructions must be used. Indicate whether conditional or unconditional.

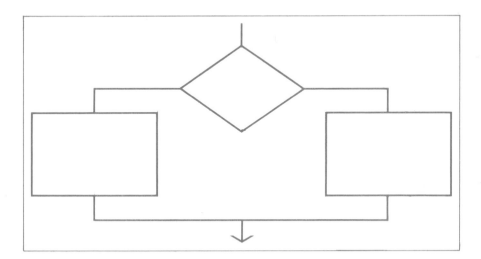

▌ EDITING

When read into the computer, data may not be in a proper form for computational use. After computation, the data is not usually in the form desired for output—no commas separate the thousands or millions, and there is no decimal point. The purpose of the editing instructions is to rearrange data words, alter individual digits or bits, convert from external form to internal processing form, and set up the data in a suitable form for printing or punching. The editing instructions, for discussion purposes, are divided into four major types—shifting, logical or bit alteration, data conversion, and output editing.

SHIFTING

Shift instructions are used in fixed word length computers to rearrange digits in a word. For example, in a 10-digit fixed-length word, 0763497621, the programmer may wish to use only digits 3 through 7, i.e., the word to be used is 0000063497. Shift instructions provide for the rearranging and eliminations required to assemble the word into the desired form. Such instructions are not necessary in a variable word length computer because by varying the address and length specification, the desired digits can be obtained.

Shift instructions use one or two registers and typically provide for several variations as shown in the margin.

The difference between an algebraic shift and a logical shift is the treatment of the sign bit. In the algebraic shift, the sign is not part of any shifting; in the logical shift, the sign bit moves as a regular bit. In a binary computer a word of, say, 36 bits will consist of a sign bit as the first bit and 35 data bits. If the word holds character codes, the word will be divided into bytes (say six 6-bit bytes), each of which encodes one alphanumeric character. The sign bit is, in this case, used as a data code bit. When shifting, the sign bit will need to move, whereas in the binary word shifting bits into the sign position would not be appropriate. Other coding, such as Boolean codes, may also use the sign bit as a regular data bit.

When shifting occurs, zeros enter the vacated spaces, and digits shifted out are lost. If, however, a double-register shift is used, digits pushed out of the first register of the pair will enter the second register, causing a shift of its contents. A variation is a circular shift in which the digits pushed out at the end (say the right end) reenter the other end (left end). The shift may be either left or right.

To illustrate the use of shifting, assume a 10-digit binary coded decimal word in the form | 3 | 7 | 6 | 5 | 7 | 8 | 4 | 8 | 9 | 4 | . The use of a decimal word is for ease in explanation. The same principle applies to a binary word.

EXAMPLE 1

Two words 3765 and 784894 were combined in a single word to conserve storage—they are to be disassembled for computational purposes into two words 0000003765 and 0000784894.

Algebraic
Single register — Double register
Left · Right · Left · Right

Logical
Single register — Double register
Left · Right · Left · Right

Algebraic left shift
lost ← | s | ← zeros

Algebraic right shift
zeros → | s | → lost

Logical left shift
lost ← | | ← zeros

Logical right shift
zeros → | | → lost

Double-register algebraic right shift
zeros → | s |
| s | → lost

Curricular right shift
| s |

Register 1

Load word in register 1 | 3765784894 |

                                   Register 1   Register 2

Use double-register right | 0000003765 | | 7848940000 |
shift to shift 6 places
Shift single-register 2 | 0000784894 |

EXAMPLE 2

The middle four digits are to be put into a register in the form 0000005784.

Load word into register 1 | 3765784894 |

Shift 3 places to left | 5784894000 |

Shift 6 places to right | 0000005784 |

LOGICAL OR BIT ALTERATION

The bit instructions, frequently referred to as filtering or masking, operate on a word to alter the bits. The bit instructions use two words—the word with the bits to be altered and the control word (called a mask) which determines how the first word is to be altered. Each of the bits is operated upon independently of the other bits in the word. The matching of each data bit with a corresponding bit in the control word determines the state of the data bits after the instruction is executed.

The instructions for bit manipulation will usually provide for logical AND, logical OR, and logical exclusive OR. The results of these operations are:

Result word	AND	Both data bit and mask bit are 1
will have a	OR	Either or both data bit or mask bit are 1
1 bit if:	Exclusive OR	Either (but not both) data bit or mask bit are 1

Otherwise the result bit will be zero. For example, the table of outcomes for an AND operation is:

AND

DATA	MASK	RESULT
0	0	0
0	1	0
1	0	0
1	1	1

These instructions can be used to erase bits in the data word, to add bits to the data word, or to combine two data words. As an example, a data word contains a code, only part of which is used for a routine. In order to extract the needed part of the code, the unneeded portion is erased. Assume the code is in the form XXXXXXXX, where each X stands for four bits, i.e., these are in hexadecimal notation. The portion of the code that is needed consists of 000XX0XX. By combining the data word using AND with a mask consisting of 000FF0FF (remember F in hexadecimal is 1111), the result will save the desired bits and erase the others. B stands for an unknown digit—either 1 or 0.

Data word	BBBB	BBBB	BBBB	BBBB	BBBB	BBBB	BBBB	BBBB
Mask word	0000	0000	0000	1111	1111	0000	1111	1111
Result	0000	0000	0000	BBBB	BBBB	0000	BBBB	BBBB

DATA CONVERSION

In binary computers and in some character computers, data in the input/output code is not suitable for arithmetic computation. When the data is read into the computer, it is in a character code. It must be converted to binary (or in some cases to a packed decimal) before it can be used in arithmetic. When data is to be output, it must be converted to character coding. Typical instructions will convert from character coding to binary and from binary to character. The IBM System/360, for example, uses binary or packed decimal for computation and an 8-bit character coding for input and output. There are two pairs of instructions:

1 Pack (PACK) converts from character coding to packed decimal.
   Convert to binary (CVB) converts from packed decimal coding to fixed word binary coding.
2 Convert to decimal (CDV) converts from binary word to packed decimal coding.
   Unpack (UNPK) converts from packed decimal to character coding.

Computers using binary coded character for computation do not need these instructions. A computer using numeric binary coded decimal for computation and a pair of digits—one zone and one numeric—for input and output will need an instruction to strip the zones from input data to obtain numeric coding for computation and an instruction to fill numeric coding by inserting zone coding. For example:

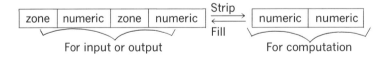

OUTPUT EDITING

In order to make meaningful printed output, leading zeros need to be suppressed (replaced with blanks), commas need to be inserted to separate groups of digits, a period needs to be inserted to mark the decimal point, and other characters need to be inserted, such as * or $. This editing can be performed by shifting, masking, inserting, etc., but most computers have special editing instructions to simplify this task.

The usual procedure for editing uses two fields—(1) the field to be edited and (2) a pattern field containing symbols which control the editing. The edited result replaces the pattern field. The programmer defines the pattern field as a word to be stored in the computer as part of the program. A simple editing instruction is used to illustrate this concept. Similar instructions are found in most computers.

EXAMPLE 1

A data field consisting of the digits 937421 is to be printed out as $9,374.21. A pattern or control field is stored in the computer in the form $b,bbb.bb where b stands for a blank. The instruction is given to move the characters in the data field to the control field and edit. This causes the two to be combined and the result stored in place of the control field.

Data field	937421
Control field	$b,bbb.bb
Result field	$9,374.21

EXAMPLE 2

A data word in the form 0000194 is to be printed out as 1.94. The edit word is bbb0b.bb. This causes the leading zeros to be suppressed (i.e., replaced by blanks) so that the result will be printed as 1.94.

▮ SUMMARY

The basic instruction repertoire for a computer includes instructions to move data, to perform arithmetic, to transfer control, and to edit data words or fields. In addition to the basic instructions described in this chapter, there are instructions used primarily for instruction modification and instructions for input and output. These are presented in Chapters 12 and 13.

A major problem in programming arithmetic operations is the necessity for keeping track of the location of the decimal point. The programmer can use a method such as the scale factor method to calculate and remember the scaling of data words. The computer can also be used to calculate the scale factor and keep track of the location of the decimal point. This is called floating point arithmetic and may be implemented either by special hardware features or by software programs.

▮ ANSWERS TO SELF-TESTING QUIZZES

SELF-TESTING QUIZ 11–1

1 *a* L   3, ALPHA
    ST   3, BETA

```
      b  L    6, ALPHA
         ST   6, D1 ⎫
         ST   6, D2 ⎪   Since the operation is a
         ST   6, D3 ⎬   copying, the contents may be
         ST   6, D4 ⎭   copied more than once
2  a  SW   BETA
   b  SW   BETA-2
   c  SW   DATA1-3
      MCW  DATA1, DATA5
```

SELF-TESTING QUIZ 11-2

```
1  a  L    3, BETA
      A    3, ZETA
      ST   3, SUM1
   b  L    4, ALPHA
      A    4, ALPHA
      ST   4, EX12
2  a  A    B2, X4
   b  MCW  B2, X4
      A    G1-3, X4      (watch scaling)
3  AP BX, AX
```

SELF-TESTING QUIZ 11-3

```
1  SR   2, 2         Clear register 2
   L    3, HOURS     Load multiplicand
   M    2, RATE      Multiply by RATE
   ST   3, GPAY      Store result in GPAY
2  ZAP  MULTAREA, DATAX    Move multiplicand into multiplier
                           area and zero out rest of area
   MP   MULTAREA, DATAY    Multiply by DATAY
```

SELF-TESTING QUIZ 11-4

```
1  L    3, ALPHA   Load dividend
   SR   2, 2       Clear register 2 for use in division
   D    2, BETA    Divide ALPHA by BETA
   ST   3, RSLT    Store quotient
2  ZAP  DAREA, GRADES     Move GRADES into divide area and
                          zero out rest of field
   DP   DAREA, CREDITS
```

SELF-TESTING QUIZ 11-5

	Number	*Scale factor*	
1	0.4701	2	
	$\times$ .11	$\underline{1}$	
	0.051711	3	$= 51.711$

$$\begin{array}{r} 0.401 \ (2) \\ \textbf{2} \quad 0.25\overline{)0.10025} \end{array}$$

(1)   (3) $3 - 1 = 2$

3 *Number*	*Scaling*	*Scaling as adjusted for addition*	
0.3801	2	0 . 0 3 8 0 1	3
0.3801	1	0 . 0 0 3 8 0 1	3
0.3801	3	$\underline{0 . 3 8 0 1}$	3
		0 . 4 2 1 9 1 1	3

SELF-TESTING QUIZ 11-6

Two branching instructions are needed. The first chooses between sequence A and sequence B based on a comparison. If sequence A is written first, it needs an unconditional branch to transfer control around sequence B in order to get to the instructions following the two sequences.

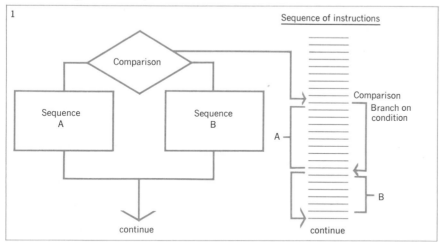

EXERCISES

1 What are the reasons for having the following types of instructions:
   a Unconditional transfer of control

    b   Suppress leading zeros

    c   Data movement

    d   Shifting

2   Why does the programmer have to keep track of the decimal point (scaling) in fixed point arithmetic?

3   Using the scale factor method, calculate the decimal point in the result for each of the following:

    a 21.48×554.55 *d* $1492.1 - 9.21$

    b $0.00891 \div 0.013$ *e* 0.007×0.003

    c $4530.1 + 1.76$ *f* $3.17 \div 0.002$

4   Describe the computational steps the computer must perform when using floating point arithmetic.

5   Assuming a computer is using excess-50 notation for the exponent and the "between zero and one" scaling of the fraction, interpret the following:

    a   50375625   *d*   53100000

    b   48290101   *e*   58250000

    c   45100000

6   Define the following terms:

    a   branching   *e*   arithmetic precision

    b   characteristic   *f*   packing

    c   word mark   *g*   interrupt

    d   overflow

7   Given a fixed word computer and an instruction LD1 (load register 1 with contents of operand address) and ST1 (store register contents in operand address), what is accomplished by the following coding:

```
LD1     FIRST
ST1     S1
ST1     S2
ST1     S3
```

8   Describe the two methods for defining field size for variable word length computers.

9   Perform the following division by successive subtraction, keeping a tally of the number of times subtraction is performed.

    a $12\overline{)50}$

    b $0.03\overline{)10}$

    c $40\overline{)120}$

10   Assuming the availability of a right shift and a left shift—either one or two registers and either logical or arithmetic—indicate the shifts to make the following changes:

	Original	To be changed to
a	+0XXXX000	+0000XXXX
b	XXX00XXX	00XXXXXX
c	X0X0X0X0	XXXX0000

11 Using a hexadecimal notation, what will be the result of the following logical instructions?

	OPERATION	DATA WORD	MASK WORD
a	AND	3741	FFFF
b	AND	2148	00FF
c	OR	1930	F011
d	OR	1028	0000
e	Exclusive OR	5510	F040

12 How does the output pattern or control word simplify output editing?

❚ ALTERING AN INSTRUCTION
THE ARITHMETIC METHOD
INDEX REGISTERS
SELF-TESTING QUIZ 12–1

❚ LOOPING
ARITHMETIC LOOP MODIFICATION
INDEX REGISTER LOOP MODIFICATION
SELF-TESTING QUIZ 12–2

❚ SWITCHES IN PROGRAMMING
HARDWARE SWITCHES
PROGRAMMED SWITCHES

❚ TABLE LOOK-UP

❚ INDIRECT ADDRESSING
SELF-TESTING QUIZ 12–3

❚ SUBROUTINES

❚ PROGRAM MODIFICATION IN MULTIPROGRAMMING
RELATIVE ADDRESSING AND RELOCATION
STORAGE PROTECTION
PURE PROCEDURES AND REENTRANT SUBROUTINES

❚ SUMMARY

❚ ANSWERS TO SELF-TESTING QUIZZES
SELF-TESTING QUIZ 12–1
SELF-TESTING QUIZ 12–2
SELF-TESTING QUIZ 12–3

❚ EXERCISES

PROGRAM
MODIFICATION

A distinguishing feature of electronic computers is the possibility of modifying the program during the execution of the instructions. The general form of the modification must be planned by the programmer, but the exact modification to be made at execution time can be dependent upon the data being operated upon or on specification data inserted by the computer operator when the program is run.

The purpose and value of program modification techniques are illustrated by the following situations.

SITUATION	WITHOUT PROGRAM MODIFICATION	WITH PROGRAM MODIFICATION
Sum 1,000 quantities stored in 1,000 separate but consecutive locations	Requires up to 1,001 separate instructions	Requires only a few (say from 2 to 12) instructions
Locate an entry in a table of 150 entries	May require up to 451 separate instructions	Requires only a few (say from 3 to 20) instructions
Calculate the square root of a quantity at six separate places in the program sequence	Requires that the square root computation be written six separate times	Requires that the square root computation routine be written only once and then used by each of the places needing it

Program modification consists of the altering of one or more instructions in a set of instructions during the running of the program, thereby changing the processing to be performed. The primary reason for using program modification techniques is to reduce the number of instructions required for a program. Other reasons are that it allows a program to be written so that its execution is dependent on data not available until the program is run. In some cases, the writing of programs may be simplified by modification techniques.

The modification methods to be discussed are the arithmetic method and the index register method. The modification procedure is necessary for the following programming techniques which will be discussed in the chapter:

1 Looping
2 Switches
3 Table look-up
4 Indirect addressing
5 Subroutine

▌ ALTERING AN INSTRUCTION

An instruction can be altered in two ways—by operating upon it as if it were data, or by special hardware features which alter it. The first way might be termed the arithmetic method, since in most cases the program performs arithmetic operations on the instruction in order to modify it. Of the possible hardware features for program modification purposes, the most common is the index register.

THE ARITHMETIC METHOD

As far as the computer is concerned, an instruction stored in memory is not different from a data item. Consider the possible contents of two locations in storage, location 375 and location 738, each of which holds 16 bits. The bit representations stored in these two locations may be identical, but they can mean entirely different things.

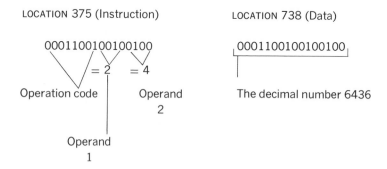

LOCATION 375 (Instruction)   LOCATION 738 (Data)

0001100100100100   0001100100100100

= 2   = 4

Operation code   Operand   The decimal number 6436
                        2

        Operand
          1

The instruction might be interpreted as "compare the contents of two registers (2 and 4)." Suppose by some error that the data in location 738 was used as an instruction, the result would be identical with the use of the instruction in location 375. Since they are the same, location 738 can be an instruction and location 375 can be data. Suppose that the computer adds the contents of location 654, which contains 0000000000000001, to the contents of data location 738 and stores the results back in the same spot. The data storage location will then hold the number 6437. Suppose the same operation is performed on the instruction stored at location 375. The result will be an altered instruction which in this case states: "Compare the contents of registers 2 and 5 (rather than 2 and 4)." It follows that any part of the instruction can be altered by performing arithmetic operations (add, subtract, multiply, erase, etc.). For example, adding the contents of a location in the form 0000000100000000 to the contents of 375 will alter the operation code of the instruction to make it say, "Add (rather than compare) the contents of two registers." If an instruction modification operation such as this produces an invalid instruction code or an invalid operand address, the computer will reject it when execution is attempted. If a data word which has the form of a valid instruction is incorrectly used as an instruction, it will be executed. In short, instructions are no different from data until they are used as instructions. All operations (arithmetic, move, comparison, etc.) which can be performed on data can also be performed on an instruction word.

The general procedure for arithmetic modification is:

COMPUTER USING REGISTERS	COMPUTER USING STORAGE-TO-STORAGE
1 Load an arithmetic register with the instruction (found in a storage location).	1 Perform operations, such as setting word marks, to define the portion of the instruction to be modified, if the method of addressing requires it.
2 Perform arithmetic as if register held a data word.	2 Perform arithmetic on the instruction field as if it were data.
3 Store altered instruction back in its memory location.	3 Use the altered instruction by specifying the location where it is stored as the address of the next location.
4 Use the altered instruction by specifying the location where it is stored as the address of the next instruction.	

Note that the stored instruction is altered. If the program were stopped and control returned to the beginning of the program in order to rerun it, the modified instruction would not be in the proper form. Only by reloading could the original form of the instructions be obtained. For this and other operating reasons, it is considered good programming practice to set all instructions to be modified to their initial form at the beginning of the program, or alternatively, to restore a modified instruction to its original form at the conclusion of a modification use.

INDEX REGISTERS

Index registers are registers which can be used for purposes such as address modification. In some computers, these are separate registers designed for use only as index registers; in other computers, general registers can be used as index registers. Almost all advanced computers have several registers for index register uses. Index registers are sometimes not found on small business-oriented computers.

Recall from the discussion in Chapter 6 that an instruction to be executed is moved out of storage into special registers for decoding—the operation code into an operation register and the operand address in an address register. Index register modification is performed by combining the contents of the index register with the contents of the address register holding the operand address. This addition (or subtraction) occurs during the instruction cycle after the instruction has been copied from its storage location into the address register, but prior to its execution, so that the instruction in storage is not altered by the index register modification. Nor does the modification alter the contents of the index register.

000346	← Address from instruction

Contents of address register holding operand address prior to index register modification

000003

Contents of index register

Contents of address register holding operand address after index register modification completed

00349   ← Address to be used (effective address)

If the instruction using the above address specified the addition of the contents of location 346 to the contents of an accumulator register, the actual execution, under the index register modification shown, would result in the contents of location 349 being used rather than 346.

Index register modification is specified by the use of a code in the instruction. In symbolic coding, the use of an index register is usually specified by a separate code identifying the index register to be used. The following are representative symbolic instructions for two different computers:

SYMBOLIC INSTRUCTION	EXPLANATION
ADD DATA, 3	Add to the contents of the accumulator register the contents of the location determined by taking the location address assigned to DATA and adding to the address the contents of index register 3.
A 2, DATA (3)	Add to general register 2 (used as an accumulator) the contents of a storage location obtained by taking location DATA and modifying it by adding the contents of general register 3 (used as an index register).

If DATA refers to location 3764 and register 3 contains 20, the instructions, when executed, will add the contents of location 3784 to the register used as an accumulator register.

In a computer with index registers, there must be instructions for loading an index register with an initial value, for incrementing or decrementing its contents, and for testing its contents. In addition to these, there may be special instructions which perform a sequence of instructions useful in programming techniques such as looping.

SELF-TESTING QUIZ 12-1

1 Assume that the operation code of an unconditional branch is 00. If the computer were referred to a data location containing all zeros as the address of the next instruction, what would happen?

2 Using operation codes of L, A, and ST for load, add and store, an instruction stored in a location with symbolic address NEXT1 and a constant of 4 in symbolic location FOUR, what will be the effect of the following sequence of instructions?

OP. CODE	REGISTER	OPERAND
L	2,	NEXT1
A	2,	FOUR
ST	2,	NEXT1

3   Suppose that instruction NEXT1 in question 2 needs to be in its original form later in the program. What should be done?

4   Assuming the following instruction format and instruction (add the contents of

OP. CODE	REGISTER	OPERAND	INDEX REGISTER
A	3,	TABLE1	(8)

TABLE1 to register 3 with TABLE1 modified by contents of register 8), answer the following questions:

    a   If index register 8 is zero and TABLE1 refers to storage location 1936, what will the instruction do?

    b   If index register 8 has a contents of 4, what will the instruction do?

    c   After executing the instruction in part b above, what does the instruction look like in storage?

    d   If the programmer wishes the next execution of the instruction to be "add the contents of TABLE1 + 8 (i.e., 1944) to register 3," what type of instruction(s) will make this modification?

▌ LOOPING

The technique of looping is basic to programming. The objective of a loop is to use the same set of instructions over and over again rather than having to write and store many instructions. This can be illustrated by a program segment which sums 100 quantities stored in locations 1000 to 1099 (each word is of fixed length). Assuming the use of addressable arithmetic registers, the straight line coding to sum 100 numbers requires 101 separate instructions. The first instruction is a "load accumulator register," the next 99 are "add to accumulator register" instructions, and the final instruction is a "store the register used as the accumulator." Given the first data location as 1000, and symbolic operation codes of LDA for load accumulator, ADD for add to the accumulator register and STO for store accumulator register, the coding would be as follows:

SYMBOLIC CODING	ABSOLUTE ADDRESS	CONTENTS OF ACCUMULATOR
LDA DATA	1000	Contents of location 1000
ADD DATA + 1	1001	Contents of 1000 + 1001
ADD DATA + 2	1002	Contents of 1000 + 1001 + 1002
ADD DATA + 99	1099	Contents of 1000 + 1001 + 1002 + ... + 1099
STO SUM		

In terms of speed of execution the straight line coding cannot be improved, but it requires storage locations for 101 instructions. Since the only change in each of the add instructions is an increment of 0001 in the address portion, a loop is indicated.

The general steps for programming a loop are the following:

1   Initialization

2   Execution

3   Modification

4   Test for termination

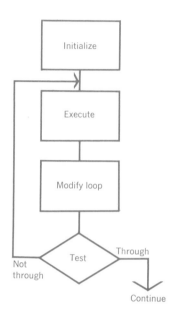

The order of the execution, modification, and testing steps can be changed. Also, the loop may be restored at the end rather than being initialized at the beginning. A programmer will usually choose one of the possible sequences and use it for all his programs in order to avoid having to rethink the procedure each time. Although the examples use register instructions, the same concept applies to storage-to-storage instructions.

ARITHMETIC LOOP MODIFICATION

If the computer being used does not have index registers or if the index registers are not available for some other reason, the arithmetic method is used for producing the modifications necessary to make a loop procedure. The arithmetic method is also useful for understanding the looping technique.

The loop using the arithmetic method will, in general, consist of the following program steps:

STEPS	COMMENTS
1 Initialization	
a Set instructions to be modified to initial condition.	This assures a proper start and allows program to be rerun without reloading.
b Define increment constant and termination constant.	The increment constant will be used for modifying the instruction. The termination constant, in the form the instruction will have when the last data word has been processed, is used to determine when the loop should be terminated, i.e., when the modified instruction is greater than (or equal to, depending on logic of loop) the termination constant.
c Zero out location used for operations having an "add to previous contents" logic.	The necessity for this step is explained later in chapter.
2 Execution	The instruction as modified is executed.
3 Modification	An instruction sequence is written to add a constant to the address portion of the instructions being modified and store the modified instructions back in their storage locations.
4 Test for termination	
a Make comparison.	The test consists of comparing the instruction, as modified, with a constant which is in a form equal to the form the modified instruction will have when it has been modified for the last time.
b Branch back to execution instructions or go out of loop to next program segment, depending on results of test.	Control should loop back to the execution instructions until the test indicates the termination has been reached.

The form of the termination constant and the condition (equal, greater than, less than, etc.) on which branching occurs must be planned with care. Otherwise, it is possible that the loop may terminate too soon or may execute an extra number of iterations.

Clearing (putting zeros into) the register or storage locations used as the accumulator is necessary whenever the loop has an "add to accumulator" form. This form is used when members are to be summed without loading (moving) the first number into the summing register or location. The result will not be correct unless the accumulator is first set to zero. This is analogous to clearing an adding machine by totaling before beginning to add a new set of numbers. An example will illustrate this concept.

Assuming that the quantities to be added are stored in locations 1000 through 1099, that the add instruction has a machine-language operation code of 70, and that parentheses indicate the contents of the location specified inside the parentheses, the form of the instruction and the contents of the accumulator are as follows:

NUMBER OF TIMES THROUGH LOOP	FORM OF INSTRUCTION BEFORE EXECUTION	CONTENTS OF ACCUMULATOR BEFORE EXECUTION
	Op. address	
0	701000	Zeros
1	701001	(1000)
2	701002	(1000) + (1001)
3	701003	(1000) + (1001) + (1002)
.	. . . . . .	. . . .
.	. . . . . .	. . . .
.	. . . . . .	. . . .
99	701099	(1000) + (1001) + . . . + (1098)
100	701100	(1000) + (1001) + . . . + (1099)

Note that the loop should terminate before executing 701100, because the last data word is in 1099. This would indicate that the test for termination should branch out of the loop after the instruction is modified to 701100 but before it is executed.

INDEX REGISTER LOOP MODIFICATION

It is difficult in a few simple examples to convey the usefulness of index registers in loop modification. In the simplest case, the difference between the two forms may not appear too great. In more complex loops, the index register approach has substantial advantages. Suppose, for example, that the execution steps in a loop require 150 instructions and that 40 of these refer to storage addresses which must be incremented. Using the arithmetic method, there would have to be 40 separate modification procedures for 40 separate instructions to be modified. If it required three instructions to complete an arithmetic modification, the modification procedure, not including initializing and testing, would require 120 instructions. Using the index register method, each of the instructions to be modified is given a code which indicates that the operand address is to be modified by the contents of an index register. In order to modify the entire sequence, all that is necessary is to change the contents of the referenced index register. This involves a single instruction.

The program steps in a loop using register modification are:

1 Initialization
   a Set index register to initial value, such as 0 or 1.
   b Clear accumulator locations if add-to-accumulator logic is used.
2 Execution
   Instructions to be modified are coded with the number of the index register to be used.
3 Increment index register
4 Test index register to see if the loop has been executed the required number of times.

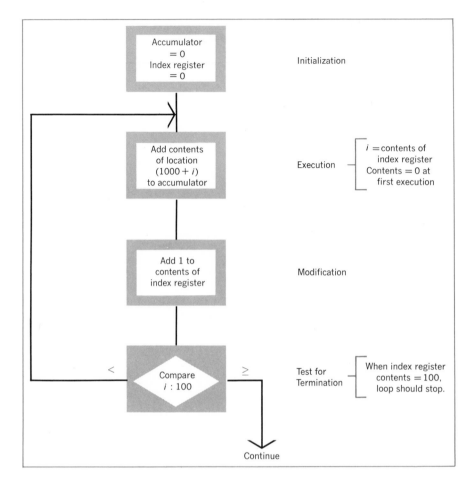

Many computers have special instructions to facilitate the increment and text steps. A single instruction may increment and test. If the test indicates the loop is to continue, control branches to the execution instructions; if the looping is completed, control transfers to the instruction following the loop. Figure 12–1 shows a flowchart for index register modification for the problem of summing 100 numbers stored in locations 1000 to 1099.

SELF-TESTING QUIZ 12–2

1 Draw a flowchart for a loop to tally the number of quantities stored in a table which are over 100.00. The table contains 90 quantities stored in locations TABLE1 to TABLE1 + 89. Use the arithmetic method. Symbolic location TALLY will be used to hold the result.

2 Draw a flowchart for question 1, but using the index register method.

3 How would it change the loop in question 1 if the test for termination were written before the modification? Is this acceptable?

▌ SWITCHES IN PROGRAMMING

There are two types of switches in programming: (1) hardware switches, which may be sensed by a program instruction, and (2) programmed switches, which provide for delayed transfer of control.

HARDWARE SWITCHES

Some computers have external switches (toggle or other type) on the CPU control panel which are set by the operator and whose position may be sensed by a program instruction. Often termed "sense switches," they may be used as a method of selecting a program option at the time the program is to be executed. For example, a program to prepare a payroll may be programmed to print out a separate special analysis following the preparation of the payroll checks only if sense switch 2 is set "on." If the analysis is desired, the operator is instructed to set the switch on; otherwise it is set off and the analysis is not printed.

PROGRAMMED SWITCHES

A programmed switch is a technique for programming a delayed transfer of control. When an analysis at one point in a program establishes the branching that is to take place later in the program, the programmed switch may be used to handle the delayed selection. In some cases, the original test can be repeated, but it may be more efficient to use a switch technique. In other cases, the original information is no longer available. Several techniques may be used, and some computers have instructions which facilitate programming switches. Some of these techniques are:

1 Current modification of the operation code or address of an instruction to be executed later. For example, modifying an operation code to the code for "no operation" will cause the instruction to be skipped; changing to another operation code will cause an operation to be performed.
2 Loading a factor into an index register which is used to modify a later sequence.
3 Setting an indicator or storing a constant in a storage location, the value of indicator or constant to be tested with a compare instruction later in the program.

A single example (Figure 12–2) will illustrate the switch concept in programming. Records containing the physical characteristics of a sample of American males over 21 years of age are processed. At one step in the processing, it is necessary to find out which height class the man is in. Later in the program the records of all men with heights between 6 ft and 6 ft 1 in. or 5 ft and 5 ft 1 in. are to be written on a magnetic tape. During the height determination process, a switch is set which will cause the

276

FIGURE 12-2 Illustration of use of programmed switch

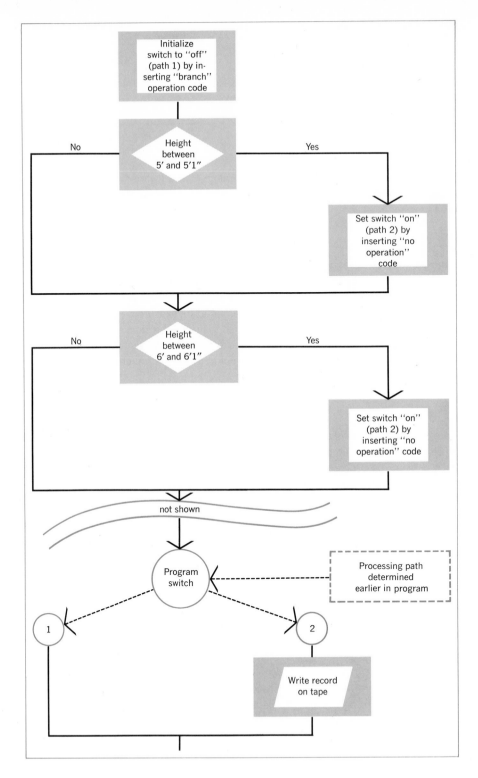

program to branch to a write tape sequence if the man is in one of the specified height classes. The setting of the switch may use any of the techniques mentioned; assume that it uses an operation code modification. Setting the switch to an initial "off" position (path 1) is performed by inserting a "branch" operation code to branch around the write tape instruction. Setting the switch to the write position involves the replacing of the branch instruction code with the code for "no operation," which means the program will not branch and will therefore write the record on tape (path 2).

▌ TABLE LOOK-UP

There are many processing problems in which a data item or other factor to be used in processing must be obtained from a table in storage. There are many methods of table look-up, but the essence of these methods is to operate upon a given input data item in order to establish a correspondence between the data and the address of the memory location needed for processing. In direct address table look-up, for example, a base address plus some element from the data gives the address of the item to be obtained from the table.

An example of direct address table look-up is the computation of a payroll in which there is a shift pay differential for the different shifts. To determine the shift differential it is necessary to multiply the pay before the shift differential by the shift differential percentage. If the shift differential percentages are stored in a table with addresses such as the following, a simple look-up procedure can be used. Note that the percentage is stored in location (3070 + the shift number). In order to obtain the address of the factor from the table, the shift number is added to a base address of 3070.

SHIFT WORKED	MEMORY LOCATION OF SHIFT PERCENTAGE
1	3071
2	3072
3	3073
4	3074
5	3075

▌ INDIRECT ADDRESSING

Up to this point, an effective address (i.e., the address after modification) represents the address to be referenced. This addressing is direct. In indirect addressing, the effective address refers not to the address of the operand but to an address whose contents are the operand address. To illustrate, assume that location 3458 contains

004762, then direct and indirect addressing will be interpreted as follows for an "add to accumulator register" instruction, ADD 3458.

DIRECT ADDRESSING	INDIRECT ADDRESSING
"ADD 3458" means to add the quantity found at location 3458 (i.e., 004762) to the contents of the accumulator register.	"ADD 3458" means to ADD the quantity found at the location specified by the contents of 3458. In other words, the instruction to be executed is ADD 4762.

Indirect addressing is not available on all computers. When available, it is implemented by a special code in the instruction. Multilevel indirect addressing is usually possible, i.e., the address referenced by the contents of the first address may also be an indirect address, the contents of that location in turn may be an indirect address, and so on.

The value of indirect addressing lies in the capability for modification of a large number of common address references by a single change. This process may be compared to a person who moves frequently and changes his telephone number. Rather than informing everyone of his new number each time he moves, he has everyone call a single number which has a recorded message specifying his current telephone number. By merely changing the contents of this message, he informs all callers of his altered location. In terms of programming, all sequences of instructions in a program which reference the same, changeable address may be modified by having the instructions reference, with indirect addressing, a location which contains the address to be used.

INSTRUCTIONS
Op. Address

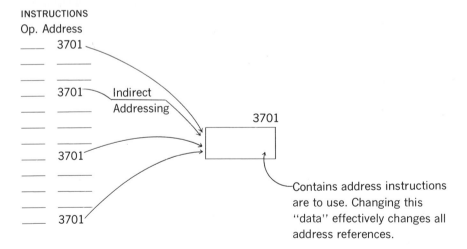

Contains address instructions are to use. Changing this "data" effectively changes all address references.

SELF-TESTING QUIZ 12–3

1   Explain what the switch technique accomplishes in the problem flowcharted in Figure 12–3. The "master" referred to is a master file, and the "detail" is a detail

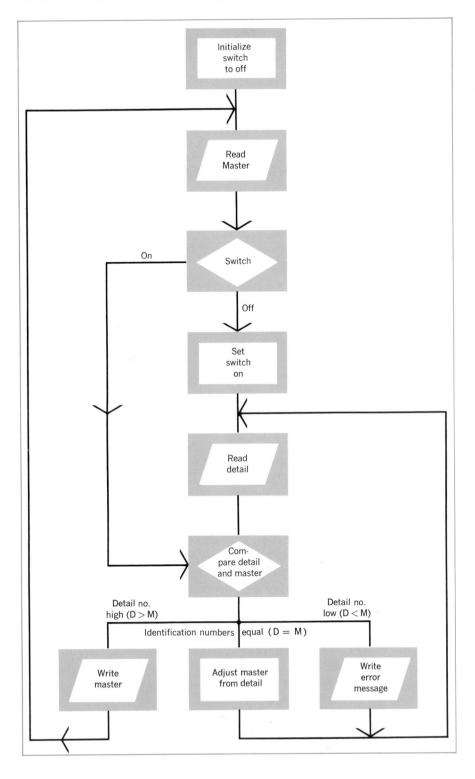

FIGURE 12–3 Flowchart of switch for
Self-testing Quiz 12–3, question 1

file containing transactions to be used to update the corresponding master record. The files are in order by a common field (say, account number). There may be one or more transactions for a single master record, there may be no transactions for a master record, or there may be transactions that do not match (an error condition).

2 What is the effect of the following sequence of instructions if the instructions marked * use indirect addressing? Assume the following contents of storage locations:

STORAGE LOCATION	CONTENTS
3752	3848
3840	3924
3848	3840
3924	1000

INSTRUCTIONS	
LDA* 2, 3752	Load accumulator register
ADD* 2, 3840	Add to accumulator register
ADD 2, 3924	Add to accumulator register
STO* 2, 3848	Store accumulator register

▌SUBROUTINES

Frequently, a mathematical computation such as obtaining a square root or a data processing operation such as sorting a table must be performed at different places in a program. A programming technique which can reduce the number of instructions in the program is the use of subroutines. A subroutine is essentially a program within a program. The main program transfers control to the subroutine, which accepts the necessary data, performs its function, and returns control back to the point in the main program from which it came. A distinction is sometimes made between open and closed subroutines. The open subroutine is essentially a prewritten program segment spliced into and made part of the main program. The closed subroutine, the type usually meant by the term, is written so that it may be used independently by any part of the main program. The closed subroutine is profitably used whenever a set of calculations is required at two or more places in the same program. It also aids in debugging programs by allowing the program to be written in separate modules.

The subroutine is written as a separate program and, if desirable, may be assembled and tested separately. Since the subroutine is to be used by the main program, there must be provisions for transferring control to (entering) the subroutine and for returning to the main program. If the subroutine needs data, there must be a means for identifying its location and results obtained by the subroutine (Figure 12–4). The linkages can be accomplished either by the use of regular instructions or by the use

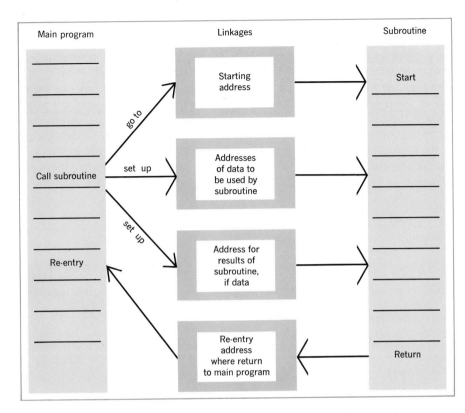

FIGURE 12–4 Linkages in use of subroutines

of special linkage instructions which simplify the programming. There are many variations in technique, and a programmer (or perhaps an entire programming group) will usually settle on a standard technique in order to make it easier to review the coding at a later date. Some possible methods of subroutine linkage are:

LINKAGE REQUIRED	METHOD OF DOING
Transfer from main program to starting address of subroutine.	Use of either a regular branch instruction or a special subroutine branch instruction.
Set up data to be used by subroutine.	Either the data is put into specific registers and storage locations to be referenced by the subroutine, or the addresses where the data is to be found are stored for reference by the subroutine.
Make results for subroutine available to main program.	Either a specific register or storage location is defined for holding the results, or the address to be used is stored for reference by the subroutine.
Set up reentry address to which control should return after the subroutine.	A reentry address is stored in a register or a specified storage location.

In addition to the linkages, it may sometimes be necessary to save (by storing) all register contents before beginning the subroutine and to restore them before re-entry to the main program. The specific method of performing the subroutine linkages is determined by the instructions and features of the computer being programmed and the preferences of the programming installation. In order to get an idea of the possible methods, a simple procedure using index registers will be explained. The main program, when it transfers control, loads an index register with the address of the current instruction (i.e., the transfer instruction). The data for use by the subroutine is located in storage positions following this instruction. The subroutine uses the index register to locate both the data and reentry since these can be defined as the current address in the main program plus 1, 2, 3, etc. locations

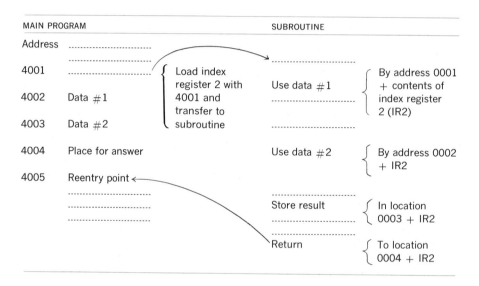

▌ PROGRAM MODIFICATION IN MULTIPROGRAMMING

In multiprogramming, two or more independent programs are handled simultaneously by overlapping or interleaving their execution. Switching from one program to another is usually controlled by the operating system for the computer. This attempts to optimize the overall performance of the computer system in accordance with a set of scheduling rules and the priority of the different jobs. For example, assume that there are four jobs to be run and that three of them fill the available storage. The operating system selects the three programs that will fit in storage, loads them into sections of the main memory, and monitors and controls their execution.

1   Programs 1, 3, and 4 are loaded into storage.

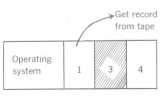

2   Program 1 begins execution.

3   Program 1 must obtain a record from a magnetic tape. While waiting, control is turned over to problem 3 for execution.

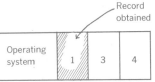

4   Program 3 is interrupted when program obtains record. Execution of 1 continues. Execution continues, shifting between the three programs until one of them (say 3) is completed.

5   Program 2 is put into storage space occupied by program 3.

Note that until the different programs were to be loaded for execution, the exact storage locations to be used were not known. The program must therefore be written so that it can fit any place in storage, and there must be provisions to prevent one program from intruding in the storage allocated to another program.

RELATIVE ADDRESSING AND RELOCATION
A program which may be placed in different sets of locations in storage each time it is executed cannot use absolute addresses such as 4015 because the referenced location may be 4015 one time, 1402 another time, etc. Instead, the program is written in a relative form. The instructions and all storage references are written as if the program started at location zero (0000). Thus the first instruction will be stored at 0000, the second at 0001, etc.

When the program is loaded into storage, the base quantity or starting location (say 2100) is added to every address to locate where it should be stored. All storage references in the instructions themselves must be modified by adding the base quantity to the instructions when they are loaded into storage, or an index register called a base register may be used to modify all instructions by the amount of the base address. Thus an instruction to branch to 0150 and a base address of 2100 will be interpreted as branch to 2250 where the referenced instruction is located.

If two or more programs are in storage at the same time, an incorrect modification by one program may cause it to store data in the set of locations occupied by another program, thereby destroying an instruction or data in the second program. In order to prevent this from happening, computers used in multiprogramming have some method (usually hardware) for memory protection. The typical approach is for each block of data to have a storage key. Each program segment using this block of storage has an instruction which sets an identical storage key. If one of the instructions, after modification, attempted to store outside the boundaries assigned to it, the program key and data block key would not agree, and the instruction would not be executed. Instead, an error condition would be signaled.

PURE PROCEDURES AND REENTRANT SUBROUTINES

If a program is interrupted in order to transfer control to another program, the register contents, etc., can be stored for later restoration when the interrupted program is again worked on. What happens, however, if two or more programs share the same subroutine and, after the first program is interrupted, a second program enters the subroutine? In order for this to work correctly, the subroutine must be written so that it cannot modify the contents of any of its own locations, and the program using the routine must supply any necessary temporary storage. Such subroutines are called pure procedures or reentrant routines. They are very useful in multiprogramming because only one copy of a routine need be in storage regardless of the number of programs which are concurrently using it.

▮ SUMMARY

If all computer programs had to be written in straight-line coding, most programs would have too many instructions to fit in the primary storage. Program modification techniques provide a means for reducing the number of instructions required to code a program.

An instruction can be altered for program modification either by operating upon the instruction as if it were data or by the use of hardware features such as index registers. In index register modification, the operand address of the instruction is modified in the instruction cycle just prior to execution by automatically adding to it the contents of a specified index register. Arithmetic modification can be performed on any computer. Index registers are, on some smaller or older equipment, an extra cost option. They are standard on most newer computers.

The modification techniques discussed in the chapter are looping, switches, table look-up, indirect addressing, and subroutines. Looping is a basic method for handling repetitive computation. Subroutines are useful when a set of instructions must be used by two or more places in the same program. It is a subsidiary program for use by a main program. Switches and table look-up are programming techniques; indirect addressing is a hardware feature which simplifies certain types of program modification.

The problems of programming and program modification in a multiprogramming environment have led to the use of relative addressing, memory protection, and re-entrant subroutines. These features allow a program to be located at any place in storage, to have its execution interleaved with other programs also in storage, and to share subroutines—all without getting the programs mixed up.

▌ ANSWERS TO SELF-TESTING QUIZZES

SELF-TESTING QUIZ 12-1

1 The computer will attempt to use the data as if it were an instruction. This means it will branch to location zero, since 00 in the data word is interpreted as branch and the location address portion of the data word being used as an instruction is zero.

2 The instruction located at NEXT1 will be altered to increase the operand address by 4. If the instruction were A 3, DATAX, it will now be A 3, DATAX + 4. If the operand address in machine code for DATAX were 3792, this address will now be 3796.

3 Either the instruction should be set to its initial form before the second set of uses, or it should be restored to its original form after the sequence requiring the modified use is complete. These both require that the original form of the instruction be stored elsewhere (say in location TEMP) and then the original restored by a sequence such as   L 2, TEMP
                            ST 2, NEXT 1

4 *a* It will execute A 3, TABLE1 (i.e., add contents of location 1936 to register 3).

   b It will execute A 3, TABLE1 + 4 (i.e., add contents of location 1940 to register 3).

   c It is the same A 3, TABLE1 (8) because index register modification occurs during the instruction cycle after the instruction has been copied from storage. The instruction in storage is not affected.

   d By adding 4 to the contents of index register 8, the instruction when executed will automatically execute TABLE1 + 8.

SELF-TESTING QUIZ 12–2

1

Initialization

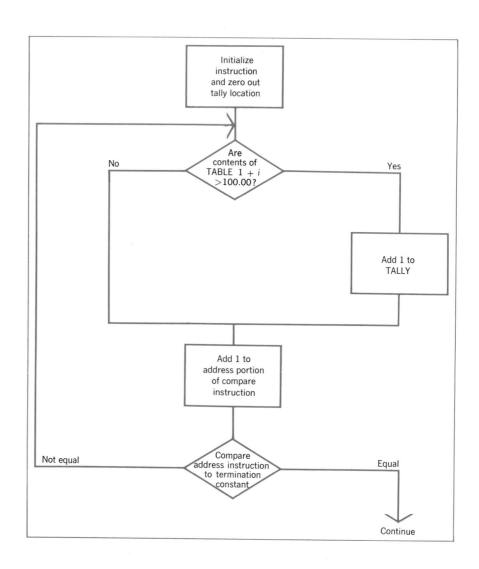

Execution. TABLE1
+ *i* is address,
''*i*'' being the
accumulated
modification.
At first execution
i = O. At second
execution *i* = 1,
etc.

Modification

Test for termination

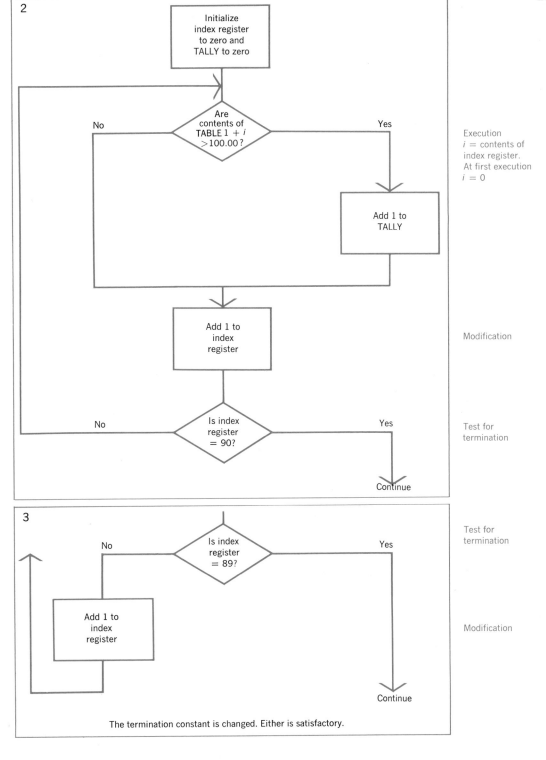

The termination constant is changed. Either is satisfactory.

SELF-TESTING QUIZ 12-3

1   The first master record is read in. A switch was initially set to "off." This causes the program to read a detail record. The identifying field of the detail is compared to the same field on the master. If these are equal, the master is updated and a new detail record is obtained. If this has a higher identification number, there is no more processing on the master and it is written out. A new master record is read. A new detail record is not needed because the last one was not used. The switch which was set "on" after the first master record was read provides for this branching around the "read detail." In other words, the switch allowed the initial master record read to be followed by a detail record read. Thereafter, the master record is compared to the prior detail record already read.

2   (1)   Load contents of 3848   3840
       (2)   Add contents of 3924   1000
                                           ————
                                           4840
       (3)   Add contents of 3924   1000
             (no indirect addressing)
                                           ————
                                           5840
       (4)   Store results in location 3840

EXERCISES

1   What is the difference between straight-line coding and looping with respect to (a) the number of instructions in the coded program and (b) the number of instructions executed to perform the processing?

2   What is the difference between the arithmetic method and the index register method of instruction modification with respect to (a) the form of the instruction in storage and (b) the testing for termination?

3   What difference does it make in the form of the termination test if the test for termination is performed before or after the iteration in a loop?

4   A computer has one instruction to load an index register and a second instruction to increment and compare the contents with a constant. How would these two instructions be used in a loop?

5   What is a switch in programming? How is it used?

6   What conditions must exist for the direct address table look-up method to be used?

7   What is indirect addressing? If location 0704 contains 0800 and location 0705 contains 0704, how is the program segment interpreted (with indirect addressing specified by an asterisk)? (Careful!)

       ADD   0704 *
       ADD   0705 *
       Store   0704
       Branch   0704 *

8 What is the reason for using subroutines?

9 What linkages are necessary between a subroutine and the main program?

10 What is a relative address? Why is it used for programs to be run in multiprogramming mode?

11 What is a reentrant subroutine? Why is it needed in multiprogramming?

12 Assume a computer with several registers used both for accumulation and as index registers and with instructions to:

    a Clear a register [SR register, register (both same)].

    b Add to a register (A register, storage).

    c Increment a register used as an index register (A register, constant in storage).

    d Compare an index register to a constant (C register, constant in storage).

    e Branch if the comparison showed the register contents are less than the constant (BL instruction location).

    f Store a register (ST register, storage).

Write the instruction sequence using index register modification, for adding 100 numbers and storing the result in SUM. Make side notations to explain what each instruction is doing.

▌ OVERVIEW OF INPUT/OUTPUT
INPUT/OUTPUT DEVICES
INPUT/OUTPUT INSTRUCTIONS

▌ TRANSFER OF DATA BETWEEN INPUT/OUTPUT
MEDIA AND THE COMPUTER
THE INPUT/OUTPUT CYCLE
RELEASED CYCLE TIME
BUFFER STORAGE
DATA CHANNELS

▌ INPUT/OUTPUT INSTRUCTIONS
MACHINE-LEVEL INSTRUCTIONS
FILE DEFINITIONS AND MACRO INSTRUCTIONS

▌ PUNCHED CARD INPUT AND OUTPUT
READING CARDS
PUNCHING CARDS

▌ PRINTED OUTPUT

▌ MAGNETIC TAPE INPUT/OUTPUT
THE FUNCTIONING OF THE EQUIPMENT
PROGRAMMING CONSIDERATIONS
EVALUATION OF MAGNETIC TAPE

▌ MAGNETIC DISC INPUT/OUTPUT
THE FUNCTIONING OF THE EQUIPMENT
PROGRAMMING CONSIDERATIONS
EVALUATION OF DISC STORAGE

▌ OTHER INPUT/OUTPUT EQUIPMENT
OPTICAL CHARACTER RECOGNITION EQUIPMENT
MAGNETIC INK CHARACTER READERS
GRAPH PLOTTERS
VISUAL DISPLAYS
AUDIO RESPONSE UNIT
PUNCHED PAPER TAPE

▌ OTHER DEVICES FOR SECONDARY STORAGE
MAGNETIC DRUM
MAGNETIC CARD STORAGE
MASS CORE STORAGE

▌ SUMMARY

▌ EXERCISES

CHAPTER

13

INPUT/
OUTPUT
PROGRAMMING

Up to this point in the text, the instructions have operated on data that is already in the internal memory, and the results of the processing have been stored in main memory storage locations. In data processing applications the data to be processed is rarely all stored in the computer memory at the same time. Usually the data is stored on some auxiliary storage media and read into the main memory when required, and the results of computer processing are either written onto a machine-readable medium (such as magnetic tape) for later use by the computer, or written or displayed in a form that is readable by persons receiving the data. This chapter explains how data is brought into the computer from input media such as punched cards, magnetic tape, magnetic disc, etc., and how data may be written from primary, internal storage onto a medium such as printer output or onto an auxiliary storage file such as magnetic tape or disc. The chapter surveys both the equipment (input/output and secondary storage) and also the programming of the input and output operations.

▌ OVERVIEW OF INPUT/OUTPUT

An input operation begins with a program instruction from the central processor which sends a command to an input device to read a record. Reading takes place by having an input medium (punched card, magnetic tape, etc.) move through the input device. Information is read and converted to the code used by the computer system. The coded information is transmitted to the internal storage and stored in locations assigned to hold the input record. The data is then available for use by the processing instructions.

An output operation is essentially the reverse of the input procedure. The data to be written is arranged by program instructions in storage locations assigned for this purpose. An instruction to perform output causes the data from the output storage locations to be copied and transmitted to the input/output device.

An input or output device is directed by a control unit. The control unit decodes the input/output command from the central processor and effects operation of the device or devices. Other functions are coding, decoding, and checking of data transmitted between the CPU storage and the device.

The connection between the central processor and the control unit is, in most third-generation equipment and much second-generation equipment also, via a channel. The channel is essentially the control unit for one or more input/output device control units. It controls the input/output paths by which data is brought into or out of the primary storage. There may be several channels. The relationship of the central processor, the channel, the control unit, and the device is illustrated in Figure 13–1.

INPUT/OUTPUT DEVICES

The devices for input and output and the media involved are summarized in Table 13–1. The media and devices can be classified into two categories based on their

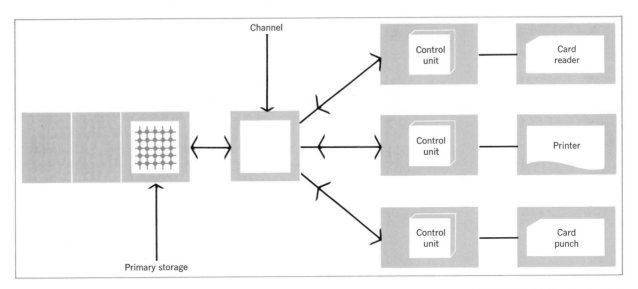

FIGURE 13–1 Relationship of central processor, channel, control unit, and input/output device

orientation: input and output and secondary storage. The input devices read input media which are normally prepared when data is recorded in machine-readable form; the output devices are used for both intermediate and final output. Although some of the output media such as punched cards can be used for auxiliary storage, the trend is toward secondary storage based on magnetic recording. As shown by Table 13–2, the read-write speed of secondary storage devices is on the order of 100 to 10,000 times faster than input/output devices. For individual devices, the speed of the fastest model compared to the slowest is from two to ten times faster.

INPUT/OUTPUT INSTRUCTIONS

Input/output programming ranges considerably in complexity depending on the complexity and versatility of the computer system. Programming may be handled at the symbolic level using three different approaches:

1 Symbolic instructions
2 Macro instructions
3 Input/output control system (IOCS)

The symbolic instruction level of programming is used for simple input/output situations or where the input/output for the computer is quite simple. The latter condition usually applies to computers with restricted input/output capabilities.

The input/output macro reduces the coding requirements. The manufacturer may supply input/output macros with the symbolic assembly system, or the programmer or programming installation may write their own. The programmer writes the macro name and related specifications as a line of coding, and the assembly system inserts a prewritten set of instructions in the program when it is assembled. The macros usually provide for the complete set of instructions to obtain a record from a device and move it into storage or the reverse for output. The macros can be fairly simple or can cover a wide range of input/output control.

The input/output control system (IOCS) is an extension of the macro instruction concept. It was developed to reduce the complexity of input/output programming and at the same time to provide an efficient and well-controlled management of the input/output functions. When using IOCS, the programmer can program as if the input/output records were being read or written one at a time even though they may

TABLE 13-1   Table of Media and Devices for Input/Output

INPUT AND OUTPUT

MEDIA	DEVICE	INPUT	OUTPUT	UNIT OF MEASUREMENT	TYPICAL RATES OF SPEED		
					LOW	MEDIUM	HIGH
Punched cards	Card reader	X		Cards/minute	300	600	1,200
	Card punch		X	Cards/minute	100	300	500
Paper tape	Tape reader	X		Characters/ second	350	500	1,000
	Tape punch		X	Characters/ second	20	100	150
Magnetic ink	Reader	X		Documents/ minute	750	1,200	1,600
Paper	Optical scanner	X		Documents/ minute	100	200	400
	Printer		X	Lines/minute	300	600	1,500
	Typewriter	X	X	Characters/ second	6	8	16
Cathode ray tube	Display	X	X	Characters/ second	250	1,000	10,000

SECONDARY STORAGE

MEDIA	DEVICE	TYPICAL RANGE OF STORAGE CAPACITY	RANGE OF TRANSFER RATES, THOUSANDS OF CHARACTERS PER SECOND
Magnetic tape	Tape drive	1–20 million characters per tape	15–350
Magnetic disc	Disc file	2–20 million characters per pack	100–225
Magnetic drum	Drum storage unit	1–4 million char- acters per high- speed drum	275–1,200
Magnetic strip	Strip storage unit	100–400 million characters per handler	25–45
Magnetic core	Mass core unit	1–2 million characters	250–2,000

TABLE 13-2   Range of Typical Read or Write Speed (in characters per second)

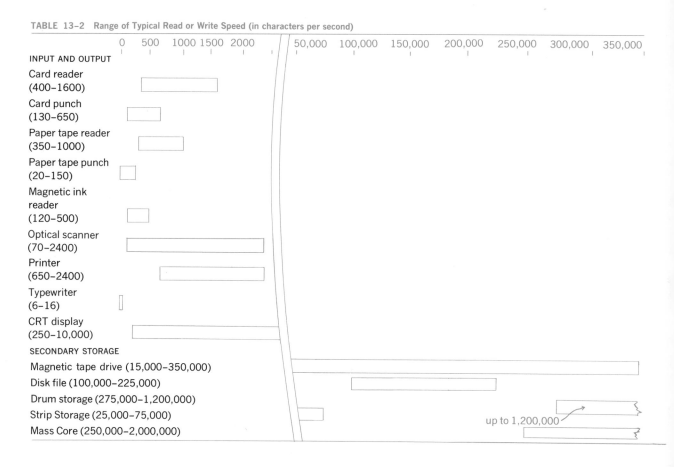

be blocked several records to a block. The IOCS is implemented by the programmer by writing a file definition which provides the IOCS system with the necessary information to function correctly. When a record is needed for processing, the programmer merely writes GET and the file name; when a record is ready to be written, the instruction is PUT file name. In addition to the GET and PUT macros, two macros are used for specifying the operations to get a file ready for use (the OPEN macro) and to terminate the use of a file (the CLOSE macro).

Although more common to card equipment or electronic card processors, there are a few input/output units which are programmed by means of a wired board attached to the unit.

TRANSFER OF DATA BETWEEN INPUT/OUTPUT MEDIA AND THE COMPUTER

The data to be used by a program must be encoded onto a machine-readable file medium such as punched cards, magnetic tape, or magnetic disc. The reading of this data and its transfer into computer memory and the reverse output process are major elements in the data processing cycle.

The input/output device consists of (1) a transport mechanism to hold and move the machine-readable media and (2) a read-write mechanism which reads or writes. The mechanical movements of the media and/or the read-write mechanism put a rather low upper limit on the speed of the devices. To provide a rough understanding of the speed of input/output devices relative to internal processing speed, a high-speed card reader reads at up to 1,200 cards per minute or 20 cards per second. This is one card every 50,000 microseconds. An average medium-size third-generation computer will be able to execute from 5,000 to 10,000 instructions in the same period of time. The efficiency of the system is therefore increased if the input and output operations can be overlapped or performed simultaneously with computation. Following a description of the input/output cycle, three approaches to the handling of input/output will be explained—released cycle time, buffer storage, and data channels.

THE INPUT/OUTPUT CYCLE

The cycle of activity for an input has a sequence approximately as follows (the output cycle is similar):

1 The computer decodes instructions to read contents of one block (also called a physical record), using a specified input device.
2 A signal is sent to the control unit for the device which starts the device in operation. If the device is busy or inoperable, an interrupt or conditional transfer of control is executed (depending on the way the program is written).
3 The device reads the contents of the physical record and encodes it into electrical signals.
4 The control unit codes the data signals and checks them.
5 The data is transmitted to the specified storage locations in main memory, usually via a channel.
6 A signal is transmitted to the central processor that the input operation is completed.

The control over the input/output device may be by a separate control unit (perhaps housed in the cabinet of the device or in a separate cabinet), or the control function, in some small systems, may be part of the central processor operations. The connection or boundary between parts of a data processing system (or between interconnecting systems) is termed an *interface*, and this term is also applied to the connection between an input/output unit and a central processor.

RELEASED CYCLE TIME

A typical data processing procedure consists of three phases—input, processing, and output. Data is read from one or more devices, the data is processed, and the results

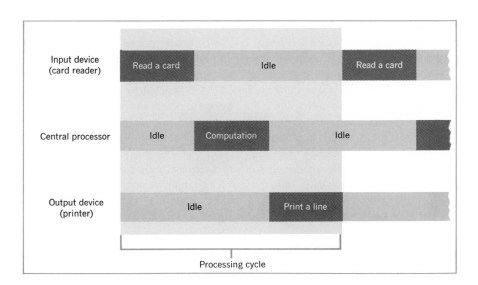

FIGURE 13-2 Processing cycle with no simultaneous operations

are written using one or more output devices. In the absence of any provisions for simultaneous operation of CPU and input/output units, the CPU would be idle a good part of the time (Figure 13–2).

In many small and medium-size second-generation installations, the facilities of the central processor are used for managing the transfer of data between the input/output device and the main storage. This means that after an instruction initiates an input/output operation, the central processor is interlocked, i.e., it cannot be used for any other purposes. Fortunately, the CPU is not interlocked for the entire input/output cycle. When released from the interlocked condition, the computer may perform processing steps (Figure 13–3). To keep the I/O devices operating at top speed, the CPU must, after a specified interval, specify a new input/output instruction. A slight delay in returning may cause a relatively long delay in initiating the next I/O operation and a consequent reduction in device operating speed.

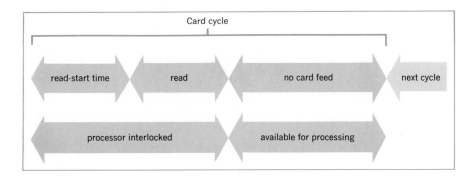

FIGURE 13-3 Diagram of card cycle with only part of cycle available for processing

BUFFER STORAGE

The buffering concept is an important one in computer operations. A buffer is a temporary storage used to compensate for the rather slow rate of operation of the I/O device compared to the high rate of operation of the central processor. In the case of input and output, the buffer is special storage used by the input device to store the data being read and by the output device to obtain the data needed to write an output record. The use of buffers allows the CPU to initiate an I/O instruction (say a read), return to computation, and after a suitable interval, accept from the read buffer the data that has been read during that interval. The transfer of data from buffer storage to main memory is very fast. Several buffers may be used, thereby allowing the simultaneous operation of several input/output devices (Figure 13–4). Buffer memories are typically not addressable except in total and are therefore not available for general use. The amount of data handled is limited to the size of the buffer.

The released cycle time and buffer approaches are based on synchronous operation. The timing of the action of an input/output device is set when the instruction is executed by the central processor. This action will occur in a fixed sequence of time beginning with the instruction cycle. This mode of operation is difficult to use when there are many I/O devices to be operated concurrently. The alternative is asynchronous operation using data channels.

DATA CHANNELS

A data channel is a separate and independent information path. It consists of hardware circuitry which controls the movement of data between the primary storage and the input or output devices. It can be thought of as a separate, small processing unit used only for managing the transfer of data. This transfer of data occurs independently of computing. Each channel has facilities for accepting input/output instructions, addressing I/O devices, obtaining its control information from storage,

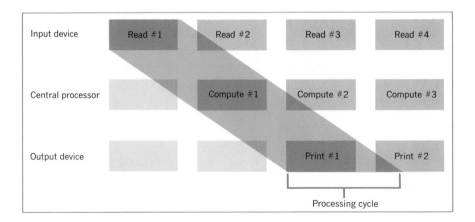

FIGURE 13–4 Processing cycle with simultaneous operations

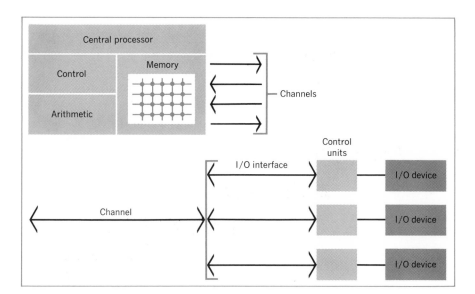

FIGURE 13–5   Use of channels for input and output

directing and buffering information transfer, and similar functions necessary for an orderly transfer of data. Normally the channel is connected not to an input/output device itself but to the control unit which matches the channel interface (connection) to the internal requirements of the device.

The data channel is activated by an input/output instruction which identifies the channel and device. The instruction also identifies the location in storage of a channel command word. There may be one or more of these command words which have been stored for use by the channel. These tell the channel what to do (read, write, control, etc.), and if the command involves a data transfer, the command word specifies the storage locations to receive the input or from which output is to be taken. After the CPU has activated the channel and identified the command word, it is free to continue other processing. Once started, the channel will control the quantity and destination of the data transmitted between main storage and the input/output devices without further supervision by the central processing unit. Several channels may be operating simultaneously because each is an independent unit.

Channels use an interrupt procedure. When the data transfer is complete, the channel interrupts the central processor to indicate completion of the transfer. The channel will also interrupt processing if an error condition is detected in the input/output device or channel. When the interrupt occurs, the central processor halts processing, examines the channel state, takes appropriate action (such as an error-handling routine) if there is an error, or provides a new channel command word if the interrupt signals the completion of the previous command and there is more input/output to be performed. The simultaneous operation of several channels means that there is the possibility of a number of interrupts occurring simultaneously and other conflicts among the channels. These conflicts are handled by a preestab-

FIGURE 13–6   Modes for channel operation

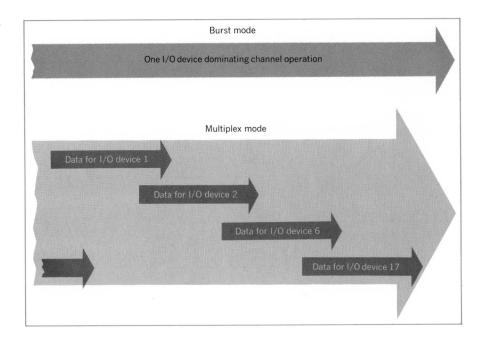

lished priority procedure and the setting up of a waiting line of requests to be serviced.

Although some channels, referred to as selector channels, can service only one device, it is not always necessary to have a separate data channel for each separate device to be operated simultaneously. A high-speed device will monopolize a channel (sometimes termed a ''burst'' mode), but slower devices such as card reader, printer, etc. can share a channel. The shared channel, frequently called a multiplexor channel, has a number of subchannels, each of which can sustain an input/output operation. In this mode, sets of data from several devices are interleaved together in the channel. The channel keeps track of these different segments and sends each to its proper destination.

The number and capacity of channels supplied with a computer are important elements affecting the capabilities of the computer system. The number of channels is important because this determines the number of devices which can be operated simultaneously. The capacity of a channel is significant because some devices provide a very high rate of data transfer (such as a magnetic drum) and therefore need a high-capacity channel.

▌ INPUT/OUTPUT INSTRUCTIONS

The input and output instructions vary in number and complexity for different computers. The trend is to simultaneous input/output using channels; the resulting necessity for a procedure for handling conflicts, assigning channels, servicing interrupts, etc., has led to the extensive use of input/output control systems for managing input/output. Input/output control routines are usually part of the routines under the operating system. When the input/output control system is available, the programmer uses input/output definitions and macro instructions rather than writing a complete set of symbolic, machine-oriented instructions. From the definitions and macros, the assembly routine prepares the necessary machine-level instructions plus the linkages to the I/O control routine.

MACHINE-LEVEL INSTRUCTIONS

The input/output instructions will specify or imply:

1. The input or output command
   a The device to be used
   b Whether read or write
   c Channel to be used
   d The memory locations to be used
2. Control operations such as backspacing, rewinding, positioning
3. Sensing for errors or unusual conditions and transfer to an error routine to handle them

Two sets of machine-level instructions will illustrate the types and forms of typical input/output instructions.

1. IBM 1401 (Preassigned memory locations for read, punch, and print; no channels)

Error condition code for condition being tested (optional) or control information.

Address to branch to if no error code. If error code specified, location to branch to if error is detected (optional).

Operation code to read or write from permanently assigned memory locations using a device specified by the operation code. No channel used. Also used for control operation code.

As an example, "R" means to read a card and transfer its contents into locations 1 to 80 in main storage. These locations are permanently assigned to the card reader.

2. IBM System/360 (channels)

The normal input/output uses a single instruction "Start I/O." This, in turn, refers to a channel address word found in a permanently assigned location. This

Op code

Identifies channel, subchannel, and device

address directs the computer to fetch a channel command word previously stored in memory and provide the word for use by the channel. This command word identifies storage to be used and contains codes to direct the channel to read, write, control, or sense for error conditions. When the I/O operation is terminated, an interrupt occurs and a channel status word containing codes describing the status of the channel is automatically stored in a permanently assigned location where it can be examined for the cause of the interrupt. This sequence means that the channel address word and channel command must be defined and stored prior to the "Start I/O" instruction.

INSTRUCTION WORD	IDENTIFIES
Start I/O	Channel, subchannel, and device
Channel address word	Address of command word
Channel command word	Operation to be performed, address and amount of storage to be used, and action to be taken when transfer completed

Three other instructions are used for special purposes: "Test I/O" to test state of a channel or device, "Halt I/O" to terminate I/O prior to completion, and "Test channel" to test a channel for availability and mode.

FILE DEFINITIONS AND MACRO INSTRUCTIONS

In the input/output control system approach to programming of input and output, each file to be read is described in a file definition. The type of file (input, output, or both), the device to be used, the record form (fixed, blocked, or unblocked), the storage area name, etc. are examples of the information included in the file definition. Figure 13-7 is an example of a file definition for records to be read from punched cards.

The file is opened before use and closed following its last use. A macro "OPEN file name" handles the reading and checking of header labels and performs other checking and housekeeping to get the device on which the file is found ready to operate. The "CLOSE file name" macro performs any housekeeping to terminate the use of a file such as writing trailer labels. Labels will be discussed in further detail in connection with magnetic tape.

A record is obtained from the file by merely writing GET and the file name; a record is written on the file by the macro PUT and the file name. Control is performed by a control macro (commonly CNTRL) which specifies the file name and control codes.

An important distinction in using macro instruction is the difference between a logical record and a physical record. A physical record is the unit read and/or written by the input/output unit. This might be a tape block, a punched card, or a line of printing. A logical record is the record used for data processing; there may be one or more of these on one physical record, or a logical record may require more than one physical record (Figure 13-8).

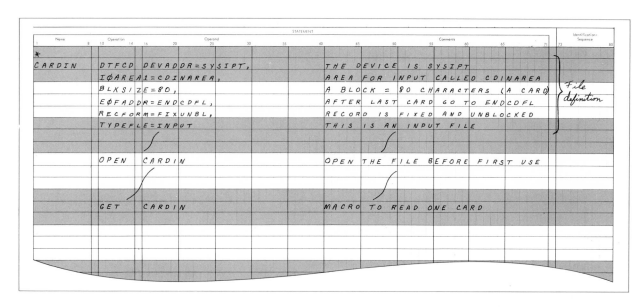

FIGURE 13–7 File definitions for input (IBM System/360)

In using macros for input and output, the input macro makes available one logical record (using one, several, or a part of a physical record), and the output macro puts one logical record into position for the physical record. Suppose, for example, that a physical record, such as magnetic tape, contains ten logical records. The first use of the input macro will cause the reading of the entire block of records and the moving of the first record into position for use by the program. The next use of the GET or READ macro will move the second record into the location where the record is to be used. A second physical record is not read because it is not yet necessary.

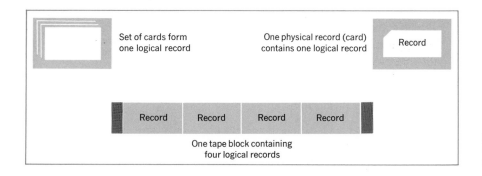

FIGURE 13–8 Three examples of relationships between logical and physical records

In summary, a sequence of macros used for all files (cards, printed output, magnetic tape, etc.) might be as follows:

File definition entries
OPEN file name

Write once before file is used

GET file name

Repeated for each logical record to be obtained

GET file name

PUT file name

Repeated for each logical record to be written

CLOSE file name

After last use of the file

▌ PUNCHED CARD INPUT AND OUTPUT

The most common input medium for introducing data into computer systems is the Hollerith 80-column punched card. Punched card output is used extensively in systems with cards as file storage; for systems having magnetic tape or magnetic disc storage, punched card output is less frequently used. Cards are read by a card reader and punched by a card punch. These two units may be housed in the same or separate cabinets.

READING CARDS

The reading of cards requires the following steps:

1   The cards with data punched in them are placed in the read hopper of the card reader.
2   On a command from the computer, a punched card is moved past two separate sensing stations (although some readers use only one).
3   The configurations of punches and no-punches are read by the two stations and are compared to detect read errors.
4   The configuration of punches and no-punches is converted to internal computer code and transmitted to the computer for storage.
5   The card is deposited in an output stacker.

The reason for two read stations is to detect possible errors in reading. Two error detection approaches are used. In the first, both read stations read the entire contents of the card and the two images are compared (usually automatically) to detect any differences. The second approach uses the first read station to develop a hole count for each column (or row) and the second read station to read the image for transferring to the primary storage. A hole count is also made by the second station and compared automatically with the first hole count. Sometimes only one read station is used, and alternative methods are applied for error detection and control.

Card readers may use two different methods of sensing the existence of punches—wire brushes or photoelectric cells. In the brush-type reader, the card is passed between a wire brush and a metal roller. If there is a punch, the brush makes electrical contact with the roller thereby sensing a punch. The card travels at a predetermined speed so that a single row (or column) is under the brushes at a given point in time. This allows the sensing mechanism to determine exactly the location of a punch which is read. The photoelectric type of reader operates on the same principle as the brush type, except that punches are detected by photoelectric cells activated by light passing through the punches.

In programming the reading of cards, the read-a-card instruction reads one card, translates to computer code, and transfers the card image to a set of locations in storage. Provisions must be made, either by an interrupt system or specific test, to check for off-normal conditions in the equipment or error conditions. Examples of these conditions are read error, input hopper out of cards, full output stacker, card jam, etc.

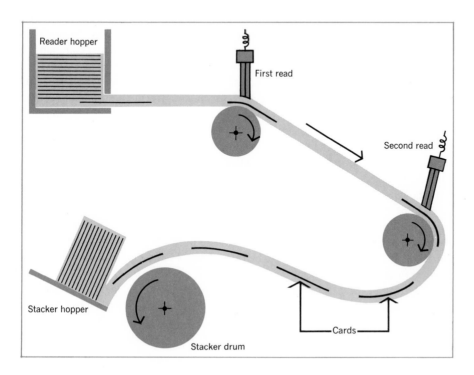

FIGURE 13–9 Card reader mechanism

The punching of cards under computer control requires an online punch. Depending on the model of punch, the unit may punch only in blank cards or may also be programmed to read a previously punched card and then punch additional data in the card.

Most punches punch a row or a column at a time as the card moves under a set of punch dies. Once punched, the card is moved into an output stacker. Card punching is normally much slower than card reading because of the additional mechanical action required.

The programming of card punching involves the preparing of the output characters in a print area of memory. The punch instruction takes the data from the punch area, translates it into external punch codes, moves a card from the input hopper into position, and activates the appropriate punch dies as the card moves under them. The checking of the punched card for erroneous punching may be either programmed or automatically performed by the equipment. Examples of machine error conditions are no cards in input hopper and output stacker full.

▌ PRINTED OUTPUT

There are two types of high-speed printers—impact printers, which print by means of a type bar or wheel pressed against a paper and ribbon, and non-impact printers, which form an image by chemical or photographic means. Almost all printers use the impact approach. There are several different methods in use; the most common are the chain printer and the print drum. In the chain printer, the print characters are mounted on a chain which moves horizontally in front of the paper. The chain may contain several sets of the print characters. As the character to be printed passes in front of each position on the paper where it is to be printed, a magnetically controlled hammer behind the paper presses the paper against the type face to print the character. Moving one character set of the chain past the paper is thus sufficient to print a line. The entire process for printing a line takes from one-fifth to one-twentieth of a second depending on the speed of the printer. The chain is removable, so that more than one type face and set of special characters may be used.

The print drum method uses a metal drum with rows of characters engraved on it. During printing, the drum revolves, moving each row of characters (for example, the row containing A's) past the print hammers. The print hammer for a position is activated when the row of characters to be printed passes and the hammer presses the paper against the drum to print the character.

The vertical spacing of the paper is typically controlled by a plastic or paper loop on the printer. The loop contains several rows or channels. Punches in these columns designate the positioning of the paper. The tape loop control is activated by a character placed in the first position of the print line. This character is sensed (but not

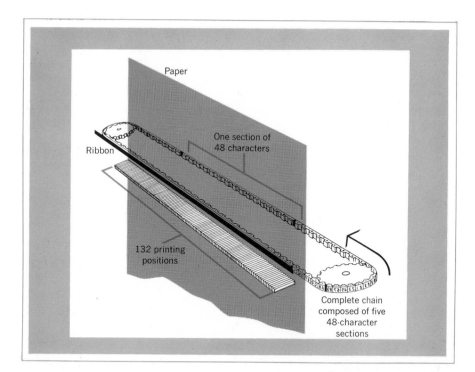

FIGURE 13–10   Print chain

FIGURE 13–11   Print drum (Courtesy of Data Products Corporation)

printed) by the printer, and it activates vertical spacing. The punched tape loop will position the paper at the top of a page and at different vertical positions on the page (required, for example, by a preprinted form). The tape loop is similar in concept to the tab stops for horizontal movement on a typewriter.

The print-a-line instruction causes the contents of the print area in storage to be printed as one line on the paper. This means that the program must have put the data in the print area into the exact form it is to be printed in. The codes for blanks must be inserted for those positions not to be printed and all editing performed. This will include the inserting of dollar signs, periods, commas, suppressing of leading zeros, etc. As with other input/output instructions, the detection of off-normal conditions such as out-of-paper, printer not turned on, etc. must be handled either by an interrupt method or by a conditional transfer of control test.

▍ MAGNETIC TAPE INPUT/OUTPUT

Magnetic tape consists of a plastic base coated with an iron oxide coating. Tape measuring ½ in. wide is most common, but some high-capacity tapes are 1 in. wide. A reel of tape is normally 2,400 ft in length, but smaller sizes are also used. Magnetic tape is very effective and inexpensive storage. A single tape can store several million characters.

THE FUNCTIONING OF THE EQUIPMENT

The recording of data on magnetic tape is similar in concept to a home tape recorder. Writing (recording) on the tape destroys the previous contents; reading (playback) may be repeated, since it does not alter the contents. For data recording purposes, the tape is divided into channels which run parallel to the edge of the tape. A single character (or part of a word) is encoded on a vertical frame or column. A typical seven-channel tape will contain four numeric bit positions, two zone positions, and

FIGURE 13–13 Recording of data on magnetic tape

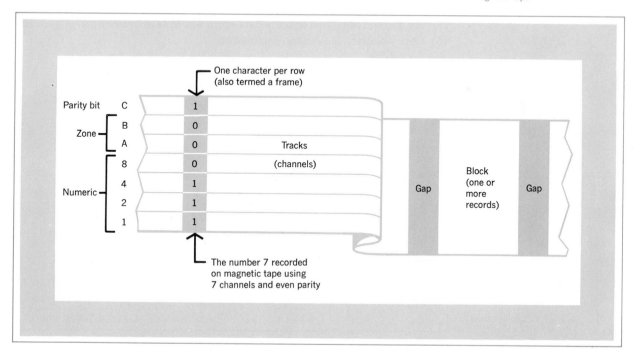

the parity position. A nine-channel tape contains four zone positions instead of two. There is a read-write head for each channel.

The tape density is the number of frames per inch of tape. The most common densities are 200, 556, and 800. The effective transmission rate is the tape speed (36, 75, and 112.5 are common) per second times the density per inch. Increasing the speed and density reduces the time that a frame will be under the read-write head and increases the need for precise positioning and timing. Tapes written on one model of a computer may not be able to be read on another model computer because of difference in channels, density, speed, recording method, etc. Where necessary, special tape-to-tape converters are available to handle this task.

Several methods, all quite similar, are used to drive the tape past the read-write heads and to permit the tape to be started and stopped quickly. A vacuum-operated tape unit is illustrated in Figure 13–14.

The physical beginning and end of a reel of magnetic tape are identified by reflective spots or other markings sensed by photoelectric cells. The one at the front of the tape, the load point (Figure 13–15), provides the positioning point for starting to read the tape. The one at the end of the tape indicates that no further information should be written on it. The end of a file on the tape may be signaled by a special tape mark character written following the last block of data.

The read-write head can be single-gap or two-gap. The two-gap has separate parts of the head (called gaps) to read and write. The advantage of the two-gap head is that data that has been written on the tape by the write gap may be immediately read by the read gap and compared with the data which was to have been written (Figure 13–16). Most tape units use the two-gap method.

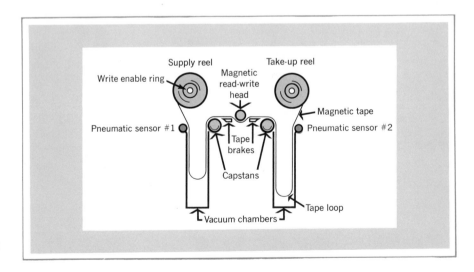

FIGURE 13–14 Vacuum-operated tape unit

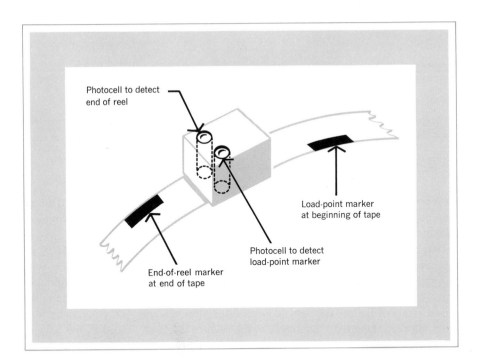

FIGURE 13–15 Photosensing markers for beginning of tape and end of reel

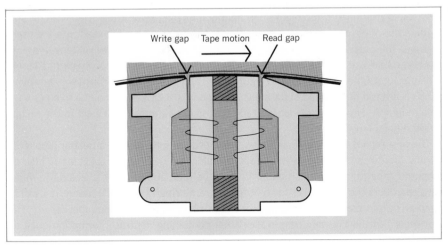

FIGURE 13–16 Two-gap read-write head

PROGRAMMING CONSIDERATIONS

Data records are written on a magnetic tape in a sequence determined by a key associated with each record. This key might be a part number, customer number, em-

FIGURE 13–17 Blocking of records on magnetic tape

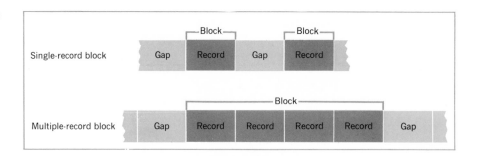

ployee number, etc. There is no tape address. When a record is to be found, the tape records are read sequentially, and the key for the record to be located is compared with the key of each record until there is a match.

Data is physically stored on the tape in blocks. The blocks are separated by an interblock gap (also called an interrecord gap). The most common gap length is ¾ in. The tape drive reads a block when a tape read instruction is given. The interblock gap allows the tape drive to detect the end of the block and also to accelerate to the speed required for reading and to decelerate after reading. Some magnetic tape units will read while the tape moves in the reverse direction as well as the forward direction.

The start and stop time associated with the end of a block means that reading time for a file is shortened if the blocks can be made as long as possible. One limit on size is the amount of memory space available for the block when it is read into the main storage. Although some computers use only fixed block sizes, most tape systems use a variable-size tape block which allows the putting of several records into a single tape block for tape read purposes (Figure 13–17). For processing purposes, however, each record will be handled separately. The records themselves may be fixed or variable in length. For a variable-length record, it is common to use a field in the record to identify its length.

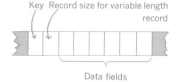

The first record on a file of magnetic tape records is frequently a header label containing identification information about the file. The OPEN macro for input files on magnetic tape will cause this header label to be read and perform checking to make sure the file is the one called for by the program. When the OPEN macro is used to open an output file on magnetic tape, it will write a standard header label record. The last record of the file may be a trailer label containing control information such as record count, control totals, etc.

If input/output macros are used, the macro GET will get one logical record and the PUT macro will store one logical record. If blocking of several records is required, the input/output control system will take care of blocking the records into a physical record and the writing of the physical record. The reverse procedure will be followed on input. If an input/output control system is not used, a tape read instruction will read a physical record into storage, and the write instruction will write the contents

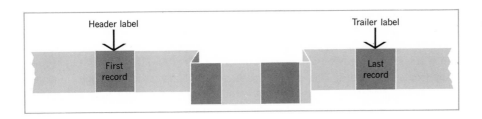

FIGURE 13-18 Use of header and trailer labels

of an area of storage onto magnetic tape. The control instructions for magnetic tape include "backspace" and "rewind." The tape instructions identify the tape drive to be used.

EVALUATION OF MAGNETIC TAPE

The advantages of magnetic tape over punched cards, evidenced by its extensive use in data processing, are as follows:

Speed The transfer of data from magnetic tape to internal memory or from memory to tape is performed at a much higher speed than with punched cards.

Convenience Tape is more compact than cards and easier to handle.

Capacity A single tape can hold several million characters. The equivalent of tens of thousands of punched cards may be stored on a reel of tape.

Low cost A reel of magnetic tape (at about $20) costs less than the punched cards it can replace, and it is reusable.

The major disadvantages of magnetic tape relative to punched cards are that it can be read only by machine (whereas punched cards can be read visually without machine interpretation) and that it is not divisible. When written on magnetic tape, a file of 100 punched cards will require one reel of tape the same size and cost as one used to hold a file of 30,000 cards. An erroneous card can be removed from a file of punched cards and replaced without disturbing the rest of the file. If an error is found in a magnetic tape, the entire reel may need to be rewritten in order to correct a single record. A disadvantage of both punched card and magnetic tape processing is the necessity to access records sequentially since there is no effective means for random access.

When comparing the performance of tape units, the effective speed and capacity of the units depend on a combination of the following operating characteristics:

1 Tape density (characters per inch) ⎫
2 Tape speed (inches per second) ⎬ Define transfer rate
3 Size of interrecord gap   ⎭
4 Start-stop delay time
5 Rewind speed
6 Ability to read or write in both directions

▌ MAGNETIC DISC INPUT/OUTPUT

A magnetic disc unit consists of rotating metal discs on which data may be stored. The disc unit is frequently referred to as random access or direct access storage because any storage position can be read or written directly without having to sequentially locate the record. This direct access, although not strictly random in access time, allows processing to be handled without sorting the input data and without having to process any records not related to the transactions.

THE FUNCTIONING OF THE EQUIPMENT

A magnetic disc file consists of a stack of discs rotating on a common shaft. There are from 5 to 100 discs measuring 1½ to 3 ft in diameter. In appearance, the disc file suggests a stack of phonograph records (Figure 13–19). The disc units may be classed according to the number of read-write heads (or arms) and the removability of the stack of discs as follows:

FIGURE 13–19   Magnetic disc storage (Courtesy of International Business Machines Corporation)

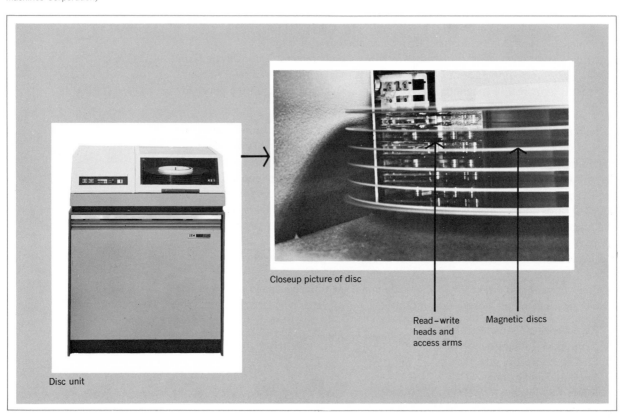

Closeup picture of disc

Read–write heads and access arms

Magnetic discs

Disc unit

1 Heads
   a Moving (single head serves more than one track)
      (1) In one direction (in and out a single disc)
      (2) In two directions (in and out, and up and down the stack)
   b Fixed (head per track)
2 Stack
   a Fixed
   b Removable (disc pack)

The most common method in terms of numbers of units installed is the moving head with one arm per track and a removable disc stack.

The access arm for a disc contains two read-write heads—one for the top and one for the underside of the disc. To read or write a record, an access arm must be positioned on the disc over the location to be used. The arm (if a moving head) moves in and out to locate itself in the correct spot. If there is not an arm for each disc, the arm must move out from the stack of discs, up or down and in on the correct disc. Having more than one arm reduces the average time required to read or write a record since access time depends on how far the arm must move from the previous position and how far the disc face must rotate. A read-write head for each disc means that a cylinder of records extending vertically through the file can be accessed (Figure 13–20). Some disc units are available with a read-write head for each recording track. This arrangement eliminates arm movement altogether. Disc units can have fixed discs or portable, replaceable disc packs. The storage capacity of units varies, but a fixed-disc unit may store several hundred million characters while each re-

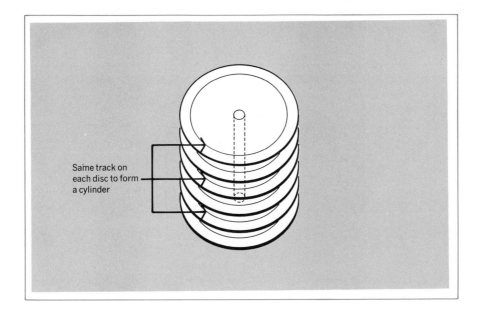

Same track on each disc to form a cylinder

FIGURE 13–20 Accessing of a cylinder using a read-write arm for each disc

placeable disc pack will store in the 2 to 20 million character range. More than one disc unit may be connected to the computer to provide additional direct access storage.

PROGRAMMING CONSIDERATIONS

Storage locations on the magnetic disc have an address. For addressing purposes, the discs are identified by disc face, track on the disc face, and sectors of the track. By means of these three identifiers, each storage segment of the disc has a unique address. This entire segment is usually read or written by a read or write command; alternatively an instruction may read or write an entire track rather than a sector on the track.

A major system design and programming consideration with disc files is the identification of a transaction item with the record on the disc to be used in processing. If, for example, the inventory records are maintained on a disc file, a withdrawal transaction will be used to update the balance-on-hand for the item. This transaction must somehow identify the storage location on the disc where the master inventory record is found. Most transactions carry some identifying number, such as part number, account number, or salesman number, but these do not usually correspond to the disc file addresses. Four different approaches are commonly used to obtain the disc file address when there is a record identification number.

1   Identification number same as disc address. This would be the ideal arrangement, but it can seldom be used because of the difficulty of assigning new numbers, the lack of significance of the number for other purposes, and the problems in reassigning numbers for records dropped from the file (as, for example, when an item is no longer carried in inventory).

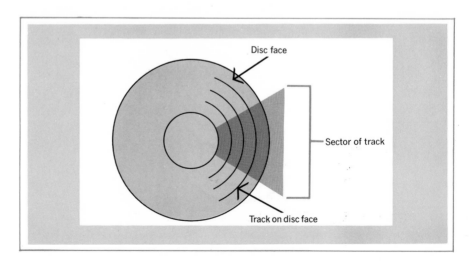

FIGURE 13–21   Disc file address identification

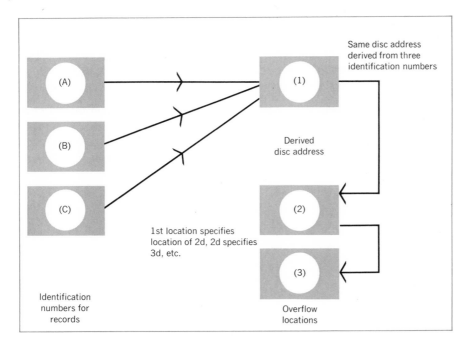

Same disc address derived from three identification numbers

Derived disc address

1st location specifies location of 2d, 2d specifies 3d, etc.

Identification numbers for records

Overflow locations

FIGURE 13–22   One method of using overflow locations in disc addressing

2   Derivation of disc address from arithmetic operations on the identification num- ber. Given an existing numbering system, it is possible to derive a disc file address by performing arithmetic on the identification number. If this method produces cases in which the same disc address is derived from more than one identification number, one of the records may be stored in this position with the other records stored in overflow positions referenced by the first record (Figure 13–22). This means that when a record is sought, it may be necessary to examine more than one before finding the right one. As long as this occurs infrequently, it is not ob- jectionable.

3   Use of an index. An index may be used at various points in the process of obtain- ing a disc address. An index may be used for the entire disc file, for a cylinder, a disc face, or a track. For example, a track number may be derived from the record identification number, and an index stored on the track used to identify the cor- rect sector in the track.

4   Use of disc file address in addition to identification number. This method has the disadvantage of requiring more coding, keypunching, checking, etc. than is nec- essary with a single identifier, but it eliminates derivation or indexing techniques.

The programming of disc file input/output commonly involves the following in- structions:

1   A seek instruction to position the access arm at the proper track before reading or writing.

2   A read instruction to read a record from the disc into an area in the main memory, or a write instruction to write a record from the main memory onto the disc.
3   Instructions for error detection and control. An example of error control instructions is an instruction to read the record just written and to compare with the record as contained in main memory in order to detect any errors in recording.

If the programmer uses macro instructions, these will be similar to those already presented. In addition, the manufacturer will usually provide utility programs to perform disc file maintenance. This includes programs to clear disc storage, to transfer disc storage to or from magnetic tape or punched cards, and to delete obsolete records from the file.

EVALUATION OF DISC STORAGE

A disc file can be used exactly like a magnetic tape having all records in sequence and processing batches in a batch-sequential processing mode. However, the advantage of having files on magnetic disc is that alternative processing modes may also be used which take advantage of the direct access characteristics of the device—the ability to obtain any record directly without reading through the file.

1   Transactions can be processed without sorting.
2   Transactions and inquiries on file status can be processed as they occur in an online realtime mode if the computer system is equipped with hardware and software to support this type of operation.
3   Several different but related disc files may all be stored on disc files, thereby allowing a transaction to be processed against all relevant files at the same time. As an example, when a customer order is processed, the inventory record, the accounts receivable record, and the sales analysis record may all be updated at the same time.

By comparison with magnetic tape, the disadvantages of magnetic disc storage are:

1   Disc files are more expensive than magnetic tape (about twenty times more for removable disc packs having a storage capacity one-fourth as great as a reel of tape up to about the same as a reel of tape).
2   For many applications, sequential batch processing is just as acceptable and perhaps more efficient than direct access processing of batched transactions in random order or of unbatched transactions when they occur. There is, for example, rarely any need to process payroll in random order.
3   In a magnetic tape updating routine, a new tape is created and the old master tape remains unaltered. In direct access processing using a disc, the record is read, updated, and written back on the disc. If there are errors, the processing trail is not as clear as with magnetic tape, and special error detection and error reconstruction provisions must be made.
4   In the event of a system failure, a fixed-disc file cannot be moved. Magnetic tape or removable disc packs may be moved to another location for processing.

▌ OTHER INPUT/OUTPUT EQUIPMENT

The preceding discussion of input/output equipment was not exhaustive, since only the more important input/output devices were described. This section deals with some additional input/output devices which, while less important, are of general interest.

OPTICAL CHARACTER RECOGNITION EQUIPMENT

A device to read numbers and letters directly from a printed, typed, or handwritten document is especially desirable because it removes the requirement for keypunching data. Optical mark readers are a restricted type of optical reader in which the reader senses marks made in designated positions. There are severe difficulties in reading printed characters because of the diversity of printed styles, the differences in quality of printing, etc. Handprinted characters present an even greater diversity for recognition purposes. The technical difficulties are being overcome, and optical readers are becoming an important method for original input of data. Examples of documents to be scanned optically are shown in Figure 13–23.

An optical character reader consists of a document transport, a scanner unit, and a recognition unit. The result of the reading operation is a machine-readable recording on punched cards, magnetic tape, or paper tape, or direct input into the computer (Figure 13–24).

In all optical reading machines, the characters to be read are scanned by some kind of photoelectric device. The photoelectric cells convert the symbols on the document into an analog or digital representation that is analyzed by the recognition unit.

The recognition unit matches patterns from the scanner against internally stored reference patterns. Patterns which cannot be identified cause the document to be rejected. There are a number of different methods for recognition. Some of the more common are:

1. Matrix matching. This method of total character recognition compares individual elements of the scanned character with the elements of all characters which can be identified by the reader. A character is recognized when it matches exactly or quite closely one of the reference patterns. Any type font may be programmed.
2. Feature or stroke analysis. A character is recognized on the basis of the stroke or line formation of each character. The technique requires a special printing font.
3. Curve tracing. Especially suited for recognizing handwritten characters which vary in size and shape, a spiraling spot of light follows the outline of a character. Characters are identified by observations as to vertical lines, horizontal lines, etc.

Reading speeds range from 70 to 2,400 characters per second. Reader reliability is important. Two measures of reliability are the reject and error rates. The reject rate is the percentage of documents (currently running from 2 to 10 percent) which the reader cannot read. The error rate (currently less than 1 percent) is the percentage of documents on which a character has been incorrectly identified.

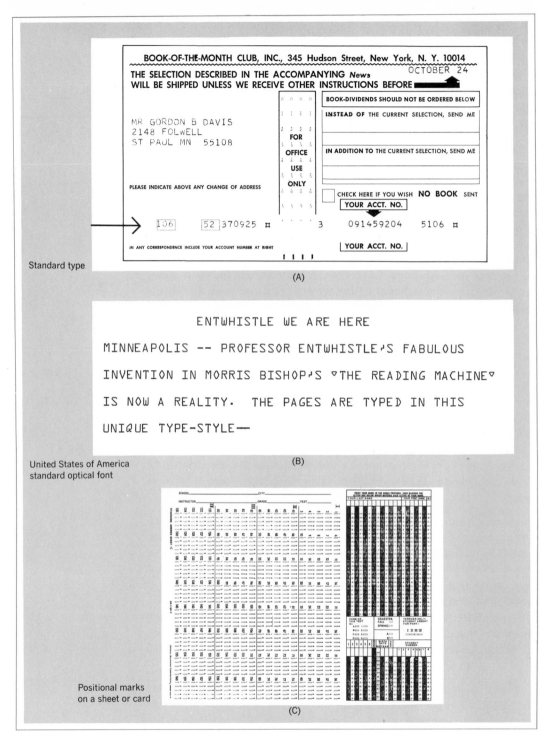

Standard type

(A)

United States of America
standard optical font

(B)

Positional marks
on a sheet or card

(C)

FIGURE 13–23 Documents which can
be read using optical scanning

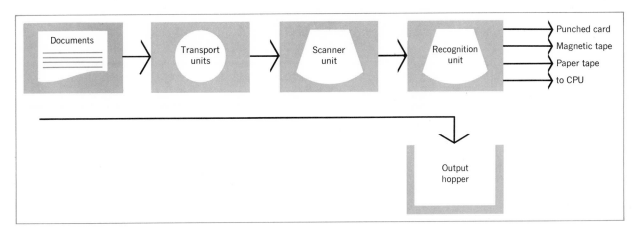

FIGURE 13-24 Elements of an optical character reader

Optical character recognition equipment is sufficiently expensive that an installation must have a volume range of over 10,000 input documents per day (say eight to twelve keypunch operators) before optical character recognition equipment is likely to be economical.

The future of optical recognition appears very promising. Reject rates are expected to be reduced, speeds will certainly increase, and the cost is expected to be reduced.

MAGNETIC INK CHARACTER READERS

The banking industry in the United States has adopted magnetic ink characters as the approach to machine-readable documents. The magnetic ink characters use a standard type form established by the banking community. The standard characters, consisting of numbers plus some special characters, are visually readable by banking personnel. The reader senses the magnetic pattern formed by the characters. A character can be read even if crossed over, creased, or otherwise made illegible for visual reading. An example of this coding is given in Figure 13-25.

GRAPH PLOTTERS

A graph plotter is a device for drawing graphs. Both point plots and smooth graphs are possible. A swimsuit manufacturer, for example, uses the graph plotter to draw different size patterns based on the standard pattern of the swimsuit designer. Figure 13-26 shows the use of the graph plotter for plotting data.

VISUAL DISPLAYS

Data display devices use a cathode ray tube (CRT) to display data in much the same form as on a television tube (Figure 13-27). The advantage of the CRT display is

FIGURE 13–25 Magnetic ink characters on bank check

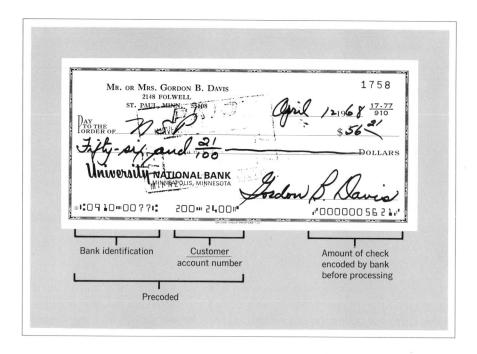

FIGURE 13–25 Magnetic ink characters on bank check

that an entire record can be displayed instantly. A typewriter device, by way of contrast, must type the record a character at a time. CRT data displays are likely to be the dominant device in online systems having remote inquiry stations. Airlines already have made extensive use of them in their online realtime reservation systems.

Display devices may allow input via a keyboard, a light pen, or sensitized points on the tube which the person using the device activates by touching the answer chosen. If a permanent record is required of data displayed on the CRT, a command may be given to write the answer on the printer or other device.

AUDIO RESPONSE UNIT

A stockbroker, wanting the latest quotation for a security listed by the New York Stock Exchange, dials a special code number. The response is immediate as a voice speaks the quotation over the telephone. The entire transaction is handled by a computer using a voice response unit. The computer interprets the input code number, obtains the answer from storage, and transmits the answer to the audio response unit. This unit selects, from a magnetic drum, words and phrases of prerecorded vocabulary which then form a spoken reply. The reply is limited to a relatively small number of words and phrases, but the inquiries and responses can make use of an

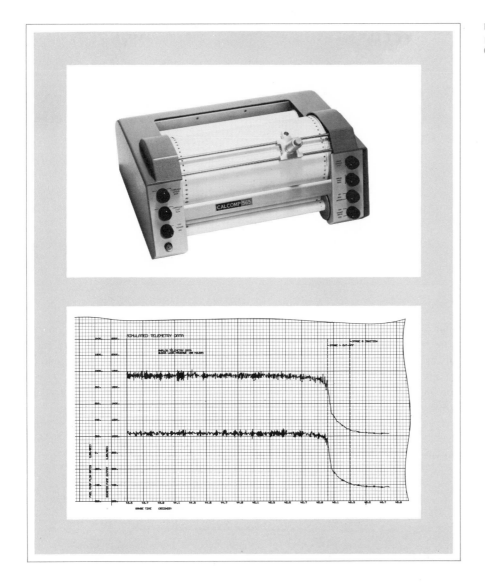

FIGURE 13.26 Graph plotter and output from graph plotter (Courtesy of California Computer Products, Inc.)

ordinary telephone. The response unit is suited for applications such as credit inquiry, inventory status, etc., where the reply can be standardized.

PUNCHED PAPER TAPE

Punched paper tape is a widely used input/output medium for computer systems. It consists of a paper tape punched with 10 characters per inch. Speeds for reading

FIGURE 13–27 Unretouched photo-graph of data display output (Courtesy of Control Data Corporation)

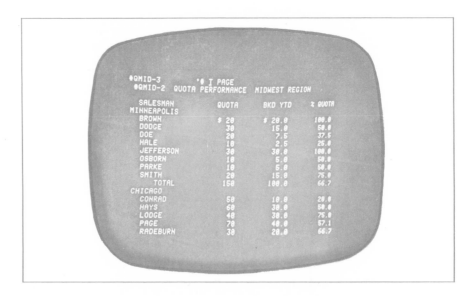

range from 10 to 2,000 characters per second. Both eight-channel and five-channel codes are in use. In concept, it can be thought of as being a continuous punched card. This presents advantages such as the fact that no individual record can be lost or put out of sequence because all are on the continuous tape. However, paper tape is more difficult to correct and is less flexible for sorting, etc. A paper tape is corrected during punching by adding deletion characters and repunching the data.

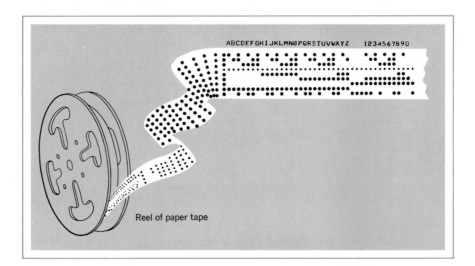

FIGURE 13–28 Punched paper tape using United States of America stand-ard code for information exchange (ASCII)

The paper tape punch is less expensive than a card punch, and it is well adapted as an attachment to business machines to produce a punched paper tape record as a by-product of some other operation such as typing. The paper tape input is frequently transcribed to magnetic tape in a paper tape to magnetic tape run before further processing is performed on the data.

▌ OTHER DEVICES FOR SECONDARY STORAGE

The major devices for input or output with secondary storage are magnetic tape and magnetic discs; others are magnetic drums, magnetic cards, and mass core.

MAGNETIC DRUM

The magnetic drum is similar in concept to a fixed-stack magnetic disc. Read-write heads read or write as the drum revolves at high speed. The advantage of a drum over a disc is generally in access time. This means that drums will tend to be used for high-speed direct access secondary storage and discs will be used for slower speed requirements. However, there are large, slower drums which compete directly with magnetic disc units.

MAGNETIC CARD STORAGE

Known under various trade names such as CRAM (Card Random Access Memory—NCR) and Data Cell (IBM), the magnetic strip or magnetic card storage device is slower than disc storage, but the file device is inexpensive, has large capacity (tens of millions of characters per holder), and allows direct access. Magnetic card storage consists of an oxide-coated plastic strip on which data may be recorded. A number of these strips are mounted in a cartridge holder. On an instruction from the computer, the selected strip drops out of the holder, moves under a read-write head where the selected record is read or written, and then is replaced in the holder. The cartridges are removable in much the same way as a removable disc pack.

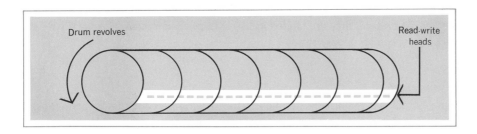

FIGURE 13–29 Operation of drum storage

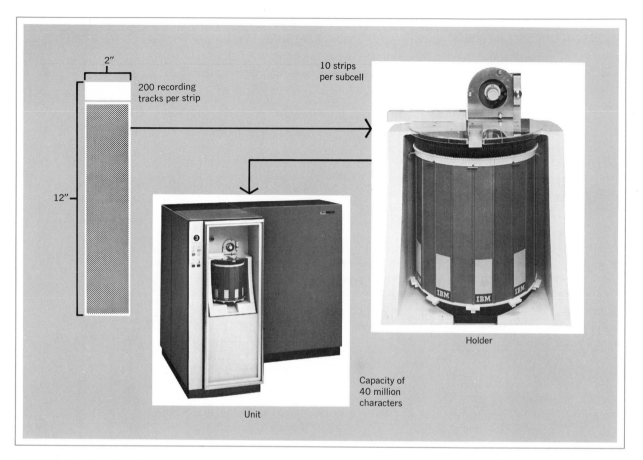

2″

200 recording
tracks per strip

10 strips
per subcell

12″

Holder

Unit

Capacity of
40 million
characters

FIGURE 13–30 Magnetic strip storage—IBM Data Cell (Courtesy of International Business Machines Corporation)

MASS CORE STORAGE

Core storage has many advantages for direct access because there is no movement
of the storage medium, thereby eliminating a major source of operating delay and
difficulty. However, core is much more expensive than other media and has been
restricted to CPU internal memory. Recent developments in fabrication of core storage have resulted in a large-capacity core storage unit designed for use as secondary
storage. At present, they are limited in use to large-scale systems having a need for
very high speed secondary storage.

▌ SUMMARY

Input/output is a major consideration in the design of a computer system. Closely
connected to input/output are the secondary storage devices used by the system.

The type of file device will determine whether processing must be restricted primarily to batch-sequential mode or whether it can also include direct processing of unsequenced or unbatched transactions.

In all but the simplest data processing system, there must be a method for buffering between the input/output unit and the central processor. The most common approach with newer equipment is the data channel. The data channel, operating independently of the central processor, manages the transfer of data between the main storage and the input/output device. The data channel is started by an instruction from the central processor, which then proceeds to other processing steps. When the channel detects an error or when it is through with the transfer, it interrupts the central processor.

The trend in programming for input and output is toward the use of macro instructions. These make use of input/output control routines which manage reading, writing, the handling of interrupts, errors, etc.

The chapter discussed several devices in some detail—card reader and punch, line printer, magnetic tape unit, and disc file. These devices represent the major input/output and secondary storage equipment. Other input/output and secondary storage devices were discussed in less detail.

▌ EXERCISES

1 Define each of the following terms:

    a File   *d* Item

    b Record   *e* Logical record

    c Field   *f* Physical record

2 Arrange the following list of devices in order by access speed (use maximum speeds for ordering purposes):

    a Card reader   *f* Magnetic card

    b Magnetic tape drive   *g* Paper tape reader

    c Printer   *h* Card punch

    d Magnetic ink character reader   *i* Optical scanner

    e Magnetic drum

3 Arrange the following list of online file storage devices in order by storage capacity (use top figure in typical range):

    a Fixed-stack disc file

    b Magnetic drum

    c Magnetic card

    d Removable-stack disc file

    e Mass core unit

4 Fill in the following table:

ALTERNATIVE DESIGNS OR METHODS (some entries may be blank)

ITEM		1	2	3	4
a	Methods for simultaneous operation of I/O device and CPU				
b	Obtaining disc file address for an item				
c	Printer mechanism				
d	Sensing of punches on card reader				
e	Methods of optical character recognition				

5   Define each of the following terms:
   a   Interface
   b   Data channel
   c   Interrupt
   d   Recording channel

6   Define or explain the following with respect to magnetic tape processing:

   a   Load point   *f*   Density
   b   Interrecord or interblock gap   *g*   Speed
   c   Blocking   *s*   Transfer rate
   d   Header label   *i*   Two-gap head
   e   Trailer label

7   What types of storage devices are likely to be used under the following circumstances?
   a   A small retailer using punched card billing forms.
   b   A manufacturer interested in up-to-the-minute inventory status information.
   c   A large credit-granting agency with need for rapid access for active accounts and slower speed access to other accounts.
   d   A large retailer sending out bills monthly.

8   What do the following letters, abbreviations, or acronyms stand for?
   a   IOCS   *c*   MICR
   b   OCR   *d*   I/O

9   Explain the following with respect to disc file processing:
   a   Track   *d*   Cylinder
   b   Sector   *e*   Index
   c   Face   *f*   Stack

10   Explain how a disc may be used for sequential batch processing using a sequenced master file on disc and a sequenced transaction file on punched cards.

11   Explain how a disc address might be obtained for accessing employees' records stored on a disc file. There are 5,000 employees.

12 Under each of the following situations, what will be the effect of a GET macro when there is an input/output control system and the file definition is appropriate to the situation?

  a Transaction data is to be read, one transaction per card.

  b Records are on magnetic tape, five to a block.

13 What is the purpose of the OPEN and CLOSE macros?

■PROGRAM COMPILERS
ELEMENTS OF A COMPILER SYSTEM
USING A PROCEDURE-ORIENTED LANGUAGE
EVALUATION OF PROCEDURE-ORIENTED LANGUAGES

■THE COBOL LANGUAGE
OVERVIEW OF COBOL
COBOL IDENTIFICATION DIVISION
COBOL ENVIRONMENT DIVISION
COBOL DATA DIVISION
COBOL PROCEDURE DIVISION
EVALUATION OF COBOL
SELF-TESTING QUIZ 14–1

■THE FORTRAN LANGUAGE
OVERVIEW OF FORTRAN
ARITHMETIC ASSIGNMENT
FORTRAN INPUT-OUTPUT
SPECIFICATION STATEMENTS
CONTROL STATEMENTS
SUBPROGRAM STATEMENTS
EVALUATION OF FORTRAN
SELF-TESTING QUIZ 14–2

■THE PL/I LANGUAGE
OVERVIEW OF PL/I
EVALUATION OF PL/I
SELF-TESTING QUIZ 14–3

■REPORT PROGRAM GENERATOR
OVERVIEW
SAMPLE PROGRAM IN RPG
EVALUATION OF RPG

■OTHER PROCEDURE- AND PROBLEM-ORIENTED
LANGUAGES
ALGOL
BASIC
JOVIAL
APT
SIMULATION LANGUAGES

■SUMMARY

■ANSWERS TO SELF-TESTING QUIZZES
SELF-TESTING QUIZ 14–1
SELF-TESTING QUIZ 14–2
SELF-TESTING QUIZ 14–3

■EXERCISES

CHAPTER

14

PROCEDURE-
AND
PROBLEM-
ORIENTED
LANGUAGES

Procedure- and problem-oriented languages, user-oriented and largely machine-independent, are also referred to as higher-order languages. Rather than having the programmer adapt himself to the individual computer, these languages adapt the computer to the programmer. The coding rules are designed to assist the programmer to define the computer processing to be performed. The translation of this coding into a machine-language program is performed by a set of routines called a compiler.

Higher-order languages can be divided into types—procedure-oriented and problem-oriented, although this distinction is not always maintained and both types are often referred to as problem-oriented languages or by the abbreviation POL. When used precisely, procedure-oriented refers to a language with which the programmer describes the set of procedures by which the problem is solved. Examples of these languages are COBOL, FORTRAN, and PL/I. With the problem-oriented language, the programmer uses the language to describe the problem itself and the compiler translates this description into suitable computational procedures. Examples are report program generators and simulation compilers.

There are many different compiler languages. Each language consists of a set of allowable words and symbols and a set of rules for using this vocabulary to define problems or problem-solving procedures. Some of the common languages with their acronyms are:

ACRONYM	MEANING OR TYPE OF ORIENTATION
COBOL	Common Business-oriented Language
FORTRAN	Formula Translator
PL/I	Programming Language, version one
ALGOL	Algorithmic Language
MAD	Michigan Algorithmic Dialect
JOVIAL	Jules Own Version of the International Algebraic Language
BASIC	Beginner's All-purpose Symbolic Instruction Code
LISP	List Processor
APT	Automatically Programmed Tooling

The purposes of this chapter are (1) to acquaint the reader with the major languages so that a program written in one of them can be recognized and (2) to provide a feel for the use to which each language is best suited and for its advantages and disadvantages.

PROGRAM COMPILERS

A POL language is designed for the programmer. Some of them are suited for relatively untrained persons programming for their own problems; others are primarily for professional programmers. In both cases, the programmer writes programs with little or no awareness of the specific equipment on which the problem will be run. The languages, as far as the programmer is concerned, are machine-independent. This is not completely true, because what the programmer wishes to do may be dependent on the availability of storage, I/O units, etc., but, in general, the concept is for machine-independent programming. The same POL program may therefore be compiled and run on different computer systems with little or no change in the program. A separate compiler, written especially for each of the computers, is required. Compilers for the major languages are usually furnished by the manufacturer as part of the software support for the computer. Compilers take up a fair amount of storage, and therefore a small, minimum-memory-size computer may not be able to use a compiler. Some manufacturers provide different compilers with a range of levels of sophistication for use by different memory size configurations.

ELEMENTS OF A COMPILER SYSTEM

To implement a language using the compiler concept requires three elements—specifications for the language; a translator routine to interpret statements written in the language and convert them to appropriate machine language instructions; and a library of subroutines which these instructions can call upon.

The source program, written in specific language, must follow the rules for that language. These rules specify the form, structure, and terms used in writing instructions. Certain words, called reserved words, have precisely defined meanings when used in source program statements. These words cannot be used for any other purpose or the statements will be misinterpreted. The specifications essentially describe a limited-purpose language. Learning such a language can be compared to learning a foreign language. One has to learn both reserved words and symbols, which are like a foreign language vocabulary, rules of grammar for using the vocabulary, and punctuation symbols to produce statements. In addition to reserved words and symbols, the language provides for names chosen by the programmer to designate input data items, results obtained during processing, etc.

The use of language specifications is illustrated by the following statements using two common procedure-oriented languages to specify the computation $x = a - b - c$.

LANGUAGE	STATEMENT
FORTRAN	$X = A - B - C$
COBOL	SUBTRACT B AND C FROM A GIVING X.

In both cases, X, A, B, and C are names assigned by the programmer. In the FORTRAN statements the minus sign is interpreted by the translator program as meaning subtraction. In the COBOL statement, the words SUBTRACT, AND, FROM, and GIVING have specified meanings the same or similar to those associated with the terms in ordinary English.

The translator, sometimes called the processor, is a computer program which reads the source language statements one at a time and prepares a number of machine language instructions to perform the operations specified or implied by each source statement. Typically the preparation of a set of instructions does not involve the compiler writing all of the required machine-level steps. In many cases, the compiler merely writes linkage instructions so that the object program can make use of subroutines provided by the compiler library of subroutines. For example, a FORTRAN statement to solve the problem $x = \sqrt{y}$ is written as X = SQRT(Y). The translator interprets the different symbols and letters and then generates instructions to obtain the value of a variable designated by Y from a storage location, to transfer this value to a subroutine which calculates the square root, to return control back to the main program and to store the results of the square root computation in a memory location associated with the variable name X.

The prewritten subroutines are contained in the compiler library. The object language statements generated by the computer are an incomplete program until they are combined with the appropriate routines from the library. Two approaches are used. In one method, all subroutines needed by the object program are written out with the rest of the object program. In the other approach, the library routines are added when the object program which includes the subroutine linkages is loaded for execution.

The process of translating a source statement so as to compile a program requires that the computer program identify:

1 The memory location associated with each quantity used in the program
2 The operations to be performed
3 The proper order for processing

The translator keeps a table for identifying names which refer to quantities and the memory locations associated with them, and a table of reserved words and symbols. The computer can compare each symbol, name, or other word in a source statement with those in the table and thereby identify its meaning. The proper order of processing is specified by the rules of the language.

The design of a translator routine will vary with the computer on which it will be used. A typical sequence of actions a translator routine might follow are:

1 The source statement is read character by character until a complete variable name, reserved word, or operation symbol has been detected.
2 A comparison is made of the variable name, reserved word, or operation symbol with tables of these symbols until an identification is made.
3 The combination of variable names and operation identifiers is translated into an ordered sequence of actions based on the order rules of the language and the form of the statement.
4 The translator writes the machine language statements onto the output medium to be used. The instructions are either operating instructions or linkages to subroutines.

As an example, suppose that the translator reads a statement such as X = A + B − 3.5, the translator compares "X" with a list of identifiers and finds that X has been assigned to a location such as 3407 so it sets up the final instruction as a "store result in location 3407." The locations for A and B are found from the same list as being perhaps 3804 and 3812. A value of 3.5 is stored in a table of constants to be used by the program, say in location 2412. The translator also identifies the plus and minus by comparing these characters to a list in storage. The compiler now constructs a sequence of instructions to:

1   Add contents of locations 3804 and 3812 and hold result in a temporary location
2   Subtract contents of location 2412 from temporary location used to store A + B
3   Store result of step 2 in location 3407

These three steps may involve many instructions because of scaling considerations, error checking, etc.

USING A PROCEDURE-ORIENTED LANGUAGE

In Chapter 8, the steps in preparing a computer program were defined as:

1   System design
2   Planning the program
3   Coding
4   Translation (assembly or compilation)
5   Debugging
6   Documentation

The use of a higher-order language affects the performance of all steps except system design. The entire process of using a procedure-oriented language is summarized in Figure 14–1.

After the problem has been defined and the system designed, the next step is the preparation of a description of the computer procedures required to perform the required processing. A program flowchart is usually the most convenient method of preparing this description. The program flowchart is prepared in the same way as for a symbolic language program, except that less detail may be required for describing higher-order program steps.

The program preparation activity continues with the coding of the logic described in the flowchart into procedure-oriented statements in the language being used. These are usually written on coding paper designed for the particular language (Figure 14–2). These source language statements are keypunched into punched cards, one line of coding into a card. The resulting deck of punched cards forms the source program deck.

The translation phase begins with the loading of the translator routine of the compiler into the computer memory. This routine reads the source program cards, interprets their meaning, and produces an object program on some machine-readable output medium such as punched cards, magnetic tape, or magnetic disc. A listing of the

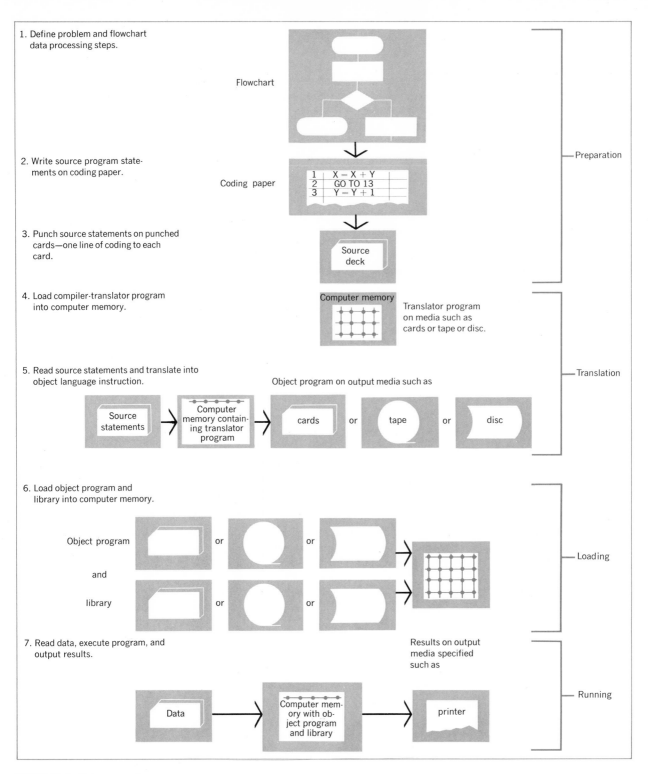

1. Define problem and flowchart data processing steps.

Flowchart

2. Write source program statements on coding paper.

Coding paper

1	X = X + Y
2	GO TO 13
3	Y = Y + 1

3. Punch source statements on punched cards—one line of coding to each card.

Source deck

4. Load compiler-translator program into computer memory.

Computer memory

Translator program on media such as cards or tape or disc.

5. Read source statements and translate into object language instruction.

Object program on output media such as

Source statements → Computer memory containing translator program → cards or tape or disc

6. Load object program and library into computer memory.

Object program or or

and

library or or

7. Read data, execute program, and output results.

Results on output media specified such as

Data → Computer memory with object program and library → printer

Preparation

Translation

Loading

Running

FIGURE 14–1   Using a compiler

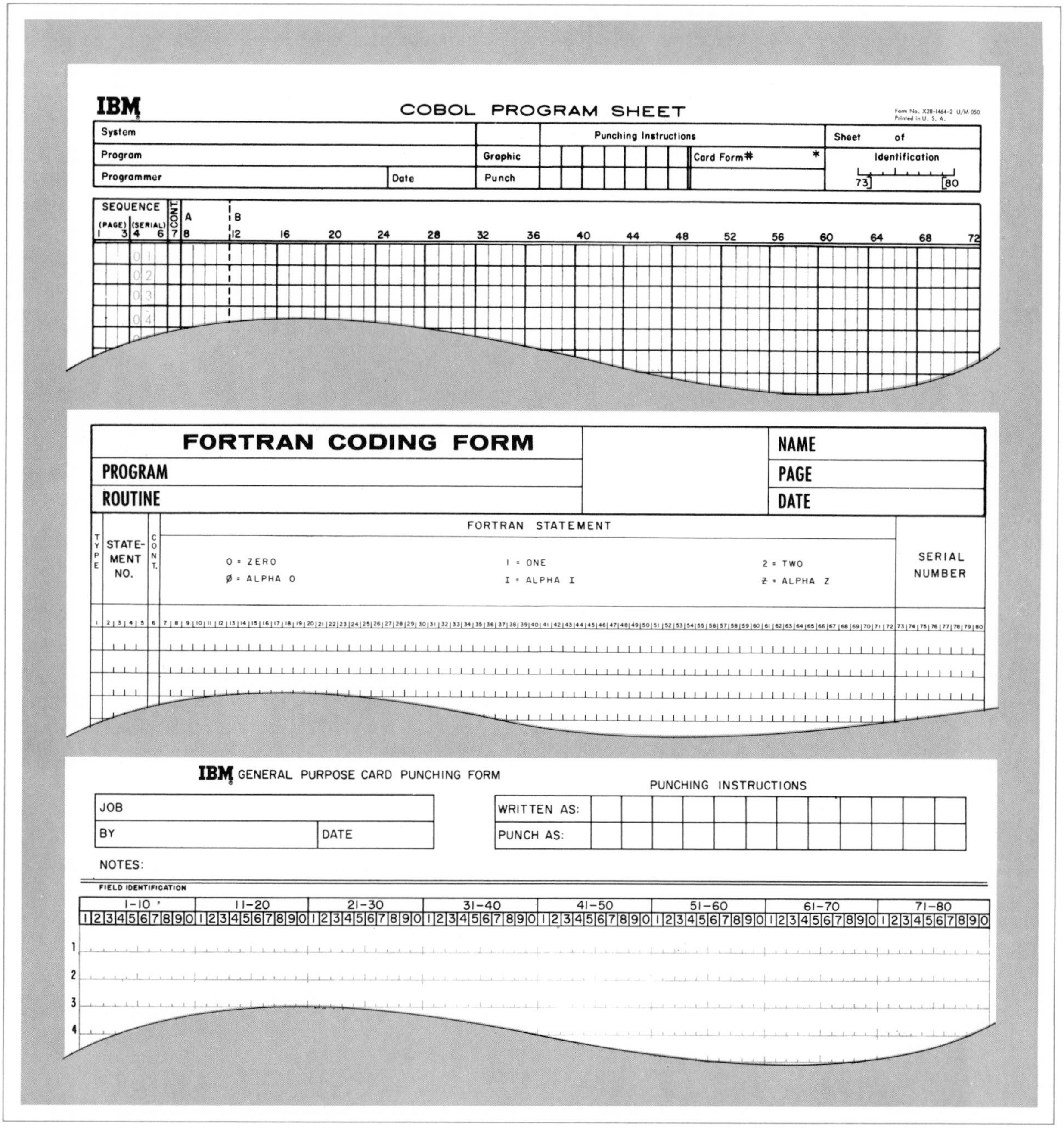

FIGURE 14-2 Coding paper for procedure-oriented languages (COBOL, FORTRAN, and PL/I)

program is printed on the line printer or typewriter. This listing includes any error diagnostics which the translator routine detected. The errors which can be detected are mainly textual errors involving the misuse of the language. If errors are found, these must be corrected and the translation process repeated.

Debugging is usually simplified by a higher-order language. The coding is normally not as lengthy and the logic of the program is easier to follow. The programmer should do desk checking of his program, tracing through the logic to see if it does what he intended. The program is then ready for a test run. If it does not run correctly, corrections are made in the source deck and the program is translated again.

Documentation is made easier using a compiler language because the coding itself forms a somewhat understandable description of the procedures being performed. The program listing is not sufficient documentation, however, and complete documentation should be provided.

After debugging, the program is ready to be used. The running of the object program to perform processing requires that library subroutines called for by the program either be copied into the object program prepared by the translator or loaded separately when the object program is loaded. For the purpose of illustration in Figure 14–1, the common FORTRAN practice of combining the library routines with the object program at the time of program loading is assumed. The program is then ready to read data, perform computations, and output results.

EVALUATION OF PROCEDURE-ORIENTED LANGUAGES

The suitability of procedure-oriented languages relates both to cost and to installation management considerations. Assuming the system analysis cost to be constant, the cost of using a computer for an application is divided into the cost of programming and the cost of running the resulting program. In general, the use of a compiler language relative to the use of alternative one-for-one symbolic coding will have the following relationship in terms of personnel and machine time expended.

COST ELEMENT	POL COMPARED TO SYMBOLIC ASSEMBLY LANGUAGE	
	PERSONNEL TIME	MACHINE TIME
Programming		
Program analysis	Less	—
Coding	Much less	—
Debugging	Less	Same or less
Documentation	A little less	—
Running	—	More, depending on efficiency of compiler

There is a tradeoff in compilers between programming cost and machine time cost. This relationship suggests that a POL program is indicated for programs meeting one of the following criteria:

1   The program is run infrequently, so that running time is not a significant cost relative to programming.
2   The program is to be used on more than one model of computer. A standard POL need be written only once to be run, usually with little modification, on different computers.
3   The program will be changed frequently. The POL program is easier to change, especially if the person making the change is not the original programmer.

The tradeoff between programming cost elements and running time means that, as compilers become more efficient, they are preferred over symbolic coding. This is happening, especially with large-scale systems. On some large systems, the running time efficiency of compiler-produced programs is as good as that of symbolic programs prepared by the average programmer. A clever programmer can always produce a more efficient code than a compiler because the compiler must be somewhat general, but if a program is limited in speed by input/output, the extra efficiency in coding may not affect the rate at which processing occurs.

Managerial considerations influence the use of higher-level languages. The coding of programs in a standard POL such as COBOL makes the installation less dependent on one manufacturer. If the installation wishes to change computers, the conversion of programs is handled by recompiling on the new computer. The changes in coding are typically minor. The same principle applies when an installation changes from one model to a noncompatible model by the same manufacturer.

Personnel management problems are lessened by the use of a compiler language. It is easier to train programmers in a POL than a machine-oriented language. If a programmer leaves in the middle of a programming job, it is easier for another programmer to complete the project if a POL is used. Documentation is usually improved because the POL coding is more understandable than symbolic coding. Control is improved because it is difficult to make changes in a compiler-generated object program. This means that it is more difficult to make unauthorized, undocumented changes in POL programs because changes must usually be made in the source program which is then recompiled.

Four languages will now be described—COBOL, FORTRAN, PL/I, and RPG. These descriptions are not designed to provide any programming skill. They are, however, intended to survey the major elements and to provide a feel for these important languages.

▌ THE COBOL LANGUAGE

COBOL (an acronym from COmmon Business-Oriented Language) is a procedure-oriented language designed for coding of business data processing procedures. The specifications for the COBOL language were developed by the CODASYL (Conference on Data Systems Languages) committee composed of representatives from several large users, the Federal government, computer manufacturers, and other interested parties. Their report, issued in 1960, contained the first version, called COBOL-60. A maintenance committee was formed to initiate and review recommended changes in order to keep the language up to date. Additional reports were issued in 1961, 1964, and 1965. The material in this section is based on COBOL-65, the latest version at the writing of the text. The revisions of basic content have not been substantial, and the major difference in later versions is the addition of new features. Early versions of COBOL were divided into two parts—required and elective. This distinction is not found in COBOL-65. A further standardization of COBOL by defining standard COBOL instruction sets has been approved by the United States of America Standards Institute.

The major impetus for COBOL in the early stages of its development came from the Federal government, which had sponsored CODASYL, and which required that COBOL compilers be available for all Federal government computers of a size large enough to handle a business compiler. Acceptance by the business community came slowly. Early compilers in business installations had long compile times and long running times relative to symbolic coding. Compile times for third-generation equipment are much faster, and running times tend to be satisfactory. The use of COBOL has increased until it is now the major higher-order business language.

OVERVIEW OF COBOL

COBOL provides a standard method for expressing solutions to business data processing problems. A basic characteristic of these problems is the existence of master files which are updated continuously or periodically. Business-type problems also tend to involve large volumes of input and output.

A COBOL program always consists of four parts called divisions—Identification, Environment, Data, and Procedure—which are arranged in that order. These four divisions form a complete description of the program, including: (1) an identification of the program, (2) a description of the equipment to be used, (3) the form and format of the data files, and (4) the processing steps to be performed. Each division has a specified form. In general the hierarchy of structure is:

Division
Section
Paragraph
Sentence or independent clause

The Procedure division contains the processing instructions. These instructions are interpreted in the context of the equipment described by the Environment division and the files and records described by the Data division. The Procedure division is machine-independent, which means that it can be written without reference to the computer on which it will be run. The Data division describes the format of the data and is machine-independent, except in those cases where the characteristics of the computer used affect the way data is described. The Environment division specifies the equipment to be used and assigns files to file storage equipment. It is a link between the machine-independent Procedure division and the specific physical characteristics of the computer system being used. It must be rewritten if the problem is to be run on another computer. The Identification division is for documentation purposes and does not affect the object program. Although the Procedure and Data divisions are machine-independent, a basic knowledge of the way the particular computer being used operates and the way it stores data is helpful in writing COBOL so that it will be compiled into most efficient object coding. Each computer on which COBOL is implemented has a manual which describes the compiling procedures and details the way all computer-dependent features have been implemented for that computer. This manual is essential when using a computer to write, compile, and run a problem written in COBOL.

As an overview, the program in Figure 14–3 is a simple but complete COBOL program to compute gross pay. Hours worked and rate of pay are read from a punched card. The gross pay is computed as hours worked times rate of pay for up to 40 hours of work. Hours worked beyond 40 are paid at one-and-a-half times the regular rate. The output will show the hours worked, the rate of pay, and the gross pay as illustrated in the margin.

Columns 1-4	5-11	12-21
40	3.756	$150.24
45	3.756	$178.41
47	3.756	$189.68
32	1.860	$59.52
48	1.890	$98.28
Hours Worked	Pay rate	Gross pay

COBOL ENVIRONMENT DIVISION

This division is for identification purposes only. It does not affect the object program. A minimum Identification division is:

    IDENTIFICATION DIVISION.
    PROGRAM-ID.   Name.

Other optional clauses may be used to expand the identification. Note the use of periods to indicate the end of each item.

COBOL IDENTIFICATION DIVISION

This division has two sections—the Configuration section and the Input/output section.

The Configuration section specifies the computer on which the program is to be compiled (source computer) and the computer on which it is to be run (object computer). These may not be the same. An optional paragraph may be used to assign special names to equipment items, such as sense switches, printer and card reader.

The Input/output section relates to transmission and handling of data between the computer and data files. The File-control paragraph associates files with the devices on which they are to be read or written and specifies the processing mode. An I/O paragraph, which is optional, defines special control techniques to be applied by the object program.

The Environment division in the sample program in Figure 14–3 is simple but complete. A few comments on this sample will help to clarify this division. Note the dependence of this division on the names and characteristics of the computer being used.

```
     LINE NO. SEQ. NO.              SOURCE STATEMENT              CBD CL2-5 06/14/68        PAGE    1

          1          IDENTIFICATION DIVISION.
          2          PROGRAM-ID.  'PAY'.
          3          REMARKS. PROGRAM TO READ HOURS-WORKED AND RATE-OF-PAY AND COMPUTE
          4              GROSS-PAY.
          5          ENVIRONMENT DIVISION.
          6          CONFIGURATION SECTION.
          7          SOURCE-COMPUTER. IBM-360.
          8          OBJECT-COMPUTER. IBM-360.
          9          INPUT-OUTPUT SECTION.
         10          FILE-CONTROL. SELECT PAYROLL-CARD-FILE ASSIGN TO 'SYS011'
         11              UNIT-RECORD 2540R.  SELECT PRINT-FILE ASSIGN TO 'SYS013'
         12              UNIT-RECORD 1403.
         13          DATA DIVISION.
         14          FILE SECTION.
         15          FD PAYROLL-CARD-FILE LABEL RECORD IS OMITTED RECORDING MODE IS F
         16              DATA RECORD IS PAYROLL-CARD.
         17          01  PAYROLL-CARD.
         18              02 HOURS-WORKED PICTURE IS 99.
         19              02 RATE-OF-PAY PICTURE IS 9V999.
         20              02 FILLER PICTURE 9(74).
         21          FD  PRINT-FILE LABEL RECORD IS OMITTED RECORDING MODE IS F DATA
         22              RECORD IS PRINT-LINE.
         23          01  PRINT-LINE.
         24              02 HOURS-PRINT PICTURE IS ZZ99.
         25              02 RATE-PRINT PICTURE IS ZZ9.999.
         26              02 GROSS-PRINT PICTURE IS $$$$$$9.99.
         27              02  FILLER PICTURE IS X(111).
         28          WORKING-STORAGE SECTION.
         29              77 GROSS-PAY PICTURE IS 999V99.
         30              77 EXCESS PICTURE IS 99V9.
         31          PROCEDURE DIVISION.
         32          START. OPEN INPUT PAYROLL-CARD-FILE OUTPUT PRINT-FILE.
         33          PROCESSING. READ PAYROLL-CARD-FILE RECORD AT END GO TO FINISH.
         34              IF HOURS-WORKED IS GREATER THAN 40 GO TO OVERTIME.  MULTIPLY
         35              RATE-OF-PAY BY HOURS-WORKED GIVING GROSS-PAY ROUNDED. GO TO
         36              PRINT-OUT.
         37          OVERTIME.  COMPUTE EXCESS = (HOURS-WORKED - 40) * 1.5. ADD 40 TO
         38              EXCESS. MULTIPLY RATE-OF-PAY BY EXCESS GIVING GROSS-PAY
         39              ROUNDED. MOVE SPACES TO PRINT-LINE. MOVE HOURS-WORKED TO
         40          PRINT-OUT. MOVE SPACES TO PRINT-LINE. MOVE HOURS-WORKED TO
         41              HOURS-PRINT. MOVE RATE-OF-PAY TO RATE-PRINT MOVE GROSS-PAY TO
         42              GROSS-PRINT. WRITE PRINT-LINE. GO TO PROCESSING.
         43          FINISH. CLOSE PAYROLL-CARD-FILE, PRINT-FILE. STOP RUN.
```

FIGURE 14-3 Simple but complete COBOL program to compute gross pay

ENTRIES	COMMENTS
ENVIRONMENT DIVISION.	
CONFIGURATION SECTION.	
SOURCE-COMPUTER. IBM/360.	The program is to be compiled on an IBM System/360.
OBJECT-COMPUTER. IBM/360.	
INPUT-OUTPUT SECTION.	
FILE CONTROL.	
SELECT PAYROLL-CARD-FILE ASSIGN TO 'SYS011' UNIT-RECORD 2540R.	A file of transactions on punched cards, called Payroll-Card-File, is assigned to be read by a card reader, called 2540R on this computer.
SELECT PRINT-FILE ASSIGN TO 'SYS013' UNIT-RECORD 1403.	The printed output, called Print-File, is assigned to be written out using a 1403, which is the number given to the printer.

COBOL DATA DIVISION

The Data division describes the data to be processed by the program. There are four sections, but all of them need not be used in a particular program.

SECTION OF DATA DIVISION	EXPLANATION
FILE SECTION	Contains a description of each input or output file—the physical structure, identification, and record names. Data description entries specify the characteristics of each item of data in the file.
WORKING-STORAGE SECTION	Describes records and individual data items which are not part of input or output file but are developed and processed internally.
CONSTANT SECTION	Describes data items whose values are assigned by the programmer and do not change during processing.
REPORT SECTION	Describes the content and format of reports to be generated by the COBOL report generator.

The File section (without the data description entries) from the sample program illustrates the file description entry:

FILE SECTION.
FD PAYROLL-CARD-FILE LABEL RECORD IS OMITTED RECORDING MODE IS F
    DATA RECORD IS PAYROLL-CARD.

FD identifies this as a general file rather than a file to be sorted or a file using random processing. The name of the file is PAYROLL-CARD-FILE. There is no label record at the beginning of the card file which identifies the file. In practice, a label record is more common with magnetic tape files. The records are of fixed length (80 characters) so the recording mode is specified as F (fixed). There is only one type of data card in the file. It has the record name of PAYROLL-CARD.

The entries for the Working-storage and Constant sections consist of the section name followed by the data entries. This overview of COBOL will not describe the report section entry, but it is similar. Each data item is assigned a name by which it is identified in the program. This name can be up to 30 characters in length and can contain hyphens. The data is assumed to be structured into a hierarchy. The first level of 01 is used for full records. Items formed from the first level are given a level number of 02. These items may in turn be composed of other items. The lowest level for each record is termed an elementary item. For example, a record may contain all information with respect to a sales invoice. A second-level item might be the date of the invoice. The date might be further divided into day, month, year.
In COBOL the level numbers would be:

    01 SALES-RECORD
        02 DATE
            03 DAY
            03 MONTH
            03 YEAR

An entry name FILLER is used to indicate unused portions of the record. This is necessary since the entire record must be accounted for. Level number 77 is used for individual items not part of a record, and 88 is used for an entry naming the values an item can take.

The data description entries must also identify the form of the data—how many characters, type of characters, decimal point location, etc. The most convenient method for accomplishing this is the Picture clause. The form of this clause requires the word PICTURE or PICTURE IS followed by characters which form a picture of the data item. The following characters are used for input items, working storage items, and constants.

PICTURE CHARACTER	REPRESENTS
9	A numeric digit
A	Alphabetic character
X	Alphanumeric character
V	Assumed decimal point (for scaling of data)

A character is repeated by placing number of times to be repeated inside parentheses following the picture character. Thus 9(4) is the same as 9999. The following entries in the sample program can now be understood:

```
01  PAYROLL-CARD.
    02 RATE-OF-PAY  PICTURE  IS  9V999.
    02 RATE-OF-PAY  PICTURE  IS  9V999.
    02 FILLER  PICTURE  9(74).
```

An output picture must provide for dollar signs, decimals, commas, etc., and for suppressing of leading zeros (changing them to blanks). The characters to be inserted are placed in the picture in the position they should occupy in the actual output. The most common insertion symbols are $, *, comma, and period. A repeat of the letter Z will cause a suppression of leading zeros (replacing with blanks) over the digits represented by the Zs. A repeat of $ means that the dollar sign will move (float) so that it will print next to the first nonzero leading digit. The following pictures illustrate how the picture for output is interpreted:

DATA	PICTURE	AS PRINTED
647ᵥ54	$999.99	$647.54
0003ᵥ10	$$$9.99	$3.10
847ᵥ652	$9,999.99	$8,476.52
00001	ZZZ99	01

COBOL PROCEDURE DIVISION

The Procedure division consists of sections, paragraphs, and sentences. Each section or paragraph has a name, and each sentence ends with a period. The words which may be used to describe what is to be done are limited to a specific list, but all are English words having a common meaning.

The input/output instructions are quite simple because all of the specifications for the data and equipment have been included in the Environment and Data divisions. Files must be opened before the first use and closed at the end of the run (note these sentences in Figure 14–3). Once opened, a simple READ file statement makes a record available to the program. A WRITE record statement causes output to be performed.

Two sentences from the sample COBOL program illustrate two methods of writing arithmetic statements—the use of words and the use of the compute verb (* means to multiply):

MULTIPLY RATE-OF-PAY BY HOURS-WORKED GIVING GROSS-PAY ROUNDED.
COMPUTE EXCESS = (HOURS-WORKED − 40) * 1.5.

In the first, the result of the multiplication of data found at storage locations identified with RATE-OF-PAY and HOURS-WORKED will be stored at a location identified as GROSS-PAY. The result will be rounded before being stored. If the COMPUTE verb had been used, the statement would read COMPUTE GROSS-PAY = RATE-OF-PAY * HOURS-WORKED. In other words, the COMPUTE verb is an alternative which is most suitable for formula-type computations.

To understand the paragraph PRINT-OUT in the sample program in Figure 14–3, it is important to remember that computational data in the computer has no decimal points, dollar signs, etc. Therefore, the computational data must be converted into an output form and edited before being printed out. This conversion in COBOL is programmed by moving (copying) the contents of a computational field into an output field. This is the reason for sentences such as MOVE HOURS-WORKED to HOURS-PRINT. Since only part of the print line is being set up with data items, spaces must be put in the rest of the line. This is performed in the sample program by first moving spaces into the entire line and afterward moving the data items into the positions they will occupy.

The transfer of control concept in COBOL is carried out by transferring control to a paragraph (or section) identified by a name. Branching is applied in three sentences in the sample program. Overtime, Processing, and Finish are paragraph names.

IF HOURS-WORKED IS GREATER THAN 40 GO TO OVERTIME.
GO TO PROCESSING.
READ PAYROLL-CARD-FILE RECORD AT END GO TO FINISH.

The first sentence is a conditional transfer of control based on a comparison; the second is an unconditional transfer of control to the paragraph named Processing; and the third is an example of a conditional transfer based on a file condition, namely the end of the file of input cards.

EVALUATION OF COBOL

COBOL is not a language designed for the inexperienced user to write his own programs. It is a programmer's language and assumes an understanding of processing concepts and principles of programming computers. As a programmer's language, it has an important benefit in the amount of documentation inherent in the source program itself. Generally, the quality and quantity of documentation produced by the use of COBOL is superior to that of other languages. However, the documenting qualities causes the programming to be "wordy" compared to other languages. Data names of up to 30 characters allow the use of descriptive names which are excellent for documentation but are also long to write.

The organization of the COBOL program is logical, and the language imposes some discipline on the programmer. COBOL started out with a magnetic tape orientation, but direct access features have now been added. The language itself is more difficult to learn than, say, FORTRAN, but easier to learn than the machine-oriented symbolic language. It is a common, universal language, and this reduces training requirements for programmers. The machine-oriented portions are small enough for COBOL programs to be easily adapted for compiling and running on computers of different manufacturers. This is an advantage when replacing equipment.

A disadvantage of COBOL when it was first implemented was excessive compile times and inefficient object programs. This objection has been overcome, in most cases, by the compilers for third-generation equipment, which are quite efficient. Over three-fourths of all installations having COBOL capability have now adopted COBOL as the major language for programming of data processing applications.

SELF-TESTING QUIZ 14-1

1 What are the four divisions in COBOL, and in what order do they appear in a COBOL program?
2 Which divisions in COBOL are dependent on the machine being used?
3 What will the data look like on the output line if they are edited by the following pictures?

DATA	PICTURE
37654	$999.99
00452	ZZ999
00452	$$9.99

4 What will each of these COBOL statements cause the computer to do?
   a ADD A, B, C GIVING TOTAL.
   b MOVE HOURS-IN TO HOURS-OUT.
   c WRITE PRINT-LINE.

 d READ CARD-IN.

 e MULTIPLY UNITS BY COST GIVING TOTAL-COST ROUNDED.

▌ THE FORTRAN LANGUAGE

FORTRAN (an acronym for FORmula TRANslator) is the most widely used procedure-oriented language. Almost every computer with memory size sufficient to implement FORTRAN has done so. The orientation of FORTRAN is toward problems which can be expressed in terms of arithmetic procedures or mathematical formulas. It is not suitable for business-type problems such as file maintenance, editing of data, and production of documents. It works well for research and analytical problems in science, engineering, and business. It is simple enough to be used by the nonprofessional programmer to program his own problem solutions.

Unlike COBOL, which resulted from specifications prepared by a committee, FORTRAN has evolved slowly. Developed in 1957 by a group from IBM, it was soon implemented by other manufacturers. Different versions were FORTRANSIT, FOR-TRAN, FORTRAN II, and FORTRAN IV. These were all similar, but each version added new features. Although all FORTRANs as implemented by different manufacturers have been very similar, each has had its own special features. To introduce uniformity in order to facilitate training and program interchange, the United States of America Standards Institute (see Appendix IV) codified existing FORTRAN specifications into two standard FORTRAN languages—FORTRAN and a subset of FORTRAN termed Basic FORTRAN. USASI FORTRAN is similar to FORTRAN IV, and Basic FORTRAN is very similar to the popular FORTRAN II but is altered slightly to be compatible with FORTRAN. Most new compilers are implementing USASI Basic FORTRAN or USASI FORTRAN.

OVERVIEW OF FORTRAN

FORTRAN is machine-independent. The FORTRAN programmer need not understand any of the details of the computer to be used. The language consists of a vocabulary of symbols and words and a grammar of rules for writing procedural instructions. The symbols, words, and rules utilize many common mathematical and English-language conventions, thereby making the language easy to learn.

Two simple examples will illustrate the FORTRAN language (Figures 14–4 and 14–5). Merely examine them now—they will be explained later in the section. The first is the problem which was coded in COBOL (Figure 14–3). In this problem, the computer reads data on punched cards (hours worked in columns 1–2 and rate of pay in columns 3–6), computes gross pay (overtime over 40 hours), and prints out the hours worked, the rate of pay, and gross pay. No dollar signs were included in the output. This could have been done, but somewhat awkwardly. The second example is a simple FORTRAN program to compute a table of squares and square roots for the numbers from 1 to 10.

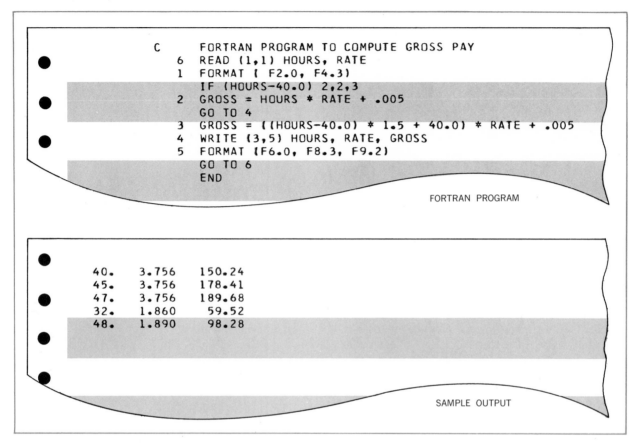

```
      C       FORTRAN PROGRAM TO COMPUTE GROSS PAY
      6       READ (1,1) HOURS, RATE
      1       FORMAT ( F2.0, F4.3)
              IF (HOURS-40.0) 2,2,3
      2       GROSS = HOURS * RATE + .005
              GO TO 4
      3       GROSS = ((HOURS-40.0) * 1.5 + 40.0) * RATE + .005
      4       WRITE (3,5) HOURS, RATE, GROSS
      5       FORMAT (F6.0, F8.3, F9.2)
              GO TO 6
              END
```

FORTRAN PROGRAM

```
      40.    3.756    150.24
      45.    3.756    178.41
      47.    3.756    189.68
      32.    1.860     59.52
      48.    1.890     98.28
```

SAMPLE OUTPUT

FIGURE 14–4 Simple FORTRAN program to compute gross pay and sample results

The statements in a FORTRAN program can be classified as follows:

CLASSIFICATION	PURPOSE	EXAMPLES FROM SAMPLE PROGRAMS
Arithmetic assignment	To perform arithmetic and assign result to a designated variable (i.e., to store result in a location associated with a variable name)	GROSS=HOURS*RATE+.005 $$J = I**2$$
Input/output	To direct the computer to obtain data from an input device or to write data using an output unit	READ (1, 1) HOURS, RATE WRITE (3, 2) I, J, Z
Specification	To declare properties of variables and to describe format of data for input and output	1 FORMAT (F2.0, F4.3)
Control	To direct the flow of the program	GO TO 4 DO 2 I = 1, 10
Subprogram	To define subprograms	

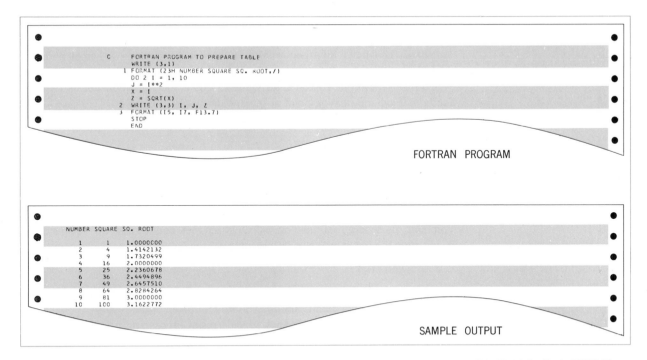

```
        C    FORTRAN PROGRAM TO PREPARE TABLE
             WRITE (3,1)
           1 FORMAT (23H NUMBER SQUARE SQ. ROOT,/)
             DO 2 I = 1, 10
             J = I**2
             X = I
             Z = SQRT(X)
           2 WRITE (3,3) I, J, Z
           3 FORMAT (I5, I7, F13.7)
             STOP
             END
```

FORTRAN PROGRAM

```
    NUMBER SQUARE SQ. ROOT

       1      1    1.0000000
       2      4    1.4142132
       3      9    1.7320499
       4     16    2.0000000
       5     25    2.2360678
       6     36    2.4494896
       7     49    2.6457510
       8     64    2.8284264
       9     81    3.0000000
      10    100    3.1622772
```

SAMPLE OUTPUT

FIGURE 14-5 Simple FORTRAN program to prepare table of squares and square roots and sample results

ARITHMETIC ASSIGNMENT

A FORTRAN arithmetic assignment statement $X = A + B$ means to compute the value of $A + B$ and assign it to X. This is not the same as equality, since $X = X + 1$ is a valid statement and it is not an equaltiy. X, A, and B are variable names. A variable name begins with a letter and has up to six alphabetic or numeric characters in it. X2, MOM, AI9, etc. are all valid variable names. A name can refer to an array, a list, or a matrix, in which case there must be a subscript enclosed in parentheses to identify which item in the list or matrix is being referenced. For example, if the sales by week are all referred to as SALES and each week's sales is stored separately, the first week's sales is identified as SALES (1) and the 40th week's sales as SALES (40).

Variable names can refer to different types of data—real, integer, complex, and logical (Boolean). The most common types are real (also called floating point) or integer (sometimes termed fixed point). A real variable can have a fractional part; an integer variable can only be a whole number. These two types are specified in two ways: (1) by the first letter of the variable name and (2) by a type statement which overrides the specification of the first letter. If the first letter is I, J, K, L, M, or N, it refers to an integer variable; all others refer to real variables.

Constants are written as ordinary numbers except that real constants (which are used in conjunction with real variables) must have a demical point. 5, 10, 3.0, 0.5 are all valid constants. An exponent form is used for very large or very small numbers. 4.3E10 means to move the decimal 10 places to the right to scale the number; −E10 would mean moving it 10 places to the left. This is the same concept as the scale factor method and floating point arithmetic discussed in Chapter 11.

Arithmetic operators are:

+ addition
− subtraction and negative sign
* multiplication
** exponentiation (raising to a power)

There are also arithmetic functions to perform common computations. The most common, the square root function, will illustrate their use. To take the square root of Y and store the result in X, the statement is written as:

X = SQRT(Y)

Any expression can be inside the parentheses. X = SQRT(Y + Z) would mean that Y + Z should be added and then the square root taken of the result.

The order of computation follows specific rules. Proceeding from left to right all exponentiation is first, all multiplication and division follows next, and addition and subtraction are last. Computations inside parentheses are performed first, using these order rules. Thus, the following are equivalent:

X = Y**2 + 3.0/X−4.0
X = (Y**2) + (3.0/X)−4.0

This short explanation should be sufficient to understand the following arithmetic assignment statement from the sample programs:

GROSS = HOURS*RATE
GROSS = ((HOURS−40.0)*1.5 + 40.0)*RATE + .005.
J = I**2
X = I
Z = SQRT(X)

The last two statements show the problem of real versus integer variables. It is convenient to have these types, but the rules do not allow the taking of the square root of an integer. The argument (i.e., the expression inside the parentheses) for SQRT must be a real variable. The expression X = I is one method of creating a real variable (X) which is the real equivalent of the integer designated by I.

FORTRAN INPUT/OUTPUT

FORTRAN input is normally from punched cards, and output is usually on a printer. There is usually little need for complicated report formats. Input and output is programmed by a pair of instructions—the I/O statement and the FORMAT specification

List of names applied to the data to be read (or written)

READ (1, 1) HOURS, RATE

Device to be used (card reader = 1)

Statement number of FORMAT statement to be used

statement. The I/O statement specifies the device to be used, the list of variables to be input or output, and the FORMAT statement to be used. READ is used for input and WRITE for output. In FORTRAN II, READ means read a card, and PRINT is used for specifying printed output.

The FORMAT specification statement describes the form of the input or output data and specifies control such as skipping of records.

The general form of a data specification is *tw.d*, where *t* is the type of data, *w* is the number of positions in the field (i.e., its width), and *d* is the number of positions in the field to the right of the decimal point. The three most common specifications refer to integer data, real data, and the exponent form of real data.

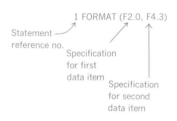

SPECIFICATION	DESCRIPTION	EXAMPLE
Iw	An integer field of *w* characters	I5
Fw.d	A real field of *w* characters and *d* digits to the right of the decimal	F9.7
Ew.d	An exponent field of *w* characters and *d* digits to right of decimal	E15.7

In most cases, data is right justified in a field (i.e., any blanks are to the left). Assuming the following variables to be printed as shown, the WRITE and FORMAT statements are:

```
    WRITE (3, 3) IX, Y, Z1
  3 FORMAT (I7, F6.2, E16.8)
```

```
     I7          F6.2        E16.8
      ↙           ↙            ↙
   ⏜⏜⏜⏜⏜   ⏜⏜⏜⏜   ⏜⏜⏜⏜⏜⏜⏜⏜⏜⏜
    66763        1.75      0.95476215E  15
```

Descriptive headings may be written by using a Hollerith specification. A slash means to skip a record and *w*X means to skip over *w* characters of the record. The statement from the sample program to write a heading for the table and then skip one line illustrates these features.

```
    WRITE (3, 1)
  1 FORMAT (23H NUMBER  SQUARE  SQ.  ROOT,/ )
```

23H means to print, exactly as written, the next 23 characters in the FORMAT statement itself.

SPECIFICATION STATEMENTS

Many of the specification statements are beyond the scope of an overview such as this (the FORMAT specification was covered in the input/output discussion). A common specification worth mentioning is the DIMENSION statement. It declares the maximum size of a list or a matrix referred to by a single name plus subscripts. This is to allow the compiler to assign storage to it. The following statement reserves 100 storage assignments for the array X and 15 storage assignments (5 rows and 3 columns) for the array B:

DIMENSION X(100), B(5, 3)

CONTROL STATEMENTS

Note that some of the statements in the sample programs have statement numbers preceding them; others do not. These are essentially a reference number. The FORMAT statement, for example, must have one because it is referenced by the input/output statement. Another reason for a statement number is for transfer of control branching.

FORTRAN statements are normally executed sequentially. If this sequence is to be changed, the branching statement specifies the statement number to which control is to be transferred. The most common transfer-of-control statements are the GO TO unconditional transfer and the IF conditional transfer. The form of the first is GO TO s, where s refers to a statement number. The transfer is unconditional; the next step in the program is the statement number s. The form of the conditional transfer statement is:

IF (e) s_1, s_2, s_3

where e refers to an expression (a variable name or an arithmetic computation to be made), and the s_1 s_2 s_3 refer to statement numbers. If the value of the expression e is negative, go to s_1; if 0, go to s_2; and if positive, go to s_3. If the test is to go to s_1 if X is greater than Y, s_2 if they are equal, and s_3 if X is less than Y, the statement can be written as:

IF (Y − X) s_1, s_2, s_3

If Y − Y = 0, they are equal; if Y − X < 0, then X is greater than Y, etc.

In the sample payroll program, both types of transfer statements are used.

IF (HOURS−40.0) 2, 2, 3

2　GROSS = (regular computation)

　GO TO 4

3　GROSS = (overtime computation)

4　WRITE − − − − −

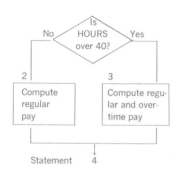

Note that the IF statement was used to decide which path to follow. When the first path (regular pay) was chosen, the second computations (overtime) had to be skipped over, hence the need for the unconditional GO to 4.

Another type of control statement is the DO statement, which controls a loop. The general form of the DO statement is:

DO s $i = m_1, m_2, m_3$

where s is a statement number of the last statement in the loop, i is the index variable, m_1 is the initial value of the index, m_2 is the value of the index variable when the loop should terminate, and m_3 is the increment by which the index variable is to be changed each time through the loop (if it is 1, it need not be written). The DO statement is a command to execute repeatedly the statement that follows, up to and including the statement numbered s. The index i is initialized at the value m_1

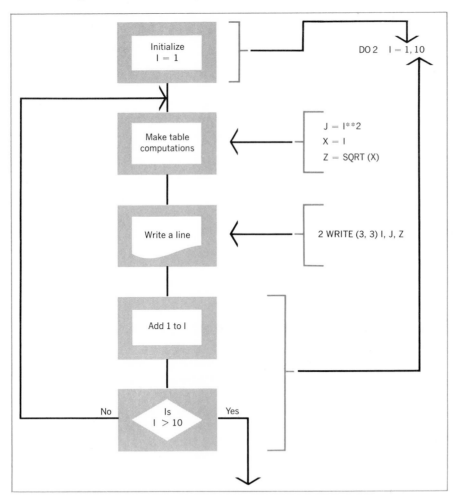

FIGURE 14–6 Example of DO statement

for the first execution and is incremented by m_3 each time until i is equal to the highest value that does not exceed m_2. The index may be used in computations inside the loop.

In the sample program to prepare a table, a DO loop is used. The loop is executed ten times. Note that the DO statement specifies many of the steps in the flowchart (Figure 14–6).

Other common control statements used in the sample programs are STOP, which terminates the program, and END, which defines that there are no more statements in the program.

SUBPROGRAM STATEMENTS

It is frequently desirable for the FORTRAN program to be written with subprograms. These are subroutines and programmer-written functions. A subprogram is written like a regular program except that it begins with a declaration which specifies whether the subprogram is a subroutine or function. A return statement is used to indicate a return from the subprogram back to the main program. For example, in a subroutine, the general approach is:

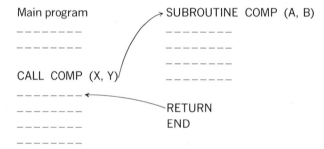

EVALUATION OF FORTRAN

Of the three procedure-oriented languages presented in this chapter, FORTRAN is the easiest to learn. It is adapted to the nonprofessional programmer. The student, the engineer, the researcher can effectively learn and use FORTRAN without a background in computers and data processing. FORTRAN is for this reason most widely used of the three languages.

Basic FORTRAN is rather simple, but the language has many extended features not covered here which give it considerable versatility and power for use by professional programmers as well as by the novice. The language has evolved and incorporated many features from other more sophisticated languages.

The evolutionary growth of FORTRAN has allowed changes to be made as features were found to be desirable, yet there are standards for what should be in FORTRAN— the USASI Basic FORTRAN and USASI FORTRAN.

FORTRAN is well suited for problems involving arithmetic procedures. It is not well adapted to business-type file management problems. There is no means for describing a hierarchy in a data structure and no facilities for doing many data editing and output tasks.

A person who may need to use a computer for occasional research or computational tasks (such as rate of return analysis, statistical analysis, tabulation) will find FORTRAN to be a suitable language.

SELF-TESTING QUIZ 14–2

1   How does FORTRAN specify an input operation?
2   What will the data look like in output using the following format specifications?

	Data	Specifications
a	376$_\wedge$	F6.0
b	376$_\wedge$	F6.2
c	3$_\wedge$76	E15.8
d	376	I3

3   What will each of the following FORTRAN statements instruct the computer to do?
   a   IF (PAY-DEDUCT) 3, 3, 5
   b   DO 3 JIX = 1, 7
   c   GO TO 15
   d   X = A + B + C
   e   Y = X * B
   f   Z = A**2

THE PL/I LANGUAGE

OVERVIEW OF PL/I

PL/I (Programming Language, version I) is a relatively new procedure-oriented language first introduced by IBM in connection with their 360 family of computers. It has been adopted by some other manufacturers as well.

PL/I is designed as a general-purpose language combining the major features of both COBOL and FORTRAN and introducing features not found in either. The language has facilities for the realtime programmer and the systems programmer in addition to the traditional commercial and scientific programming features.

One of the difficulties of a sophisticated language is the fact that many users do not need the advanced features and do not find it useful to be trained in their use. PL/I handles this problem through a modular design and a default interpretation of specifications.

Modularity means that the language is divided in modules or subsets for different applications and different levels of complexity. A programmer using one subset need not even know about the other modules. The reason the programmer can ignore the advanced modules is the default interpretation given to every specification. If the programmer does not state a choice among the various alternative specifications, the compiler automatically chooses the default interpretation. In each case, the default specification is the one most likely to be required by the programmer who is not using the advanced features.

PL/I allows the programmer considerable freedom. For example, there are no special indentations or reserved columns on the coding sheet—the format is free form. More than one statement can be written on a line, and although PL/I uses different data types (integer, real, etc.), these may be mixed in an expression and the compiler will prepare coding to make the appropriate conversions to produce a proper result.

A PL/I program is constructed from program elements. The basic program element is the statement. Statements are combined into larger elements—the group and the block. A group is a number of statements with an identifying label (name) for control purposes. It is similar to a paragraph in COBOL. A block (normally a procedure block) also has a name and defines a program region (section) for data definition purposes. It may be thought of as a subprogram.

A statement in PL/I is a string of characters terminated by a semicolon. The statements are similar to FORTRAN except that additional operators are available and names may be up to 31 characters in length. A break character (_) is used instead of the hyphen to provide a COBOL-like name. The additional operators are:

Comparison operators	Bit-string (Boolean) operators
$>$ greater than	$\neg$ not
$> =$ greater than or equal	ε and
$<$ less than	$\mid$ or
$< =$ less than or equal	
$\neg$ not equal to	

Some typical PL/I statements are:

```
A = B**2;
X = Y/3 + 5;
IF HOURS > 40 THEN GO TO OVERTIME;
ELSE GROSS-PAY = HOURS * RATE;
```

Data in PL/I can be either numeric or string. String data consists of a group of characters or bits. Data can be grouped into arrays as in FORTRAN and in structures (hierarchies) as in COBOL. A DECLARE statement is used to specify the array or structure attribute of the data. For example a 2×3 matrix referred to as X is defined by the statement:

DECLARE X(2, 3)

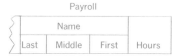

A payroll record with the structure shown in the margin would be defined by the statement:

DECLARE 1 PAYROLL, 2 NAME, 3 LAST, 3 MIDDLE, 3 FIRST, 2 HOURS;

The numbers 1, 2, and 3 correspond to level numbers in COBOL.

The programmer has considerable flexibility in input and output. Input/output is either record input/output which consists of discrete records or stream input/output which is a continuous stream of characters. The input/output for records uses READ and WRITE statements while stream input/output uses GET and PUT statements. In the following examples, the READ and WRITE statements will be used; the sample programs use the GET and PUT statements. The READ and WRITE statements are not available in some versions of PL/I. For the examples, assume data names of HOURS and RATE (hours worked and rate of pay) to be read from cards. Three methods of designating the form of the data are data-directed, list-directed, and edit-directed.

METHOD	FORM OF DATA ON CARD	EXPLANATION
Data-directed	HOURS=42, RATE=4.253;	Each data item is written with its data name. The read statement is: READ DATA (HOURS, RATE);
List-directed	42, 4.253;	The items are listed in order and separated by a space or commas. The read statement is: READ LIST (HOURS, RATE);
Edit-directed	424253	The items are listed in order. The form of the data is defined by a format list. The read statement is: READ (HOURS, RATE) (F(2), F(5, 3));

For output, the three methods are again available:

METHOD	STATEMENT	FORM OF OUTPUT
Data-directed	WRITE DATA (HOURS, RATE);	HOURS = 42 RATE = 4.253
List-directed	WRITE LIST (HOURS, RATE);	42 4.253
Edit-directed	WRITE (HOURS, RATE) (F(3), F(7, 3));	42 4.253

In the data-directed output each variable is printed out with its name. A space is automatically inserted between the entries. The list-directed output places the output in predetermined-fields (which the programmer can override if he wishes). The edit-directed output specifies the form of the output, as in FORTRAN. A picture declaration similar to the picture clause in COBOL is used to edit data by inserting dollar signs, commas, etc.

Other important features of PL/I are specifications by which the programmer can direct the computer to work on more than one procedure concurrently, as in multi-

FIGURE 14-7 PL/I program to compute gross pay and sample edit-directed output from program

```
/*PL/I PROGRAM TO COMPUTE GROSS PAY*/
PAY: PROCEDURE OPTIONS(MAIN);
   A1: GET EDIT (HOURS,RATE) (F(2),F(4,3),X(74));
   IF HOURS <= 40 THEN GROSS =
   HOURS*RATE + .005; ELSE
   GROSS = ((HOURS - 40) * 1.5 + 40) * RATE + .005;
     PUT EDIT (HOURS,RATE,GROSS)  (SKIP(1),F(10), F(10,3), F(10,2));
   GO TO A1;
END PAY;
```

```
40      3.755     150.24
45      3.755     178.41
47      3.755     189.68
32      1.859      59.52
48      1.889      98.28
```

programming. There is a sort verb by which the programmer can specify the file to be sorted, the sort key, and the order. Storage allocation is also very flexible.

The two simple examples already written in FORTRAN and COBOL have been written in PL/I. These do not illustrate the power or versatility of the language but do show its general form. Figure 14–7 shows the program to compute gross pay. Figure 14–8 is a sample program to prepare a mathematical table.

EVALUATION OF PL/I

PL/I is the most versatile of the major languages. It incorporates in one language the main features of both FORTRAN and COBOL. It has additional features not found in either of these. Since it is considerably more extensive than either FORTRAN or COBOL, it is more difficult to learn the entire language. The modularity and default interpretation are intended to meet this objection. In addition, PL/I has omitted some of the error-prone features of FORTRAN and COBOL.

There are indications that PL/I may become quite popular over time as more installations adopt it and find it useful. Early difficulties with compilers will presumably be overcome. PL/I will be especially valuable in complex environments such as multiprogramming.

SELF-TESTING QUIZ 14–3

1 What are the three methods of specifying input and output in PL/I?
2 If a programmer omits a PL/I specification, what does the computer do?

```
/*PL/I PROGRAM TO PREPARE TABLE OF SQUARES AND SQUARE ROOTS.*/
TABLE: PROCEDURE OPTIONS(MAIN);
   PUT EDIT ('NUMBER SQUARE SQUARE ROOT') (PAGE,A(25));
   DO I = 1 TO 10;
   X = SQRT (I);
   J = I**2;
   PUT EDIT (I,J,X) (SKIP(1),F(4),F(7),E(14,5));
   END;
   END TABLE;
```

FIGURE 14–8 PL/I to prepare table of squares and square roots and sample edit-directed output from program using exponent form

Edit-directed output

NUMBER	SQUARE	SQUARE ROOT
1	1	1.00000E+00
2	4	1.41421E+00
3	9	1.73204E+00
4	16	2.00000E+00
5	25	2.23606E+00
6	36	2.44948E+00
7	49	2.64575E+00
8	64	2.82842E+00
9	81	3.00000E+00
10	100	3.16227E+00

3   What do the following PL/I statements instruct the computer to do?
   a   GO TO NEXT-CARD;
   b   IF GROSS $<=$ DEDUCT THEN GO TO ERROR-ROUTINE; ELSE NET-PAY $=$ GROSS $-$ DEDUCT;
   c   READ DATA (EMPLNO, RATE);
   d   END BILLING;

REPORT PROGRAM GENERATOR

OVERVIEW

Report Program Generator (RPG) is a problem-oriented language in which the programmer writes the specifications for the problem and the compiler generates a program from the specifications. RPG is offered by several manufacturers, but it is not standardized. Therefore although all RPGs are similar, each version is different, and RPG written for one computer may not be satisfactory for another. The explanation will be based on one of these versions—the RPG for the IBM System/360. RPG is well suited for the types of problems usually run on a small computer, so that it is an important programming aid for computers of this class.

A problem is programmed in RPG by filling out specification forms. There are four basic ones and two additional forms for special situations. Not all are required, and a specification may consist of a single line.

SPECIFICATION FORM	MAJOR USE
File description	Identifies the file as input, output, or combined. Associates file with an I/O device.
Input	Describes the records contained on the file and the location of the data fields.
Calculation	Specifies the operations to be performed and the data to be used.
Output format	Specifies the arrangement of data on the output medium.
File extension	Provides additional information for chaining, using tables, and using direct access files.
Line counter	Specifies line control if report is to be written on tape or disc for subsequent printing.

The RPG specifications provide all information for the program. Each specification is punched into a card. The set of specification cards are read by the RPG compiler, and an object program is generated.

SAMPLE PROGRAM IN RPG

1–2	3–6	Not used 7–80
HOURS	RATE	

HOURS	RATE	GROSS PAY
XX	X.XXX	$XXX.XX
XX	X.XXX	$XXX.XX
XX		

The sample program will use the simple gross pay computation already presented. Some headings will be used on the printed output. The input for the program is hours and rate on a punched card. The calculations are straight time for 40 or less hours and time-and-a-half for all hours over 40. The output is in the form shown.

The sample specification sheets are given in Figure 14–9. The file of cards containing the hours and rates is called the PDATA file. The input data fields are called HOURS and RATE. The output file is called REPORT. The result of the computations is GROSS for gross pay.

The file description form defines PDATA as an input file (I) to be read from the card reader (called READ40 for a card reader–punch on a model 40). REPORT is defined as an output file (O) on the printer.

The input specification sheet for PDATA defines the data fields as columns 1–2 for HOURS, with no decimal position, and columns 3–6 for RATE, with the decimal position three places from the right.

The first action on the calculation sheet is the test to find out whether hours exceed 40. If they do, control proceeds to the line marked with 21; if hours do not exceed 40, control goes to N21 (not 21). 21 is an arbitrary designation. For over 40 hours, the computations prepare an amount TEMP2 which is a revised hours figure giving overtime credit. The "H" means to round the result.

The output specification of the report first defines the heading line and then the form and position of the variables on the detail line. The edit word "$bbo.bb" defines a dollar sign and decimal location in the same way as a COBOL picture.

REPORT PROGRAM GENERATOR FILE DESCRIPTION SPECIFICATIONS
IBM System/360

Date _____

Program _____

Programmer _J. Weinand_

Punching Instruction — Graphic / Punch

Page 01

Program Identification RPG100

Line	Form Type	Filename	I/O/U/C	P/S/C/R/T	E	A/D	F/V	Block Length	Record Length	L/R	K/I	I/D/T	Key Field Starting Location	Extension Code E/L	Device	Symbolic Device	Labels (S, N, or E)	Name of Label Exit	Extent Exit for DAM	Comments
0 1 0	F	PDATA	I	PE			F	80	80						READ40	SYSRDR				
0 2 0	F	REPORT	O				V	132	132					OF	PRINTER	SYSLST				

IBM

INTERNATIONAL BUSINESS MACHINES CORPORATION
REPORT PROGRAM GENERATOR INPUT SPECIFICATIONS
IBM System/360

Form X24-3350-1 U/M025
Printed in U.S.A.

Date _____

Program _____

Programmer _____

Punching Instruction — Graphic / Punch

Page 02

Program Identification RPG100

Line	Form Type	Filename	Sequence	Number (1-N)	Option (O)	Resulting Indicator	Position	Not (N)	C/Z/D	Character	Position	Not (N)	C/Z/D	Character	Position	Not (N)	C/Z/D	Character	Stacker Select	Packed (P)	From	To	Decimal Positions	Field Name	Control Level (L1-L9)	Matching Fields or Chaining Fields	Field-Record Relation	Plus	Minus	Zero or Blank	Sterling Sign Position
0 1 0	I	PDATA	AA			01																									
0 2 0	I																				1	20		HOURS							
0 3 0	I																				3	63		RATE							
0 4 0	I																														

FIGURE 14-9 RPG specification sheets for program to compute gross pay and sample output from program

INTERNATIONAL BUSINESS MACHINES CORPORATION

REPORT PROGRAM GENERATOR   CALCULATION SPECIFICATIONS
IBM System/360

Form X24-3351-1 U/M025
Printed in U.S.A.

Date _____
Program _____
Programmer _____

Punching Instruction — Graphic / Punch

Page `03`   Program Identification `RPG100`

Line	Form Type	Control Level (L0-L9, LR)	Indicators And Not / And Not / Not	Factor 1	Operation	Factor 2	Result Field	Field Length	Decimal Positions	Half Adjust (H)	Resulting Indicators Plus High 1>2	Minus Low 1<2	Zero or Blank Equal 1=2	Comments
0 1	0	C	01	HOURS	COMP	40							21	
0 2	0	C	21	HOURS	SUB	40	TEMP1	41						
0 3	0	C	21	TEMP1	MULT	1.5	TEMP1	41						
0 4	0	C	21	40	ADD	TEMP1	TEMP1	41						
0 5	0	C	21	RATE	MULT	TEMP1	GROSS	62	H					
0 6	0	C	N21	RATE	MULT	HOURS	GROSS	62	H					
		C												

INTERNATIONAL BUSINESS MACHINES CORPORATION

REPORT PROGRAM GENERATOR OUTPUT-FORMAT SPECIFICATIONS
IBM System 360

Form X24-3352-1 U/M 025
Printed in U.S.A.

Date _____
Program _____
Programmer _____

Punching Instruction — Graphic / Punch

Page `04`   Program Identification `RPG100`

Line	Form Type	Filename	Type (H/D/T)	Stacker Select	Space Before / After	Skip Before / After	Output Indicators And Not / And Not / Not	Field Name	Zero Suppress (Z)	Blank After (B)	End Position in Output Record	Packed Field (P)	Constant or Edit Word	Sterling Sign Position
0 1	0	REPORT	H		2 0 1		1P							
0 2	0		OR				OF							
0 3	0										26		'HOURS RATE GROSS PAY'	
0 4	0		D		1		01							
0 5	0							HOURS			8			
0 6	0							RATE			15		'. '	
0 7	0							GROSS			26		' , $0. '	
			O											

FIGURE 14-9 (continued)

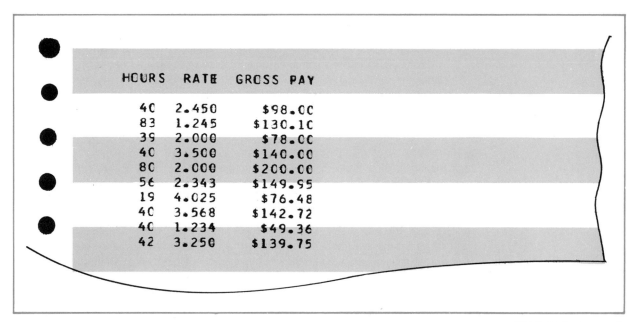

HOURS RATE GROSS PAY

HOURS	RATE	GROSS PAY
40	2.450	$98.00
83	1.245	$130.10
39	2.000	$78.00
40	3.500	$140.00
80	2.000	$200.00
56	2.343	$149.95
19	4.025	$76.48
40	3.568	$142.72
40	1.234	$49.36
42	3.250	$139.75

FIGURE 14–9 (continued).

EVALUATION OF RPG

RPG is a limited-purpose programming language. It is therefore an alternative to be considered for use in programming a particular problem. It is as easy or perhaps easier to learn than elementary FORTRAN, COBOL, or PL/I. The source language is not quite as understandable as the other languages. There is no industry standard for RPG such as there is for FORTRAN and COBOL.

The RPG language is intended for straightforward applications without complicated logic, many loops, or complicated use of files. When applied to this type of problem, it is easier to use than COBOL or PL/I and requires fewer statements. It does not usually produce a coding as efficient as one written in symbolic languages, but most problems of the type to which it is suited are limited by the speed of input and output operations, so that making the processing portion more efficient will not usually increase total throughput time.

In general, RPG is a useful language especially suited for simple report-type problems involving relatively little uncomplicated computation. RPG is also suited to small computers which do not have sufficient storage to implement COBOL, PL/I, etc.

▌OTHER PROCEDURE- AND PROBLEM-ORIENTED LANGUAGES

There are hundreds of POLs but only a few that are used widely enough to receive special mention. The major languages have been explained; some minor languages which are considered important will be briefly summarized in this section.

ALGOL

The ALGOrithmic Language is an algebraic language similar to FORTRAN. It is quite popular in Europe but has never achieved the popularity of FORTRAN in the United States. FORTRAN IV has some features adopted from ALGOL, as has PL/I. The Association for Computing Machinery uses ALGOL as a publication language for computer algorithms published in its journals. A student who has learned FORTRAN or PL/I will have little difficulty in learning ALGOL, should the need arise.

BASIC

Beginners All-purpose Symbolic Instruction Code (did they perhaps decide on the acronym BASIC first and then think up a name?) was developed at Dartmouth College. It was intended to make the computer easier to use by students for relatively simple problems. It resembles a stripped-down FORTRAN, and some error-prone features of FORTRAN have been eliminated. The language has been used extensively for writing programs at remote typewriter terminals in a time-sharing system. Its input/ output facilities are very limited and very simple. BASIC takes about half as long to learn as elementary FORTRAN. It is a language well suited for the nonprogrammer engineer, researcher, etc. who occasionally must write his own programs. The problem of preparing a table of squares and square roots is written as an illustration. Note the absence of any specification of the form of the output. The output takes a standard form, with the computer giving as many digits of precision as are available. There is no distinction between integer and real quantities. The disadvantages are its lack of advanced features should the programmer want them.

FIGURE 14–10 BASIC language program to prepare table of squares and square roots and sample output from program

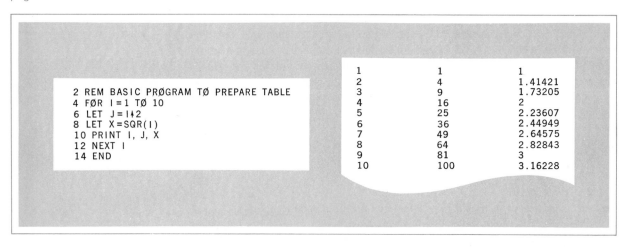

JOVIAL

Jules Own Version of International Algebraic Language is an ALGOL derivative created primarily for use in command and control networks. It incorporates abilities to express specialized command and control procedures, to accept environmental variables, and to operate efficiently in a realtime atmosphere.

APT

The Automatically Programmed Tooling system codes instructions for automatically controlled machine tools. The coded instructions are interpreted by a control system that guides machine production of parts.

SIMULATION LANGUAGES

The writing of simulations can become quite complicated. Several languages have been developed to make it easier to describe the problem and let the compiler generate the program. The most popular are SIMSCRIPT and GPSS (General Programming System Simulator). Both languages provide for describing waiting lines (queues) and the rules for service (queue discipline). For example, in a simulation of a bank's services, waiting lines develop in front of teller windows and the tellers service them on a first-in first-out basis. A simulation language would be useful in writing a computer program to study the effects of more tellers, different service procedures, etc.

▌ SUMMARY

The trend in computer programming is clearly away from machine-oriented languages to procedure- and problem-oriented languages. The efficiency of the POLs in running time has improved, and in many cases the throughput times for a program written in a POL and one written in a symbolic assembly language are the same because of input/output limitations.

The four major POLs were described in the chapter—COBOL, FORTRAN, PL/I, and RPG. The explanations provide a general understanding of the form and scope of the languages. The purposes of other minor POLs were summarized briefly.

The availability of suitable POLs is an important factor when considering a computer system. Since POLs can vary widely in efficiency with respect to compile time, diagnostic capabilities, and running time, the performance of the compilers is an important element in evaluating a computer system.

▌ ANSWERS TO SELF-TESTING QUIZZES

SELF-TESTING QUIZ 14-1

1 Identification
  Environment

Data

Procedure

2 Environment

3 $376.54

452

$4.52

4 *a* Add together A B and C and store the result in a location called TOTAL.

b It will copy the contents of HOURS-IN and store it in location HOURS-OUT. If HOURS-OUT has a PICTURE, it will edit the data being moved into that location.

c Write a record called PRINT-LINE.

d Read a record from a file called CARD-IN.

e Multiply UNITS times COST and store the result after rounding, in location TOTAL-COST.

SELF-TESTING QUIZ 14-2

1 Input is specified by a READ command and a format specification. As an example, to read data called A and B, the pair of statements would be:

READ (1, 1) A, B

1 FORMAT (F10.0, F10.0)

2 *a* 376.   *c* 0.37600000E 01

b 3.76   *d* 376

3 *a* If DEDUCT is greater than PAY, or equal to PAY, the next statement to be executed is 3; if PAY is greater, the next statement is 5.

b All statements between this DO statement and statement 3 are to be executed seven times, i.e., JIX starts with a value of 1 and is increased by 1 each time through the loop. When JIX = 7 has been executed, the loop is terminated.

c Branch to statement 15 and continue execution with that statement.

d Add the values of A, B and C and store the results in a location called X.

e Multiply the value of X and B and store the result in location Y.

f Square the value of A and store it in location Z.

SELF-TESTING QUIZ 14-3

		Example
1 *a*	Data-directed	READ DATA (NO, COST);
b	List-directed	READ LIST (NO, COST);
c	Edit-directed	READ (NO, COST) (F(4), F(8, 3));

2 Uses a default specification written into the compiler.

3 *a* Transfers control to a procedure called NEXT-CARD.

b Compares GROSS and DEDUCT. If GROSS is less than or equal to DEDUCT, the program goes to a procedure called ERROR-ROUTINE. If not (i.e., GROSS is larger), the NET-PAY is computed.

    c Reads data-directed input. The form of the data will be as shown in the following example:

        EMPLNO = 13764, RATE = 4.375;

    d Defines the end of a procedure called BILLING.

▎ EXERCISES

1 What is the difference between a procedure-oriented and a problem-oriented language?

2 What do the following acronyms stand for?

    a COBOL   *d* PL/I

    b FORTRAN   *e* JOVIAL

    c ALGOL   *f* BASIC

3 Describe the steps in solving a problem using a POL.

4 Outline the conditions which suggest the use of a POL.

5 How are library routines used by a compiler?

6 Name the four divisions in a COBOL program, and describe the purpose of each.

7 Which of the four COBOL divisions are machine-independent?

8 Identify the following statements as COBOL, FORTRAN, or PL/I:

    a X = Y**2

    b X = Y**2;

    c COMPUTE X = Y**2.

    d ADD A, B GIVING C.

    e C = A + B

    f C = A + B;

    g IF GROSS-PAY > 300 THEN GO TO ERROR-1;

    h IF (GROSS − 300.0) 2, 2, 3

    i READ DATA (X, Y);

    j READ (3, 1) X, Y

    k READ PAYROLL-FILE RECORD.

9 In most POLs, statements or groups of statements need to be identified for reference purposes. How is a referenced statement identified in FORTRAN, COBOL, and PL/I?

10 Describe the purpose of each of the specification sheets used in the RPG version illustrated in the text.

11 What is the difference between USASI Basic FORTRAN and FORTRAN?

❚ ELEMENTS OF A COMPUTER FILE
RECORD KEY
DATA HIERARCHY
CROSS REFERENCING

❚ FILE MANAGEMENT ACTIVITIES

❚ CONSIDERATIONS IN FILE DESIGN
FILE ACCESS METHODS
FILE SIZE
ITEM DESIGN
COST
FILE MAINTENANCE, PROCESSING, AND INQUIRY REQUIREMENTS
NEED FOR DATA BASE
FILE PRIVACY NEEDS

❚ SEQUENTIAL FILE DESIGN
DESCRIPTION OF THE FILE
A SEQUENTIAL FILE UPDATE RUN
HANDLING A FILE INQUIRY
EVALUATION OF SEQUENTIAL FILE DESIGN

❚ DIRECT ACCESS FILE DESIGN
DESCRIPTION OF THE FILE
ADDRESSING A DIRECT ACCESS FILE
UPDATING A DIRECT ACCESS FILE
HANDLING A FILE INQUIRY
EVALUATION OF DIRECT ACCESS FILE DESIGN

❚ ORGANIZATION OF FILES IN ADVANCED SYSTEMS

❚ SORTING TRANSACTIONS FOR FILE PROCESSING

❚ SUMMARY

❚ EXERCISES

METHODS
FOR
ORGANIZING
AND
PROCESSING
COMPUTER FILES

The end result of data processing is a document or a report; the processing of these, in most cases, makes use of files maintained for this purpose. A file is defined as a collection of related records containing data needed for subsequent data processing. Files are created when the need for a collection of records is recognized. This need may come from the requirements in preparing a regular report or from the need to facilitate data retrieval in response to inquiries and requests for special analysis. The processing of files is the major factor in the workload of a data processing installation. This chapter will discuss the design and maintenance of files plus the related activity of sorting files for processing.

▋ ELEMENTS OF A COMPUTER FILE

Files are kept for a variety of purposes. Four main types are usually identified:

TYPE	PURPOSE	EXAMPLES
Master file	Relatively permanent records containing statistical, identification, and historical information which is used as a source of reference.	Accounts receivable file Personnel file Inventory file
Transaction file	Also called detail file. Collection of records of transactions resulting from the processing of transactions. Usually used to update a master file.	Sales invoice file Purchase file Material received file
Report file	Records extracted from data in master files in order to prepare a report.	Report file for taxes withheld Report file for delinquent customer accounts Report file for analysis of employee skills
Sort file	A working file of records to be sequenced. This may be the original or a copy of a transaction file, a master file, or a report file.	

RECORD KEY

Each record in a file is identified by an identification field. A customer account number, an employee identification number, and a part number are examples of identification. This identification field, used as the basis for sequencing and searching the file, is frequently called the record key. This key can be numeric, such as a social security number, or alphabetic, such as a name. There can be more than one key, and a record may therefore be sequenced on one key in one file and on another key in a second file.

Employee no.	Name	Street address	City and state	Gross wages, etc.
984321	Thomas Grant	115 Crowther	New York, N.Y.	

Key for record

DATA HIERARCHY

A record consists of data items, also termed fields, which may themselves be formed from two or more items. This process of subdivision can be continued, the last items being termed *elementary items*. For example, an item DATE may be formed from three elementary items, MONTH, DAY, and YEAR.

DATE

10	12	1967
MONTH	DAY	YEAR

When the item DATE is specified, the entire item is obtained. MONTH will refer only to the MONTH portion of DATE. The relationship of items in a file thus forms a hierarchical or tree form:

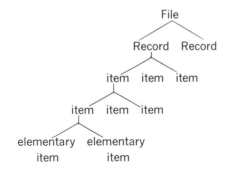

Some records may be divided into two parts: a master record and detail or trailer records. For example, a customer accounts receivable record may be divided into the master portion containing the name, address, credit rating, etc., and several trailer records each containing the data on an unpaid invoice. The trailer records are often termed *detail records* or repeating records.

Master record	Detail	Detail	Detail	Detail

Customer record

In addition to the items themselves, the records may contain cross-referencing aids called pointers, chains, and links. These establish a relationship between the record, or an item in the record, and other records or items. They are especially applicable for files in direct-access storage. The terms are often used interchangeably because they are conceptually similar.

TERM	DESCRIPTION
Pointer	A reference in the item, record, or index which tells the computer where to go next to obtain the data or more data.
Link	A reference in a record to another related record.
Chain	A set of references in a record which provide the circular connection between the master record and the trailer or detail records which are stored in different locations. By using the chain one can trace through all the trailers and back to the master record (Figure 15–1).

FILE MANAGEMENT ACTIVITIES

File management refers to all activities relating to the creation, updating, and use of files. These activities can be classed as:

1   File creation
2   File processing and maintenance
3   Selection (retrieval)
4   Extraction

File creation can refer to the establishing of an entirely new file or to the conversion of an existing file in non-computer form to a computer file medium. The conversion of existing files is one of the difficult problems of converting to a computer system or from one computer system to another.

File maintenance is the updating of a file to reflect the effects of nonperiodic changes by adding, altering, or deleting data. To maintain a master file, new records are added and obsolete or erroneous records are removed. Maintaining a program library entails the addition of new programs and the replacing of existing programs with revised versions when changes are made. File processing, on the other hand, is the periodic updating of a master file to reflect the effects of current data, often transaction data in a detail file.

Selection refers to the retrieval of a record from the file. This search process is very straightforward with a sequential file organization but can become quite complex when using direct access storage equipment.

Extraction is the copying of selected records from a file to form a new file for analysis, report preparation, etc. For example, from the file of all employees, the records

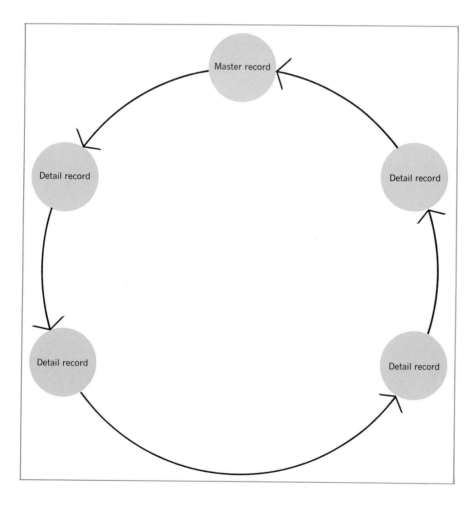

FIGURE 15-1 Chaining of records

of employees with over 20 years of service may be extracted in order to perform an analysis of the characteristics of these employees.

CONSIDERATIONS IN FILE DESIGN

The objectives of a file organization are:

1 To provide a means for locating records for processing, selection, or extraction
2 To facilitate file creation and maintenance

In working toward these objectives, the file organization should be designed to use to advantage the characteristics of the equipment, the data, and the processing system. Some of the key considerations in file design are:

1   File access method
2   File size
3   Item design
4   Cost
5   File maintenance requirements
6   File processing requirements
7   File inquiry requirements
8   Need for data base
9   File privacy needs

FILE ACCESS METHODS

File access methods will be discussed in some detail in the next sections of this chapter because of the importance of this factor in file design and file processing. The two major methods of access are sequential access and direct access (also termed random access). Sequential access is illustrated by magnetic tape and punched cards; the most common direct access equipment unit is a disc file. The fact that the disc or other direct access device has direct access capabilities does not mean that the records must be accessed randomly. A disc file can access records in either a sequential manner or randomly. This means that the two equipment capabilities provide four methods of access and processing:

Sequential access–sequential batch processing
Direct access–sequential batch processing
Direct access–random batch processing
Direct access–random online processing

FILE SIZE

The size of a file in terms of storage requirements is affected by the number of records, record size, block size, and the method for storing the data on the file medium. The record size is dependent on the number of items in the record and the item design. The block size will affect the storage requirements because putting several records in a block reduces the number of interblock gaps on magnetic tape and reduces the unused storage space on a medium such as disc files, where there are fixed-size storage areas. The effect of blocking on tape utilization is shown below:

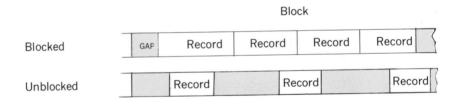

The blocking of records also affects total throughput time because starting and stopping at the interblock gap takes considerable time relative to the usual processing time. Bringing in more records at a time reduces the total start and stop tape time.

Where file size becomes quite large because of substantial numbers of large-size records, one solution is to make a smaller record containing the information which changes frequently and a second, complete file. The abridged file is processed frequently; the unabridged file is updated less often.

ITEM DESIGN

Item design refers to the planning of the form in which fields will be stored in a record. There are two major considerations—the way information is arranged in a record and the item size. The item design may affect the throughput time because of its effect on the editing necessary to prepare an item for processing, and it will usually affect the total storage required.

Not all items in a record contain information. A personnel file may contain data about some employees which is not relevant for other employees. An accounts receivable file which stores data on individual invoices not yet paid will have a different number of invoices for each customer. The field size requirements are not the same for all items. If the field is for a name, the names differ in length. These considerations lead to either a fixed item size approach or a variable item size approach. With fixed item size, each record is designed with space for every field. Those spaces not pertinent to the record or subfield are filled with blanks or some other fill character. The other approach is to have each record contain only those fields with significant information and omit those fields not needed. The item size is allowed to be variable.

In order to implement the variable item size approach, the variable-size record usually contains a special fixed field identifying the fields present in the item. If there is a variable size for the field itself, this may be specified by a special-length subfield or by a special symbol.

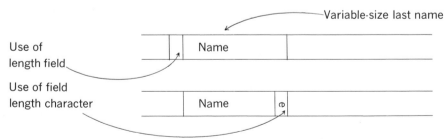

Fixed item size is easier to handle for the programmer, and there is no need to have the extra computer operation to identify the field, field size, etc. Therefore, fixed item size is indicated for small-volume files where space is not a consideration, for jobs where the data is quite similar as to fields and field sizes, and for high-activity jobs where efficiency of processing may be important. Variable item size is indicated if there is considerable variability in the data such that variable design will reduce significantly the storage requirements.

COST

The file size and cost considerations are closely related. Magnetic tape is usually favored for large files because it is relatively inexpensive (say $20 per reel), is reusable, and can be expanded indefinitely. The storage capacity of a tape will vary depending on recording mode, density, record gap, etc. A rough range is from 3 to 6 million characters of storage for each tape. By way of contrast, disc storage devices hold from about 2 to 100 million, and this figure may be increased by the use of several disc drives. Magnetic strip files have capacities ranging in the hundreds of millions of characters. In general the cost of a file medium is highest for fast-access and lowest for slow-access devices. If direct access is not vital and storage requirements are large, magnetic tape is favored. If direct access is necessary, disc storage is generally used for files needing medium-speed access.

FILE MAINTENANCE, PROCESSING, AND INQUIRY REQUIREMENTS

Master files must be maintained in an up-to-date condition if they are to supply current information. Obsolete items must periodically be purged from the file, and, depending on the file organization, it may need to be reconstructed to reflect changing requirements of the organization. File maintenance may be performed either in conjunction with file processing runs or as a separate run. File processing is performed either periodically as batches are accumulated or immediately when the transaction first occurs (as in online systems). The frequency of batch processing for the batch approach must balance the extra cost of more frequent processing runs against the reduced timeliness of data in the file if the processing interval is longer. As shown by the following graphs, the average age of the batch of data to be processed is one-half of the time interval between processing runs.

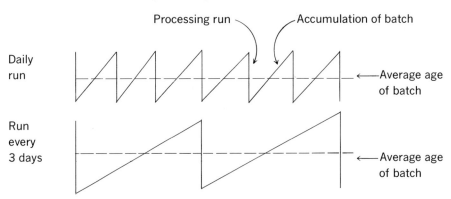

The file is always out-of-date by a factor equal to the age of the items in the batch being accumulated. In some cases, this lack of an up-to-the-minute file is not serious, such as for a payroll file for employees who are paid periodically. In other cases, an up-to-the-minute file is vital to operating decisions, and the existence of unprocessed transactions would make the file information unsatisfactory for decision purposes. If the file consists of records on available space on airline flights, the space cannot be sold if the person making the sale does not know whether or not the seat has already been sold and the transaction not yet recorded. Online immediate processing is then called for, and its cost is justified by the value of up-to-the-minute results in making operating decisions.

The major use for a file can be regular analyses and reports or random inquiry. A file that is designed for ease of processing regular reports may be very difficult to use for inquiry processing. The balancing of these two considerations is one of the major problems of file design.

NEED FOR DATA BASE

The typical approach to file design has been to set up a separate file for each data processing application. This provides a satisfactory file for that application but leads to several files with similar data which must be separately maintained and which are not necessarily compatible. The payroll file and the personnel file have much data which is common, but where there are separate files, they may not be the same even for the same data items because of different delay factors for updating or because an updating entry may be initiated by the payroll department but not reported to the personnel department. This arrangement of data files makes it difficult to obtain an answer to any management inquiry which crosses the lines between applications. An alternative is an organization-wide data file or data base. A data base for a bank, for example, would store in a single file, suitably linked together, all information about an individual's dealings with the bank—as a depositor, saver, borrower, safety deposit box holder, endorser, etc. The objectives of data base systems are user-oriented. The files should be structured to increase user control over the creation of, maintenance of, and access to data. The information processing support should aid the decision-making and creative investigation process. Data base systems require considerable software support which fortunately is becoming available with third-generation systems.

FILE PRIVACY NEEDS

When a user-oriented data base file is used, privacy becomes a consideration. Unless safeguards are established, any person will be able to access any information in the data base. In most organizations, there is confidential information in the files which should be restricted—salary data, for example. There is no method of completely restricting access, because any safeguards which are programmed can be changed through programming. The user restrictions can be quite effective, however, through the use of provisions such as:

1   A ''lockword'' or ''password'' which the user must provide in order for file access
    to be accomplished.
2   A catalog of eligible users which is checked before access.
3   Scrambled data fields for confidential information. The data field is unscrambled
    for users who establish a need to know through a password. Other users who may
    accidentally obtain access get only meaningless data.

The security provisions on access apply equally to safeguards over the making of
changes to the files.

▌SEQUENTIAL FILE DESIGN

The sequential file is the most common design, in part, because of the popularity of
sequentially accessed punched cards and magnetic tape—the most common file
media. But this media dependence should not obscure the inherent advantages, in
many cases, of this approach. A magnetic tape file will be used to illustrate sequential
file processing.

DESCRIPTION OF THE FILE

A sequential file is organized around complete records. All the data in the payroll file
regarding an individual is part of the record for that person. If there are master records with detail records, the detail records follow immediately behind the master
record. There may be cross-referencing entries to other records, but there is no need
to chain the master and detail records. If the records are of variable length, a fixed
field at the beginning of the record is often used to specify the record length.

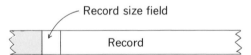

The sequential file is ordered in ascending or descending order by a key field which
may be numeric (such as a customer account number) or alphabetic (such as customer name). Since the records are physically ordered by the key field, there is no
location identification. The identification is by the key, not by the fact that the record
is the 113th on the tape. There may be gaps in the numbering of the records; no
blank records are necessary on the tape to accommodate the missing numbers.

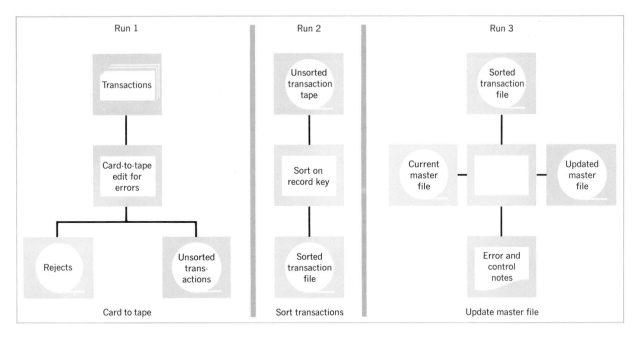

FIGURE 15–2   Runs to update a magnetic tape file from input transactions on punched cards

A SEQUENTIAL FILE UPDATE RUN

In order to update a sequential file, the transactions must be sorted into the same order on the same key as the master file. A magnetic tape file update from punched card input is really the third of three separate computer runs (Figure 15–2). Note that in sequential processing the entire master file is passed through the computer. Even if there are only a few transactions, the entire file is copied to make a new file incorporating the changes. This means that it is desirable to hold transactions until a reasonable-size batch of transactions can be processed. The sequential processing mode is therefore batch-oriented. The card-to-tape and sort times are related to the number of records, but there is a setup time, so that by comparison with direct processing it is inefficient to process in the batch-oriented sequential manner if there are few transactions. However, rarely will all records in the file have activity. In most files of any size, a 10-percent activity rate (transactions affecting 1 of 10 master records) represents a substantial level of activity.

HANDLING A FILE INQUIRY

If the file is organized sequentially and there are inquiries for information found in the file, how is this handled? It depends on the type of inquiry. Consider the following examples for a personnel file sequenced on employee identification number:

1   Selection inquiry—list and tally all employees over 45 years in age who have worked for the organization for less than 5 years.

2　Extraction inquiry—obtain and list the records for the employees in department 13.

3　Extraction inquiry—obtain the records for employees with identification numbers 37965 and 94326.

In the first case, every record in the file is read with two fields being examined. Any record meeting the requirements is listed and tallied. In the second case, the entire file must be searched because the file is not sequenced by department. The third example requires only that the key be examined. The file must be searched only until the indicated records are obtained. If these are the first two records, the search is then over; if they are the last two, the entire file will be searched. The second example points up the problem of the key. If there is processing to be performed or considerable inquiry based on a key other than the primary sequencing key, a second file may be created and sequenced on another key (say, department number). Note that two files must be maintained. The second file must either be maintained through an updating using the transactions or it must be recreated from the first file and sorted before every use.

EVALUATION OF SEQUENTIAL FILE DESIGN

Keep in mind that a sequential file medium, e.g., magnetic tape or cards, can in a practical sense be used only with a sequential file structure, but that one can also use a sequential file design with a direct access device. The advantages of low cost and expandability are characteristics of magnetic tape rather than the file design. However, the hardware characteristics cannot be completely divorced from the evaluation.

The advantages and disadvantages of sequential design (assuming batch processing) for updating master files are:

ADVANTAGES	DISADVANTAGES
File design is simple—locating a record requires only a sequence key.	Entire file must be processed no matter how low the activity rate.
If activity rate is high, the simplicity of the key as method for accessing makes for efficient processing.	Transactions must be sorted.
	File is never up-to-the-minute.

If there is sufficient level of activity and transactions can be batched, the sequential design is favored for master file updating. This design encounters problems, however, for accessing data to answer inquiries.

In the examples of inquiry handling with sequential files, a selection inquiry examining several characteristics requires looking at every record in any case, so the sequential design is optimal for this type. In the other two instances, the sequential file must pass the entire file, whereas with direct access and proper indexing the desired records can be obtained without reading other records. Also, responses to inquiries can never be up-to-the-minute because the transactions in the batch waiting to be processed may affect the result. These batched but unprocessed transactions are difficult to routinely locate and examine should this be desirable.

▌ DIRECT ACCESS FILE DESIGN

The direct access file device allows methods of processing not available with the sequential type. Direct access processing is required in the case of online realtime systems and for any system which must respond quickly to requests for up-to-the-minute information. The direct access file design is influenced by the characteristics of the file device, so that this must also be considered.

DESCRIPTION OF THE FILE

A direct access or random access file is kept on a drum, disc, strip file, or mass core. Except for mass core, these involve a rotational movement to move the media past the read-write head. The reading or writing in the file requires the obtaining of the storage address of the record and the accessing of the location. The accessing steps will be discussed first, followed by a description of the address-locating problem.

The time to access a record on a rotational direct access file consists of the seek time and the rotational time.

1 *Seek time.* This is the time required to position a movable read-write head over the recording track to be used. If the read-write head is fixed, this time will be zero.
2 *Rotational time.* This is the rotational delay, also termed latency, to move the storage medium underneath the read-write head.

Drum and disc files are cyclic—the disc or drum revolves past the read-write head at fixed intervals. If the read or write instruction is not given and executed at that time, there is a delay while the disc or drum again revolves into position (Figure 15–3). This cyclic action means that while each record is accessible without reading other records, the time intervals required to access different records are not equal but are dependent on the location of the read-write head and the position of the disc or drum surface. The seek time can be especially significant, so that an improvement in the structuring of a file to improve the seek time is frequently the most productive action that can be taken to improve the overall throughput time. For example, one popular disc file takes a maximum of 170 msec to position and revolve. If the arm is positioned over the correct track, the maximum delay due only to rotation is reduced to 25 msec. By way of contrast, a 100-character record, once positioned, is read or written in less than 1 msec.

In a tape file, each file is put on separate tape reels. In direct access, more than one file may be put on a single device. As explained in Chapter 13, each storage loca-

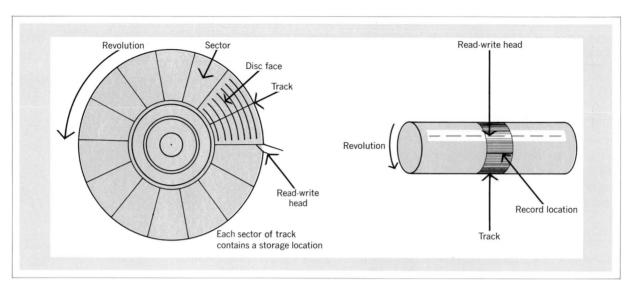

FIGURE 15–3   Storage on a revolving-medium direct access file

tion has an address. On a disc file the address identifies the disc face, track, and sector. This address must be specified in some way in order to retrieve data stored at that location. The record itself is similar to a record on magnetic tape except that subfields are frequently not stored next to the master record. When stored elsewhere, these records are associated with the master record via links or pointers.

ADDRESSING A DIRECT ACCESS FILE

As discussed in Chapter 13, the major problem with direct access processing is identifying the address where the record is stored. This addressing was not a problem with magnetic tape because the file was sequenced on the key—no tape address was required. Suppose the personnel record for Bill Smithers, employee number 387654, is to be updated. Where is his record located in the file? Only by knowing the address can it be found. The address can be obtained in several different ways:

1   Identification same as address
2   Address supplied as separate identification field
3   Address derived from identification (randomizing)
4   Address located from an index

The use of the address as the identification field is usually not feasible. It means renumbering all records, because purging obsolete records leaves an unused location and the address is not always suitable as an identification number. The problem of obsolete records can be illustrated by a part number. To avoid confusion a part should not be assigned the part number belonging to another, even if the first is obsolete.

The second method of making an additional address field in the data to be processed is feasible but has the disadvantage of adding to the coding requirement. It is a number which is nonmeaningful to persons doing the coding of input data, and therefore the coding of the field tends to be error-prone.

The use of the identification number to derive a storage address has the advantage that no new identification keys need be coded. Arithmetic performed on the regular identification number results in a derived storage address. If, for example, the storage addresses for a 10,000-item file range from 50000 to 59999 and the identification numbers run sequentially from 3000 to 12999, each identification key has 50,000 added and 3000 subtracted to arrive at the storage address. This is a one-for-one transformation, and no duplicate addresses will be generated. Numbering systems are frequently arranged sequentially, and, if they are, there are gaps of varying length in the numbering to allow the insertion of new items. The individual portions of the record key may have significance such as territory code, subassembly code, etc. To arrive at a suitable arithmetic procedure to transform this number into a storage address requires some ingenuity. The procedure is often termed *randomizing* because transformation of the nonsequential numbers to storage addresses is based on the uniform distribution of random digits. If, for example, 100,000 storage locations are to be assigned, and one tallies the occurrence of the digits 0 to 9 in each position of the storage addresses, there will be 10,000 ones, 10,000 twos, etc. This suggests that a procedure which can take all or part of the identification number and produce a random number will generate storage addresses falling uniformly in range of the assigned storage. An analysis of the arithmetic procedures for generating a set of somewhat random digits from a given number are beyond the scope of this text. The procedures used, however, can be quite simple. The number may be divided by a divisor equal to the number of available storage locations. The remainder is saved as the storage address. The randomness of the remainder is usually improved if the prime number nearest in value to the number of storage locations is used as the divisor. A second approach is to multiply part or all of the key and then extract the middle digits as the storage address. There are also randomizing procedures which use addition to obtain a set of random digits.

The difficulty with the randomizing procedure is that two or more keys may produce identical addresses. In that event one of the records, termed a *synonym,* is stored at the location with a link to the second record stored in an overflow location; a third synonym is linked to the second, etc. When locating a record, the program first derives the address from the key and if the record at that location does not have the same key, the program looks at the link and goes to the overflow location for the record. It is also necessary to keep track of unused locations in order to be able to assign them.

The index method uses a table to find the address. The table lists the reference numbers of data items along with the addresses where the records are stored. The computer searches the table until it locates the address of the record. There may be a hierarchy of tables to reduce search time. For example, the first table gives the entry in the second table, which then gives the location in storage. The table look-up can also be used in connection with a derived address. The track on a cylinder where the record is located is derived from the address, and the record is then located by means of a small index associated with the track or cylinder.

UPDATING A DIRECT ACCESS FILE

A direct access file may be updated continuously as transactions are recorded or periodically after a batch of transactions has been accumulated. Continuous processing is also termed online or random access processing. Online processing is particularly appropriate in those cases where the file needs to be completely up to date at all times, such as with airline reservation records, or needs to be updated with very little delay, as with inventory records. The direct access device has distinct advantages over sequential access for processing inquiries; for regular reports, the advantage may not be great.

If transactions are batched before processing, they may be processed in random input order or sequenced to reduce file access time. If a file is randomized, the transactions cannot be sequenced, but the most active records can be stored together on the file so that overall seek time is reduced. If processing is performed periodically and there is activity for a fairly large percentage of the file, a sequential file design and sorting of transactions may be most efficient. For small numbers of transactions, direct processing without sorting eliminates the sort run.

In updating a direct access file, the record to be updated is copied into primary storage and altered, then written out into the same location from which it was ob-

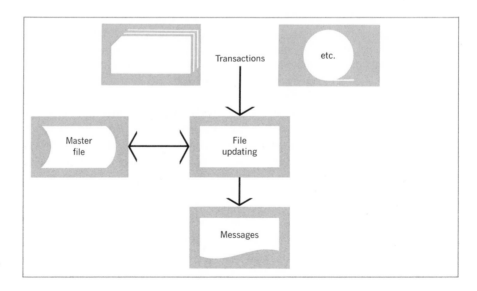

FIGURE 15-4 Direct access processing

tained. This destroys the prior contents of the location. If the updating was in error, the record prior to updating is no longer available. This is in contrast to the approach of creating a whole new file when using sequential media such as punched cards and magnetic tape. Especially in online processing, the direct access file is exposed to the risk of incorrect updating. This is handled by careful editing by the computer of all input transactions, the recording of all inputs, the use of programs to reverse faulty transactions, etc. These and other security provisions are detailed in Chapter 17.

One of the processing economies achieved in direct access processing is the concurrent processing of several files. When a sale is recorded, the account receivable can be posted, the inventory withdrawal written, etc., at the same time. In magnetic tape processing, this would require several different runs.

HANDLING A FILE INQUIRY

The three inquiry examples discussed in connection with sequential file devices will be examined in the context of a file stored on a direct access device.

1 *Selection inquiry*—List and tally all employees over 45 years in age who have worked for the organization for less than 5 years.
2 *Extraction inquiry*—Obtain and list the records for the employees in department 13.
3 *Extraction inquiry*—Obtain the records for employees with identification numbers 37965 and 94326.

In the first case, every record in the personnel file must be examined unless there are indexes based on age and length of service. The latter is unlikely. If the file is arranged in some sequential fashion, the processing is made more efficient since there is no need to seek randomly.

The second case will depend on how the file and its indexes are organized. If considerable processing is performed by department, the records will either be grouped together for easy access or there will be an index to locate employees by department.

In the third example, the records can be located directly if their disc addresses are known. If not known, the disc addresses can be derived by one of the methods described.

Another possibility in file inquiry is an inquiry involving more than one file. With several files located online in direct access equipment, processing which begins with the personnel file can cross-reference data in the payroll file, etc., in order to provide a complete response. With sequential files, each of these represents a separate run which must process each of the separate files.

EVALUATION OF DIRECT ACCESS FILE DESIGN

A direct access device is flexible. The records can be arranged either sequentially or randomly. Processing can be performed with sorted, sequenced batches of transactions or with one or more unsorted ones. Processing can be integrated to concurrently update several files affected by a transaction or inquiry. With a direct access file, online processing is possible and inquiry response is improved.

Direct access storage is more costly, and the amount of storage is limited, whereas the number of tapes which can be stored is for practical purposes unlimited. On the other hand, online storage of 100 billion characters is now available in some systems, so that size is not a factor at present. If one wished, he could organize his disc file exactly like the tape file and, after sorting the data, pass it against the file to perform the updating. The problems which arise have therefore to do with using the file to process unsequenced data. These problems center on the organizing of the file and the file accesses to reduce seek time and the obtaining of the storage address when fetching a record for processing. The several methods described all add to the processing effort and usually to the amount of storage. The tape records are closely packed—when a record is dropped, the space on the tape is closed up. When a disc record is dropped, the location may go unused because the method for assigning and locating addresses cannot use it without reorganizing the entire file. Randomizing techniques will rarely completely pack the file. The result is that direct access storage locations have a packing factor (occupancy rate) of less than 100 percent, and tables are maintained to keep track of unused locations.

Processing punched cards or magnetic tape automatically provides a backup file for reconstruction purposes as a by-product of the method of processing. Special provisions must be made for backup and reconstruction when direct access files are used. This will be discussed further in Chapter 17.

ORGANIZATION OF FILES IN ADVANCED SYSTEMS

The trend in file design in advanced data processing systems is to integrated files stored in a hierarchy of storage devices. The hierarchy of devices allows the system to take advantage of the capabilities of each and yet provide extensive storage. Figure 15–5 illustrates this concept.

In some of the advanced systems, designers are finding that the interrelationship between files requires a central control of the data files and data definitions. The organization-wide data file is an attractive concept difficult to implement. Software is being provided by the manufacturers, but substantial design work is required by the organization taking this approach. This work includes the making of a central definition of all data to be stored or processed and the organizing of data so that it can be used both for routine production runs and for inquiries. The orientation of data to provide user-oriented files means that data must be able to be retrieved by content rather than by specifying a key. This is accomplished by setting up a series of indexes based on content identifiers. A user specifies content words and the computer retrieves data identified by this content.

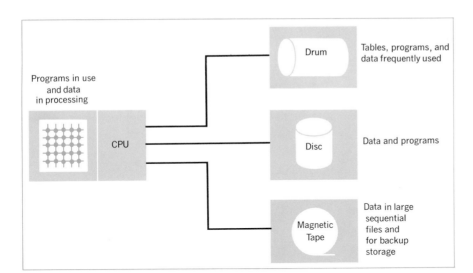

FIGURE 15-5 Hierarchy of storage devices

▌ SORTING TRANSACTIONS FOR FILE PROCESSING

Sorting is basic to the processing of sequential file media. The sorting of punched cards was explained in Chapter 2; this section will describe the sorting of records on magnetic tape. Sort routines are provided as a part of the software furnished by the manufacturer, so that the individual installation need not usually write the sort programs. The sort routine is used by specifying the key on which the file is to be sorted, the record length, and similar characteristics.

There are two steps in sorting a tape file. The first is establishing the initial sorting strings, and the second is the merging of these strings into a single sequenced string. A string is a group of records which have been sequenced. The merging process will be explained first.

If we have two strings of records sequenced on a key, the two strings can be merged into a sequenced string by looking at the keys of only two records at a time. In other words, no matter how long the two strings, only the next two records need be in main memory for the sort comparison. This merging of strings will be illustrated for two strings of four records (Figure 15-6).

The two merging strings come from two different input magnetic tape drives, and the merged string that results is written on one of two output tapes. The next pair of strings are merged and written on the other output tape. When the input tapes have been completely read, the output tapes become input for the next merge. Suppose that there are 15,360 records to be sorted and that there are 512 initial strings each 15 words in length.

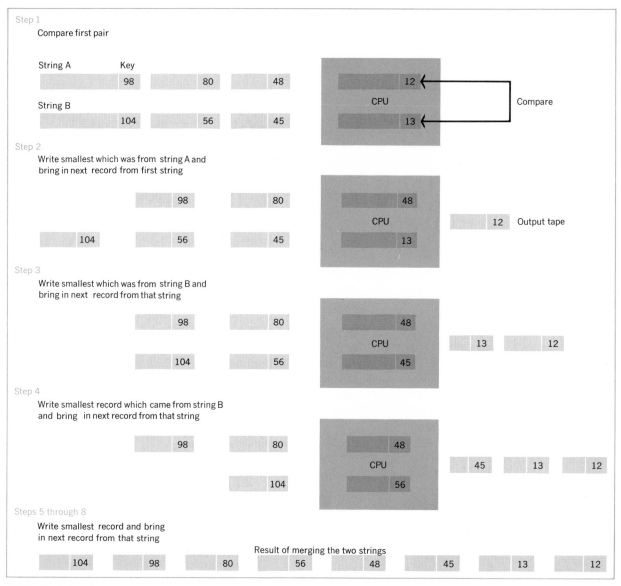

FIGURE 15-6   Merging of two strings

The initial strings are usually established by reading in a group of records and sorting them inside the computer. By doing this, the number of sorts can be substantially reduced. For example, in the case of the 15,000-record file, initial strings of 60 instead of 15 reduce the number of passes by 2, a 20-percent reduction in sorting time. The size of the initial sort is limited by the size of the memory since the records are held there during the sorting. The internal sort can take several forms. The methods are illustrated by exchange sorting (Figure 15–7). Starting with the first record in a list, the key of that record is compared, one at a time, with those following. If any key for a record lower in the list has a higher key (for an ascending sort), the records exchange places in the list and the new record key is used to continue comparing to the end of the list. The first item is now the largest in the list. The second item is then compared with the third, etc., until the second largest key with its record is in the second position. The process continues as shown for a list of four keys in Figure 15–7. If the data is somewhat in order, the exchange procedure can be improved by comparing successive pairs of keys and exchanging. When there are no exchanges, the list is in order.

PASS NUMBER	STRING LENGTH AT END OF PASS	NUMBER OF STRINGS ON EACH TAPE
1	30	256
2	60	128
3	120	64
4	240	32
5	480	16
6	960	8
7	1,920	4
8	3,840	2
9	7,680	1
10	15,360	1 on final tape

Note that in tape sorting the key length does not, for practical purposes, affect the length of time for the sort. In card sorting, the number of sorts was dependent on the length of the key. An advantage of tape sorting is the fact that the final sequence is checked by the final merge. This is not true of a card sort.

Since the setting up of the initial string is time consuming, this step is often combined with other processing runs such as the card to tape edit run. The tape sort requires four tape units to sort without having to switch tape reels. If additional tape units are available, the sort procedure can be further refined.

STEP	1	2	3	4	5	6	FINAL
RECORD KEYS	82 98 49 87 Exchange	98 82 49 87 No exchange	98 82 49 87 No exchange	98 82 49 87 No exchange	98 82 49 87 Exchange	98 87 49 82 Exchange	98 87 82 49

FIGURE 15–7 Exchange sorting

▌SUMMARY

The types of file storage devices in an installation, the methods of file organization, and the processing approaches to be used are fundamental and interrelated decisions. This chapter has presented many of the considerations in file design and has discussed in some detail sequential and direct access file structures. The chapter also discussed the method of sorting data on magnetic tape, an essential processing step before updating master files maintained on magnetic tape.

▌ EXERCISES

1　Define the following terms:
   a　Master file　　　　e　Data base
   b　Record key　　　　f　Latency
   c　Pointer　　　　　　g　Rotational delay
   d　Link　　　　　　　h　Seek time
2　Describe file management activities.
3　Describe a sequential file update run. What run must have preceded it?
4　What is the major difficulty with handling a limited inquiry when the data is on magnetic tape?
5　Compare the advantages and disadvantages of a magnetic tape sequential file with a direct access disc file.
6　Explain the different methods for obtaining the disc address for locating a record.
7　Why is the randomizing procedure used to assign disc addresses?
8　Assuming an eight-digit disc address, square the account number 8943764843 and save the middle eight digits. How can this be used to obtain a disc address?
9　If a merge sort for a file of 6,000 records starts with strings of 30, how many passes will it take to sort the file?
10　What influence does the key size have on the sort time with magnetic tape?
11　How is the length of a variable-length record specified?
12　How is the length of a variable-length field identified?
13　A processing job involving 1,000 records of a maximum length of 200 characters is to be processed once a month. The fields vary in length. Should the item sizes be fixed or variable? Explain.

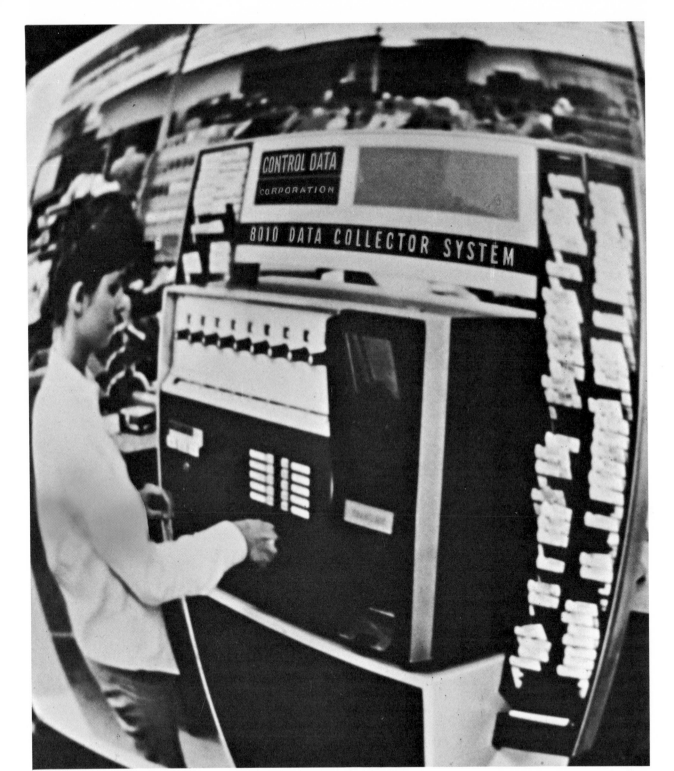

CHAPTER 16

▍ APPLICATIONS OF DATA COMMUNICATIONS

DATA COLLECTION
INQUIRY PROCESSING
COMPUTER TIME SHARING
MESSAGE SWITCHING

▍ DATA TRANSMISSION

▍ COMMUNICATIONS FACILITIES

MODES OF OPERATION
CLASSES OF FACILITIES
TYPES OF SERVICE
TYPEWRITER TERMINAL DEVICES
TRANSMISSION CODES

▍ ERROR CONTROL IN DATA COMMUNICATIONS
SYSTEMS

CAUSES OF ERRORS
ERROR DETECTION AND CORRECTION TECHNIQUES

▍ ANALYSIS FOR THE USE OF DATA
COMMUNICATIONS

ANALYSIS OF DISTRIBUTION OF MESSAGE TRAFFIC
ANALYSIS OF VOLUME AND URGENCY
ANALYSIS OF TERMINAL DEVICE REQUIREMENTS AND COMPUTER
  COMMUNICATION CAPABILITIES
DESIGN OF ALTERNATIVE SYSTEMS AND SELECTION OF A SYSTEM

▍ SUMMARY

▍ EXERCISES

DATA COMMUNICATIONS IN DATA PROCESSING SYSTEMS

A data communications system consists of a group of functional units which transfer digital data between two or more terminals. It is an important element in most advanced data processing systems, and its use is expected to increase. American Telephone and Telegraph has estimated that by 1970 revenue from long-distance data transmission will exceed the revenue received from long-distance voice communications. The technical requirements and specifications of data communications equipment are beyond the scope of this chapter. Instead, the chapter will survey the most important applications, the way data is transmitted, the facilities available, the error control problem, and major selection considerations.

APPLICATIONS OF DATA COMMUNICATIONS

Data communication is employed to reduce the time required to move data from a point of origin to the computer and from the computer to a point of use. It reduces the time requirements from the hours or days involved in mail or messenger transportation to the few seconds or minutes for electrical transmission. Data communication should be considered whenever the benefit from this immediate movement of data is expected to exceed the extra cost of the communication. Data communication is used in a wide variety of applications, four of which will be described briefly as an indication of its usefulness.

DATA COLLECTION

In data collection applications, data from a remote station is transmitted to a central processing facility. The remote input units may be located on the factory floor, in branch or regional sales offices, at geographically separated manufacturing plants, and at other outlying facilities. The advantage of data collection is that it provides timely information through the prompt transmission of data from remote points. This direct transmission also reduces the number of times data must be handled, thereby reducing handling errors and manual processing costs.

An example of data collection with data communications is a system which employs recording devices on the factory floor. As a worker begins a job, he inserts his plastic identification badge and a punched job card into a data collection device. The data collection device transmits this data to a central computer facility. When the job is completed, the worker repeats the process and keys in the actual number of units produced. By this means, data on the location of each job, job time, and amount produced in the shop is made known immediately to the central computer (Figure 16–1).

INQUIRY PROCESSING

Many organizations find it desirable or necessary to establish central data files and to provide a means by which many remote locations can obtain access to the data. Each remote location has an inquiry device connected via communications lines to

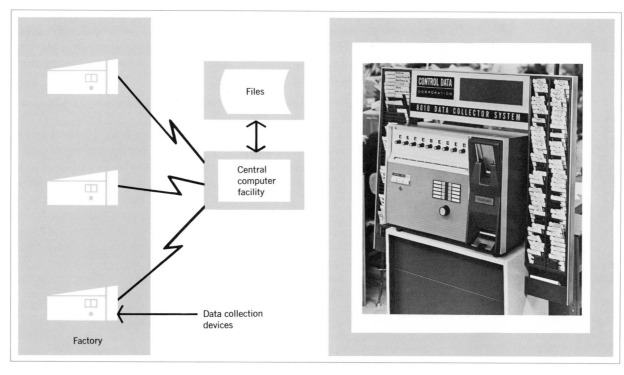

FIGURE 16–1   Example of data collection system (Courtesy of Control Data Corporation)

the central computer. Inquiries are transmitted to the computer, which processes them and, when required, prepares response messages which are transmitted back to the inquiring terminals. An inquiry may involve the realtime updating of the file to reflect the data received. The file is kept up to date at all times by immediately processing all transactions as they are recorded.

Examples of online inquiry and processing systems utilizing communications to connect a network of remote terminals to a central processing facility are brokerage firms, airlines, hotels, savings and loan associations, and banks. A common factor in these examples is a benefit from being able to service immediately a customer inquiry or transaction from any location in the system.

COMPUTER TIME SHARING

A time-shared computer system consists of a central computer facility which is accessed by a number of remote user terminals, each capable of input or output. Although some terminals may be close enough to make use of direct cable connections, the typical system will use communications links for most of the remote devices. Time sharing is discussed further in Chapter 21.

A variation on computer time sharing is the connecting via communications of two or more geographically dispersed computers and the transmission of data between these computers in order to balance the work load. For example, a company with two computers in two separate locations may transmit jobs from the one if it is overloaded to the other if it has available time.

MESSAGE SWITCHING

An organization which has a number of widely separated locations will normally have a communications network to handle the transmission of messages from one location to one or more other locations. An efficient method of handling this message traffic is to have two-way communication between each remote location and a central message switching center. The switching center receives messages, stores them, and transmits them to the designated receiving terminals. A switching center may be operated with manually operated or mechanical equipment, or a realtime computer may be used. For example, a large manufacturer uses a computer to control message switching for a nationwide network of 100 teletypewriter stations. This switching is performed concurrently with data processing. The computer receives the message from the sending station, stores it, and forwards it to the receiving station when an outgoing line becomes available.

▮ DATA TRANSMISSION

In order to understand the discussion of communications facilities, equipment, and error problems, it will be helpful to have an understanding of how data can be transmitted by electrical or electronic means.

Data is transmitted by an electrical signal or wave form which is defined by the strength of the signal (*amplitude*) and its duration in time (*phase*). The *frequency* of a wave form is the number of times the form is repeated during a specified interval. These three characteristics are diagrammed in Figure 16–2. If the basic shape of a wave form is known, a few measurements at selected time intervals (in other words, a sampling) provide the receiving instrument with enough data to identify the signals.

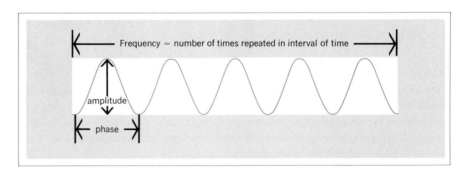

FIGURE 16–2   Diagram of wave form

For a given wave form there is a minimum frequency and a maximum frequency required to define a "state." Changing only one of these characteristics provides a different signal to encode a state. For example, if the pulse representing a "1" bit were represented by a signal having one amplitude, phase, and frequency, the "0" bit pulse could then be represented by a signal having the same amplitude and phase but a different frequency. The complete transmission of a message will have many changes of state to represent the bits which encode it. The length of time the signal must stay in one state for the receiving instrument to interpret it is dependent on the technique used by the receiver. The receiver must take a sampling during the interval of time a bit is transmitted (bit time). In order to sample within a bit time, the receiving terminal must be synchronized with the sending terminal. In general, a high-frequency state can be identified in a shorter time than a low-frequency state.

A transmission medium is usually separated into many independent bands or data paths, each consisting of a range of frequencies assigned to it. Band width is an important consideration in data communications. This refers to the range of frequencies accommodated within a band on a transmission medium. When bands are used, there is a device to convert the constant-level direct current pulses of the computer equipment into signals suitable for transmission and to perform the reverse process for the receiving terminal. The conversion is called *modulation* and *demodulation*. The device is referred to as a *modem* or *data set*.

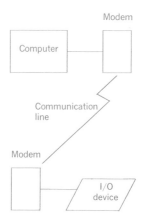

When pulses are sent by a transmitting station, the receiving station must be in synchronization with the sending device in order to interpret correctly the signals received. In order to visualize this problem, consider that a pulse for a defined time interval represents a 1-bit and a period of no-pulse represents a 0-bit. The 8-bit ASCII representation for an S would appear as shown:

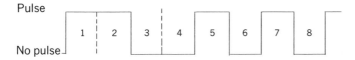

If the receiving terminal does not start at the proper point or does not maintain the same time interval, the interpretation of the coded pulses will not be correct. Two commonly employed techniques for keeping the sending and receiving devices in step are start/stop synchronization and synchronous transmission.

In the start/stop method, a start signal is transmitted at the beginning of a group of data (say for a character) and a stop signal at the end of the group. When the start signal is recognized, the receiving terminal sets up a timing mechanism to time the arrival of the data bits. This technique allows for irregular transmission of data, but it requires an extra two bits with each set to act as the start and stop signals.

In the synchronous or bit stream method, the receiving and transmitting stations are synchronized by transmitting synchronizing characters at the beginning of a message or during idle periods. During the transmission, the receiving station is kept in step with the transmitting station by a special timing circuit.

▍ COMMUNICATIONS FACILITIES

Some of the types of communications facilities are telephone and telegraph cables, radio, and microwave. Although under certain circumstances an organization may install its own communications facilities, most communication utilizes the facilities of the public telephone and telegraph companies, the largest of these in the United States being the American Telephone and Telegraph Company (Bell System) and Western Union.

MODES OF OPERATION

There are three modes of operation for communications facilities—simplex, half duplex, and full duplex (Figure 16–3).

MODE	DESCRIPTION
Simplex	Communication in only one direction. Used, for example, for a remote device which receives but does not send.
Half duplex	Communications in both directions, but in only one direction at a time.
Full duplex	Communications in both directions at the same time.

CLASSES OF FACILITIES

Service can be divided into three classes based on the band width. Band width determines the maximum transmission speed because the width of a band affects the frequency range that can be accommodated and a high-frequency state provides for faster communication. The three classes of band width therefore represent three classes of capacity.

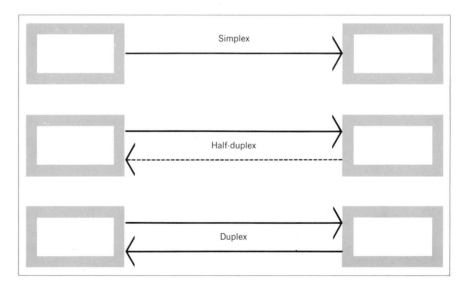

FIGURE 16–3 Modes of communication

CLASS	DESCRIPTION
Narrow band	Communications facilities capable of transmitting data in the range up to 300 bits per second. Typical speeds are 45, 57, 75, and 150 bits per second depending on service used. The Bell System TWX (Teletypewriter Exchange Service) and the Western Union TELEX fall into this class.
Voice band	Channels used for human voice communications which have a band width of 3,000 cycles for the public lines and 4,000 cycles for leased lines. Maximum speeds range up to 2,400 bits per second, although some higher speeds can be obtained and slower speeds are frequently used.
Broad band	Communication facilities having a higher band width than voice band width and therefore used for communication involving high data transfer rates.

TYPES OF SERVICE

The services available to a user from the communications companies include leased lines or public switched lines (the term "lines" commonly refers to all types of communications facilities even though they may use nonwire methods such as microwave). Leased lines provide the user with a specific communications path dedicated to his use only. The switched line (also termed dial-up), on the other hand, provides access to the communications network. For the switched line, the path of connections and routing of a message may vary from use to use because the automatic switching equipment in the network selects a path from the many available connections and lines when the connection is dialed. The leased line is more expensive, but its quality is known and it is available for use at any time. The switched line is less expensive, but it must be connected for each use (through dialing), and the quality of the connection may vary considerably from time to time.

The services offered by the Bell System companies are marketed under the following trade names:

NAME	DESCRIPTION OF SERVICE
Data-Phone	Data transmission using dial-up telephone voice band service. The Data-Phone data set (modem) usually has a telephone associated with it (Figure 16–4). There are several grades of service ranging from speeds of 250 to 2,500 words per minute.
Wide Area Telephone Service (WATS)	A flat rate service for long-distance calls. WATS lines may also be used for data transmission together with Data-Phone.
Teletypewriter Exchange Service (TWX)	A communications network for teletypewriter messages and low-speed business machines.
Data-Speed	For sending and receiving data in punched tape form. Operates at 1,050 words per minute, ten times the speed of standard teletypewriter tape transmission.
Telpak	Private line service providing large communication capacity. One Telpak channel may be equivalent to 12, 24, 60, or 240 voice circuits, according to user requirements.

FIGURE 16–4 DATA-phone data set (Courtesy of Northwestern Bell Telephone Company)

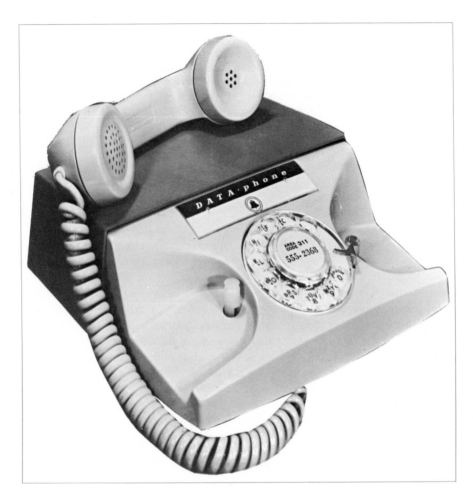

In many cases, an alternative to the telephone company is service offered by Western Union, also a regulated carrier for data communication services. The following services are offered:

NAME	DESCRIPTION OF SERVICE
TELEX	A dial-up network for low-speed communications similar to TWX.
Broadband Exchange Service	A network connecting various cities and providing subscribers with connections for two-way voice or data communication.

TYPEWRITER TERMINAL DEVICES

There are a number of new terminal devices currently being introduced. However, the extensive use of typewriter-like terminals makes it desirable to survey them briefly. The most commonly used typewriter terminal devices are Teletypes. A second important device is IBM's 1050 Data Communication System typewriter. These products illustrate the available capabilities for input and output by typewriter.

The Teletype equipment consists of a typewriter having either a 3- or 4-row keyboard (Figure 16–5). There are different models which operate in one of three modes:

RO   Receive only (remote typewriter output)

KSR   Keyboard send-receive (keyboard input and output)

ASR   Automatic send-receive (keyboard plus option to send from prepunched paper tape and to receive message on paper tape)

Generally, Teletype equipment operates for output at a maximum speed of 100 words per minute. Typewriter input is at the speed of the operator.

FIGURE 16–5 Teletype model 35 ASR
(Courtesy of Teletype Corporation)

FIGURE 16–6 IBM 1050 Data Communication System (Courtesy of International Business Machines Corporation)

FIGURE 16–6 IBM 1050 Data Communication System (Courtesy of International Business Machines Corporation)

An example of a computer manufacturer's remote typewriter is IBM's 1050 Data Communication System, which operates at 14.8 characters per second (about 150 words per minute). The system can also include slow-speed punched card, punched tape, or edge-punched input and output (Figure 16–6).

TRANSMISSION CODES

There are five codes commonly used in data communications. These are:

1. Baudot 5-level code
2. Binary coded decimal 6-level code
3. Teletypesetter 6-level code
4. Field Data 7-level code with provision for a compatible 8-level code
5. American Standard Code for Information Interchange (ASCII) 7-level code with provision for compatible 8-level code

The two most important of these are the Baudot and ASCII codes.

The 5-level code was devised late in the nineteenth century by Jean Baudot, an engineer in the French telegraph service. With a 5-level code, 32 combinations are possible. By using a shift code, to shift from a code for numbers to a code for alphabetics and special characters, it is possible to code 62 combinations (Figure 16–7). The term *baud* (pronounced bôd), referring to a unit of signaling speed, is also named after Baudot. A baud is equal to one pulse or code element per second.

The Baudot code is too limited for efficient high-speed data communications. An 8-bit code (7-level plus parity level) is used on most new equipment. The most common 7-level codes are the Field Data code specified by the Department of Defense and the USA standard code for information interchange. These codes provide for 128 combinations, some of which are shown in Figure 16–7.

Because a data communications system may use several different codes, an important equipment selection consideration for a computer to use with data communications is a hardware or adequate software capability for rapid code conversion.

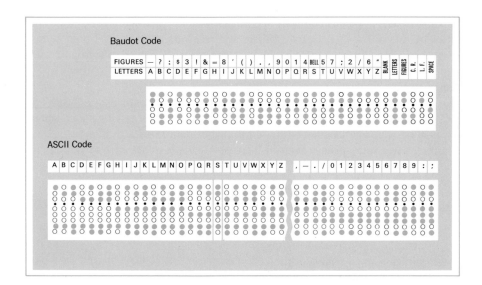

FIGURE 16-7 Transmission codes (Baudot and ASCII)

ERROR CONTROL IN DATA COMMUNICATIONS SYSTEMS

No data communications system is free of errors. Therefore, it is important to understand why errors occur, the methods of detecting them, and the methods for overcoming them.

Studies of error rates in data processing indicate the following rates for undetected errors:[1]

[1] Edgar C. Gentle, Jr., "Keeping Management up to the Minute," Computers and Data Processing, May, 1964, p. 12.

ERROR PERFORMANCE

PROCESSOR	UNDETECTED ERROR RATE
Human typists or clerks	1 error in 1,000 characters
Mechanical devices including telephone lines	1 error in 10,000 characters
Electronic devices	1 error in 100,000 characters
Electronic device with simple parity check and telephone line with error detection and correction equipment	1 error in 10,000,000 bits
Electronic device with two-dimensional parity check	1 error in 100,000,000 bits

CAUSES OF ERRORS

The causes of errors can be classed as noise, fading, and distortion. "Noise" refers to random fluctuations which interfere with the transmitted signal. This may be a rather steady background called Gaussian noise or impulse noise. The background noise, which is annoying in voice communications, is not usually a problem in data transmission. Impulse noise results from a disturbance (for example, lightning) which causes a burst of short-duration pulses.

Fading occurs in connection with microwave facilities in which signals are transmitted by sets of line-of-sight transmitters and receivers miles apart. Under certain atmospheric conditions, there is a fading in the received signals. Distortion occurs because signals which travel different paths and signals at different portions of the frequency spectrum will arrive at different times.

In general, a leased line has a lower rate of errors than a switched network line because leased lines are not subject to the variability of the switched connections and may be specially conditioned to permit higher data rates with a lower number of errors. Error rates usually tend to increase as the distance of transmission increases.

ERROR DETECTION AND CORRECTION TECHNIQUES

There are a number of techniques for detecting and correcting errors. System cost and complexity are increased by measures which improve reliability, so that the system designer must evaluate the cost of improved reliability achieved by a particular method against the benefits of the method. It is a fairly simple task to detect most errors; it requires a more complex and expensive technique to correct the detected errors. The techniques for error detection include a constant-ratio code, character parity, and combination of longitudinal and character parity.

A constant-ratio code is one in which every character is represented by the same number of 1 bits and the same number of 0 bits but in different combinations. The codes are simple to generate and to check and relatively good at detecting errors. A disadvantage of the constant-ratio code is that it increases the number of bits required to represent a given set of characters. For example, a 4-of-8 (four 1 bits) constant-ratio code provides 70 combinations, whereas a normal binary coding for 8 bits (7 bits plus parity bit) allows 128 combinations.

Parity checking is commonly used in data communications. The parity check may be only for each character, or it may be combined with a longitudinal parity bit to form a two-dimensional parity checking. This is described further in Chapter 17. The simple parity check does not allow for error correction and will not detect errors involving an even number of bits. Two-dimensional checking provides better detection—up to a total of three errors in each data block. It also allows the use of automatic error correction techniques.

There are a number of codes designed to allow efficient detection and correction of data transmission errors. However, because they require a large number of redundant bits and complex equipment, they are not widely used. Some equipment using two-dimensional parity also provides for correction of the detected errors. However, the most common method of error correction is the retransmission of erroneous messages or segments of messages. In this approach, the message is tested for parity and other characteristics as it is received. After each block, a signal is transmitted back to the sending station either confirming a no-error condition or requesting a retransmission.

▌ ANALYSIS FOR THE USE OF DATA COMMUNICATIONS

Data communications will usually cost more than slower communications methods such as mail. On the other hand, the advantages from reducing the time required to obtain information frequently more than offset the extra cost. As part of the analysis for data processing system design, there should be a cost and benefit analysis for proposed data communication. The information characteristics to be considered in the analysis of data communication needs are the distribution, volume, urgency, and terminal devices.

ANALYSIS OF DISTRIBUTION OF MESSAGE TRAFFIC

The analysis of distribution covers the information which is transmitted between different locations in the organization. This analysis may be summarized in a message grid chart (Figure 16–8) based on the grid analysis form explained in Chapter 9.

To From	Headquarters	Factory	Sales office, NYC	Sales office, SF
Headquarters		Inquiries and administrative messages	Credit status and administrative messages	Credit status and administrative messages
Factory	Shipment, production, and inventory reports		Order status and inventory position	Order status and inventory position
Sales office, NYC	Credit inquiry	Inquiries on stock and order status		None
Sales office, SF	Credit inquiry	Inquiries on stock and order status	None	

FIGURE 16–8 Grid analysis of flow of messages in a data communications system

FIGURE 16–9 Basic communication distribution patterns

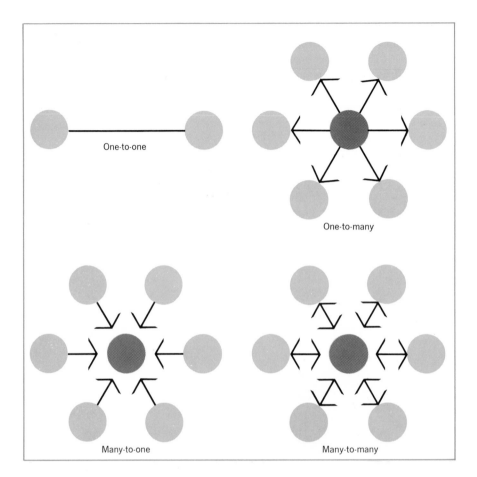

FIGURE 16–9 Basic communication distribution patterns

The distribution analysis also indicates the network of connections and the direction of data movement. These can be summarized into the four patterns diagrammed in Figure 16–9, based on the direction of calling. The one-to-one pattern involves only two points. The flow may be in one direction (one-way), in one direction at a time (half duplex), or in both directions simultaneously (full duplex). The one-to-many network involves a central station which calls to many outlying locations. The outlying offices may be able to transmit, but only when called by the central office. The many-to-one configuration allows the outlying locations to call a central facility to make inquiries, etc. The many-to-many pattern is a network in which any station may call any other station. This may be by direct wires between all offices or by each office being connected to a central switching facility which routes the messages. There are many variations of these patterns. For example, a regional switching center may service offices in a region and also connect with other regional offices.

ANALYSIS OF VOLUME AND URGENCY

The volume of information to be handled at each location should be calculated, both in total and for periods of peak volumes. The steps in this analysis are:

1 Calculate the number of messages flowing to and from every point in the system.
2 Calculate the average characters per message.
3 Calculate the total transmission time, using the data from 1 and 2 plus the transmission speed of the type of communication being analyzed.
4 Calculate the volumes for the peak periods.

The method of analysis followed where data is available is to select a sample of a number of days and calculate the number of messages for this period. The number of characters per message is estimated by counting the characters in a sample of messages. Non-printing characters such as control characters are included in the count. Peak period volume is calculated by tallying messages by time of transmission and arrival during the day.

If every remote location must transmit and receive with little possibility of delay, there will need to be more terminal facilities, faster speeds, or more lines than in a situation where delays are allowed. The analysis of urgency requirements may result in procedures to transmit messages having a low urgency during periods of low volume, thereby increasing the capacity available for peak periods.

ANALYSIS OF TERMINAL DEVICE REQUIREMENTS AND COMPUTER COMMUNICATION
CAPABILITIES

The terminal devices (a typewriter, CRT display, paper tape reader, punch card reader, etc.) represent an important consideration. Different devices have different codes and speed of operation. The process of converting data to machine-readable form is expensive and the source of a good many errors. Careful selection of devices and planning of forms, procedures, etc. to utilize effectively the characteristics of the terminal chosen are therefore important.

The facilities of the computer should include sufficient storage to hold incoming and outgoing messages. The hardware capabilities (channels, interrupts, etc.) and software support (communication software, multiprogramming, etc.) should be adequate. A computer system should be equipped with sufficient storage and hardware and software to be able to handle the peak load for data communications and still carry on other required activities such as processing programs.

DESIGN OF ALTERNATIVE SYSTEMS AND SELECTION OF A SYSTEM

Having obtained information on the characteristics and requirements of the system and having projected these figures to reflect future growth, the next step is to design alternative systems and analyze their cost and operating characteristics. These tentative designs will show the type of terminal devices, the type and speed of communication service, the number of circuits, the code, and similar specifications. Costs for the system should include estimated personnel expense, supplies for the system, space required, hardware purchase or rental, maintenance, etc.

The system to be implemented should be selected from the alternatives using criteria of effectiveness in meeting the objectives set for data communications and effectiveness in meeting specifications as to performance and cost.

▌ SUMMARY

Data communication is already an important consideration in many data processing systems; it will be an increasingly important element in future systems. Improved communication facilities and faster, more versatile terminal devices are now in development.

The uses for data communications cover a wide range of applications. They can be summarized in four major uses:

Data collection or distribution
Inquiry processing
Computer time sharing
Message switching

Data communication is carried out largely over the facility of communication carriers such as Western Union or a telephone company. Facilities range from narrow to wide band and include both public, dial-up lines and dedicated, leased lines.

Error control is an important consideration in data communications. Errors do occur, but a proper set of hardware and software controls can hold the undetected error rate at a very low level.

The analysis for data communication facilities includes analysis of distribution of traffic, the volume of messages, the urgency of transmission and receipt, the terminal device requirements, and the communications capability of the computer. Based on this data, alternative systems can be designed and evaluated in terms of cost and performance.

▌ EXERCISES

1   The formula for the number of combinations available for representing characters in a constant-ratio code is $n!\ p!g!$ where n stands for the total number of bits and p and g represent the number of 1 and 0 bits. Compare the number of characters which can be represented by a binary representation with a parity bit and the same number of bits with a constant-ratio code for 5, 6, 7, 8, and 9 bits.
2   Explain the two terms named after Emile Baudot.

3 Define the following data communications terms:

   a Data-phone   *e* Modem

   b Data set   *f* TWX

   c ASCII   *g* Telpak

   d Modulation   *h* TELEX

4 Explain the difference between the three different modes of operation for communication facilities.

5 Explain the two methods of keeping the sending and receiving stations synchronized.

6 Define the three classes of service based on band width.

7 What do the following abbreviations mean with respect to teletype equipment?

   a RO   *c* ASR

   b KSR

8 A voice band is used to transmit data to be printed on a line printer which has 132 characters per line. The code used is a 7-level code with an added parity bit for each character. Ignoring synchronization characters, how many lines per minute can be transmitted if the line will handle 2,400 bits per second?

▌ CONTROL IN A COMPUTER PROCESSING SYSTEM
TOP MANAGEMENT RESPONSIBILITY
DATA PROCESSING MANAGEMENT RESPONSIBILITY
THE CONTROL FUNCTION
PROCESSING CONTROLS
EVALUATING ERROR CONTROLS

▌ CONTROL OVER INPUT AND OUTPUT
PROCEDURAL CONTROLS AND DATA REVIEW
VERIFICATION OF CONVERSION TO MACHINE-READABLE FORM
CHECK DIGIT
INTERNAL FILE LABEL
TESTS FOR VALID DATA
CONTROL TOTALS
MOVEMENT AND HANDLING CONTROLS
OUTPUT CONTROLS
EXAMPLE OF USE OF INPUT CONTROLS—DEPARTMENT STORE
ACCOUNTS

▌ HARDWARE FEATURES FOR CONTROL OVER
   EQUIPMENT MALFUNCTIONS
REDUNDANT OR PARITY CHARACTER
DUPLICATE PROCESS
ECHO CHECK
VALIDITY CHECK
EQUIPMENT CHECK

▌ PROGRAMMED CONTROL OVER PROCESSING
LIMIT AND REASONABLENESS TEST
CROSSFOOTING TEST
CONTROL FIGURES

▌ CONTROL OVER COMPUTER PROGRAMS
ORGANIZATION OF DUTIES
APPROVAL AND DOCUMENTATION OF CHANGES
AUDITING

▌ PROTECTION OF COMPUTER RECORDS AND FILES
PHYSICAL SAFEGUARDS
PROCEDURAL CONTROLS
RETENTION AND RECONSTRUCTION PLAN
INSURANCE

▌ SUMMARY

▌ EXERCISES

CHAPTER

17

CONTROL OVER
QUALITY OF
COMPUTER
PROCESSING

Computer processing is all too often carried out with a higher error rate than is desirable because top management does not insist on proper quality control. On the other hand, error control is not without cost, and the manager who understands the problems of quality control and its methods is able to evaluate the value of tighter control compared to its cost. With computer processing there are control problems not found in manual data processing, but there are also unique, new control methods because of the capabilities of the computer.

▌ CONTROL IN A COMPUTER PROCESSING SYSTEM

There is a hierarchy of control in a computer data processing system. The outer level of control is provided by the company organization management and procedures. Within this framework there operates the organization and management of the data processing activity. A component part of this activity is the control function which monitors the quality of processing. The computer processing operations are subject to departmental control activities. This hierarchy of control is illustrated in Figure 17–1.

TOP MANAGEMENT RESPONSIBILITY

Top management has the overall responsibility for data processing. This consists of:

    Authorization of major systems additions or changes
    Post-installation review of actual cost and effectiveness of systems projects
    Review of organization and control practices of the data processing function
    Monitoring of performance

Top management responsibility for authorizing major systems work means that each such major addition or change must be presented to management as a proposal to be evaluated in terms of its cost and the benefits to be derived from it. A new or improved data processing system is similar to a large expenditure for an addition to the plant or equipment and should receive careful scrutiny before resources are committed to the project. Also, since data processing systems work will affect both the data handling requirements of other departments and the information available to them, top management understanding of the addition or change and top management approval are necessary for adequate control over data processing. Requiring top management approval also enforces adequate preplanning by data processing management.

There is a tendency among data processing personnel to underestimate both the cost and difficulty of implementing new or improved data processing systems. It is a part of the responsibility of management to follow up on project proposals and to evaluate the reasons for deviations from planned cost, planned schedule, and estimated benefit. The assessment of performance on the post-installation review will aid in evaluating future systems requests.

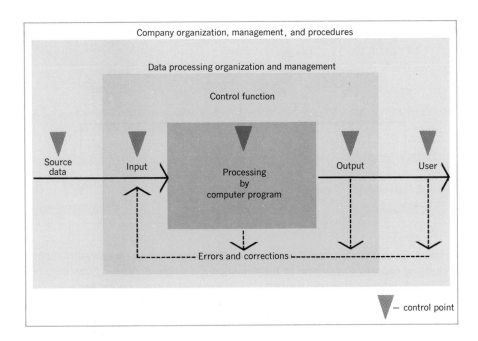

FIGURE 17–1   The control framework for a computer data processing system

Top management has the responsibility for employing competent, adequately trained data processing management personnel and for reviewing the organization and control practices of the data processing function. Day-to-day control is the responsibility of the data processing management, so that poor organization and inadequate control procedures indicate a weakness at this level of management.

The monitoring of performance requires a performance plan or standard and the reporting of deviations from this expected level of performance. The plan and variation reporting should cover three types of performance:

1   Cost of data processing activities compared to planned cost
2   Frequency and duration of delays in meeting processing schedules
3   Error rates for errors detected at various control points

DATA PROCESSING MANAGEMENT RESPONSIBILITY

In the organization of the data processing activity, it is desirable both from an operating standpoint and a control standpoint to separate the three functions of (1) system design and programming, (2) operating, and (3) control. If possible, it is frequently advantageous also to separate system design and programming. In larger installations control over data files and programs may be increased by the use of a separate file librarian. Figure 17–2 is an organization chart showing this division of functions. A suitable plan of organization and resulting division of duties are internal control features which protect the organization against the consequences of incompetence

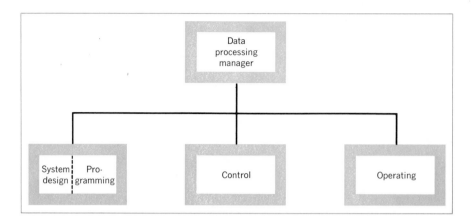

or fraud. The small number of people in computer processing compared to manual processing exposes the system to manipulation if a single person is given both programming and operating responsibility. As an example, a programmer for a company servicing a bank sometimes acted as an operator. One of the applications he had programmed was a listing of accounts which were overdrawn. While serving as computer operator he inserted a "patch" in the program to cause it to ignore overdrafts in his account when printing the overdraft report. The fraud was discovered when, because of a computer breakdown, the report was prepared manually.

Control practices associated with data processing organization and management are:

Documentation (described in Chapter 10)
Program change controls
Scheduling of personnel
Procedures for reviewing error logs, time log, etc.
Maintenance of an adequate processing reference trail (also called an audit trail)
Provision for file protection

As with manual data processing, there should be established procedures for authorization of transactions. The authorization may take the form of signatures or initials on documents from which the input is prepared. If input data may be introduced directly into the computer system without the preparation of documents, there must be alternative means for authorization, such as some form of physical control over access to the input devices or access to the means by which they can be activated.

Authorization of programs and program changes is as important as authorization of input data since both are an integral part of the processing operations in computer applications. Evidence of proper authorization of programs and program changes is normally included in program documentation.

The application of management principles to computer data processing operations will typically involve the preparation and use of a systems and procedures manual which describes standard operating procedures. The contents of the manual will usually include:

1   Standard programming procedures
2   Standard operating procedures
3   Control procedures
4   Organization and personnel duties

As with systems and procedures manuals used in other areas of activity, the manual is useful in training, supervision, and evaluation of performance.

THE CONTROL FUNCTION

The plan of organization and the operating procedures should provide for a control function. The control function can be divided into two types: (1) processing control internal to data processing and (2) independent, outside checks. The internal processing control, a function of the data processing department, is concerned with monitoring accuracy of processing and ensuring that no data is lost or mishandled within the department during processing. For example, if a detail transaction file is processed with the current master file to produce an updated master file, the sum of the transaction file and the related master file records should equal the total of the records on the updated master file. The person charged with the processing control function is responsible for making or reviewing the results of such a comparison. In very small installations, the data processing manager may perform the control activities; in others, a control clerk will perform this task.

The activities of the control clerk or control group are specified both in the systems and procedures manual and in the description of control activities for each computer application. The control function will include duties such as the following:

1   Logging of input data and recording of control information
2   Recording progress of work through the department
3   Reconciling computer controls with other control information
4   Supervising distribution of output
5   Scrutiny of console logs and control information in accordance with control instructions
6   Liaison with users regarding errors, logging of correction requests, and recording corrections made
7   Scrutiny of error listings and maintenance of error log or error report

Independent, outside checks can take several forms, but they are basically concerned with an independent check of the functioning of the data processing department. This check may be performed by a user department. If the general ledger, for instance, is maintained on the computer, the accounting department may keep a control total of all debits and credits to be posted by the computer. This control can be compared against the debits and credits from the computer run. Another possibility is an independent quality control evaluation group in a user department where the volume of data to be controlled is large. As an example, a large corporation has a payroll processing control group responsible for evaluating the payroll data produced by the computer.

PROCESSING CONTROLS

Computer data processing requires new controls for detecting and controlling errors arising from the use of EDP equipment. Examples of these controls are:

Verification of conversion of input data to machine-readable form
Control totals to detect the loss or non-processing of data items
Program steps or manual procedures to guard against the misuse of files stored on machine-readable media
Hardware features to detect hardware malfunctions
Program checks to guard against operator error

The computer system requires new controls, but it also provides new methods of control which substitute for human controls. In a manual system, internal control relies upon such factors as human alertness, care, acceptance of responsibility, and division of duties. By concentrating the data processing activity, many controls based on human judgment or division of duties are no longer available. However, the computer program provides an alternative for many manual checks. For example, the lowest-level clerk will normally react when she receives a shipping document on which to insert prices and cannot find the item on the price list. In a computer operation, a non-match such as this must be programmed. Once programmed, however, it will be faithfully executed. In most instances, the computer checks can be more extensive than those performed manually.

EVALUATING ERROR CONTROLS

There are error control procedures to prevent or detect almost any type of error. Despite the availability of these methods, one still hears about payroll checks being written for $1 million instead of $100. In these cases, elementary control features have not been used. On the other hand, error controls, like all other controls, require an expenditure of resources. Programmed controls take up valuable memory positions, and when a programmer is trying to conserve storage locations in order to fit a large program into main memory, it may be necessary to omit some desirable though not critical programmed controls. In other words, controls need to be part of the data processing system, but they have a cost associated with them; therefore, before implementing a control, the system designer or programmer should evaluate its merits by asking such questions as:

How frequently might this error occur?
What are the monetary consequences of the error not being detected?
What are the nonmonetary consequences of the error not being detected?

What is the cost of detecting these errors?

If the error is missed at this point in processing, will it be detected at a later stage? What are the consequences of late rather than early detection?

The control points at which specific data processing controls are applied to prevent or detect errors are shown in Figure 17–1. These are the controls on original document preparation, on conversion to machine-readable form, on computer processing, on distribution of output and controls based on uses of the output. It is noteworthy that only one of these control points involves machine errors or program errors. This illustrates the fact that data processing controls must include controls over the human errors in source data preparation, conversion, output, and use, as well as controls over the operation of the equipment or programs. The system designer should consider the entire set of controls which apply to an application and the organizational and management environment in which they are applied rather than viewing individual controls in isolation. For the purpose of this chapter, these control points will be discussed under the following topics: control over input and output, hardware features for control over equipment malfunctions, and programmed control over processing. Two additional control problems—the control over computer programs and the protection of computer records and files—will also be covered.

CONTROL OVER INPUT AND OUTPUT

Input data is the weakest link in the chain of data processing events. A study of 100 computer installations showed input errors to be the major operating problem. Good system design should therefore make provisions to assure the quality of the input into the system.

The input data for a program may be in error for one of four general reasons: (1) it may be incorrectly recorded at the point of inception; (2) it may be incorrectly converted to machine-readable form; (3) it may be incorrectly read or otherwise entered into the computer; or (4) it may be lost in handling. Input controls should therefore be established at the point of data creation and conversion to machine-readable form, at the point where the data enters the computer, and at points when the data is handled, moved, or transmitted in the organization. Table 17–1 presents an inventory of methods from which the system designer selects in order to achieve the level of error control required for an application. Each of these will be discussed in this chapter.

Before data is used in updating files or other processing, it is usually tested for errors to the extent possible or appropriate in the light of the consequences of input errors. A separate input validation run or input editing run is usually performed in systems where the data is batched and transferred to a file medium such as magnetic tape before processing.

If errors are detected by this run or during subsequent processing, the erroneous transaction or record found to contain an error is shunted aside rather than stop-

TABLE 17–1   Methods for Input Data Error Control

AT POINT DATA IS CREATED AND CONVERTED TO MACHINE-READABLE FORM	AT POINT DATA IS FIRST PUT INTO THE COMPUTER	AT POINTS DATA IS HANDLED, MOVED, OR TRANSMITTED
Procedural controls	File label (internal)	Transmittal controls
Data review	Tests for validity:	Route slip
Verification	Code	Control total
Check digit	Character	External file labels
	Field	
	Transaction	
	Combination of fields	
	Missing data	
	Check digit	
	Sequence	
	Limit or reasonableness test	
	Control total	

ping the computer to make corrections. It will usually be written on a temporary file to be examined later, and information will be written on the console typewriter or printer explaining why the item was rejected. There will thus usually be a file of rejects and an error listing indicating the reason for rejection (Figure 17–3). Items which are rejected by the input editing run should be carefully controlled to make sure they are corrected and reentered at a later run.

PROCEDURAL CONTROLS AND DATA REVIEW

Standard clerical practices and well-designed data forms impose procedural controls on the creation of data. For example, if a part number is to be written on a document, boxes may be printed which contain the exact number of spaces required for the part number. Any clerk writing a part number containing less or more digits than the required number of characters will notice the error. Where direct input devices are used, templates over the keys, identification cards, and other procedural aids help to reduce input errors.

Some installations make a review examination of input data (especially codes which identify part number, product etc.) before it is converted to machine-readable form. This checking may be performed in connection with the addition of information, or it may be an entirely separate step.

VERIFICATION OF CONVERSION TO MACHINE-READABLE FORM

When data is punched into cards, the accuracy of the data conversion can be tested by mechanically verifying the keypunching operation. Two separate keydriven machines are used—a card punch and a verifier. The data is first punched by a keypunch operator. The punched cards and original data are then given to a verifier

```
BG // JOB BETTY
BG 00.00.06
BG BEGIN UNEARNED INCOME REPORT
BG ALLSTORES CORP.
BG OP11I  I  DATA CHECK SYS001=181
        CCSW=02100031680E000000 SNS=085203C00000 CCB=003128
BG NO MATCH CARD 021602R3
BG NON NUMERIC FIELD  02980452
BG DUP 03110004
BG TERMS NOT EQUAL ACCOUNT 03200024 TB 48 CARD 36
BG NON NUMERIC FIELD  03910053
BG DUP 03910087
BG TERMS NOT EQUAL ACCOUNT  04610200  TB 08  CARD 36
BG TERM NOT GREATER THAN ZERO OR REMAINING PAYMENTS IS NEGATIVE 04610200
BG NON NUMERIC FIELD  04660002
BG DUP 06510011
BG TRIAL-BALANCE READ ERRORS 000001
BG END UNEARNED INCOME REPORT
BG EOJ BETTY
BG 00.07.25
```

FIGURE 17-3 Sample output from input validation run

operator, who inserts the punched card in the verifier and rekeys the punches using the original source documents. The verifier does not punch but instead compares the data keyed into it with the punches already in the card. If they are the same, the punched card is presumed to be correct. A common indication that this check has been performed is for the verifier to notch over the column containing the difference. This was illustrated in Chapter 2 (Figure 2–14). The incorrect cards are returned to the keypunch operator for repunching and reverification.

Similar verification is used with a magnetic tape encoder, where data is keypunched and recorded directly on a magnetic tape. The same device is used (at separate times) both to record data and to verify it. The verification process includes the correction of errors.

Verification is a duplicate operation and therefore doubles the cost of data conversion. Various methods are used to reduce the amount of verifying. One method is to verify only part of the data. Some data fields are not critical, and an error will not affect further processing. Examples are descriptive fields containing vendor name, part description, etc. which, under most circumstances, are not critical. The use of prepunched cards, prepunched stubs, and duplication of constant data during key-punching may allow verification to be restricted to the variable information added by the card punch. A second approach used with statistical data is to verify only if the card punching error rate is above an acceptable level. Each operator's work is checked on a sample basis. If her error rate is acceptable, no verification is made; if not, there is complete verification.

Verification can also be conducted by visual inspection of the printing on the card or a visual review of a listing of the cards. Other control procedures to be explained may be substituted for verification, e.g. a check digit on an account number or a batch control total.

Other techniques for data conversion produce a punched card or a punched paper tape as a by-product of another operation. For example, the typing of an invoice may, by the use of a device hooked up to the typewriter, automatically produce a punched card or punched paper tape for inventory control, sales analysis, etc. Proofreading of the invoice serves also to verify the punched card by-product, although not to the same extent as mechanical verification.

CHECK DIGIT

In most applications involving an identification number, the identification number may be verified for accuracy by a check digit. A check digit is determined by performing some arithmetic operation on the number. The arithmetic operation is performed in such a way that the typical errors encountered in transcribing a number will be detected. There are many possible procedures. For example, a simple check digit procedure might be as follows:

1   Start with a number without the check digit.

2   Take every other digit and multiply these by two.

3   Sum the digits in the resulting numbers plus the digits not multiplied.

4   Subtract sum from next higher number ending in zero.

5   Add check digit to number (at end or elsewhere).

Note that a check digit procedure is not completely error-proof. For this example method, 57846 or 54678 gives the same check digit. It is unlikely, however, that transpositions of this form will occur. The check digit does not guard against assignment of an incorrect but valid code, such as the assignment of the wrong but valid identification code to a customer.

The checking of the code number for the check digit may either be performed by the input device, such as a keypunch or a paper tape punch, or be programmed into the computer. The use of the check digit as part of the input device has the advantage that an incorrect code is detected before it enters the computer process and a field checked by a check digit does not need to be verified. Examples of uses are charge account numbers, employee pay numbers, and bank account numbers.

INTERNAL FILE LABEL

A file label is a record at the beginning and also possibly the end of the file which records identification and control information. They are used to ensure that the proper transaction or master file is used and that the entire file has been processed. At the beginning is the header label, which identifies the file. Typical contents are:

Name of file
Creation date
Purge date
Identification number
Reel number (for magnetic tape)

The trailer label is the last record and summarizes the file. Contents normally include:

Record count
Control totals for one or more fields
End-of-file or end-of-reel code

TESTS FOR VALID DATA

The data, once read by the computer, can be subjected to programmed tests to establish that it is within the limits established for valid data. Some examples of checking which can be done are:

1 *Valid code.* If there is only a limited number of valid codes, say for coding expenses, the code being read may be checked to see if it is one of the valid codes.
2 *Valid character.* If only certain characters are allowed in a data field, the computer can test the field to determine that no invalid characters are used.
3 *Valid field size, sign, and composition.* If a code number should be a specified number of digits in length, the computer may be programmed to test that the field size is as specified. If the sign of the field must always be positive or always negative, a test may be made to ensure that there is not an incorrect sign. If the field should contain only numerics or only alphabetics, a test may be made to determine that the field does indeed contain a proper composition of characters.
4 *Valid transaction.* There is typically a relatively small number of valid transactions which are processed with a particular file. There is a limited number, for example, of transaction codes which can apply to accounts receivable file updating. As part of input error control the transaction code can be tested for validity.
5 *Valid combinations of field.* In addition to each of the individual fields being tested, combinations may be tested for validity. For example, if a salesman code may be associated with only a few territory codes, this can be checked.

6 *Missing data test*. The program may check the data fields to make sure that all data fields necessary to code a transaction have data in them.

7 *Check digit*. The check digit is checked on identification fields having this control feature.

8 *Sequence test*. In batch processing the data to be processed must be arranged in a sequence which is the same as the sequence of the file. Both the master file and the transaction file may be tested to ensure that they are in a proper sequence, ascending or descending as the case may be. The sequence check can also be used to account for all documents, if these are numbered sequentially.

9 *Limit or reasonableness test*. This is a basic test for data processing accuracy. Input data should usually fall within certain limits. For example, hours worked should not be less than zero and should not be more than say 50. The upper limit may be established from the experience of the particular firm. Input data may be compared against this limit to ensure that no input error has occurred or at least no input error exceeding certain preestablished limits. Examples are:

The total amount of a customer order may be compared with his average order amount. If this order exceeds say three times the amount of his average order, then an exception notice may be printed.

A material receipt which exceeds two times the economic order quantity established for the particular item might be subject to question.

A receiving report amount may be compared with the amount requested on the purchase order. If there is more than a small percentage variance, then there is an assumption of an error in the input data.

In a utility billing, consumption is checked against prior periods to detect possible errors or trouble in the customer's installation.

CONTROL TOTALS

Control totals are a basic method of error control to determine whether or not all items in a batch have been received and processed. The control total procedure requires that a control figure be developed by some previous processing and that the current data processing recompute this amount, comparing the resultant total with the previous total. Control totals are normally obtained for batches of data. The batches are kept to a reasonable size so that errors can be easily isolated. For example, the sales slips to be processed by computer are first added on an adding machine to arrive at a control total for the sales in the batch. A control total for payroll might be the number of employees for whom checks should be prepared. Control figures may be financial totals, hash totals, or document or record counts.

Financial totals. Financial totals are totals such as sales, payroll amounts, inventory dollar amounts, etc., which are normally added together in order to provide financial summaries.

Hash totals. Hash totals are totals of data fields which are typically not added. The total has meaning only as a control and is not used in any other way in data processing. To determine that all inventory items are processed, a control total might be developed of the inventory item numbers, and this would be compared with the sum of the item numbers obtained during the processing run.

Document or record count. In many cases, rather than obtaining a financial total or hash total, it may be sufficient merely to obtain a count to ensure that all documents or records have been received and processed.

Control totals prepared prior to computer processing are furnished to computer processing as an input data item. The computer is then programmed to accumulate control totals internally and make a comparison. A message confirming the comparison should be printed out even if the comparison did not disclose an error. These messages are then subject to review by the control clerk (Figure 17–4).

FIGURE 17–4   Use of control totals

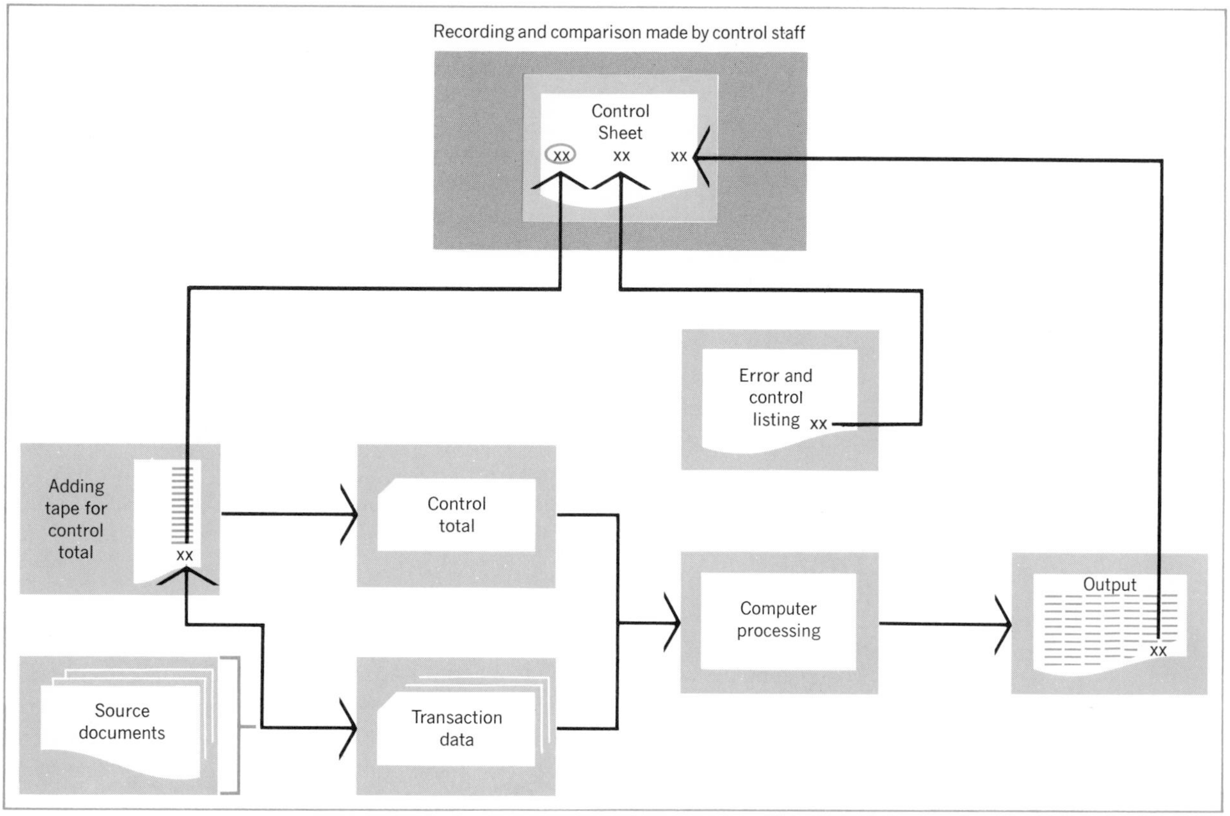

FIGURE 17-5 Batch control ticket to accompany source documents

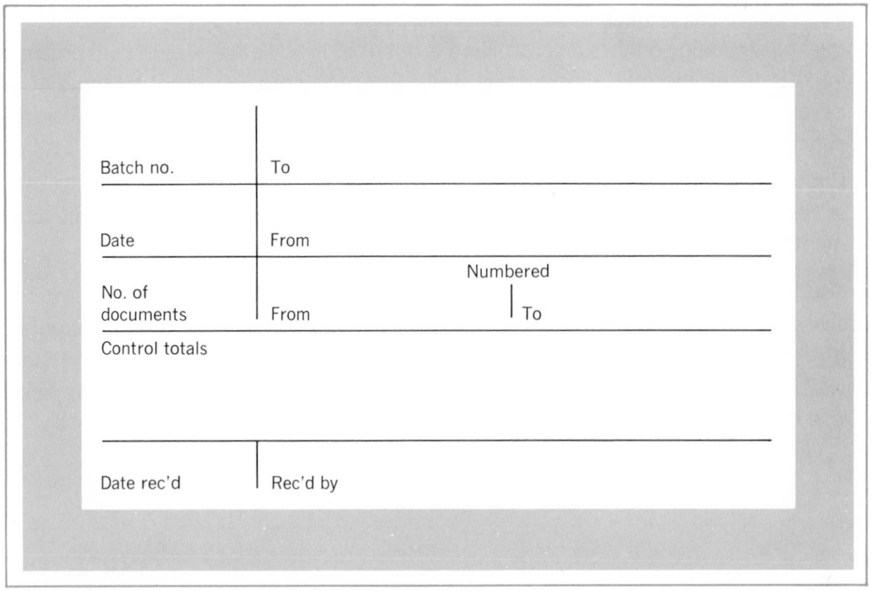

Batch no.	To	
Date	From	
No. of documents	From	Numbered To
Control totals		
Date rec'd	Rec'd by	

MOVEMENT AND HANDLING CONTROLS

Transmittal controls, route slips, control totals, and external file labels are examples of controls over the internal handling and movement of input data. Control totals have already been explained, and external file labels are described in connection with file safeguards. The transmittal controls and route slips are discussed in this section.

When data is moved about through an organization, there is always a possibility that it may be lost or otherwise diverted from the proper processing channels. To ensure proper identification of data as it moves through the company, and more especially as it moves through the data processing steps, it is customary to use some form of status identification. As they enter the data processing center, batches of data may be logged on a listing showing the data received. As each batch passes a data processing station it is registered, recording the fact that the batch has been processed. The batch itself usually carries a route slip which indicates the path of processing which it should follow and a record of processing performed (Figure 17–5).

OUTPUT CONTROLS

The distribution of output should be controlled to ensure that only those authorized to receive reports do so. The output should be reviewed for completeness and agreement with controls and screened for obvious errors. Persons receiving the output are an important error detection control point, and provisions should be made in the system design for error feedback from recipients of output.

In this example of accounts receivable input preparation procedure for a department store, the use of a control total plus a check digit eliminates the need for separate verification.

1 A clerk writes the sales slip containing the description of the sale, amount, customer number, date, etc. The credit sale is also entered in a cash register.
2 The sales from the department are batched and visually checked; a control total for the batch, prepared on an adding machine, is attached to it.
3 The batch goes to data processing, where a paper tape punch operator first enters the control total for the batch into her machine and then prepares a punched tape of transactions by punching:
   a Customer account number. This is checked automatically by the tape punch device using a check digit procedure.
   b Amount of sale.
   All other data such as the date, department number, etc. is constant, and is entered only once for the batch.
4 At the completion of punching the batch, the dollar sales amounts just punched are checked in total by being compared automatically with the batch total. If they are the same, the batch of input data is considered to be correct.
5 The control total for the batch is included as part of the input data to be used for computer input and processing controls.

▌ HARDWARE FEATURES FOR CONTROL OVER EQUIPMENT MALFUNCTIONS

A computer system consists of both electronic elements and mechanical parts. The central processing unit, for example, consists almost entirely of electronic elements such as transistors, resistors, and diodes, whereas most input/output equipment and file storage devices contain both electronic components and parts which move mechanically. Failure in the system can therefore result from the malfunction of one of the mechanical parts or through the failure of an electronic element.

The electronic portion of the computer system operates with electrical pulses which are created, counted, delayed, transmitted, etc. The electronic circuitry of the computer is designed to control the timing, shape, strength, and frequency of these pulses. Failure of an electronic element such as a transistor, resistor, diode, etc., may cause a change in the timing, shape, strength, or frequency of the pulses and lead to an error. Some of the reasons for deterioration of an electronic element are extremes of heat or humidity, power disturbances, mishandling, and normal wear.

Quality control in manufacture, built-in equipment checks, and programs of periodic preventive maintenance have made the electronic portion of the computer system very reliable. Preventive maintenance procedures usually detect elements which are getting out of adjustment or are close to failure and allow adjustments or replacements to be made. Preventive maintenance is performed daily on complex computer systems and less frequently on simple configurations.

Mechanical operation is required in almost all input/output and file storage equipment. Two mechanisms with mechanical actions are generally used:

1   A transport mechanism to move the media (input/output or file storage) past the reading or writing mechanism
2   Mechanism to read or write

These actions occur at high rates of speed. For example, a card reader must transport, say, 1,100 cards a minute past the read mechanisms (brushes or photoelectric cells) at a precise speed and in a precise position. A printer which turns out 1,000 lines of 136 characters per minute requires as many as 136,000 individual print mechanism movements per minute.

A machine error can be caused by a failure in the timing, speed, and movement of a transport mechanism or through a malfunction of the read/write units. This can result from the devices getting out of adjustment, operator mishandling, wear, etc. Failures can also be traced to faulty media, such as warped cards, magnetic tape with surface defects, and poor-quality paper stock.

Equipment controls are usually based on the concept of redundancy. This concept has received much attention in communication theory but is also applicable elsewhere as a general basis for error control. Redundancy, with respect to error control, means that an element is added to a process or the code for an item for the sole purpose of detecting any error which may occur. If there was no possibility of error, the redundancy would usually be eliminated.

Equipment controls can be divided into five types: a redundant or parity character, a duplicate process, an echo check, a validity check, and an equipment check. These all involve a separate operation which provides a check on the results of the main operation.

REDUNDANT OR PARITY CHARACTER

A redundant character is one attached to a data item for the purpose of providing for error detection. The most common is the parity bit. A separate parity bit or check bit, when used, is associated with each separately identified group of bits which is moved as a separate unit through the computer. This unit may be a large, fixed set of bits, as in a computer word, a smaller set which can encode a single alphanumeric character, or a byte which is a separately identified part of a larger fixed word. The parity of the binary word, character set, or byte is made even or odd when the data is first converted to binary from input items or when data is formed from a computation or other manipulation. The number of bits is summed, and a 1-bit or a 0-bit is placed in the parity bit position to make the total number of bits odd if an odd parity check is used or even for an even parity check. Figure 17–6 illustrates the parity bit in a 6-bit binary coded character bit set. Each time this basic group of bits is moved in the computer, the parity of the group is checked. If the parity bit, as newly computed,

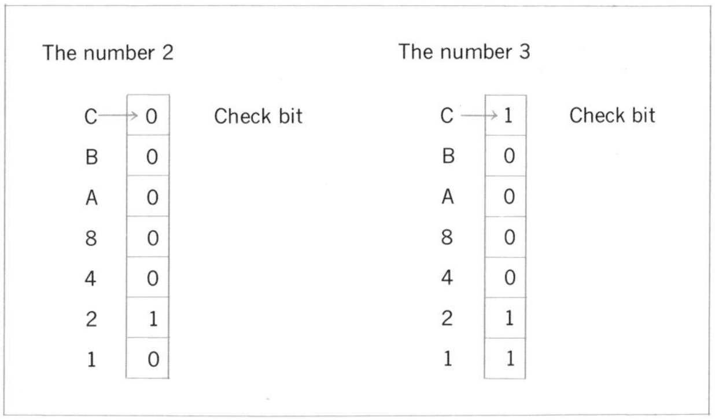

FIGURE 17-6 Illustration of odd parity bit for a computer using a 6-bit binary coded character bit set

is different from the parity bit previously computed, a bit has been destroyed. This test is not infallible in the sense that the alteration of two bits will leave the parity bit unchanged, but the probability of this happening is very low.

DUPLICATE PROCESS

Another type of equipment control is to have the same process performed twice and then compare the results of the two operations. Any difference between the first operation and the second will signal an error. This is used by most card readers which have two read stations. The duplicate process may also be a complementary action, such as reading after writing to check what was written.

ECHO CHECK

In an echo check the central processor sends a command to an input or output device to perform an operation. The device returns a signal which verifies that the proper mechanisms for performing the actions have been activated. This verifies that the equipment was activated rather than testing the actual results obtained. This check is frequently used for checking the printer and the card punch.

VALIDITY CHECK

Since on many operations only certain results (e.g. data character codes) can be considered correct, one method of checking is for the computer system circuitry to compare the result attained against all valid results. Any results not fitting into this set of valid results are considered incorrect. This is used with some card readers and in data communications.

EQUIPMENT CHECK

In this control, the computer checks the equipment to see if it is functioning properly rather than checking the results from the operation. It is not a positive check, since the equipment may be working properly, with defective media or other factors never-theless giving an improper result. An example is a card reader using photoelectric sensing which tests the photoelectric cells to make sure they are on and working.

▮ PROGRAMMED CONTROL OVER PROCESSING

Assuming that there are proper input controls so that the input data is considered to be correct and that there are proper equipment controls to detect equipment errors, what is the need for programmed control over internal processing? A program will perform exactly as written. If properly debugged and tested, there should be no pro-gram-based errors. However, large programs are sufficiently complex to harbor latent errors which may not show up for weeks, months, or even years after the program has been accepted. For example, a large payroll program worked well for several years but failed when required to process name changes for two newly married female employees whose names were on adjacent records in the master file. The program was not able to handle this somewhat unusual situation. Another reason for pro-grammed controls over processing is the possibility of improper modification of a program, intentionally or accidentally, while the data is being processed. It therefore makes sense to put various error control features into the program.

The types of program controls which test computer processing are the limit and reasonableness test, the crossfooting or crosstesting check, and control figures.

LIMIT AND REASONABLENESS TEST

As with input data, a control over processing can be exercised by program steps test-ing the results of processing by comparing them with predetermined limits, or by comparison with flexible limits testing the reasonableness of the results. In a payroll application, the net pay can be checked against an upper limit. The upper limit is an amount such that any paycheck exceeding the limit is probably in error. In a billing operation for a relatively homogeneous product, such as steel bars and plates, the weight of the shipment may be divided into the billing in order to develop a price per pound. If the price per pound exceeds the average by more than a predetermined percentage, a message will be written for subsequent followup to determine if the billing is in error.

CROSSFOOTING TEST

It is frequently possible to check computer data processing in a manner similar to the manual method of crossfooting. Individual items are totaled independently and then a crossfooting total developed from the totals. For example, in a payroll appli-cation the totals are developed for gross pay, for each of the deduction items, and for net pay. The total for net pay is then obtained independently by taking the total for gross pay and deducting the totals for each of the deduction items. If this crossfooting does not yield identical figures, there has been some error in the program of processing.

CONTROL FIGURES
Control figures developed in a manner similar to the input control totals can be used for testing the data processing within the machine. For example, the number of items to be invoiced in a billing run may be used as a control total and compared with the number of items billed on invoices.

CONTROL OVER COMPUTER PROGRAMS

Computer programs are a valuable product of the data processing programming staff. Copies should be protected from fire or other destruction. There should also be controls to prevent unauthorized changes. Controls include those based on organization of duties, approval and documentation of program changes, and auditing.

ORGANIZATION OF DUTIES

As mentioned earlier in the chapter, it is feasible in most installations to segregate the systems and programming responsibility from the computer operating responsibility. Access to the complete documentation of the run manual should be restricted, where possible, and the operators given only the operator instructions. Under these circumstances, the operator is less likely to attempt unauthorized changes (whether desirable or not) than when he is also a programmer and has access to the complete documentation.

APPROVAL AND DOCUMENTATION OF CHANGES

Before a program is put into use, it should be reviewed by a supervisor to check whether or not it performs as specified and to check for adequacy of testing and completeness of documentation. After being approved and put in use, there will be a need for program changes. These should be approved by the program manager or data processing manager and a record of the change made and filed with the Run Manual for the program (Figure 17–7).

The program change record is useful in keeping documentation current. It is very time consuming to correct all documentation each time a program change is made. Instead, a change record is included with the documentation, and unless there is a rather substantial rewrite of the program, the flowcharts are not redrawn. The original documentation plus the change records form the current documentation.

AUDITING

The primary purpose of auditing control practices for computer programs is to evaluate both the adequacy of the controls and the manner in which they are operating.

FIGURE 17–7   Program change notice

FIGURE 17–7   Program change notice

DATA PROCESSING PROGRAM CHANGE RECORD

Program name or
description

Change number _____

Date
change effective _____

Program number

Change initiated by _____ Date _____
Change request approved by _____ Date _____

Description of purpose or reason for change

Description of changes made (and effect on this and other programs)

Change made by _____ Date _____
Change tested by _____ Date _____
Change posted to run manual _____ Date _____
Change posted to operator instructions _____ Date _____
Review of changes _____ Date _____

Audit tests are designed to detect breaches of established procedures and other practices which may lead to errors or fraud. Besides checking compliance with procedures
such as preparation of change records, the auditor may test the program itself for
unrecorded changes. One approach is for the auditor to maintain a control copy of the
program which he updates with all approved changes. He then compares this control

program with the program in use. Another testing procedure is the running of major programs using test data for which the answer is known.

▌ PROTECTION OF COMPUTER RECORDS AND FILES

A data processing installation should establish and follow procedures to safeguard the program and data files from loss or accidental destruction. If loss or destruction does occur, advance provisions should have been made for reconstruction of the records. The protection of computer records and files involves physical safeguards, procedural controls, a retention plan, a reconstruction plan, and insurance.

PHYSICAL SAFEGUARDS

These may be classified as fire protection, security protection, and off-premises storage. Tape files, card files, disc packs, etc. are more subject to fire damage than the printed or written records available with manual or tabulating systems. A small fire which may char only the edges of paper or books can melt a magnetic tape or warp a disc. The National Fire Protection Association has made extensive recommendations with respect to computer installations.[1] These call for housing the computer in a noncombustible environment, storage of vital records in storage cabinets having a class C rating (one hour at 1700° F), separate air conditioning and power controls, carbon dioxide fire extinguishers, etc.

When confidential corporate information is kept in a machine-readable format, it should be subject to the same security precautions which are applied to written records.

Off-premises storage is used to provide a further safeguard for essential data processing records. Space can be rented in a secure, fireproof location, or another storage location in the same company can be used.

PROCEDURAL CONTROLS

Procedural controls can be used in the management of a computer center in order to minimize the possibility that an operator error will result in the destruction of a data or program file. Some common methods are external labels, magnetic tape file protection rings, and tape library procedures.

Files should be clearly labeled so that the operator will know the file contents. Punched card files are usually labeled on the top of the deck with a felt marking pen. File name, identification, and date are commonly written. The first and last cards are also labeled. A paper label should be attached to magnetic tape reels and disc packs (Figure 17–8).

A physical safeguard used to prevent writing on a magnetic tape and destroying information prior to the release date for the tape is a removable plastic or metal ring, the presence or absence (depending on the computer manufacturer) of which will

[1] *Standard for the Protection of Electronic Computer Systems*, Bulletin no. 75, National Fire Protection Association, 60 Batterymarch Street, Boston, Mass., 1964.

FIGURE 17–8   External magnetic tape label

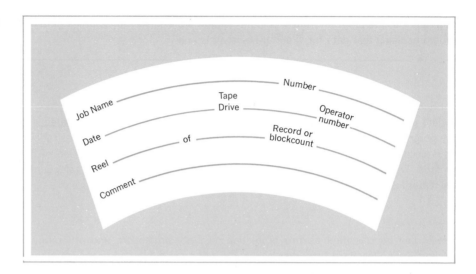

prevent writing on the tape. The most common method is the insertion of the ring to allow writing and its removal to inhibit writing (Figure 17–9). The ring is used in conjunction with the external label as an added protection. The procedure for writing a file will include instructions as to the external label and a reminder to remove the file protection ring.

Tape library procedures provide for record keeping to maintain a log of the use to which tape reels have been put and for systematic methods for storage of reels to allow the tapes to be easily located or replaced in the storage racks.

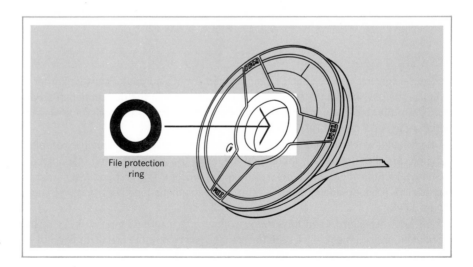

FIGURE 17–9   Magnetic tape file protection (or write enable) ring

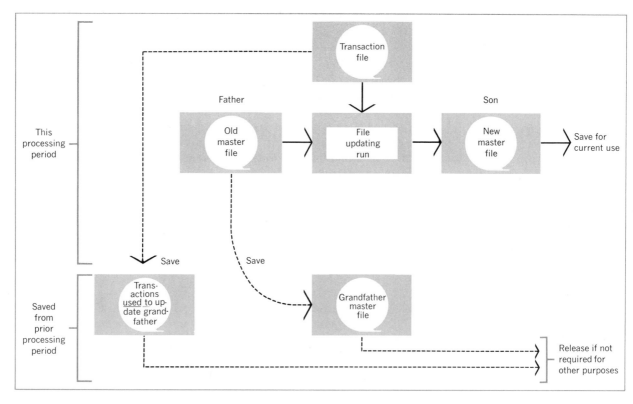

FIGURE 17–10   Son-father-grandfather concept for retention of magnetic tape files

RETENTION AND RECONSTRUCTION PLAN

The retention plan of a data processing department provides a means for record or file reconstruction. Source documents are retained at least until the computer file has been proved and balanced with its controls. However, other considerations may require a longer storage period for these documents. Copies of important master files or cards should be reproduced and a copy maintained in secure storage, preferably off the premises.

A retention plan for magnetic tape is usually accomplished by the use of the son-father-grandfather concept (Figure 17–10). The files retained under this concept on a Wednesday (assuming daily processing) would be:

Wednesday's file   (son)
Tuesday's file   (father)
Monday's file   (grandfather)

If, during processing on Thursday, the Wednesday tape was destroyed, Tuesday's tape would be processed again with Wednesday's transactions to recreate Wednesdays's master tape. If no other processing or retention considerations require keeping the tape longer, the old grandfather can be released when a new one is produced.

Disc file processing, unlike magnetic tape, does not automatically produce a duplicate, update copy of the file. To provide for reconstruction, the disc must be duplicated to provide a reference point and all transactions saved until the next reference file copy is made. The reference copy can be put onto another disc or magnetic tape. The "dump" to another disc or magnetic tape provides good reconstruction capabilities. If a second disc or magnetic tape is not available, the disc may be copied onto punched cards or even printed out. These are the least satisfactory methods because of the difficulty of reloading the file from punched cards or having to repunch the entire file from a printout.

The file protection plan requires not only a retention plan but also a plan for reconstruction in the event of loss of a file or destruction of equipment. The plan will include backup facilities either through the manufacturer, a service center, or another user, and special programs, if required, to facilitate reconstructing of files.

INSURANCE

Insurance should be part of the protection plan of a data processing installation. The major risk is fire, unless work is performed for others, in which case there should be liability insurance for errors or omissions in doing the work. The ordinary fire insurance policy is limited in its coverage of risks associated with losses connected with data processing. Therefore, many organizations take special data processing insurance coverage.

Although the number of losses arising from the dishonesty of data processing employees is apparently quite small, the risks associated with the concentration of the data processing function on a relatively small number of people suggest that bonding (fidelity insurance) of data processing employees is a desirable practice.

▌ SUMMARY

A major problem with computer data processing systems is control over the quality of the processing. The responsibility for quality extends from top management down to the control function in the data processing department. Top management should require adequate justification before projects are approved and should follow up with reviews of performance. The data processing department should be organized to provide for division of responsibility and a clear assignment of duties, including the control function. Documentation and other desirable management practices should be included.

The control over input is very important because most errors occur at this point in the processing. The equipment on the other hand is very reliable and, in general, has adequate controls. Programmed controls over processing can detect some program errors. The programs themselves should be controlled to prevent unauthorized changes. Also, a protection plan for computer records and files should be part of the operations of a computer installation.

This chapter has surveyed the major techniques and major considerations associated with the different control points. Adequate controls have a cost associated with them. Therefore, data processing management should understand control practices and evaluate their use based on the cost of the control versus the consequences of an error being undetected at that point in the data processing cycle.

▌ EXERCISES

1 As financial vice-president with executive responsibility for the computer data processing center, what should be your role in the following:
   a   A decision to change to a new model of computer
   b   A decision to add disc-processing capabilities to a tape-oriented system
   c   A decision to purchase 50 new tapes (cost is $1,000)
   d   A decision to hire an added programmer (there are four programmers already)
   e   The decision as to which programmer applicant to hire
   f   The center budget for the next year
   g   A decision as to programming a shop-scheduling application (requiring 5 man years of work)
   h   A decision to alter slightly the processing program for preparation of sales invoices
2 What performance reports should the top executive over data processing have in order to carry out his responsibility?
3 What is the purpose of the control function? What duties might be assigned to a control clerk?
4 How do computer control problems differ from manual system control problems?
5 Evaluate, using the criteria given, the merits of controls to:
   a   Prevent item quantities on purchase orders prepared by the computer from exceeding certain limits
   b   Prevent shipping order errors
   c   Prevent billing errors
   d   Prevent sales analysis errors
   e   Prevent overpayment of wages to an employee
6 How might an error in keypunching of input data get past the verification process?
7 What is the purpose of an input validation run?
8 What input controls might be used to detect the following input data errors:
   a   Transcription error creating wrong customer account number
   b   Pricing error—wrong price used

   c Quantity written as number of pounds but issued in tons, not pounds

   d Wrong plant coded in shipment instructions—plant does not stock item

   e Seven-digit salesman code used instead of eight-digit product code

   f No price entered

9 Use the check digit procedure to find the check digit to attach to:

   a 137654

   b 949321

10 If reliance is placed on a check digit and this field is not verified, what errors might not be detected?

11 How might control totals be used in the preparation of payroll and the related updating of the payroll master file?

12 Why is a hash total used?

13 What errors will the parity bit procedure detect? Which will it not detect?

14 What is an echo check?

15 An installation prepares good documentation but is never up to date because of the time required to redraw flowcharts, etc. Suggest an alternative procedure making use of program change forms.

16 The master payroll file on magnetic tape was inadvertently written over by another processing run.

   a What elementary operating control procedure was not used?

   b How can the installation recreate the master file?

17 Fill in the table with methods, procedures, or techniques for error detection and control. Not all entries need be used.

PROBLEM	METHODS					
	1	2	3	4	5	6
a Machine malfunctions						
b Errors in input data						
c Errors in program						
d Unauthorized program changes						
e File protection						

▌ ORGANIZATION
JOB DESCRIPTIONS
ORGANIZATION CHART
THE CONTROL FUNCTION
SELECTION OF PERSONNEL

▌ THE USE OF STANDARDS IN THE MANAGEMENT OF
THE DATA PROCESSING FUNCTION
STANDARD PROCEDURES
PERFORMANCE STANDARDS

▌ STEPS IN MANAGING THE PROGRAMMING AND
RUNNING OF AN APPLICATION

▌ RUNNING A PROGRAM
THE COMPUTER CONSOLE
LOADING THE PROGRAM INTO MEMORY
STARTING THE PROGRAM
SUCCESSFUL AND UNSUCCESSFUL TERMINATIONS

▌ OPERATING SYSTEMS
MANAGING OF ASSEMBLY AND COMPILATION
MANAGING OF SCHEDULING AND MULTIPROGRAMMING

▌ COMPUTER MAINTENANCE

▌ SUMMARY

▌ EXERCISES

OPERATION AND
MANAGEMENT
OF THE COMPUTER
INSTALLATION

A computer installation is significant in the overall organization not only because of the expense of the equipment and personnel but also because of its role as a service department which accepts input data, performs processing and storage, and provides information. If the function is not well managed, it can seriously impair the activities of the entire organization.

▌ ORGANIZATION

A data processing installation should be organized and managed using the same methods which have proved effective in other segments of the organization. There should be a plan of organization and clear assignments of responsibilities. In managing the operations, there should be written procedures and standards of performance against which accomplishment may be measured. This chapter assumes a general knowledge of management principles, so that the discussion will cover organization features and operating procedures which are more or less unique to computer data processing. Some of these unique features are the job descriptions, the organization chart, the control function, and the selection of personnel.

JOB DESCRIPTIONS

Job descriptions should be prepared which identify job titles and clearly describe all job functions. Although titles vary between installations, the following abbreviated, general job descriptions cover the most common data processing positions other than those at the managerial level.

TITLE	DESCRIPTION
Systems analyst	Analyzes the requirements for information, evaluates the existing system, and designs new or improved data processing procedures. He outlines the system and prepares specifications which guide the programmer.
Programmer	Flowcharts the logic of the computer programs specified by the system designed by the system analyst. Codes the logic in the language of the computer. Debugs the resulting program. Prepares documentation.
Computer operator	Operates the computer according to the operating procedures for the installation and the detailed procedures for each program described in the Computer Operator Instructions. Also called a console operator.
Keypunch operator	Prepares data for machine processing by keypunching into cards. Operates a card punch (also called a keypunch).
Unit record equipment operator	Also called a tabulating equipment operator. Operates the non-computer punched card equipment such as sorter, collator, reproducer, accounting machine, etc.

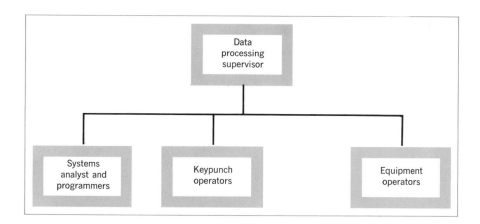

FIGURE 18-1 Organization chart—small data processing installation (equipment rental less than $4,000 month)

In general, the analyst is the position requiring the broadest background and highest qualifications. The programmer follows next in this hierarchy of qualifications with the computer operator requiring the least training and experience of the three. The unit record equipment operator position requires roughly the same level of ability and training as the computer operator job in a relatively uncomplicated computer installation. Keypunch skills are similar to those of a typist.

ORGANIZATION CHART

Figures 18-1 to 18-3 are sample organization charts for small, medium, and large data processing installations. These organization charts do not show the location of the computer data processing in the overall organization plan. The most common approach is to have data processing report to the chief financial or accounting officer such as financial vice-president, treasurer, or controller. There is a growing tendency, however, to move the data processing executive to a higher position in the organization. In cases where the computer acts as a service center for many departments, the possibility of conflict over the scheduling of the computer and the design of common files requires that the data processing executive be on the same level organizationally as the department heads of the units being serviced.

Figure 18-1 shows an organization chart for a small installation. Note that the systems analysis and programming function have been combined.

Figure 18-2 illustrates a medium-scale installation. Of interest is the separation of systems analysis from programming and the addition of an internal control clerk. In the expanded organization, there may also be opportunities for a hierarchy of supervision, e.g., senior programmer and programmer.

Figure 18-3 is an organization chart for quite a large installation. There is further specialization, with systems analysts being separated completely from programmers, under different supervisors. Programming includes a separate documentation librar-

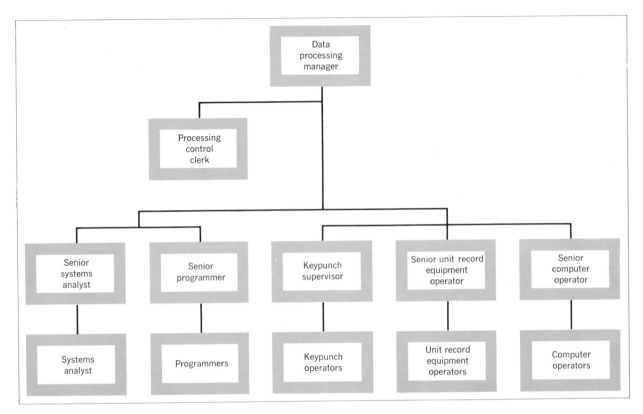

FIGURE 18–2 Organization chart—medium-size data processing installation ($4,000 to $15,000 monthly equipment rental)

ian; there is a separate data communications function; and operations now has a separate position of tape librarian responsible for custody of the magnetic tapes.

THE CONTROL FUNCTION

The plan of organization and operating procedures should provide for a control function. The control function can be divided into two types:

1 Processing control internal to data processing
2 Control external to data processing

Internal processing control is a function of the data processing department and is concerned with ensuring that processing is performed correctly and that no data is lost or mishandled within the department. The procedures for doing this were explained in Chapter 17. This control is usually the responsibility of the manager in charge of data processing operations. Depending on the volume of activity, one or more subordinates may be assigned to perform control activities. It is desirable, from a control standpoint, for the persons assigned to the control function not to have other data processing responsibilities such as programming or operating.

The functions of systems analyst and programmer are frequently performed by the same person or by persons in the same organizational unit. It is considered good practice to keep the three major functions (systems analysis–programming, operation, and control) separate and distinct. This separation of duties results in operational efficiency since the functions require differing standards of training and skill. In addition, the division of duties is important to internal control. The small number of people and high mechanization of a computer system expose the system to manipulation and fraud if a single person has operational knowledge plus easy access to procedures and programs at all levels. In one instance, for example, a former timekeeper was involved in both programming and machine operation. He was able to

FIGURE 18-3 Organization chart—large data processing installation (more than $25,000 monthly equipment rental)

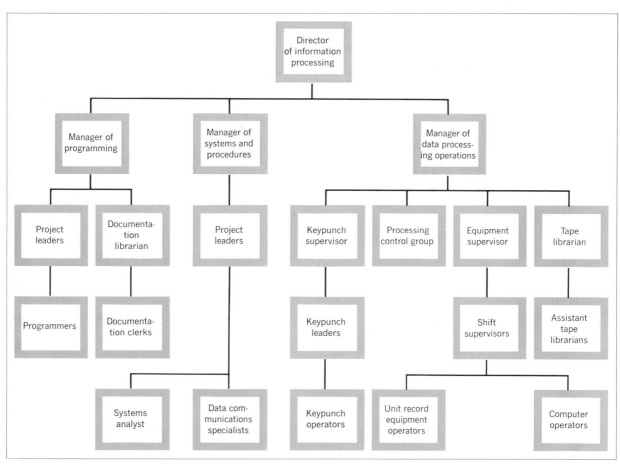

draw on his varied skills to manipulate payroll data in his favor without affecting the payroll control totals.

Outside control can take several forms but is basically concerned with establishing an independent check on the functioning of the data processing department. This checking may be performed in user departments or by a special control group set up in the accounting finance or other department to perform an independent and critical review of performance.

The quality of data processing is highly dependent upon the quality of personnel in the installation. Even though programming and systems analysis can be learned, there are large differences in individual aptitude for performing these activities. There are several aptitude tests, including some developed by the equipment manufacturers, which can be used to evaluate prospective employees. These are especially helpful for new or relatively inexperienced applicants. A second approach to evaluation, useful where the candidate for a position has training or experience, is to have the applicant sketch a simple system design or write a short program. The time required and the results achieved can provide a basis for evaluating potential performance on the job.

Companies converting to the use of computers frequently will train company personnel who have interest and aptitude to take positions in the new installation. Manufacturers typically provide training for their customers' personnel. Other sources of trained personnel vary considerably in depth and quality of training.

SOURCE	EVALUATION
Colleges and universities	May provide good background but typically do not develop a working proficiency.
Technical schools	Vary considerably in quality. With qualified instructors, good access to equipment, and "hands on" instruction, proficiency obtained may be good.
Self-study programs	Programmed instruction texts have proved very useful for some topics. Achievement of working knowledge usually requires additional "hands on" experience under a qualified instructor. Correspondence courses which do not provide the discipline of having programs run on the computer are not likely to develop any working proficiency.

▌ THE USE OF STANDARDS IN THE MANAGEMENT OF THE DATA PROCESSING FUNCTION

The same management principles which apply to general business management also apply to data processing. One of the most effective management techniques is the use of standards. As used here, standards refer both to procedures or methods standards which state the way a job should be done as well as to performance standards which state the amount and quality of work to be expected.

STANDARD PROCEDURES

Procedural standards are established by defining clearly and exactly how each job is to be done. This provides each person with a clear description of what he is expected to do and the methods and techniques he is to use. The standard methods provide a discipline to the data processing operations, which reduces training difficulties, increases the effectiveness of review and supervision, minimizes the effect of personnel turnover, and provides a basis for performance evaluation. The lack of standard procedures leads to operating difficulties. As an example, if a programmer is allowed to program, debug, and document a program in his own nonstandard fashion, it is difficult for a supervisor to review his work, and if the programmer leaves the employ of the company, it is very difficult for another programmer to understand his work when a change becomes necessary in the program. In addition, the computer operators may have trouble following operating instructions if each set has its own nonstandard format, terminology, etc.

In order to implement standard procedures, a standard operating procedure manual is prepared which specifies for all personnel the standard methods to be used in that installation. This will include standard procedures for systems analysis, programming, and operating. The manual may also include organization charts and job descriptions. An outline of the contents of a standard operating procedures manual is given in Figure 18-4.

The need for standard procedures can be seen by the seemingly trivial matter of differentiating between alphabetic letter O and zero in programming and in writing instructions. Several conventions are in common use:

METHOD	ALPHABETIC O	ZERO
Slash alphabetic	Ø or Θ	O
Slash number	O	Ø or Θ
Underline alphabetic	O̲	O

A standard procedures manual would designate one of these conventions for use by all persons in the installation. Where USA standards have been adopted by the United States of America Standards Institute, these standards should be used, if feasible. See Appendix IV for description of national and international standards activities.

PERFORMANCE STANDARDS

Performance standards aid in planning, in controlling costs, and in evaluating performance. They can be developed for both equipment and personnel.

FIGURE 18-4 Outline of contents of a standard operating procedures manual

STANDARD OPERATING PROCEDURES MANUAL

TABLE OF CONTENTS

Organization and Personnel
    Organization charts
    Job descriptions
    Performance evaluation

Standard Procedures for Systems Analysis
    Methods for systems analysis
    Flowcharting symbols and other standard notation
    Methods for describing the form of documents and files

Standard Programming Procedures
    Methods for describing program logic
    Rules for programming performance of housekeeping tasks in programs
    Rules for coding
    Standard control methods
    Testing standards
    Standard documentation
    Procedures for initiating and documenting program changes

Standard Computer Operating Methods
    Library procedures
    Procedures for scheduling computer time
    Machine operating procedures
    Procedures for recording and reporting results of operations

Equipment standards for each separately operated unit specify the amount of time the equipment should be devoted to setup, production, scheduled maintenance, and unscheduled maintenance. The production time is available for jobs. Based on the speed of the equipment, the production time gives an estimate of the total quantity of work that may be obtained from the unit. The rated speed of the equipment can frequently not be used as the performance standard for production because of handling time, error stops, etc. For example, a card sorter may be rated at 1,000 cards per minute, but the actual throughput will be less because of card handling, card jams, etc. The performance standards for a unit of equipment provide a basis for scheduling work, evaluating operator performance, spotting units to be replaced or repaired, etc.

Performance standards for systems and programming personnel are more difficult to establish than equipment standards because of the problems in estimating a task that has a substantial element of creativity. However, performance estimates can usually be made sufficiently close for management purposes. In one approach to estimation, each assignment is divided into tasks. For example, a programming job may be divided into the following tasks:

    Flowcharting overall logic
    Flowcharting detailed logic

FIGURE 18-5 Estimating programming time

Problem name: *Accounts Receivable Aging, Analysis and Report*
Language: *COBOL*   Level of difficulty: *Medium*
Estimated number of pages of coding: *6*

	Man days
Flowcharting system and preparation of layouts	2
Flowcharting detailed program logic	2½
Coding	3
Desk checking	1½
Compilation and testing	2
Documentation	2
Estimated time in man days	13

FIGURE 18-5 Estimating programming time

Coding
Desk checking
Assembly or compilation
Testing
Documentation

The assignment is evaluated in terms of its size and complexity. Preestablished times for size and complexity categories are then applied to arrive at time estimates for performing each individual task using the standard methods for the installation (Figure 18–5). Once a performance standard has been estimated, it provides a basis for scheduling work and evaluating individual progress and performance. This approach is useful for both systems analysis and programming. Equipment operators' jobs are machine-paced, and therefore operator scheduling is based on machine standards.

▍STEPS IN MANAGING THE PROGRAMMING AND RUNNING OF AN APPLICATION

In order to visualize the management of a computer installation, the steps in programming and running an application will be surveyed.

STEPS	COMMENTS
Problem recognition and definition	When the need for a computer program is recognized, a systems analyst is assigned to work on the project. He is assigned a project name and/or number for keeping track of time devoted to the project. After a preliminary investigation, he will be given a time budget for completion of the systems analysis phase. Using a Gantt-type bar chart, the work of the systems analysts and programmers is scheduled by the supervisor for this activity (Figure 18–6).

STEPS	COMMENTS

Systems analysis	As work proceeds, the systems analyst reports the time spent on each element of the job on a time sheet and makes an estimate of time to completion. For example, he may report time by the following basic tasks:
	    Problem definition
	    Job specifications
	    Layout of reports and files
	    System flowchart
	The supervisor reviews progress and approves the work when it is completed.

Programming	The job is then assigned to a programmer who is given the systems analysis specifications, a job number, and a time budget (see Figure 18–5). The job is scheduled as with the systems analysis. The programmer records his time by each phase of the job, such as:
	    Program flowcharting
	    Coding
	    Desk checking
	    Assembly, compiling, or testing
	    Documentation
	The hours are summarized by the clerical staff and compared with the time budget. The job, when completed, is analyzed by the supervisor for programming evaluation purposes. The supervisor reviews the program before it is released for production use. Based on either delays or early completion, the programmer schedule is revised. The data processing executive is furnished with a periodic summary of program status for managerial review.

Running of program	The operations supervisor prepares a production schedule showing the jobs to be run, the expected running time, and the time each job is to be completed. A new job is inserted in this schedule. When the time arrives for the job to be run, the operator obtains the program and any data files from the program and file library. Using the Operator Instructions for the run as a guide, he obtains any special forms and loads the program, forms, and data files into the equipment. The program is then run. The running time is recorded either automatically by the computer or by the operator. The times are summarized by job and by major operating category and reviewed by the data processing management. A record of delays, errors, and other conditions which required corrective action is made and summarized for management review purposes.
Control and distribution of output	The control clerk logs in any control figures prepared when the data was recorded or converted. The control clerk records the computer control totals and checks for any discrepancy. The clerk examines the output for obvious errors and then has it distributed according to the distribution instructions in the run manual documentation. Any errors reported by the users are logged in, investigated, and corrected. A report of such errors is made periodically to the data processing management.

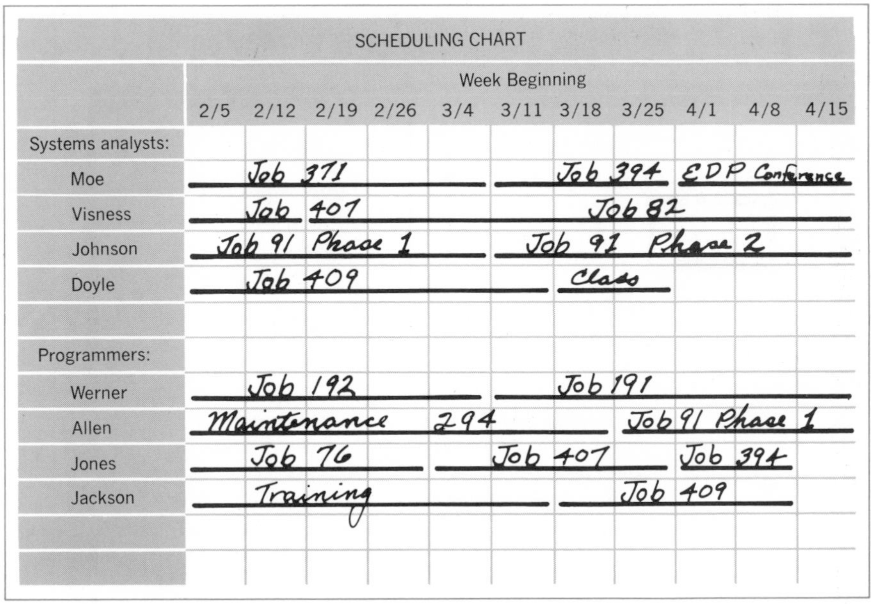

SCHEDULING CHART											
	Week Beginning										
	2/5	2/12	2/19	2/26	3/4	3/11	3/18	3/25	4/1	4/8	4/15
Systems analysts:											
Moe		Job 371					Job 394		EDP Conference		
Visness		Job 407					Job 82				
Johnson		Job 91 Phase 1					Job 91 Phase 2				
Doyle		Job 409					Class				
Programmers:											
Werner		Job 192					Job 191				
Allen		Maintenance		294					Job 91 Phase 1		
Jones		Job 76				Job 407			Job 394		
Jackson		Training						Job 409			

FIGURE 18–6 Scheduling of systems analysts and programmers

From the reports prepared for the operating supervisors in data processing, a summary report is prepared for top management summarizing the performance of the data processing department.

▌ RUNNING A PROGRAM

Once assembled or compiled into the object language of the computer, the program must be loaded into computer storage in order for it to be run. When loaded into storage the computer must be directed to the first instruction of the sequence. From that point on, the program takes control. There are, of course, differences in the procedures followed with different computers for loading a program and transferring control to the first instruction of the program, but the procedures typically require the use of the computer console and, on most advanced computers, the use of a set of programs called an operating system.

THE COMPUTER CONSOLE

The computer console (Figure 18–7) contains a control panel for the operator to monitor the action of the computer. The console may be mounted on the cabinet housing the central processor, or it may be a separate unit. Usually associated with

FIGURE 18–7 Computer console (IBM System 360/30)

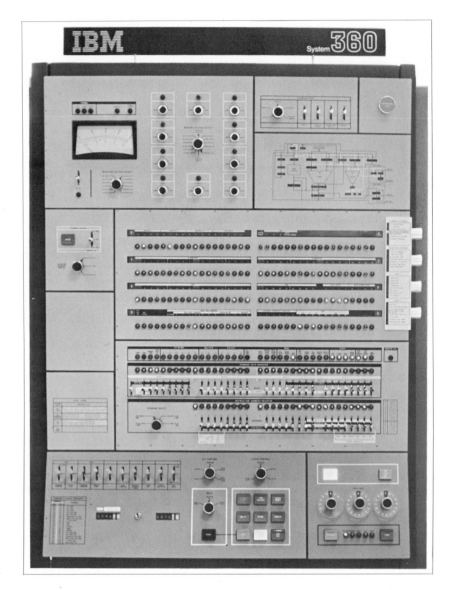

the console is a low-volume input/output device, such as a typewriter. The control panel lights, switches, dials, and the console typewriter are used to:

1 Manually instruct the computer
2 Display the condition and status of the computer equipment and the input/output devices

3 Display the contents of registers
4 Alter the operation of the equipment
5 Alter the contents of registers or other storage locations
6 Diagnose equipment malfunctions (by maintenance personnel)

The small incandescent lights on the panels of many computer consoles usually display the contents of the various registers. During the running of the program, the lights change too rapidly for the contents to be read. During debugging or when the computer halts, the register contents are often a valuable aid in determining what has happened. The display is usually in the code used by the computer but with markings to assist the operator to read the display in terms of octal, hexadecimal, binary coded character, etc.

Various lights indicate the operation or condition of important assemblies in the central processor and in peripheral equipment. For example, there may be an overflow light, parity-error indicator, temperature warning light, indicators to display the results of program comparison tests, and lights to indicate off-normal conditions for peripheral equipment. Each item of equipment will have on it a small number of buttons and lights. The buttons will be to start, stop, reset, etc., while the lights indicate off-normal conditions. For example, a light on a printer may indicate it is out of paper.

Frequently, there are console switches called sense switches which are interrogated by the program. The operator sets these switches as specified by the operator instructions before running the program.

On all but the smallest computers the console typewriter is used by the programs to send messages to the operator and by the operator to respond. For example, a program may require the date for program purposes. The typewriter will type out a request to the operator to type in the current data and the format he is to use: "TYPE TODAYS DATE IN FORMAT DD-MM-YY". The operator types 02-10-67 if the day is October 2, 1967, and the program proceeds. The typewriter also gives instructions and error messages. Frequently, but not in all cases, manual intervention to change the running of a program is handled through the console typewriter.

LOADING THE PROGRAM INTO MEMORY

When the source program is assembled or compiled, the result is a machine language program on some machine-readable media such as punched cards or magnetic tape. Since each instruction must be stored in memory, it is assigned to a separate memory location. This assignment may be made in two ways:

1 *Absolute assignment.* The assembly program assigns a specific memory location to each instruction. When the program is loaded into memory, the same instruction will always be put in the same location.

2   *Relative assignment.* The instructions are given a relative or base address rather than being assigned to specific locations. This assignment is performed when the program is loaded into storage, and therefore the location used may vary from one use to the next. In essence, the relative address is altered by adding a constant to it when the program is loaded to provide an absolute address.

In both cases, there is an address associated with each instruction. If, for example, the instructions are punched one per card, the card will have both the address where the instruction is to be placed in memory and the instruction itself. If more than one instruction is punched into a card, only the instruction of the first need be specified since the others will be stored sequentially following the first one. The same concept is applied if the instructions are on magnetic tape or other media.

Instructions will not automatically place themselves in the designated locations. There must be a procedure to take each instruction and place it in the location specified for it. This is accomplished by a load program. The load program may be a separate program which must be in memory in order to read and store the program to be loaded, or a load routine may be part of each program to be loaded. In the latter case, a bootstrap technique is used. The first instruction entered into memory loads the next one, which loads a third, and so on until a small number of instructions are loaded. These few instructions then load the remaining instructions. A special load button on the console is usually available to read the first record into memory to start the bootstrap operation.

STARTING THE PROGRAM

The load program, as its last step, will usually transfer control to the operating program just loaded. There may be a standard starting address used by all programs, or it may be completely variable. The load program may set up a pause and give the operator a message, after which he must press "run" for the program to start, or the program may be automatically started without further operator intervention. An informational console message may be typed out, but no operator action requested except in the case of errors in starting.

The computer console provides some means for specifying a starting address and transferring control to it. This is necessary in order to allow the operator to start or restart a program at a point other than the beginning. The branching may be done through console switches, dials or console typewriter.

When loading and starting the computer, the operator must also prepare the peripheral input/output units. The printer must be loaded with blank paper or paper forms, magnetic tapes or disc packs must be mounted, and all required units must be turned on. External sense switches, if used, must be placed in proper positions. The operator instructions tell the operator how to set up the equipment. A program will often be written to check for proper setup before processing is started. If the equipment and switches are not properly set, an error condition is reported via the console typewriter.

Once started, a program may be terminated for one of several reasons:

1 Successful completion
2 Programmed error halt
3 Continuous loop
4 Invalid operation

In the case of successful completion of a program, this is indicated explicitly by a console message or by console lights. The operator instructions will specify how the operator knows the program has been completed. Programmed error halts are each associated with a specified console message or pattern of display on the console lights. By reference to his instructions, the operator can determine the exact reason for the error halt. A program may occasionally get into a continuous loop (executes a sequence of steps over and over again) from which there is no exit. If allowed to continue, the computer would never stop performing the same loops. The reason for this is an error in programming. A loop of this sort may sometimes be spotted by a recurrent pattern on the console lights, but in most cases it is detected because of excessive running time. The expected maximum running time for a program is part of the operator instructions. If the program exceeds this limit, a loop is assumed and the run is aborted. Many computer centers automatically apply limits to small problems written in FORTRAN or similar languages; unless the writer of the program specifies a longer running time, the automatic limit is used. A program may also hang up because of an invalid operation or location. For example, a program instruction may send control to a location which contains data. The computer will attempt to use the data as an instruction and, if this is impossible, will halt. Improper instruction modification is also a cause of invalid instructions.

OPERATING SYSTEMS

An operating system, also called a supervisor, monitor, or executive, is a set of routines to manage the running of the computer. Operating systems range in complexity from simple systems which manage only basic functions to very complex ones. In general, the more sophisticated the computer system, the more complex the operating system required to manage its use. The philosophy underlying the operating system is that the computer should perform those operator tasks which it can do faster and more accurately and that the computer should be kept operating as continuously and as effectively as possible.

Consider the steps required to compile and run a program written in FORTRAN, both with and without an operating system.

OPERATOR ONLY	OPERATOR AND OPERATING SYSTEM
1 Operator examines program and determines that it is a FORTRAN program. 2 Operator records start time, operator, and program name on a log. 3 Operator locates copy of FORTRAN compiler. 4 Operator loads FORTRAN compiler into storage (manual start). 5 Operator starts FORTRAN compilation (manual start). 6 At completion, operator examines program printout to see if successful compilation. 7 If yes, operator loads FORTRAN program into storage (manual start). 8 Operator determines if all input/output units are properly loaded with input data, cards, paper, tapes, etc. 9 Operator starts execution of program (manual start). 10 At completion, operator decides if it is a successful termination. If so, he unloads all input/output media associated with program. 11 Operator writes time of completion on computer log and notes errors or other conditions. 12 Operator examines programs to be run and chooses next one to work on.	Operator: Put program into card reader along with other jobs. Job and control cards are included with each program deck. Operating system automatically: 1 Determines that program is FORTRAN program to be compiled. 2 Loads compiler and starts compilation. 3 Checks for successful compilation. 4 Loads object program and starts execution. 5 Provides messages to operator regarding any duties he may have. 6 Prepares a record of the time taken by the program, records error conditions, and updates operating statistics. 7 At successful completion goes on to next program.

As indicated by this comparison, the operating system performs all tasks associated with loading programs and monitoring their execution. When certain error conditions occur, the operating system will automatically undertake error diagnosis and recovery techniques.

The operating system manages the assembly, compilation, and running of programs based in part on data furnished with each program. These job cards specify the type of program (FORTRAN, COBOL, ASSEMBLY LANGUAGE, etc.), the job to be performed (compile and execute, compile only, etc.), the input/output units to be used, etc. Job cards for a COBOL compile and execute are illustrated in Figure 18–8. These are used with the operating system of one manufacturer for one computer system. Other operating systems will differ, but the principles are the same.

Some of the tasks typically performed by an operating system are:

Program loading
Interrupt handling

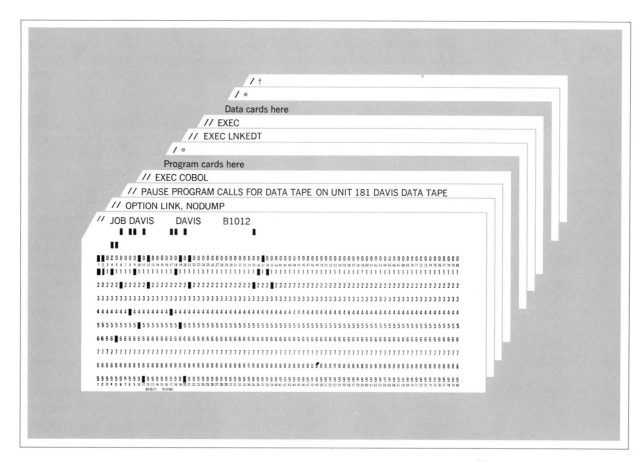

FIGURE 18–8 Example of job cards utilized by an operating system for compiling and executing a COBOL program (on IBM System/360)

Scheduling of input/output operations
Operator communications
Job-to-job communications
Job accounting
Job scheduling and management

The scheduling of input/output may include the use of an input/output control system which will perform label verification, assignment of buffer areas in memory for use in input and output, error checking and recovery during I/O operations, etc.

MANAGING OF SCHEDULING AND MULTIPROGRAMMING

The job scheduling and management activity of the operating system can become quite complex. Their purpose is to provide a steady flow of work to the computer.

Scheduling can be divided into two types—sequence scheduling and concurrent scheduling. A sequence-scheduling supervisory program selects the next program to be run based on such factors as time of day, priority rankings of the programs in the job stack, and availability of input data. Only one program is scheduled into memory at a time.

The concurrent-scheduling program not only schedules the sequencing of programs but also directs the concurrent processing of two or more programs. This technique for having the computer handle several programs concurrently is known as *multiprogramming* or *parallel processing*. The programs are placed in different sections of memory, and the operating system switches control from one to the other. For example, a program to read cards and print their contents may be run concurrently with a program to update a file. The control routine in the operating system first gives control to the read/print program. This initiates a read-a-card instruction. Control is then shifted to the file update program. When the card for the first program has been read, the second program is interrupted and control is passed back to the first program, and so on. Since the read/print routine can proceed no faster than the reader and printer can operate, the central processing unit would be idle much of the time if multiprogramming were not used. The term multiprocessing is often applied to multiprogramming, but it applies especially to a system with more than one arithmetic and logic unit. Several programs can be run simultaneously because more than one processing unit can be in use at the same time. A configuration with two or more CPUs with common primary storage and common peripherals is, by this definition, a multiprocessor system.

When a computer is operating in multiprogramming mode, several programs will be in memory and several jobs will be in a queue (on a magnetic disc or other medium) waiting to be processed. When one of the jobs in memory is finished, a job is taken from the queue of jobs and put into main memory for execution. This means that the jobs in the queue must not have absolute addresses which specify where they must be placed. Instead, the program is in a relocatable form, which means that it can be placed in memory in any free section. The relative or base addressing is done by the assembler; the load routine in the operating system performs the relocation to the available space by adding a constant to the relative address. For example, if a program taking 2,000 locations is to be loaded into 42,000 to 43,999, the instructions, assembled as if they were to be loaded into 0 to 1,999, will be located into the available section by adding a relocation factor of 42,000 to each address.

For simple, second-generation systems, the operating system was a convenience; for third-generation systems, it is essential to efficient operation. The reason is that the new computers are designed with complex interrupt systems and input/output facilities which operate without constant supervision by the central processor. These features mean that it is usually desirable to do multiprogramming and that it is not feasible to have the human operator doing the detailed scheduling. Even without multiprogramming operations, the use of an operating system reduces operator duties, the necessity for operator intervention, and operator-based errors.

❚ COMPUTER MAINTENANCE

In the management of an installation, the steps to protect against interruption of service will include regular maintenance of the equipment and backup physical facilities.

Most rental contracts with manufacturers include regular maintenance in the monthly rental fee. If the equipment is purchased, the user has the option of buying a maintenance contract from the manufacturer or of hiring his own service engineer. For large installations, preventive maintenance is carried out each day, a specific time being allotted for this purpose. Service personnel are usually assigned full time to large installations so that they are available immediately for emergency maintenance. Smaller installations will receive either regular preventive maintenance calls or be on an ''on call'' basis, obtaining maintenance only if there is equipment malfunction.

The task of preventive maintenance is to identify and replace electronic components which are likely to fail and to keep the input/output equipment adjusted properly. Maintenance programs are run which utilize the system more completely than most processing routines in order to spot trouble before it can cause a breakdown during processing.

One of the developments in computer design is a semiautomatic fault location procedure which identifies the faulty module when there is a failure. The modular design of the circuitry usually means that within a few minutes the module containing the faulty element can be pulled out and another plugged in.

If it is important that the computer operate without interruption, two computers may be installed—one acting as a backup to the other. This arrangement is common in critical realtime installations. The two computers are both connected to the same storage and input/output devices. If one computer fails, the second one takes over. The changeover is so rapid there is no interruption of service. However, the second computer does not sit idle waiting for a breakdown of the first; it is used for batch processing jobs which can be interrupted and delayed when necessary.

For the ordinary user, the two-computer approach is much too expensive. The reliability of computers is very high, but nevertheless breakdowns do occur. It is therefore desirable to make advance arrangements for the use of backup facilities. These may be at a data processing service center, at test facilities maintained by the manufacturer, or at an installation of another user.

❚ SUMMARY

The management of the data processing organization can make effective use of traditional management methods. These include job descriptions, organization charts, standard procedures, and performance standards.

The control function is especially important in data processing. It is found in the processing center in the job of the processing control clerk or processing control group. Control is also exercised by having formal or informal review in user departments.

In order to give a feel for the way a data processing department is managed, the chapter describes the steps in managing the programming and running of a new application. The steps in running a program are surveyed with emphasis on the computer console, loading the program into memory, starting the program, and program stops. The operating system, basic to third-generation computers, is also described.

❚ EXERCISES

1 Define the following job functions:

    a　Systems analyst   *e*　Unit record equipment operator
    b　Programmer   *f*　Tabulating equipment operator
    c　Computer operator   *g*　Tape librarian
    d　Console operator

2 Define the following terms:

    a　Computer console   *c*　Multiprocessing
    b　Multiprogramming   *d*　Operating system

3 What is the difference between standard procedures and performance standards? How are each used?

4 How is a program loaded into memory? After it is loaded, how is it started?

5 For what reasons may a program be terminated?

6 What is the purpose of an operating system?

7 What is the purpose of job cards? Explain their use.

8 How can an operator determine that a program is in an endless loop?

9 What are the usual arrangements for computer maintenance?

10 On what basis are analysts and programmers scheduled? How does their scheduling differ from operator scheduling?

11 How does the data processing management know whether or not a programming job is on schedule?

12 What difficulties are encountered in evaluating programmer performance?

▌ GENERAL CONSIDERATIONS

COST OF A COMPUTER FACILITY

TIME REQUIRED FOR INSTALLATION

GENERAL GUIDELINES FOR SUCCESS IN USING A COMPUTER

▌ CRITERIA FOR EVALUATING THE DESIRABILITY OF
A COMPUTER DATA PROCESSING SYSTEM

▌ AN APPROACH TO INVESTIGATION AND DECISION
MAKING

THE STUDY GROUP

THE FEASIBILITY STUDY

PREPARATION OF MANUAL OF SPECIFICATIONS

▌ DECIDING ON THE COMPUTER EQUIPMENT

INVITING PROPOSALS FROM MANUFACTURERS

COMPARING THROUGHPUT PERFORMANCE

OTHER SELECTION CONSIDERATIONS

▌ CONVERTING TO A COMPUTER SYSTEM

SITE PREPARATION AND TRAINING

PREPARATION OF INITIAL APPLICATIONS AND CUTOVER

POSTINSTALLATION REVIEW

▌ FINANCING USE OF COMPUTER EQUIPMENT

RENTAL FROM THE MANUFACTURER

PURCHASE OF EQUIPMENT

LEASING OF COMPUTERS

▌ SUMMARY

▌ EXERCISES

EVALUATING AND
INSTALLING
A PROPOSED
COMPUTER SYSTEM

The installation of a computer system is a major capital expenditure. Not only does this decision require a substantial initial outlay of resources; it also changes the structure of data processing and may alter the operations and management of the organization. Such an expensive and important decision should be made only after careful analysis. The system itself should be installed according to a plan and with due regard for its impact on people in the organization and for its impact on operations. Special precautions should be taken to guard against disruptions of operations during installation. The specific process of evaluating a computer system, selecting equipment, and installing the system must of course be tailored to fit the characteristics of each organization doing it. This chapter presents general considerations affecting the process and describes an approach to use in evaluation and selection.

▌ GENERAL CONSIDERATIONS

It is helpful to have some general concept of the dimensions of a computer selection decision and rough guidelines as to probable cost and time required for implementation. This section discusses these factors and outlines the general guidelines for a successful evaluation and installation process.

COST OF A COMPUTER FACILITY

Acquiring a computer is similar to purchasing an automobile. The price of the automobile, as advertised in the newspaper, is for the stripped-down model. Features such as automatic transmission, radio, etc. are extra-cost items. After purchase, there are operating costs such as gasoline, repairs, for example. The value of the car in the used car market drops rapidly over time as the car gets older.

The computer system is priced unit by unit, and many necessary features are extra-cost options. Therefore, the same computer system as configured by two different users may have a considerable difference in price. The following figures are therefore rough guidelines.

	SMALL	MEDIUM	LARGE
Cost of purchase of computer system	$100,000–250,000	250,000–1,000,000	Over 1 million
Monthly rental, including maintenance	$1,000–4,000	4,000–15,000	Over 15,000

The cost of computer equipment has been dropping steadily since computers were introduced, or, stated another way, there has been a striking improvement in performance for the same cost. For the years 1963–1966, the improvement in performance for computers costing the same was 115 percent per year for scientific computations and 160 percent per year for commercial processing operations.[1]

[1] Kenneth E. Knight, "Evolving Computer Performance 1963–1967," *Datamation*, January, 1968, pp. 31–35.

The cost of the computer itself is only a fraction of the cost of the computer data processing facility. During the late 1950s and early 1960s, a rule of thumb was that equipment rental would be about half the costs of running the facility. Now this figure is between 30 and 40 percent. The reason is that the cost of the equipment has been going down but the cost of support personnel has been increasing. The cost elements for continued operation after implementation are now approximately the following:

OPERATING COST ITEM	PERCENT OF TOTAL COST	
Systems planning and programming	30	(25–35)
Equipment rental	35	(30–40)
Other operating expenses	35	(30–40)

The startup costs to get the system installed, tested, and ready to run will vary depending on circumstances. A rough guide is that this cost will approximate one year's expected operating costs. In other words, a small commercial computer installation renting for $2,000 a month might have the following costs associated with it:

Operating costs	Month
Systems analysis and programming	$1,700
Equipment rental	2,000
Other operating expenses—operators, supplies, supervision, maintenance of programs, etc.	2,000
	$5,700 per month
Installation and conversion costs	$65,000 one-time costs

TIME REQUIRED FOR INSTALLATION

Installing a computer data processing system in a proper manner requires many months of preparation prior to the moving in of the equipment. As a rough guide, installing a batch-oriented data processing system requires from 12 to 24 months from the point in time that the decision is made to investigate the feasibility of the computer system until the system is running satisfactorily with the first applications. Figure 19–1 gives a reasonable approximation of minimum times. However, the total elapsed time may, in some cases, be reduced by performing some tasks simultaneously in parallel fashion rather than one after another. Even so, a year of selection and preparation activity is probably a minimum, and, for an inexperienced organization, two years is more reasonable. Adequate planning and preparation time from the final selection of equipment until it is installed ranges from 8 to 15 months depending on the experience of the organization, complexity of the system, etc. A more complex online realtime system requires from two to three years from feasibility analysis to actual operation.

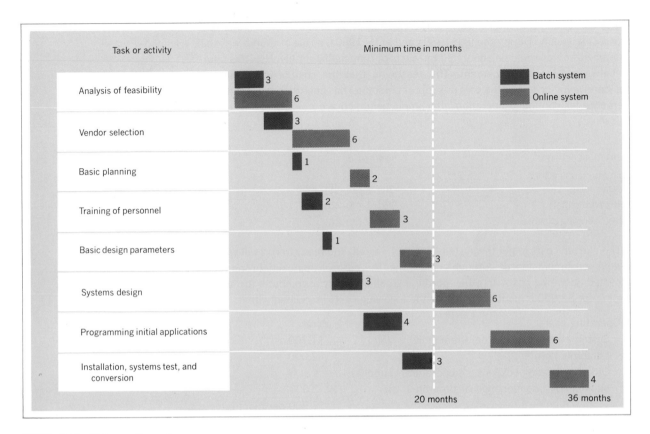

FIGURE 19–1 Minimum times for implementing a computer data processing system. Adapted from letter to editor by D. H. Brandon, *Datamation,* December, 1966, p. 14

GENERAL GUIDELINES FOR SUCCESS IN USING A COMPUTER

Some computer installations have been very successful; others have been plagued by trouble. What is the difference? Equipment problems are rarely to blame for the troubles of a computer installation. Failure of the manufacturer to deliver software on schedule or failure of the software to meet specifications may be quite disruptive, but the major elements of success are within the company. These are:

1   Top management participation and support
2   Adequate planning and control
3   Adequate consideration of human problems caused by the introduction of the computer and a program of action to handle the problems

Top management participation and support is a necessary condition for success. Since the installation of a computer can be disruptive to the organization, the entire organization must understand that top management is solidly behind the new system.

Lower levels of management will tend to support what is clearly being supported by top management. The top management also needs to be involved in deciding on the broad outlines of the new system. The design, as far as top management is concerned, must be "our design" and "our system" not "your design" and "your system."

The installation of a computer system extends over a long period of time. If it is not properly planned and controlled, the different activities will not be achieved on time and the different parts of the system will not mesh correctly. The planning and control of the steps in installing a computer system should utilize standard management techniques. This means that responsibility should be defined, criteria and objectives should be specified, schedules and deadlines should be established, work assignments should be made, and procedures should be established for spotting deviations from this plan and for bringing these to the attention of top management.

▌ CRITERIA FOR EVALUATING THE DESIRABILITY OF A COMPUTER DATA PROCESSING SYSTEM

The fundamental criterion for deciding whether or not to install a computer system in a business organization is whether or not the system will help to produce greater profits. For a nonprofit or government organization, the criterion is whether or not the computer will result either in reduced operating costs or in significantly improved ability to provide service to customers, clients, or the public.

In the early days of computer usage, most computers were justified on the basis of direct clerical cost reduction. In a large percentage of cases, these cost reductions were not achieved. Today, the emphasis is on increasing profits through the use of the computer. The latter criterion is more nebulous than direct cost reductions but should not be ignored. Some businesses could not return to manual processing even if they wished; the large clerical staffs which the computers replaced may no longer be available. The processing of checks, for example, is now so completely computerized that it would be virtually impossible for an individual bank in a large city to process manually. These and other similar considerations influence a computer system decision.

The criteria for decision cover both reduced costs and better service. These should be identified and a dollar value estimate made for each element. Examples of items which may be included are:

Decreased operating costs
    Reduction in personnel
    Less inventory (and therefore reduced costs for carrying inventory)
    Less stockouts and shortages (and therefore reduced costs or reduction in lost sales)
    Improved scheduling of production (less lost time, or improved utilization of machines and personnel)

Reduction in time to bill customers (and therefore faster collections)
Reduction in space requirements
Improved service
　　To customers:
　　　　Less inventory stockouts
　　　　Improved delivery time
　　　　Improved response time to customer service inquiries
　　To management:
　　　　More timely reports for planning and control
　　　　Improved analysis for decision making
　　　　Improved ability to respond to requests for special analysis

Studies have shown that companies which have aggressive and alert managements have tended to be in the forefront in the use of computers. An executive of a company making extensive use of computers stated this view:[2]

> "Our real goal is to make sure that we achieve more benefits from computers than our competitors do." This kind of aggressive, competitive thinking has doubtless played a large part in speeding the development of computer systems. It also spells a real threat for laggards in such development, for it means that the gap between effective users, on the one hand, and ineffectiveness, on the other, will widen ever more swiftly. The day may not be far distant when those who analyze annual business failures can add another category to their list of causes—failure to exploit the computer.

This association of the computer with progress should not stampede an organization into an uneconomical computer installation or cause a firm to move into a more sophisticated installation than it can effectively utilize. Only after careful analysis should an organization install a computer or move into a larger, more sophisticated system.

[2] Neal J. Dean, "The Computer Comes of Age," *Harvard Business Review*, January-February, 1968, p. 91.

❚ AN APPROACH TO INVESTIGATION AND DECISION MAKING

A general approach to the analysis of the desirability of a computer system consists of the following steps which are carried out or supervised by a study group:

Feasibility study
Preparation of manual of specifications
Obtaining of equipment proposals
Selection

The first two steps are described in this section of the chapter; the last two in the next section.

THE STUDY GROUP

A recommended approach is to form a committee or task group to direct the evaluation study. For most organizations, the committee should consist of middle management personnel who represent the principal functions of the business plus an executive from the systems function. One of the major problems in systems design is understanding the requirements of the different portions of the organization. The use of middle management personnel who are reasonably high in the organization and can speak authoritatively about the requirements of their functions gives authority and scope to the work of the group. They can also be freed from part of their responsibilities in order to allow adequate time for this assignment. Although the members of the study group do not have to be technically proficient, they should have a reasonable overall understanding of data processing. A short training course for the committee may therefore be desirable. The task group must be provided with technical staff support. For an organization with a computer installation which is studying the value of a new or expanded system, the staff support can come from the data processing systems staff. For an organization without prior experience, the use of outside consultants is frequently advisable. If used, consultants should work with, guide, assist, and otherwise aid the study group by providing the experience and technical expertise which the committee may not have. It is not usually advisable to turn the entire evaluation process over to outside consultants without having them work with an internal group.

A question which may arise is the use of manufacturer's representatives in the investigation phases. Many concerns let the manufacturer's sales and systems representatives perform most of the analysis and system formulation. By following this seemingly cost-free approach of letting a willing and eager manufacturer's representative do the job, these organizations abdicate their responsibilities. To be sure, the training provided to these representatives is usually quite good, and the support provided by their companies is substantial. However, they are not independent in their advice and suggestions. The proper approach is to use them as one source of information for a company-conducted study. Their suggestions may, for example, be valuable in bringing methods and equipment to the attention of the study group.

THE FEASIBILITY STUDY

The purpose of the feasibility study is to investigate the present system, evaluate the possible application of computer-based methods (and also non-computer methods), select a tentative system, evaluate the cost and effectiveness of the proposed system, evaluate the impact of the proposed system on existing personnel, and ascertain the need for new personnel.

To define an improved information system, the study group must understand the information requirements of the organization. This understanding may be obtained by the dual process of examining the existing data processing system to determine what is currently being done and of investigating through interviews and analysis what information needs to be provided that is not being furnished by the existing system. Data on the cost of operating the current system needs to be collected in order to make a cost/benefit analysis for a new system.

FIGURE 19-2 Considerations in analysis of existing data processing system

PREPARATION AND PROCESSING
Who originates source data?
Who prepares documents?
How often is processing performed?
Where is processing performed?
What equipment and supplies are used?
How many copies are prepared? Who receives them?
Is there additional processing capacity?
What is volume of documents—maximum, minimum, and average?
What is expected growth in volume?

FORM AND TIMELINESS OF DOCUMENTS
Is document in a useful form?
Is exception reporting used, if feasible?
Can two or more documents be combined?
Is greater accuracy needed?
Can lesser accuracy be tolerated?
Is faster reporting desired? Is it needed?

USE OF DOCUMENT
Who receives the document?
Does the document cause action?
What decisions are made based on the document?
Is there a part of the document that is ignored?
What additional information is needed?
What processing is performed by the user of the document?

STORAGE AND RETRIEVAL
Is the document filed? Where?
How long is it retained?
How often is it retrieved?
How large is file (in number of records and average size per record)?
What is growth rate for file?
Is there a chance for integrating different files?

COST
What is the cost of processing the document?
What is change in cost by a change in frequency or accuracy of processing?
How much of present costs of processing will be eliminated by computer processing?
What is the cost of storage and retrieval?

The data collection procedure consists of interviews with management, an analysis of the decision processes, an analysis of document flow, reports, files, and records, and an analysis of system objectives. Questions to consider in data collection are summarized in Figure 19-2. The result of the data collection will be:

1 Description of events which lead to data processing and the response time and accuracy needed by the system user.
2 Samples of all input, output, and file documents.
3 Description of use of information and the processing performed by each person receiving or issuing documents.
4 Information and document flow within the organization.

5   Description of all files. The description includes the rate of growth, the inquiry rate (why and by whom), and the frequency of updating (if a master file).

From this documentation of events, documents, information flow, and files, a description of the existing system can be organized and new systems laid out. Techniques for the system design are system flowcharting, grid charts, networks, specification sheets, layouts, etc.

When conducting interviews, the staff of the study group should seek to discover the information and data processing requirements not satisfied by the current system and to find out what information is needed. In this phase, it should be recognized that many persons do not know what they need or can use. Some analysis is then required to help the user to perceive what information would be useful.

From the information obtained in the feasibility survey, the study group formulates one or more tentative systems, then makes rough estimates of their cost and their ability to meet system objectives. From these tentative systems, one of which should usually be a modified version of the present system, a system is selected as the best solution and is then analyzed further in terms of personnel impact, cost/benefit, and suitability in terms of the needs to be met. Care should be taken to design the system to take advantage of the computer rather than merely computerizing an existing system.

The personnel impact portion of the feasibility study assembles data on the impact on company personnel of the proposed system. Rough plans are formulated for orienting, training, counseling, and adjusting the work force to the computer system. Estimates are made of the cost of the adjustment.

The cost/benefit study summarizes the benefits to be expected from the computer, the expected cost, and expected savings, if any. Figure 19–3 shows a summarized

```
                          COST ANALYSIS
Estimated initial cost of new computer system
   Cost of site preparation                                 $XX
   Analysis and programming of initial applications           XX
   Cost of training, parallel operation, etc.                 XX
      Total one-time costs                                          $  XX

Annual estimated operating costs:
   Computer and related equipment rental, including maintenance  $XX
   Computer personnel                                          XX
   Supplies, power, etc.                                       XX
                                                                     XX

Annual savings (annual operating costs using present system minus
annual operating costs expected with new system)
                                                                     XX

Rate of return (rate at which present value of savings equals present
value of one-time investment)
                                                                     XX%

Other non-cash or intangible savings (list)
```

FIGURE 19–3 Preliminary cost/benefit analysis

analysis. This would be supported by an analysis showing more detail. The figures are rough because specific equipment has not yet been selected. For the purposes of an investment analysis, the life of a system is probably about five to eight years. Six years is probably a satisfactory compromise unless added facts are available which dictate otherwise.

The results of the feasibility study together with the recommendations of the study groups are summarized and presented for top management approval. If the project is approved, the next step is to prepare a manual of specifications for use in procurement.

PREPARATION OF MANUAL OF SPECIFICATIONS

The manual of specifications is a statement of requirements which defines specifically what is to be accomplished by the proposed computer. It is a fairly detailed document. Most of the data needed for it is collected in the feasibility study. The document serves both as a summary of the proposed system for internal purposes and as a statement for use in inviting equipment proposals from vendors of data processing equipment. The system specifications will usually include the elements listed in Figure 19–4.

```
1   Introduction
    a   Description of organization and what it does
    b   Summary of requirements
    c   Current equipment
    d   The selection process—criteria to be used, form of responses, etc.
2   System requirements
    a   Hardware features required
    b   Software required
        (1)   Compilers (FORTRAN, COBOL, RPG, etc.)
        (2)   Utility packages (e.g., sort routine)
        (3)   Application packages (e.g., linear programming)
        (4)   Operating system
    c   Support required
        (1)   System designers provided by vendor
        (2)   Backup facilities
        (3)   Test time and facilities
    d   Constraints
        (1)   Planned delivery date for equipment and software
        (2)   Time constraints on processing
    e   Desirable features not required to meet specifications
    f   Capability for future growth
3   Major applications (for each, the following)
    a   System description
    b   File description including current size and growth rate
    c   Input data specifications and volume of input
    d   System flowcharts for each run and run descriptions giving
        (1)   frequency of processing
        (2)   volume of transactions
        (3)   suggested method of processing
```

FIGURE 19–4   Elements in a manual of specifications

The rather complete specifications of the system requirements should not be used to discourage innovative suggestions by the vendors. Rather, they are a base from which the manufacturer preparing a proposal may wish to suggest alternative or improved methods.

▌ DECIDING ON THE COMPUTER EQUIPMENT

The selection process consists of two major steps: the obtaining of proposals from manufacturers and the evaluation of these proposals to select one of them. The underlying concept in the decision process is that the company should define its requirements (in the manual of specifications) and that the vendor proposals will be measured against these specifications. If this is not done, the company is at the mercy of a computer manufacturer's assessment of what the system should be and what the equipment should do.

INVITING PROPOSALS FROM MANUFACTURERS

Based on a preliminary screening, four or five vendors may be invited to submit proposals. Each vendor is provided with a copy of the manual of specifications and the rules for submitting proposals. Normally, 60 days should be allowed for vendor response, although shorter times are frequently possible. During this period there will be followup interviews with vendors to clarify any misunderstandings or uncertainties in the specifications.

When the proposals are ready, the manufacturer's representative is usually provided with an opportunity for a presentation to the study group. At this meeting, he will summarize the proposal and answer questions. The manufacturer's proposal should normally contain the points listed in Figure 19–5.

After the proposals have been received and questions about items have been resolved, the staff can prepare an evaluation and recommendation for the study group to consider.

COMPARING THROUGHPUT PERFORMANCE

The study group should make an analysis of the applications timings furnished by the manufacturer and conduct an independent analysis of the computer capabilities. There is no foolproof method for selecting the best computer system; there are too many uncertainties. However, a combination of the stated system times for the applications contained in the specifications and independent evaluation of throughput provide a reasonably good basis for decision.

If the programs have not yet been written, how can a valid time estimate be made? For some computer runs using utility packages such as the sort routine, the times can be estimated with a high degree of precision. Some jobs are input/output bound, so that as long as the computational steps stay within the bounds of the input/output

FIGURE 19-5 Outline of information normally found in a manufacturer's proposal

1 Proposed equipment configuration
   a Equipment units
   b Equipment operating characteristics and specifications
   c Options or alternative configurations
   d Ability of the system to expand (modularity)
   e Special requirements as to site and other installation costs
2 Cost of proposed configuration
   a Rental and purchase price by unit
   b Extra shift rental
   c Maintenance contract if a unit is purchased
3 Software availability for specified software and special software packages
4 Systems support
   a Systems analysis included
   b Programming services included
   c Customer maintenance engineer availability
   d Education support
   e Backup availability
5 Terms
   a Acceptance of specified delivery date or proposed alternative delivery date
   b Payment terms
   c Lease-purchase and other options
   d Amount of test time to be provided
6 System performance for specified applications
   a Changes in design if different from that specified in requirements
   b Timings (how long each application takes)
   c Changes in timings using optional equipment
7 Other information

FIGURE 19-5 Outline of information normally found in a manufacturer's proposal

times, these times can be used. Other routines can be estimated by estimating number of instructions required and multiplying by an average time per instruction. The proposal should be checked to ensure that all estimating procedures are specified. The time estimates should include handling and setup time where required and should show the timing for each unit of the configuration for each run; these times should be summarized by day. This shows the peak requirements since some runs are daily, others weekly or monthly, etc. This provides an estimate of the peak load of the system.

There should also be some independent evaluation of the manufacturer's times. This can be performed using data from computer information services and by specially constructed kernel or benchmark problems. The information and analysis services which are available for this purpose range from a computerized analysis, which makes independent timings for a specified list of computers and compares them for decision making purposes, to comparisons based on instruction times or standard benchmark problems.

In using evaluation techniques, it should be kept in mind that the real criterion for measuring system performance is throughput. The comparisons that are made are in lieu of the complete throughput analysis, which cannot be made in advance because all programs would have to be written and running. The following frequently used methods of comparison are listed together with comments on their effectiveness:

COMPARISON TECHNIQUES	COMMENTS
Core cycle time	Extremely gross measure. Unreliable because systems differ in organization. Useful only for systems with same organization.
Add time	Extremely gross measure. Perhaps useful when comparing computers with same word organization.
Instruction times	Very gross measure since the frequency of instruction use must be considered.
Instruction mix times (average for a mix of instructions)	An average instruction time based on the expected frequency with which each instruction is used for different types of applications. Gross measure, but better than unweighted instruction time. At best, it is a measure of raw internal computing power.
Kernel problem	Sample problems are coded with the system's own instructions and timed. Especially useful for standardized mathematical applications. Gives a measure of internal performance. Does not reflect the effect of input/output, multiprogramming, operating system, etc.
Standard benchmark problems	Standard problems of a type normally performed. The problem is coded, and time to perform the standard task is estimated or measured by running it. Standard benchmark problems usually reflect the type of jobs done but are not a sample of the complete processing system as it will operate.
Simulation	The characteristics of the proposed system are compared with the characteristics of available computers, and the performance of the different systems is simulated by a computer program. A commercial service using this technique is called SCERT.[3]

[3] Fred C. Ihrer, "Computer Performance Projected through Simulation," *Computers and Automation*, April, 1967, pp. 22–27.

OTHER SELECTION CONSIDERATIONS

The major question, other than relative cost, is whether or not the proposed equipment will do the job in the time allowed and whether or not it has sufficient flexibility to expand as more applications are added. A system should allow for growth—in file size, in number and scope of applications, and in volume of transactions. Most systems can provide for growth by the addition of equipment options. For example, a stripped-down, minimum-memory-size computer may have its power increased by adding faster input/output units, more storage, special instruction packages, etc. A compatible family of computers allows the user to move from one computer in the family to a larger size without reprogramming.

The software and other support offered by the equipment manufacturer is another important consideration. A computer without proper software will lead to higher programming and operating costs for the user of that computer. It is necessary to evaluate not only the existing software but the probability of promised software being available when promised. There has been a general tendency in the industry not to meet scheduled software delivery dates.

In evaluating hardware and software, it is desirable to program and run a test problem to try out the effectiveness of the software and to evaluate the operating problems. The manufacturer will usually provide time for testing. Frequently, an order must be placed before any test machine is available. But the practice in the industry is to use the initial sales order as a basis for scheduling machine delivery. When the delivery time is close (say six months), the order is firmed. Thus, there is usually sufficient time to evaluate by test runs the equipment which may not have been available when the initial order was placed.

In making the selection, different criteria will receive a different weight with different users. The following list is in the order of importance assigned by a sample of computer users:[4]

[4] Norman F. Schneidewind, "The Practice of Computer Selection," *Datamation,* February, 1967, pp. 22–25.

Most important	Hardware performance
	Software performance
	Cost
	Manufacturer support
	Compatibility with present hardware and software
	Growth potential of system (modularity)
Least important	Delivery date
	Availability of application programs

When the evaluation is completed, the final cost estimates are presented to management with a recommendation for action. During this time, a contract is negotiated with the selected manufacturer. The final cost analysis will contain the contract price of the equipment and other cost estimates which have become more detailed and refined during the evaluation process. The final cost analysis might include the items listed in Figure 19–6.

The contract with the manufacturer is usually based on a standard contract form used by him. However, there are still many points for negotiation. For example, the assistance to be provided by the manufacturer—number of systems analysts who will get the system going, number of hours of free test time, etc., may vary from installation to installation depending on the negotiations.

▌ CONVERTING TO A COMPUTER SYSTEM

Rarely is a computer delivered shortly after the order is signed. Usually there is a lapse of several months. Sometimes as much as two years go by between the signing of the initial order and the installation of the equipment. Within the limits of possible delivery dates, the installation date should be planned for when the organization is prepared for delivery rather than having this date set by the manufacturer. The conversion to a new computer is a major project and should therefore be carefully scheduled and coordinated. Planning and scheduling tools useful for this purpose are bar charts and critical path networks. The conversion must be supervised, preferably by

FIGURE 19-6 Items in final cost analysis for computer system

Development costs
    Hiring and training of programmers and systems analysts
    Salaries of personnel during developmental period
    Disruption of normal operations
    Retraining of displaced personnel or termination costs
    Site preparation
Hardware costs (either monthly lease or purchase)
    Central processor
    Storage devices
    Input/output devices
    Peripheral equipment
    Preparation equipment (keypunches, magnetic tape encoders, etc.)
    Equipment maintenance
Operating expenses
    Programmers
    Systems analysts
    Operators
    Keypunchers
    Supervisory and control staff
    Utilities
    Supplies

the new data processing manager (if a new system) or by the current manager (if a replacement computer). The installations may be assisted by the study group. Some of the preparatory activities are site preparation, training, preparation of initial applications, and cutover to the new system.

SITE PREPARATION AND TRAINING

A computer will usually require some special site preparation. There are both engineering and esthetic considerations, since many companies use their computer center as a showplace. The manufacturer will provide complete specifications for the electrical, space, air conditioning, and other needs of the equipment. A site planning engineer from the vendor will usually be available for assisting in this aspect of site planning.

Although smaller computer configurations can get by without special air conditioning, it is required for medium- and large-scale systems. The air conditioning is required not only because operating in too warm an environment is damaging to the equipment but also because of the need for humidity control. Punched cards, for example, swell and jam in the reader if there is too much humidity. Raised computer room floors are used to allow the cables which connect the equipment to be run underneath the floor. Otherwise these cables impede free movement of traffic.

Initial training of staff in programming and using the equipment will typically be provided by the manufacturer. However, the amount and type of training should be agreed upon when the contract is negotiated. Programmed instruction manuals for self-instruction purposes are also frequently available. Manuals and other instructional materials are normally provided by the vendor.

PREPARATION OF INITIAL APPLICATIONS AND CUTOVER

The initial applications to be run on the computer should be written and debugged prior to delivery of the equipment. In other words, when the computer is working and turned over to the organization, the first applications should be programmed, debugged, and ready to run. As part of the agreement to rent or purchase the equipment, the user should have negotiated with the computer manufacturer for a certain number of hours of time on that model computer at the manufacturer's test facilities. Additional time may of course be purchased. This provides the customer with computer time to assemble or compile, debug, and test programs prior to the installation date. The customer's personnel can also gain experience in operating the equipment.

Prior to the beginning of processing, all master files must be prepared. For a completely new installation, this will normally involve extensive conversion of data to punched cards and then to magnetic tape or disc. This must be done with care and with a substantial amount of control and checking, so that the initial file is correct. If the conversion is from one model computer to another, the old files may be able to be run on the new equipment without change. If not, a conversion program may be necessary, or special equipment such as a tape-to-tape converter may be used.

When converting from one computer system to another, various methods are used to ease the problem of rewriting programs.

METHOD	EXPLANATION
Emulation	An extra-cost hardware feature (actually a special wired program in read-only storage) which executes the instructions of the old computer on the new one by interpreting each old instruction into its equivalent in the new instructions. Programs do not run as fast under emulation as when they are rewritten in the language of the new computer.
Simulation	Does the same function as the emulator except that it is software instead of hardware. Consists of a program which interprets each instruction and executes the equivalent instructions in the new machine. Generally slower than emulation.
Conversion routines	Routines which produce source programs for the new computer from the source program for the old system. Used both for symbolic languages and for making required changes for various higher-order languages such as FORTRAN or COBOL.

An installation may use a combination of methods. Some applications may be reprogrammed immediately; others may be emulated or simulated until such time as they can be reprogrammed. In some cases, the frequency with which a job is run may not justify reprogramming, and it will continue to be run in emulation or simulation mode.

During the startup for a new system, it is often difficult to obtain a proper cutoff. Also, unforeseen difficulties may arise in the processing programs. For these reasons, it is usually a good idea to run both old and new systems in parallel until the new system is found to be operating satisfactorily (say, two to four weeks). A cutoff point is then established, the files are updated to the cutoff point, and all transactions initiated after that point are recorded using only the new system.

Computer user organizations may be a useful source of information for the user. These organizations are operated by the participating user of the same equipment but are supported by the manufacturers. Each manufacturer will have one or more user groups. For example, SHARE is the IBM large-scale computer users group. The user groups share information, exert pressure on the manufacturer, establish standards, etc.

POSTINSTALLATION REVIEW

In preparing for a computer system, cost and benefit estimates are made. But it often happens that the cost savings are not realized and the benefits are not as great as projected. A computer system disturbs existing jobs and procedures, and frequently the personnel will duplicate the work of the computer because they do not trust the new system or do not understand the new procedures.

A postinstallation review is a desirable procedure to detect unrealized benefits, cost reductions not made, and lack of adherence to the new system. Measures may then be taken to improve performance. If there are substantial deviations in cost or performance by the computer processing group, this should be reviewed in order to appraise the reasons for it and to assess possible courses of action. Plans for a post-installation review probably improve the planning and estimating performed in deciding on the computer. If it is known that there will be a followup, estimates and plans are likely to be made more carefully than if such appraisal is not done.

▌ FINANCING USE OF COMPUTER EQUIPMENT

There are three major approaches to financing the use of computer equipment—rent or lease from manufacturer, purchase, or lease from an independent leasing firm. The terms which can be negotiated under each of these methods will depend on the manufacturer, the leasing agent, and the negotiating strength of the user.

RENTAL FROM THE MANUFACTURER

This is the most common financing method. There is a rental price which includes maintenance for using each piece of equipment. There are differences in rental agreements used by different manufacturers, but the most common calls for a base rental for 176 hours of actual use per month. This represents one 8-hour shift per day for the average month of 22 working days. Hours above 176 are charged at a lower rate (a common percentage is 30 percent of the implied hourly rate for the first 176 hours). The trend in computer rental terms is to reduce the second- and third-shift rental charges. The use of computers on a rental agreement can usually be canceled by the user on fairly short notice (say two to three months). Many manufacturers offer a reduced rental rate for companies which sign a long-term lease (three to five years) for the equipment. Users can also rent with options to purchase.

The major advantages of renting are the absence of a large capital outlay, the assumption by the manufacturer of all maintenance, and the removal of the risk of obsolescence for the user. The latter risk is not entirely removed, since a user has large amounts invested in special site preparation, training, programming, and other costs, which are lost if the computer must be replaced by one of another manufacturer. The major disadvantage of rental is the higher total cost. The manufacturers have tended to base rentals on a five-year life, but computers now being installed are likely to be used longer than this—probably closer to eight or nine years.

PURCHASE OF EQUIPMENT

The major incentive for purchase is the savings to be had over the life of the equipment. There is also a tax advantage because of the investment credit provisions of income tax law. The purchaser assumes a risk with respect to the reliability of the equipment, amount of maintenance, and obsolescence.

If the equipment is purchased, separate arrangements must be made for maintenance. Several possible arrangements are:

1   Maintain equipment using own personnel
2   Purchase a complete parts and. labor maintenance agreement from the manufacturer
3   Pay for maintenance personnel on an hourly rate when needed, and pay for parts as used

The maintenance risk varies for different units in the computer configuration. For example, central processors are very reliable, while disc files or magnetic tape units, because of the precision required in their moving parts, are more likely to require frequent maintenance. Therefore, some installations will purchase part of their equipment and rent the rest.

One consideration in a maintenance program is the need for a continuing relationship with the manufacturer. As weak points are discovered or improvements are found desirable, the manufacturer usually makes field changes in the equipment. Since these occur throughout the life of the equipment, a purchaser will want to be aware of them so that a decision can be made as to whether or not they should be made.

An impediment to purchase is the risk of obsolescence. This may occur because of the introduction of substantially improved equipment, because the equipment will not handle the volume of work, or because new systems concepts require a different kind of equipment configuration. Although the possibility of obsolescence because of new equipment with enhanced capabilities is very real, it requires several years leadtime to accomplish. The possibility of outgrowing a system can be guarded against by acquiring a system with considerable growth possibilities, both in the basic system and in available options for adding equipment.

When the risk of obsolescence has been considered, the problem of purchase or rental becomes a standard problem in capital expenditure analysis. A rough rule of thumb frequently cited is that a computer installation with a useful life of more than five years should be purchased rather than rented. However, in any specific case, the breakeven point is dependent on such factors as the number of shifts the equipment is used, so that specific analysis should be made. This analysis will frequently favor purchase. For example, the Federal government began in 1964 a program of analysis for computer acquisitions which is resulting in the purchase of much equipment previously rented.

LEASING OF COMPUTERS

A company which has examined the obsolescence and reliability problems and has concluded that purchase is the best alternative may not have funds available, or it may be that using the funds for purchasing computers will restrict future sources of funds. Under these circumstances, the possibility of leasing from an independent leasing company should be examined.

A lease typically provides for the purchase by a leading company of the specific equipment configuration desired by the user. The leasing company then leases it to the user. Lease agreements vary, but usually they have provisions such as the following:

1 User agrees to lease for a minimum period, say five years, with purchase and trade-in options.
2 The lease payment includes a maintenance contract and other charges.
3 There is no additional charge for second- or third-shift operations (except perhaps some additional maintenance charges).
4 After the minimum period, the lease charges drop to a lower rate.

If the lease is terminated before the minimum period is up, the user must pay a termination charge. This sometimes takes the form of a guaranteed sale price. The lease payments and termination payments amortize the cost of the equipment. These provisions apply to a "full payout" lease. A less common form is the equity lease, which has higher payments but no termination penalty. In both cases, the user obtains the investment-credit tax benefit just as if the equipment were purchased.

▌ SUMMARY

The major criteria for converting to a computer system are reduction in operating costs or an improvement in the information system. A typical approach to evaluating the desirability of a system is to form a study group to direct an investigation of information and data processing requirements. From possible system designs, a system is selected and described in a manual of specifications. This manual specifies the different processing runs, the volumes and frequencies of processing, the format of data, the documents and reports required, and other information relative to the organization's processing needs.

The computer manufacturers selected to bid on equipment for the proposed system are given the specifications for the system. The manufacturers respond with a suggested equipment configuration, together with estimates of the time required for the system to do the processing tasks specified. Evaluating the manufacturers' proposals includes an evaluation of hardware capabilities, future expandability of equipment, software, and other support.

Converting to a computer is a complex task that should be planned and scheduled with care. Before the equipment is installed, programs for major applications should have been prepared and tested. During the conversion to the new system, it is wise to run both systems in parallel until all major problems in operating the new system have been solved. After installation, there should be a followup review to appraise how well the system is meeting the planned objectives.

Although most computer equipment is currently being rented from the manufacturer on short-term leases, there is a growing trend to long-term leases, outright purchase, or to lease from an independent leasing company. The impediments to purchase or long-term lease are the questions of equipment reliability and technological obsolescence. Since reliability is now very high and risk of obsolescence may be estimated and taken into consideration, this trend to purchase or long-term lease is likely to continue.

▌ EXERCISES

1   An executive in a company with a successful computer installation was called by a friend, an executive in another organization, who asked if he might come and have a chat. He stated, ''We are getting our computer in a couple of months and are looking for ideas on how to use it.'' Evaluate the position of the company making the inquiry.

2   What criteria can be used to evaluate the following proposals?

    a   Proposal to obtain a computer primarily for payroll processing now being done by a large number of clerks.

    b   Proposal to obtain a computer primarily for production scheduling and inventory control. It would replace clerks using manual methods and would also allow the use of advanced methods.

    c Proposal to obtain a small scientific computer for linear programming applications.

    d Proposal to put remote inquiry stations at all sales offices. Salesmen would be able to make direct inquiries about status of inventory, items scheduled into production, shipments, etc.

3 What is the advantage of a middle management study group committee?

4 Under what circumstances in evaluating new systems is it appropriate to rely on manufacturers' representatives?

5 The manufacturer of one computer states that programs written for the current computer can be emulated on the new computer; a second manufacturer says that his computer has both a simulator and a conversion routine. Evaluate the relative merits of the two approaches.

6 Two young men from the Boise Cascade Company in Idaho wrote a program to convert IBM 1401 programs to System/360 programs after IBM said it could not be done (did IBM mean they preferred not to do it?). This conversion routine is being rented to users for a fee. Since IBM 1401 programs can be emulated, why would a company pay to have a conversion routine?

7 Suggest the applicability of the various methods of comparing computer performance for the following situations:

    a Comparing two models in the same family of computers.

    b Comparing two computers with similar word organization.

    c Comparing several computers for use on a wide range of scientific problems.

    d Comparing several computers for rather standard data processing tasks— mostly sorting, file updates, and reports.

    e Comparing several computers for all-round use.

8 A company's officials stated that they would buy their computer equipment only from company X since they were a supplier of services to that company and did not wish to offend their customer. How should this decision affect their evaluation and equipment selection procedures?

9 What methods of financing a computer are used? Under what conditions is each method appropriate?

10 What should be included in the manual of specifications? Of what use is this set of requirements inside the organization?

11 What information should be included in a run description?

12 How can a manufacturer estimate times for runs which are not yet written?

13 Why is there a need for running the old and new systems in parallel?

14 What should the installation do in order to have a set of applications ready to run when the computer is installed?

15 During the post installation review, a company discovers that the computer system is just barely breaking even on a month-to-month comparison of computer system costs with costs displaced by the computer. It appears that the substantial costs of conversion will never be recovered. What action should the company take?

▌ DESCRIPTION OF DATA PROCESSING SERVICE
ORGANIZATIONS
DEFINITION

REASONS FOR USE

CLASSIFICATION

METHOD OF OPERATION

▌ CONSIDERATIONS IN UTILIZING A SERVICE CENTER
PREPARATION OF MACHINE-READABLE INPUT

HANDLING OF INPUT ERRORS

STORAGE OF FILES

SECURITY OVER FILES AND DATA

SPECIAL PROGRAMS VERSUS GENERAL-PURPOSE PROGRAM

OWNERSHIP OF SPECIAL PROGRAMS

METHOD OF CHARGING FOR SERVICE

PROVIDING FOR INTERRUPTION OF SERVICE

▌ SELECTING A DATA PROCESSING SERVICE
ORGANIZATION
PREPARING A REQUEST FOR PROPOSALS

EVALUATING A PROPOSAL

COMPLETING THE NEGOTIATIONS

▌ CONTROL OVER IMPLEMENTATION
CONTROL OVER CONVERSION

OPERATING PROCEDURES

▌ PURCHASE OF BLOCK TIME

▌ SUMMARY

▌ EXERCISES

DATA PROCESSING
SERVICE CENTERS

This chapter is extracted in part from a reference article by this author and reprinted by permission from "The Selection and Use of A Data Processing Service Center," *AUERBACH Computer Notebook for Accountants*, Philadelphia, March, 1967. Copyright 1967 by AUERBACH Corporation and AUERBACH Info, Inc. All rights reserved. This reference is available from the American Institute of Certified Public Accountants, New York.

If an organization can benefit from the use of punched card or computer processing methods for one or more applications but cannot do the processing internally, a commercial data processing service may be the answer. The data processing service center is a way for an organization to share the facilities of a computer or punched card system without taking over the entire expense of the system and without the problems of organizing and managing a center. In most service centers, the processing is performed periodically in batch mode on data turned over to the center. An alternative approach involving continuous online access to a remote computer will be discussed in Chapter 21.

▌ DESCRIPTION OF DATA PROCESSING SERVICE ORGANIZATIONS

DEFINITION

A data processing service center or service bureau is an organization which provides data processing service to outside clients on a fee basis. This service may be provided continuously or only as needed. The equipment used may range from unit record equipment to computers. There is considerable diversity in the data processing service center industry, but established firms tend to be able to provide a complete data processing service rather than merely renting equipment time. A typical well-established data processing service organization has qualified personnel to analyze customer requirements, write programs, etc. as well as having control over appropriate equipment.

REASONS FOR USE

A data processing service can be used either in place of manual processing or to supplement an existing internal machine data processing installation. A data processing service center should be considered for an application if the center can perform the processing at a lower cost or on a more timely basis than can be done in-house. An application which can profitably be turned over to a service center will usually have one or more of the following characteristics:

1   The volume of records is significant.
2   Considerable computation is required.
3   The data must be rearranged in several ways to obtain different tabulations or to perform different computations.
4   The time available for processing is too short for the regular in-house processing staff, or there are insufficient personnel.
5   The application requires specialized knowledge not available in-house but found in the data processing center.

Even if an organization has its own data processing equipment, it may still use a service center for reasons such as the following:

1 Special or periodic overloads
2 Projects requiring specialized handling, specialized knowledge, or special equipment
3 Need for experience and assistance in connection with a conversion to new equipment

CLASSIFICATION

The diversity of service center organizations makes it somewhat difficult to categorize them. Table 20–1 summarizes the different ways in which a data processing service center may be classified. These are by ownership, control of equipment, type of equipment, and type of service.

The ownership of a data processing center provides a useful background for understanding the data processing service industry. Most of the major computer manufacturers have their own data processing centers. In fact, the largest data processing service organization, in terms of number of offices and volume of work, is Service Bureau Corporation, a wholly owned subsidary of IBM. The independents vary in size, with the larger ones having offices in major cities. A significant portion of the costs of a computer installation are fixed costs. Therefore, many business organizations which have installed a computer for their own use but have not fully utilized the available time find it advantageous to enter into a part-time service bureau arrangement. In some cases, this arrangement involves only the sale of blocks of time to outside users, the outside organizations providing their own programming, staff, operators, etc. In other cases, organizations such as banks with large computer installations have organized rather complete data processing services and sell these in competition with the manufacturer-owned and independent data processing organizations.

The control of equipment classification is based upon the fact that the availability of off-shift time on computers has made it possible for a person to set up a service

TABLE 20–1   Classification of Data Processing Service Centers

OWNERSHIP	CONTROL OF EQUIPMENT
Manufacturer	Owner or prime lessee
Independent	Block time lessee
Organization-affiliated	
University	

TYPE OF EQUIPMENT	TYPE OF SERVICE
Unit record equipment	Commercial
Computer	Scientific
Time-sharing computer	Industry-specialist
	Full-line

center without owning or leasing his own equipment. He leases a block of time from one or more computer installations, operating these computers with his own personnel.

The type of equipment found in some service centers is limited to unit record (i.e., card) equipment; others have a full range of equipment, including a computer. The computer equipment may range from small to large. Several service centers have been organized which specialize in time sharing, and these have computers especially suited for time-sharing applications. This will be described in Chapter 21.

Data processing centers tend to specialize. Some, especially smaller ones, have specialized in commercial processing of accounting-type applications. Others have specialized in scientific processing and have personnel with mathematical and analytical ability in the computer solution of scientific problems. Within these commercial and scientific processing specialties, industry specialists have also developed. For example, one service bureau concentrates primarily in the retail business, while another one handles only data processing for automobile dealerships. Even where there is no announced specialty, the expertise a service bureau obtains allows it to compete most effectively in the industry where it has developed programs and solved problems.

METHOD OF OPERATION

The functions in a data processing service organization are illustrated in Figure 20–1. Although the organizational structure for a center may vary, there tend to be three major functions: sales, consulting/programming, and production.

The sales function is carried on by sales representatives who call upon customers to explain the services offered by the organization. They analyze customer requirements and present proposals for performing services.

The purpose of the consulting and programming function is to perform system analysis and prepare specialized system designs for each customer's unique requirements. If the system is accepted by the client, the service organization also prepares programs.

The production department performs the data processing activity for the firm. This is typically divided into three separate areas: keypunch, quality control, and data processing. The quality control activity is concerned with controlling customer records and ensuring that the work is done correctly and on time. An account representative or account supervisor in the quality control group is assigned the responsibility for customer contact regarding the data processing.

Another way of describing how a service center operates is to trace the handling of a continuing commercial data processing contract such as preparation of a payroll, preparation of accounts receivable, etc. The salesman who first calls on the customer may work out the solution and make an estimate, especially if the system is relatively uncomplicated and fits standard procedures already developed by the center. If the system is complicated or unique, he will call on the systems analysts, who will prepare layouts, system flowcharts, programs, etc. Once the system is agreed upon and programs have been prepared, the client's files are converted to machine-readable

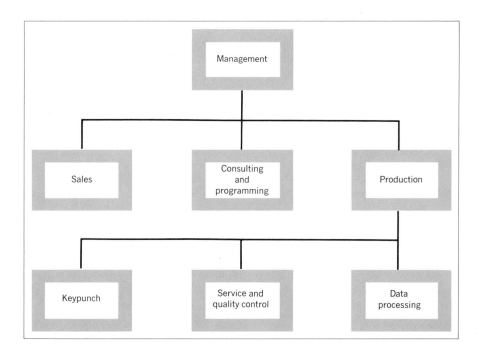

FIGURE 20–1 Functions in a data processing service organization

form in order to get the system started. These files are then stored at the service center. Thereafter, documents received from the client are logged in by the data processing center, checked for appropriateness by the control unit, then keypunched and key-verified. The data processing group obtains the master file from the quality control group, runs the program, and turns the results back to quality control. The account representative examines the master records and the processed reports for completeness and accuracy and returns the master file to the storage area. The completed reports are either picked up by the client or are transmitted by messenger service or mail. An error listing accompanies the reports. The client is advised through the error listing or through a call from the account representative as to the procedures to be followed to take care of the errors in the next data processing cycle.

▌ CONSIDERATIONS IN UTILIZING A SERVICE CENTER

There are various options available to the user of a data processing service center. Several of the key considerations in utilizing an outside service center are described in this section. These are:

1   Preparation of machine-readable input
2   Handling of input errors
3   Storage of the files

4   Security of files and data
5   Use of a special program versus a general-purpose program
6   Ownership of special programs
7   Method of charging
8   Providing for interruption of service

PREPARATION OF MACHINE-READABLE INPUT

One of the options open to the user of the service center is to perform the conversion of the data to machine-readable form himself, rather than have the service center do it. The advantage of the user preparing the input data himself is the control that can be exercised. Questions arising because of illegible documents, invalid or missing codes, etc. can be handled immediately by company personnel familiar with the company operations. The machine-readable input can frequently be prepared as a by-product of other data processing steps by company personnel. As examples, a paper tape punch can be attached to a cash register used for recording retail sales, an adding machine or cash register can be equipped with print mechanisms which print characters readable by optical scanners, and punched tape or punched cards can be prepared automatically by special equipment when a document is typed or an account posted.

The disadvantages of data conversion by the user are the expense of equipment just described and the fixed expense and management problems of an in-house keypunching staff.

Keypunching is usually not considered a profitable operation by many service centers, but they offer it as a necessary part of the total service. Since it is an important cost element, it is helpful to have some knowledge of this factor. Keypunch operators punch from 4,000 to 10,000 characters or strokes per hour, depending on the type of punching. As a rough guide, an average keypunch operator rate of speed for pricing purposes is 6,000 numeric strokes or 4,000 mixed alphabetic and numeric strokes per hour if reading from good source documents. The actual cost for keypunching or verifying will depend on the legibility and format of the documents, the number of punches per card (since it takes less time to punch 80 characters on one card than it does to punch one character on 80 separate cards) and the amount of intermixing of alphabetic and numeric characters. A rough rule of thumb for a quick estimate is $1 per card column per one thousand cards. Depending on the characteristics of the job, the rule will tend to give a figure a little on the high side, but it is useful for rough estimates. For example, assume a business had the following information to be punched from a document into punched cards:

ITEM	DIGITS
Product code	4
Quantity	4
Dollar amount	6
Total	14

Using the rule of thumb, the original keypunching would cost approximately $14 for each 1,000 documents because there are 14 columns to be punched. The key verification of the punching would cost an additional $14.

HANDLING OF INPUT ERRORS

The account representative at the service bureau is responsible for all communications with the client regarding errors or failure in data processing, resulting either from problems at the data processing center or problems with respect to the input furnished to the center. When an error is detected by the computer, it will typically print an error message and eliminate the item from the processing run. The user must process these items manually if processing must be done before the next processing cycle as is the case, for example, with a payroll check. He then prepares a change record which is included with the next service center run in order to update the files at the service center with the effect of the manually processed item. If the account representative detects an error resulting from improper processing by the data center, he will arrange for the job to be rerun before the results are sent to the client. If an error is not detected until it reaches the client, the client may reject the run if the errors affect so many parts of it that the results are not usable. Otherwise, he may accept the run, make manual adjustments, and send in corrections with the next input batch to be processed.

STORAGE OF FILES

Two approaches are taken with regard to storage of user files. In the first, the client keeps his files in his custody and takes them to the service center at processing time. If practical, the user representative may remain at the service center while the data is processed and take the files back with him. The second approach is for the service center to keep all files on their premises. The first approach is used where there is material of a highly confidential nature or where the data processing center has inadequate storage facilities to maintain security and protection against destruction.

SECURITY OVER FILES AND DATA

Assuming that the data processing center stores the files and receives documents for processing, then a question to be considered is the security over these files and over the data transmitted to the center. This consideration may be important in the case of confidential material or because of the consequences of loss or destruction. In the former case, security may be maintained by using codes rather than names for such items as payroll processing. Typically this is not considered necessary but is available as a method should it be deemed desirable. In order to guard against loss or destruction, the client may use his own messenger service and may store his own files (although this presents many practical problems). The security arrangements at the data processing center should include fireproof storage, procedures governing access to records and files, and insurance to pay claims which may arise. In the case of data being transmitted to the center, the user should always keep a copy of this data or have some means of reconstructing it in the event of loss.

SPECIAL PROGRAMS VERSUS GENERAL-PURPOSE PROGRAM

The customer's application may be run either with a special program written specifically for that customer or on a generalized program to which the customer's system has been adapted. The generalized or packaged program is used for a number of customers and is written with that objective in mind. There are good economic reasons for the use of package programs. The general program spreads the costs of programming over many users, therefore greater programming effort can go into making it a superior package. Having a program already available makes the system design work with the client easier, because the user's system is adapted to the program rather than the reverse; however, most generalized programs do allow for options with respect to such items as format in order to suit the individual preferences of clients. Cost estimates are more certain because of the experience from running similar problems using the generalized program. Against the use of package programs is the fact that, being written with no single client in mind, the program fits no user exactly and therefore does not completely please anyone. Even though the recommended approach is to adapt the customer's system to the general program, it may turn out that this is not feasible, and the service center then adapts the program to the customer by making changes in the program itself.

OWNERSHIP OF SPECIAL PROGRAMS

If a client pays for the writing of a special program, the ownership of the program would seem to be his. In actual practice this does not automatically follow, and therefore the question should be decided explicitly beforehand. In such cases where ownership does reside with the client, then progress documentation is obtained as a basis for progress payments to the center, and the final documentation, including a copy of the program in machine-readable form, is obtained by the client. Provision should also be made in the contract for restricting, licensing, or otherwise allowing the use of the program by other users.

METHOD OF CHARGING FOR SERVICE

There are three basic approaches to charging for data processing center services. These are:

1   Fixed price
2   Time and materials at standard rate
3   Cost plus fixed fee or percentage

The fixed fee is preferred in most cases, with the understanding that changes not agreed on in advance can cost extra. It is well suited for standard program packages or for those cases where specifications for the customer's system are firm and few changes are to be anticipated. The fixed price contract may take the form of a fixed fee plus a charge for each item processed. There is usually a minimum charge for each processing period for recurring jobs. The minimum reflects the fact that there is an administrative cost associated with each client no matter how small the job.

The "time and materials at a standard rate" is suitable where the problem and procedures are well defined but the running time, number of runs, or number of transactions are not known. It is also a useful method of charging in cases where the client's own program is being used. The "cost plus fixed fee or percentage" is applicable where the problem or procedures are not well defined.

As a general principle, reruns due to erroneous input data or errors caused by the customer will be charged to him. Reruns caused by the program being unable to handle conditions which were not excluded when the contract was taken are presumably the responsibility of the service center. In all cases, however, these should be discussed beforehand rather than after the fact.

PROVIDING FOR INTERRUPTION OF SERVICE

The service center should itself have made specific arrangements for backup service in the event of equipment failure or other interruption of service. It is up to the user to satisfy himself that these provisions are adequate. If the user has a copy of a program and the related files, he can, of course, at any time switch to another service center having similar or compatible equipment. If the user has paid for a special program, he should also have arranged for a copy of the program. However, the general programs provided by the data processing center are considered proprietary and are usually not available to their clients. The ownership of the customer files should be clearly spelled out so that if the service center user terminates his relationship for any reason, all master files and data files maintained by the service center will be returned to him.

▌ SELECTING A DATA PROCESSING SERVICE ORGANIZATION

In a survey of a group of users of data processing service organizations,[1] the following difficulties were mentioned:

Slow service
Lack of accuracy in reports and excessive reruns
Reports in a format confusing to client
Insufficient knowledge of accounting by EDP center
Insufficient planning and preparation
Data transmission difficulties
Additional service costs
Auditing difficulties
Overselling by the centers

[1] American Institute of Certified Public Accountants Computer Research Studies, "Computer Applications to Accounting Operations," 1966.

Such difficulties can be minimized through a proper approach to the selection of a data processing bureau and through control over implementation of this decision.

There are three major steps in selecting a data processing center: (1) preparing a request for proposals, (2) evaluating the proposals, (3) completing the negotiations. Considerations in the implementation of the decision are covered in the next section. The discussion to follow is oriented toward the use of a data processing center for a continuing data processing service rather than for a one-time tabulation or a one-time scientific computation. For the latter case, the general approach is similar but the amount of investigation is substantially less because of the one-time nature of the processing. The extent of the evaluation procedure should, of course, be compatible with the size and complexity of the job to be performed—a large and important data processing job should receive more careful evaluation than a small job which is less important.

PREPARING A REQUEST FOR PROPOSALS

The basic idea underlying the request for proposals is that the prospective user of the data processing service should define his own data processing requirements using his own staff or professional adviser. The request should be specific but should allow the proposals submitted by service centers to suggest alternative means for processing and alternative report layouts in order to achieve economies or efficiency in processing. The request document should include the following:

1   Purpose of the processing
2   A layout of the final reports, if the format is important, or a complete description of content if the format itself is not vital
3   A copy of the input documents (a blank one as well as a sample filled in) with a description of the information fields; or a layout of the input data if machine-readable media will be furnished by the user. If the size of a data item is variable, a range should be given.
4   Number of records to be included in the master file and the expected growth factor. The estimate should give a range if there is considerable difference in activity during different periods.
5   Handling of exceptions to normal processing
6   Specifications for frequency of processing
7   Specifications for timeliness of processing
8   Special requirements—for example:
    a   Extra copies
    b   Special reports required
    c   Conversion specifications, including time limits, problems, etc.
    d   Special security and control specifications
    e   Accuracy specifications
    f   Alternative methods allowed
9   Acceptance testing requirements, such as a test run

The request for proposals is sent to those organizations[2] which have passed an initial screening test based on their experience with similar problems, reputation, financial ability, etc. A week to ten days is usually sufficient for a data processing center to respond.

If the data processing problem is standard and well defined, the request for proposal can be used for obtaining firm proposals from service centers. If the problem is such that a center must do considerable system design work before being able to make a proposal, the request for proposals approach may be used to select a suitable organization with which to work rather than to try and get price bids. The reason for this is that a center can be expected to make a suitable proposal if the job is well defined in the request, but it may not be willing to invest large amounts of design time to make a competitive proposal unless the job is large enough to justify the risk.

EVALUATING A PROPOSAL

Based on the initial screening, a visit to the data processing center, and the responses to the request for proposals, a service organization can be chosen. The following are examples of possible criteria:

Experience with similar problems
Availability of general program packages
Reputation and recommendations
Financial stability
Quality of staff
Quality of sales representative and account representative
Availability of control safeguards
Backup provisions
Proximity and convenience
Quality of proposal
Amount of work they subcontract
Time-of-completion quotation
Cost quotation
Ability to meet time and price quotation
Potential for handling requirements in future

Note that the integrity and professional character of the service center are as important as its price proposal. For a continuing job, there will be special reports to be prepared, reruns, changes, etc., and the user should have confidence in the service organization if there is to be this continuing relationship.

COMPLETING THE NEGOTIATIONS

Some service centers prefer a formal contract; others use a simple memorandum of understanding. In either case, the agreement should explicitly cover the respon-

[2] Two directories of data processing organizations are useful in locating service centers. The Association of Data Processing Service Organizations (ADAPSO) issues a biannual directory of members. The organization is limited to for-profit organizations which utilize their own equipment on their own premises, assume full responsibility for the finished product, and have completed one full year of successful operation. This directory therefore excludes organizations (such as banks) which are only part-time service organizations, and others not having their own equipment. Members must subscribe to a code prescribing standards of conduct. ADAPSO membership is one indication of a stable, bona fide organization. The directory is available from ADAPSO, 947 Old York Road, Abington, Pa. The second directory is contained in the July issue of *Systems* magazine.

sibilities of both parties—the processing to be performed, schedule of charges, renewal and cancellation, etc.

▌ CONTROL OVER IMPLEMENTATION

When a decision has been made to accept a data processing organization's proposal, decisions must be made regarding:

1 Scheduling of the conversion to the new system
2 Conversion of the master files to machine-readable form
3 Procedure for acceptance testing
4 Period of parallel operation
5 Operating procedures

These are very similar to the steps in implementing the decision to install an in-house computer system.

CONTROL OVER CONVERSION

A schedule of events and dates for completion in order to achieve the conversion is prepared and should be then used as a basis for reporting progress.

One of the major jobs to be undertaken is the conversion of paper document files to machine-readable files. This involves substantial keypunching. In some cases it may require extracting information from the documents and writing it on special forms for the keypunch operators. As with the normal operating procedures, irreplaceable files are not to be transmitted to the data center unless there are ample provisions for reconstructing the documents in case of loss. If these provisions do not exist, copies are made, and these are sent to the data center for keypunching.

One of the procedures necessary during the conversion period is the processing of a sample run in order that any difficulties may be resolved before processing begins on a regular basis. The processing of a sample run is especially important where a special-purpose program has been written.

It is typically not feasible to transfer to the new system without a break-in period during which both the old and new system are operating. Except for the simplest case, a period of dual processing is necessary in order to instruct personnel properly in the new procedures and to become acquainted with error procedures, the new report formats, and other questions which may arise. The period of parallel operation is usually from two to three processing periods.

OPERATING PROCEDURES

The operating procedures for personnel of the user organization will include instructions covering the following responsibilities:

1 Form of data to be prepared; editing procedures to ensure completeness and legibility
2 Time schedule for preparation
3 Type of control figures and transmission controls
4 Person responsible for preparing controls
5 Person responsible for all contacts with the service bureau
6 Procedures for handling errors in input data
7 Procedures for checking output received against control totals and person responsible for it
8 Procedures for handling delays, errors, or failures in data processing

▌ PURCHASE OF BLOCK TIME

An alternative to the use of a full-service data processing organization is the rental of a computer system by the hour. In this arrangement, sometimes called block time, the seller provides no service or programs but simply rents the use of his computer system for a stipulated period of time. The user writes and debugs his own programs, provides his own operators, prepares his own data, maintains his own files, is responsible for his own supplies, etc. The user thus takes on substantially the same responsibilities as when operating his own computer except for the installation and maintenance of the equipment.

Block time is available from a number of sources:

Regular service centers
Service centers especially designed for block time users
Organizations having time available on their computers and offering it for rent

The economics of computers make it attractive for many organizations to offer block time for sale. An organization may be able to justify having its own computer and yet use only a fraction of the time available on it. Even if the system is being leased from the manufacturer, the typical contract calls for rental of at least a full shift. Added shift rentals are at a fraction of the first-shift cost. The sale of block time allows an organization offering such time to share the cost of its computer system without having to provide services as well. The seller may need to provide storage and work space for the user and may wish to furnish operators as well, but otherwise he does not become involved with the data processing being performed.

Some of the reasons a buyer of block time may find it desirable to take this "do-it-yourself" approach rather than make use of the capabilities of a data processing service organization are:

The organization may be going to install a computer and may use block time as a means of getting experience with one or more applications. If he has a computer on order, the user will rent time on the same type of computer.

A regular service organization may not be readily available. In a small city, there may be several computer installations which will rent block time but no regular data processing center.

The using organization may wish to maintain high control or close security over programs and data and therefore may prefer that its personnel do the processing. An organization may have exceeded the capacity of its own computer system and use block time for the extra work.

▍ SUMMARY

An organization may obtain the benefit of automated data processing by sharing the use of a data processing system. Two approaches are presented in this chapter—the use of a data processing service center and the purchase of block time. The difference between these approaches is that the data processing service center provides full service, while block time agreements cover only the rental of equipment facilities and require the user to furnish his own programs and personnel support.

The major emphasis of the chapter is on the selection and use of a data processing service center. The recommended approach is for the user to define his data processing needs and then request data processing organizations to make proposals to meet these needs. Based on selection criteria and the proposals received, a service organization can be selected.

▍ EXERCISES

1   What is the recommended approach to selecting a data processing service organization
    a For a recurring data processing job?
    b For a one-time data processing job?
2   What special consideration might be important in selecting a center to do a linear programming computation?
3   What is the significance of the control of equipment classification in locating a service center?
4   What is the purpose of the quality control function in a data processing service center?
5   In talking with three different service centers about an application three different replies were received. Evaluate them, considering all other factors equal:
    a Center A has a general-purpose program which they have prepared and which is used by several clients.
    b Center B has a similar program written for another client which they will revise to do your processing.
    c Center C has no such program, but will write a special program for you.

6 What method of charging for data processing would be most applicable to:
   a Payroll
   b Accounts receivable
   c Writing a modification of an existing program
   d Providing services to investigate an unusual data processing application
7 What are the reasons a user might use block time?
8 To whom does a special program belong, if:
   a The client paid all costs of preparation.
   b The client shared the cost with the service center.
9 What precautions need to be taken during a file conversion?
10 How does the service center usually handle input errors?

▌ DESCRIPTION OF TIME SHARING
BASIC CHARACTERISTICS
TYPES OF TIME SHARING
TERMINAL DEVICES
PREPARATION OF USER PROGRAMS

▌ A USER'S VIEW OF TIME SHARING
A SIMPLE SCIENTIFIC TIME-SHARING SYSTEM
A BUSINESS-ORIENTED TIME-SHARING SERVICE

▌ A LOOK AT TIME-SHARING SYSTEM HARDWARE
   AND SOFTWARE
SHARING THE MAIN MEMORY
SHARING THE CENTRAL PROCESSOR
PROBLEMS IN TIME-SHARING COMPUTER OPERATIONS

▌ PROGRAMMING A TIME-SHARED COMPUTER

▌ CONTROL FEATURES

▌ AN EVALUATION OF TIME SHARING
COST FACTORS
NON-COST FACTORS

▌ SELECTING A TIME-SHARING SERVICE

▌ SUMMARY

▌ EXERCISES

TIME
SHARING
A REMOTE
COMPUTER

Time sharing is the concurrent use of a single computer system by many independent users, each user having his own programs, each expecting fast response, and each operating independently without an awareness of the use of the facility by others. Time sharing is popular for universities and for certain types of scientific and engineering computation. It is quite limited for commercial use. Time sharing is expected to grow in popularity in the future.

▌ DESCRIPTION OF TIME SHARING

BASIC CHARACTERISTICS

Time sharing may be viewed as an extension of multiprogramming in which the computer works on several programs concurrently, going from one to another for the purpose of maximizing the use of the system hardware. In time sharing, the additional notion is added of servicing all programs frequently enough so that a user does not become discouraged with the waiting time. The direct access to the computer by many users is the reason that a time-sharing system is also referred to as multiple-access system.

Time sharing may be used internally within an organization or by a data processing service center. A university, for example, may have a central computer facility with remote input/output stations at various points on the campus from which many faculty members and students simultaneously make use of the computer. A data processing service center which offers time sharing provides continuous access to the computer. This differs significantly from the approach described in Chapter 20.

A time-sharing computer arrangement will typically have the following characteristics:

1   Each user has one or more input/output devices connected to the central computer by communication lines (Figure 21–1). The most common input/output (terminal) device is a typewriter. The most common communication connection is over the facilities of a telephone company.
2   Each user acts independently of the others who are connected to the system. He sends data and instructions from his terminal, acting as if he were the sole user.
3   The central computer accepts the data and instructions arriving simultaneously from many users and, by giving each user a small but frequently repeated segment of computer time, services all users concurrently. For most problems, the computer can send the requested output back almost immediately.
4   The user's data files are maintained at the central computer center. The user instructions to the computer identify the files to be used. The system is designed to prevent one user from making unauthorized access to the files of another user.
5   Each user has his own private set of programs plus access to a set of public programs.

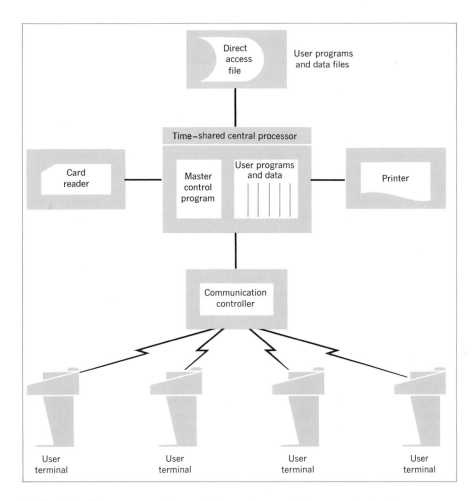

FIGURE 21–1 A time-sharing computer system

6 The data files, program files, and input/output devices are all directly connected
to the computer, so that processing can be performed at random as transactions
occur or requests are made.

TYPES OF TIME SHARING

Time-sharing systems may be classified by orientation as either scientific (computational procedures) or business (data processing procedures). Most of the time-sharing
systems currently operating are classed as scientific and are best equipped for problems that can be solved by a set of computational procedures. This class of problems
is characterized by very little input/output relative to the computations. By contrast,
the business data processing application is characterized by problems of file management, data preparation, report layout, and somewhat specialized programming.

Time-sharing users are online and typically operate within the instantaneous or near-instantaneous response conditions of realtime processing. The processing mode may be fixed-procedure or interactive. In the fixed-procedure mode the input is inserted in a specific order, the computation is run, and the output is received according to a procedure preestablished by the user. In the interactive mode (also called the conversational mode), the user carries on a conversation with the computer by inserting data or keywords, to which the computer responds with intermediate results, questions, or answers to questions. The user's responses to these outputs cause additional computation to take place. This process, which may also be used in programming and debugging of programs, continues until the answer is finally determined and printed out.

Another useful distinction in time-shared systems is the difference between a fixed set and an open set of programs. In the system with a fixed set of programs, the user prepares (or has prepared) a set of programs to do the required processing. Except for necessary updating, improving, etc., the programs remain the same from day to day. The fixed set of programs approach is suitable for most commercial data processing applications. In the open set, there may be new programs written each day, some of which will be saved for future use, while others will be run only once then discarded. This approach is suited to university, research, and engineering computation needs where each day there are new problems requiring different or modified computational procedures.

TERMINAL DEVICES

From the time-sharing user's standpoint the operation of the central time-shared computer facility is of little concern. Except for an assurance that proper controls exist, he does not need to understand the programming or hardware that is required at the computer center. The user operates only with his input/output device which is connected by communication lines to the computer. For him, the access device represents the computer. He inserts data into the device and receives operating messages and instructions and the output from it. Devices for time sharing may be conveniently divided into three categories—typewriter terminals, multifunction terminals, and visual displays.

Typewriter devices have a keyboard very similar to that of a regular typewriter and can be operated with very little instruction by anyone who can type. Figure 21–2 shows a popular teletype terminal. Many of the typewriter devices can produce punched paper tape as a by-product and can also act as punched paper tape readers. The input speed for a typewriter is limited to the speed of the operator. The output speeds are in the range from 6 to 16 characters per second. For comparison purposes, a good typist will type in the range of 5 to 7 characters per second.

For many data processing applications, a typewriter or paper tape typewriter combination may not be sufficiently versatile. There are also available a few devices that combine reasonable speed printout and card reading with the use of a typewriter and paper tape input/output. Figure 21–3 shows an example of one of these—a UNIVAC

FIGURE 21–2 Model 35 Teletype teletypewriter (Courtesy of Teletype Corporation)

DCT 2000 printer, card reader, and card punch. It prepares and sends data via telephone lines to a central computer. The reader-punch is capable of operating at 200 cards per minute for reading and 75 cards per minute for punching; the printer is capable of operating at 250 lines per minute. Although slow by comparison with the high-speed computer-attached input/output devices, the speed of the printer and the reader approach the limit which can be transmitted over a standard voice-grade telephone line, and these speeds are sufficient to support the average time-sharing user.

Visual displays, also called CRTs, were explained in Chapter 13. In time sharing, the keyboard is used for typing inputs. During typing, the input characters are displayed on the screen so that there is an opportunity to scan them for errors. Outputs

FIGURE 21–3   UNIVAC DCT 2000 remote input/output unit

are transmitted back to the CRT and shown on the screen. The input speed of the display device is no greater than the operator speed, but the output speed is extremely fast since a large number of characters can be instantly displayed. The display has other advantages when used in an interactive mode. Questions may be posed on the screen and the answers given via the keyboard. If the device is equipped with a light pen (a photoelectric cell for "writing" on a display), the question is displayed in a format similar to a multiple-choice question and the light pen is used to elect the appropriate response. Hard-copy printed output is not usually produced by a CRT device, because that capability adds substantially to the cost of the unit.

PREPARATION OF USER PROGRAMS

The time-sharing subscriber may make use of standard programs available to all subscribers, or he may write his own programs. Examples of "public" programs are mathematical and statistical programs such as multiple regression, data analysis, or linear programming. The subscriber specifies that he wishes a particular "public program," and the computer replies by first asking the user to select certain program options and then insert the necessary data. In such cases the user does no programming but depends completely upon programs previously written and inserted into the library of the time-sharing center.

Private programs suited to the individual user can be written either by the time-sharing service or by the subscriber's personnel. When programming for a time-shared computer, the programmer can perform online programming and debugging. In this approach the user inserts his program via his terminal. The program is immediately compiled, and error diagnostics are returned through the terminal. The subscriber then makes changes, recompiles, etc., until the program runs. The program is then added to the subscriber's private library of programs and can be called out at any time thereafter by specifying the name he assigned to it.

▌ A USER'S VIEW OF TIME SHARING

The remote user of a time-shared computer is in a position with respect to the computer center itself that is somewhat analogous to the relationship of a telephone subscriber to the telephone company transmission and switching facilities. The telephone user does not need to understand the operation of the telephone exchange; all he needs to know is how to operate the telephone furnished to him. He expects the service to be available on demand. Similarly, the time-sharing user is primarily concerned with what happens at his terminal. The terminal is, for his purposes, the computer. However, the user's understanding of responses at his terminal is enhanced if he understands how the central computer facility operates. This knowledge, plus an understanding of necessary controls in a time-sharing system, is necessary for choosing among competing time-sharing services. By way of contrast, the telephone user does not usually have a choice of concerns. If he did, he might be more interested in factors at the telephone company facilities which are important for achieving a satisfactory level of service.

A SIMPLE SCIENTIFIC TIME-SHARING SYSTEM

Scientific computation–oriented time sharing is available from service centers located in most large cities, and users from any location may be connected to these centers via communication facilities. In the typical approach, the user is furnished with a typewriter terminal which is connected to the computer over the dial-up switched telephone network.

The individual using this type of service must define his own problem, design his own computational procedure, and either use a standard library program or write his own. The programming is relatively simple because the time-sharing computer will accept one or more procedure-oriented programming languages.

As an illustration, the steps in using a popular scientific time-sharing service will be presented in sequence. The computer printout is shown in Figure 21–4. The computer questions are in color and explanatory comments have been added.

1   The subscriber turns on the typewriter and dials the computer telephone number.
2   When the hookup is made, the computer sends a message signaling a successful connection.
3   The user identifies himself and supplies information such as whether he is running a new or old program, the programming language, etc.
4   The user, if writing a program, types the statements.
5   At the completion of the program, the execute command is given. (In this case, the term RUN is typed.) If the program is executable, it is run and the results

```
Typewriter printout                                    Comments
(not given)                              Answering code after dialing
HELLO                                    User command to request service
UOFM SCH BUS

ON AT  15:48  FRI.   06-14-68

USER NUMBER--P53437                      Request for user identification number
SYSTEM--BASIC                            Inquiry as to language to be used
NEW OR OLD?                              Is it a new program or one previously saved?
NEW    NAME--DEPR                        We will call the program DEPR
READY.                                   Computer is ready to accept program


10 PRINT "ENTER THE VALUES OF N,C,S"
15 INPUT N,C,S
20 PRINT
25 PRINT "YEAR", "DEPRECIATION", "BALANCE"
30 LET R=C
35 LET F=N*(N+1)/2                       Program to compute depreciation
40 FOR I=N TO 1 STEP -1.0                and undepreciated balance using
45 LET D=(I/F)*(C-S)                     sum-of-years-digits method
50 LET R=R-D
55 PRINT I,D,R
60 NEXT I
65 END


RUN


DEPR      15:51  FRI.   06-14-68

ENTER THE VALUES OF N,C,S                 User input
?5,  9348.00,  1100.00                    of data

YEAR           DEPRECIATION   BALANCE
5              2749.33        6598.67
4              2199.47        4399.2     Computer
3              1649.6         2749.6     printout
2              1099.73        1649.87    of answer
1              549.867        1100.

TIME:  2 SECS.
```

FIGURE 21-4 Output from programming and running a sample problem on a time-sharing service (computer responses in color)

typed on the typewriter according to the program instructions. If there is a programming error, the program is not executed and diagnostic error messages are printed out instead.

6 The program may be saved for later use. If not saved, it is immediately released.

The sample program shown in Figure 21–4 computes the amount of depreciation and undepreciated balance for the "sum of the years digits" method of depreciation. In this method, the digits for each of the years in the life of the item are summed. The amount of depreciation to be taken is the cost times a fraction formed from the sums of the digits as the denominator and as the numerator the life in years minus one less than the number of prior years in service. For example, if as shown in Figure 21–3 the life is 5 years, the denominator is 15 $(5+4+3+2+1)$. A formula to compute this sum is $n(n+1)/2$ where $n =$ the number of years. The fraction for computing depreciation for the first year is thus $5/15$, for the second $4/15$, and so on.

A BUSINESS-ORIENTED TIME-SHARING SERVICE

When a business-oriented time-sharing service is used for routine tasks such as invoice preparation, updating inventory records, accounts receivable accounting, etc., the person using the terminal must follow preestablished procedures. Therefore, the processing steps must be stable and not change every day. Forms must be prepared, controls established, etc. Under these conditions, the set of regular processing programs is likely to be quite stable and subject to change infrequently and only after proper authorization.

The steps followed by one of the business-oriented time-sharing services[1] when establishing a new subscriber are:

1 Define data processing and file requirements, and design the system. This is accomplished by working with the subscriber.
2 Write program(s) to perform processing.
3 Place customer records on computer file media.
4 Install terminal devices at user location.
5 Train subscriber personnel.

A complete system design and programming service is provided. Each customer has a unique program or set of programs that are written specifically for him. No programming language is normally available to the customer, and he does no programming.

The terminal devices used are a teletypewriter and an auxiliary printer. They are connected to the computer by leased teletype lines operating in full duplex mode, which allows typing of new information on the keyboard while other data is being printed by the typing mechanism. There is no need to dial the computer to begin processing, because the leased line provides a continuous connection to it. The data keyed in by the operator is not printed directly but is transmitted to the computer, checked, and transmitted back to the printing mechanism, thus assuring that invalid

[1] Keydata Corporation, Cambridge, Mass.

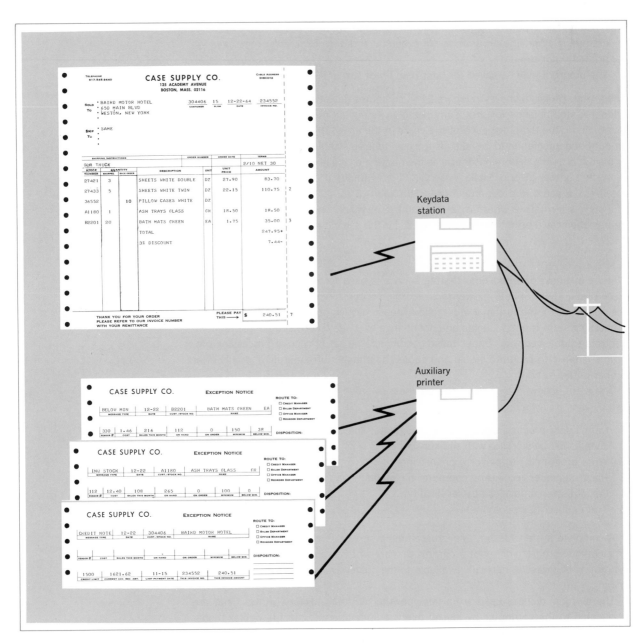

FIGURE 21-5 Invoicing application using a time-sharing service (Courtesy of Keydata Corporation)

lines are not typed. If an operator discovers an error before she completes an entry, she can erase it before transmission by hitting a control key.

In a typical invoicing application (Figure 21–5) the operator types a customer number, and the typewriter then automatically types the customer name, address, and other heading information. For each item on the invoice, she types only the product code and quantity. The computer sends back the item description and price extension and automatically signals the operator if there is an error in the input data or if there is insufficient available inventory. When all items have been typed, the computer automatically prepares the totals and computes any discounts. The computer can automatically do the following:

Put heading on invoice
Check input data to see if valid
Check customer credit
Check inventory availability and post issue if available
Price, extend, discount, and total the invoice
Record data for preparation of a sales journal

▎ A LOOK AT TIME-SHARING SYSTEM HARDWARE AND SOFTWARE

Although the user of a time-sharing system need not understand the complexities of computer operations, it is helpful to understand the broad requirements imposed on the equipment and the general organization of a time-sharing computer system. Consider first what the computer must do in a time-sharing environment:

1 Communicate at irregular intervals with a number of remote devices
2 Hold programs and data in secondary storage until they are ready to be run
3 Decide the order in which programs should be run
4 Put the program to be run next and its associated data into the main memory
5 Run the problem and transmit the results back to the proper terminal

In time sharing, the computations associated with a problem typically are not run continuously until the answer is obtained, because this might mean that a program requiring a long running time would cause an excessive delay for other users. Instead, each user is given a small amount of computer time with such frequency that the access appears to be continuous.

In implementing this sharing arrangement, there are two problems: sharing the main memory and sharing the central processor. Sharing the main memory is a problem, since there is a limit on the size of storage such that all of the program sharing the processor cannot be in memory at once. Sharing the central processor presents difficulties because the computer must switch between programs, giving each a share of the time so that no program is noticeably delayed.

SHARING THE MAIN MEMORY

There are many schemes for sharing the main memory (Figure 21–6). These may be classified as (1) paging and (2) memory swapping. In paging, each program is broken into small sets of instructions called pages. These may range from a fairly small number of instructions to quite a large segment of a program. For example, one large scientific system uses pages of 1,000 computer words, while another business-oriented service uses pages of only 64 words. When a program is to be run, a single page (or a small number of pages) is brought into memory and executed. Any reference by this page to another page in the program will necessitate bringing that page into memory. The previous page is no longer needed, and its memory space can be released. Pages from many programs may be in memory simultaneously, thereby allowing the computer to switch between programs.

In the memory-swapping approach, the entire program is moved in or out of main memory. Only one program is in memory at a time, and it is allowed only a very short residence before it is rolled out in favor of the next program. Both alternatives require a sophisticated program to supervise the operation and high-speed transfer rate from secondary storage.

SHARING THE CENTRAL PROCESSOR

If pages from many programs are in memory at the same time, the computer shares the processing time among them. Two methods may be used for deciding when to switch between them. One method is to switch at the end of a very short time slice. Each program gets its slice of time, if it can use it. This is very useful in scientific processing where the time for any one problem is not known. The other method is to switch each time the program being executed has to wait for a direct access file reference or for an input/output operation. A program may thus execute and wait many times before its execution is complete. If memory swapping is used, each program gets a small amount of processing time before being moved from memory to be replaced by the next one. The program then waits its turn, repeating the cycle until it is finished.

PROBLEMS IN TIME-SHARING COMPUTER OPERATIONS

Moving programs in and out of memory and allowing each program to use only a small slice of each time segment results in a considerably higher overhead in a time-sharing computer system than the regular batch-processing system. The overhead in a computer system consists of that time which is taken in putting programs into memory, switching between programs, recording program time usage, deciding which program should be run next, etc. If a computer is not specifically designed for multiple access, the overhead required to do time sharing may run quite high. The use of special hardware features in computers designed for time sharing reduces the overhead, but this is still a substantial factor in the operating time of the computer system. The speed required to service many terminals without an individual user being

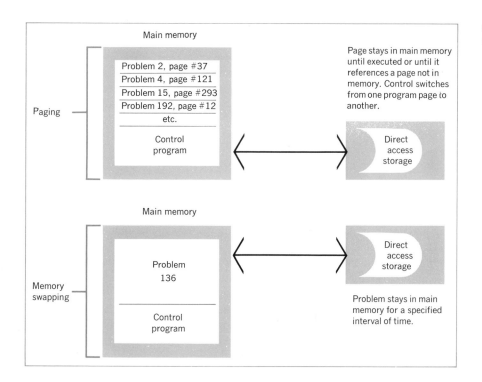

FIGURE 21–6 Methods for sharing main memory in time sharing

Paging

Main memory

Problem 2, page #37
Problem 4, page #121
Problem 15, page #293
Problem 192, page #12
etc.

Control program

Page stays in main memory until executed or until it references a page not in memory. Control switches from one program page to another.

Direct access storage

Memory swapping

Main memory

Problem 136

Control program

Direct access storage

Problem stays in main memory for a specified interval of time.

particularly aware of the others or being aware of the overhead requirement means that the time-shared computer is usually a medium- to large-scale processor.

Because of the speed with which programs have to be moved in and out of main memory and the speed with which decisions must be made as to the proper program to enter main memory for processing, the computer itself must make all of these decisions, and no operator intervention can be required. The time-sharing operating system for doing this is considerably more complex than the normal operating system used in batch processing.

Another problem in a time-sharing system is the amount of storage. If many users are sharing a computer system, only a very small number of them may have their current program or part of their current program in memory simultaneously. The remainder of the programs or remaining part(s) of the program(s) must be stored elsewhere. In order to quickly obtain the most commonly used computer programs, a hierarchy of storage is usually provided, as described in Chapter 13. The fastest storage is the main storage of the computer. The next fastest is a bulk core storage or a magnetic drum. The third level, slower in operation, is the magnetic disc. Little-used programs and larger volumes of data are stored on magnetic tape or magnetic strips.

Some of the considerations in running a time-sharing computer center are the length of the time slice which is given to each program, the scheduling algorithm (the rules for deciding which program will enter memory next), and the organization of storage. These are also of interest to a prospective user, since time-slice size and the scheduling algorithm will affect response time, and the storage organization and backup method are important in protecting user files from destruction. These control features are discussed later in this chapter.

▌ PROGRAMMING A TIME-SHARED COMPUTER

As previously indicated, programs for using the computer may be written (1) by the time-sharing service for use by all subscribers, (2) by the time-sharing center for the use of one subscriber, or (3) by the subscriber himself. The new element in programming introduced by time sharing is the online conversational mode of writing and debugging programs.

In the conversational mode the subscriber types in his program statements, and these are examined by the computer. In true conversational mode, each statement is examined individually; in a variation of this, the computer does not examine any statements until the entire program is written. The computer may ask questions or print error diagnostics. The user then responds with answers, questions, or corrected statements. This dialog continues until a correct program has been written. This eliminates the turn-around time usually experienced in debugging programs in batch systems which operate according to a schedule.

Programming is usually done in a procedure-oriented language. The most commonly used are BASIC, FORTRAN, ALGOL, and COBOL. Special compilers must usually be written to accommodate time sharing because compilation of a program may need to be interrupted to allow compilation to proceed on another. The technique of pure procedures and reentrant routines, described in Chapter 12, are used. In these approaches, the translator routine of the compiler remains independent of the programs which it is translating, and all information necessary to the compilation is attached to the program. If interrupted in compilation, the translator program can work on other programs, then return later and pick up the compilation at the point of interruption.

▌ CONTROL FEATURES

A time-sharing subscriber need not know how the equipment operates, but he must be assured of controls and protections in the operation of the time-sharing service, such as:

1   Protection against alteration or destruction of his program
2   Control against unauthorized access to his data files
3   Protection against the loss or destruction of data files

4 Provision for file reconstruction
5 Provision for recovery from an equipment failure
6 Control against unauthorized use of his proprietary programs

Methods used by time-sharing services include memory protect hardware, identification codes, a hierarchy of file preservation, and internal subscriber audit controls.

If more than one program is in the main memory of the computer at the same time, a memory protect feature described in Chapter 12 is used to prevent one program from entering the memory space reserved for another. This is accomplished through the addition of a memory key to all instructions of each program. If an instruction of one program attempts to enter the memory domain of another program, the mismatching of the memory key will prevent the instruction from being executed.

In order to prevent unauthorized access to both data files and proprietary programs, a code may be associated with all inquiries into the system and the supervising control program will match this code against the code for the files and programs being examined. If the inquiry code provided to the computer is not a valid one for the files, the request will not be honored (Figure 21–7).

There is always the possibility that there may be a destruction of program and data files. The time-sharing system should therefore provide for copying data and program files on to another file medium from which a reconstruction can take place. This is especially true for commercial processing performed in time sharing.

The time-sharing service should, for proper internal control, furnish the user with checking features through which he can audit his application. Some examples are:

Control totals for batches of processing and for time periods

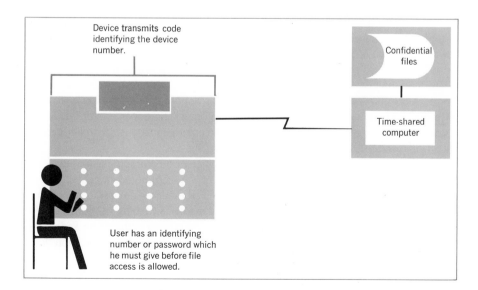

Device transmits code identifying the device number.

Confidential files

Time-shared computer

User has an identifying number or password which he must give before file access is allowed.

FIGURE 21–7 Controlling access to confidential files

Transaction listings for reference purposes
Transaction numbering
File printout and analysis

▌ AN EVALUATION OF TIME SHARING

In evaluating time sharing, the discussion will use the comparison of a computer installation which provides a scheduled, batch service at periodic intervals of time.

COST FACTORS

The hardware cost of using a time-sharing service consists of three major elements:

1 Cost of computer system use. This may be a flat time charge or may be divided into a charge for time (or transaction) and a charge for the amount of file storage used.
2 Cost of terminal device.
3 Cost of communication.

In addition the user must provide for supplies, personnel, and programming.

The charges for different time-sharing services vary and can be compared adequately only if information is available on characteristics of the system. Some services charge for connect time (the time during which the terminal device is hooked in and being used to send or receive from the computer). Others charge on the basis of the actual time the central processing unit of the computer takes in processing. The latter is usually only a fraction of the connect time.

The terminal cost depends on the device used. Monthly rental for a remote typewriter terminal ranges from $50 to $115 per month without an attached paper tape device, and from $75 to $175 with paper tape capabilities. A multipurpose input/ output terminal which can read and punch cards and also print will cost from $400 to $600 per month. Costs of renting a visual display range from $125 to $400 per month. A communications controller required for remote operation adds extra cost, so that a single remote time-sharing terminal will be at the upper end of this range. If several displays are used at a location, a single communications controller can frequently be used for all of them, thereby reducing the cost.

Since communication is usually over the facilities of a common carrier such as a telephone company or Western Union, the cost of wire communications depends on the tariff of the common carrier being used and whether or not the connection is over a line dedicated to the user or through the regular switching network used for telephone calls. If a switched toll service is used, the charge is the same as for telephone service. Long-distance charges apply for long-distance communication, local rates for local communications.

A time-sharing terminal is usually an alternative to the use of a batch-oriented service center, where data must be taken to the service center to be run on a fixed schedule and the results picked up later. The cost comparison must therefore be viewed in the light of the different characteristics of the system. Because the time-sharing user must pay for a remote access device, for communication line charges, and for access to the computer (which cannot operate as efficiently in a time-sharing mode as it can in a sequential batch processing mode), the time-sharing user incurs an additional cost for being in this mode. The minimum differential per month for a simple terminal connected to a local computer over a switched, toll line is about $100. In practice, the differential is apt to be closer to $400 or $500 per month. If the basic charge for computer time is considered to be approximately the same, the user of a regular service center who spends approximately $1,000 per month on services will probably have to spend $1,500 to receive the same amount of service on a time-sharing basis.

NON-COST FACTORS

Though the cost may be higher, the time-sharing unit offers a new dimension in data processing. It is online to the user's office. There is immediate and continuous access to the computer and to all the files. There is the possibility of immediate inquiry and immediate response.

Another advantage of time sharing is that small problems which would not justify a trip to the computer center or the setup time required to arrange for processing can be run economically in a time-sharing system. The immediate response is especially attractive for small processing problems which are likely to arise at irregular intervals, and a delay while the problem is sent to and returned from a service center is likely to mean a delay in the progress of the work. For this reason, the scientific time-sharing system is very popular with engineers, scientists, and others who find a need to utilize the computer for their problems. By having a terminal device readily accessible to the user, a whole new class of problems too large for slide rules or mechanical calculators and too small for regular batch processing can be put on the computer. There is little question but that time sharing will dominate this type of processing need.

The time-sharing terminal provides a relatively inexpensive entry into the computer field. Besides providing processing, its use has training possibilities. The time-sharing service may also assist the user in a small town, since a person who is located at a great distance from a service center can make use of a computer via a time-sharing terminal.

In evaluating time sharing it is well to keep in mind that time sharing is in its infancy. There is not yet sufficient experience to judge the future course of events. Special time-sharing hardware is being introduced, new terminal devices are planned, and new communications facilities and rate schedules can be expected. In addition to the possibilities inherent in the sharing of a large-scale computer system, time sharing may offer the opportunity to be part of future cooperative arrangements to share statistics for industry comparisons, retrieve information, etc.

▌ SELECTING A TIME-SHARING SERVICE

If it appears desirable to use a time-sharing service, the following are some of the selection considerations:

1   *Response time.* A time-sharing system can become overloaded if too many users are connected to the system. Certain times of the day may present a serious problem. An investigation should be made into the response time and the times of the day when overload is likely to occur.

2   *Terminal devices.* Virtually all time-sharing services provide typewriter input/output. If the user requires higher input or output speeds, it is necessary to make sure that the particular computer system will accept a higher speed device.

3   *Programming languages.* If the primary purpose of the installation is to do problems that can be expressed as a set of algebraic procedures, it is most important to have access to an algebraic compiler language such as FORTRAN, ALGOL, or BASIC. If the service center does the programming, cost estimates should be obtained. The number of standard packages available to facilitate programming is important. If the processing is primarily of a research nature, then it is important to have statistical routines so that programming will not be required for these. If the processing is primarily commercial, then the existence of prewritten commercial data processing programs is desirable. However, it frequently happens that a general-purpose program is unsatisfactory for a particular user; therefore, it is important to examine whether or not it is possible to easily modify a standard routine furnished by the service center.

4   *Assistance in systems design.* The typical scientific user of a time-sharing terminal requires little assistance. A small amount of training is all that is necessary for him to be able to work out his formula-type problems at a time-sharing terminal. In the case of commercial data processing, this will not usually be true. There are forms design, handling procedures, special programs, input/output problems, error recovery procedures, and other problems which require assistance by the service center. The amount and quality of assistance furnished by the time-sharing service is therefore an important consideration.

5   *Control features.* Before committing himself to a service center and entrusting data files to it, the user should be satisfied that proper precautions have been taken to protect against file destruction and against unauthorized use. He should also be satisfied that, in the event of system failure, there is adequate provision for file reconstruction. When beginning to use the service center, the same principle applies as in other computer installations. There should be a period of dual operation during which manual reconstruction will be possible in the event of a failure of the computer system. This dual operation should not continue for any extended period of time but should be available during a break-in period of two to four weeks.

6   *Financial integrity.* As with conventional data processing services, the failure of

a time-sharing operation will endanger files and future processing, so there should be an assurance that the operation is properly funded and is likely to continue in operation.

SUMMARY

Time sharing a remote computer has many advantages. Many users may concurrently use the computer without any awareness of the other users. Through time sharing, one is able to purchase direct access to a remote computer, storage units, and processing time. Servicewise, it is an extension of the service center concept to provide service on a demand basis rather than the scheduled basis of the regular service center.

The sharing by remote users introduces new cost elements because of the need for terminal devices and communications lines. It also results in added operating time at the computer center because of the time required to switch programs in and out of main memory and to switch from processing one program at a time to processing many programs, each for a short but frequently repeated interval of processing time.

If a time-sharing arrangement is deemed advisable, some of the selection considerations are response time, terminal devices used, programming language, amount of systems assistance provided, control features, and stability. It appears that time sharing will come to dominate in the field of "short" problems—student, research, and engineering-type computations where immediate response speeds the other work of the user. The extent to which time sharing will be used for commercial processing is not yet clear and may depend on improved input/output devices and more suitable communications rates.

EXERCISES

1   What is time sharing? How does it differ from multiprogramming? How does it differ from multiaccess computing?
2   What are the characteristics of a time-sharing arrangement?
3   What might make a user aware of the existence of other users? How does this differ from the use of a telephone?
4   What types of terminal devices are available? What are the advantages and disadvantages of each?
5   What must the system do in order to operate in time-sharing mode?
6   What is the difference between paging and swapping? What difference does it make how big the pages are?
7   What controls should be present in a time-sharing system?

8   A time-sharing service allows an access to a section of a subscriber's file only if two keys are matched: (1) the device code which is automatically checked and (2) a personal identification code given to each person with a need to have access. Under what circumstances can these controls fail to stop unauthorized access?

9   What are some important considerations in selecting a time-sharing service?

10   Which of the following are likely possibilities for time sharing:

    a   Students studying operations research

    b   An engineer who routinely performs engineering computations

    c   An analyst doing economic evaluations requiring frequent computations of rate of return

    d   A company with 100,000 active accounts which issues 5,000 invoices per day

    e   A CPA having a number of small write-up clients, some of whose accounts are prepared by a regular data processing service center

    f   A physician whose receptionist performs bookkeeping for 150 transactions per day

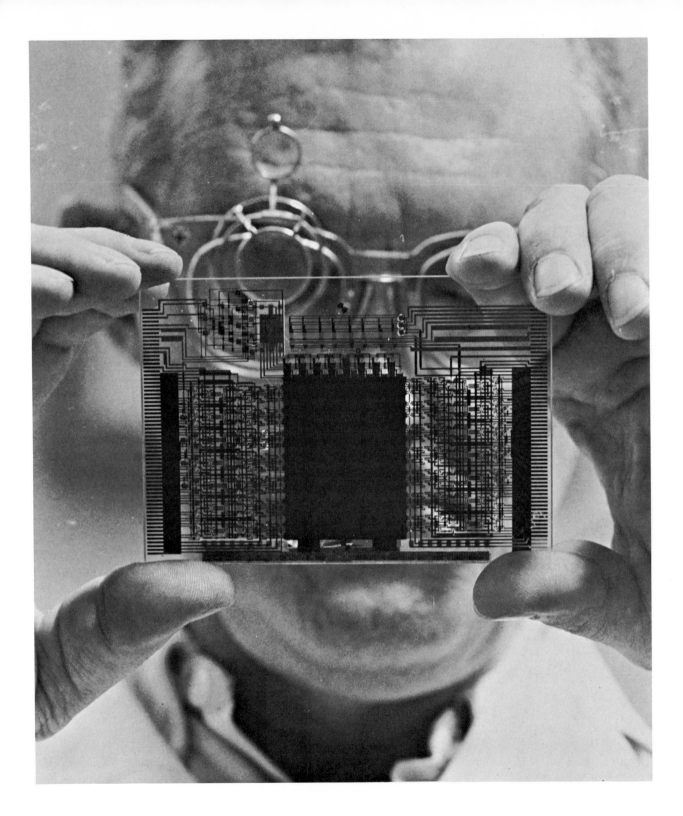

▮ DEVELOPMENTS IN HARDWARE
LARGE-SCALE INTEGRATION (LSI)
PHOTODIGITAL STORAGE
ASSOCIATIVE MEMORIES
CRYOGENICS
IMPROVED INPUT AND OUTPUT
IMPROVED DATA COMMUNICATIONS
HEURISTIC AND ADAPTIVE COMPUTERS

▮ DEVELOPMENTS IN SOFTWARE
IMPROVED PERFORMANCE
STANDARDIZATION
FIRMWARE (STORED LOGIC)
SEPARATE PRICING OF HARDWARE AND SOFTWARE

▮ DEVELOPMENTS IN SYSTEMS

▮ IMPACTS OF COMPUTERS ON ORGANIZATION AND
MANAGEMENT
NEW APPROACHES TO PLANNING AND CONTROL
IMPACT ON STRUCTURE OF ORGANIZATIONS
EFFECT ON THE MANAGER

▮ SOCIAL IMPLICATIONS OF COMPUTER UTILIZATION
TECHNOLOGICAL UNEMPLOYMENT
ETHICS, PRIVACY, AND FREEDOM IN THE USE OF
CENTRAL DATA BANKS

▮ SUMMARY

▮ EXERCISES

LOOKING AHEAD: IMPACT OF CURRENT AND PROSPECTIVE DEVELOPMENTS IN HARDWARE/ SOFTWARE AND SYSTEMS

This chapter attempts to look ahead and anticipate new developments. Some of the items described are clearly imminent or may have already been implemented in a few advanced situations. Other developments are less certain, and it is possible that events will show such predictions were wrong. At this point in time, hardware developments are more clearly predictable than the impact of computers on organizations. The chapter surveys new hardware developments, trends in software, new systems concepts, the impact of computers on organization and management, and the social problems of the computer revolution.

▌ DEVELOPMENTS IN HARDWARE

Hardware will be faster and smaller. The techniques of microelectrics are bringing about these changes and, at the same time, reducing production costs. Memories will become larger, faster, and less expensive. Billion- or even trillion-bit online memories are even now beginning to be implemented. There is a clear trend to modularity in hardware design and to the concept of a compatible family of computers. The use of stored logic (described under software) makes this feasible. The hardware developments discussed in this chapter are large-scale integration, photo-digital mass storage, associative memories, cryogenics, improved input/output, improved data communications, and heuristic computers.

LARGE-SCALE INTEGRATION (LSI)

Large-scale integration (often termed LSI) refers to the batch fabrication of logical circuits and memory elements. A complex array of switching circuits is manufactured on a silicon chip. This is done by depositing films of conducting and semiconducting materials onto the chip. A mask causes the material to be deposited in a pattern. The superimposed pattern from many (say 10 to 12) deposits make up a complete circuit including all components and interconnections (Figure 22–1). The advantages of LSI for logic circuits are reduced cost, smaller size, and greater speed. LSI means that an increased amount of logic hardware (say three times as much) can be used for the same cost as regular hardware. This changes the tradeoff between functions assigned to hardware and software. The LSI circuit can be used for memories as well. It will probably be used only in high-speed control memories or special-purpose storage because it is volatile, i.e. there is a loss of information when power is turned off.

PHOTODIGITAL STORAGE

A device first installed in 1967 uses a small film chip to store data. Data is recorded on the film by an electron beam exposure. Each tiny light or dark spot on the film records a 1-bit or a 0-bit. After exposure, the film chip is developed. It is read by a tiny flying spot scanner. Once exposed and developed, the chip cannot be erased

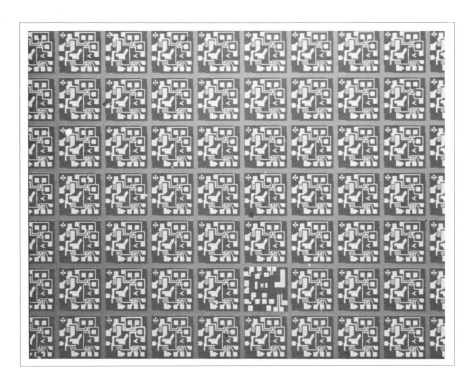

FIGURE 22–1 Large-scale integrated circuits (Courtesy of Control Data Corporation)

and reused. The read and write rates are reported to be very fast (½ million and 2½ million bits per second respectively). This device can provide more than a trillion bits of online storage.

Laser techniques appear to offer a potential for very dense storage on a media such as film. In one technique, a film chip is divided into infinitesimally small squares, each of which can be used for a 1-bit or 0-bit. The laser (a very tiny and very concentrated beam of light) records a 1-bit by "burning" the emulsion. It is read by sensing the black and white spots. The probable packing densities are very high— perhaps 1 million bits per square inch. A second laser-based memory uses a magnetic-coated mylar tape wrapped around a drum. The packing density is 13 million bits per square inch, which is 1,000 times greater than conventional magnetic tape. A laser beam makes a hole in the metallic coating to record a 1-bit. Readout is accomplished by reducing the laser power; beam reflection or non-reflection then indicates holes or non-holes.

ASSOCIATIVE MEMORIES

An associative memory is one in which data is addressed on the basis of a portion of its contents rather than by a numeric address. It is also termed content-addressed memory or search memory. Data is located by association rather than by specific

FIGURE 22–2 Operation of associative memory

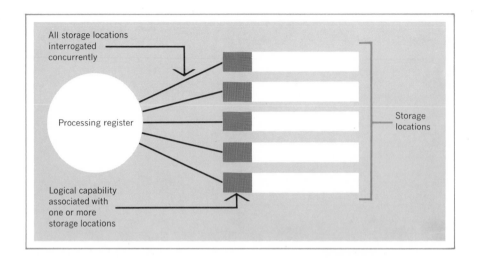

All storage locations interrogated concurrently

Processing register

Logical capability associated with one or more storage locations

Storage locations

memory address. All storage locations are searched simultaneously in order to locate desired data. The search is based upon part or all of the contents of each storage location and may be based upon criteria such as equality, greater than, less than, etc. If, for example, the storage contained payroll data for 100 employees, an instruction to fetch the record of employee 736201 would cause the logic circuits associated with each storage location or set of locations to examine the portion of each memory location containing the employee number. That storage location which was found to contain the data would be transferred to a register for processing.

Associative memories are quite expensive relative to regular storage. Barring some unforeseen technological change, the high cost probably precludes its use as the main memory. However, the use of a small associative memory in conjunction with a large-capacity direct access storage device appears to be practical. In this application, the associative memory is used for locating entries in indexes and tables which contain storage location addresses for the data in storage files.

CRYOGENICS

Cryogenics is the study of physical phenomena at very low temperatures. The phenomenon which is of primary interest to computers is the superconductivity of metals, alloys, and other materials at temperatures near absolute zero, i.e. $-450°$ F. Superconductivity was discovered in 1911 by Kammerlingh Onnes, only three years after he had successfully liquefied helium. This scientist found that the electronic resistance in many metals drops to zero when the metals are at the temperature of liquid helium. It was also discovered that an externally applied magnetic field can cause the material in its superconductive state to return to its normal resistive state. For each material, there exists a critical temperature and a magnetic-field point defining a sharp break beween superconductivity and normal resistance. With this property, superconductive materials can be used for switching, storage, and amplifying currents by varying the magnetic field. The cryotron, a superconductive computer component, is, in its simplest form, a short piece of straight wire with a single winding wire around it for control. Current in the control winding creates a magnetic field which can cause the central wire to change from superconductivity to normal resistance at a temperature near the critical temperature. With this device, a small current can control a large one.

Superconductive computer components have many important advantages. Most components such as the cryotron are easily made and inexpensive. They are very reliable, and they are very small. With these components, a computer could be made which would occupy only 1 cu ft, not including the refrigeration components and terminals. Also important is the fact that many materials such as glass, tape, and glue are not affected by the low temperature. In fact, many metals become stronger. The full possibilities and advantages of using superconductive components are not yet known. At the present time, however, there are major disadvantages. The principal impediment is the development of an efficient refrigeration system to reach a temperature near $-450°$ F. This will probably be a system using liquid helium. Despite intensive interest, a cryogenic computer, at this point, is a research development and must await further technological advances.

IMPROVED INPUT AND OUTPUT

Input is usually the most pressing data processing operating problem—most errors occur at this point, and conversion for computer input is relatively expensive. Although card readers are likely to be made to operate faster, an important development is the encoding of data directly on magnetic tape rather than using punched cards. The magnetic tape can then be read at magnetic tape speeds, which are much faster than card read speeds. This approach still requires keying of data to encode it. In order to bypass this keying step, optical reading recognition appears most promising.

Optical reading is becoming more accurate and more versatile, so that the reading of any style of numeric printing is possible with advanced models. Recognition of alphabetic characters is also to be expected. Recognition of hand-printed characters is already feasible; more progress can be expected.

Voice recognition appears to be possible, but not in the near future. Perhaps a simple device to recognize spoken terms such as no, yes, and the numerals might be made operational first.

CRT displays are likely to be used more and more for output. In addition, they may be used for input through an attached typewriter, by light pens, or by making the face of the tube sensitive to the heat of the finger. In the latter application, the display provides questions or data, and the user selects or responds by touching the tube on a spot next to the question or data. This response becomes an input to the system.

Output speeds for impact printers will probably be increased, but the major improvements will probably be in other types of output devices such as visual displays and remote I/O devices for time sharing. Improvements in voice output devices will promote the use of this method of response.

IMPROVED DATA COMMUNICATIONS

The hardware of the central processor has consistently outpaced the input and output devices. This disparity in speed of performance has been compensated for by the use of data channels and other methods for allowing independent operation of the I/O units and the CPU. In the case of communications, the telephone network—designed for voice communication—is proving to be a barrier to centralized data processing systems which send and receive data from many remote locations. The mechanical switching which makes up most of the voice-grade telephone system is much too slow for high-speed data processing.

Developments now under way indicate that new communications networks will be developed to meet the needs for data communications. New schedules for pricing data communications are also to be expected.

HEURISTIC AND ADAPTIVE COMPUTERS

Digital computers use a predetermined program for problem solving. The computer does only what it is instructed how to do. The human brain is not like a computer, because the computer does not have adaptive and heuristic (discovering) ability. It has been proposed, however, that computers be designed with at least partial heuristic and adaptive ability. A heuristic computer would, in essence, write its own program for problem solving and analysis based on the results of previous processing. In the case of a chess game, for example, the computer would "learn" from its past errors and successes and would, over a period of time, "discover" an approach to playing chess. It would take into account the probabilities of successful strategies and would react to changes in the strategy of its opponents.

An adaptive computer is programmed by having it attempt to perform a task several times. Each success reinforces the processing path taken, and a failure causes the path to be inhibited. In much the same way that a path or road that is worn smooth by much use becomes the established route for walking, the repeated attempts finally establish one or more successful paths. Special electronic devices are used which can be regulated to establish such a processing sequence. As an example, an adaptive computer at Stanford University was "taught" to play black-jack. The computer, named Adeline, was furnished certain arbitrary information about card values, but was not given the strategy of the game. Every time she won a hand she was "rewarded" by having her responses reinforced. Whenever she lost, she was "punished" by having her responses diminished. After several hundred hands she developed a blackjack strategy quite close to theoretical optimum.

Although heuristic and adaptive computers are not in the status of current developments and current research has not achieved the necessary technological breakthrough, such developments may be possible and may affect the use of computers in the future.

▌DEVELOPMENTS IN SOFTWARE

Hardware improvements have been spectacular and rapid; software development has lagged behind the promises made by its designers and, when implemented, has not lived up to advance specifications. The software is so important that a company selecting a computer for use with an advanced business system must place more emphasis on software than hardware. Current and prospective software developments are improved performance, standardization, firmware, and separate pricing of hardware and software.

IMPROVED PERFORMANCE

Software can be improved by being more general, more economical of internal memory, faster in execution, and easier and less error-prone to use. All of these developments are taking place with newer versions of software packages.

If a problem is defined specifically and the processing requirements do not change, a very rigid, specific software suited to that problem is most desirable. But the only thing constant about most systems is change. Therefore, generalized software packages which can accommodate change are to be preferred over specific, rigidly defined ones. The trend to generalized software can be expected to continue.

Early versions of software tend to be very wasteful of storage. After some experience has been obtained, the software programming is then streamlined and the memory requirements reduced. In FORTRAN compilers, this trend has been marked. When FORTRAN was first introduced, a computer needed a large memory to handle it. Over time, the coding of FORTRAN compilers was made more efficient so that almost all computers, even quite small in storage capacity, have a FORTRAN compiler.

The rapid increase in hardware speeds has made general software more attractive. If a generalized system requires, say one-third more instruction executions than a specific program, the extra time becomes less significant as internal speeds reach the nanosecond range. The I/O speeds and other considerations become much more critical.

Experience with software is bringing improvements which will make it easier to use and less error-prone. The newer specification formats are more user-oriented than before. As an example of reduction in error possibilities, one of the error-prone features of FORTRAN was the prohibition of mixed types in expression. $X = A + I$ was invalid because A and I referred to two different types of numbers. This restriction was a common source of errors. Newer compilers relax this restriction and adjust automatically for mixed-type expressions.

STANDARDIZATION

The standardization of certain types of computer software allows greater interchange of software and allows software packages to be designed which have a large market. The standardization is most apparent in the language area where FORTRAN and COBOL have been standardized. The dominance of IBM (more than two-thirds of the market) means that there is a certain amount of de facto standardization. In fact, several manufacturers have put out hardware which is almost identical to IBM System/360 series. This makes software compatibility easier to achieve.

FIRMWARE (STORED LOGIC)

Firmware, stored logic, and microprograms are terms which refer to a special control program which serves the same function as additional computer circuitry. The microprogram is stored in a read-only storage. The program is loaded as part of the computer manufacturing process and is not normally available to the user. Stored logic allows the computer to accept instructions which are not included in the circuitry. When an instruction is decoded, a microprogrammed routine is entered which directs the computer to perform a number of the elementary steps which are included in the circuit design. The execution of a set of these microinstructions has the same effect as if the computer circuitry were designed to handle the instruction itself. In other words, the computer is designed to execute a relatively small number of very elementary operations; the programmer is allowed to write normal instructions. The microprogram is a program stored in the control memory which directs the computer to carry out a set of micro instructions in order to execute each of the program instructions.

This technique is used in many third-generation computers. A family of computers such as IBM's System/360 has an extensive set of instructions which can be executed by any of the computers in the family ranging from a fairly small model 25 to a large-scale model 75. This is accomplished by using a microprogram in read-only storage to allow the smaller machines in the family to execute the full set of instructions. This results in hardware compatibility. Read-only stored programs are also used in emulators. In this technique, one computer will execute the instructions written for another computer (for example, the System/360 model 30 can execute, via emulation, instructions written for an IBM 1401). Basically, an emulator is an interpretive simulator which uses a microprogram to interpret the operation codes and direct the steps to be performed by the processor.

The success in the use of stored logic in third-generation computers suggests that it may receive expanded use in fourth-generation equipment, but this will depend on other factors affecting fourth-generation hardware. In fourth-generation computers, for example, it is possible that the computer will be constructed with no order set and no data structure. The computer would be specialized for the use to which it is to be put by a replaceable microprogram. Many of the functions now relegated to software would be included in the firmware.

SEPARATE PRICING OF HARDWARE AND SOFTWARE

The prevailing practice in the computer industry is for the manufacturer to provide all software without additional charge. Presumably, the software support is included in the hardware price. A frequently discussed point is the desirability of separate pricing for hardware and software. This would allow users to purchase only the software they were interested in and to choose between manufacturer software and competing software from independent organizations.

While it appears unlikely that hardware and software will be completely separated for pricing purposes, there have been indications of a trend to separate pricing for special-use software. For example, Control Data sells a mathematical programming software package for the CDC 6600 computer as an extra-cost option, and Scientific Data Systems charges extra for a COBOL compiler for the SDS scientific-oriented computer.

Independent software houses are becoming increasingly aggressive. Flowcharting programs for preparing flowcharts from source coding, payroll programs, file management systems, and specialized compilers are examples of software now being offered by independent software firms.

▌ DEVELOPMENTS IN SYSTEMS

The new systems that will be installed in the next few years are already outlined in concept. Some of these were described in Chapter 4, and time-shared systems were described in Chapter 21. Most advanced computer applications for management purposes center on a concept variously described as an integrated system, a total system, or a management information system (MIS). These systems take so long to implement that one person in the industry was prompted to observe that "a management information system is like a purple cow. I haven't seen one yet, but I will recognize it when I do." There are many organizations that are working on advanced systems for computer-assisted management. Some of the more advanced ones have implemented partial MIS systems and have made substantial progress toward a full MIS system.

As the term is coming to be used, a management information system refers to a computer-based system for providing information for management. Its analytical framework includes statistics, operations research, and management principles. The management information system usually includes the concept of a comprehensive data base maintained by computer and available for analysis, processing, and decision-making purposes by the entire organization. Processing is integrated to avoid duplication of effort and duplication of files. The use of the system is designed to support the management process by providing analysis and information both routinely and on request. The system integrates planning with current operations and provides a dynamic mechanism for the planning and control of the organization.

An organization is not modular. What the sales department does affects production, which affects inventory, which affects accounting, which affects the financial requirements of the organization. There is a dynamic interaction, which is not recognized by batch processing facilities. This dynamic interaction can be captured only if there is a total MIS system. In the total system, all transactions, wherever they occur in the organization, and all environmental changes affecting the organization are captured in machine-readable form immediately upon their occurrence and are transmitted into a central computer facility. They are processed immediately, then, using predetermined decision rules, the computer sends out, on an exception basis, reports which are necessary for decision making. Where appropriate, the computer program makes necessary decisions and sends the instructions required by these decisions to the proper individuals. For example, suppose a salesman hears that a customer in another state is going to accept delivery of a competitor's product. This information is relayed immediately to the computer system, which first examines the available information about the customer to determine if this fact has previously been reported. If the fact has not previously been reported, the system records the information and transmits it not only to the salesman who has responsibility for the account, but also to others who should know about this development. As a second illustration, a customer places an order for delivery on a certain date, and the order with delivery requirements is transmitted to the computer. When the computer adds this order to the scheduled production program, it finds that certain raw materials must be ordered immediately. The raw material procurement requisition is automatically prepared and printed in a form suitable to be sent to the supplier. A confirmation of the order and a confirmation of the scheduled completion date are then prepared and transmitted to the customer. If difficulties arise requiring human decision making, the necessary facts will be transmitted to the person responsible for making such decisions.

Such a comprehensive management information system will make use of point-of-transaction inputs, remote inquiry and display units, transmission and communications equipment, mass random access storage, parallel processing, and complex operating systems. The emphasis on multiprocessing, input/output, and multiple access to files means that the core of future EDP systems may not be the central processor but a switching center which directs the operating of the many devices connected to the system, one or more of these devices being processors.

IMPACT OF COMPUTERS ON ORGANIZATION AND MANAGEMENT

Our ability to speculate about how computers will change organization and management is greater than our ability to produce such change. In other words, there has been considerable talk about what will happen, but it is taking place very slowly. It is too soon to tell if the predictions of change are correct, but certainly a technological innovation of the magnitude of the computer is bound to have an impact. This section will review what these changes appear to be.

NEW APPROACHES TO PLANNING AND CONTROL

In Chapter 4, some of the uses for computers which were surveyed included critical path analysis, forecasting, and system simulation. These three uses have an impact on planning and control because they make the process more flexible and more responsive to changing conditions. The reason a formal plan should be prepared is that an organization is usually too complicated for a planner to consider all variables in his head and come up with a well-coordinated plan. Instead, the individual forecasts must be made, interrelationships specified, the parts examined for consistency, and so on as the plan evolves. This means that some of the constraints on planning are the forecasts and the putting together of a consistent plan based on resource constraints that exist. The computational and processing demands of planning restrict the range of planning activity and the economical frequency of updating. The use of computer techniques can remove these restrictions, but to do so requires a quantification of the planning and budgeting procedure. The latter is not easily done, and this may account for the slowness with which the planning and budgeting process has been computerized. Planning illustrates the concept of man/machine systems in which man's ability as a heuristic reasoner and his ability to make judgments based on incomplete data is supplemented by the computer, which provides computational and processing capabilities. The planner can ask "what if" questions, and the computer can provide the computation which translates the questions into financial statements, requirements, etc. for review. One of the consequences of the computer planning and scheduling methods is to give the top executive the ability to inquire more deeply into these processes and exercise more control over his subordinates as they perform them.

In implementing projects, the time scheduling is very important. PERT and other network methods assist the executive to calculate the consequences of delays in the completion of individual activities. For large, complex projects, computer processing is an important element in making frequent planning and rescheduling practical.

IMPACT ON STRUCTURE OF ORGANIZATIONS

In the speculation as to the impact of computers on the organizational power and status structure, most attention has been concentrated on the middle management level. The reasoning is that computers provide top management with a greater span of control and that many of the judgmental decisions usually handled by middle management will be programmed into the computer. Therefore, less middle management will be required, and its power and status will decline.

However, one might argue that most of the time of middle management personnel is spent on tasks which are motivational or which require unstructured decision making or heuristic reasoning. Therefore, although some of the decisions may be taken from them and central planning may further restrict their range of decision making, all other functions will remain. The problem of managing people and related human relations is still critical and is not computerized. Furthermore, the frequency of change may make it more difficult than was thought to routinize many middle management decisions.

The question of whether or not complex computer systems will cause organizations to centralize operations that have been decentralized is not yet answered. In a decentralized organization, planning and decision making at the individual plant or other facility is delegated to the local manager. In a centralized organization, all important decisions are made by a central staff at the headquarters. It is clear that some individual decisions are being centralized—an example is centralized inventory control, in which a computer system keeping track of all inventory at all locations is usually able to make better decisions than the individual managers. On the other hand, the economic and managerial considerations which have prompted some organizations to decentralize are still strong. Examples are the need for local response to changing conditions and enhanced motivation.

On balance, it seems quite clear that the computer has already had some impact on organization and management and will have greater impact as more complex systems are implemented. More and more decisions will be taken over by the computer. It is likely that the most successful systems will be man/machine systems rather than fully automated systems. In a man/machine system, the decisions made by the man are the unstructured, difficult ones. And even computer decisions will need to be monitored. It would take an executive with more faith in computer programs (written by mere mortal programmers) than he should have to let important decisions be handled automatically by a computer without human review.

EFFECT ON THE MANAGER

If the computer-based systems emphasize a man/machine interaction, the manager must understand the computer. He must know how to evaluate the promises of programmers and systems designers. He must know what he can reasonably expect from the computer.

The man/machine system puts more responsibility on the manager because it clearly indicates what is expected of him. The system becomes machine-paced. Just as an assembly line paces the speed of workers on the line, computer-assisted management is likely to be computer-paced management.

▌ SOCIAL IMPLICATIONS OF COMPUTER UTILIZATION

The computer is clearly one of the most important technological innovations of this generation. It ranks on a par with atomic energy and automation in its impact on society. As the final topics in the text, it is well to turn to the social implications of computers—whether they will enhance or detract from the freedom and well-being of individuals in society. Two important aspects of this problem are technological unemployment and the effect of central data banks on privacy and freedom.

TECHNOLOGICAL UNEMPLOYMENT

The computer industry has created a number of new jobs—software specialist, systems analyst, programmer, customer engineer, computer operator. On balance, these new jobs are well paid and challenging. In the main, the jobs the computer has displaced have been lower paid, menial, repetitive, and generally uninteresting.

The growth in clerical jobs has begun to decline as computers have become common. Because the computer is extending the scope of work performed, total employment may not have changed drastically—the jobs displaced by computers are probably offset by jobs created by the computer industry. At the same time however, the jobs created require education and training at a fairly high level; the jobs displaced used fairly low-level, minimally trained people. In other words, the computer is reducing job opportunities for the poorly trained. However, many of the displaced jobs are not challenging, and, in the long run, society is probably better off to put its human energies to other tasks. In the short run, computers have compounded the problem of employment for the marginally educated and unskilled.

ETHICS, PRIVACY, AND FREEDOM IN THE USE OF CENTRAL DATA BANKS

A data bank is a central file containing all information about an organization or an individual. A financial institution such as a savings and loan association might, for example, establish a single file containing all information about a customer, instead of having separate files for his different activities with the association, e.g. as depositor, savings account holder, mortgagee, borrower on auto loan, safety deposit box rentee. If any action is being considered by the savings and loan association, all information regarding his standing at the association can be evaluated. For an individual company to have a data bank does not have significant social implications, but suppose that all government agencies cooperate to centralize all information about each individual in the country? The establishment of such a computer-based dossier is abhorrent to the basic concepts of a democratic society.

A recent proposal by a task force recommended a national statistical data bank in which statistics, but not other data, would be maintained for statistical analysis only, without identifying individuals. Despite protestations to the contrary, many people felt the proposal would lead to a computer-based dossier.[1]

Files about individuals exist in various different organizations; the computer makes it feasible to centralize these files. Does the existence of one file or many files make any difference with regard to privacy and freedom? With separate files, imperfectly maintained, it is only with much effort that all the information about an individual can be assembled. Much information is lost and much of it is discounted in its value because of the imperfect file maintenance. With a central computer file, these cost and quality deterrents to prying and spying are removed. The normal deterioration which takes place in manually maintained files (data being lost, misfiled, misplaced, thrown away, etc.) does not necessarily take place. This means that the computer system is less forgiving (forgetful).

What must be recognized is that the absence of a central governmental file does not mean there will be no central data banks. When, for instance, the credit bureaus which operate in different cities install a complete data interchange system, there will exist a privately operated data bank. The existence of such large-scale data banks raises serious questions—the possible harm from erroneous or improperly interpreted information is much greater than with less extensive manual systems.

[1] *The Computer and Invasion of Privacy, Hearings before a Subcommittee of the Committee on Government Operations*, 89th Cong., 2d Sess., July 26–28, 1966.

[2] Two bills were introduced in the Ninetieth Congress to give individuals control over their credit dossiers—HR 15495 by Wright Patman and HR 15627 by Clement Zablocki.

Perhaps there needs to be legislation to give each individual the right to examine his own record in such files and to request corrections, and new legal liability for erroneous or uncorrected data may need to be defined.[2]

This discussion of social implications points up one of the benefits from studying computers. One may never need to program one or to design a system using one. But to be an intelligent employee and an intelligent citizen in a world of computer-based data processing, it is helpful to have a general understanding of computers and to understand why one should not "fold, mutilate, or spindle."

▌SUMMARY

This chapter looks ahead at developments which are now new or appear to be imminent. By surveying them in a separate chapter, attention is focused on the dynamic and rapidly changing technology. Hardware changes quite rapidly; trends and long-term developments are more meaningful for software and systems.

The changes in hardware can be easily summarized—faster and smaller, with bigger storage. Some developments which support this view are large-scale integration, photodigital storage, improved I/O, and improved communications. Other developments to watch are associative memories, cryogenics, and heuristic computers, because, if the requisite breakthrough should come, they will have a great impact on the field.

Developments in software center on improved performance standardization and the marriage of software and hardware by the use of stored logic. There is also some evidence of a trend toward separate pricing of hardware and software by some companies.

Data processing systems are becoming more comprehensive. The distinction between batch and realtime systems may disappear as systems are designed which operate in the appropriate mode, both being available. The trend is to comprehensive systems which build computers into the information decision structure. The tools of analysis—statistics and operations research—are also designed into the system. Such a comprehensive total system has been termed a management information system. It is easier to describe than to implement, so that there is likely to be an evolution in the growth of such designs rather than having them spring forth full-grown.

The impact of computers on organization and management is often discussed but difficult to perceive as yet. On balance, the impact will probably be to make top management people better able to make the organization responsive to their plans and to reduce the scope of decision making but not the need for middle management personnel.

A technological innovation of the size and scope of the computer cannot help but have social implications. It causes a dislocation in employment and provides a tool which, if misused, would support the information processing needs of a ''big brother is watching you'' type of society. For this reason, an understanding of computer technology has utility beyond its application to business or scientific processing.

▌ EXERCISES

1   The U.S. Patent Office patented the first computer program in 1964. The patentability of computer programs has been the subject of much discussion and additional legislation. Discuss the potential impact on separate pricing of software of a decision against patentability of computer programs.

2   What might be the impact of LSI on the design of a new computer?

3   How can a laser be used to store and retrieve data? *Note:* Refer to an up-to-date encyclopedia for information on how a laser beam is obtained.

4   Why would an associative memory be useful in information retrieval?

5   Why has there been difficulty in building an economical cryogenic computer? What advantage would there be in such a computer?

6   How would one program an heuristic computer? For what types of problems might it be useful?

7   What is stored logic used for? One writer has suggested that firmware will be as important as hardware and software in fourth-generation equipment. What is the role of firmware compared to hardware and software?

8   IBM prices are sometimes higher than their competitors, but one of the advantages IBM is reported to have is an abundance of software and other support for prospective users. How might separate pricing of hardware and software affect them?

9   Assume you are a plant manager of a multiplant organization. How do you feel it would affect your power and status in the organization if the following decisions formerly made by your subordinates were now made by a central computer?

    a   Inventory reorder decisions
    b   Scheduling of jobs through the production line
    c   Payment of invoices
    d   Billing for shipments made

10 The profit plan for the coming year, based on an estimated sales volume, has just been finished. The president storms into your office and says that sales estimates must be revised upward by 10 percent, sales prices downward by 4 percent, wages for factory workers up from 5–6 percent instead of 4 percent depending on classification, and other employees up 5 percent instead of 3 percent. What would be your reaction:

    a   If the profit plan were prepared manually and required several days merely to work out the computations
    b   If the profit plan were prepared using a computer model

11   Considering the fact that most people are honest and law-abiding, what difference does it make to the average person whether there is a computer-maintained dossier on him or not? What about a privately maintained dossier by a credit bureau versus a government dossier?

12   The benefits of computer technology accrue to the firms using them; the social costs of displaced employees, etc. are born by the entire society. What would be the economic consequences to computer users of a special tax on computers to defray the social costs of technologically displaced workers?

▎ PUNCHING WITHOUT USE OF AUTOMATIC FEATURES

▎ PUNCHING WITH AUTO FEED

▎ PUNCHING WITH A PROGRAM CARD

▎ OTHER KEYS AND CONTROLS

APPENDIX

HOW
TO USE
THE
CARD
PUNCH

Students of computer data processing frequently need to be able to operate the key-driven card punch, either to keypunch their programs or to make corrections in previously punched card decks. The purpose of this appendix is to aid the student in these activities, therefore it covers only the basic elements of using the card punch. There are many features for facilitating its use which will not be explained. Therefore, a person learning to be a keypunch operator needs additional training information not contained here.

The two most common card punches are the IBM model 26 and the IBM model 29 printing card punches (Figure I–1). The model 26 has been the standard card punch for many years; the model 29 was introduced in conjunction with IBM's System/360 computers.

The model 26, which has only 11 special characters, has either a commercial or a scientific keyboard. The difference between the keyboards is in four of the special characters. These are as follows:

COMMERCIAL	SCIENTIFIC (FORTRAN)
#	=
@	+
%	(
□	)

FIGURE I–1　IBM card punches (Courtesy of International Business Machines Corporation)

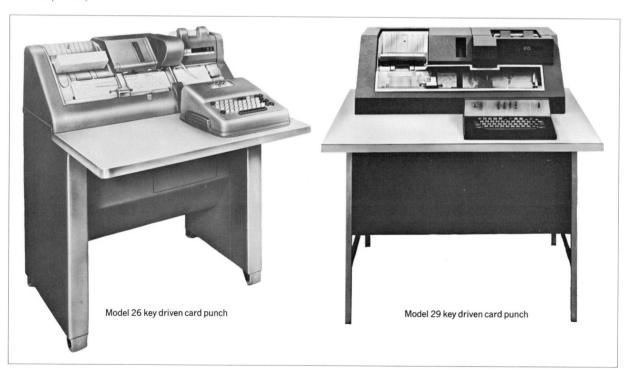

Model 26 key driven card punch

Model 29 key driven card punch

FIGURE I-2   Keyboards of IBM model 26 and IBM model 29 card punches

Model 26 keyboard with scientific characters shown on keytops

Model 29 keyboard

The punches are the same for either of each pair of characters; the difference is only in the keytop character and in the printing character which is printed on top of the card when it is punched. This means that a user needing to punch the FORTRAN statement X = Y + (A/B) can get the correct punches from a commercial keyboard by punching X # Y & % A/B □. On a model 29, there are different punches for each of 28 special characters, and each has a unique position on the keyboard. However, a model 29 can be equipped with a keyboard and printing mechanism which identify only 12 special characters, and for all practical purposes this makes the 29 look like a 26. Figure I-2 shows the keyboards of a model 26 and a model 29.

The alphabetical characters on the keyboard are identical to those on a typewriter. This means that a person who can type can keypunch alphabetics without learning any new keying. The numbers 1 to 9 are arranged so they can be punched with three fingers of the right hand. The arrangement is the reverse of a 10-key adding machine. For the special characters, the novice user can usually "hunt and peck."

The use of the card punch is facilitated by features which perform functions that otherwise must be done manually. The beginner may wish to start out by doing his punching without using these features and then, as more proficiency is developed, begin to use these aids to punching speed. The use of the card punch will therefore be described at three levels:

1 Punching without making use of automatic features
2 Punching using the automatic feed but not using a program card
3 Punching with a program card

▌ PUNCHING WITHOUT USE OF AUTOMATIC FEATURES

The on-off switch for the card punch is at the upper left in the card stacker for a model 26, and on the inside of the right leg for the model 29. The 26 requires a warmup period before it will operate.

On the panel directly above the keytops, there are three toggle switches on a model 26 and six switches on a 29 (Figure I-3). Turn the AUTO SKIP DUP and AUTO FEED switches off (down). Turn the PRINT switch on. On a model 29, the LZ print should be on; the PROG SEL and CLEAR are not used. In the upper part of the card punch, directly below the window showing a cylinder (program drum), there is a small program control lever. Depress this lever to the right to deactivate the program card mechanism.

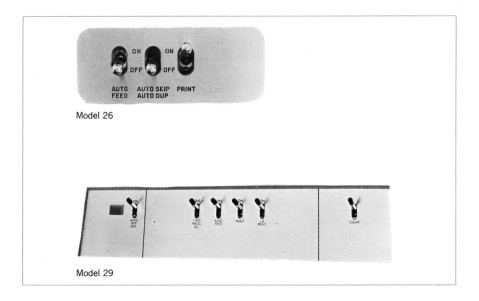

Model 26

Model 29

FIGURE I-3 Functional control switches for card punch model 26 (top) and model 29 (bottom) (Courtesy of International Business Machines Corporation)

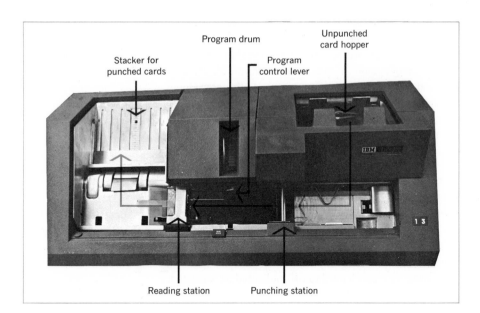

FIGURE I-4   Path of the card through the card punch

Blank cards to be punched are placed in the card hopper at the upper right; cards which have been punched are moved by the card punch into a card stacker at the upper left from which they can be removed. The path of a card through the card punch is shown in Figure I-4.

Note in Figure I-2 the three keys at the right-hand side of the keyboard labeled REL, FEED, and REG. These are the release, feed, and register keys. Using these keys, punching a card is performed as follows:

1   Press FEED key to move one card from the card hopper to the entrance to the punching station.
2   Press REG key to move the card into position for punching.
3   The card is punched serially (column by column) by striking the proper keys. The keyboard operates normally in alphabetic mode (the bottom character is punched if more than two are shown on a keytop). To obtain the upper character, which includes all the numerics, the numeric shift key at the lower left of the keyboard must be depressed while striking the keys. Columns may be skipped by depressing the space bar.
4   When all punching has been performed, the card is moved to the reading station by pressing REL.
5   If only one card is to be punched, immediately pressing REL and REG will move the card from the reading station to the card stacker where it can be removed.

If a card needs to be corrected, a damaged card needs to be replaced, or a card is to be duplicated, the card to be reproduced is manually inserted against the reading station, leaving only a slight space. A blank card is brought from the card hopper by depressing FEED (or a card is inserted manually at the punching station). Pressing the REG key will then register both cards. Depressing the DUP (duplicate) key will cause the punches in the card at the reading station to be punched into the card at the punching station. If one or more columns are to be omitted or altered from what is found in the card being reproduced, the operator depresses the space bar or keyboard characters instead of the duplicate key for the columns to be omitted or altered. The next column to be punched or duplicated is read from the column indicator in the opening which contains the program control drum.

▌ PUNCHING WITH AUTO FEED

If many cards are to be punched, the feeding of cards can be speeded up by using the AUTO FEED option. When this is on, it causes a new card to be automatically fed and registered each time the card being punched is released. Since this provides a continuous supply of cards at both the punching and reading stations, it is turned off in order to insert a card to be duplicated or corrected.

▌ PUNCHING WITH A PROGRAM CARD

In punching applications, there are repetitive operations—for example, the starting of the punching of a field at a certain column, the duplication of certain information from the prior card, or the switching to numeric or alphabetic for a group of columns. The program card allows these functions to be done automatically.

The program card is a regular punched card which is wrapped around the program drum. Control punches in the top five rows are read by program star wheels (Figure I–5) and cause certain functions to be automatically performed. On a model 29 a second program may be punched lower in the same card. The second program is selected by the PROG SEL switch. This should be on ONE to use the control cards explained here. A small lever on the keypunch is depressed to the left to activate the program card and to the right to deactivate it. Some common control punches are:

PUNCH	FUNCTION	
none	Beginning of field to be manually punched.	
1	Shifts keyboard to alphabetic mode with program control; the keyboard is in numeric unless this control punch is used.	
0	Starts automatic duplication.	AUTO SKIP DUP toggle switch must be "on" for duplication or
11	Start automatic skipping.	skipping.
12	Defines the columns for which the preceding punches apply.	

FIGURE I–5   Program drum (left) and program drum in place (right) (Courtesy of International Business Machines Corporation)

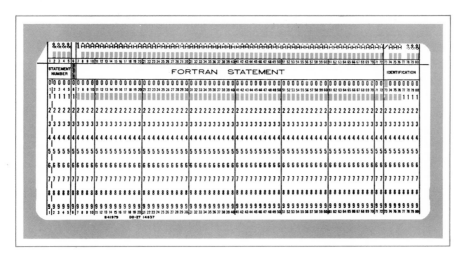

FIGURE I–6   Example of program card for card punch

An example will illustrate the use of a control card. In punching a FORTRAN program, the first five columns are for a statement number (numeric). Column 6, indicating a continuation of a statement, is rarely used. Columns 7–72 are for alphanumeric punching, with alphabetics the most common. Columns 73–80 are for identification.

The identification in this example is assumed to be a four-character alphabetic program identifier to be duplicated in every card and a four-digit numeric sequence number. The program card should therefore put the card punch in numeric mode for columns 1–5, in numeric mode for column 6, and in alphabetic mode for columns 7–72, should duplicate columns 73–76, and should put the punch in numeric mode for columns 77–80. The control card is illustrated in Figure I–6. Remember that the use of the control card shifts the punch to numeric mode. When punching FORTRAN under program card control (and AUTO SKIP DUP switch on), there will be no need to manually space the card to column 7 (if there is no statement number to be punched); merely pressing SKIP twice will position the card at the third field (7–72). If the FORTRAN statement is completed at column 61, pressing SKIP will move the card to column 73 and will duplicate column 73–76. The keypuncher can then punch the card number in column 77–80. If there were to be no identification in columns 73–80, the program card would use an 11 punch in column 73 and 12 punches in 74–80. The punch will automatically skip over these columns when the column to be punched is 73. For a model 29, the PROG SEL switch must be set to ONE.

▌ OTHER KEYS AND CONTROLS

The MULT PCH (multiple punch) key is for use when a punch combination not found for the machine is to be punched. If, for example, an 11, 5, 8 punch combination is to be punched on a model 26, the MULT PCH key (and NUMERIC if necessary) is depressed, and 11, 5, and 8 are punched. The multiple punch key keeps the card from advancing to allow the three keys to punch in one column.

The backspace control is a small rectangular button between the reading station and the punching station. Depressing the control backspaces one column.

On a model 29, but not on the 26, there are two additional switches not normally used by the student. If the LZ PRINT is OFF, it suppresses the printing of leading zeroes in a field. The switch should usually be on for the student user. The CLEAR switch is a spring switch which causes all cards then in process to be moved through to the stacker without feeding any new cards.

▌ COMPUTER ORGANIZATIONS

▌ PERIODICALS

GUIDE
TO COMPUTER
ORGANIZATIONS
AND
PERIODICALS

▌ COMPUTER ORGANIZATIONS

AMERICAN FEDERATION OF INFORMATION PROCESSING SOCIETIES (AFIPS)

This is a federation of societies representing the information processing community. AFIPS represents the United States in a similar international group (IFIPS). The major activity of AFIPS is to sponsor the spring and fall joint computer conferences. These usually consist of sessions at which papers are presented and a large equipment show at which manufacturers display their latest equipment. Proceedings of the conference are published. The spring meeting is traditionally located in the eastern part of the United States and the fall computer conference is in the West. A person receives AFIPS notices by being associated with one of its member societies—ACM, IEEE, AICPA, etc.

ASSOCIATION FOR COMPUTING MACHINERY (ACM)

211 East 43d Street, New York, N.Y. 10017. This organization, founded to advance the science and arts of information processing, publishes three journals, holds an annual meeting (usually in August), sponsors special interest groups on various topics, organizes seminars, and publishes three journals—*Journal of the Association for Computing Machinery* (quarterly), *Communications of the ACM* (monthly), and *Computing Reviews* (monthly). ACM tends to be oriented toward scientific problems, algorithms for solutions, etc. ACM chapters are active in many cities and on a number of college campuses. Annual dues include subscriptions to the three journals. There is a special student membership rate.

ASSOCIATION FOR EDUCATIONAL DATA SYSTEMS (AEDS)

1201 16th Street N.W., Washington, D.C. Founded by professional educators, membership consists of individuals interested in exchanging information about the impact of modern technology upon the educational process. The Association provides a monthly publication, a quarterly journal, a national convention, regional chapters, etc., and operates the AEDS National Center for Educational Data Processing.

ASSOCIATION OF DATA PROCESSING SERVICE ORGANIZATIONS (ADAPSO)

947 Old York Road, Abington, Pa. An association of those commercial organizations which utilize their own equipment on their premises to offer data processing services. Publishes an annual directory.

BUSINESS EQUIPMENT MANUFACTURERS ASSOCIATION (BEMA)

235 East 42d St., New York, N.Y. This is an association of the manufacturers of computing equipment and is the sponsoring organization for standards for computers and information processing (see Appendix IV).

DATA PROCESSING MANAGEMENT ASSOCIATION (DPMA)

505 Busse Highway, Park Ridge, Ill. 60068. The membership of this organization is concerned mainly with business methods and their mechanization. The association has local chapters, publishes a monthly journal, holds an annual Data Processing Conference and Business Exposition, publishes the proceedings of this conference, sponsors educational programs, and administers the DPMA certificate program (see Appendix III).

INSTITUTE OF ELECTRICAL AND ELECTRONICS ENGINEERS (IEEE)

The orientation of this organization, composed largely of engineers, is toward the problems of hardware design.

SYSTEMS AND PROCEDURES ASSOCIATION (SPA)

7890 Brookside Drive, Cleveland, Ohio 44138. A national organization of persons interested in systems work. It has local chapters, publishes a journal, promotes educational programs, and holds an annual meeting with an accompanying equipment exposition.

▌ PERIODICALS

BUSINESS AUTOMATION

Business Press International, Inc., Elmhurst, Ill. Published monthly. Covers topics related to business data processing. Free to qualified executives directly involved with their organization's information handling activities. Available on subscription basis to others. September issue is a reference issue summarizing various equipment items related to computer data processing.

BUSINESS AUTOMATION NEWS REPORT

OA Business Publications, New York, N.Y. Nontechnical weekly newsletter covering items of interest to the business data processing user.

COMMUNICATIONS OF THE ACM

A monthly journal of ACM.

COMPUTER CHARACTERISTICS QUARTERLY

Charles W. Adams Associates, Inc., Bedford, Mass. Surveys the salient characteristics of all digital computers and related peripheral devices commercially available, both United States and foreign.

COMPUTER DIGEST

Detroit, Mich. 48226. A monthly digest of articles from over 400 journals and other publications in computers.

COMPUTERS AND AUTOMATION

Newtonville, Mass. This monthly publication has articles on hardware, software, and systems. A regular monthly feature is a computer census. A subscription can include a *June Computer Directory and Buyers' Guide*.

COMPUTING REVIEWS

A monthly publication of ACM devoted to reviews of books and papers in the computing field.

DATAMATION

New York, N.Y. Circulated without charge to individuals (by name and title) who qualify. Also available on a subscription basis. It is a basic source of information on current and prospective developments in the computer field.

DATA PROCESSING DIGEST

Los Angeles, Calif. A monthly service which reviews publications relevant to business data processing.

DATA PROCESSING MAGAZINE

North American Publishing Co., Philadelphia, Pa. Contains general and semitechnical articles.

EDP WEEKLY

Industry Reports, Inc., Washington, D.C. Nontechnical reports on current developments in data processing.

ELECTRONIC NEWS

A weekly newspaper on events in the field of electronics.

INFORMATION PROCESSING JOURNAL

Cambridge Communication Corporation, Washington, D.C. 20006. Abstracts of articles, reports and books in information processing.

JOURNAL OF THE ASSOCIATION FOR COMPUTING MACHINERY

Baltimore, Md. A quarterly publication devoted to research papers.

JOURNAL OF DATA MANAGEMENT

Park Ridge, Ill. Published monthly by DPMA. Articles are oriented to business data processing.

MANAGEMENT SERVICES

American Institute of Certified Public Accountants, New York, N.Y. Articles in the area of planning, computers, and systems.

SOFTWARE AGE

Evanston, Ill. Devoted largely to software at a nontechnical level. Distributed free to qualified readers.

SYSTEMS & PROCEDURES JOURNAL

Cleveland, Ohio. Monthly publication of the Systems & Procedures Association. Contains articles on a variety of topics related to analysis and design of information and management systems.

APPENDIX

THE
DATA PROCESSING
MANAGEMENT
ASSOCIATION
CERTIFICATE
IN
DATA PROCESSING

▌ EDUCATION

▌ EXPERIENCE

▌ EXAMINATION

▌ HOW TO APPLY

▌ EVALUATION OF CERTIFICATE

Most data processing personnel have trained themselves in unstructured programs of instruction ranging from manufacturer's courses to self study. Under these conditions, it is desirable to have some independent means for establishing a satisfactory level of competence. In order to have a data processing profession it is necessary to provide some means for confirming that a person has adequate competence to be part of the profession.

The Data Processing Management Association (DPMA) is an organization of personnel dedicated to the advancement of the art of data processing. The orientation of the organization is toward business data processing. The Certificate in Data Processing, administered by DPMA, is intended to establish recognized professional standards in data processing. It is not limited to members of DPMA.

The certificate is designed to meet the following objectives:

1 To establish high standards for data processing personnel by emphasizing a broad educational framework and practical knowledge in the field
2 To develop a method for recognizing a corps of individuals as having the knowledge considered important in data processing
3 To lay a firm foundation for the continued growth of the data processing field

The Certificate in Data Processing (CDP) is awarded to persons of high moral qualification and professional attitude who satisfy requirements as to education and experience and pass the examination. Up to 1966, education requirements were waived.

▌ EDUCATION

The candidate must have completed at least two years (60 semester hours or equivalent) from accredited college level institutions. This may include home study courses. As of 1972, the academic requirement will be increased to four years or the bachelor's degree.

The 60 semester hours must include or be supplemented by at least two courses directly related to computers and data processing.

▌ EXPERIENCE

All candidates for the examination must have had three years direct experience in the field of data processing (or its equivalent in part-time work). These need not be consecutive years. Data processing teaching, systems, and programming experience while employed by data processing equipment manufacturers, service centers, management consulting firms, or educational institutions are also applicable toward meeting the requirement. Clerical, keypunch, or direct sales experience may not be applied.

EXAMINATION

The four-hour examination is offered each year (normally in February) at a number of university and college test sites. The questions are multiple choice for ease in machine scoring. Candidates are notified only of pass or fail, and failing candidates are told in which sections they scored below passing. Scores are not released. A person may retake the examination.

The test encompasses a wide range of subjects which are considered mandatory for professional competence in the field of data processing and management information systems. Candidates must score at passing level in each of the four major categories:

1 Automatic data processing equipment
2 Computer programming and software systems
3 Data processing systems and management—concepts, design, and implementation
4 Quantitative methods
    a Accounting
    b Mathematics
    c Statistics

The examination is not a test of programming knowledge or ability, but a familiarity with electronic computer programming concepts and techniques is considered an essential requisite for the data processing profession. Questions requiring a detailed knowledge of any specific machine are not asked.

HOW TO APPLY

Applications, a study guide, and test center information are available from DPMA International Headquarters, 505 Busse Highway, Park Ridge, Ill., or from any local DPMA chapter. Deadline for filing is ten weeks before the test date (about November). The examination fee is $50. The fee for retaking the examination is $30.

EVALUATION OF THE CERTIFICATE

The certificate program is useful because it establishes a minimum level of competence and academic work experience. The statistics on the examination indicate that success is correlated highly with education and that experience beyond the mandatory three years does not help in passing.[1]

The pass rate for candidates with adequate educational and experience requirements has been reasonably high—60 to 80 percent. The pass rate for the marginally qualified, as evidenced by the passing percentage for retakes, is low—about 20 percent pass on retake.

[1] Herman Roemmich, "A Descriptive Analysis of Candidates for the 1966 Certificate in Data Processing Examination," *DPMA Quarterly*, October, 1966, pp. 3–24.

Although the examination is short compared with professional examinations for CPAs, architects, etc., and does not yet have the prestige attached to these, the Certificate in Data Processing is a significant element in establishing a professional attitude among data processing personnel. One can anticipate that it will become an increasingly important mark of competence in the field.

STANDARDS
FOR COMPUTERS
AND
INFORMATION
PROCESSING

▮ THE UNITED STATES OF AMERICA STANDARDS IN-
STITUTE (USASI)

▮ THE X3 SECTIONAL COMMITTEE ON COMPUTERS AND
INFORMATION PROCESSING

There are some 30 American manufacturers of computers and a similar number of foreign companies. These manufacturers are supplemented by hundreds of suppliers of computer components and computer operating supplies.

Each manufacturer's equipment has unique characteristics, yet at the same time some connection with equipment and supplies provided by others. There is frequently a need to exchange data between different systems. Not everyone uses the same words to mean the same things. These and other considerations make it desirable to develop industry-wide standards. In the United States, industry standards are usually the responsibility of the United States of America Standards Institute.

▌ THE UNITED STATES OF AMERICA STANDARDS INSTITUTE (USASI)

Formerly called the American Standards Association (ASA), the United States of America Standards Institute is a private, voluntary federation of about 150 trade associations and professional societies plus over 2,000 member companies interested in developing standards.

USASI acts as a facilitating and coordinating agency in the development of voluntary standards. A standard is approved only if it is supported by consensus of all national groups substantially concerned with its scope and provisions. Standards prepared under USASI auspices typically have wide acceptance. More than 2,000 standards in the fields of engineering, industry, safety, and consumer goods have been developed and approved under its procedures. In short, a "USA standard" is a voluntary, national standard arrived at by common consent and available for voluntary use.

Through USASI, the United States is represented in the International Organization for Standardization (ISO), the International Electrotechnical Commission (IEC), and in the Pan American Standards Committee (PASC). USASI thus is the focus for both United States standards and United States participation in international standards.

USA standards are proposed through two basic methods:

1. *Existing standards*. An existing standard which originated within a technical society or group may be submitted for approval as a USA standard. Approximately one-third of the standards have come through this channel.
2. *Developed standards*. A technical society or group may develop a proposed standard on assignment by the USASI. This is typically performed by a sectional committee. A sectional committee is composed of representatives of all groups or organizations substantially concerned with the scope of the standards project. The sectional committee is the method used most frequently for computers and data processing.

▌ THE X3 SECTIONAL COMMITTEE ON COMPUTERS AND INFORMATION PROCESSING

The sectional committee for computers is designated as X3, "Computers and Information Processing." Each sectional committee has one or more organizations designated as sponsors to give administrative support and direction to the committee. The sponsor is responsible for the administration and direction of the standards project. The sponsor organization for the X3 sectional committee is the Business Equipment Manufacturers Association (BEMA). The scope of X3 is "Standardization related to systems, computers, equipments, devices, and media for information processing." The ISO counterpart is Technical Committee 97, Computers and Standardization.

Membership in X3 is by national association, society, or organization and is divided equally into three groups of members: general interest, consumers, and producers. Each member is entitled to one vote. The committee has eight subcommittees responsible for the technical work of considering standardization (Figure IV-1). In general, membership on these subcommittees is by individual rather than by organization.

The following USA standards have received final approval and are available in published form from the United States of America Standards Institute, 10 East 40th Street, New York, N.Y. 10016.

NUMBER

X3.1–1962	USA Standard Signaling Speeds for Data Transmission
X3.2–1963	USA Standard Print Specifications for Magnetic Ink Character Recognition
X3.3–1963	USA Standard Bank Check Specifications for Magnetic Ink Character Recognition
X3.4–1963	USA Standard Code for Information Interchange
X3.5–1966	USA Standard Flowchart Symbols for Information Processing
X3.6–1965	USA Standard Perforated Tape Code for Information Interchange
X3.7–1965	USA Standard Interchange Perforated Tape Variable Block Format for Positioning and Straight Cut Numerically Controlled Machine Tools
X3.8–1966	USA Standard Interchangeably Perforated Tape Variable Block Format for Contouring and Contouring/Positioning Numerically Controlled Machine Tools
X3.9–1966	USA Standard FORTRAN
X3.10–1966	USA Standard Basic FORTRAN
X3.11–1966	USA Standard Specification for General Purpose Paper Cards for Information Processing
X3.12–1966	USA Standard Vocabulary for Information Processing
X3.13–1966	USA Standard for Parallel Signaling Speeds for Data Transmission
X3.15–1966	USA Standard for Bit Sequencing of the USA Standard Code for

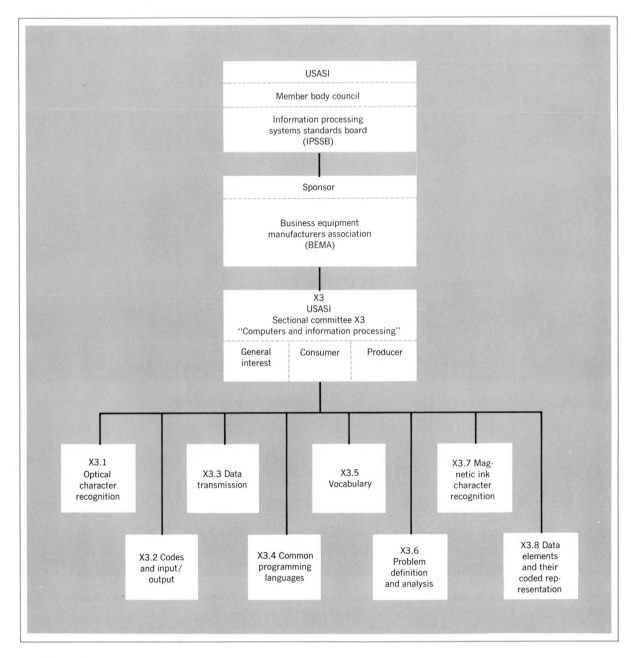

FIGURE IV–1   Organization of United
States of America Standards Institute
X3 Committee

Information Interchange in Serial-by-Bit Data Transmission (Low Order)

X3.16–1966	USA Standard for Character Structure and Character Parity Sense in Serial-by-Bit Data Communication in the USA Standard Code for Information Interchange
X3.17–1966	USA Standard Character Set for Optical Character Recognition
X3.18–1967	USA Standard One-inch Perforated Paper Tape for Information/ Processing
X3.19–1967	USA Standard Eleven-sixteenths Inch Perforated Paper Tape
X3.20–1967	USA Standard Take-up Reels for One-inch Perforated Tape for Information Interchange
X3.21–1967	USA Standard for Rectangular Holes in Twelve-row Punched Cards
X3.22–1967	USA Standard Recorded Magnetic Tape (800 cpi, NRZI)
X3.23–1968	USA Standard COBOL
X3.24–1968	USA Standard Signal Quality at Interface between Data Processing Terminal Equipment and Synchronous Data Communication for Serial Data Transmission
X3.25–1968	USA Standard Character Structure and Character Parity Sense for Parity-by-Bit Data Communication in the USA Standard Code for Information Interchange

GLOSSARY

[1] Where used, the glossary terms are with the permission of AUERBACH Info, Inc., Philadelphia, Pa., publishers of *AUERBACH Standard EDP Reports* and related looseleaf reference services. These services, available on a subscription basis, contain independent data on the characteristics and performance of most computer systems, peripheral equipment and related items.

The glossary contains selected terms used in the field of computers and data processing. Almost all the entries in this glossary are taken from or adapted from the glossary contained in the *AUERBACH Standard EDP Reports*,[1] which is one of the most complete (over 700 terms) and most readable glossaries available. It is consistent with and, in many cases, makes use of definitions contained in two glossaries having official status and a widely used glossary prepared by the Bureau of the Budget. Although not as readable as the Auerbach glossary, these are useful references for personnel in the field of computers and data processing.

IFIP/ICC (International Federation for Information Processing and International Computation Centre), *IFIP/ICC Vocabulary of Information Processing*, North-Holland Publishing Company, Amsterdam, 1966.

USA Standards Institute, *American Standard Vocabulary for Information Processing*, USA Standard X3.12–1966, New York, 1966.

U.S. Bureau of the Budget, *Glossary of Automatic Data Processing*, December, 1962.

The Bureau of the Budget glossary was reprinted as the *Datamation EDP Glossary* and also served as the basis for the Honeywell, Inc. *Glossary of Data Processing and Communications Terms*.

The present glossary is arranged in natural order (e.g., "absolute coding" rather than "coding, absolute"). In the case of terms with two or more meanings, the meanings are numbered sequentially, and the first meaning listed is the most common or most general one. Examples and comments follow the formal definitions to clarify the meanings, usage, and significance of the terms defined.

Several different types of cross references are used. Their meanings are as follows:

Same as—indicates that the referenced term has the same meaning as the term containing the reference and that the referenced term is the preferred one.

Synonymous with—indicates that the referenced term has the same meaning as the term containing the reference and that the term containing the reference is the preferred one.

Contrast with—indicates that the referenced term is a related term that has a meaning significantly different from that of the term containing the reference.

See also—indicates that the referenced term is a related term whose definition will provide additional background or clarification.

See—indicates that the referenced term is an alternative or qualified form of the term containing the reference.

A

▌ ABSOLUTE ADDRESS

An address that is permanently assigned by the machine designer to a particular storage location. For example, the addresses 0000, 0001, and 0002 might be assigned to the first three locations in a computer's storage.

▌ ABSOLUTE CODING

Coding that uses machine instructions and absolute addresses; therefore, it can be directly executed by a computer without prior translation to a different form. Contrast with *symbolic coding.*

▌ ACCESS TIME

The time interval between the instant when a computer or control unit calls for a transfer of data to or from a storage device and the instant when this operation is completed. Thus, access time is the sum of the waiting time and transfer time. Note: In some types of storage, such as disc and drum storage, the access time depends upon the location specified and/or upon preceding events; in other types, such as core storage, the access time is essentially constant.

▌ ACRONYM

A word formed from the initial letter or letters of the words in a name or phrase; e.g., ALGOL from ALGOrithmic Language, COBOL from COmmon Business Oriented Language.

▌ ADDRESS

A name, numeral, or other reference that designates a particular location in storage or some other data source or destination. Note: Numerous types of addresses are employed in computer programming; see, for example: *absolute address, base address, direct address, effective address, immediate address, indirect address, relative address, symbolic address.*

▌ ADDRESS MODIFICATION

An operation that causes an address to be altered in a prescribed way by a stored-program computer. Note: The address upon which modification is performed is called the presumptive address, and the address that results is called the effective address. See also *index register* and *indirect address*—the two most common methods for address modification.

▌ ADP (Automatic Data Processing)

Data processing performed largely by automatic means, i.e., by a system of electronic or electrical machines which require little human assistance or intervention.

▌ ALGOL (ALGOrithmic Language)

A standard procedure-oriented language for expressing computational algorithms developed as a result of international cooperation. ALGOL is designed to serve as a means for communicating computational procedures among humans, as well as to facilitate the preparation of such procedures for execution on any computer for which a suitable ALGOL compiler exists. Note: The basic elements of ALGOL are arithmetic expressions containing numbers, variables, and functions. These are combined to form self-contained units called assignment statements. Declarations are noncomputational instructions which inform the compiler of characteristics such as the dimensions of an array or the class of a variable. A sequence of declarations followed by a sequence of statements, all enclosed within "begin" and "end" instructions, constitutes an ALGOL program block. ALGOL is not widely used in the United States but is very popular in Europe.

▌ ALGORITHM

A set of well-defined rules for the solution of a problem in a finite number of steps; e.g., a full statement of a procedure for computing a rate of return. Contrast with *heuristic*.

▌ ALPHAMERIC

Same as *alphanumeric*.

▌ ALPHANUMERIC

Pertaining to a character set that includes both alphabetic characters (letters) and numeric characters (digits). Note: Most alphanumeric character sets also contain special characters (dollar signs, commas, etc.).

▌ ANALOG COMPUTER

A computer that operates on data represented in the form of continuously variable physical quantities (e.g., voltage or angular position) by performing physical processes on the data. Contrast with *digital computer*.

▌ APPLICATION PACKAGE

A computer routine or set of routines designed for a specific application (e.g., inventory control, online savings accounting, linear programming, etc.). Note: In most cases, the routines in the application packages are necessarily written in a generalized way and must be modified to meet each user's own specific needs.

▌ ASCII (American Standard Code for Information Interchange)

A 7-bit (or 8-bit compatible) USA standard code adopted to facilitate the interchange of data among various types of data processing and data communications equipment.

▌ ASSEMBLE

To prepare a machine language from a program written in symbolic coding by substituting absolute operation codes for symbolic operation codes and absolute or relocatable addresses for symbolic addresses. For example, the symbolic instruction ADD TAX might be assembled into the machine instruction 24 1365, where 24 is the operation code for addition and 1365 is the address of the storage location labeled TAX. Contrast with *compile* and *generate*.

▌ ASSEMBLER

A computer program that assembles programs written in symbolic coding to produce machine language programs. Note: Assemblers are an important part of the basic software for most computers and can greatly reduce the human effort required to prepare programs.

▌ ASSOCIATIVE MEMORY

A storage device whose storage locations are identified by their contents (rather than by names or positions, as in most computer storage devices). Synonymous with *content-addressable memory*. Note: Associative memories can facilitate programming and increase computer efficiencies by eliminating the need for item-by-item search operations, but the high cost of implementing such memories limits their current use to specialized functions such as holding small, frequently referenced tables.

▌ ASYNCHRONOUS COMPUTER

A computer in which each operation starts as a result of a signal generated by the completion of the previous operation or by the availability of the equipment required for the next operation. Contrast with *synchronous computer*.

▌ AUDIT TRAIL

A means (such as a trail of documents, batch and processing references) for identifying the actions taken in processing input data or in preparing an output. By use of the audit trail, data on a source document can be traced to an output (such as a report), and an output can be traced back to the source items from which it was derived.

▌ AUXILIARY STORAGE

Storage that supplements a computer's primary internal storage. Note: In general, the auxiliary storage has a much larger capacity but a longer access time than the primary storage. Synonymous with *mass storage*. Same as *secondary storage*.

B

▌ BACKGROUND PROGRAM

A program, usually of the batch processing type, that can be executed whenever the facilities of a multiprogramming computer system are not required by realtime programs or other programs of higher priority. Contrast with *foreground program*.

▌ BACKUP

Pertaining to equipment or procedures that are available for use in the event of failure or overloading of the normally used equipment or procedures. Note: The provision of adequate backup facilities is an important factor in the design of all data processing systems and is especially vital in the design of realtime systems, where a system failure may bring the entire operation of a business to a virtual standstill.

▌ BASE ADDRESS

A specified address (often held in a "base address register") which is combined with a relative address (usually contained in an instruction) to form the absolute address of a particular storage location.

▌ BATCH PROCESSING

A technique in which items to be processed are collected into groups (batched) to permit convenient and efficient processing. Note: Most business applications are of the batch processing type; the records of all transactions affecting a particular master file are accumulated over a period of time (e.g. one day), then they are arranged in sequence and processed against the master file.

▌ BATCH TOTAL

A sum of a set of items in a batch of records which is used to check the accuracy of operations involving the batch.

▌ BAUD

A unit of signaling speed equal to the number of discrete conditions or signal events per second. Note: In the case of a train of binary signals one baud therefore equals one bit per second.

▌ BAUDOT CODE

A 5-bit code used in telegraphy for more than 100 years and still widely used in data communications and punched tape. Note: The Baudot code has two significant disadvantages: the limitation to 5-bits per character (i.e., 32 code combinations) requires frequent shifts between the "letters" and "figures" cases, and there is no provision for a parity check. The Baudot code is gradually being replaced by ASCII and other codes.

▌ BCD (Binary Coded Decimal)

Pertaining to a method of representing each of the decimal digits zero through 9 by a distinct group of binary digits. For example, in the "8–4–2–1" BCD notation, which is used in numerous digital computers, the decimal number 39 is represented as 0011 1001 (whereas in pure binary notation it would be represented as 100111).

▌ BINARY

Pertaining to the number system with a radix of 2, or to a characteristic or property involving a choice or condition in which there are two possibilities. For example, the binary numeral 1101 means:

$$(1 \times 2^3) + (1 \times 2^2) + (0 \times 2^1) + (1 \times 2^0)$$

which is equivalent to decimal 13. Note: The binary number system is widely used in digital computers because most computer components (e.g., vacuum tubes, transistors, flip-flops, and magnetic cores) are essentially binary in that they have two stable states.

▌ BINARY CODED DECIMAL

See *BCD*.

▌ BIT

A binary digit; a digit (0 or 1) in the representation of a number in binary notation.

▌ BLOCK

A group of words, characters, or digits that are held in one section of an input/output medium and handled as a unit; e.g., the data recorded on a punched card, or the data recorded between two interblock gaps on a magnetic tape.

▌ BLOCK DIAGRAM

See *program flowchart*.

▌ BLOCKING

Combining two or more records into one block usually to increase the efficiency of computer input and output operations. For example, the effective data transfer rates of most magnetic tape units can be greatly increased if the need for frequent tape stops and starts is reduced by combining multiple short records into long blocks.

▌ BOOTSTRAP LOADER

A form of loader whose first few instructions are sufficient to bring the rest of itself into the computer's storage from an input device.

▌ BRANCH

(1) Same as conditional transfer. (2) A set of instructions that are executed between two successive conditional transfer instructions.

▌ BREAKPOINT

A specified point in a program at which the program may be interrupted by manual intervention or by a monitor routine. Note: Breakpoints are generally used as an aid in testing and debugging programs; they facilitate halting a computer or triggering a printout at a particular point so that specific conditions can be examined.

▌ BUFFER

A storage device used to compensate for differences in the rates of flow of data or in the times of occurrence of events when transmitting data from one device to another. For example, a buffer holding the characters to print one line is associated with most line printers to compensate for the difference between the high speed at which the computer transmits data to the printer and the relatively low speed of the printing operation itself.

▌ BUG

A mistake in the design of a program or a computer system, or an equipment fault.

▌ BYTE

A group of adjacent bits operated on as a unit and usually shorter than a word. Note: In a number of important current computer systems, this term stands specifically for a group of eight adjacent bits that can represent one alphanumeric character or two decimal digits.

C

▌ CALL

In computer programming, to transfer control to a subroutine, usually by supplying the required parameters and executing a jump to the entry point of the subroutine.

▌ CALLING SEQUENCE

A specified set of instructions and data necessary to call a given subroutine.

▌ CATHODE RAY TUBE

An electronic vacuum tube containing a screen on which information can be displayed. The abbreviation CRT is frequently used.

▌ CENTRAL PROCESSOR

The unit of a computer system that includes the circuits which control the interpretation and execution of instructions. Synonymous with *CPU* (central processing unit) and *main frame*.

❚ CHANNEL

A path or group of parallel paths for carrying signals between a source and a destination. See also *input/output channel*.

❚ CHECK BIT

A binary check digit. See also *parity check*.

❚ CHECK DIGIT

A digit associated with a word or part of a word for the purpose of checking for the absence of certain classes of errors. See *residue check*.

❚ CLOCK

(1) A timing device that generates the basic periodic signal used to control the timing of all operations in a synchronous computer. (2) A device that records the progress of realtime, or some approximation of it, and whose contents are available to a computer program (frequently in a special register); the clock may also be capable of initiating a program interrupt when a specified period of time has elapsed.

❚ COBOL (Common Business Oriented Language)

A procedure-oriented language developed to facilitate the preparation and interchange of programs which form business data processing functions. Note: Designed in 1959 by a committee representing the U.S. Government and several computer manufacturers, COBOL has evolved through several versions (e.g., COBOL-60, COBOL-61, COBOL-61 Extended, COBOL-65). Every COBOL source program has four divisions, whose names and functions are as follows: (1) Identification Division, which identifies the source program and the output of a compilation, (2) Environment Division, which specifies those aspects of a data processing problem that are dependent upon the physical characteristics of a particular computer, (3) Data Division, which describes the data that the object program is to accept as input, manipulate, create, or produce as output, and (4) Procedure Division, which specifies the procedures to be performed by the object program, by means of English-like statements such as: "SUBTRACT TAX FROM GROSS-PAY GIVING NET-PAY." "PERFORM PROC-A THRU PROC-B UNTIL X IS GREATER THAN Y."

❚ CODING

(1) An ordered list or lists of the successive instructions which will cause a computer to perform a particular process. See also *absolute coding* and *symbolic coding*. (2) The act of preparing a coding.

❚ COLLATE

Same as *merge* (i.e., to form a single sequenced file by combining two or more similarly sequenced files).

▌ COLLATING SEQUENCE
The ranking, or precedence with respect to each other, of all the *characters* in a *character set* that can be used to constitute a key used for sequencing purposes. Note: Most collating sequences are arranged so that the digits 0 through 9 and the letters A through Z fall into their natural sequences. However, either the digits or letters may come first, and the handling of special characters varies widely.

▌ COMPILE
To prepare a machine language program (or a program expressed in symbolic coding) from a program written in another programming language (usually a procedure-oriented language such as COBOL or FORTRAN). The compilation process usually involves examining and making use of the overall structure of the program and/or generating more than one object program instruction for each source program statement. Contrast with *assemble* and *generate*.

▌ COMPILER
A computer program that compiles. Note: Compilers are an important part of the basic software for most computers permitting the use of procedure-oriented languages which can greatly reduce the human effort required to prepare computer programs.

▌ CONDITIONAL TRANSFER
An instruction that may or may not cause a jump (i.e., a departure from the normal sequence of executing instructions) depending upon the result of some operation, the contents of some register, or the setting of some indicator. Contrast with *unconditional transfer*. Note: Conditional transfer instructions are the basic means for implementing decision-making processes in stored-program computers.

▌ CONSOLE
A portion of a computer that is used for communication between operators or maintenance engineers and the computer, usually by means of displays and manual controls.

▌ CONSOLE OPERATOR
A computer operator.

▌ CONTENT-ADDRESSABLE MEMORY.
Same as *associative memory*.

▌ CONTROL CARD
A punched card that contains input data required for a specific application of a general routine such as a generator or operating system; e.g., one of a series of cards that direct an operating system to load and initiate execution of a particular program.

▌ CONTROL CLERK

A person having responsibility for performing duties associated with the control over data processing operations. Note: Such duties usually include the checking of control totals, the checking of run-to-run controls, the checking of output before distribution, etc.

▌ CONTROL PROGRAM

A routine, usually contained within an operating system, that aids in controlling the operations and managing the resources of a computer system.

▌ CONVERSATIONAL MODE

A mode of operation that implies a "dialog" between a computer and its user, in which the computer program examines the input supplied by the user and formulates questions or comments which are directed back to the user.

▌ CPU (Central Processing Unit)

Same as *central processor*.

▌ CRT

Cathode ray tube display device.

▌ CRYOGENICS

The study and use of devices which utilize the properties assumed by materials at temperatures near absolute zero. Note: Certain materials become "superconductive" at very low temperatures; i.e., their resistance falls to zero, so they can maintain (i.e., store) a current indefinitely. Cryogenic techniques have found little practical application in computer design to date, but they represent a promising area for research and development.

▌ CYCLE TIME

The minimum time interval between the starts of successive accesses to a storage location. Contrast with *access time*. For example, if it takes 2 microseconds to read a word out of a core storage unit and 3 more microseconds to rewrite the word before another read operation can be initiated, then the unit has a read access time of 2 microseconds and a cycle time of $2 + 3 = 5$ microseconds.

D

▌ DATA BASE

Data items that must be stored in order to meet the information processing and retrieval needs of an organization. Note: The term implies an integrated file of data used by many processing applications in contrast to an individual data file for each separate application.

▌ DEBUG
To trace and eliminate mistakes in a program or faults in equipment. The process is often assisted by a diagnostic routine.

▌ DECISION TABLE
A table listing all the contingencies to be considered in the description of a problem, together with the corresponding actions to be taken. Note: Decision tables permit complex decision-making criteria to be expressed in a concise and logical format. They are sometimes used in place of flowcharts for problem definition and documentation. Compilers have been written to convert decision tables into programs that can be executed by computers.

▌ DEMODULATOR
A device that receives signals transmitted over a communications link and converts them into electrical pulses, or bits, that can serve as inputs to a data processing machine. Contrast with *modulator*.

▌ DENSITY
See *recording density*.

▌ DESK CHECKING
A manual checking process in which representative data items, used for detecting errors in program logic, are traced through the program before the latter is checked on the computer.

▌ DETAIL FILE
A file containing relatively transient information; for example, records of individual transactions that occurred during a particular period of time. Synonymous with *transaction file*. Contrast with *master file*.

▌ DIAGNOSTIC ROUTINE
A routine designed to perform diagnostic functions. See also *dump, postmortem routine, snapshot,* and *trace routine* (commonly used types of diagnostic routines).

▌ DIGITAL COMPUTER
A computer that operates on digital data by performing arithmetic and logical operations on the data. Contrast with *analog computer*.

▌ DIRECT ACCESS
See *random access*.

❚ DIRECT ADDRESS

An address that specifies the storage location of an operand. Contrast with *indirect address*.

❚ DOCUMENTATION

Preparation during programming of documents that describe the program and document its preparation, its approval, and any subsequent changes. Usually assembled in a run manual.

❚ DOUBLE PRECISION

Pertaining to the use of two computer words to represent a number in order to gain increased precision. Note: Double-precision arithmetic operations may be implemented in various ways, e.g., by means of standard instructions, optional hardware facilities, or subroutines.

❚ DUMP

(1) To copy the contents of a set of storage locations, usually from an internal storage device (such as core storage) to an external storage medium (such as magnetic tape), and usually for diagnostic or rerun purposes. (2) The data that results from the process as defined in (1). See also *postmortem routine, selective dump, snapshot.*

❚ DUPLEX

(1) Pertaining to a twin, a double, or a "two-in-one" situation. (2) A channel which allows simultaneous transmission in both directions. (3) A standby unit to be used in the event of equipment failure.

❚ DYNAMIC RELOCATION

The movement of part or all of an active (i.e., currently operating) program from one region of storage to another, with all necessary address references being adjusted to enable proper execution of the program to continue in its new location. Note: Dynamic relocation helps to ensure effective utilization of internal storage in a multiprogramming environment.

E

❚ EAM (Electrical Accounting Machine)

Pertaining to data processing equipment that is predominantly electromechanical, such as keypunches, collators, mechanical sorters, and tabulators. Note: EAM equipment is still widely used in lieu of, or in support of, electronic digital computers. (The computers themselves are classified as "EDP equipment" rather than "EAM equipment.")

▌ EBCDIC (Extended Binary Coded Decimal Interchange Code)

An 8-bit *code* that represents an extension of a 6-bit "BCD" code that was widely used in computers of the first and second generations. Note: EBCDIC can represent up to 256 distinct characters and is the principal code used in many of the current computers.

▌ ECHO CHECK

A check upon the accuracy of a data transfer operation in which the data received (typically, by an output device) is transmitted back to the source (typically, a control unit) and compared with the original data. Note: An echo check on an output operation usually can only verify that, for example, the proper print hammers or punch pins were actuated at the proper instants; it cannot ensure that the proper marks were actually recorded on the output medium.

▌ EDIT

To modify the form or format of data. May involve the rearrangement of data, the addition of data (e.g., insertion of dollar signs and decimal points), the deletion of data (e.g., suppression of leading zeros), code translation, and the controls of layouts for printing (e.g., provision of headings and page numbers).

▌ EDP (Electronic Data Processing)

Data processing performed largely by electronic equipment, such as electronic digital computers.

▌ EFFECTIVE ADDRESS

The address that is derived by performing any specified address modification operations (e.g., indexing or indirect addressing) upon a specified address (called the presumptive address) and that is actually used to identify the current operand.

▌ EMULATOR

A device, generally used in conjunction with special routines, that enables a computer to execute machine language programs written for another computer of dissimilar design, without prior translation. Note: Emulation is an important technique for achieving program compatibility between certain current computers and earlier computers produced by the same or different manufacturers. An emulator usually consists of stored logic, in a read-only storage unit, that interprets and simulates the functions of each instruction in the original computer's programs. Functions that cannot be handled conveniently by stored logic, such as input/output operations, are performed by the associated special routines.

▌ EXECUTIVE ROUTINE

A routine designed to organize and regulate the flow of work in a computer system by initiating and controlling execution of programs. A principal component of most operating systems. Synonymous with *supervisory routine*.

❚ EXTERNAL LABEL

An identifying label attached to the outside of a file media holder identifying the file; for example, a paper sticker attached to the side of a reel containing a magnetic tape file.

F

❚ FIELD

(1) In a punched card, a group of columns whose punchings represent one item. (2) A subdivision of a computer word or instruction; e.g., a group of bit positions within an instruction that hold an address. (3) A subdivision of a record; that is, an item.

❚ FILE

A collection of related records, usually (but not necessarily) arranged in sequence according to a key contained in each record. Note: A record, in turn, is a collection of related items; an item is an arbitrary quantity of data that is treated as a unit. In payroll processing, an employee's pay rate forms an item; a group of items relating to one employee form a record, and the complete set of employee records forms a file.

❚ FILE LABEL

A label identifying the file. Note: An internal label is recorded as the first or last record of a file and is machine-readable. An external label is attached to the outside of the file holder and is not machine-readable.

❚ FILE MAINTENANCE

The updating of a file to reflect the effects of nonperiodic changes by adding, altering, or deleting data; e.g., the addition of new programs to a program library on magnetic tape.

❚ FILE PROCESSING

The periodic updating of master files to reflect the effects of current data, often transaction data contained in detail files; e.g., a weekly payroll run updating the payroll master file.

❚ FIXED-LENGTH RECORD

A record that always contains the same number of characters. The restriction to a fixed length may be deliberate, in order to simplify and speed processing, or it may be dictated by the characteristics of the equipment used. Contrast with *variable-length record*.

▌ FIXED POINT

Pertaining to a number system in which each number is represented by a single set of digits and the position of the radix point is implied by the manner in which the numbers are used. Contrast with *floating point*. Note: Fixed point representation is generally used in business data processing, while floating point representation is frequently used in scientific applications because it allows convenient representation of a wide range of magnitudes—though usually at a higher cost in equipment complexity and execution times.

▌ FIXED WORD LENGTH

Pertaining to a machine word or operand that always has the same number of bits or characters. Contrast with *variable word length*. Note: Most scientific computers are of the fixed word length type for maximum computational speeds, while many business-oriented computers have variable word lengths to permit efficient handling of items and records of varying sizes. Some computers have both types of instruction.

▌ FLOATING POINT

Pertaining to a number system in which each number is represented by two numerals (i.e., two sets of digits), of which one (the fixed-point part) represents the significant digits and the other (the exponent) indicates the position of the radix point. The number represented is equal to the fixed-point part multiplied by the radix raised to the power of the exponent. Algebraically, the relationship is $x = a(r^b)$, where x is the number represented, a is the fixed-point part, b is the exponent, and r is the radix (a positive integer which is usually not represented explicitly). Contrast with *fixed point*. Note: Floating point allows the representation of a wide range of magnitudes to a given precision using a limited number of digits; therefore, it is frequently used in scientific applications. Floating point arithmetic operations may be implemented by means of either standard instructions, optional hardware facilities, or subroutines.

▌ FLOWCHART

A diagram that shows, by means of symbols and interconnecting lines, (1) the structure and general sequence of operations of a program (program flowchart) or (2) a system of processing (system flowchart).

▌ FOREGROUND PROGRAM

A program that requires realtime responses or has a high priority and therefore takes precedence over other concurrently operating programs in a computer system using multiprogramming techniques. Also called a priority program. Contrast with *background program*.

▌ FORTRAN (FORmula TRANslator)

A *procedure-oriented language* designed to facilitate the preparation of computer programs that perform mathematical computations. Note: Designed by IBM in the 1950s to use symbols and expressions similar to those of algebra, FORTRAN was not originally intended to be a common language. However, it has evolved through several basic versions (e.g., FORTRAN, FORTRAN II, FORTRAN IV) plus numerous dialects, has become largely machine-independent, and has been approved as a USA standard programming language in two versions (FORTRAN and Basic FORTRAN). FORTRAN is now by far the most widely used procedure-oriented language in the United States and is being effectively employed in certain business as well as scientific applications. The essential element of the FORTRAN language is the assignment statement; e.g., $Z = X + Y$ causes the current values of the variables X and Y to be added together and their sum to replace the previous value of the variable Z.

▌ FULL DUPLEX
Pertaining to the simultaneous, independent transmission of data in both directions over a communications link. Synonymous with *duplex*. Contrast with *half duplex* and *simplex*.

G

▌ GAP
See *interblock gap*.

▌ GENERATE
To use a generator to prepare a machine language program from a set of specifications. Contrast with *assemble* and *compile*.

▌ GENERATOR
A computer program designed to construct other programs for performing particular types of operations; e.g., a report program generator. Based upon parameters supplied to it, the generator typically selects from among various alternatives the most suitable method for performing the specified task, and adjusts the details of the selected method to produce a program matched to the characteristics of the data to be handled by the generated program.

H

▌ HALF DUPLEX
Pertaining to the alternate, independent transmission of data in both directions—but in only one direction at a time—over a communications link. Contrast with *full duplex* and *simplex*.

▌ HEADER LABEL
A machine-readable record at the beginning of a file containing data identifying the file and data used in file control.

▌ HEURISTIC

Pertaining to exploratory methods of problem solving in which solutions are discovered by evaluating the progress made towards the final result; i.e., a guided trial-and-error approach. Contrast with *algorithm*.

▌ HEXADECIMAL

Pertaining to the number system with a radix of 16, or to a characteristic or property involving a choice or condition in which there are 16 possibilities. Synonymous with sexadecimal. Note: Hexadecimal numerals are frequently used as a "shorthand" representation for binary numerals, with each hexadecimal digit representing a group of four bits (binary digits); e.g., the binary numeral 1001 0111 0100 can be represented as hexadecimal 974.

▌ HIGH-ORDER

Pertaining to the digit or digits of a number that have the greatest weight or significance; e.g., in the number 53276, the high-order digit is 5. Contrast with *low-order*.

▌ HOLLERITH CODE

A widely used *code* for representing alphanumeric data on punched cards, named after Herman Hollerith, the originator of punched card tabulating. Each card column holds one character, and each decimal digit, letter, and special character is represented by one, two, or three holes punched into designated row positions of the column.

▌ HOUSEKEEPING

Pertaining to operations in a program or computer system which do not contribute directly to the solution of users' problems, but which are necessary in order to maintain control of the processing.

▌ IDP (Integrated Data Processing)

Data processing by a system that coordinates a number of previously unconnected processes in order to improve overall efficiency by reducing or eliminating redundant data entry or processing operations. An example of IDP is a system in which data describing orders, production, and purchases is entered into a single processing scheme that combines the functions of scheduling, invoicing, inventory control, etc.

▌ IMMEDIATE ADDRESS

Pertaining to an instruction whose address part contains the value of an operand rather than its address. Thus, an "immediate address" is not an address at all, but an operand supplied as part of an instruction. Note: The capability to use "immediate addressing" is available only in certain computers, and usually only with certain types of instructions.

INDEX REGISTER

A register whose contents can be added to or subtracted from an address prior to or during the execution of an instruction. Note: Indexing (i.e., the use of index registers) is the most common form of address modification used in stored-program computers. Indexing can greatly simplify programming by facilitating the handling of loops, arrays, and other repetitive processes. Some computers have many index registers, some have only one, and others have none.

INDIRECT ADDRESS

An address that specifies a storage location that contains either a direct address (i.e., an address that specifies the location of an operand) or another indirect address. Note: Indirect addressing (also called "multilevel addressing") is a form of address modification possible in many, but not all, digital computers; it can simplify programming and increase execution speeds in certain applications by permitting the effective addresses of many instructions to be modified by changing the contents of a single storage location.

INITIALIZE

To set the variable items of a process at initial values before the process is started; e.g., to set counters, indicators, and addresses to the appropriate starting values at the beginning or other prescribed points of a computer program.

INPUT/OUTPUT

A general term for the techniques, devices, and media used to communicate with data processing equipment and for the data involved in these communications. Depending upon the context, the term may mean either "input and output" or "input or output." Synonymous with I/O.

INPUT/OUTPUT CHANNEL

A channel that transmits input data to, or output data from, a computer. Note: Some channels can transmit data to or from only one peripheral device at a time. Others, called multiplexor channels, can service a number of simultaneously operating peripheral devices. See multiplexor channel and selector channel.

INPUT/OUTPUT CONTROL SYSTEM

See IOCS.

INSTRUCTION

A set of characters that specifies an operation to be performed and, usually, the value or locations of one or more of its operands. Note: In this context, the term *instruction* is preferable to the terms *command* and *order,* which are sometimes used synonymously.

▌ INTEGRATED CIRCUIT

A complete, complex electronic circuit, capable of performing all the functions of a conventional circuit containing numerous discrete transistors, diodes, capacitors, and/or resistors, all of whose component parts are fabricated and assembled in a single integrated process. The resultant assembly cannot be disassembled without destroying it.

▌ INTEGRATED DATA PROCESSING

See *IDP.*

▌ INTERBLOCK GAP

The distance on a magnetic tape between the end of one block and the beginning of the next. Note: Within this distance the tape can be stopped and brought up to normal speed again. Since the tape speed is not constant when stopping or starting, no reading or writing is permitted in the gap. Synonymous with *interrecord gap* and *record gap,* though the use of these two terms is not recommended because of the important distinction between blocks and records.

▌ INTERFACE

A shared boundary; e.g., the boundary between two systems, or between a computer and one of its peripheral devices.

▌ INTERLOCK

A protective facility that prevents one device or operation from interfering with another; for example, the locking of a console typewriter's keys to prevent manual entry of data while the computer is transferring data to the typewriter.

▌ INTERPRETIVE ROUTINE

A routine that deals with the execution of a program by translating each instruction of the source language into a sequence of machine instructions and executing them' before translating the next instruction. Thus, each instruction must be translated every time it is to be executed—an inherently inefficient process. See also *simulator.*

▌ INTERRECORD GAP

Same as *interblock gap.*

▌ INTERRUPT

A signal, condition, or event that causes an interruption; e.g., completion of an input or output operation, detection of incorrect parity, or an attempt to execute an illegal instruction or to write in a protected location.

▌ INTERRUPTION

A temporary suspension of the execution of a sequence of instructions resulting from the occurrence of some prescribed event or condition. Note: The interrupt usually triggers a transfer to a predetermined location, where a special routine (usually part of an operating system) determines the cause of the interruption, takes the appropriate action, and then transfers control back to the point where the program was interrupted—or, in some cases, to another program of higher priority. Effective interruption facilities are a vital factor for computers that are to operate in a multiprogramming or realtime mode.

▌ I/O

Same as *input/output*.

▌ IOCS (Input/Output Control System)

A standard routine or set of routines designed to initiate and control the input and output processes of a computer system, thereby making it unnecessary for users to prepare detailed coding for these processes.

▌ ITEM

An arbitrary quantity of data that is treated as a unit. Note: A record, in turn, is a collection of related items, while a file is a collection of related records. Thus, in payroll processing, an employee's pay rate forms an item, all of the items relating to one employee form a record, and the complete set of employee records forms a file.

K

▌ KEY

One or more characters associated with a particular item or record and used to identify that item or record, especially in sorting or collating operations. The key may or may not be attached to the record or item it identifies. Contrast *label* and *tag*.

L

▌ LABEL

A name attached to or written alongside the entity it identifies; e.g., a key that is attached to the item or record it identifies, or a name written alongside a statement on a coding sheet.

▌ LATERAL PARITY CHECK

Same as *row parity check*.

▌ LIBRARY ROUTINE

A tested routine maintained in a program library (in contrast to a routine written especially for a particular job).

▌ LINKAGE

Coding that connects two separately coded routines; e.g., the coding that links a subroutine to the program with which it is to be used. See also *calling sequence*.

▌ LOAD-AND-GO

An operating technique in which the loading and execution phases of a program are performed in one continuous run. The "loading" phase frequently includes performance of the functions of an assembler, compiler, or generator. Note: The load-and-go technique is especially effective when a program must be compiled or generated for a one-time application, such as the production of a special report.

▌ LOADER

A service routine designed to read programs into internal storage in preparation for their execution.

▌ LOG

A record of the operations of data processing equipment, listing each job or run, the time it required, operator actions, and other pertinent data.

▌ LONGITUDINAL PARITY CHECK

A parity check performed on the bits in each track of magnetic tape or punched tape. For this check, the parity bits generated for each of the tracks are recorded simultaneously at the end of each block in the form of a "longitudinal check character," which is regenerated and checked when the block is read. Synonymous with *track parity check*.

▌ LOOK-UP

See *table look-up*.

▌ LOOP

A sequence of instructions that can be executed repetitively, usually with modified addresses or modified data values. Each repetition is called a cycle. Cycling continues until a specified criterion is satisfied (e.g., until a counter reaches a predetermined value). Note: The use of loops greatly facilitates the coding of any iterative process.

▌ LOW-ORDER

Pertaining to the digit or digits of a number that have the least weight or significance; e.g., in the number 53276, the low-order digit is 6. Contrast with *high-order*.

M

▌ MACHINE ADDRESS
Same as *absolute address*.

▌ MACHINE INSTRUCTION
An instruction that a computer can directly recognize and execute.

▌ MACHINE LANGUAGE
A language that is used directly by a computer. Thus, a "machine language program" is a set of instructions which a computer can directly recognize and execute, and which will cause it to perform a particular process.

▌ MACHINE-ORIENTED LANGUAGE
A language in which there is a general (though not necessarily strict) one-to-one correspondence between the statements of the source program and the instructions of the object program (which will normally be a machine language program ready for execution on a particular computer). Note: The input to an assembler is usually expressed in a machine-oriented language. Contrast with *procedure-oriented language*.

▌ MACRO INSTRUCTION
An instruction written in a machine-oriented language that has no equivalent operation in the computer and is replaced in the object program by a predetermined set of machine instructions. Note: Macro instruction facilities can ease the task of coding in a machine-oriented language by precluding the need for detailed coding of input and output operations, blocking, format control, checking for errors, etc.

▌ MAIN FRAME
Same as *central processor*.

▌ MANAGEMENT INFORMATION SYSTEM
A system designed to supply the managers of a business with the information they need to keep informed of the current status of the business, to understand its implications, and to make and implement the appropriate operating decisions.

▌ MAP
A list that indicates the area of storage occupied by various elements of a program and its data.

▌ MARK SENSING
A technique for detecting pencil marks entered by hand in prescribed places on punched cards or other documents. The marked data may be converted into punched

holes in the same cards, recorded on another medium, or transmitted directly to a computer.

▌ MASK
A machine word containing a pattern of characters or bits that is used to extract or select parts of other machine words by controlling an instruction which retains or eliminates selected characters or bits.

▌ MASS STORAGE
Same as *secondary storage* or *auxiliary storage*.

▌ MASTER FILE
A file containing relatively permanent information which is used as a source of reference and is generally updated periodically. Contrast with *detail file*.

▌ MERGE
To form a single sequenced file by combining two or more similarly sequenced files. Note: Merging may be performed manually, by a collator, or by a computer system for which a "merge routine" is available. Repeated merging, splitting, and remerging of strings of records can be used to arrange the records in sequence; this process, called a "merging sort," is frequently used as the basis for sorting operations on computer systems.

▌ MESSAGE SWITCHING
A technique for controlling the traffic within a data communications network that involves the following: the reception of messages from various sources at a switching center, the storage of each message until the proper outgoing communications link is available, and the ultimate retransmission of each message to its destination or destinations.

▌ MICR (Magnetic Ink Character Recognition)
The automatic reading by machine of graphic characters printed with magnetic ink.

▌ MICROPROGRAMMING
A method of operation of the control unit of a computer in which each instruction, instead of being used to initiate control signals directly, starts the execution of a sequence of "micro instructions" at a more elementary level. The micro instructions are usually stored in a special read-only storage unit. Note: The instruction repertoire of a microprogrammed computer can be altered to suit particular requirements by simply changing the stored micro instructions.

▌ MICROSECOND
One-millionth of a second, abbreviated μsec or μs.

▌ MILLISECOND
One-thousandth of a second, abbreviated msec or ms.

▌ MNEMONIC
Pertaining to a technique used to assist human memory. Note: Most symbolic assembly languages use mnemonic operation codes, which are typically abbreviations such as MPY for multiply and SUB for subtract.

▌ MODEM (MOdulator-DEModulator)
A device that provides the appropriate interface between a communications link and a data processing machine or system by serving as a modulator and/or demodulator.

▌ MODULATOR
A device that receives electrical pulses, or bits, from a data processing machine and converts them into signals suitable for transmission over a communications link. Contrast with *demodulator*.

▌ MODULO N CHECK
Same as *residue check*.

▌ MONITOR ROUTINE
(1) A routine designed to indicate the progress of work in a computer system. (2) Sometimes used to refer to an *executive routine*.

▌ MULTIPLEX
To transmit two or more messages simultaneously over a single channel or other transmission facility. This can be accomplished either by splitting the channel's frequency band into two or more narrower bands ("frequency-division multiplexing") or by interleaving the bits, characters, or words that make up the various messages ("time-division multiplexing").

▌ MULTIPLEXOR
A device that makes it possible to transmit two or more messages simultaneously over a single channel or other transmission facility.

▌ MULTIPLEXOR CHANNEL
A special type of input/output channel that can transmit data between a computer and a number of simultaneously operating peripheral devices.

▌ MULTIPROCESSING
The simultaneous execution of two or more sequences of instructions in a single computer system. Frequently refers to simultaneous execution accomplished by the use of a system with more than one central processor.

▌ MULTIPROGRAMMING

A technique for handling two or more independent programs simultaneously by overlapping or interleaving their execution. The overlapping or interleaving of the execution of the various programs is usually controlled by an operating system which attempts to optimize the overall performance of the computer system in accordance with the priority requirements of the various jobs.

N

▌ NANOSECOND

One-billionth of a second (i.e., 10^{-9} second), abbreviated nsec or ns.

O

▌ OBJECT LANGUAGE

A language that is an output from a translation process. Contrast with *source language*.

▌ OBJECT PROGRAM

A program expressed in an object language (e.g., a machine language program that can be directly executed by a particular computer).

▌ OCR (Optical Character Recognition)

The automatic reading by machine of graphic characters through use of light-sensitive devices.

▌ OCTAL

Pertaining to the number system with a radix of 8 or to a characteristic or property involving a choice or condition in which there are eight possibilities. Note: Octal numerals are frequently used as a ''shorthand'' representation for binary numerals, with each octal digit representing a group of three bits (binary digits); e.g., the binary numeral 110 101 010 can be represented as octal 652.

▌ OFFLINE (or OFF-LINE)

Pertaining to equipment or devices that are not in direct communication with the central processor of a computer system. Note: Offline devices cannot be controlled by a computer except through human intervention. Contrast with *online*.

❙ ONLINE (or ON-LINE)

Pertaining to equipment or devices that are in direct communication with the central processor of a computer system. Note: Online devices are usually under the direct control of the computer with which they are in communication. Contrast with *offline*.

❙ OPERAND

A unit of data upon which an operation is performed. Note: The operand of a computer instruction may also be an equipment item such as an indicator, switch, or peripheral device.

❙ OPERATING SYSTEM

An organized collection of routines and procedures for operating a computer. These routines and procedures will normally perform some or all of the following functions: (1) scheduling, loading, initiating, and supervising the execution of programs; (2) allocating storage, input/output units, and other facilities of the computer system; (3) initiating and controlling input/output operations; (4) handling errors and restarts; (5) coordinating communications between the human operator and the computer system; (6) maintaining a log of system operations, and (7) controlling operations in a multiprogramming, multiprocessing, or time-sharing mode. Note: Among the facilities frequently included within an operating system are an executive routine, a scheduler, an IOCS, utility routines, and monitor routines.

❙ OPERATION CODE

A code used to represent the specific operations of a computer.

❙ OVERFLOW

In an arithmetic operation, the generation of a quantity beyond the capacity of the register or storage location which is to receive the result.

❙ OVERHEAD

A collective term for the factors which cause the performance of a device or program to be lower than it would be in the ideal case; e.g., the start and stop times which can cause a magnetic tape unit's effective speed to be far lower than its rated speed, and the time and storage space required by an operating system to perform its functions.

❙ OVERLAY

To transfer segments of program from auxiliary storage into internal storage for execution, so that two or more segments occupy the same storage locations at different times. Note: This technique makes it possible to execute programs which are too large to fit into the computer's internal storage at one time; it is also of great importance in multiprogramming and time-sharing operations.

P

PACK
To store several short units of data in a single storage cell in such a way that the individual units can later be recovered; e.g., to store two 4-bit BCD digits in one 8-bit storage location.

PADDING
Dummy characters, items, or records used to fill out a fixed-length block of information.

PAGE
A segment of a program or data, usually of fixed length, that has a fixed virtual address but can in fact reside in any region of the computer's internal storage. Note: The division of every program and its data into pages can facilitate the control of time-sharing operations by permitting straightforward "swapping" of pages belonging to various programs between internal storage and secondary storage.

PARALLEL
Handling all the elements of a word or message (e.g., the bits or characters) simultaneously. Contrast with *serial*.

PARITY BIT
A bit (binary digit) appended to an array of bits to make the sum of all the 1-bits in the array either always even ("even parity") or always odd ("odd parity"). For example:

	Even parity			Odd Parity		
	0	1	1	0	1	1
	0	1	0	0	1	0
Data bits	0	1	0	0	1	0
	0	1	1	0	1	1
	0	1	1	0	1	1
	1	1	0	1	1	0
Parity bit	1	0	1	0	1	0

PARITY CHECK
A check that tests whether the number of 1-bits in an array is either even ("even parity check") or odd ("odd parity check"). See also *row parity check* and *longitudinal parity check*.

PASS
One complete cycle of input, processing, and output in the execution of a computer program. For example, a "one-pass compiler" reads the source program, compiles

it, and writes the object program without intermediate input/output operations or human intervention.

▌ PATCH
To correct or modify a program in a rough or expedient way by adding new sections of coding.

▌ PERIPHERAL EQUIPMENT
The input/output units and secondary storage units of a computer system. Note: The central processor and its associated storage and control units are the only parts of a computer system which are *not* considered peripheral equipment.

▌ PICOSECOND
One-thousandth of a nanosecond (i.e., 10^{-12} second), abbreviated psec.

▌ PL/I (Programming Language I)
A procedure-oriented language designed to facilitate the preparation of computer programs to perform both business and scientific functions. Note: Developed jointly by IBM and the SHARE users' organization between 1964 and 1966, PL/I represents an attempt to combine the best features of existing programming languages (such as ALGOL, COBOL, and FORTRAN) with a number of facilities not available in previous languages.

▌ PLUGBOARD
A perforated board used to control the operation of some automatic data processing equipment. The holes in the board (called "hubs" or "sockets") are manually inter-connected, in a manner appropriate to the job to be performed, by means of wires terminating in plugs (called "patchcords").

▌ POSTMORTEM ROUTINE
A diagnostic routine, often a dump, that is used after a program has failed to operate as intended.

▌ PRECISION
The degree of discrimination with which a quantity is stated. For example, a three-decimal-digit numeral permits discrimination among 1,000 possible values. Precision should be carefully distinguished from accuracy, which is the degree of freedom from error. For example, a six-digit numeral is more precise than a four-digit numeral, but a properly computed four-digit result may be more accurate than an improperly computed six-digit result.

▌ PRESUMPTIVE ADDRESS
An address that is altered through address modification to form an effective address which is actually used to identify an operand.

▌ PRIVILEGED INSTRUCTION

A computer instruction that is not available for use in ordinary programs written by users; its use is restricted to the routines of the operating system. Note: Input/output, priority control, and storage protection instructions are in the "privileged" category in many of the current computers.

▌ PROBLEM-ORIENTED LANGUAGE

A language whose design is oriented toward the specification of a particular class of problems, such as numerical control of machine tools. Sometimes used as a general term to describe both procedure- and problem-oriented languages.

▌ PROCEDURE-ORIENTED LANGUAGE

A language designed to permit convenient specification, in terms of procedural or algorithmic steps, of data processing or computational processes. Examples include ALGOL, COBOL, and FORTRAN. Contrast with *problem-oriented language* and *machine-oriented language*.

▌ PROCESSOR

A device or system capable of performing operations upon data. Note: The terms may refer to either hardware (see *central processor*) or software (an assembler or compiler is sometimes referred to as a "language processor").

▌ PROGRAM

(1) A plan for solving a problem. (2) To devise a plan for solving a problem. (3) A computer routine, i.e., a set of instructions arranged in proper sequence to cause a computer to perform a particular process. (4) To write a computer routine.

▌ PROGRAM FLOWCHART

A flowchart diagramming the processing steps and logic of a computer program. Contrast with *system flowchart*.

▌ PROGRAMMER

A person who devises programs. Note: The term "programmer" is most suitably applied to a person who is mainly involved in formulating programs, particularly at the level of flowchart preparation. A person mainly involved in the definition of problems is called an analyst, while a person mainly involved in converting programs into coding suitable for entry into a computer system is called a coder. In many organizations, all three of these functions are performed by "programmers."

▌ PROGRAMMING LANGUAGE

An unambiguous language used to express programs for a computer.

▌ PSEUDO INSTRUCTION

An instruction that has the same general form as a machine instruction but is not directly executable by a computer. Pseudo instructions are commonly used in machine-oriented languages to control the operation of a translator.

R

▌ RADIX POINT

In a number system, the character (usually a dot) or implied character that separates the integral part of a numeral from the fractional part; e.g., decimal point, binary point.

▌ RANDOM ACCESS

Pertaining to a storage device whose access time is not significantly affected by the location of the data to be accessed; thus, any item of data which is stored online can be accessed within a relatively short time (usually less than one second). Same as *direct access*. Contrast with *serial access*.

▌ READ-ONLY STORAGE

A storage device into which data cannot be written by the computer with which it is used. Note: In some computers, portions of the core storage or drum storage can be made "read-only" by temporarily effecting manual or programmed write lockouts. Permanent read-only storage (ROS) is used in many current computers to implement emulators and microprogramming.

▌ REALTIME (or REAL-TIME)

(1) Pertaining to the actual time during which a physical process takes place. (2) Pertaining to fast-response online computer processing, which obtains data from an activity or a process, performs computations, and returns a response rapidly enough to control, direct, or influence the outcome of the activity or process. For example, realtime operation is essential in computers associated with process control systems, message switching systems, and reservation systems.

▌ RECORD

A collection of related items of data. Note: In payroll processing, for example, an employee's pay rate forms an item, all of the items relating to one employee form a record, and the complete set of employee records forms a file. See also *fixed-length record* and *variable-length record*.

❚ RECORD GAP
Same as *interblock gap*.

❚ RECORDING DENSITY
The number of useful storage cells per unit of length or area; e.g., the number of rows (or characters) per inch on a magnetic tape or punched tape, or the number of bits per inch on a single track of a tape or drum. Note: The most common recording densities in current use are 10 rows per inch for punched tape and 200, 556, 800, or 1,600 rows per inch for magnetic tape.

❚ REDUNDANCY CHECK
A check based on the transfer of more bits or characters than the minimum number required to express the message itself, the added bits or characters having been inserted systematically for checking purposes. Note: The most common type of redundancy check is a parity check

❚ REENTRANT
Pertaining to a routine that can be used by two or more independent programs at the same time. This means that the reentrant routine cannot modify the contents of any of its own locations, and that any required temporary storage must be supplied along with each program using the reentrant routine. Note: Reentrant routines have two significant advantages in multiprogramming or time-sharing environments: (1) they conserve storage space because only one copy of a routine needs to be present regardless of the number of programs which are simultaneously using it; (2) since they are never modified, they do not need to be rewritten in secondary storage when displaced from internal storage by another program.

❚ REGISTER
A device capable of storing a specified amount of data, such as one word, and usually intended for some special purpose. Note: Among the registers included in many computers are an accumulator, index registers, instruction register, and sequence counter.

❚ RELATIVE ADDRESS
An address (usually contained in an instruction) that is combined with a base address to form the absolute address of a particular storage location.

❚ RELOCATABLE CODING
Coding existing in a form that permits it to be loaded and executed in any available region of a computer's internal storage. Note: The object programs produced by most of the current assemblers and compilers are in relocatable form to permit flexibility in storage allocation.

▌ REPORT PROGRAM GENERATOR (RPG)

A generator designed to construct programs that perform routine report-writing functions; e.g., to accept input data from punched cards or magnetic tape and produce printed reports, often with headings, subtotals, etc.

▌ RESIDUE CHECK

A check of numeric data or arithmetic operations in which each number, A, is divided by the modulus, N, and the remainder, B, accompanies A as a check digit or digits. For example, in a modulo 4 check, B will be either 0, 1, 2, or 3; if the remainder formed when A is divided by 4 does not equal B, an error is indicated. Synonymous with *modulo N check.*

▌ ROUTINE

A set of instructions arranged in correct sequence to cause a computer to perform a particular process. Note: in this context, the term "routine" is somewhat more precise than the more general (and more commonly used) term "program."

▌ ROW PARITY CHECK

A parity check performed on the bits in each row of magnetic tape or punched tape. Synonymous with *lateral parity check.*

▌ RUN

A performance of a specific process by a computer on a given set of data; i.e., the execution of one routine or of several routines which are linked to form one operating unit, during which little or no human intervention is required.

▌ RUN MANUAL

A manual documenting the processing system, program logic, controls, program changes, and operating instructions associated with a computer run.

S

▌ SCALE FACTOR

A number used as a multiplier to scale one or more quantities so that they will fall within a prescribed range of values. For example, to scale the values 96, 43.2, -9, and -75.6 to fall between $+1$ and -1, a scale factor of $1/100$ could be used, resulting in the scaled values 0.96, 0.432, -0.09, and -0.756 respectively.

▌ SECONDARY STORAGE

Storage that supplements a computer's primary internal storage. Synonymous with *auxiliary storage.*

SELECTOR CHANNEL

A term used in certain computer systems for an input/output channel that can transfer data to or from only one peripheral device at a time. Contrast with *multiplexor channel*.

SEQUENTIAL PROCESSING

Same as *batch processing*.

SERIAL

Handling the elements of a word or message (e.g., the bits or characters) one after another. Contrast with *parallel*.

SERIAL ACCESS

Pertaining to a storage device in which there is a sequential relationship between the access times to successive locations, as in the case of magnetic tape. Contrast with *direct access* or *random access*.

SETUP TIME

The time between computer runs or other machine operations that is devoted to such tasks as changing reels of tape and moving cards, forms, and other supplies to and from the equipment.

SIMPLEX

Pertaining to a communications link that is capable of transmitting data in only one direction. Contrast with *full duplex* and *half duplex*.

SNAPSHOT

A dynamic dump of the contents of specified storage locations and/or registers that is performed at specified points or times during the running of a program.

SOFTWARE

A collection of programs and routines associated with a computer (including assemblers, compilers, utility routines, and operating systems) which facilitate the programming and operation of the computer. Contrast with *hardware*.

SOLID STATE

Pertaining to electronic components whose operation depends on the control of electric or magnetic phenomena in solids; e.g., transistors, crystal diodes, ferrite cores.

SOURCE LANGUAGE

A language that is an input to a translation process. Contrast with *object language*.

❚ SOURCE PROGRAM
A program written in a source language (e.g., written in COBOL, FORTRAN, or symbolic coding for input to a compiler or assembler).

❚ SPECIAL CHARACTER
A character that is neither a letter nor a digit; it may be a punctuation mark (e.g., comma) or a character that causes a particular operation to be performed (e.g., carriage return).

❚ STATEMENT
In computer programming, a meaningful expression or generalized instruction in a programming language.

❚ STORAGE ALLOCATION
The assignment of specific programs, program segments, and/or blocks of data to specific portions of a computer's storage.

❚ STORAGE PROTECTION
Protection against unauthorized writing in and/or reading from all or part of a storage device. This may be implemented by manually set switches or by automatic hardware facilities, usually in connection with an operating system. Note: Effective storage protection is a vital element in multiprogramming and time-sharing systems both for ensuring privacy and for preventing concurrently operating programs from interfering with one another.

❚ STRAIGHT-LINE CODING
Coding in which the use of loops and/or closed subroutines is avoided by repetition of parts of the coding when required.

❚ SUBPROGRAM
A part of a larger program. Usually the subprogram can be converted into machine language independently of the remainder of the program.

❚ SUBROUTINE
A routine that can be part of another routine. A closed subroutine is stored in one place and connected to the program by means of linkages at one or more points in the program. An open subroutine is inserted directly into a program at each point where it is to be used. Note: A great deal of coding effort can be saved through judicious use of subroutines to handle tasks which are encountered repetitively, such as the control of input/output operations, the evaluation of mathematical functions, and the handling of checking and error recovery procedures.

▌ SUPERVISORY ROUTINE
Same as *executive routine*.

▌ SWITCH
(1) In a program, an instruction or parameter that causes selection of one of two or more alternative sequences of instructions. The selection, once made, persists until it is altered. (2) In hardware, a device that can be placed in one of two or more distinct settings by a human operator or an instruction.

▌ SYMBOLIC ADDRESS
An address expressed in symbols convenient to the programmer, which must be translated into an absolute address (usually by an assembler) before it can be interpreted by a computer. For example, the storage location that holds an employee's gross pay might be assigned the symbolic address GPAY.

▌ SYMBOLIC CODING
Coding that uses machine instructions with symbolic addresses. Contrast with *absolute coding* and *relative coding*. Note: The input to most assemblers is expressed in symbolic coding. Mnemonic operation codes are usually employed along with the symbolic addresses to further simplify the coding process. For example, a two-address instruction that subtracts an employee's taxes from his gross pay might be written SUB TAX GPAY.

▌ SYNCHRONIZATION CHECK
A check that determines whether a particular event or condition occurs at the proper moment; e.g., whether the print hammers in a drum printer were activated at the moment when the appropriate character slugs on the drum were in the proper position.

▌ SYNCHRONOUS COMPUTER
A computer in which each operation starts as a result of a signal generated by a clock. Contrast with *asynchronous computer*.

▌ SYSTEM
A set or arrangement of entities that forms, or is considered as, an organized whole. Note: This term is a very general one that is applied to both hardware and software entities; therefore, it must be carefully qualified to be meaningful (e.g., computer system, management information system, number system, operating system).

▌ SYSTEM ANALYSIS
The examination of an activity, procedure, method, technique or business to determine what needs to be done and how it can best be accomplished.

SYSTEM FLOWCHART
A flowchart diagramming the flow of work, documents, and operations in a data processing application. Contrast with *program flowchart.*

T

TABLE LOOK-UP
A procedure for using a known value (the argument) to locate an unknown value in a table. Note: Special instructions for table look-up operations are provided in some computers; in others, the procedure must be programmed using regular instructions.

TABULATING EQUIPMENT
Data processing machines which use punched cards and are predominantly electromechanical, such as tabulators, collators, gang punches, interpreters, reproducers, and sorters. Note: The name "tabulating equipment" resulted from the fact that the main function of these machines for many years prior to the introduction of electronic computers was to produce tabulations of information by sorting, listing, selecting, and totaling data on punched cards.

TAG
One or more characters attached to a particular item or record and used to identify that item or record. Note: The tag can be removed from the item or record by a simple operation, but it then loses its significance. Contrast with *key.*

TELECOMMUNICATIONS
The transmission of signals over long distances, such as by radio or telegraph. See also *data communications.*

THIN FILM
A layer of magnetic material, usually less than one-millionth of an inch in thickness and deposited by a vacuum process on some "substrate" such as a flat plate or wire. Note: Magnetic thin films are being used for both storage and logic elements.

THROUGHPUT
The total amount of useful work performed by a data processing system during a given period of time.

TIME SHARING
(1) The use of a given device by a number of other devices, programs, or human users, one at a time and in rapid succession. (2) A technique or system for furnishing

computing services to multiple users simultaneously, providing rapid responses to each of the users. Note: Time-sharing computer systems usually employ multiprogramming and/or multiprocessing techniques and are often capable of serving users at remote locations via a data communications network.

▌ TRACE ROUTINE

A diagnostic routine designed to check or demonstrate the operation of a program; its output usually includes some or all of the instructions in the program being checked and the immediate results of those instructions, arranged in the sequence in which the instructions are executed.

▌ TRACK

That part of a data storage medium that is influenced by (or influences) one head; e.g., the ring-shaped portion of the surface of a drum associated with one non-movable head, or one of several divisions (most commonly seven or nine) running parallel to the edges of a magnetic tape.

▌ TRACK PARITY CHECK

Same as *longitudinal parity check*.

▌ TRAILER RECORD

A record that follows another record or group of records and contains pertinent data related to that record or group of records.

▌ TRANSACTION CODE

One or more characters that form part of a record and signify the type of transaction represented by the record (e.g., in inventory control, the types of transactions would include deliveries to stock, disbursements from stock, orders, etc.).

▌ TRANSACTION FILE

Same as *detail file*.

▌ TRANSLATOR

A device or computer program that performs translations from one language or code to another; e.g., an assembler or compiler.

▌ TRAP

An unprogrammed jump to a preset location, activated automatically upon the occurrence of a particular condition (e.g., upon an attempt to execute an instruction that is not in the computer's instruction repertoire). The location from which the jump occurred is recorded, so that normal execution of the program can be resumed after the condition that activated the trap has been dealt with.

U

▌ UNCONDITIONAL TRANSFER

An instruction that always causes a jump (i.e., a departure from the normal sequence of executing instructions). Contrast with *conditional transfer*.

▌ UNIT RECORD

(1) A record that is similar in form and content to other records but is physically separate; e.g., a record on a punched card. (2) Pertaining to equipment or techniques for dealing with unit records as described in (1), especially to punched card equipment.

▌ UNPACK

To separate short units of data that have previously been packed; i.e., to reverse a packing operation.

▌ UPDATE

To incorporate into a master file the changes required to reflect recent transactions or other events.

▌ UTILITY ROUTINE

A standard routine used to assist in the operation of a computer by performing some frequently required process such as sorting, merging, report program generation, data transcription, file maintenance, etc. Note: Utility routines are important components of the software supplied by the manufacturers of most computers.

V

▌ VARIABLE-LENGTH RECORD

A record that may contain a variable number of characters. Contrast with *fixed-length record*. Note: In many cases where the equipment would permit the use of variable-length records, the records are nonetheless held to a fixed length to facilitate both programming and processing.

▌ VARIABLE WORD LENGTH

Pertaining to a machine word or operand that may consist of a variable number of bits or characters. Contrast with *fixed word length*. Note: Many business-oriented computers are of the variable word length type for efficient processing of items and records of varying sizes.

▌ VIRTUAL ADDRESS

An address in a machine instruction that refers to a particular page which may be located in any region of the computer's internal storage; thus, every time the instruction is executed, the virtual address must be translated to the proper absolute address, usually through the use of an associative memory and/or a page directory. Note: Virtual addresses are used in many time-sharing computer systems.

▌ WORD

A group of bits or characters treated as a unit and capable of being stored in one storage location. Note: Within a word, each location that may be occupied by a bit or character is called a "position."

▌ WORD LENGTH

The number of bits or characters in a word.

▌ WORD MARK

A symbol (e.g., a special character or a single bit) used in some variable word length computers to indicate the beginning or end of a word or item.

▌ WORKING STORAGE

A storage section set aside by the programmer for use in the development of processing results, for storing constants, for temporarily storing results needed later in the program sequence, etc.

▌ X PUNCH

A punch in the X row (or 11 row) of an 80-column punched card, often used to indicate a negative number or for control or selection purposes.

▌ Y PUNCH

A punch in the Y row (or 12 row) of an 80-column punched card, often used to indicate a positive number or for control or selection purposes.

Z

▌ ZERO SUPPRESSION

The suppression (i.e., elimination) of nonsignificant zeros in a numeral, usually before or during a printing operation. For example, the numeral 0006304, with zero suppression, would be printed as 6304.

SELECTED
REFERENCES

For the student who wishes to explore certain topics in more depth, the following selected references should be useful. The emphasis in the references is toward books rather than journal articles because the former tend to be more readily available.

▮ GENERAL REFERENCES

Arnold, Robert R., Harold C. Hill, and Aylmer V. Nichols: *Introduction to Data Processing,* New York, John Wiley & Sons, Inc., 1966.

Awad, Elias M. and DPMA: *Automatic Data Processing,* Englewood Cliffs, N.J., Prentice-Hall, Inc., 1966.

Bernstein, Jeremy: *The Analytical Engine: Computers—Past, Present and Future,* New York, Random House, Inc., 1964.

Chapin, Ned: *An Introduction to Automatic Computers,* 2d ed., Princeton, N.J., D. Van Nostrand Company, Inc., 1963.

Davis, Gordon B.: *An Introduction to Electronic Computers,* New York, McGraw-Hill Book Company, 1965.

Gregory, R. H. and R. L. Van Horn: *Automatic Data Processing Systems,* 2d ed., Belmont, Calif., Wadsworth Publishing Company, 1963.

Martin, Wainright E., Jr.: *Electronic Data Processing: An Introduction,* rev. ed., Homewood, Ill., Richard D. Irwin, Inc., 1965.

Sanders, Donald H.: *Computers in Business: An Introduction,* New York, McGraw-Hill Book Company, 1968.

Scientific American, September, 1966: *Information,* San Francisco, W. H. Freeman and Company, 1966.

▮ PUNCHED CARD PROCESSING

There are a large number of IBM publications covering punched card equipment and processing methods. These publications include programmed learning texts for punched card equipment.

IBM Personal Study Program, No's 320–1443 to 320–1449: *Punched Card Data Processing Principles,* International Business Machines Corporation, 1961.

Levy, Joseph: *Punched Card Data Processing,* New York, McGraw-Hill Book Company, 1967.

Salmon, Lawrence J.: *IBM Machine Operation and Wiring,* Belmont, Calif., Wadsworth Publishing Company, Inc., 1962.

▌ THE USES OF COMPUTERS

Boore, William F. and Jerry R. Murphy: *The Computer Sampler: Management Perspectives on the Computer,* New York, McGraw-Hill Book Company, 1968.

Burck, Gilbert and the Editors of *Fortune: The Computer Age and Its Potential for Management,* New York, Harper & Row, Publishers, Incorporated, 1965.

Mizc, Joe H. and Grady J. Cox: *Essentials of Simulation,* Englewood Cliffs, N.J., Prentice-Hall, Inc., 1968.

Naylor, Thomas H., Joseph L. Bolintfy, Donald S. Burdick, and Kong Chu: *Computer Simulation Techniques,* New York, John Wiley & Sons, Inc., 1966.

Schoderbek, Peter P., (ed.): *Management Systems,* New York, John Wiley & Sons, Inc., 1967.

Withington, Frederic G.: *The Use of Computers in Business Organizations,* Reading, Mass., Addison-Wesley Publishing Company, Inc., 1966.

▌ COMPUTER ARITHMETIC AND CIRCUITRY

Burroughs Corporation: *Digital Computer Principles,* New York, McGraw-Hill Book Company, 1962.

Evans, David C.: "Computer Logic and Memory," *Scientific American,* September, 1966.

Flores, Ivan: *The Logic of Computer Arithmetic,* Englewood Cliffs, N.J., Prentice-Hall, Inc., 1963.

▌ ANALYSIS, DESIGN AND IMPLEMENTATION OF DATA PROCESSING SYSTEMS

Chorafas, Dimitris N.: *Selecting the Computer System,* London, Gee & Co. Limited, 1967.

Laden, H. N. and T. R. Gildersleeve: *System Design for Computer Applications,* New York, John Wiley & Sons, Inc., 1963.

Meadow, Charles T.: *The Analysis of Information Systems,* New York, John Wiley & Sons, Inc., 1967.

Optner, Stanford L.: *Systems Analysis for Business Management,* 2d ed., Englewood Cliffs, N.J., Prentice-Hall, Inc., 1968.

Radamaker, T.: *Business Systems,* vols. I and II, Cleveland, Ohio, Systems and Procedures Association, 1963.

Salton, Gerald: *Automatic Information Organization and Retrieval,* New York, McGraw-Hill Book Company, 1968.

USA Standard Flowchart Symbols and Their Usage in Information Processing (X 3.5—1968), New York, United States of America Standards Institute, 1968.

Wilson, Ira G. and Marthann E. Wilson: *Information, Computers, and System Design,* New York, John Wiley & Sons, Inc., 1965.

▌ COMPUTER PROGRAMMING

There are a number of books which cover programming for specific machines. In addition the manufacturers normally supply training materials.

Chapin, Ned: *360 Programming in Assembly Language,* New York, McGraw-Hill Book Company, 1968.

Computer Usage Company: *Programming the IBM System/360,* New York, John Wiley & Sons, Inc., 1966.

Germain, Clarence B.: *Programming the IBM 360,* Englewood Cliffs, N.J., Prentice-Hall, Inc., 1967.

Martin, James: *Programming Real-time Computer Systems,* Englewood Cliffs, N.J., Prentice-Hall, Inc., 1965.

Walnut, Francis K.: *Introduction to Computer Programming and Coding,* Englewood Cliffs, N.J., Prentice-Hall, Inc., 1968.

Wegner, Peter: *Programming Languages, Information Structures, and Machine Organization,* New York, McGraw-Hill Book Company, 1968.

▌ PROCEDURE- AND PROBLEM-ORIENTED LANGUAGES

Because of the number and availability of FORTRAN texts, these will not be listed. All major publishers have one or more FORTRAN books. In selecting a FORTRAN text for study, preference should be given to those which use American Standard FORTRAN.

Bates, Frank and Mary L. Douglas: *Programming Language/One,* Englewood Cliffs, N.J., Prentice-Hall, Inc., 1967.

Baumann, Richard, F. L. Bauer, K. Samelson, and M. Feliciano: *Introduction to ALGOL,* Englewood Cliffs, N.J., Prentice-Hall, Inc., 1964.

Farina, Mario V.: *COBOL Simplified,* Englewood Cliffs, N.J., Prentice-Hall, Inc., 1968.

Kemeny, John G. and Thomas E. Kurtz: *BASIC Programming,* New York, John Wiley & Sons, Inc., 1967.

COBOL, Edition 1965. Washington, D.C., U.S. Government Printing Office, 1965.

McCameron, Fritz A.: *COBOL Logic and Programming,* Homewood, Ill., Richard D. Irwin, Inc., 1966.

Rosen, Saul (ed.): *Programming Systems and Language,* New York, McGraw-Hill Book Company, 1967.

USA Standard FORTRAN (X3.9–1966) and *USA Standard Basic FORTRAN* (X3.10–1966), New York, United States of America Standards Institute, 1966.

▌ OPERATION, MANAGEMENT, CONTROL, AND AUDITING OF THE COMPUTER INSTALLATION

Brandon, Dick H.: *Management Standards for Data Processing,* Princeton, N.J., D. Van Nostrand Company, Inc., 1963.

Brown, Harry L.: *EDP for Auditors,* New York, John Wiley & Sons, Inc., 1968.

Canning, Richard G. and Roger L. Sisson: *The Management of Data Processing,* New York, John Wiley & Sons, Inc., 1967.

Davis, Gordon B.: *Auditing & EDP,* New York, American Institute of Certified Public Accountants, 1968.

Lecht, Charles Philip: *The Management of Computer Programming Projects,* New York, American Management Association, Inc., 1967.

Porter, W. Thomas: *Auditing Electronic Systems,* Belmont, Calif., Wadsworth Publishing Company, Inc., 1966.

Wofsey, Marvin M.: *Management of Automatic Data Processing,* Washington, D.C., Thompson Book Company, 1968.

▌ REALTIME SYSTEMS AND DATA COMMUNICATIONS

Desmonde, William H.: *Real-time Data Processing Systems,* Englewood Cliffs, N.J., Prentice-Hall, Inc., 1964.

Gentle, Edgar C., Jr. (ed.): *Data Communications in Business,* New York, American Telephone and Telegraph Company, 1966.

Head, Robert V.: *Real-time Business Systems,* New York, Holt, Rinehart and Winston, Inc., 1964.

IBM: *Data Communications Primer,* International Business Machines, Form C20–1668.

Martin, James: *Design of Real-time Systems,* Englewood Cliffs, N.J., Prentice-Hall, Inc., 1965.

Sprague, Richard E.: *Electronic Business Systems: Management Use of On-line–Real-time Computers,* New York, The Ronald Press Company, 1962.

▌ TIME SHARING AND DATA PROCESSING SERVICE CENTERS

Barnett, C. C., Jr. and Associates: *The Future of the Computer Utility,* New York, American Management Association, 1967.

Carter, Byron L.: *Data Processing for Small Business,* New York, MacFadden-Bartell Corporation, 1966.

Sanders, Donald H.: *Introducing Computers to Small Business,* Park Ridge, Ill., Data Processing Management Association, 1966.

Ziegler, James R.: *Time-sharing Data Processing Systems,* Englewood Cliffs, N.J., Prentice-Hall, Inc., 1967.

▌CURRENT AND PROSPECTIVE DEVELOPMENTS IN HARDWARE/SOFTWARE AND SYSTEMS

Amdahl, G. M. and L. D. Amdahl: "Fourth-generation Hardware," *Datamation,* January, 1967, pp. 25–26.

Drucker, Peter F.: "What the Computers Will Be Telling You," *Nation's Business,* August, 1966, pp. 84–90.

Emory, James C.: "The Impact of Information Technology on Organization," *Proceedings of the Academy of Management,* 24th Annual Meeting, December, 1964.

Farina, Donald E.: "Large-scale Integration: A Status Report," *Datamation,* February, 1968, pp. 22–29.

Higginson, M. Valliant: *Managing with EDP—AMA Research Study 71,* American Management Association, 1965.

Hobbs, L. C.: "The Impact of Hardware in the 1970's," *Datamation,* March, 1966, pp. 36–44.

Leavitt, Harold J. and Thomas L. Whisler: "Management in the 1980's," *Harvard Business Review,* November-December, 1958, pp. 41–48.

Lee, Hak Chong: *The Impact of Electronic Data Processing upon Patterns of Business Organization and Administration,* State University of New York at Albany, 1965.

Mayne, David: "What's Next in Memories?" *Datamation,* February, 1968, pp. 30–32.

Meyers, Charles A. (ed.): *The Impact of Computers on Management,* Cambridge, Mass., The M.I.T. Press, 1967.

Patrick, R. L.: "Computing in the 1970's," *Datamation,* January, 1967, pp. 27–30.

Perlman, Justin A.: "Centralization vs. Decentralization," *Datamation,* September, 1965, pp. 24–28.

Schoderbek, Peter P. (ed.): *Management Systems,* New York, John Wiley & Sons, Inc., 1967.

Sprague, Richard E.: "The Browsing Era," *Business Automation,* June, 1967, pp. 53–56, 70.

"The Next Generation," *Datamation,* January, 1967, pp. 31–34.

Absolute address, 181–183, 283, 452, 563
Absolute coding, 181–183, 186, 563
Absolute value in number system, 113
Access time, 563
Accounting machine, 30, 45
Accounts receivable processing, example, 9–14, 48–53
Accumulator, 147
Acronym, 63, 563
Adder, 147–148
Addition, 119, 242–245
Address, 162–163, 563
    for direct access file, 316–317, 382–383
Address modification, 266–280, 563
ADP (Automatic Data Processing), 563
Aiken, Howard, 62–63
ALGOL (ALGOrithmic Language), 364, 564
Algorithm, 564
Alphameric, 564
Alphanumeric, 127–131, 564
Altering an instruction, 266–269
Amplitude, 396–397
Analog computer, 58, 564
Analytic engine, 60–61
Application package, 189, 564
APT language, 365
Arithmetic:
    in binary, 118–123
    in COBOL, 345
    in FORTRAN, 350
Arithmetic method of modification, 267–268, 271–273
ASA [see United States of America Standards Institute (USASI)]
ASCII (American Standard Code for Information Interchange), 402–403, 564
Assemble, 177, 183–185, 454, 565
Assembler, 183–185, 565
Assembly system, 222–228
Associative memory, 523–524, 565
Asynchronous computer, 149–150, 565
Audio response unit, 322–323
Audit trail, 414, 565
Auxiliary storage, 565
    (See also Secondary storage)

Babbage, Charles, 60–61
Background program, 566
Backup, 434, 566
Balance-forward statement, 48–49
Band, 397–399
Base of member system, 113–114
Base address, 283, 566
BASIC, 364, 505–506

INDEX

Batch processing, 566
average age, 376–377
random, 78
sequential, 77
total, 422–424, 566
Baud, 402, 566
Baudot code, 402–403, 566
BCD (binary coded decimal), 112–113, 126–131, 567
Benchmark problem, 473
Binary coded decimal (BCD), 112–113, 126–131, 567
Binary system, 112–113, 115–118, 567
arithmetic, 118–123
Bit, 112, 115, 567
storage circuit, 146
Block, 312, 374–375, 567
Block diagram, 567
(See also Program flowchart)
Block time, 495–496
Blocking, 312, 374–375, 567
Bookkeeping machine, 9–11
Boole, George, 61
Boolean algebra, 61–62, 143–145, 257–258
Bootstrap loader, 452, 567
Branch, 567
instructions, 251–255
Breakpoint, 568
Broadband Exchange Service, 400
Buffer, 298, 568
Bug, 177, 228–230, 568
Byte, 128–131, 568
addressable storage, 164–165

Calculator, 30, 44–45
Call, 280–282, 568
Calling sequence, 568
Capacitor, 142
Card layout, 194
Card punch, 30–34, 74–75, 294–295, 306, 538–544
Card punching, cost, 488–489
Card reader, 72, 294–295, 304–305
Cathode ray tube (CRT), 74, 294–295, 321–324, 568
Central processor (CPU), 67–70, 568
Certificate in data processing (CDP), 551–554
Chain, 372–373
Channel, 292–293, 296, 298–302, 569
printer, 306–307

Channel:
tape, 309–310
Character, 4–5
Check bit, 427–428, 569
Check digit, 420–421, 569
Circuitry, 142–146
Clock, 146, 569
Close macro, 302, 304
COBOL (COmmon Business Oriented Language), 339–346, 569
CODASYL committee, 340, 569
Coding, 177, 222–225, 569
Collate, 37–41, 569
Collating sequence, 129, 570
Collator, 30, 38–41
Communication (information) theory, 5–6
Communications system, 103
Comparator, 149
Compile, 177, 454, 570
Compiler, 186, 332–339, 570
Complement subtraction, 122–123
Complementer, 149
Computer:
capabilities of, 88–90
configurations, 79–82
cost, 462–463
data processing, 13–14, 65–67, 73–79
definition, 58
equipment, 67–74
history, 60–65
importance, 59–60
orientation, 59
selection, 471–474
Computer-assisted instruction, 107–108
Computer program, 174–189
Concurrent scheduling, 456
Conditional transfer, 251–256, 570
Console, 449–451, 570
Console operator, 440–444, 570
Console typewriter, 72
Content-addressable memory, 523–524, 570
Control:
evaluation of, 416–417
framework, 413
function, 415–416, 442–444
practices, 414–434
required by EDP, 416
sheet, 49–50
in time sharing, 512–514
total, 422–423
Control card, 454–455, 570
Control clerk, 440–444, 448, 571
Control panel, 41–44

Control program, 455–456, 571
Control unit (input-output), 292–293, 296
Conversational mode, 502, 571
Conversion programs, 189–190, 476
Converting to computer, 474–477
Cost:
    of computer system, 461–462, 469–470
    of service center services, 490–491
    of time sharing, 514–515
CPU (central processing unit), 67–70, 571
CRAM, 325
Critical path analysis (PERT/CPM), 96
Crossfooting test, 428–429
CRT, 74, 294–295, 321–324, 571
Cryogenics, 524–525, 571
Current information selection, 99–100
Curve tracing, 319
Cycle time, 473, 571
Cyclic action storage, 381

Data, 5–6
Data bank, 17, 533–534
Data base, 377, 571
Data cell, 71, 325–326
Data collection terminal, 76, 394–395
Data communications, 394–408
Data conversion, 258
Data division (COBOL), 343–344
Data-Phone, 399–400
Data preparation equipment, 69, 73, 75–76
Data processing:
    cycle, 6–8
    mechanization of, 8–16
    service centers, 483–497
    system, 6–8
    tasks, 6–8
Data processing management association
    certificate in data processing, 551–554
Data representation, 112–113, 127–131
Data set, 397
Debug, 177, 228–230, 572
Decimal system, 113–114
Decision table, 210–212, 572
Decoder, 148–149
Demodulator, 397, 572
Density, 310, 572
Desk checking, 228, 572
Detail file, 370, 572
Diagnostic routine, 229, 572
Difference engine, 60–61
Digit, 4–5

Digital computer, 58, 572
Diode, 142
Direct access, 78, 572
    file design, 381–385
    processing, 78–79, 384–386
Direct address, 277–278, 573
Disc address, methods for locating, 316–317,
    382–384
Disc file, 294–295, 314–318
Division, 246–247
    in binary, 121
Documentation, 177, 230–233, 573
Double dabbling, 116–117
Double precision, 166, 241–242, 573
Drum storage, 71, 294–295, 325–326
Dump, 229, 434, 573
Duplex, 398, 573
Dynamic relocation, 456, 573

EAM (Electrical Accounting Machine), 9–10,
    573
EBCDIC (Extended Binary Coded Decimal
    Interchange Code), 574
Echo check, 427, 574
Eckert, J. Presper, 63
Edge-punched cards, 32–33, 574
Edit, 255–259
    in COBOL, 344
    instructions to, 255–259, 308
EDP (electronic data processing), 574
EDSAC, 63
EDVAC, 63
Effective address, 265–269, 574
Elections, prediction of, 107
Electronic card processor, 46
Emulator, 476, 528, 574
Encoder, 148–149
End of reel marker, 310–311
ENIAC, 63
Environment division (COBOL), 341–342
Errors:
    in data communication, 403–404
    handling of, by service center, 489
    reasons for, in input/output, 417
Evaluating computer system, 465–466, 471–
    473
Executive routine, 453–456, 574
Expenses of computer, 463
Exponentiation, 113
External label, 431–432, 575
Extraction, 380, 385

Feasibility study, 466–470
Field, 4–5, 370–371, 575
File, 4–5, 370–386, 575
    design, 373–374
    maintenance, 6–7, 372, 575
    processing, 372–373, 575
File label, 312–313, 371, 421, 575
File protection ring, 431–432
Film chip, 522–523
Financing computer equipment, 477–479
Firmware, 528
Fixed-length record, 375, 575
Fixed point, 249–250, 576
Fixed word length, 163, 166–167, 179–180, 576
Flip-flop, 146
Floating point, 250–251, 576
Flowchart, 176, 198–209, 576
    standard symbols, 198–204
    standard usage, 204–205
Forecasting models, 97
Foreground program, 576
FORTRAN (FORmula TRANslator), 347–355, 576
Frequency, 396–397
Full duplex, 398, 577

Gang punching, 47
Gap, 312, 577
Gates, 144–145
Gaussian noise, 403
Generate, 577
Generator, 189, 359–363, 577
Gentle, Edgar C., Jr., 403
GET macro, 302–304, 312
GPSS, 365
Graph plotter, 74
Grid charts, 197–198, 405
Grouping of cards, 35

Half duplex, 398, 577
Hardware controls, 425–428
Hash total, 422–423
Header label, 312–313, 421, 577
Heuristic, 90, 520, 578
Hexadecimal, 125–126, 578
High-order, 578
Higher-order languages, 332–365
Hole count, 304–305
Hollerith, Herman, 22

Hollerith card (see Punched card data processing)
Hollerith code, 24–25, 578
Housekeeping, 578
Hub, 41–42
Hybrid circuits, 142
Hybrid computer, 58

IAS computer, 63
IBM, 22
IBM card (see Punched card data processing)
Identification division (COBOL), 341
IDP (integrated data processing), 104–105, 337, 578
Immediate address, 178, 578
Impact of computers, 530–532
Impact printer, 306–308
Index for disc addressing, 317
Index register, 268–269, 273–274, 282, 579
Indirect address, 277–278, 579
Industrial dynamics, 99
Information, 5–6, 220
Information retrieval, 99–101
Information systems, 2–6
Information theory, 5–6
Initialize, 270–274, 579
Input:
    cycle, 296
    data processing cycle, 6–8
    preparation, 7
Input/output, 291–327, 579
    in COBOL, 343–344
    controls, 417–425
    devices, 69–72, 294–295, 304–327
    in FORTRAN, 350–351
    instructions, 293–295, 300–304
    in PL/I, 357
Input/output channel, 292–293, 296, 298–302, 579
Input/output control system (IOCS), 294–295, 302–304, 579
Input validation run, 417–419
Installation, time for, 463–464
Instruction, 579
    coding of, 181–187
    form of, 177–181
    storage for, 168–169
    times, 473
Instruction modification (see Program modification)

Instructions, types of: arithmetic, 240–251
    editing, 255–259
    move, 236–240
    transfer of control, 251–255
Insurance, 434
Integrated circuit, 142–144, 580
Integrated data processing, 104–105, 377, 580
Interblock gap, 312, 580
Interface, 296, 580
Interlock, 297, 580
Interpreter, 30, 46–47
Interpretive routine, 580
Interrecord gap, 312, 580
Interrupt, 299, 580
Interruption, 455–456, 581
International Organization of Standardization (ISO), 556
    flowchart standards, 202–203
Inverter, 146
I/O (see Input/output)
IOCS (input/output control system), 294–295, 581
Item, 4–5, 343, 370–371, 581
Item design, 375–376

Job cards, 454–455
Jobs in computer data processing, 67, 440–444
Jules Own Version of International Algebraic Language (JOVIAL), 365

K (thousands), 79
Kernel problem, 473
Key, 370–371, 383, 581
Keydata Corporation, 507–509
Keypunch (see Card punch)

Label, 183, 312–313, 421, 581
Large-scale integrated circuits, 142, 522–523
Laser beam, 423
Lateral parity check, 426–427, 581
Layout charts, 194–197, 221
Leasing of computers, 479
Library routine, 188, 280, 338, 582
Limit test, 428
Linear programming, 96
Link, 372

Linkage, 280–282, 582
Literals, 224–225
Load-and-go, 452, 582
Load-point marker, 310–311
Loader, 452–453, 582
Log, 582
Logical circuits, 143–145
Logical record, 302–304
Longitudinal parity check, 426–427, 582
Look-up, 277, 582
Loop, 270–274, 582
    in FORTRAN, 353–354
Low-order, 582

Machine address, 181–182, 583
Machine instruction, 181–182, 583
Machine language, 181–182, 226, 583
Machine-oriented language, 181–186, 222–225, 583
Macro instruction, 185–186, 293–294, 302–304, 583
Magnetic core, 157–160
Magnetic disc, 71, 294–295, 314–318
Magnetic ink character reader, 72, 294–295, 321–322
Magnetic ink enscriber, 76
Magnetic recording, 161–162
Magnetic strip, 71, 294–295, 325–326
Magnetic tape encoder, 75
Magnetic tape unit, 72, 294–295, 309–313
Main frame, 67–70, 583
Maintenance, 457
Management of data processing, 440–457
Management information system, 105–106, 529–530, 583
Manual of specifications, 470–471
Map, memory, 229, 583
Mark I calculator, 62–63
Mark sensing, 32–33, 583
Mask, 257–258, 584
Mass core storage, 294–295
Mass storage (see Secondary storage)
Master file, 370, 584
Matrix matching, 319
Mauchly, John W., 63
Memory swapping, 510–511
Merge, 37–41, 387–389, 584
Merge sorting, 387–389
Merging, 29, 37–41
Message switching, 396, 584

614

MICR (magnetic ink character recognition), 321–322, 584
Microprogramming, 528, 584
Microsecond, 142, 584
Millisecond, 142, 585
Mnemonic, 182–183, 585
MODEM (MOdulator-DEModulator), 397, 585
Modulator, 397, 585
Modulo N check, 420, 585
Monitor routine, 453–454, 585
Monolithic integrated circuit, 142
Move instructions, 236–240
Multiplex, 585
Multiplexor, 585
Multiplexor channel, 300, 585
Multiplication, 245–246
  in binary, 120–121
Multiprocessing, 456, 585
Multiprogramming, 282–284, 456, 500–517, 586

Nanosecond, 142, 586

Object language, 586
Object program, 185, 333–338, 451, 586
OCR (optical character recognition), 319–321, 586
Octal, 124–125, 586
Offline, 101–103, 586
One-address instruction, 179–180
Online, 101–103, 586
OPEN macro, 302, 304, 312
Operand, 178–181, 587
Operating cycle, 149–150
Operating system, 190, 453–457, 587
Operation code, 178, 587
Operator instructions, 230–233
Operator notation, 123–126
  hexadecimal, 125–126
  octal, 124–125
Optical character encoder, 76
Optical scanner, 72, 294–295, 319–321
Organization:
  of data processing, 413–416, 440–444
  of service center, 486–487
Output cycle, 6–8
Output devices, 73–74
Overflow, 248–249, 587
  in disc addressing, 316–317

Overhead, 510–511, 587
Overlay, 587

Pack, 168, 258, 588
Padding, 588
Page, 510–511, 588
Paper tape unit, 72, 74, 294–295, 323–325
Parallel, 588
  operations, 147
  processing, 456
Parity bit, 130, 588
Parity check, 426–427, 588
Pass, 588
Patch, 231, 589
Pattern, 259
Payroll processing, 91–95
Performance standards, 446–447
Peripheral equipment, 69–74, 589
Personnel, 440–444
Phase, 396–397
Physical record, 302–304
Picosecond, 142, 589
PL/I (Programming Language I), 353–359, 589
Plated wire memory, 160–161
Plugboard, 41–44, 589
Pointer, 372
POL, 332–365
Powers, James, 22
Primary storage, 154–161
Printing, 29, 306–309, 589
Port-A-Punch, IBM, 32
Position value in number system, 112–113
Postmortem routine, 589
Precision, 166, 241–242, 589
Presumptive address, 266–269, 589
Print chain, 306–307
Print drum, 306–307
Printer, 74, 294–295, 304–309
Printer layout, 196
Privacy, 377–378
Privileged instruction, 590
Problem-oriented language, 186–188, 332–365, 590
Procedure division (COBOL), 344–346
Procedure-oriented language, 186–188, 332–365, 590
Procedures manual, 445–447
Process control, 102–103
Processing methods, computer, 73, 77–79, 101–103

Processor, 590
Program, 66, 174–176, 590
  controls over, 429–431
  generator, 189
Program card, 542–543
Program flowchart, 205, 207–209, 335, 590
Program modification, 266–285
  arithmetic method, 267–268, 271–273
  index register method, 268–269, 273–274
  indirect addressing, 277–278
  in multiprogramming, 282–284
  subroutines, 280–282
  switches, 275–277
  table look-up, 277
Programmer, 440–444, 590
Programming language, 181–187, 332–365, 590
Pseudo instruction, 225, 591
Punched card data processing, 12–13, 22–53
  edge-notched card, 25–26
  edge-punched card, 27–28
  equipment, 28–48
    accounting machine, 30, 45
    calculator, 30, 44–45
    card punch, 30–34, 538–544
    collator, 30, 38–41
    control panel, 41–44
    interpreter, 30, 46–47
    reproducer, 30, 47
    sorter, 30, 35–37
    summary punch, 30, 47–48
    verifier, 30, 34
  procedures, 28–53
    calculating, 29, 44–46
    collating, 37–41
    merging, 29, 37–41
    printing, 29, 45
    sorting, 29, 35–37
Pure procedure, 284
PUT macro, 302–304, 312

Quality control over EDP, 413–435

Radix point, 113–114, 591
Random access, 78, 591
  processing, 73, 78–79, 384–386
Randomizing, 383
Read-only storage, 476, 528, 591
Read-write head, 310

Realtime, 101–103, 591
Record, 4–5, 343–344, 370–371, 591
Record gap, 312, 592
Record keeping, 91–95
Recording density, 310, 592
Redundancy check, 425–426, 592
Reentrant, 284, 512, 592
Register, 146–147, 149–150, 165–166, 179–180, 592
  for arithmetic, 239–251
  for clear, 239
  for move, 237–238
Relative address, 283, 452, 592
Released cycle time, 296–297
Relocatable coding, 283, 452, 592
Report file, 370
Report preparation, 7
Report program generator (RPG), 189, 359–363, 593
Reproducer, 30, 47
Residue check, 420, 593
Resister, 142
Retention plan, 433–434
Roemmich, Herman, 553
Rotational delay, 381
Route slip, 424
Routine, 593
Row parity check, 426–427, 593
Run, 93–95, 221, 593
Run manual, 177, 230–233, 593
Running a program, 4, 449–453

Scale factor, 249–250, 593
Scaling, 240–251
Scheduling:
  of jobs, 455–456
  of personnel, 448–449
Second generation computer, 64
Secondary storage, 69–71, 155, 294–295, 593
Security, 377–378, 489–490
Seek time, 381
Selecting:
  of cards, 35
  of records, 379–380, 385
Selection:
  of a computer, 471–474
  of a data processing service center, 491–494
  of a time-sharing service, 516–517
Selector channel, 300, 594

Sense switch, 275, 451
Sequence scheduling, 456
Sequencing of cards, 35
Sequential file design, 378–381, 594
Serial, 147, 166, 594
Serial access, 378–381, 594
Service center, 483–497
Setup time, 594
Shifting, 256–257
Simplex, 398, 594
Simscript, 365
Simulation, 97–99
    for conversion, 189–190, 476
    for selection, 473
Snapshot, 594
Software, 66, 188–190, 527–529, 594
Solid logic technology, 142–143
Solid state, 65, 494
Son-father-grandfather concept, 433–434
Sort file, 370
Sorter, 30, 35–37
Sorting, 29, 35–37, 387–389
Source language, 185, 333–338, 451, 594
Source program, 185, 333–338, 451, 595
Spacecraft, guidance and control, 106
Special character, 24–25, 127–128, 595
Specifications, manual of, 470–471
Sperry Rand Corporation, 22
Standards, 444–447, 555, 559
State in representing information, 114–115
Statement, 595
Storage, 154–170
    access, 155–156
    comparing sizes, 167–169
    definition, 225
    devices and media, 70–71, 156–157, 294–
        295
    primary, 154–161
    secondary, 155
Storage allocation, 456, 509–510, 595
Storage layout, 196–197
Storage protection, 284, 595
Storage-to-storage design, 166–167
    for arithmetic, 239–251
    for clear, 239
    for move, 238–239
Stored logic, 528
Straight-line coding, 270–271, 595
String sorting, 387–389
Stroke analysis, 319
Study group for evaluation and selection,
    466–467

Subprogram (see Subroutine)
Subroutine, 188, 280–282, 354, 595
Subtraction, 242–245
    in binary, 119–120
    using complements, 122–123
Summary punch, 30, 47–48
Supervisory routine, 453–456, 596
Switch, 275–277, 596
Symbolic address, 225, 596
Symbolic assembly system, 183–185, 222–
    229
Symbolic coding, 181–187, 222–228, 596
Symbolic logic, 61–62
Synchronization check, 427–428, 596
Synchronous computer, 149–150, 596
System, 5, 529–530, 596
System analysis, 176, 220–222, 448, 596
System design, 176, 335
System flowchart, 205–206, 221, 597
System simulation, 97–99, 473
Systems analyst, 440–444

Table look-up, 277–278, 597
Tabulating equipment, 28–48
Tag, 183, 597
Tape layout, 195
Tape loop, 306, 308
Telecommunications, 394–408, 597
Teletype, 401, 502–503
Telex, 400
Telpak, 399
Termination of program, 453
Test for termination, 270–274
Test data, 229
Thin film, 160–161, 597
Third-generation computer, 64
Throughput, 472–473, 597
Time for installing computer, 463–464
Time sharing, 395, 500–517, 597
Trace routine, 229, 598
Track, 316, 598
Track parity check, 426–427, 598
Trailor record, 312–313, 371, 421, 598
Training, sources of, 444
Transaction code, 598
Transaction file, 370, 598
Transaction processing, 7
Transfer of control, 251–255
    in COBOL, 345–346
    in FORTRAN, 352–354
Transistor, 142

Translator, 334–336, 598
Trap, 255, 598
Trigger, 146
Truth tables, 61–62, 145
Two-address instruction, 179–180

Unconditional transfer, 251–253, 599
Unit record, 12–13, 28–29, 599
United States of America Standards Institute
    (USASI), 555–559
  flowchart standards, 198–209
  FORTRAN, 347
  optical font, 320
UNIVAC I, 63–64
Unpack, 168, 258, 599
Update, 6–7, 372, 599
Utility routine, 189, 599

Valid data tests, 421–422
Variable-length record, 375, 599
Variable word length, 163–164, 166–167,
    179–180, 599
Vendor selection, 471, 474
Verification, 418–420

Verifier, 30, 34, 75
Virtual address, 283–284, 510–511, 600
von Neumann, John, 63

W-2 report processing, 38–40
WATS, 399
Wave form, 396–397
Wiring diagram, 41–43
Word, 163–167, 600
Word length, 163–167, 600
Word mark, 130, 164, 238–239, 243–244,
    600
Working storage, 343, 600
Write enable ring, 431–432

X punch, 600
X3 Sectional Committee on Computers and
    Information Processing, 555–559

Y punch, 600

Zero suppression, 258–259, 601
Zone, 258